NP 68

EAST COAST OF THE UNITED STATES PILOT VOLUME I

East Coast of the United States from Great Wass Island to Barnegat Inlet

TWELFTH EDITION
2006

PUBLISHED BY THE UNITED KINGDOM HYDROGRAPHIC OFFICE

Previous Editions covering this area

Ports on the east coast of the United States
 First published 1858
 2nd Edition 1874
 3rd Edition 1882

East coast of United States
 First published 1899
 2nd Edition, Part I 1909
 3rd Edition, Volume I 1922
 4th Edition 1934
 5th Edition 1949
 6th Edition 1960
 7th Edition 1975
 8th Edition 1995
 9th Edition 1998
 10th Edition 2001
 11th Edition 2004

PREFACE

The Twelfth Edition of the East Coast of the United States Pilot, Volume I, has been prepared by Captain R D Peddle, Master Mariner. The United Kingdom Hydrographic Office has used all reasonable endeavours to ensure that this Pilot contains all the information obtained by and assessed by it at the date shown below. Information received or assessed after that date will be included in *Admiralty Notices to Mariners* where appropriate. If in doubt, see *The Mariner's Handbook* for details of what *Admiralty Notices to Mariners* are and how to use them.

This edition supersedes the Eleventh Edition (2004), which is cancelled.

Information on climate and currents has been based on data provided by the Met Office, Exeter.

Information on ice has been based on data provided by the Scottish Association for Marine Science, Oban.

The following sources of information, other than UKHO publications and Ministry of Defence papers, have been consulted.

United States
 Charts.
 United States Coast Pilots:
  Volume 1. Atlantic Coast: Eastport to Cape Cod 36th Edition 2006
  Volume 2. Atlantic Coast: Cape Cod to Sandy Hook 35th Edition 2006
  Volume 3. Atlantic Coast: Sandy Hook to Cape Henry 39th Edition 2006

Other publications
 Fairplay World Ports Directory 2006
 Lloyds Ports of the World 2006
 The Statesman's Yearbook 2006
 Whitaker's Almanack 2006

Mr M S Robinson
Chief Executive

The United Kingdom Hydrographic Office
Admiralty Way
Taunton
Somerset TA1 2DN
England
12 October 2006

PREFACE

to the Eighth Edition (1995)

The Eighth Edition of the East Coast of the United States Pilot, Volume I, has been prepared by Commander R. Perceval Maxwell RN, and contains the latest information received in the United Kingdom Hydrographic Office to the date given below.

This edition supersedes the Seventh Edition (1975) and supplement No 11 (1994), which are cancelled.

Information on climate, currents and ice has been based on data provided by the Meteorological Office, Bracknell.

The following sources of information, other than UKHO publications and Ministry of Defence papers, have been consulted.

United States
Charts.
United States Coast Pilots:
Volume 1. Atlantic Coast: Eastport to Cape Cod. 1995 Edition.
Volume 2. Atlantic Coast: Cape Cod to Sandy Hook. 1994 Edition.
Volume 3. Atlantic Coast: Sandy Hook to Cape Henry. 1994 Edition.

Other publications:
Encyclopædia Britannica. Fifteenth Edition.
Fairplay Worlds Port Directory 1995.
Guide to Port Entry 1995.
Lloyds Maritime Guide 1995.
Lloyds Ports of the World 1995.
Lloyds Shipping Information Services 1991.
The Statesman's Yearbook 1994-95.
Whitaker's Almanack 1995.

N R ESSENHIGH
Rear Admiral
Hydrographer of the Navy

United Kingdom Hydrographic Office
Taunton
Somerset
England
11th November 1995

CONTENTS

APPENDICES AND INDEX

EXPLANATORY NOTES

Admiralty Sailing Directions are intended for use by vessels of 150 gt or more. They amplify charted detail and contain information needed for safe navigation which is not available from Admiralty charts, or other hydrographic publications. They are intended to be read in conjunction with the charts quoted in the text.

This volume of the Sailing Directions will be kept up-to-date by the issue of a new edition at intervals of approximately 3 years, without the use of supplements. In addition important amendments which cannot await the new edition are published in Section IV of the weekly editions of *Admiralty Notices to Mariners*. A list of such amendments and notices in force is published quarterly. Those still in force at the end of the year are reprinted in the *Annual Summary of Admiralty Notices to Mariners*.

This volume should not be used without reference to Section IV of the weekly editions of Admiralty Notices to Mariners.

References to hydrographic and other publications

The Mariner's Handbook gives general information affecting navigation and is complementary to this volume.

Ocean Passages for the World and *Routeing Charts* contain ocean routeing information and should be consulted for other than coastal passages.

Admiralty List of Lights should be consulted for details of lights, lanbys and fog signals, as these are not fully described in this volume.

Admiralty List of Radio Signals should be consulted for information relating to Maritime and port radio stations, radio details of pilotage services, radar beacons and radio direction finding stations, meteorological services, radio aids to navigation, Global Maritime Distress and Safety System (GMDSS) and Differential Global Positioning System (DGPS) stations, as these are only briefly referred to in this volume.

Annual Summary of Admiralty Notices to Mariners contains in addition to the temporary and preliminary notices, and amendments and notices affecting Sailing Directions, a number of notices giving information of a permanent nature covering radio messages and navigational warnings, distress and rescue at sea and exercise areas.

The International Code of Signals should be consulted for details of distress and life-saving signals, international ice-breaker signals as well as international flag signals.

Remarks on subject matter

Buoys are generally described in detail only when they have special navigational significance, or where the scale of the chart is too small to show all the details clearly.

Chart index diagrams in this volume show only those Admiralty charts of a suitable scale to give good coverage of the area. Mariners should consult NP 131 *Catalogue of Admiralty Charts and Publications* for details of larger scale charts.

Chart references in the text normally refer to the largest scale Admiralty chart but occasionally a smaller scale chart may be quoted where its use is more appropriate.

Firing, practice and exercise areas. Submarine exercise areas are mentioned in Sailing Directions. Other firing, practice and exercise areas maybe mentioned with limited details. Signals and buoys used in connection with these areas maybe mentioned if significant for navigation. Attention is invited to the Annual Notice to Mariners on this subject.

Names have been taken from the most authoritative source. When an obsolete name still appears on the chart, it is given in brackets following the proper name at the principal description of the feature in the text and where the name is first mentioned.

Tidal information relating the daily vertical movements of the water is not given; for this *Admiralty Tide Tables* should be consulted. Changes in water level of an abnormal nature are mentioned.
Time difference used in the text when applied to the time of High Water found from the *Admiralty Tide Tables*, gives the time of the event being described in the Standard Time kept in the area of that event. Due allowance must be made for any seasonal daylight saving time which may be kept.

Wreck information is included where drying or below-water wrecks are relatively permanent features having significance for navigation or anchoring.

Units and terminology used in this volume

Latitude and Longitude given in brackets are approximate and are taken from the chart quoted.

Bearings and directions are referred to the true compass and when given in degrees are reckoned clockwise from 000° (North) to 359°
Bearings used for positioning are given from the reference object.
Bearings of objects, alignments and light sectors are given as seen from the vessel.
Courses always refer to the course to be made good over the ground.

Winds are described by the direction from which they blow.

Tidal streams and currents are described by the direction towards which they flow.

Distances are expressed in sea miles of 60 to a degree of latitude and sub-divided into cables of one tenth of a sea mile.

Depths are given below chart datum, except where otherwise stated.

Heights of objects refer to the height of the object above the ground and are invariably expressed as "... m in height".

Elevations, as distinct from heights, are given above Mean High Water Springs or Mean Higher High Water whichever is quoted in *Admiralty Tide Tables*, and expressed as, "an elevation of ... m". However the elevation of natural features such as hills may alternatively be expressed as "... m high" since in this case there can be no confusion between elevation and height.

Metric units are used for all measurements of depths, heights and short distances, but where feet/fathoms charts are referred to, these latter units are given in brackets after the metric values for depths and heights shown on the chart.

Time is expressed in the four-figure notation beginning at midnight and is given in local time unless otherwise stated. Details of local time kept will be found in *Admiralty List of Radio Signals Volume 2*.

Bands is the word used to indicate horizontal marking.

Stripes is the word used to indicate markings which are vertical, unless stated to be diagonal.

Conspicuous objects are natural and artificial marks which are outstanding, easily identifiable and clearly visible to the mariner over a large area of sea in varying conditions of light. If the scale is large enough they will normally be shown on the chart in bold capitals and may be marked "conspic".

Prominent objects are those which are easily identifiable, but do not justify being classified as conspicuous.

ABBREVIATIONS

The following abbreviations are used in the text:

AIS	Automatic Identification System		km	kilometre(s)
ALC	Articulated loading column		kn	knot(s)
ALP	Articulated loading platform		kW	kilowatt(s)
AMVER	Automated Mutual Assistance Vessel Rescue System		Lanby	Large automatic navigation buoy
ASL	Archipelagic Sea Lane		LASH	Lighter Aboard Ship
			LAT	Lowest Astronomical Tide
			LF	low frequency
°C	degrees Celsius		LHG	Liquefied Hazardous Gas
CALM	Catenary anchor leg mooring		LMT	Local Mean Time
CBM	Conventional buoy mooring		LNG	Liquefied Natural Gas
cm	centimetre(s)		LOA	Length overall
CDC	Certain Dangerous Cargo		LPG	Liquefied Petroleum Gas
CVTS	Co-operative Vessel Traffic System		LW	Low Water
DF	direction finding		m	metre(s)
DG	degaussing		mb	millibar(s)
DGPS	Differential Global Positioning System		MCTS	Marine Communications and Traffic Services Centres
DW	Deep Water			
DSC	Digital Selective Calling		MF	medium frequency
dwt	deadweight tonnage		MHz	megahertz
DZ	danger zone		MHHW	Mean Higher High Water
			MHLW	Mean Higher Low Water
E	east (easterly, eastward, eastern, easternmost)		MHW	Mean High Water
EEZ	exclusive economic zone		MHWN	Mean High Water Neaps
ELSBM	Exposed location single buoy mooring		MHWS	Mean High Water Springs
ENE	east-north-east		MLHW	Mean Lower High Water
EPIRB	Emergency Position Indicating Radio Beacon		MLLW	Mean Lower Low Water
ESE	east-south-east		MLW	Mean Low Water
ETA	estimated time of arrival		MLWN	Mean Low Water Neaps
ETD	estimated time of departure		MLWS	Mean Low Water Springs
EU	European Union		mm	millimetre(s)
			MMSI	Maritime Mobile Service Identity
feu	forty foot equivalent unit		MRCC	Maritime Rescue Co-ordination Centre
fm	fathom(s)		MRSC	Maritime Rescue Sub-Centre
FPSO	Floating production storage and offloading vessel		MSI	Marine Safety Information
			MSL	Mean Sea Level
FPU	Floating production unit		MV	Motor Vessel
FSO	Floating storage and offloading vessel		MW	megawatt(s)
ft	foot (feet)		MY	Motor Yacht
g/cm³	gram per cubic centimetre		N	north (northerly, northward, northern, northernmost)
GMDSS	Global Maritime Distress and Safety System			
GPS	Global Positioning System		NATO	North Atlantic Treaty Organization
GRP	glass reinforced plastic		Navtex	Navigational Telex System
gt	gross tonnage		NE	north-east
			NNE	north-north-east
HAT	Highest Astronomical Tide		NNW	north-north-west
HF	high frequency		No	number
hm	hectometre		nrt	nett register tonnage
HMS	Her (His) Majesty's Ship		NW	north-west
hp	horse power			
hPa	hectopascal		ODAS	Ocean Data Acquisition System
HSC	High Speed Craft			
HW	High Water		PEL	Port Entry Light
			PLEM	Pipe line end manifold
IALA	International Association of Lighthouse Authorities		POL	Petrol, Oil & Lubricants
			PSSA	Particularly Sensitive Sea Areas
IHO	International Hydrographic Organization		PWC	Personal watercraft
IMO	International Maritime Organization			
ITCZ	Intertropical Convergence Zone		RCC	Rescue Co-ordination Centre
			RMS	Royal Mail Ship
JRCC	Joint Rescue Co-ordination Centre		RN	Royal Navy
			Ro-Ro	Roll-on, Roll-off
kHz	kilohertz		RT	radio telephony

S	south (southerly, southward, southern, southernmost)		UKHO	United Kingdom Hydrographic Office
			ULCC	Ultra Large Crude Carrier
SALM	Single anchor leg mooring system		UN	United Nations
SALS	Single anchored leg storage system		UT	Universal Time
SAR	Search and Rescue		UTC	Co-ordinated Universal Time
Satnav	Satellite navigation			
SBM	Single buoy mooring		VDR	Voyage Data Recorder
SE	south-east		VHF	very high frequency
SPM	Single point mooring		VLCC	Very Large Crude Carrier
sq	square		VMRS	Vessel Movement Reporting System
SRR	Search and Rescue Region		VTC	Vessel Traffic Centre
SS	Steamship		VTMS	Vessel Traffic Management System
SSE	south-south-east		VTS	Vessel Traffic Services
SSW	south-south-west			
SW	south-west		W	west (westerly, westward, western, westernmost)
SWATH	small waterplane area twin hull ship			
			WGS	World Geodetic System
teu	twenty foot equivalent unit		WMO	World Meteorological Organization
TSS	Traffic Separation Scheme		WNW	west-north-west
			WSW	west-south-west
UHF	ultra high frequency		WT	radio (wireless) telegraphy
UKC	under keel clearance			

NOTES

xi

Chapter Index Diagram

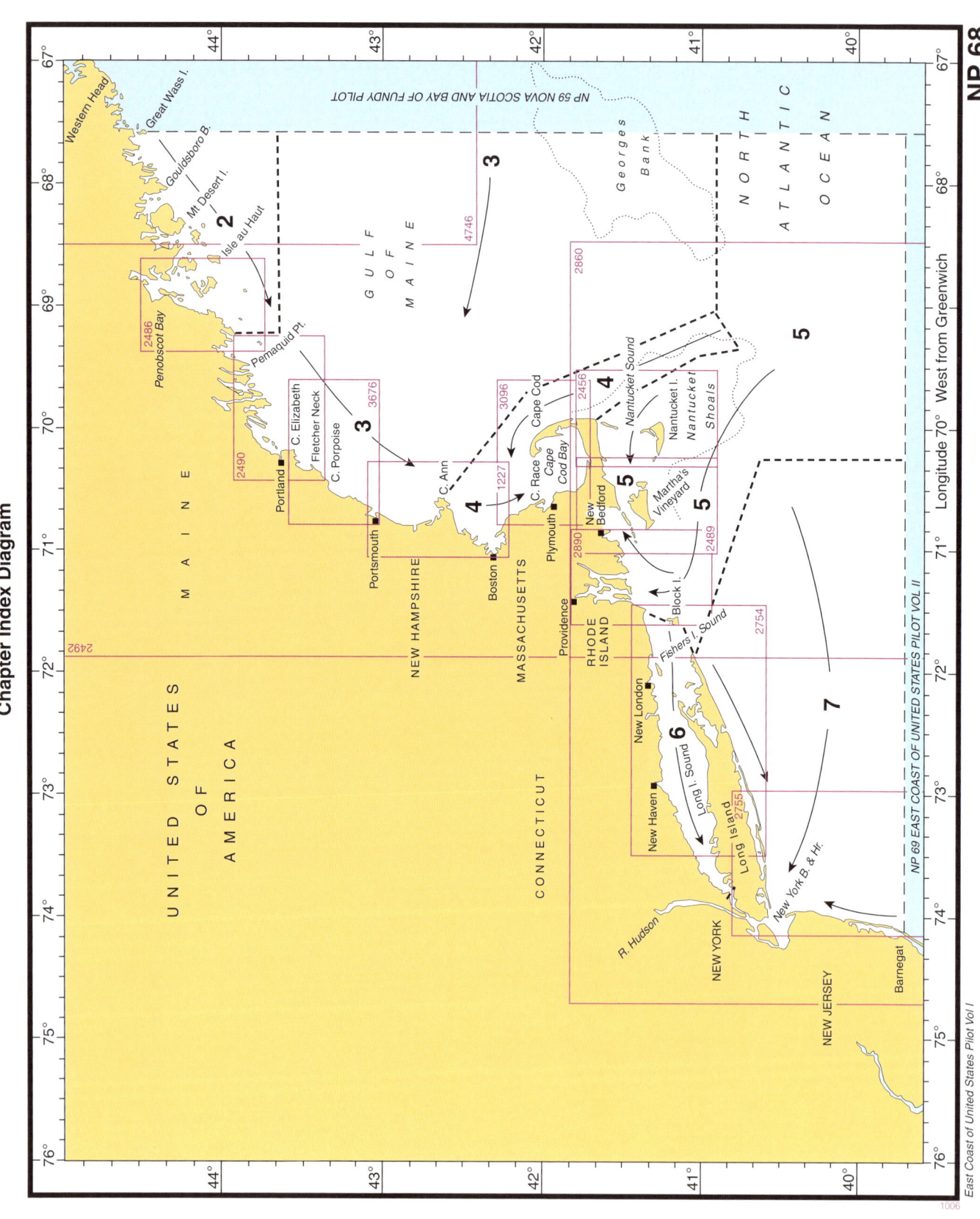

EAST COAST OF THE UNITED STATES PILOT

VOLUME I

CHAPTER 1

NAVIGATION AND REGULATIONS
COUNTRIES AND PORTS
NATURAL CONDITIONS

NAVIGATION AND REGULATIONS

LIMITS OF THE BOOK

Chart 2670
Area covered
1.1

1   This volume contains Sailing Directions for the NE coast of the United States between Great Wass Island, about 40 miles from the Canadian border and Barnegat Inlet, 60 miles S of New York, and for the sea area contained within the limits defined below:

	Lat N	Long W
From Great Wass Island	44°27′	67°35′
Thence S to position:	39°45′	67°35′
Thence W to Barnegat Inlet:	39°45′	74°06′

Thence NE along the coast of the United States to Great Wass Island.

NAVIGATIONAL DANGERS AND HAZARDS

Coastal conditions

Outlying dangers
1.2

1   The principal outlying dangers are Georges Bank (3.1) and Nantucket Shoals (5.19). Both these dangers should be entirely avoided.

There are also a number of other shoals in the Gulf of Maine, but only Ammen Rock (3.5) is a danger. There are no outlying dangers in the approaches to New York, to the SW of Nantucket Shoals.

Coastal dangers
1.3

1   In the Gulf of Maine there are a number of coastal dangers lying off the coast. In clear weather the land will be distinguished before these dangers are encountered, but in fog caution is required.

Natural conditions
1.4

1   **Ice.** See 1.121.
Strong winds. See 1.139.
Fog. See 1.145.

Former mined areas
1.5

1   The only former mined area in the waters covered by this volume is in the approaches to New York Harbor where mines were laid during the war of 1939-45. Due to the lapse of time this area is considered safe for surface navigation, but a very real risk still exists with regard to anchoring, fishing or any form of submarine or sea-bed activity. See 7.11.

Overhead cables

1.6

1   Overhead cables are mentioned in the text where the clearance beneath them may be a hazard to navigation. Some of these cables carry high voltages and sufficient clearance must be allowed when passing underneath them. In winter, the published clearance may be varied by ice or snow conditions.

    See *The Mariner's Handbook* for information on safety clearances and the radar responses to be expected.

TRAFFIC AND OPERATIONS

Traffic

Shipping

1.7

1   Transatlantic routes for traffic to ports in the area covered by this volume are given in *Ocean Passages for the World.*

Ferries

1.8

1   There are numerous ferry routes between the mainland and the islands in Nantucket Sound, Vineyard Sound and Long Island Sound.

Pleasure craft

1.9

1   The coastal and inshore waters covered by this volume, which have many marinas and boatyards, are very popular with yachtsmen.

Fishing

General remarks

1.10

1   Fishing craft are based at most of the ports along the coast covered by this volume. There are numerous lobster and oyster fisheries, and canning factories are established in some harbours.

Fish traps

1.11

1   Lobster pots are set in the inshore waters covered by this volume, especially between Great Wass Island and Portland. The pots are marked by small buoys, the mooring lines of which are liable to foul the propellers of small craft.

Exercise areas

Naval exercises

1.12

1   Naval exercises may take place in the waters covered by this volume. They are mentioned at the appropriate place in the text. Notice of exercises giving limits of the area, nature and duration of the exercise, and specified navigation rules, are promulgated by local *Notices to Mariners* and radio navigation warnings. For signals used by warships, see 1.58.

2   For general information on such areas see the *Annual Summary of Admiralty Notices to Mariners.*

Firing practice

1.13

1   Gunnery and bombing practice may take place in the waters covered by this volume. They are mentioned at the appropriate place in the text. Notice of firing practices, giving the limits of the area, nature and duration of the practice, and specified navigation rules, are promulgated by local *Notices to Mariners* and radio navigation warnings. For signals used by warships, see 1.58.

2   For general information on such areas see the *Annual Summary of Admiralty Notices to Mariners.*

Submarine exercises

Submarine transit lanes

1.14

1   Lanes used by submerged submarines may be established in the approaches to Portsmouth (3.225), New York, and Rhode Island Sound (5.9). Their positions will be shown on the charts of the National Ocean Survey and the times of usage published in US Notices to Mariners. When the lanes are in use by submarines, ships should not tow submerged objects within them.

Submarine operating areas

1.15

1   Submarine operating areas are established in Long Island Sound (6.71). As submarines may be operating submerged in these areas, vessels should proceed with caution.

CHARTS

Admiralty charts

1.16

1   Admiralty charts give full coverage of the offshore waters and most of the coastal waters of the area covered by this volume. They also give plans of all the important harbours and most of the important anchorages.

2   Admiralty chart coverage is not adequate for entry into some of the minor harbours and bays, especially those lying in the E part of the area between Great Wass Island and Portland.

3   With the exception of one chart which largely covers Canadian waters, there are no current plans to metricate any of the Admiralty charts covering the area of this volume.

Foreign charts

1.17

1   In certain areas, where Admiralty charts show insufficient detail for navigation close inshore, these Sailing Directions have been written using foreign charts. These are not quoted as reference charts in the text, which has been written on the assumption that mariners wishing to navigate in these areas will have provided themselves with suitable charts on which to do so.

2   US charts and publications of the National Ocean Service (NOS) and unclassified charts of the National Geospatial-Intelligence Agency (NGA) can be obtained from chart agents in US and foreign ports, or by mail order from the following address:

> Federal Aviation Administration,
> National Aeronautical Charting Office,
> Distribution Division (AVN-530),
> 10201 Good Luck Road,
> Glendale, MD 20769-9700,
> USA.

3   These charts are not issued by the UKHO nor are they amended by *Admiralty Notices to Mariners*.

Datums

Horizontal
1.18

1   For the area covered by this book, Admiralty and US charts are usually referred to North American Datum 1983 (NAD 83). For practical navigation purposes this equates to World Geodetic System 1984 (WGS84).

2   On a few Admiralty charts, positions are based on North American Datum (1927) and corrections are shown to align this datum with WGS84. On some smaller scale Admiralty charts, corrections cannot be determined.

3   When transferring positions between charts with different horizontal datums, it is advisable to do so by bearing and distance from a common reference object and not by latitude and longitude.

Vertical
1.19

1   **Depths.** On Admiralty charts for the area covered by this volume the Chart Datum is MLLW.

US charts are reduced to MLLW or MLW as shown on the chart.

As a consequence, mariners using these charts (see 1.17) should be aware that predicted and actual depths less than those charted may routinely occur. See Table V of *Admiralty Tide Tables* for details.

2   **Drying heights** on Admiralty charts are shown as being above Chart Datum.

Elevations on Admiralty charts are shown as being above MHWS and on US charts are shown against MHW.

Depths

Depth terms used in US waters
1.20

1   **Project depth** is the design dredging depth of a channel. The project depth may or may not be the goal of maintenance dredging after completion of the channel.

Controlling depth is the least depth within the limits of the channel; it restricts the safe use of the channel to draughts of less than that depth.

2   **Centreline controlling depth** of a channel applies only to the centreline; lesser depths may exist in the remainder of the channel.

Mid-channel controlling depth of a channel is the controlling depth of only the middle half of the channel.

3   In this volume project depths are given where available. For the latest controlling depths charts and local harbour and pilotage authorities should be consulted.

Depths alongside wharves are usually those reported by the owner or operator of the wharf. Local authorities should be consulted for the latest controlling depths.

AIDS TO NAVIGATION

Lights
1.21

1   In the US, lights are the responsibility of the Coast Guard. Major lights are those with a nominal range of 15 miles or more.

Light structures only are described in this volume; see *Admiralty List of Lights and Fog Signals* for details.

Landmarks
1.22

1   Caution is necessary when evaluating the description of some landmarks, such as trees and buildings, that are given in this volume or on some of the older charts. New buildings may have been erected and old trees or houses destroyed, so that such marks, which may at one time have been conspicuous on account of their isolation, shape or colour, may now be difficult to identify or no longer exist.

Beacons
1.23

1   A beacon is a fixed artificial navigation mark which can be recognised by means of its shape, colour, pattern or topmark; it may carry a light, radar reflector or other navigational aid. In the US unlit aids are known as daybeacons.

Daymarks
1.24

1   The term daymark refers to a large unlit beacon but the term is also used to denote a topmark or other distinguishing mark or shape incorporated into a beacon, light-buoy or buoy.

2   Daybeacons in the US are used where navigation at night is negligible or where the conditions are such that it is impractical to operate a light. Reflective material is applied to daybeacons to improve their identification at night with the aid of a searchlight.

The lateral system for fixed artificial aids is based on that used for buoyage.

Buoys

IALA Maritime Buoyage System
1.25

1   The IALA Maritime Buoyage System Region B (red to starboard) is in use throughout the area covered by this volume, but mariners are cautioned that in minor locations, and where navigational aids are privately maintained, non-IALA buoys and marks may be encountered.

For full details of the system see *The Mariner's Handbook* and *IALA Maritime Buoyage System*.

Radar reflectors are not charted; it can be assumed that most major buoys are fitted with radar reflectors.

Ocean Data Acquisition (ODAS) buoys
1.26

1   ODAS buoys (special) may be encountered within the area covered by this volume. These buoy systems, which vary considerably in size, are used for environmental research purposes; they are marked "ODAS" with an identification number. The large systems should be given a clearance of at least 1 mile, and in the case of vessels towing underwater gear this distance should be increased to 2½ miles.

2   As the buoys have no navigational significance, and as they are liable to be moved or withdrawn at short notice, they are not normally mentioned in the text of the book.

See *The Mariner's Handbook* for further details.

Winter buoyage
1.27

1   When threatened by ice, certain lighted buoys may be replaced by lighted ice buoys having reduced candle-power or by unlighted buoys, and certain unlighted buoys may be discontinued.

During winter months buoys may prove unreliable as they may become damaged or break adrift.

PILOTAGE

General
1.28

1   Information on pilotage procedures at individual ports is given in the text at the port concerned.

See *Admiralty List of Radio Signals Volume 6(5)* for details.

United States
1.29

1   Pilotage is compulsory for all foreign vessels and, apart from a few exceptions, US registered vessels engaged in foreign trade. It is optional for US vessels in the coastal trade, provided they are under the control and direction of a pilot duly licensed by Federal Law for the waters that vessel is navigating.

See *Admiralty List of Radio Signals Volume 6(5)* for details.

RADIO FACILITIES

Position fixing systems

Loran-C
1.30

1   The entire area covered by this volume is within Loran–C coverage. See *Admiralty List of Radio Signals Volume 2* for details.

Radio aids to navigation
1.31

1   **Racons.** There are several racons in the area to aid both offshore navigation and entry into harbours. See *Admiralty List of Radio Signals Volume 2* for details.

Satellite navigation systems
1.32

1   **Global Positioning System.** The Navstar Global Positioning System (GPS), a military satellite navigation system owned and operated by the US Department of Defense, provides world wide position fixing.

The system is referenced to the datum of the World Geodetic System 1984 (WGS84) and therefore positions obtained must be adjusted, if necessary, to the datum of the chart being used.

2   **Global Navigation Satellite System.** The Russian GLObal NAvigation Satellite System (GLONASS) is similar to GPS in that it is a space-based navigation system which provides world wide position fixing.

The system is referenced to the Soviet Geocentric Co-ordinate System 1990 (SGS-90) and as for GPS positions must be adjusted, if necessary, to the datum of the chart being used.

3   **DGPS.** Differential Global Positioning System (DGPS) compares the position of a fixed point, referred to as the reference station, with positions obtained from a GPS receiver at that point. The resulting differences are then broadcast as corrections to suitable receivers to overcome the inherent and imposed limitations of GPS.

4   Within the area covered by this volume DGPS data is broadcast from the following places:

    Penobscot (44°27′N 68°46′W).
    Brunswick (43°53′N 69°57′W).
    Portsmouth Harbor (43°04′N 70°43′W).
    Acushnet (41°45′N 70°53′W).
    Moriches (40°47′N 72°45′W).
    Sandy Hook (40°28′N 74°01′W).

5   **Caution.** Satellite navigation systems are under the control of the owning nation which can impose selective availability or downgrade the accuracy to levels less than that available from terrestrial radio navigational systems. Therefore satellite based systems should not be relied upon as the sole aid to navigation.

See *Admiralty List of Radio Signals Volume 2* for details.

Radio stations
1.33

1   See *Admiralty List of Radio Signals Volume 1(2)* for full details of all the radio stations in the area covered by this volume.

Radio navigational warnings

Long range warnings
1.34

1   The waters covered by this volume lie in NAVAREA IV of the World-wide Navigational Warning Service. The Area Co-ordinator is the US and navigation warnings are issued by the National Geospatial-Intelligence Agency (NGA). Warnings are broadcast through:

    a) USCG radio station at Boston.
    b) The International SafetyNET Service via an Inmarsat Land Earth Station (LES).

See *Admiralty List of Radio Signals Volume 3(2)* for details.

Local warnings
1.35

1   Local warnings are issued by the USCG for coastal and harbour areas. These warnings are broadcast by the appropriate USCG radio station.

See *Admiralty List of Radio Signals Volume 3(2)* for details.

Radio weather reports

Warnings and bulletins
1.36

1   See *Admiralty List of Radio Signals Volume 3(2)* for full details of all radio weather services and the stations from which they are issued.

Radio medical advice
1.37

1   In US waters the USCG will respond to DH MEDICO messages by providing advice that is immediately available or by referring requests to the International Radio Medical Centre in Rome, Italy. See *Admiralty List of Radio Signals Volume 1(2)* for details.

REGULATIONS

International regulations

Submarine cables
1.38

1   Mariners are advised not to anchor or trawl in the vicinity of submarine cables. See *The Mariner's Handbook* for information on the *International Convention for the Protection of Submarine cables.*

Submarine pipelines
1.39

1   Mariners are advised not to anchor or trawl in the vicinity of pipelines. Gas from a damaged oil or gas pipeline could cause an explosion, loss of a vessel's buoyancy or other serious hazard. Pipelines are not always buried and their presence may effectively reduce the charted depth by as much as two metres. They may also span seabed undulations and cause fishing gear to become irrecoverably snagged, putting a vessel in severe danger. See *Annual Notice to Mariners No 24* and *The Mariner's Handbook.*

Pollution
1.40

1   **Pollution.** See *The Mariner's Handbook* for information concerning the *International Convention for the Prevention of Pollution from Ships 1973 (MARPOL 1973)* and the *1978 Protocol to MARPOL 1973.*

Traffic separation schemes
1.41

1   There are a number of TSS's in the area covered by this volume, all of which are IMO adopted. See the IMO publication *Ships' Routeing* and Rule 10 of the *International Regulations for Preventing Collisions at Sea (1972)* for further details.

National regulations

United States Coast Guard
1.42

1   The USCG includes amongst its duties:
Enforcement of the laws of the US, including those of navigation and neutrality, on the high seas and in the coastal and inland waters of the US and its possessions.
Administration of the Oil Pollution Act.
Establishment and administration of anchorages.
2   Inspection and documentation of vessels.
Operation of aids to navigation.
Operation of Automated Mutual Assistance Vessel Rescue System (AMVER).
Search and Rescue operations.
Publication of Lights List and Local Notices to Mariners.
3   **Coastguard Marine Safety Offices**, which combine the functions of Captain of the Port and Marine Inspection Office, in the area covered by this volume are situated at:
Portland, ME: 103 Commercial Street, 04101-4726.
Boston, MA: 447 Commercial Street, 02109-1096.
Providence, RI: 20 Risho Avenue, East Providence, RI 02914-1208.
Group/MSO Long Island Sound: 120 Woodward Avenue, New Haven, CT 06512-3698.

Code of Federal Regulations
1.43

1   The US Code of Federal Regulations (CFR) governs all marine regulatory requirements and should be consulted for detailed information on any of the following summarised regulations, or any other US Federal Regulation. CFR extracts can be found in the relevant edition of the US Coast Pilots.
Selected extracts from Titles 33 and 50 CFR are given in the Appendices to this volume.

Pollution of the sea
1.44

1   **Oil and hazardous substances**. The Federal Water Pollution Control Act, as amended, and the Fishery Conservation and Management Act of 1976, prohibit the discharge of oil or any hazardous substance into any US waters to the limits of the exclusive economic zone. Any spillage that does occur must be reported immediately to the nearest USCG station by radio, or by an established nationwide toll free telephone number, 1-800-424-8802. Vessels are required to have on board and available for inspection an International Oil Pollution Prevention Certificate verifying compliance with Marpol 73/78 and that all necessary equipment is fitted and operational, also to maintain an Oil Record Book reporting all oil transfers and discharges.
2   **Garbage and refuse**. The Refuse Act of 1899 prohibits the dumping of any refuse into US waters. Whilst within US waters all garbage and refuse matter must be contained in leak-proof receptacles for supervised off-loading at the next US port visited.
Area to be avoided. See 5.5.
3   **No-Discharge Zones (NDZ)** have been established at numerous specific locations throughout the United States. These zones, which may or may not be shown on the chart, are areas into which the discharge of sewage (whether treated or untreated) from all vessels is completely prohibited. For further details see the US Environmental Protection Agency website at www.epa.gov.

National Marine Sanctuaries
1.45

1   National Marine Sanctuaries are established over large areas of the water and are described in the text. In general terms, the purpose of the sanctuaries is to protect and preserve the ecosystems, including marine birds and mammals and other natural resources, and to ensure the continued availability of the areas as research and recreational resources.
2   Prohibited activities, consistent with international law, include hydrocarbon operations, dumping of certain substances, placing of structures on the seabed, disturbance of marine life, and the removal of historical or cultural resources.
The principal area, within the limits of this volume, is Stellwagen Bank National Marine Sanctuary (4.5).

Navigation Safety Regulations
1.46

1   The general purpose of the US Navigation Safety regulations is to set a minimum level of navigational practice and equipment, so as to reduce the risk of casualty to vessels, bridges and other structures on or in navigable waters, or any land structure or shore area immediately adjacent to those waters; and to protect the navigable waters and resources therein from environmental harm resulting from damage to a vessel or structure.

2   The regulations require all self-propelled vessels over 1600 tonnes grt navigating in US waters to carry up-to-date charts, Sailing Directions, Light Lists, Tide Tables and Tidal Current Tables. US charts and publications are not mandatory, provided up-to-date foreign government charts of an adequate scale and foreign publications containing equivalent information are carried in lieu.

3   In general Admiralty charts and publications, including *Admiralty Tide Tables* which contain Tidal Stream Tables where appropriate, meet these requirements but the chart service does not include cover of all US ports and their approaches.

    The regulations are reproduced in Appendix IV and an up-to-date synopsis of them, with explanatory notes, is published in *Annual Admiralty Notice to Mariners No 22.*

Navigation Rules for United States Inland Waters
1.47

1   **Inland Navigational Rules Act of 1980** modifies the *International Regulations for Preventing Collisions at Sea, 1972,* for use in US Inland Waters, inshore of established lines of demarcation. These rules apply in all inland waters of the US. The COLREG demarcation lines are defined in the general information of each chapter of the text, with reference to the area covered by that chapter.

2   The Navigation Rules, International-Inland (COMDTINST M16672·2 series), are published by the US Coast Guard, obtainable on request from USCG Marine Inspection offices in major US ports, or by writing to:

        Superintendent of Documents,
        US Government Printing Office,
        Washington, DC 20402-9325.

3   Any vessel intending to navigate in US inland waters should obtain a current copy of the document mentioned above.

    See Appendix VII for further information.

Shipping Safety Fairways
1.48

1   Shipping Safety Fairways may be established by the US authorities. These fairways are lanes or corridors in which no artificial island or fixed structure, whether temporary or permanent, will normally be permitted. Use of Safety Fairways is not mandatory but is recommended.

Special anchorage areas
1.49

1   Vessels not more than 19·8 m (65 ft) in length, when at anchor in any special anchorage area, shall not be required to carry or exhibit the white anchor lights or shapes required by the navigation rules.

Communication between vessels
1.50

1   For information on the US Bridge-to-Bridge Telephone Act, see Appendix I.

Notification of Arrival, Hazardous Conditions, and Certain Dangerous Cargoes
1.51

1   For extracts from US regulations concerning Ports and Waterways Safety see Appendix II.

Regulated Navigation Areas
1.52

1   Areas of regulated vessel movement designated as a Regulated Navigation Area, a Safety Zone, or a Security Zone may be established under certain circumstances by

the US Coast Guard. For further information see Appendix V and the relevant edition of the US Coast Pilot.

    In such areas described in this volume, special regulations apply and are given in the relevant text.

Danger Zones and Restricted Area Regulations
1.53

1   A number of areas covered by this book are subject to regulations concerning danger zones and restricted areas, and are described in the relevant text. For further details see Appendix VI and the relevant edition of the US Coast Pilot.

Designated Critical Habitat
1.54

1   A designated critical habitat has been established for the Northern right whale (*Eubalaena glacialis*). For details see 4.6 and Appendix VIII.

Northern right whale Mandatory Reporting System
1.55

1   A mandatory ship reporting system is established for the protection of the Northern right whale. See *Admiralty List of Radio Signals Volume 6(5)* for details.

Vessel arrival inspections
1.56

1   Vessels subject to US quarantine, customs, immigration, and agricultural quarantine inspections generally make arrangements in advance through ships' agents. Government officials conducting such inspections are stationed at most major ports. Mariners arriving at ports where officials are not stationed should contact the nearest office providing that service.

Quarantine and customs
1.57

1   **Quarantine.** All vessels arriving in the United States are subject to inspection by the Public Health Service. Vessels subject to routine boarding for quarantine inspection are only those which have had on board, during the last 15 days preceding the date of expected arrival or during the period since departure (whichever period of time is shorter), the occurrence of death or ill person amongst passengers or crew (including those who have disembarked or have been removed). The master of a vessel must report such occurrences immediately by radio to the quarantine station at or nearest the port at which the vessel will arrive. In addition, the master of a vessel carrying 13 or more passengers must report by radio 24 hours before arrival the number of cases (including nil) of diarrhoea in passengers and crew recorded in the ship's medical log during the current voyage. All cases that occur after the 24 hour report must also be reported not less than 4 hours before arrival.

2   Any death or illness occurring during a vessel's stay in a US port must be reported immediately to the nearest quarantine station.

    Specific public health laws, regulations, policies and procedures may be obtained by contacting US Quarantine Stations, US Consulates or the Chief Program Operations, Division of Quarantine, Centers for Disease Control, Atlanta GA 30333.

3   A special signal code has been adopted internationally for the transmission of Radio Pratique messages. The code, which forms part of the *International Code of Signals,* is given in the *Admiralty List of Radio Signals Volume 1(2).*

4   **Customs.** Vessels may be entered and cleared at any port of entry or customs station so described under an individual port heading. However, entry at a customs station is with prior authorisation only from the Custom Service district director.

5   Yachts of foreign countries having reciprocal agreements with the US may be granted cruising licenses, enabling them to cruise in the designated waters of the US without having to enter and clear formally at each port visited.

SIGNALS

National signals

Naval vessels
1.58

1   Certain types of US Navy vessels that cannot comply fully with the requirements as to the number and positioning of navigation lights, will comply as closely as possible in accordance with Rule 13 of the *International Regulations for Preventing Collisions at Sea 1972*. They may also exhibit other lights such as coloured recognition lights, special coloured flashing lights, or landing lights for aircraft or helicopters (details are given in US Notices to Mariners annually). When darkened during naval manoeuvres, navigation lights will be temporarily exhibited if possible on the approach of other shipping.

2   US helicopters engaged in mine-sweeping operations exhibit a red or amber rotating beacon; the amber mode is used during towing operations.

Submarine Emergency Identification Signals and Hazard to Submarines.
1.59

1   1. US Navy submarines are equipped with signal ejectors which may be used to launch identification signals, including emergency signals. Two general types of signals may be used: smoke floats and flares or stars. A combination signal which contains both smoke and flare of the same colour may also be used. The smoke floats, which burn on the surface, produce a dense, coloured smoke for a period of fifteen to forty five seconds. The flares or stars are propelled to a height of 300 to 400 ft from which they descend by small parachute. The flares or stars burn for about twenty five seconds. The colour of the smoke or flare/star has the following meaning:

2   (a) **Green or black.** Used under training exercise conditions only to indicate that a torpedo has been fired or that the firing of a torpedo has been simulated.

(b) **Yellow.** Indicates that submarine is about to come to periscope depth from below periscope depth. Surface craft terminate anti-submarine counter attack and clear vicinity of submarine. Do not stop propellers.

3   (c) **Red.** Indicates an emergency condition within the submarine and that it will surface immediately, if possible. Surface ships clear the area and stand by to give assistance after the submarine has surfaced. In case of repeated red signals, or if the submarine fails to surface within a reasonable time, she may be assumed to be disabled. Buoy the location, look for submarine buoy and attempt to establish sonar communications. Advise US Naval Authorities immediately.

(d) **White.** Two white flares/smoke in succession indicates that the submarine is about to surface, usually from periscope depth (non-emergency surfacing procedure). Surface craft should clear the vicinity of the submarine.

4   2. Submarine Marker Buoy consists of a cylindrically shaped object about 3 feet by 6 feet with connecting structure and is painted international orange. The buoy is a messenger buoy with a wire cable to the submarine; this cable acts as a downhaul line for a rescue chamber. The buoy may be accompanied by an oil slick release to attract attention. A submarine on the bottom in distress and unable to surface will, if possible, release this buoy. If an object of this description is sighted, it should be investigated and US Naval Authorities advised immediately.

5   3. Transmission of the International Distress Signal (SOS) will be made on the submarine's sonar gear independently or in conjunction with the red emergency signal as conditions permit.

6   4. Submarines may employ any or all of the following additional means to attract attention and indicate their position while submerged:
(a) Release of dye marker.
(b) Release of air bubble.
(c) Ejection of oil.
(d) Pounding on the hull.

7   5. US destroyer-type vessels in international waters engaged in naval manoeuvres will, on occasion, stream a towed underwater object at various speeds. All nations operating submarines are advised that this underwater object in the streamed condition constitutes a possible hazard to submerged submarines.

Survey vessels and buoy tenders
1.60

1   National Oceanic and Atmospheric Administration (NOAA) vessels engaged in survey operations which limit their ability to manoeuvre, and US Coast Guard vessels handling or servicing aids to navigation, each exhibit the lights and shapes required by Rule 27 of the *International Regulations for Preventing Collision at Sea 1972*.

2   Wire drags, used by the National Ocean Survey in sweeping for dangers to navigation, may be crossed by vessels without danger of fouling at any point along their lengths, except between the towing launches and the large buoys near them. Vessels passing over the drag, when it is in motion, are advised to cross it at right angles, as a diagonal course may cause the propeller to foul the supporting buoys and wires.

3   No attempt should be made to pass between the wire drag launches while the wire is being streamed or taken in, unless it would endanger a vessel to do otherwise. In streaming or taking up the wire drag, the tension on the bottom wire is released and the floats at each 30 m (100 ft) section may cause the wire to be held near the surface. At the same time, the launches are usually heading either directly towards or away from each other and the operation of taking up or streaming may be clearly seen.

DISTRESS AND RESCUE

General information

Radio monitoring
1.61

1   The radio watch on the international distress frequencies, which certain classes of ship are required to keep when at sea, is one of the most important factors in the arrangements for the rescue of mariners and other people in distress at sea.

For general information concerning distress and rescue, including helicopter assistance, see *Annual Summary of Notices to Mariners* and *The Mariner's Handbook*.

Global Maritime Distress and Safety System
1.62

1   The Global Maritime Distress and Safety System (GMDSS) enables search and rescue authorities on shore, in addition to shipping in the immediate vicinity of a vessel in distress, to be rapidly alerted to an incident so that assistance can be provided with the minimum of delay.

2   The sea area covered by this volume lies within the Boston Rescue Co-ordination Centre (RCC).

See *Admiralty List of Radio Signals Volume 5* for details.

Ship reporting system

Automated Mutual Assistance Vessel Rescue System (AMVER)
1.63

1   The AMVER system, maintained and administered by the US Coast Guard, with the co-operation of coast radio stations of many nations, is a global ship reporting system for search and rescue (SAR) which provides important aid to the development and co-ordination of SAR efforts in the offshore areas of the world. Vessels of all nations, on the high seas, are encouraged to voluntarily send movement reports and periodic position reports to the AMVER Centre located in Martinsburg, West Virginia, via selected radio stations and coast earth stations. US Maritime Administration regulations require certain US flag vessels and foreign flag "War Risk" vessels to report and regularly update their voyages to the AMVER Centre.

2   See *Admiralty List of Radio Signals Volume 1(2)* for details.

United States Coast Guard

General
1.64

1   The US Coast Guard conducts and/or co-ordinates search and rescue operations for surface vessels and aircraft that are in distress or overdue. Coast Guard Stations have search and rescue capabilities and may provide lookout, communication, and/or patrol functions for vessels in distress. The National VHF-FM Distress System provides continuous coastal radio coverage out to 20 miles on Channel 16.

2   **Coast Guard District.** The area covered by this volume lies within the First Coast Guard District, the office of which is situated in Boston.

Coast Guard Stations
1.65

1   The following Coast Guard stations are situated in the area covered by this volume:

Jonesport (44°32′N 67°37′W) (2.8).
Southwest Harbor (44°17′N 68°19′W) (2.86).
Rockland (44°06′N 69°06′W) (2.183).
Boothbay Harbor (43°51′N 69°39′W) (3.81).
South Portland (43°39′N 70°15′W) (3.220).

2   Portsmouth (43°04′N 70°43′W) (3.284).
Merrimack River (42°49′N 70°52′W) (3.299).
Gloucester (42°37′N 70°40′W) (4.27).
Cape Cod Coast Guard
  Air Station (41°38′N 70°32′W) (4.67).
Chatham (41°40′N 69°57′W) (4.67).
Boston (42°22′N 71°03′W) (4.123).

3   Point Allerton (42°18′N 70°55′W) (4.123).
Scituate (42°12′N 70°43′W) (4.129).
Provincetown (42°03′N 70°12′W) (4.158).
Brant Point (41°17′N 70°06′W) (5.45).
Woods Hole (41°31′N 70°40′W) (5.112).
Menemsha (41°21′N 70°46′W) (5.112).
Cape Cod Canal (41°46′N 70°30′W) (5.173).

4   Castle Hill (41°28′N 71°22′W) (5.244).
Point Judith (41°22′N 71°28′W) (6.11).
Montauk Point (41°04′N 71°56′W) (6.11).
Fishers Island (41°15′N 72°02′W) (6.32).
Eatons Neck (40°57′N 73°24′W) (6.91).
New London (41°21′N 72°06′W) (6.127).
New Haven (41°16′N 72°54′W) (6.155).

5   Shinnecock (40°51′N 72°30′W) (7.20).
Moriches (40°47′N 72°45′W) (7.20).
Fire Island (40°38′N 73°16′W) (7.20).
Jones Beach (40°35′N 73°33′W) (7.20).
Rockaway (40°34′N 73°53′W) (7.24).
Barnegat (39°46′N 74°06′W) (7.40).
Manasquan Inlet (40°06′N 74°02′W) (7.41).

6   Shark River (40°11′N 74°01′W) (7.43).
Fort Totten (40°48′N 73°47′W) (7.53).
Coast Guard Air Station
  Brooklyn (40°35′N 73°54′W) (7.101).
New York (40°42′N 74°01′W) (7.101).
Sandy Hook (40°28′N 74°01′W) (7.101).

COUNTRIES AND PORTS

UNITED STATES OF AMERICA

General description

1.66

1   The United States of America, including Alaska and Hawaii, comprises fifty states and the Federal District of Columbia, and extends across the North American Continent from the Atlantic to the Pacific Ocean for a distance of about 4800 km. Except for Alaska and Hawaii, they are bounded on the N by the Dominion of Canada, and on the S by the Gulf of Mexico and the Republic of Mexico. The area of the fifty states and the Federal District cover an area of about 9·2 million sq km.

2   Washington is the capital city, in the Federal District of Columbia; in 2005 the estimated population of the city was 550 521.

    States covered in this volume are Maine, New Hampshire, Massachusetts, Rhode Island, Connecticut, New York and New Jersey.

National limits

1.67

1   The US claims a limit of 12 miles for territorial waters and 200 miles for an exclusive economic zone. See the *Annual Summary of Admiralty Notices to Mariners and The Mariner's Handbook.*

History

1.68

1   The area which is now the US was first inhabited by nomadic hunters, who it is thought arrived from Asia *c.*30 000 BC. The first (failed) European colony was founded by Sir Walter Raleigh in 1585. By 1733 there were 13 British Colonies, which were made up, largely of religious non–conformists who had left Britain to escape persecution; the French and Spanish had also founded colonies.

2   The War of Independence broke out in 1775 largely because of the colonists' objection to being taxed by, but having no representation in, the British Parliament. The forces of the British government were defeated with French, Spanish and Dutch assistance. The Declaration of Independence which inaugurated the United States of America was signed on 4 July 1776; Britain recognised American sovereignty in 1783. The first federal constitution was drawn up in 1787; ten amendments, termed the Bill of Rights, were added in 1791. The 13 original states of the Union ratified the constitution between 1787 and 1790. Vermont, Kentucky and Tennessee were admitted in the 1790s but most of the states acceded in the 19th century as the opening up of the centre and the west led to the creation of new states and European or neighbouring countries ceded or sold their territories to the USA.

3   The Civil War was fought over the issue of slavery, which was integral to the economy of the southern states but was opposed by the northern states. The northern states defeated the confederacy of southern states (South Carolina, Georgia, Alabama, Florida, Mississippi, Louisiana).

4   The US emerged as a world economic and military superpower in the 20th century and played a decisive role in the two world wars. Its economic and military (including nuclear) supremacy gave the US a key role in shaping the post–war world.

Government

1.69

1   The constitution is that of a Federal Republic consisting of fifty states and the Federal District of Columbia and of the outside territories. Of the present fifty states, thirteen are original states, seven were admitted without previous organisation as territories, and thirty were admitted as organised territories.

2   By the constitution of 1787, and as subsequently amended, the government of the US is entrusted to three separate authorities; the executive, the legislature, and the judiciary. The President is elected every four years; his tenure is limited to two terms.

3   Each state manages its own affairs and has a Governor, Senate and House of Representatives, or institutions of corresponding authority.

Population

1.70

1   In 2005 the total population was estimated to be 296 410 404.

Language

1.71

1   The language spoken is English but there is a significant minority who speak Spanish.

Physical features

1.72

1   Structurally, the US mainland may be divided into three main divisions. The Appalachian Mountains to the S and E, separated from the Atlantic by a coastal plain; the Central Plains which stretch from the Arctic Ocean to the Gulf of Mexico, and the Western Highlands, or Cordillera, which take up nearly a third of the total area of the continent.

2   There are many navigable rivers, the major ones being the Hudson, Mississippi, Missouri, and Red.

Flora and fauna

Flora

1.73

1   The natural vegetation of the US has been significantly modified by human activity, but its general nature is still apparent over much of the continent. The most notable forest is the taiga, or boreal forest, an enormous expanse of mostly coniferous trees (especially spruce, fir, hemlock, and larch) that extends from Canada into Alaska. In the E part of the United States a mixed forest, dominated by deciduous trees in the N and by various species of yellow pine in the SE, has mostly been cleared or cut over, but a considerable area has regrown since the 1940s. In the W portion of the continent, forests are primarily associated with mountain ranges, and coniferous trees are dominant. In California, the redwood and giant sequoias are to be found, many of which are protected because of their great age and beauty.

Fauna

1.74

1   The native wildlife of the US was once numerous and diverse, but the spread of human settlement has resulted in contracting habitats and diminishing numbers. In general the fauna of the states is similar to that of the N areas of Europe and Asia. Notable large mammals include several kinds of bear, the largest being the grizzly; bighorn sheep; bison, now only in protected herds; caribou; moose, called elk in Europe; musk ox; and wapiti. Large carnivores include the puma and, in S regions, the jaguar; the wolf and its smaller relative, the coyote; and, in the far N, the polar bear. One species of marsupial, the common opossum, is indigenous to the continent. A few of the many reptiles are poisonous including the coral snake, pit vipers such as the rattlesnake and copperhead, and the gila monster and bearded lizard in the SW of the US, the only poisonous lizards in the world. A great variety of finfish and shellfish live in the marine waters, and many kinds of fish are found in its freshwater rivers and lakes.

Maine

General description
1.75

1   **Area.** The area of Maine, which is bounded on the W, N and E by Canada, is 30 865 square miles.
    Population. In 2005 the estimated population of Maine was 1 321 505.
    State capital. Augusta.

History
1.76

1   After several unsuccessful attempts by both the British and the French, a permanent settlement was established by the Plymouth Company in 1623, in the area that became the State of Maine. From 1652 to 1820 this area was part of Massachusetts and was admitted into the Union as a separate state on 15 March 1820.

Natural resources and industry
1.77

1   **Natural resources** consist of minerals, agriculture, forestry and fisheries.
    Industry. Paper manufacture, agriculture and tourism are important industries.

New Hampshire

General description
1.78

1   **Area.** The area of New Hampshire is 8993 square miles. The state has only 15 miles of coastline.
    Population. In 2005 the estimated population of New Hampshire was 1 309 940.
    State capital. Concord.

History
1.79

1   New Hampshire was first settled in 1623 and was one of the 13 original states of the Union.

Natural resources and industry
1.80

1   **Natural resources** consist of agriculture and forestry.
    Industry. Electronic goods, machinery and metal products.

Massachusetts

General description
1.81

1   **Area.** The area of Massachusetts is 7838 square miles.
    Population. In 2005 the estimated population of Massachusetts was 6 398 743.
    State capital. Boston.

History
1.82

1   The first permanent settlement within the borders of the present state was made at Plymouth in 1620 and in 1628 a further settlement was made at Salem. In 1630 Boston was settled. During the American War of Independence Massachusetts took a leading part in the war and in February 1788 became the sixth state to ratify the US constitution.

Natural resources
1.83

1   Natural resources consist of minerals, agriculture, forestry and fisheries.

Rhode Island

General description
1.84

1   **Area.** The area of Rhode Island is 1054 square miles. It is the smallest state in the Union.
    Population. In 2005 the estimated population of Rhode Island was 1 076 189.
    State capital. Providence.

History
1.85

1   Rhode Island was first settled in 1636 by colonists from Massachusetts who had been driven out by religious disputes. A policy of religious tolerance was followed and by 1663 the area was recognised as a separate colony. In 1790 the state accepted the federal constitution and entered the Union as the last of the 13 original states.

Industry
1.86

1   Manufacturing is the main economic activity.

Connecticut

General description
1.87

1   **Area.** The area of Connecticut is 4844 square miles.
    Population. In 2005 the estimated population of Connecticut was 3 510 297.
    State capital. Hartford.

History
1.88

1   Connecticut was first settled in 1634 and has been an organised Commonwealth since 1637. It was one of the original 13 states to ratify the US constitution.

Industry
1.89

1   Manufacturing is the main economic activity.

New York State

General description
1.90

1   **Area.** The area of New York State is 47 224 square miles.
    Population. In 2005 the estimated population of New York State was 19 254 630. It is the third most populous state in the Union.
    State capital. Albany.

History
1.91

1   In 1603 the N part of what is now New York State was explored by Samuel de Champlain and a party of French fur traders and in 1609 Henry Hudson, an Englishman in the service of the Dutch, sailed up the river that bears his name as far as the area of present day Albany.

From 1609 to 1664 the region was claimed by the Dutch and the Dutch West India Company made its first permanent settlement in 1624 at what is now the site of New York. In 1664 the area was taken over by the British.

2   In July 1788 New York ratified the constitution of the United States and became one of the 13 original states of the Union.

Natural resources and industry
1.92

1   **Natural resources** consist of minerals and agriculture.
Industry. Service industries, clothing, machinery and metal products, clothing and printing and publishing.

New Jersey

General description
1.93

1   **Area.** The area of New Jersey is 7417 square miles.
Population. In 2005 the estimated population of New Jersey was 8 717 925.
State capital. Trenton.

History
1.94

1   New Jersey was first settled in the early 1600s and was one of the original 13 states to ratify the US constitution.

Industry
1.95

1   Manufacturing is the most important economic activity.

PRINCIPAL PORTS, HARBOURS AND ANCHORAGES
1.96

Place and position	Remarks
1 **Maine**	
Bar Harbor (2.69) (44°24'N 68°12'W)	Port of entry. Summer resort and yachting centre.
Rockland Harbor (2.177) (44°05'N 69°06'W)	Port of entry. Commercial and fishing port. Anchorage.
Belfast Harbor (2.194) (44°26'N 69°00'W)	Port of entry. Fishing port and yachting centre.
2 Searsport Harbor (2.199) (44°27'N 68°54'W)	Commercial port.
Bangor (2.239) (44°48'N 68°46'W)	Port of entry. Commercial port.
Bath (3.108) (43°54'N 69°49'W)	Port of entry. Repair shipyard.
Portland (3.188) (43°39'N 70°14'W)	Port of entry. Major commercial port. Cruise ship terminal.
3 **New Hampshire**	
Portsmouth (3.250) (43°04'N 70°45'W)	Major commercial port. USN naval base.

Place and position	Remarks
Massachusetts	
Gloucester (4.15) (42°36'N 70°40'W)	Port of entry. Major fishing port. Harbour of refuge.
4 Salem (4.41) (42°31'N 70°52'W)	Port of entry. Commercial port.
Boston (4.76) (42°22'N 71°02'W)	Port of entry. Largest commercial port in New England.
Provincetown (4.151) (42°03'N 70°11'W)	Harbour of refuge. Fishing port and holiday resort.
5 Vineyard Haven (5.84) (41°28'N 70°35'W)	Harbour of refuge.
New Bedford (5.187) (41°38'N 70°55'W)	Port of entry. Commercial port.
Fall River (5.316) (41°41'N 71°10'W)	Port of entry. Commercial port.
6 **Rhode Island**	
Newport (5.255) (41°29'N 71°20'W)	Port of entry. Harbour of refuge. Summer resort. USN naval base.
Providence (5.277) (41°48'N 71°23'W)	Port of entry. Major commercial port.
7 **Connecticut**	
New London (6.97) (41°21'N 72°05'W)	Port of entry. Commercial port. USN naval base.
New Haven (6.128) (41°15'N 72°55'W)	Port of entry. Harbour of refuge. Major commercial port.
Bridgeport (6.156) (41°10'N 73°11'W)	Port of entry. Commercial port.
8 **New York**	
New York (7.78) (40°41'N 74°02'W)	Port of entry. Largest commercial port on E coast of United States.

PORT SERVICES SUMMARY

Docking facilities
1.97

1   **Rockland**
      Patent slip. Maximum size of vessel: length 68 m, 1200 tonnes (2.183).
    Portland
      Dry dock. Length 257 m width 42 m, depth over sill 14·3 m (3.216).

2   **Gloucester**
      Patent slip. Maximum size of vessel: length 44 m, 600 tonnes (4.27).
    Boston
      South Boston. Largest graving dock: length 358 m, depth over sill 10·9 m (4.119).
      Patent slip. Largest vessel: length 55 m, 1000 tonnes (4.119).

3   **Hyannis**
      Patent slip. Largest vessel: length 43 m (5.65).

New Bedford

Patent slip. Largest vessel: length 100 m (5.212).

Newport

Patent slip. Largest vessel: length 100 m, 6·6 m draught (5.262).

4 **New London**

Floating dock. Lift 10 000 tonnes; length 91 m, width 33·5 m (6.123).

New York

Brooklyn. Graving dock: length 332·8 m, width 43·6 m (7.97).

Brooklyn. Largest floating dock: Lift 16 000 tonnes; length 176·8 m, width 30·5 m (7.97).

5 Staten Island. Largest floating dock: lift 8 000 tonnes; length 147·8 m; width 35·6 m (7.97).

Other facilities

Salvage services
1.98

1 New York.

Deratting
1.99

1 Deratting services, deratting certificates and deratting exemption certificates may be obtained at:

Boston.

New York.

By special arrangement deratting certificates and exemption certificates may be obtained at certain smaller ports in the United States depending on the availability of inspectional manpower and resources.

Degaussing range
1.100

1 New London (6.124).

Measured distances
1.101

1 Whaleboat Island, Casco Bay (43°45′N 70°03′W) (3.143). Privately maintained.

Gloucester Harbour (42°35′N 70°41′W) (4.18).

Port Jefferson Harbor, Long Island Sound (40°58′N 73°05′W) (6.218).

2 Eatons Neck, Long Island Sound (40°57′N 73°26′W) (6.272).

Atlantic Highlands, Sandy Hook Bay (40°25′N 74°02′W) (7.104).

NATURAL CONDITIONS

MARITIME TOPOGRAPHY

General remarks
1.102

1   The coast of the United States covered by this volume was largely shaped by the pressure of ice during the glacial period and its subsequent retreat; the offshore islands from New York to Cape Cod are disconnected fragments of the coastal plain, the intervening strata having sunk under pressure.

Seabed
1.103

1   The continental shelf bordering this part of the coast extends between 70 and 110 miles offshore to the vicinity of the 180 m (100 fm) depth contour and then drops steeply at a gradient of about 1:7 and then more moderately at about 1:15 to the North American Basin which stretches E to the Mid Atlantic Ridge. A ridge of sea mounts, rising to a least depth of 1400 m (770 fm) extends SE from Georges Bank for nearly 600 miles.

2   The NW part of the North American Basin is comprised of mud and sand; on the continental shelf NE of Cape Cod, the bottom is mud, sand and gravel, while SW of that peninsula the bottom is mainly sand.

The continental slope and continental shelf as defined by the 180 m (100 fm) line, is penetrated by deeper water extending into the Gulf of Maine to within 20 miles of the shore in places. Farther SW the shelf is indented by numerous submarine canyons. See 5.4 and 7.7.

Seismic and volcanic activity
1.104

1   Earthquakes of shallow depth have been felt on the continental shelf NE of Cape Cod and in the vicinity of Long Island.

There are no known active volcanoes in the area covered by this volume.

CURRENTS, TIDAL STREAMS AND FLOW

General information

General
1.105

1   The currents in the area covered by this volume are generally neither strong nor constant, and are mainly the result of strong or persistent winds and the SW extension of the Labrador Current. The mean rate of the currents over the whole of the area is between ½ and ¾ kn, with less than 15% of observations reporting 1 kn and only a very few exceeding 2 kn.

Current Diagrams
1.106

1   In the current diagram (1.106), arrows indicating the predominant direction and constancy are shown, which are defined as follows:

Predominant direction. The mean direction within a continuous 90° sector containing the highest proportion of observations from all sectors.

2   **Constancy** is a measure of its persistence, eg Low constancy implies marked variability in rate and, particularly, direction.

Labrador Current
1.107

1   The predominant current over the greater part of the area is a SW extension of the Labrador Current which rounds Newfoundland and sets close inshore and parallel to the coasts of Nova Scotia and the NE States of the United States. Within the Gulf of Maine there is a weak anti-clockwise set to the current.

2   In the SE of the area, branches of the Labrador Current successively leave the SE flank of the main flow and set S and then SE to converge, outside the area of this volume, with the NW flank of the Gulf Stream.

Gulf Stream
1.108

1   On some occasions the Labrador Current to the SE of about 40°N 72°W is displaced by branches or eddies from the Gulf Stream. Due to the marked sea temperature gradients that result, currents of 1 to 2 kn setting between NE and SE may be experienced, and may persist for several weeks.

Effects of strong winds
1.109

1   After prolonged periods of strong winds from a constant direction, a wind-drift current may be generated, the rate of which varies according to the wind speed and direction. These wind-drift currents may reduce or enhance the main underlying current. For further information on how currents are influenced by wind, tropical storms, pressure gradient and topography, see *The Mariner's Handbook*.

2   Rates of 2 kn or over are possible on the relatively infrequent occasions when a hurricane or extra-tropical storm affects the area, and particularly when such a storm nears the coast.

SEA LEVEL AND TIDES

Sea level
1.110

1   Tidal, meteorological and seasonal factors acting individually or in combination, may give rise to abnormally high or low water levels. See *The Mariner's Handbook* for further details.

Tidal ranges
1.111

1   In the N half of the area covered by this volume the spring range is between 3·4 and 4·5 m. This decreases to about 1·5 m in the S half of the area.

SEA AND SWELL

General remarks
1.112

1   For general information on sea and swell see *The Mariner's Handbook*.

Sea conditions
1.113

1   Sea waves are generated locally by the wind and can be very variable in direction, especially when NE-moving mobile depressions move across the area.

2   In January, the frequency of reported combined sea and swell waves of 3·5 m and over is around 5 to 10% of occasions near the coast, but steadily increases to about 20% in the extreme SE of the area. By July, combined sea

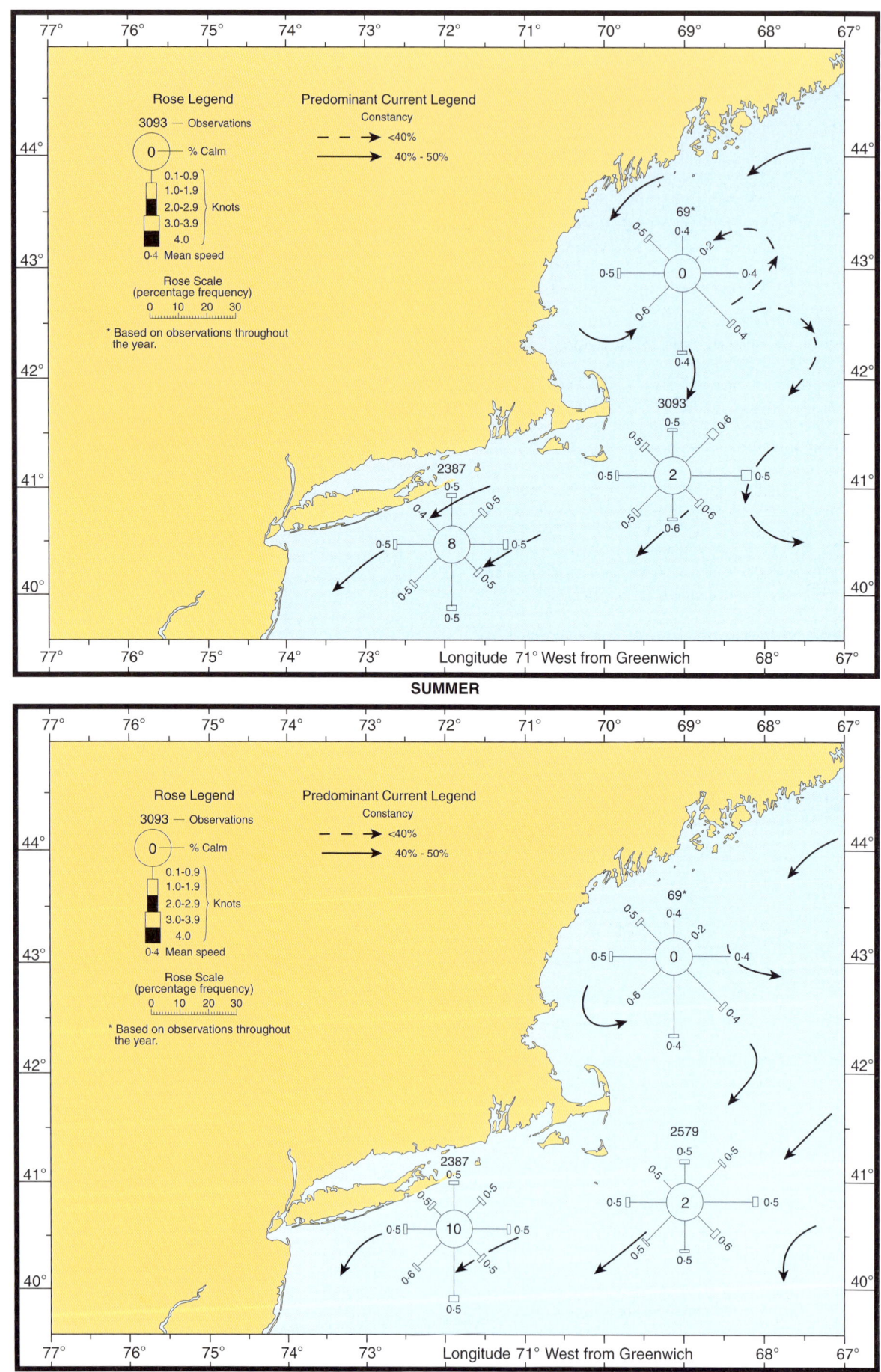

SUMMER

WINTER

Predominant currents - direction, constancy and variability (1.106)

and swell heights of 3·5 m and over are uncommon, except when a tropical storm moves towards the area from the S.

Swell conditions
1.114

1   Diagrams 1.114.1 and 1.114.2 give swell roses for January and July. The roses show the percentage of observations recording swell from a number of directions and for various ranges of wave height.

2   In winter, the swell is predominantly from the NW. Swell heights of 4 m and over are reported on less than 5% of occasions near the coast, but steadily increase to around 14% in the extreme SE of the area. By July, swell heights of 4 m and over are relatively rare, and the swell direction is mainly from between SSE and SW.

Sea and swell waves associated with tropical storms
1.115

1   Mountainous and confused seas are raised by the violent winds associated with tropical storms and hurricanes. Near the centre of a storm, groups of large waves moving in different directions, create very irregular wave heights and can combine together to give exceptionally high waves.

2   Waves travel radially outwards from the storm centre as swell waves, with the highest swell moving ahead of the storm and roughly in the same direction as the storm. When a storm approaches a coastline high tides may occur, due to the addition of the heavy swell and, later, the very high seas. These tides may cause severe flooding in low lying areas.

3   Long period swells usually indicate the approach of a tropical storm, and with increasing height as the storm nears the area.

Tsunamis
1.116

1   Tsunamis, or seismic waves, have been reported in the coastal region of Penobscot Bay, between Portland and Cape Ann and off Narragansett Bay.

SEA WATER CHARACTERISTICS

Density
1.117

1   For an explanation of density as applied to sea water, see *The Mariner's Handbook*.

2   Density values for the area covered by this volume vary across the area with isopycnics generally running parallel to the coast due to the Labrador Current setting SE and the Gulf Stream setting NE. The isopycnics do, however, turn towards the coast in the Gulf of Maine and Bay of Fundy areas. In winter values vary from 1·02550 gm/cm^3 along the coast and in the Bay of Fundy, to 1·02675 gm/cm^3 at the SE limit of the area covered by this volume. In summer the values fall to between 1·02350 gm/cm^3 and 1·02375 gm/cm^3 at the SE limit of the area.

Salinity
1.118

1   For an explanation of salinity as applied to sea water, see *The Mariner's Handbook*.

2   Salinity values for the area covered by this volume vary across the area with isohalines running parallel to the coast due to the Labrador Current setting to the SW and the Gulf Stream setting to the NE. In winter values vary from 32·00‰ along the coast to 35·00‰ at the SE limit of the area covered. In summer the values fall to 31·00‰ along the coast to 34·50‰ at the SE limit of the area.

Sea surface temperature
1.119

1   The mean sea surface temperatures for February, May, August and November are shown in the diagrams 1.119.1 to 1.119.2. Sea surface temperatures are generally at their lowest in late January and February and highest in August. The steep temperature gradient in the extreme SE of the area is the result of the proximity of the cold Labrador Current setting towards the SW and the warm Gulf Stream setting towards the ENE.

2   Mean sea surface temperatures, in winter, decrease from 10°C in the extreme SE of the area to below 4°C in coastal waters, and in severe winters to below freezing, especially in sheltered inlets and harbours in the N. By August, the mean sea surface temperatures have risen to around 10°C in the N and 22°C in the S.

Variability
1.120

1   Mean sea surface temperatures in coastal waters can be very variable in both summer and winter depending on the airstream. Due to the steep temperature gradient in the SE of the area, the day to day variability at any one position can be considerable. In addition, the occasional Gulf Stream meanders, in the SE of the area, may result in a vessel passing through alternating areas of warm and cold water that may vary by as much as 4° to 6°C above or below the mean.

ICE CONDITIONS

General information

Sea ice
1.121

1   A complete list of ice terms and their definitions, as agreed by the World Meteorological Organisation in 1969, together with photographs of typical ice formations, is given in *The Mariner's Handbook*.

2   The area in this volume lies outside the main sea ice and iceberg regions of the NW Atlantic Ocean, which extends S from Baffin Island to S of Nova Scotia. The extreme limits of this ice and the maximum extent of icebergs are shown, by months, in *Nova Scotia and Bay of Fundy Pilot*. Drift ice, which in late winter and spring is liable to spread S off Newfoundland and also SW off Nova Scotia, has not been known to extend W of 67°W or S of 42°N.

Icebergs
1.122

1   Except for very isolated cases, icebergs are not encountered W of 67°W. However at extremely rare intervals icebergs or their remnants have been reported within the area of this volume. Three such sightings are known to have occurred since 1925.

Inshore ice
1.123

1   The severity of the winters along the coasts covered in this volume varies greatly in different years. In the average winter ice forms in many rivers, estuaries, harbours, bays and other shallow inshore localities but most of the harbours remain open. In severe winters most such locations are affected by ice and only some of the harbours and anchorages are available. An account of the ice conditions of affected areas is given in the appropriate part of the body of the book.

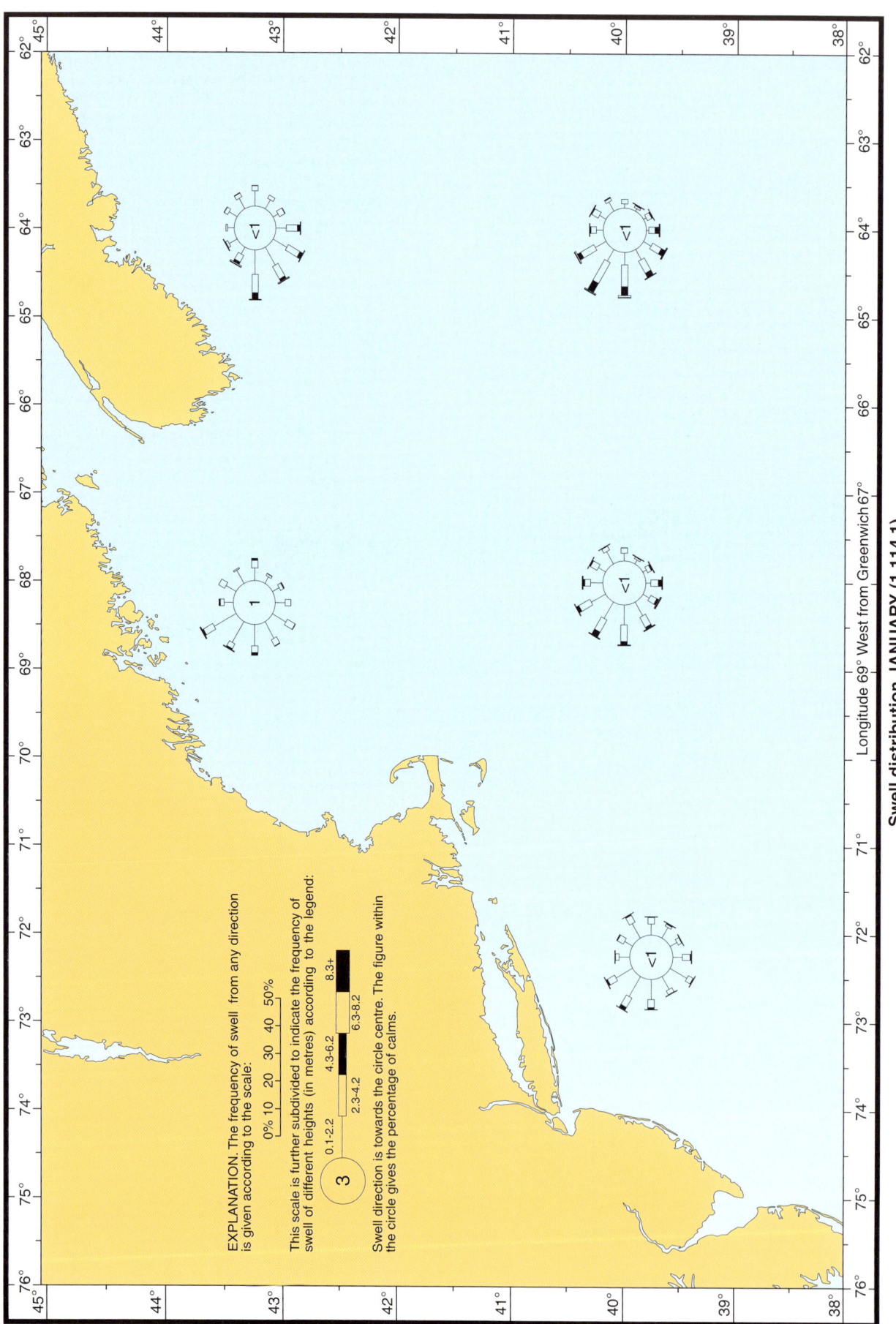

EXPLANATION. The frequency of swell from any direction is given according to the scale:

0% 10 20 30 40 50%

This scale is further subdivided to indicate the frequency of swell of different heights (in metres) according to the legend:

0.1-2.2   2.3-4.2   4.3-6.2   6.3-8.2   8.3+

Swell direction is towards the circle centre. The figure within the circle gives the percentage of calms.

Longitude 69° West from Greenwich

Swell distribution JANUARY (1.114.1)

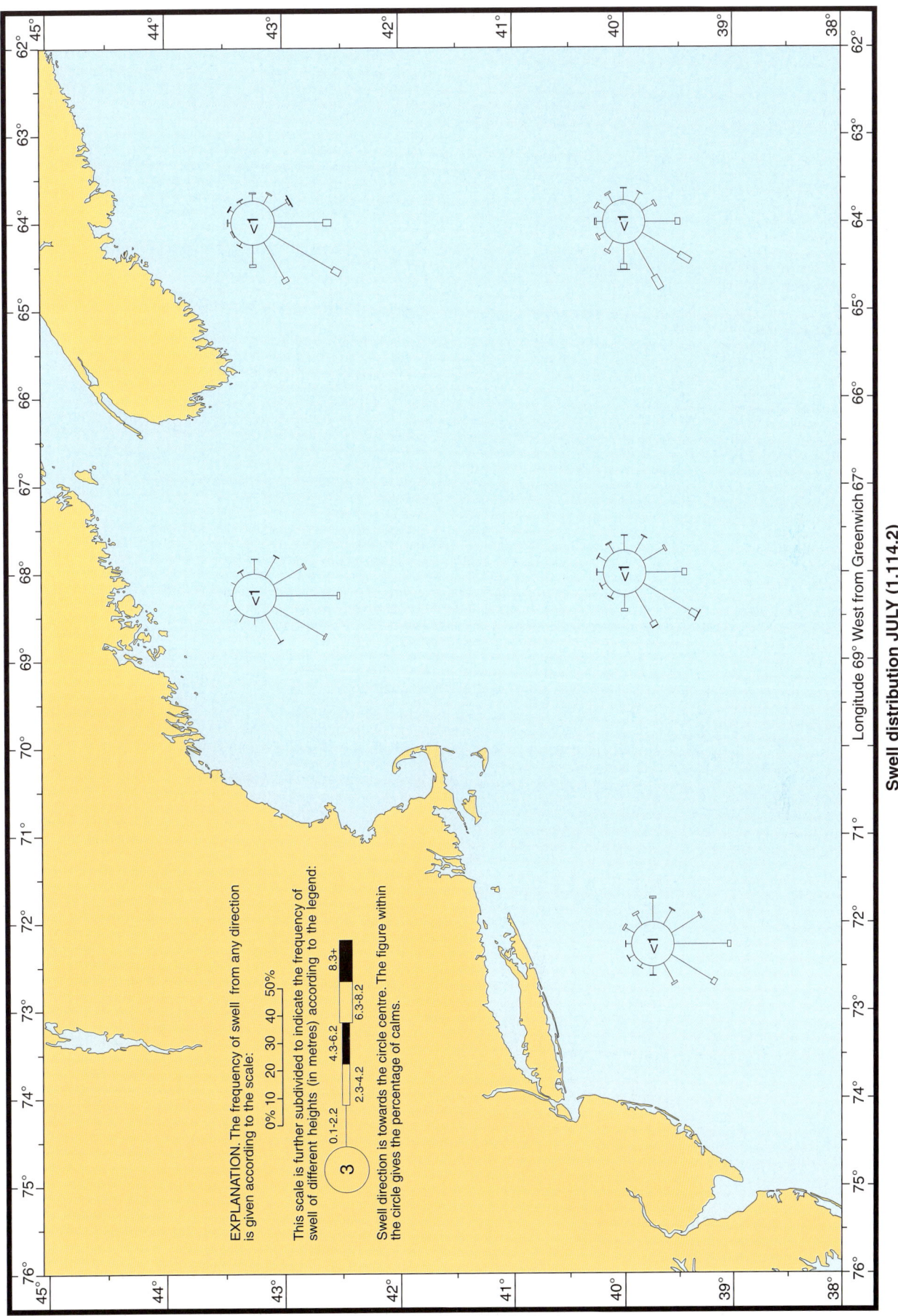

EXPLANATION: The frequency of swell from any direction is given according to the scale:

0% 10 20 30 40 50%

This scale is further subdivided to indicate the frequency of swell of different heights (in metres) according to the legend:

0.1-2.2   2.3-4.2   4.3-6.2   6.3-8.2   8.3+

Swell direction is towards the circle centre. The figure within the circle gives the percentage of calms.

Swell distribution JULY (1.114.2)

Longitude 69° West from Greenwich

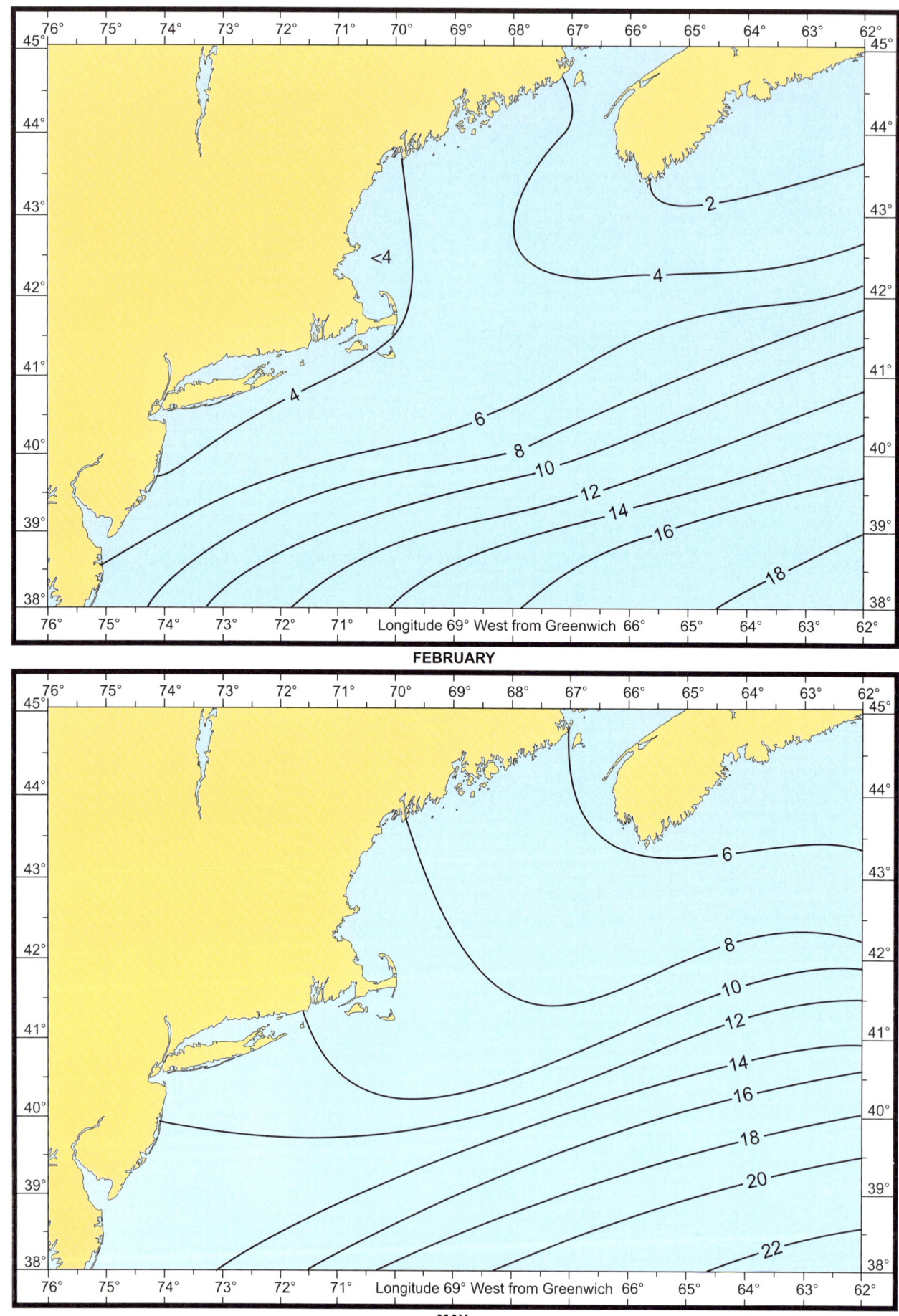

FEBRUARY

MAY

Mean sea surface temperature (°C) (1.119.1)

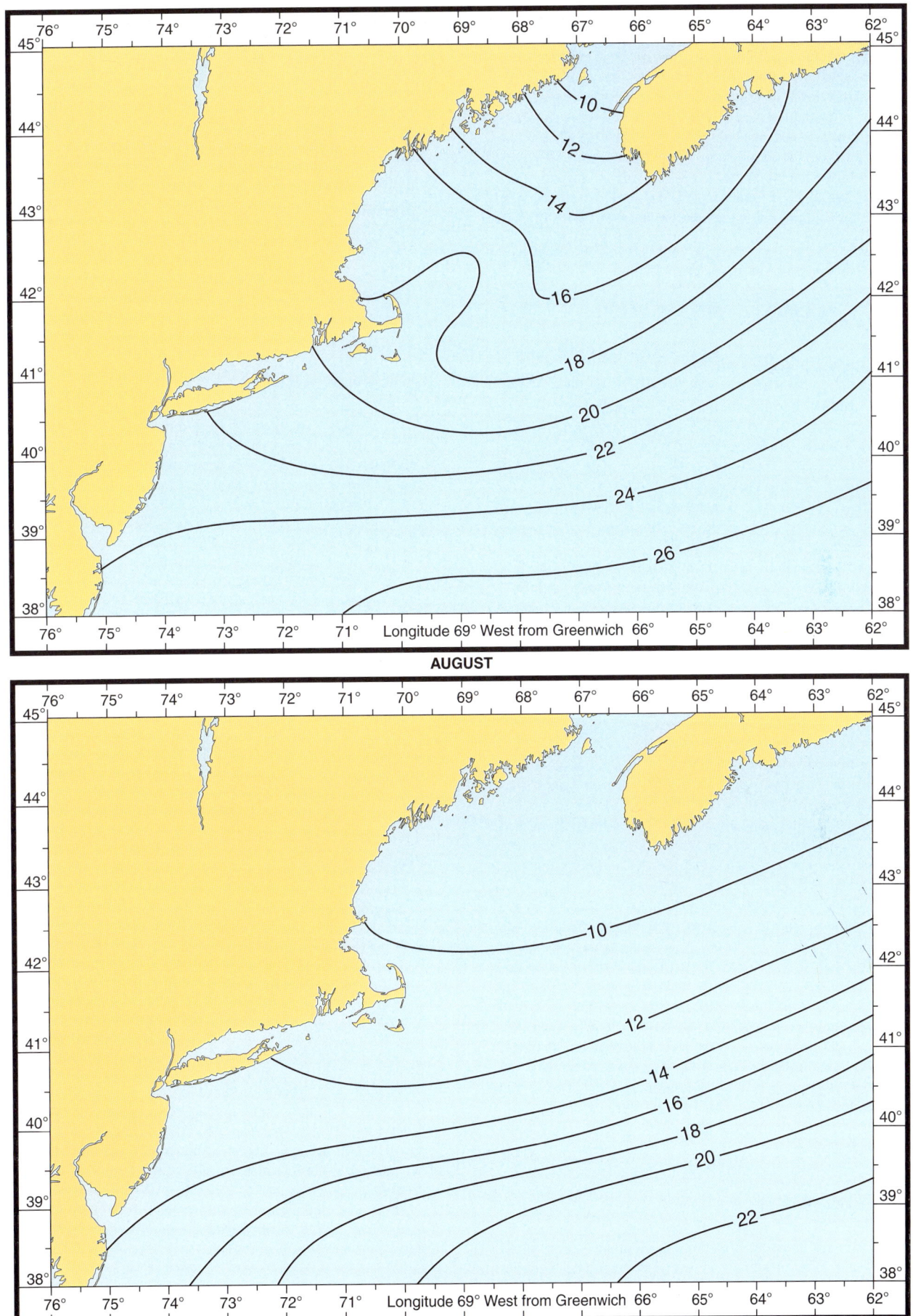

AUGUST

NOVEMBER
Mean sea surface temperature (°C) (1.119.2)

Access to ports
1.124

1   Access to the principal ports is not seriously restricted even in severe winters, but many of the smaller, more land-locked ports are liable to be closed at times. For example, Portland Harbor generally preserves an open channel due to the constant traffic. Similarly at Boston, the greater part of the harbour is sometimes frozen during a severe winter, but shipping keeps the main channel open. As an example of a smaller port, Plymouth, in Cape Cod Bay, is usually closed to navigation during a part of each winter.

CLIMATE AND WEATHER

General information
1.125

1   The following information on climate and weather should be read in conjunction with the information contained in *The Mariner's Handbook* which explains in more detail many aspects of meteorology and climatology of importance to the mariner.

2   **Weather reports** and forecasts, that cover the area, are regularly broadcast in English; see *Admiralty List of Radio Signals Volume 3(2)* for details.

3   **Ice accumulation.** In certain weather conditions, ice accumulation on hulls and superstructures of ships can be a serious danger. This is a possible hazard, in winter, particularly in the N of the area. See *The Mariner's Handbook* for details on the causes of ice accumulation and the recommended course of action.

General conditions
1.126

1   In the region covered by this volume conditions can be very variable, especially in winter, with marked fluctuations in both temperature and visibility. Mobile depressions tend to move most frequently from SW to NE across the region and are more frequent and violent in winter than summer. These depressions generally give rise to periods of stormy wet weather followed by clear dry spells.

2   Precipitation is plentiful and is highest in the NE of the area in winter. In winter, much of the precipitation in coastal areas falls in the form of snow. Fog is a problem, especially in summer, when warm moist SW air is cooled by the Labrador Current. In settled conditions in autumn and winter, radiation fog often forms over the land and may drift out over coastal sea areas, but usually clears by midday. Land and sea breezes are common in summer.

3   During the hurricane season, June to November, an occasional tropical storm or hurricane may affect some parts of the area.

Pressure

Average distribution
1.127

1   The average pressure distribution at mean sea level in January and July is shown in the accompanying diagram 1.127. Seasonal variations in the average pressure distribution are only about 3 to 4 hPa. In winter, the average pressure increases from NE to SW and, in summer, increases from NW to SE.

Variability
1.128

1   It is stressed that the diagrams depict the average pressure distribution and that the actual pressure pattern can be markedly different from the mean due to the numerous NE-moving mobile depressions that frequently parallel the coast. Changes of 20 hPa in 24 hours are common when a series of deep depressions and anticyclones cross the region.

Diurnal variation
1.129

1   The diurnal variation is about 2 hPa, and with maxima at 1000 and 2000 and minima at 0400 and 1600. This daily variation is often obscured by fast moving mobile depressions.

Anticyclones

Azores anticyclone
1.130

1   In summer, a ridge of high pressure normally extends NW from the Azores anticyclone to the vicinity of Bermuda as a semi-permanent feature. As a consequence, mobile depressions are displaced farther N. In winter, the ridge weakens and retreats E.

North American anticyclone
1.131

1   This anticyclone forms over N America in winter as the land mass cools, and, on occasions, a ridge of high pressure may extend E towards Bermuda. Whenever a ridge or high pressure cell moves towards the area in the late autumn or winter, winds turn to the W or NW and bring with them cold, or extremely cold, but relatively dry unstable air to the region. If a high pressure cell becomes slow moving over the area then NE-moving mobile depressions are either blocked or diverted farther N away from the region.

2   The anticyclone normally weakens in spring as the land warms up and the pressure falls.

Depressions

Frontal depressions
1.132

1   Depressions are most frequent and violent in winter and least frequent and intense in summer. These depressions may move into the area from the SW or develop within, or just to the E, of the area covered by this volume. Part of one of the world's densest concentration of depression tracks is to be found within the area, where the NE track parallels the NE coast of the United States between 150 and 250 miles offshore. Depressions generally move across the area, often at intervals of 2 to 3 days between November and March, and with greater speeds in winter (between 10 and 30 kn) than summer, although deep secondary depressions (see *The Mariner's Handbook* for a full description) may become slow moving within the area. As with all mobile depressions, tracks other than NE are possible.

2   In winter, depressions are most likely to bring with them gale force winds, heavy rain or snow, poor visibility and very low temperatures. Each year about 40 depressions rapidly deepen, occasionally within 24 hours, and produce waves of 7 to 15 m with hurricane force winds in exposed places. These depressions are sometimes referred to as *Hatteras* storms as they often develop to the S of the area between Cape Hatteras and Delaware Bay, and can extend

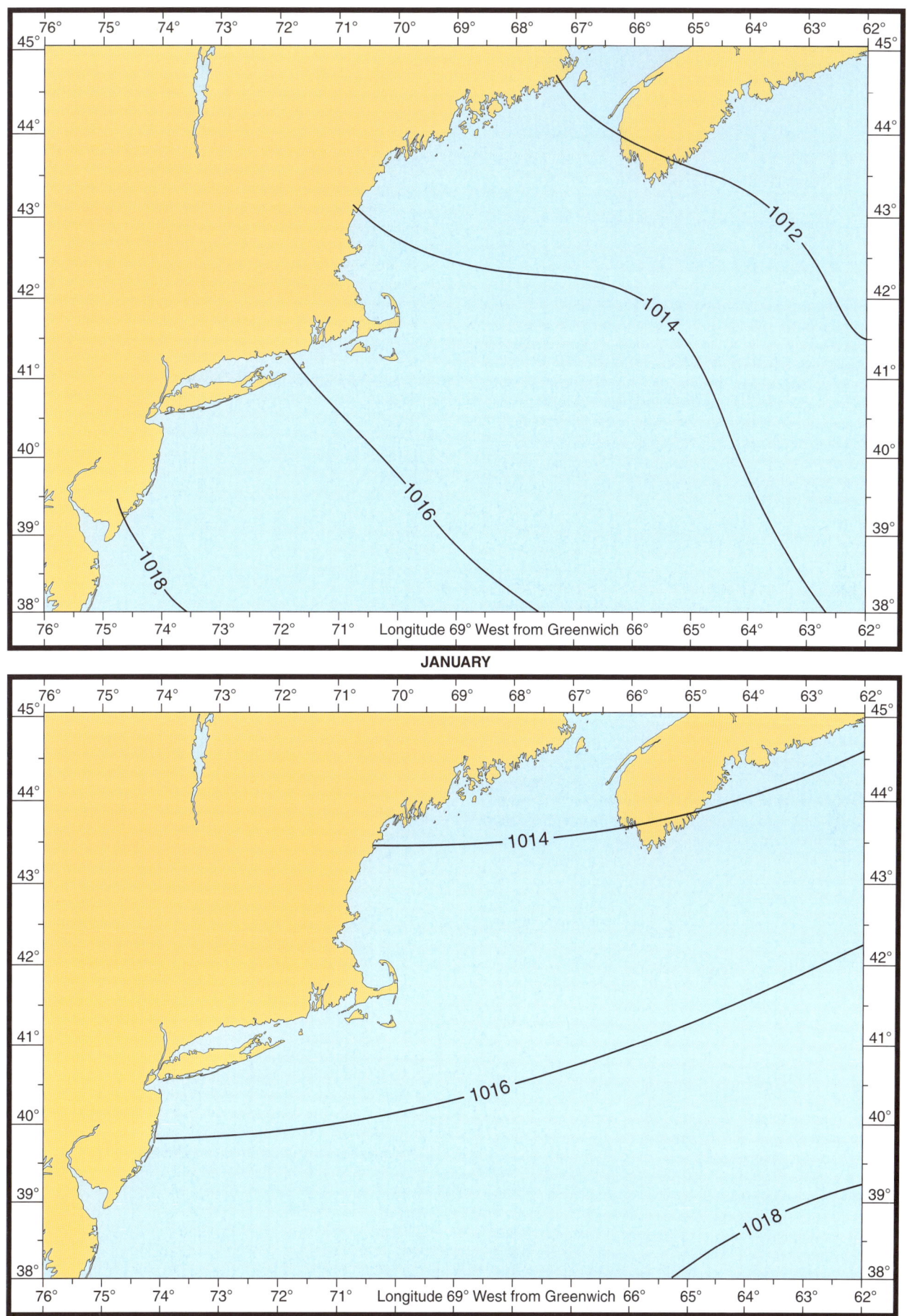

JANUARY

JULY
Mean barometric pressure (hPa) (1.127)

21

out over most of the W North Atlantic. They may give rise to storm force, or higher, NE winds in coastal waters, which often back to the SW as they move, on frequent occasions, rapidly NE.

3   Deep depressions may also give rise to storm surges which can result in unexpectedly high tides, particularly in the N.

Hurricanes and tropical storms
1.133

1   The hurricane season lasts from June to November although a few tropical storms have been recorded at other times throughout the year. The number of tropical storms generally reaches a peak during the period from August to early October. In an average season there are about 9 or 10 tropical depressions, of which five reach hurricane strength and with about two affecting the United States. Tropical storms that recurve N towards the area covered by this volume generally lose much of their strength but occasionally they may retain their original intensity. The track of any particular tropical storm can be extremely erratic but often they track NE and generally affect a smaller area than mid-latitude depressions. Tropical storms usually increase in speed to around 20 kn or more as they recurve towards the N.

2   See *The Mariner's* Handbook for a detailed description of tropical storms, signs of approach and recommended evasive action.

The Hurricane Havens Handbook for the North Atlantic Ocean which gives detailed information on the vulnerability of North Atlantic ports to hurricanes is obtainable from The National Technical Information Service, Springmead, Virginia 22161 www.ntis.gov

Fronts

Warm and cold fronts
1.134

1   Most of the mobile depressions, other than tropical storms or hurricanes, have well defined and active warm and cold fronts associated with them. The fronts mark the boundaries between the cool or very cold air of N regions and the mild or warm moist air of the sub-tropical S. They generally bring with them much cloud, rain or snow, and shifting winds. Cold fronts can move, on occasions, very rapidly with speeds of 10 to 20 kn in summer and up to 40 kn in winter.

2   See *The Mariner's Handbook* for a detailed description of the weather patterns that are usually associated with warm and cold fronts and occlusions.

Winds

Average distribution
1.135

1   Wind roses showing the frequency of winds of various directions and speeds for January and July are given in diagrams 1.135.1 and 1.135.2.

Open sea
1.136

1   Winds are predominantly from between WSW and NNW between November and March as a result of the North American anticyclone, and with the frequency of strong to gale force winds reaching a maximum during this period. Winds of force 5 and above occur on about 45 to 50% of occasions in the SW of the area and between 55 and 60% in the N and E.

2   In summer, the winds are predominantly from between S and WSW as a result of the Bermuda anticyclone, and with relatively few occasions with winds of gale force and above. Winds of force 5 and above occur on about 35 to 40% of occasions in the N of the area and around 27 to 32% in the S.

Coastal waters
1.137

1   Topography has a major influence on the strength and direction of the wind. In the more sheltered locations like New York and Providence, the offshore winds are usually greatly modified within a relatively short distance of the coast; whereas in Buzzards Bay, SW winds are often double those offshore due to funnelling. Because of this funnelling, winds in Buzzards Bay may remain SW even though the wind offshore may have veered to the W or NW.

2   See *The Mariner's Handbook* for further details on the modification of both wind speed and direction in coastal waters.

Land and sea breezes
1.138

1   Land and sea breezes affect most of the coastline. Summer sea breezes are common, particularly in the areas around New York and Portland. Depending on the prevailing wind, these breezes may reinforce or moderate the strength of the prevailing wind. Sea breezes normally set in by late morning, increase to a maximum of about force 3 to 4 by mid-afternoon and then die away by sunset. The land breeze is generally weaker and blows as a light offshore wind from around midnight to soon after dawn.

Gales
1.139

1   Winds of gale force 8 and above occur within the circulations of tropical storms and hurricanes. These storms normally develop well to the S of the area, or in the Gulf of Mexico, and can on occasions move N to affect the area.

2   Winds of force 7 or more are reported, in January, on 5 to 10% of occasions near the coast and steadily increase to about 20% in the SE of the area covered by this volume. The frequency decreases during the spring and by mid-summer the frequency falls to less than 2% across most of the area (see accompanying diagram 1.139).

3   Gales frequently develop as NE-moving mobile depressions move across the area, or when slow moving deep vigorous depressions develop in or just to the east of the area, especially during late autumn and winter. The circulations around these deep winter depressions may extend for many hundreds of miles and with winds, on occasions, to hurricane strength. Gale force winds may blow from any direction but, in winter, the most likely direction is from between SW and N and, in summer, strong winds are most frequent from between S and WSW.

Cloud
1.140

1   Due to the alternating highs and lows, that usually move NE across the area, it is uncommon for either clear or overcast skies to persist for more than a few days, except when the Azores anticyclone extends NW to Bermuda in summer to give a period of settled weather. Even then coasts may be affected by widespread summer fog, especially in the N of the area.

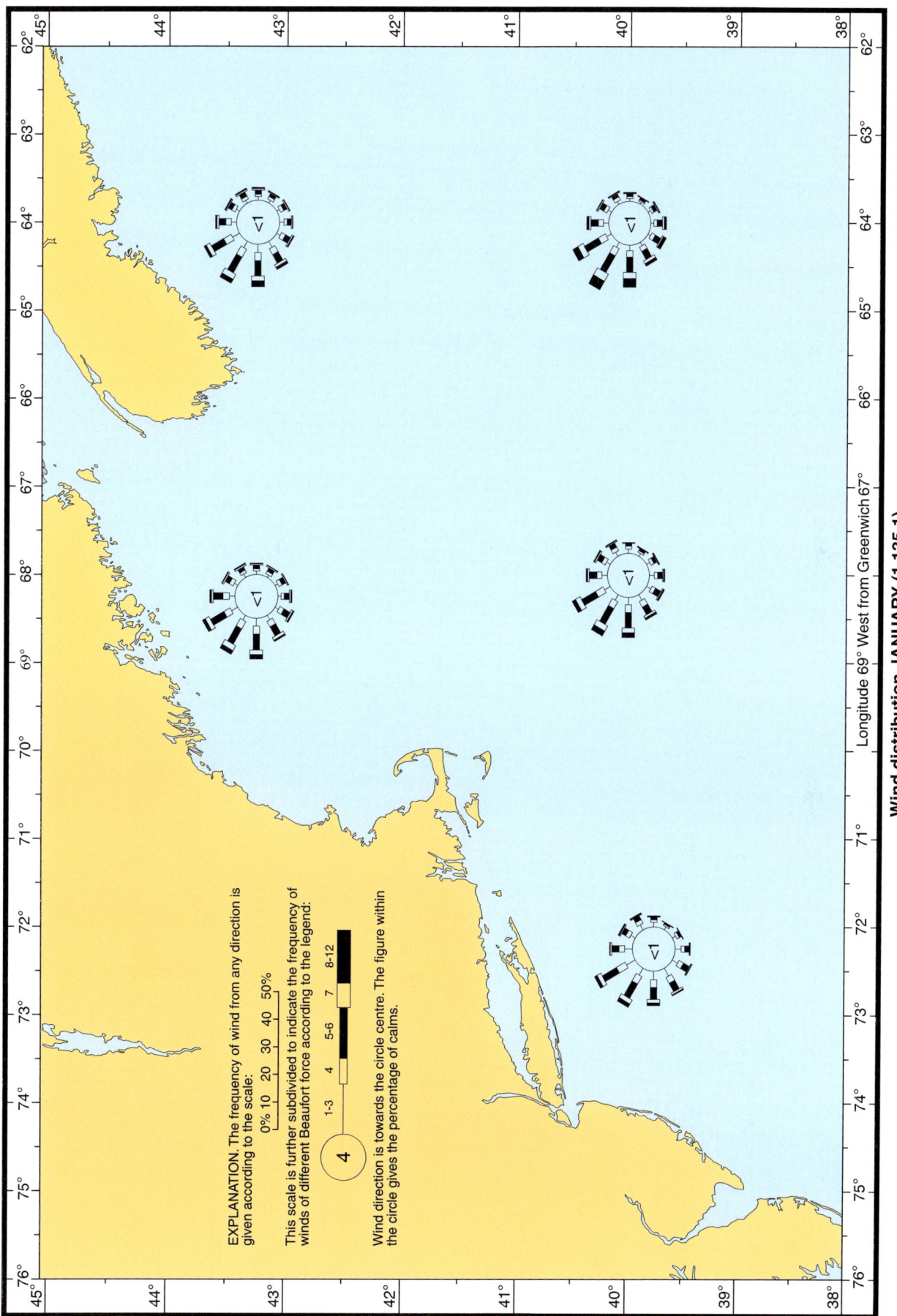

Wind distribution JANUARY (1.135.1)

Longitude 69° West from Greenwich

EXPLANATION. The frequency of wind from any direction is given according to the scale:

0% 10 20 30 40 50%

This scale is further subdivided to indicate the frequency of winds of different Beaufort force according to the legend:

1-3   4   5-6   7   8-12

Wind direction is towards the circle centre. The figure within the circle gives the percentage of calms.

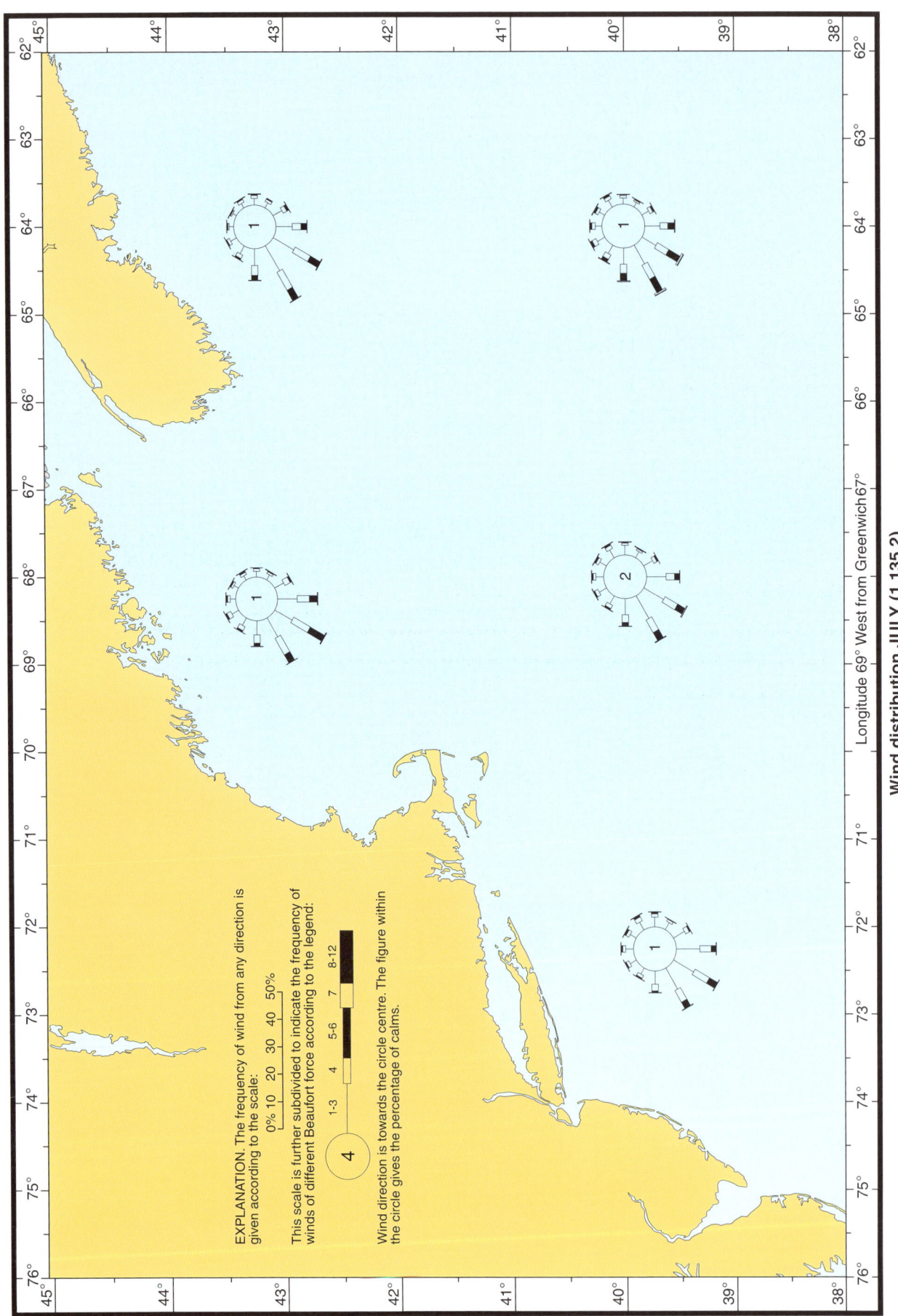

EXPLANATION. The frequency of wind from any direction is given according to the scale:

0% 10 20 30 40 50%

This scale is further subdivided to indicate the frequency of winds of different Beaufort force according to the legend:

1-3 4 5-6 7 8-12

Wind direction is towards the circle centre. The figure within the circle gives the percentage of calms.

Wind distribution JULY (1.135.2)

Longitude 69° West from Greenwich

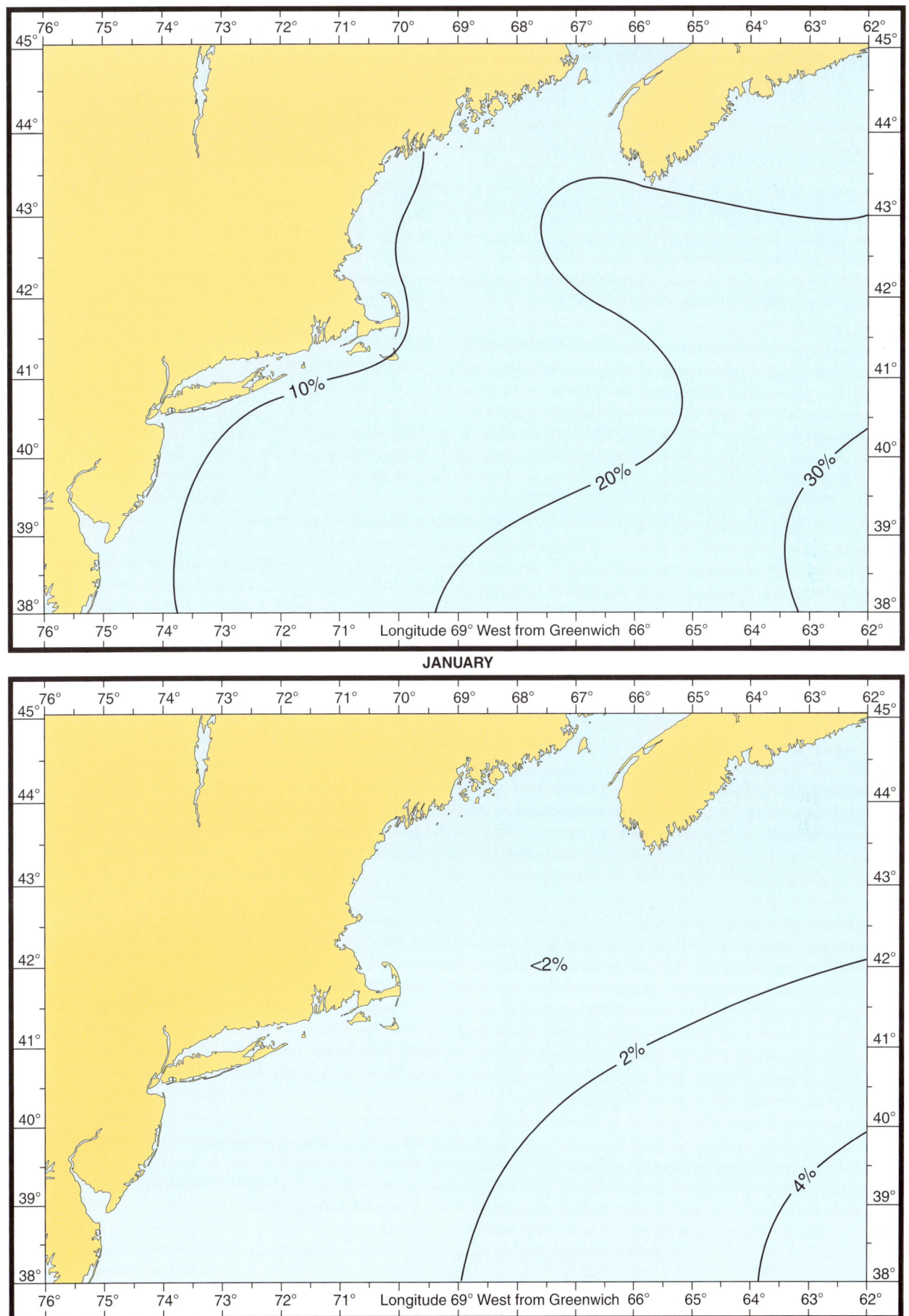

JANUARY

JULY
Percentage frequency of winds of Force 7 and above (1.139)

25

2   In mid-winter, the mean cloud amount in coastal areas is around 4 oktas in the N and 5 oktas in the SW, and increases to 6 oktas over the open waters to the SE. By July, the mean cloud amount is between 4 and 5 oktas in the N and E and decreases slightly to around 4 oktas in the SW.

Precipitation
1.141
1   The climatic tables (1.152) give the average amounts of precipitation for each month at a number of coastal stations and the mean number of days in each month when significant precipitation is recorded. In coastal areas, rainfall amounts are generally higher on wind facing coasts, and over high ground, than at sea to windward.

Precipitation
1.142
1   Rain, which often turns to snow in winter in the N of the area, can be expected in January, on about 10 to 12 days a month in the SW and 13 to 15 days in the extreme NE. In late summer and early autumn, significant rainfall is recorded on about 7 to 9 days per month in the SW and 10 to 12 days in the extreme NE.

2   Annual rainfall averages around 1000 to 1100 mm in most coastal areas and is fairly evenly spread throughout the year, although August tends to be the wettest month in the SW (Sandy Hook and New York) and the driest in the NE (Portland). The quantity and duration of any precipitation can vary significantly from one day to another and one year to another.

Thunderstorms
1.143
1   Rapidly moving thunderstorms with violent squalls are not uncommon. Around 13 to 16 thunderstorms are reported each year in the N and about 25 in the SW, but with a significantly higher frequency inland. They are relatively rare in mid-winter but steadily increase in frequency to reach a maximum in June and July. Hail is almost entirely confined to the summer months and is generally associated with thunderstorm activity. Severe thunderstorm activity may also give rise to the occasional tornado over land or waterspout over the sea.

Snow
1.144
1   Snow mainly occurs between November and April but occasionally as early as October and as late as May, especially in the N. The annual number of days with appreciable falls of snow (25 mm or more) varies from around 7 days in the SW to about 15 to 25 days in the extreme NE. Blizzard conditions are not uncommon when an active cold front moves across the area to the rear of a deep depression. The frequency of occurrence of snow over the open waters to the extreme SE of the area is about 50% of that in the SW.

Fog and visibility
1.145
1   Radiation fog often forms over low lying land on calm clear winter nights and is generally thickest towards dawn. This fog may drift out over coastal waters before dispersing by mid-morning, although on occasions it may be more persistent and extensive. For a full description of the different types of fog see *The Mariner's Handbook*.

2   Sea or advection fog affects nearly all of the area covered by this volume (see diagram 1.145) from late May to early September, although in the extreme SW, towards the W half of Long Island and Sandy Hook, the majority of fog occurs in early summer and is less persistent than that to the NE. This fog is caused by sub-tropical moist S air being cooled by the Labrador Current and is often dense and extensive.

3   The frequency of occurrence of fog increases rapidly to the N and E of Nantucket Island in summer and may persist for several days until the arrival of a relatively dry NW wind. Over the central part of the Gulf of Maine the frequency of fog is about 20% and decreases to around 3 to 5% in the extreme S of the area. In winter, sea fog is mainly confined to the N of the area with a frequency of occurrence of around 6 to 8%.

4   In settled conditions, offshore sea fog may move inshore on a flood tide or with a light sea breeze. Fog frequency often increases in summer in the approaches to Long Island Sound and Narragansett Bay; the area around Point Judith is often referred to as "the fog hole".

5   Visibility is, on occasions, reduced to near fog limits during heavy thunderstorms and on the passage of warm and cold fronts. Good visibility of over 10 miles is frequent with NW winds in both summer and winter.

Air temperature
General information
1.146
1   In general the coldest time of the year is January and February and the warmest July and August. Because of the numerous frontal depressions that affect the area, with marked changes of airstream, the temperatures can be extremely variable from one day to the next, particularly in winter. The variation between mild S air and the very cold NW winds, in winter, is more pronounced than in most other areas of the world at similar latitudes.

Open sea
1.147
1   In the extreme N of the area covered by this volume, the mean air temperature over open waters in January is about $-1.5°C$, and increases to around 4°C in the SW and 6°C in the SE. By July, the mean air temperature is about 8°C in the North and 13 to 14°C in the S. In the extreme SE of the area, the temperature gradient is most marked because of the nearness of the Gulf Stream.

Coastal waters
1.148
1   Air temperatures in the coastal waters covered by this volume, are much more variable than over the open sea. The temperature being greatly affected by land and sea breezes, and with large diurnal, latitudinal and seasonal variations. The climatic tables (1.153 to 1.160) give mean temperatures for a number of coastal stations.

2   Extreme values of 35°C are not uncommon in summer, especially in the S, and $-25°C$ in severe winters in the N. Temperatures, in mid-winter, normally remain below freezing to the N of Boston.

Relative humidity
General information
1.149
1   Humidity is closely related to air temperature and generally decreases as the temperature increases. During the early morning, when the air temperature is normally at its lowest, the humidity is generally at its highest, and falls to a minimum in the afternoon. In fog, the air is saturated with a humidity of 100%.

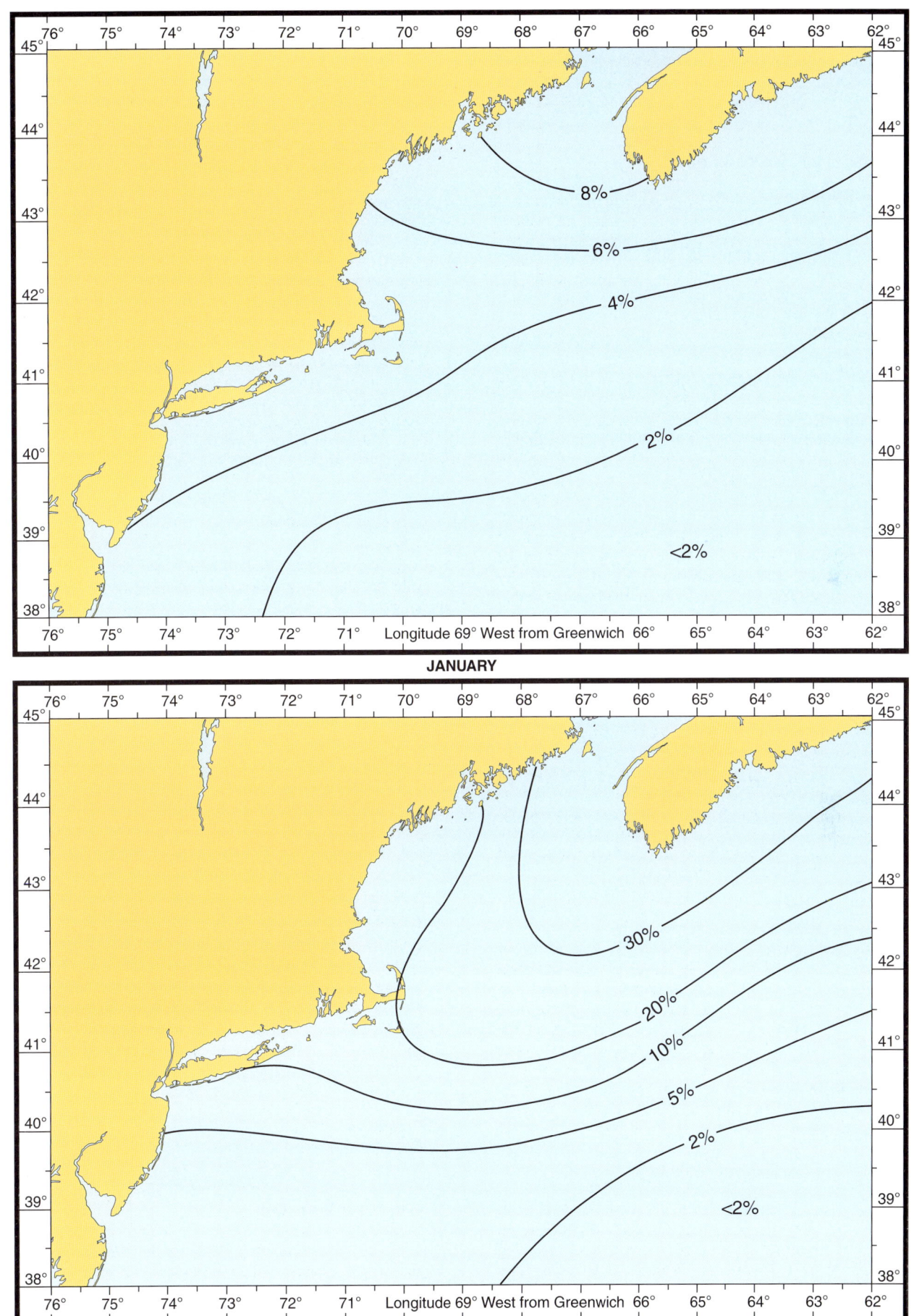

JANUARY

JULY
Percentage frequency of fog (1.145)

Open sea
1.150

1   The mean humidity is about 80% in the N of the area, in winter, and decreases to around 76% in the SW and 78% in the SE. In summer, the figures are 90, 82 and 86% respectively. Actual daily values will, however, be very dependant on the airstream and the distance from land, but with little or no diurnal variation.

Coastal waters
1.151

1   In coastal waters the mean humidity is around 80% in the early morning and 65 to 70% in the afternoon. However, large changes in humidity along the coast are possible, and will depend on latitude, the airstream, exposure to the prevailing wind, distance from the open sea and both land and sea breeze effects.

CLIMATIC TABLES
1.152

1   The climatic tables which follow give data for several coastal stations which regularly undertake weather observations. Some of these stations have been re-sited and the position given is the latest available. The positions of these coastal stations are shown on diagram 1.152.

2   It is emphasised that these data are average conditions and refer to the specific location of the observing station and therefore may not be representative of the conditions over the open sea or in approaches to ports in their vicinity. The following comments briefly list some of the differences to be expected between conditions over open sea and those at the nearest reporting station (see *The Mariner's Handbook* for further details).

3   Wind speeds tend to be higher at sea with more frequent gales than on land, although funnelling in narrow inlets can result in an increase in wind strength.

    Precipitation along mountainous wind facing coasts can be considerably higher than at sea to windward. Similarly, precipitation in the lee of high ground is generally less.

4   Air temperature over the sea is less variable than over the land.

    Topography has a marked effect on local conditions.

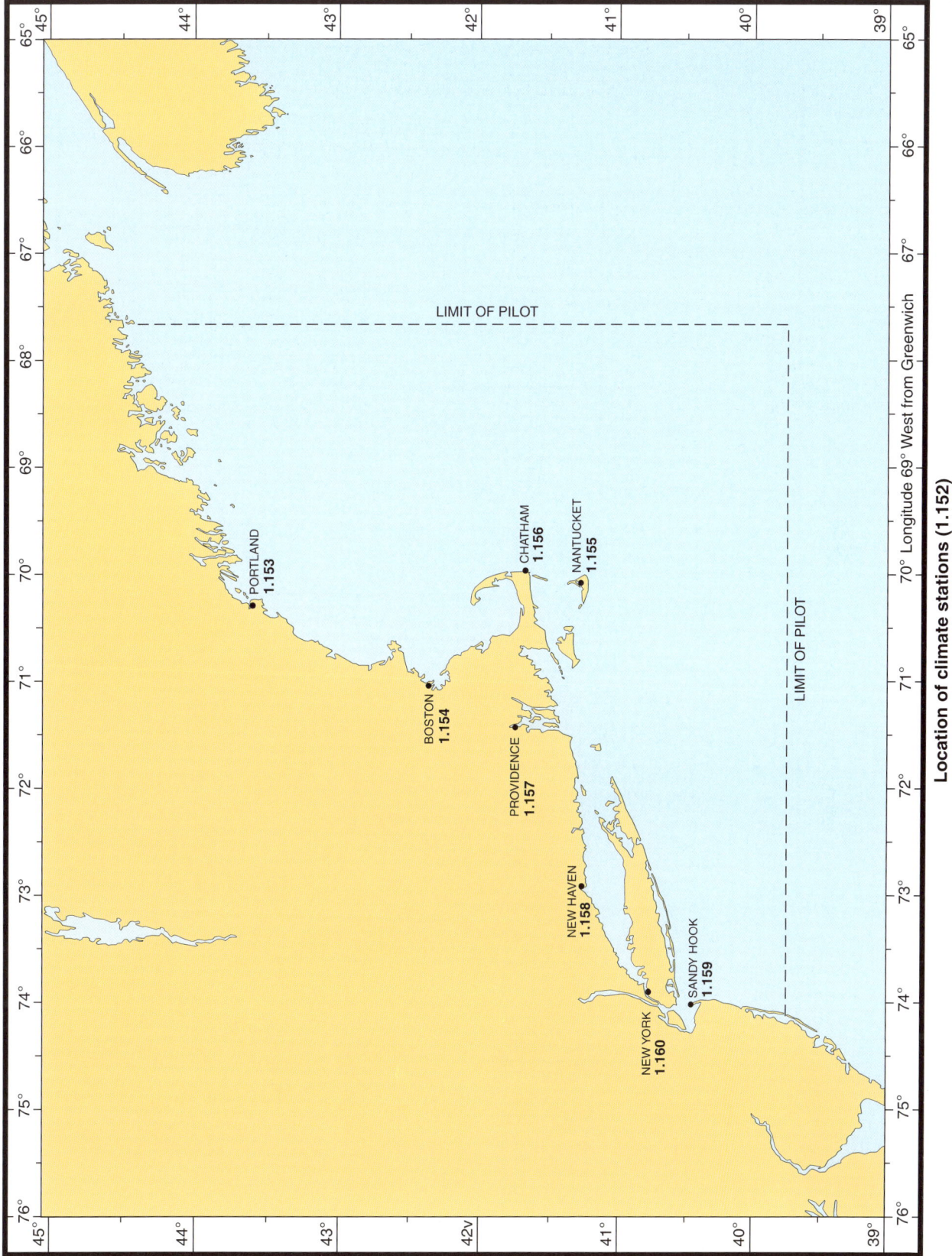

Location of climate stations (1.152)

1.153

WMO No 72606

PORTLAND (43°39'N, 70°19'W) Height above MSL – 23 m

Climatic Table compiled from 12 to 30 years observations, 1960 to 2002

Month	Average pressure at MSL (hPa)	Mean daily max (°C)	Mean daily min (°C)	Mean highest in each month (°C)	Mean lowest in each month (°C)	Humidity 0700 (%)	Humidity 1300 (%)	Cloud 0700 (Oktas)	Cloud 1300	Precip. Average fall (mm)	No. of days with 1 mm or more	0700 N	NE	E	SE	S	SW	W	NW	Calm	1300 N	NE	E	SE	S	SW	W	NW	Calm	Wind speed 0700 (Knots)	Wind speed 1300	Gale	Fog	Thunder
January	1017	0	-8	11	-21	76	59	4	4	90	9	23	5	⊕	3	5	17	22	21	6	15	7	5	5	15	12	22	19	1	6	8	1	2	⊕
February	1016	1	-7	12	-20	74	54	4	4	85	8	25	4	2	1	5	16	20	22	6	14	7	7	8	15	9	16	24	⊕	7	10	1	1	0
March	1016	5	-3	15	-14	74	56	4	5	93	9	24	9	3	3	7	11	17	21	5	13	8	10	7	28	4	11	20	⊕	7	11	1	2	⊕
April	1015	12	2	24	-5	71	54	4	5	104	9	21	15	7	6	10	11	13	15	3	7	11	16	11	34	2	6	13	⊕	8	12	1	1	0
May	1015	17	7	28	0	74	57	4	4	92	9	14	15	9	3	15	16	13	14	1	6	6	14	11	41	3	7	12	1	7	11	⊕	2	1
June	1014	23	12	32	5	76	59	4	4	87	9	14	9	8	5	11	14	22	15	4	5	4	11	11	41	6	10	12	1	6	10	⊕	3	1
July	1014	26	15	33	10	79	59	4	4	79	8	14	8	7	4	12	13	21	18	4	5	4	8	12	47	7	7	10	⊕	6	9	⊕	4	2
August	1016	26	15	32	9	82	58	3	3	73	8	18	7	6	5	11	15	17	16	6	5	3	11	11	47	3	11	9	⊕	5	9	⊕	4	1
September	1016	21	10	30	2	85	61	4	4	79	7	16	5	4	1	11	17	23	16	7	4	6	8	9	39	6	12	15	1	5	10	⊕	3	⊕
October	1018	15	4	24	-4	83	57	4	4	99	8	20	7	2	2	10	20	16	14	8	13	4	7	11	30	7	14	14	1	6	10	1	2	⊕
November	1017	9	0	19	-9	80	58	4	4	131	10	17	4	2	1	9	19	19	21	7	14	4	4	8	21	9	18	20	1	6	9	1	1	0
December	1016	3	-6	14	-15	77	58	4	4	116	10	23	4	2	1	5	21	20	18	7	19	5	4	4	12	14	21	19	2	6	9	1	1	0
Means	1016	13	3	34*	-23§	78	57	4	4			19	8	4	3	9	16	19	18	5	10	6	9	9	31	7	13	15	1	6	10			
Totals										1128	104																					8	26	5
Extreme values				37†	-28‡																													
No. of years observations	20	20				20		20		30		12									12									20		17	17	17

* Mean of highest each year
§ Mean of lowest each year

† Highest recorded temperature
‡ Lowest recorded temperature

⊕ Rare
⊙ All observations

1.154

WMO No 72509

BOSTON (42°22'N, 71°02'W) Height above MSL - 9 m

Climatic Table compiled from 12 to 30 years observations, 1960 to 2002

Month	Average pressure at MSL	Temperatures Mean daily max.	Mean daily min.	Mean highest in each month	Mean lowest in each month	Average humidity 0700	1300	Average cloud cover 0700	1300	Precipitation Average fall	No. of days with 1 mm or more	Wind 0700 N	NE	E	SE	S	SW	W	NW	Calm	Wind 1300 N	NE	E	SE	S	SW	W	NW	Calm	Mean wind speed 0700	1300	Gale	Fog	Thunder
	hPa	°C	°C	°C	°C	%	%	Oktas	Oktas	mm																				Knots	Knots			
January	1017	3	-5	15	-14	70	59	5	5	91	9	15	2	3	3	7	17	25	29	1	9	4	5	8	7	13	25	28	1	11	12	1	1	0
February	1017	3	-4	14	-14	69	56	5	5	92	8	16	5	5	3	6	18	18	30	1	10	7	9	6	5	13	26	25	⊕	11	12	⊕	2	0
March	1016	7	-1	20	-10	71	57	5	6	94	9	17	8	4	4	9	13	15	30	1	7	9	16	14	7	8	16	23	⊕	11	13	⊕	2	⊕
April	1015	13	5	26	-1	70	57	5	6	91	9	12	14	7	6	7	14	18	21	1	5	10	22	14	9	10	14	17	⊕	10	13	⊕	1	⊕
May	1015	19	10	31	5	73	59	5	6	83	9	12	15	8	7	11	14	20	13	⊕	4	9	24	22	12	9	10	12	⊕	9	13	0	3	1
June	1014	25	15	34	9	73	58	5	5	79	8	10	8	7	7	8	21	18	20	1	2	7	19	18	12	15	17	10	⊕	9	12	⊕	3	1
July	1015	27	18	35	14	74	57	5	5	72	7	10	9	4	5	10	19	22	20	⊕	3	3	20	20	11	15	19	10	⊕	8	12	0	2	1
August	1017	27	18	34	13	78	60	5	5	82	8	13	9	3	6	9	22	16	20	⊕	4	6	22	22	10	15	12	9	⊕	8	11	⊕	3	1
September	1018	22	14	31	8	79	60	5	5	78	7	15	10	6	4	7	20	17	20	1	3	7	18	16	8	19	14	15	⊕	9	12	0	1	⊕
October	1019	17	8	27	2	77	57	4	5	84	7	14	7	4	4	8	20	17	25	1	7	8	16	12	10	14	15	19	⊕	10	12	⊕	2	⊕
November	1017	11	3	22	-5	74	57	5	5	107	9	16	3	4	4	8	20	20	23	1	9	5	9	11	9	14	20	23	⊕	10	12	⊕	1	⊕
December	1017	5	-2	16	-11	69	56	5	5	102	10	15	3	3	4	6	20	20	30	1	10	6	7	7	10	14	23	26	⊕	11	12	⊕	1	0
Means	1016	15	7	36*	-16§	73	58	5	5	—	—	14	8	5	5	8	18	19	23	1	6	7	16	14	9	13	17	18	⊕	10	12	—	—	—
Totals										1055	100																					1	22	4
Extreme values	—	—	—	38†	-20‡	—	—	—	—	—	—																			—	—	—	—	—
No. of years observations	20	20				20		20		30		21									21									20		12	12	12

* Mean of highest each year
§ Mean of lowest each year
† Highest recorded temperature
‡ Lowest recorded temperature
⊕ Rare
⊖ All observations

1.155

WMO No 72506

NANTUCKET ISLAND (41°15'N, 70°04'W) Height above MSL – 15 m
Climatic Table compiled from 12 to 30 years observations, 1931 to 2002

Month	Average pressure at MSL (hPa)	Temp. Mean daily max (°C)	Temp. Mean daily min (°C)	Temp. Mean highest in each month (°C)	Temp. Mean lowest in each month (°C)	Humidity 0400 (%)	Humidity 1600 (%)	Cloud cover 0400 (Oktas)	Cloud cover 1600 (Oktas)	Precip. Average fall (mm)	Precip. No. of days with 1 mm or more	Wind 0700 N	NE	E	SE	S	SW	W	NW	Calm	Wind 1300 N	NE	E	SE	S	SW	W	NW	Calm	Wind speed 0400 (Knots)	Wind speed 1600 (Knots)	Gale	Fog	Thunder
January	1016	4	-3	12	-11	79	71	4	5	94	13	15	10	3	7	9	9	15	27	6	14	9	6	4	7	10	24	22	4	11	12	⊕	2	0
February	1016	3	-3	11	-12	80	69	4	5	87	11	23	11	6	5	4	15	12	21	3	16	14	6	4	5	14	24	14	2	11	13	0	1	0
March	1015	6	-1	13	-7	81	70	5	5	92	13	20	15	6	8	8	12	13	16	2	13	16	7	7	7	18	21	9	2	12	13	⊕	2	⊕
April	1015	11	3	18	-1	85	73	4	5	91	12	15	20	6	9	11	18	11	9	2	9	19	9	9	11	24	17	2	2	10	13	⊕	1	⊕
May	1015	16	8	23	3	88	75	4	5	88	11	11	16	7	7	11	23	18	6	2	3	16	10	7	13	29	18	4	1	9	12	0	2	⊕
June	1015	21	13	27	8	90	78	4	4	74	9	14	9	6	5	11	27	20	6	1	3	12	6	5	13	33	25	⊕	2	8	11	0	4	⊕
July	1014	23	17	28	13	93	79	3	4	78	8	12	11	6	3	12	32	17	5	3	4	9	8	4	17	34	21	1	2	7	11	0	5	⊕
August	1016	23	17	29	12	93	78	4	4	78	9	13	11	6	6	12	30	15	5	3	4	14	7	4	14	37	17	1	1	6	10	⊕	3	⊕
September	1016	21	14	27	8	90	75	3	4	84	8	16	14	10	5	9	23	13	7	3	8	18	9	6	12	24	20	4	1	8	11	⊕	2	⊕
October	1018	16	9	23	2	82	72	3	4	92	9	17	16	6	6	12	15	13	13	3	11	17	5	8	10	21	19	7	2	9	12	⊕	1	0
November	1015	11	4	18	-3	79	73	4	5	101	11	15	12	5	7	8	14	16	20	3	11	10	6	6	9	15	20	16	6	10	12	⊕	1	0
December	1015	6	1	13	-10	76	71	3	5	105	13	18	10	1	5	5	11	15	24	7	14	11	5	5	7	10	21	22	4	11	12	1	1	0
Means	1016	13	6	30*	-14§	85	74	4	5	–	–	16	13	6	6	9	19	15	13	3	9	14	7	6	11	22	21	8	2	9	12	–	–	–
Totals										1064	127																					2	25	⊕
Extreme values	–	–	–	35†	-20‡	–	–	–	–	–	–																			–	–	–	–	–
No. of years observations	20	30				20		20		30/12		12									12									20		12		

* Mean of highest each year
§ Mean of lowest each year
† Highest recorded temperature
‡ Lowest recorded temperature

⊕ Rare
⊙ All observations

1.156

WMO No 74494

CHATHAM (41°40'N, 69°58'W) Height above MSL – 16 m
Climatic Table compiled from 12 to 20 years observations, 1972 to 2002

Month	Average pressure at MSL (hPa)	Temperatures Mean daily max (°C)	Temperatures Mean daily min (°C)	Temperatures Mean highest in each month (°C)	Temperatures Mean lowest in each month (°C)	Average humidity 0700 (%)	Average humidity 1300 (%)	Average cloud cover 0700 (Oktas)	Average cloud cover 1300 (Oktas)	Precipitation Average fall (mm)	Precipitation No. of days with 1 mm or more	Wind 0700 N	Wind 0700 NE	Wind 0700 E	Wind 0700 SE	Wind 0700 S	Wind 0700 SW	Wind 0700 W	Wind 0700 NW	Wind 0700 Calm	Wind 1300 N	Wind 1300 NE	Wind 1300 E	Wind 1300 SE	Wind 1300 S	Wind 1300 SW	Wind 1300 W	Wind 1300 NW	Wind 1300 Calm	Mean wind speed 0700 (Knots)	Mean wind speed 1300 (Knots)	Gale	Fog	Thunder
January	1017	4	-3	11	-12	75	69	5	6	110		11	10	6	6	4	15	24	25	1	13	9	3	3	11	21	16	24	⊕	10	11	⊕	3	⊕
February	1016	3	-4	10	-14	75	67	5	5	100		17	11	5	5	6	13	16	26	2	20	12	5	4	7	24	11	17	1	11	12	0	2	0
March	1015	6	0	13	-8	78	71	5	6	111		16	14	5	7	7	11	14	21	3	16	18	8	6	11	15	10	13	2	11	12	⊕	4	⊕
April	1014	10	4	17	-1	80	72	5	5	99		12	15	7	9	12	16	11	16	2	12	17	9	10	13	27	5	8	⊕	11	12	0	4	0
May	1015	15	9	23	4	81	73	5	5	88		15	17	4	5	8	22	14	12	3	7	24	5	9	17	28	3	7	1	9	11	0	4	⊕
June	1014	20	14	27	10	83	75	5	5	86		8	14	4	5	9	29	13	17	2	11	16	6	4	14	39	7	5	⊕	8	10	0	5	1
July	1015	23	16	29	13	84	73	5	5	81		9	12	3	3	11	30	15	14	3	7	20	4	8	18	35	4	4	⊕	7	10	⊕	7	1
August	1016	24	17	28	13	86	73	5	4	77		13	11	4	5	13	25	10	15	4	9	19	5	6	21	29	5	4	2	7	9	0	7	⊕
September	1018	20	14	25	5	83	71	5	4	88		18	10	5	5	13	23	9	14	4	13	19	5	7	16	27	5	9	⊕	8	10	0	4	⊕
October	1018	15	9	22	3	79	68	5	4	116		18	11	4	8	13	12	15	17	2	15	13	3	10	13	25	10	10	1	9	10	⊕	3	0
November	1017	11	5	17	-4	78	68	5	5	94		15	6	4	13	9	17	18	17	1	11	10	3	7	12	22	17	18	⊕	10	11	0	2	0
December	1017	6	0	13	-10	74	66	5	5	131		14	6	4	6	8	11	21	29	⊕	16	11	4	4	6	18	10	22	2	10	12	0	2	⊕
Means	1016	13	7	29*	-15§	80	70	5	5			14	11	5	6	9	18	15	19	2	12	16	5	7	13	26	9	12	1	9	11	–	–	–
Totals										1181	–																					⊕	47	2
Extreme values				32†	-18‡																											–	–	–
No. of years observations	20	20				20		20		15		12									12									20		12	12	12

* Mean of highest each year
§ Mean of lowest each year

† Highest recorded temperature
‡ Lowest recorded temperature

⊕ Rare
⊖ All observations

1.157

WMO No 72507

PROVIDENCE (41°44'N, 71°26'W) Height above MSL – 19 m

Climatic Table compiled from 20 to 30 years observations, 1960 to 2002

Month	Average pressure at MSL (hPa)	Mean daily max (°C)	Mean daily min (°C)	Mean highest in each month (°C)	Mean lowest in each month (°C)	Avg humidity 0700 (%)	Avg humidity 1300 (%)	Avg cloud cover 0700 (Oktas)	Avg cloud cover 1300 (Oktas)	Precip. Average fall (mm)	Precip. No. of days with 1 mm or more	Wind dist ① N	NE	E	SE	S	SW	W	NW	Calm	Wind dist ① N	NE	E	SE	S	SW	W	NW	Calm	Mean wind speed ① (Knots)	Mean wind speed (Knots)	Gale	Fog	Thunder
January	1018	4	-3	14	-15	75	67	5	5	99	9										11	4	3	5	9	24	12	32	0	9	10	6	0	⊕
February	1014	7	-1	13	-15	81	58	5	5	92	8										12	6	3	5	10	22	10	32	0	9	11	4	1	⊕
March	1016	9	0	18	-10	80	57	5	6	103	9										9	8	3	7	12	22	8	31	0	7	12	6	1	1
April	1013	14	5	26	-2	70	51	5	6	104	8										9	9	5	10	13	21	9	24	0	7	11	4	1	1
May	1013	20	10	31	3	79	61	5	5	96	9										10	8	4	13	17	23	10	15	0	8	11	2	2	1
June	1011	23	15	33	8	86	69	5	6	85	8										9	6	3	13	17	24	13	15	0	6	10	1	3	3
July	1013	28	18	34	12	78	60	4	6	81	7										7	6	4	11	17	30	12	13	0	5	10	1	2	4
August	1018	27	17	34	11	84	57	6	5	92	7										9	7	4	9	18	26	10	16	0	5	10	1	2	2
September	1017	25	15	31	4	84	62	5	5	88	7										13	9	5	8	14	24	8	19	0	6	10	1	3	1
October	1019	17	7	27	-1	79	54	3	4	94	7										11	6	3	6	13	24	10	27	0	6	9	2	4	1
November	1014	10	2	21	-7	82	62	5	5	113	9										12	6	3	6	15	22	10	26	0	8	11	3	2	⊕
December	1012	5	-2	14	-14	76	58	4	4	111	10										11	5	3	4	7	22	12	36	0	7	10	4	1	⊕
Means	1015	16	7	35*	-18§	80	60	5	5												10	7	4	8	13	24	10	24	0	7	10			
Totals										1158	98																					35	22	14
Extreme values				38†	-27‡																													
No. of years observations	20	20/30				20		20		30		30																			20		30	20	20

* Mean of highest each year
§ Mean of lowest each year
† Highest recorded temperature
‡ Lowest recorded temperature
⊕ Rare
① All observations

1.158

WMO No N/A

NEW HAVEN (41°16'N, 72°53'W) Height above MSL - 2 m
Climatic Table compiled from 30 years observations, 1931 to 1960

Month	Average pressure at MSL (mb)	Temperatures Mean daily max (°C)	Mean daily min (°C)	Mean highest in each month (°C)	Mean lowest in each month (°C)	Average humidity 0700 (%)	1300 (%)	Average cloud cover (Oktas) ①	Precipitation Average fall (mm)	No. of days with 1 mm or more	Wind distribution N	NE	E	SE	S	SW	W	NW	Calm	Mean wind speed (Knots) ①	Gale	Fog	Thunder
January	1018	3	-5	12	-14	76	64	5	95	12	12	16	2	4	8	20	19	19	0	8	1	3	—
February	1017	4	-4	12	-14	79	62	5	96	11	20	18	3	6	10	13	13	19	0	8	1	2	—
March	1015	8	-1	17	-10	73	60	5	107	12	18	14	3	8	16	14	9	18	0	8	1	3	—
April	1016	13	4	24	-2	71	58	5	95	12	17	15	3	8	14	17	11	15	0	8	⊕	3	—
May	1015	19	9	29	3	72	59	5	90	12	15	13	4	10	20	17	9	12	0	7	⊕	3	—
June	1015	24	15	31	8	75	62	5	86	11	12	10	3	11	24	19	9	12	0	6	⊕	3	—
July	1015	27	18	33	12	76	62	4	106	11	14	11	2	7	24	23	8	11	0	6	⊕	2	—
August	1016	27	17	33	11	78	62	4	105	10	16	14	2	7	22	19	8	11	0	6	⊕	2	—
September	1018	23	13	31	5	79	61	4	93	9	21	17	3	7	16	17	9	10	0	7	⊕	2	—
October	1019	17	7	26	-1	78	58	4	91	9	25	11	2	4	12	15	11	20	0	8	⊕	2	—
November	1018	11	2	19	-7	78	62	5	94	10	20	12	2	2	10	23	14	17	0	8	1	2	—
December	1018	5	-3	13	-13	75	62	5	96	11	23	15	0	1	5	20	18	18	0	8	1	1	—
Means	1017	15	6	34 *	-17§	76	61	5			18	14	2	6	15	18	12	15	0	7			
Totals									1154	130											6	28	
Extreme values				38†	-26‡																		
No. of years observations	30	30				30		30	30							30				30	30		

* Mean of highest each year
§ Mean of lowest each year
† Highest recorded temperature
‡ Lowest recorded temperature
⊕ Rare
① All observations

1.159

WMO No N/A

SANDY HOOK (40°28'N, 74°01'W) Height above MSL – 7 m
Climatic Table compiled from 30 years observations, 1931 to 1960

Month	Average pressure at MSL (mb)	Temp. Mean daily max (°C)	Temp. Mean daily min (°C)	Temp. Mean highest in each month (°C)	Temp. Mean lowest in each month (°C)	Humidity 0700 (%)	Humidity 1300 (%)	Average cloud cover (Oktas) ①	Precip. Average fall (mm)	Precip. No. of days with 1 mm or more	Wind N	NE	E	SE	S	SW	W	NW	Calm	Mean wind speed (Knots) ①	Gale	Fog	Thunder
January	1019	3	-3	12	-12	78	70	5	83	11	9	11	2	3	9	19	24	22	0	14	9	4	
February	1018	3	-3	12	-12	77	70	5	78	10	10	13	6	6	10	16	20	20	0	14	8	4	
March	1015	8	1	18	-7	77	67	4	79	12	8	11	6	7	14	13	19	22	0	14	9	3	
April	1015	13	6	24	-1	75	64	5	76	11	7	12	6	9	16	16	17	17	0	13	7	2	
May	1015	19	11	29	7	77	63	4	74	11	7	11	8	10	19	17	15	13	0	11	3	2	
June	1014	24	16	32	10	79	65	4	93	11	5	8	7	11	21	20	16	12	0	10	2	3	
July	1015	27	19	34	16	80	65	4	106	11	5	10	5	9	24	22	14	11	0	10	3	2	
August	1016	27	19	33	15	81	66	4	100	10	7	13	8	9	21	22	11	9	0	10	2	2	
September	1018	23	16	31	11	80	67	4	89	9	8	14	7	11	18	19	12	10	0	11	4	1	
October	1018	17	11	26	4	78	64	4	78	9	9	11	4	5	15	22	16	18	0	12	5	2	
November	1019	11	4	19	-3	77	67	5	68	9	6	12	4	4	12	23	20	19	0	14	7	2	
December	1019	4	-2	14	-10	77	70	5	76	11	7	12	3	3	8	19	26	22	0	14	9	3	
Means	1017	15	8	34*	-15§	78	67	4			7	12	6	7	16	19	17	16	0	12			
Totals									1000	125											68	30	
Extreme values				38†	-24‡																		
No. of years observations	30	30				30		30	30		30									30	30	30	

* Mean of highest each year
§ Mean of lowest each year
† Highest recorded temperature
‡ Lowest recorded temperature
⊕ Rare
① All observations

1.160

WMO No 72503

NEW YORK/LA GUARDIA (40°46'N, 73°54'W) Height above MSL – 9 m

Climatic Table compiled from 20 to 30 years observations, 1960 to 2002

Month	Average pressure at MSL (hPa)	Temperatures — Mean daily max (°C)	Temperatures — Mean daily min (°C)	Temperatures — Mean highest in each month (°C)	Temperatures — Mean lowest in each month (°C)	Average humidity 0700 (%)	Average humidity 1300 (%)	Average cloud cover 0700 (Oktas)	Average cloud cover 1300 (Oktas)	Precipitation — Average fall (mm)	Precipitation — No. of days with 1 mm or more	0700 N	0700 NE	0700 E	0700 SE	0700 S	0700 SW	0700 W	0700 NW	0700 Calm	1600 N	1600 NE	1600 E	1600 SE	1600 S	1600 SW	1600 W	1600 NW	1600 Calm	Mean wind speed 0700 (Knots)	Mean wind speed 1300 (Knots)	Gale	Fog	Thunder
January	1019	5	-2	16	-11	68	59	5	5	77	8	13	17	5	2	4	12	20	25	3	10	14	3	2	9	12	20	31	1	11	12	⊕	1	⊕
February	1018	6	-1	17	-10	67	54	5	5	73	8	14	19	5	2	6	12	15	27	1	13	15	3	3	12	11	13	29	1	11	12	⊕	1	⊕
March	1017	9	2	22	-8	68	51	5	5	91	9	13	22	6	4	10	9	11	24	2	12	14	3	7	17	5	14	26	1	11	13	⊕	1	⊕
April	1015	16	7	27	1	69	52	5	5	96	8	10	24	5	5	10	9	11	23	3	8	13	4	8	23	8	13	23	⊕	10	12	⊕	1	⊕
May	1015	21	12	32	7	71	53	5	5	97	9	10	27	6	4	10	14	9	19	3	7	16	3	10	31	6	11	17	⊕	9	12	⊕	1	1
June	1015	27	18	34	12	71	53	5	5	91	8	9	22	3	3	10	18	11	23	2	6	12	3	9	34	8	12	16	⊕	8	11	⊕	1	2
July	1015	29	21	36	16	73	54	4	5	103	8	10	22	5	3	8	19	10	20	3	7	13	3	9	33	10	11	14	⊕	7	10	⊕	⊕	2
August	1017	28	21	35	16	76	56	4	5	95	8	13	24	4	3	11	16	10	17	2	7	13	5	8	33	10	8	15	⊕	8	10	0	⊕	1
September	1018	24	17	30	11	76	56	4	5	86	7	16	20	7	3	7	18	10	16	3	10	14	4	7	27	9	12	16	⊕	8	11	0	⊕	⊕
October	1019	18	11	27	5	74	55	4	5	77	6	16	18	4	4	8	18	11	18	2	13	11	6	6	23	11	11	18	1	9	11	0	1	⊕
November	1018	12	6	22	-1	71	57	5	5	97	8	14	14	6	3	9	17	17	20	2	8	10	5	4	16	13	17	26	1	10	12	⊕	1	⊕
December	1019	7	0	16	-8	67	57	5	5	86	9	13	13	6	2	6	13	21	24	2	10	13	5	2	11	15	17	27	1	11	12	⊕	1	⊕
Means	1017	17	9	37*	-13§	71	54	5	5	–	–	13	20	5	3	8	15	13	21	2	9	13	4	6	23	10	13	21	1	9	12	–	–	–
Totals	–	–	–	–	–	–	–	–	–	1069	96	–	–	–	–	–	–	–	–	–	–	–	–	–	–	–	–	–	–	–	–	⊕	9	6
Extreme values	–	–	–	40†	-19‡	–	–	–	–	–	–	–	–	–	–	–	–	–	–	–	–	–	–	–	–	–	–	–	–	–	–	–	–	–
No. of years observations	20	20	20	20	20	20	20	20	20	30	30	21	21	21	21	21	21	21	21	21	21	21	21	21	21	21	21	21	21	20	20	20	20	20

* Mean of highest each year
§ Mean of lowest each year

† Highest recorded temperature
‡ Lowest recorded temperature

⊕ Rare
① All observations

METEOROLOGICAL CONVERSION TABLE AND SCALES

Fahrenheit to Celsius
°Fahrenheit

	0	1	2	3	4	5	6	7	8	9
°F					Degrees Celsius					
-100	-73·3	-73·9	-74·4	-75·0	-75·6	-76·1	-76·7	-77·2	-77·8	-78·3
-90	-67·8	-68·3	-68·9	-69·4	-70·0	-70·6	-71·1	-71·7	-72·2	-72·8
-80	-62·2	-62·8	-63·3	-63·9	-64·4	-65·0	-65·6	-66·1	-66·7	-67·2
-70	-56·7	-57·2	-57·8	-58·3	-58·9	-59·4	-60·0	-60·6	-61·1	-61·7
-60	-51·1	-51·7	-52·2	-52·8	-53·3	-53·9	-54·4	-55·0	-55·6	-56·1
-50	-45·6	-46·1	-46·7	-47·2	-47·8	-48·3	-48·9	-49·4	-50·0	-50·6
-40	-40·0	-40·6	-41·1	-41·7	-42·2	-42·8	-43·3	-43·9	-44·4	-45·0
-30	-34·4	-35·0	-35·6	-36·1	-36·7	-37·2	-37·8	-38·3	-38·9	-39·4
-20	-28·9	-29·4	-30·0	-30·6	-31·1	-31·7	-32·2	-32·8	-33·3	-33·9
-10	-23·3	-23·9	-24·4	-25·0	-25·6	-26·1	-26·7	-27·2	-27·8	-28·3
-0	-17·8	-18·3	-18·9	-19·4	-20·0	-20·6	-21·1	-21·7	-22·2	-22·8
+0	-17·8	-17·2	-16·7	-16·1	-15·6	-15·0	-14·4	-13·9	-13·3	-12·8
10	-12·2	-11·7	-11·1	-10·6	-10·0	-9·4	-8·9	-8·3	-7·8	-7·2
20	-6·7	-6·1	-5·6	-5·0	-4·4	-3·9	-3·3	-2·8	-2·2	-1·7
30	-1·1	-0·6	0	+0·6	+1·1	+1·7	+2·2	+2·8	+3·3	+3·9
40	+4·4	+5·0	+5·6	6·1	6·7	7·2	7·8	8·3	8·9	9·4
50	10·0	10·6	11·1	11·7	12·2	12·8	13·3	13·9	14·4	15·0
60	15·6	16·1	16·7	17·2	17·8	18·3	18·9	19·4	20·0	20·6
70	21·1	21·7	22·2	22·8	23·3	23·9	24·4	25·0	25·6	26·1
80	26·7	27·2	27·8	28·3	28·9	29·4	30·0	30·6	31·1	31·7
90	32·2	32·8	33·3	33·9	34·4	35·0	35·6	36·1	36·7	37·2
100	37·8	38·3	38·9	39·4	40·0	40·6	41·1	41·7	42·2	42·8
110	43·3	43·9	44·4	45·0	45·6	46·1	46·7	47·2	47·8	48·3
120	48·9	49·4	50·0	50·6	51·1	51·7	52·2	52·8	53·3	53·9

Celsius to Fahrenheit
°Celsius

	0	1	2	3	4	5	6	7	8	9
°C					Degrees Fahrenheit					
-70	-94·0	-95·8	-97·6	-99·4	-101·2	-103·0	-104·8	-106·6	-108·4	-110·2
-60	-76·0	-77·8	-79·6	-81·4	-83·2	-85·0	-86·8	-88·6	-90·4	-92·2
-50	-58·0	-59·8	-61·6	-63·4	-65·2	-67·0	-68·8	-70·6	-72·4	-74·2
-40	-40·0	-41·8	-43·6	-45·4	-47·2	-49·0	-50·8	-52·6	-54·4	-56·2
-30	-22·0	-23·8	-25·6	-27·4	-29·2	-31·0	-32·8	-34·6	-36·4	-38·2
-20	-4·0	-5·8	-7·6	-9·4	-11·2	-13·0	-14·8	-16·6	18·4	-20·2
-10	+14·0	+12·2	+10·4	+8·6	+6·8	+5·0	+3·2	+1·4	-0·4	-2·2
-0	32·0	30·2	28·4	26·6	24·8	23·0	21·2	19·4	+17·6	+15·8
+0	32·0	33·8	35·6	37·4	39·2	41·0	42·8	44·6	46·4	48·2
10	50·0	51·8	53·6	55·4	57·2	59·0	60·8	62·6	64·4	66·2
20	68·0	69·8	71·6	73·4	75·2	77·0	78·8	80·6	82·4	84·2
30	86·0	87·8	89·6	91·4	93·2	95·0	96·8	98·6	100·4	102·2
40	104·0	105·8	107·6	109·4	111·2	113·0	114·8	116·6	118·4	120·2
50	122·0	123·8	125·6	127·4	129·2	131·0	132·8	134·6	136·4	138·2

HECTOPASCALS TO INCHES

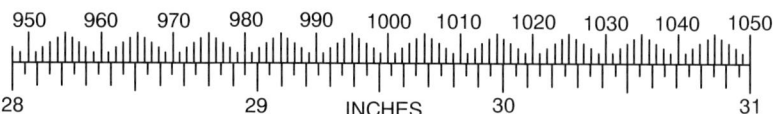

MILLIMETRES TO INCHES

(1) (for small values)

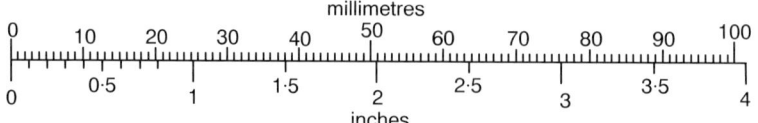

(2) (for large values)

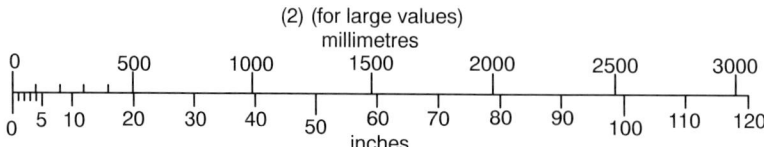

NOTES

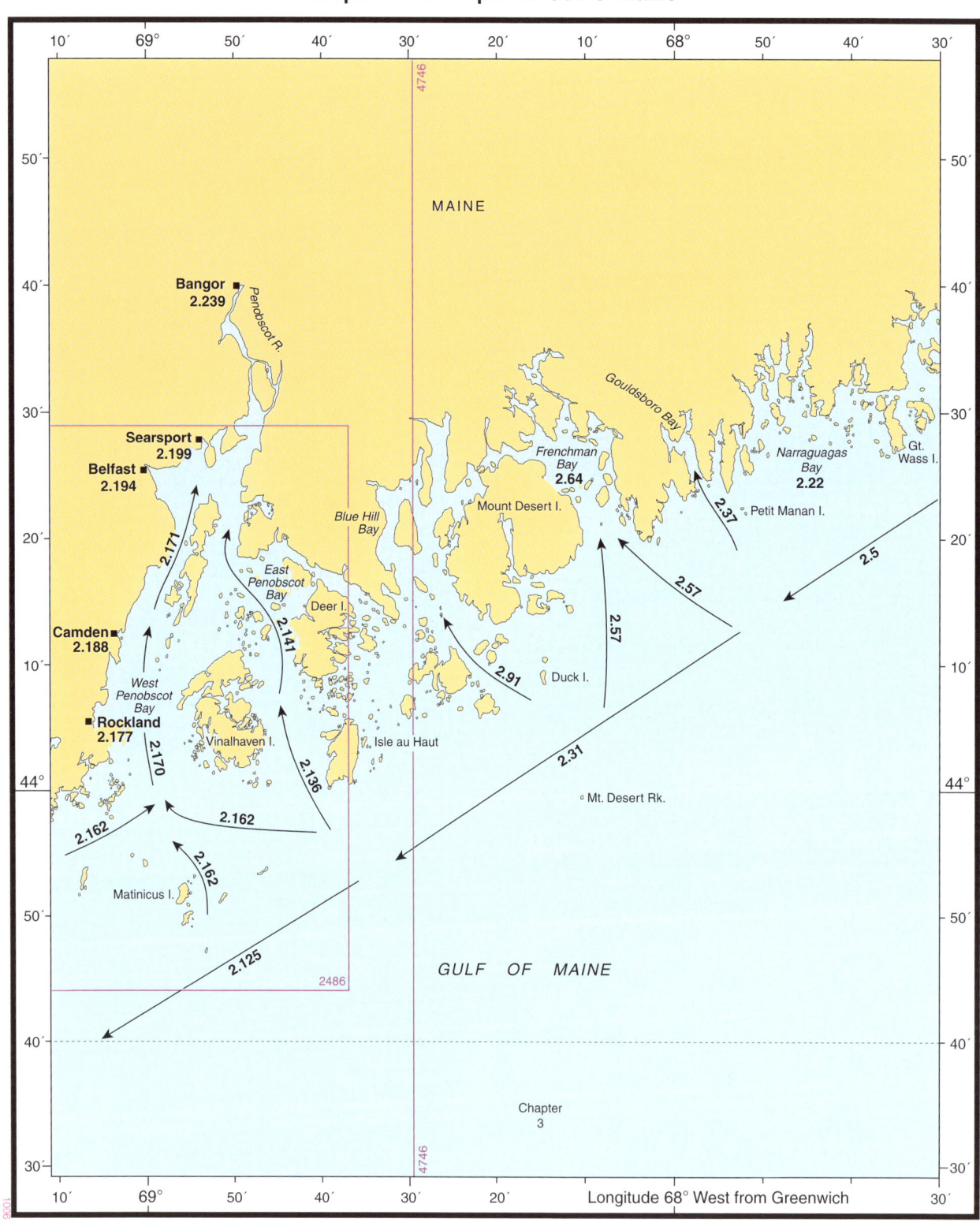

CHAPTER 2

NORTH PART OF GULF OF MAINE

GREAT WASS ISLAND TO ISLE AU HAUT

GENERAL INFORMATION

Charts 4746, 2492 (see 1.17)

Description

2.1

1   The coast of Maine between Great Wass Island (44°28′N 67°35′W) and Isle au Haut, 50 miles SW, is generally rocky and indented by bays and broken by numerous islands. Amongst these islands are inshore passages, much used by shallow draught vessels as they afford shelter and anchorage in a head wind or in thick weather. Many of the bays make excellent anchorages.

2   In its W part, this coast forms a large bight between Schoodic Head (44°20′N 68°03′W) and Isle au Haut, the centre being occupied by Mount Desert Island, which divides the bight into Frenchman Bay to the E, and Blue Hill Bay with Jericho Bay, to the W.

3   Mount Desert Island is mountainous and the highest feature on the coast of Maine. Its summits are rounded and several are nearly the same height, making it difficult to identify individual summits from a distance. Cadillac Mountain (2.57) is the highest peak.

Other features that are prominent are Pigeon Hill (44°27′N 67°53′W) (2.28), Schoodic Head and Isle au Haut.

Vertical datums and depths

2.2

1   Depths on Chart 4746 are reduced to Chart Datum which is approximately the level of LAT.

Depths on Chart 2492 are reduced to Chart Datum which is the level of MLLW in US waters.

Dangers

2.3

1   Off-lying dangers extend up to 5 miles offshore from salient points in the E part of the area, and up to 10 miles off in the W part. Mount Desert Rock (2.33), the outermost danger, is isolated and lies 22 miles S of Schoodic Head.

Caution. The numerous dangers which front this coast require the closest attention, as in many cases they rise abruptly from deep water, and sounding does not generally indicate their proximity until it is too late to avoid them.

Tidal streams

2.4

1   Tidal streams E of Mount Desert Rock are stronger than those farther W, and are more regular and conform more exactly to the rise and fall of the tides.

GREAT WASS ISLAND TO PETIT MANAN ISLAND

General information

Chart 4746 (see 1.17)

Description

2.5

1   The following paragraphs describe the coastal passage between Great Wass Island (44°28′N 67°35′W) (2.7) and

Petit Manan Island (2.7), 13 miles SW, and the inshore waters that lie between these two islands.

Directions
(continued from Nova Scotia and Bay of Fundy Pilot)

Principal marks

2.6

1   **Major lights:**
Moose Peak Light (white tower, 17 m in height) (44°28′N 67°32′W). See *Nova Scotia and Bay of Fundy Pilot.*
Petit Manan Light (grey granite tower, 36 m in height) (44°22′N 67°52′W).

Great Wass Island to Petit Manan Island

2.7

1   From a position abreast Pond Point (44°27′N 67°35′W), the SW extremity of Great Wass Island, the coastal passage leads SW, passing (with positions relative to Pond Point):
SE of Crumple Island (4 cables WSW), which is high, bare and rocky with several hummocks, thence:
SE of Egg Rock (2 miles WSW) (2.28), which is 5 m (15 ft) in height and bare, thence:

2   SE of Seahorse Rock (2½ miles WSW), which dries 1·5 m (5 ft). This rock is marked 2 cables SW by 2SR Light-buoy (starboard hand). Thence:
SE of a rock (9½ miles WSW), with a depth of 2·1 m (7 ft) over it, which is marked by DTS Buoy (isolated danger). Tibbett Rock, with a depth of 2·7 m (9 ft) over it and marked by DT Buoy (isolated danger), lies 7½ cables farther NNW. Thence:

3   SE of 6A Light-buoy (starboard hand) (12 miles SW), marking Southeast Rock, a rocky shoal with a depth of 0·6 m (2 ft) over it. A 11·6 m (38 ft) shoal lies 1¾ miles SW of Southeast Rock. Thence:

4   SE of Petit Manan Island (13 miles WSW), which is low and bare, with several buildings on it. Petit Manan Light (2.6) stands on the E extremity of the island. Simms Rock, consisting of two rocks, 2 cables apart, lies 1¾ miles SSE of the lighthouse. No 1 Buoy (port hand) is moored close NW of Simms Rock.

(Directions continue for coastal passage at 2.32)

Western Bay and west part of Moosabec Reach

Description and topography

2.8

1   Western Bay, which is entered between Pond Point (44°27′N 67°35′W) and Nash Island (2.15), 7 miles W, is encumbered with a number of groups of islands and rocks, which lie mainly in a N–S direction. Between these groups are passages, available to mariners with local knowledge, which lead to the W entrance of Moosabec Reach. For details of the E part of Moosabec Reach, E of the bridge, see *Nova Scotia and Bay of Fundy Pilot.*

2   On the E side of the entrance to the bay Fisherman Island (44°27′N 67°37′W) and Browney Island lie on foul

ground extending 2½ miles N from Crumple Island (2.7). A line of above and below-water rocks extends NE from Browney Island to Great Wass Island.

3   In the central part of the bay Outer Sand Island, 13 m (44 ft) in height and wooded, lies 2 miles W of Browney Island. Inner Sand Island, Drisco Island and Stevens Island form a group of wooded islands that lie on foul ground that extends N from Outer Sand Island in the central part of Western Bay, 3 miles W of Great Wass Island.

4   On the W side of the bay Flat Island, Green Island, both low and grassy, Plummer Island, wooded, and Ram Island (44°29′N 67°42′W), not to be confused with a larger island of the same name 3 miles E (2.9), lie in a N-S direction about 1½ miles W of the island group in the central part of the bay. Flat Island is separated from the other islands by a channel and the group is separated from Moose Neck (44°30′N 67°43′W), on the mainland NW, by Tibbett Narrows (2.10).

5   **Rescue.** Coast Guard station (44°32′N 67°37′W) is situated near the N end of the bridge over Moosabec Reach.

Passages
2.9

1   **Ram Island.** The passage that leads between Ram Island (44°29′N 67°38′W), not to be confused with a smaller island of the same name 3 miles W (2.8), and Stevens Island (2.8), though wide in its S part, is restricted by foul ground in its N part and is consequently only available to mariners with local knowledge.

Directions
2.10

1   **West approach to Moosabec Reach.** The W end of Moosabec Reach can be approached either through the passage that leads between Sands Island, Drisco Island and Stevens Island on the E and Flat Island and Plummer Island on the W, or through Tibbett Narrows (44°30′N 67°43′W). Tibbett Narrows is a narrow channel, the NE entrance of which is marked by No 27 Light-buoy and No 28 Buoy (port and starboard hand, respectively), that leads between Tibbett Island and Ram Island (44°29′N 67°42′W) (2.8). These narrows are ¾ cable wide at the narrowest part with a least depth of 11 m (36 ft).

2   **Caution.** There are patches, with depths of 8·5 and 7·6 m (28 and 25 ft), 1½ cables ESE and 4 cables ENE of the E point of Tibbett Island.

    West part of Moosabec Reach. From a position NE of Shabbit Island (44°30′N 67°41′W) the track through the W part of Moosabec Reach, which is marked by light-buoys (port and starboard hand), leads ENE, passing (with positions relative to Shabbit Island):

3   SSE of the entrance to Wohoa Bay, into the N part of which flow the West River and Indian River, thence:

    NNW of Shabbit Island Ledge (7 cables ENE), which dries 3·4 m (11 ft) at its N end and is marked by No 23 Light-buoy (port hand), thence:

4   Between Fessenden Ledge (1 mile ENE) and the N point of Hardwood Island. The former dries 0·3 m (1 ft) and is marked by No 22 Light-buoy (starboard hand). The latter is wooded and has a house on its N point. A shoal, marked by No 21 Light-buoy (port hand), extends 3 cables NE from the island. Thence:

5   NNW of Pomp Island and Norton Island (1¾ miles ENE), both of which are wooded. No 4 Beacon

marks a rock 1½ cables SW of the N point of Pomp Island. Thence:

    To the bridge crossing Moosabec Reach linking Jonesport to Beals. For further details of this area see *Nova Scotia and Bay of Fundy Pilot.*

Anchorage
2.11

1   **Wohoa Bay.** Good anchorage may be obtained in the entrance to Wohoa Bay in depths of 4 to 11 m (13 to 36 ft) between Fessenden Ledge (2.10) and Moose Neck (1¼ miles W).

Eastern Harbor
Description and topography
2.12

1   Eastern Harbor (44°30′N 67°44′W), on the W side of Moose Neck (2.8), is a secure anchorage for small vessels. The harbour is mostly occupied by flats and reefs between which there is a buoyed channel 1 cable wide.

Directions
2.13

1   From position 44°29′N 67°44′W, S of the harbour entrance, the track into Eastern Harbor leads midway between Nos 1 and 2 Buoys (lateral), marking the limits of the shoal ground on either side of the harbour entrance, and then proceeds N to the anchorage. This harbour is easily entered by day.

Berths
2.14

1   **Anchorage,** with the most swinging room, may be obtained in depths of 5 to 7 m (18 to 22 ft), 4 cables inside the W entrance point. Vessels with a draught of 2·7 m (9 ft) can anchor in depths of 3 to 5 m (9 to 15 ft) in Otter Cove on the E side of the harbour 5 cables within the entrance. Good anchorage may also be obtained, in depths of 2 to 4 m (8 to 12 ft), 1 cable NW of the fish factory pier.

2   **Alongside berth.** Pier at the fish factory, on the E side of the harbour 9 cables from the entrance, has a depth alongside of 1·5 m.

Pleasant Bay
Description and topography
2.15

1   Pleasant Bay, the entrance of which lies between Nash Island (44°28′N 67°45′W) and Flint Island (2.17) (1¼ miles WNW) is a secure anchorage. There are numerous islands and reefs in the bay but important dangers are buoyed. A channel, not less than 5 cables wide, with a least depth of 11 m (36 ft) leads up the bay to an anchorage.

Limiting conditions
2.16

1   **Navigation at night.** As there are no lighted aids to navigation N of Nash Island a vessel should not enter the harbour at night. Navigation in the bay should present no difficulty by day in good visibility.

2   **Ice** obstructs navigation in the Pleasant River from December to April. In ordinary winters ice that forms in the bay is swept out by the tide.

Directions
2.17

1   From a position SW of Nash Island (44°28′N 67°45′W) the route to the anchorages in Pleasant Bay leads N, passing (with positions relative to Nash Island):

W of NI Light-buoy (safe water) (5 cables W). The tower of a disused lighthouse stands on the W end of Nash Island. Thence:

2　W of Pot Rock (9 cables N), which is 1·8 m (6 ft) in height and bare, thence:

E of No 1 Buoy (port hand) (1½ miles NW) that marks Coles Ledge which is situated 3 cables E of Flint Island, a wooded island 23 m (75 ft) in height, which is a wildlife sanctuary. Thence:

3　Between Norton Island Ledge (2 miles NNW) and the E extremity of Dyer Island (2½ miles NW). Dyer Island is separated from Flint Island to the S by Flint Island Passage, a deep but narrow passage 1 cable wide, the S side of which is marked by No 1 Buoy (port hand). The passage should not be used without local knowledge.

Thence proceed as necessary to the anchorages.

Anchorages
2.18

1　The best anchorage, with depths of 4 to 5 m (14 to 18 ft), which is used most frequently, is situated SE and E of Birch Islands, 4 miles N of Nash Island (44°28′N 67°45′W).

Anchorage may also be found, in depths of 9 to 11 m (30 to 36 ft), W of Nightcap Island, 3½ miles N of Nash Island entrance.

In an emergency, at night, anchorage may be obtained 2¼ miles NNW of Nash Island, close inside the entrance to the bay, in depths of 18 m (60 ft).

Harrington Bay

Description and topography
2.19

1　Harrington Bay, which is entered from the NW corner of Pleasant Bay, is separated from the upper part of that bay on the E by Ripley Neck, and from Narraguagus Bay (2.22) on the W by Foster Island. The bay extends 2½ miles N from Strout Island, a wooded island which lies in the middle of its entrance.

Harrington River and Flat River enter the N end of the bay.

Ice
2.20

1　Ice very frequently forms in Harrington River and Bay between December and April as far down as Ripley Neck.

Channels and anchorages
2.21

1　The main channel leads W of Strout Island through Strout Island Narrows, and has a depth of 8·2 m (27 ft).

Anchorage is available in depths of 9 to 14 m (30 to 47 ft) on the E side of the bay, but the bay is seldom used except by local vessels.

2　**Dyer Island Narrows,** which has a depth of 2·4 m (8 ft), leads N of Dyer Island from Harrington Bay to Narraguagus Bay (2.22). The passage is buoyed but there are numerous dangers near to the fairway and the channel should not be used without local knowledge.

Narraguagus Bay

Description and topography
2.22

1　Narraguagus Bay is entered between Flint Island (44°29′N 67°47′W) (2.17) and Bois Bubert Island, which is wooded, 4 miles SW. It is a well sheltered anchorage, used as a harbour of refuge all the year round by vessels of up to 5·5 m (18 ft) draught which anchor in the lower part of the bay.

A number of islands and rocks lie in the entrance to the bay.

Directions
2.23

1　From a position SSE of Flint Island the route to the anchorages in Narraguagus Bay leads NW, passing (with positions relative to Pond Island Tower (44°27′N 67°50′W)):

NE of Black Ledge (1¼ miles SE), which dries 3·4 m (11 ft). This ledge is the N extremity of Jordans Delight Ledge, at the S extremity of which lies a pipe, marked by No 2 Buoy (starboard hand). Thence:

2　NE of Mackerel Rock (1¼ miles ESE), an unmarked rock with a depth of 3 m (10 ft) over it, thence:

NE of Pond Island, with a bare conical hill 48 m (158 ft) in height. A tower, which is a disused lighthouse, stands on its E extremity and is prominent from E and S. No 1 Light-buoy is moored off this extremity. Thence:

3　SW of Shipstern Island (1¾ miles NE), which is 29 m (95 ft) in height and wooded, with rocky bluffs on its S side, thence:

Either side of Trafton Island (2 miles N), which is 26 m (84 ft) in height and wooded. There is a good channel on either side of the island. The E channel, 5 cables wide, separates Trafton Island from Tommy Island and Western Reef. The S extremity of the latter is marked by No 2 Buoy (starboard hand).

4　Thence to the anchorages and the entrance to the Narraguagus River.

Caution. The vicinity of Black Ledge should be avoided as the bottom is very irregular and other dangers may exist.

Berths
2.24

1　**Anchorage** for vessels seeking shelter, is usually obtained in a depth of 6 m (21 ft) between Trafton Island and No 5 Buoy (port hand) marking Lower Middle Ground (1 mile NW). Good anchorage may also be obtained 4 cables NE of No 6 Beacon, marking Trafton Halftide Ledge.

2　Vessels of up to 3 m (10 ft) draught sometimes anchor in depths of 4 to 5 m (14 to 17 ft) between Trafton Island and Trafton Halftide Ledge (1 mile N).

Vessels bound for Narraguagus River (2.26) anchor in depths of 4 to 6 m (12 to 16 ft), 7 cables E of Mitchell Point (1¾ miles NNW of Trafton Island).

2.25

1　Douglas Island Harbor is formed by Pond Island, Douglas Islands, the N part of Bois Bubert Island and the mainland NW.

Anchorage may be obtained in depths of 7 to 11 m (24 to 35 ft), but is seldom used as the anchorage above

Trafton Island is better and a considerable sea enters the harbour between the Douglas Islands in heavy S weather.

Narraguagus River
2.26

1 The Narraguagus River flows into the NW corner of Narraguagus Bay.

Channel. A dredged channel, marked by buoys and a day beacon leads for 2¾ miles from a position 5 cables SE of Mitchell Point to the town of Milbridge.

2 **Depths.** In 2004 the controlling depth in the channel was 3·1 m (10·3 ft) in mid-channel to the town wharf and in 1995 depths of 2 m (5·5 ft) were available in the anchorage 6 cables below the bridge at Milbridge.

Wharf. The town wharf, with reported depths alongside of about 2·5 m, lies on the E side of the river, 2½ cables E of the bridge.

3 **Caution.** Old fish weirs, which are reported not to be visible at LW, are on either side of the channel just above No 1 Buoy at the channel entrance. Care should be taken to pass close to this buoy when heading up for the channel entrance.

4 **Ice** seldom obstructs navigation except in January and February when the river is normally frozen to the mouth.

Pigeon Hill Bay

Description and topography
2.27

1 The entrance to Pigeon Hill Bay (44°25′N 67°53′W) lies between the S end of Bois Bubert Island (2.22) and Petit Manan Point, 2½ miles SW. The bay is easy of access by day and affords good anchorage.

Directions
2.28

1 From a position N of Petit Manan Light (44°22′N 67°52′W) (2.6) the route to the anchorages in Pigeon Hill Bay leads NNW, passing (with positions relative to Petit Manan Point (44°24′N 67°54′W)):

WSW of Whale Ledge (1½ miles E), which dries 1·8 m (6 ft) and is marked on its S side by No 4 Buoy (starboard hand), thence:

2 WSW of Egg Rock (1½ miles ENE), which is 5 m in height and consists of a ledge of dark boulders, parts of which are dry. There is a narrow channel for small vessels between Egg Rock and Bois Bubert Island, the use of which requires local knowledge. Thence:

ENE of Wood Pond Point (1 mile NNE), from which a bank with depths of 2·1 to 5·2 m (7 to 17 ft) extends 8½ cables SSE, thence:

3 N of Gull Rocks (2½ miles NNE), which dry 1·8 m (6 ft).

Thence to the anchorages.

Useful mark:

Pigeon Hill 97 m (317 ft) in height (3½ miles N), a bare topped hill standing on the W side of the head of the bay.

Anchorages
2.29

1 Anchorage may be obtained in depths of 4 to 7 m (12 to 24 ft), clear of a cable area running through the centre of the bay, but is seldom used except by local fishermen.

Caution. Fish weirs extend from either side of the bay.

Channel
2.30

1 A narrow channel leads from the head of the bay to Douglas Island Harbor (2.25). **Local knowledge** is necessary to use this channel.

PETIT MANAN ISLAND TO ISLE AU HAUT

General information

Charts 4746, 2492 (see 1.17)
Description
2.31

1 The following paragraphs describe the coastal passage between Petit Manan Island (44°22′N 67°52′W) (2.7) and Isle au Haut (2.137), 40 miles SW.

Directions
(continued from 2.7)

Principal marks
2.32

1 **Major lights:**

Petit Manan Light (44°22′N 67°52′W) (2.6).
Mount Desert Rock Light (43°58′N 68°08′W).
Great Duck Island Light (44°09′N 68°15′W).

Petit Manan Island to Isle au Haut
2.33

1 From a position SE of Petit Manan Island (44°22′N 67°52′W) (2.7) the coastal passage leads SW, passing (with positions relative to Great Duck Island Light (44°09′N 68°15′W)):

2 SE of Moulton Ledge (19 miles NE). This ledge, which is awash, is marked on its W side by ML Light-buoy (preferred channel to port). Many rocky patches surround the ledge including patches with depths of 5·5 and 7 m (18 and 23 ft) over them, situated respectively, 6 cables SSE and 3 cables SE. Thence:

3 SE of Schoodic Island (15 miles NE), which is low and fringed by reefs. Its N end is grassy and S end is wooded. 2S Light-buoy (starboard hand) is moored 4 cables S of the S end of the island. Thence:

SE of Baker Island (6½ miles NNE) (2.63). This island forms the W entrance point to Frenchman Bay. Thence:

4 Clear of No 1 Light-buoy (special) (6½ miles ESE), thence:

SE of Great Duck Island, which is partly wooded and appears as two islands from a distance E or W. A light (2.32) stands on the island. Thence:

Either side of Mount Desert Rock (11½ miles SSE), which is 6 m in height. A light (2.32) stands on the rock. Thence:

5 SE of Long Island (5 miles WSW), which is 64 m (210 ft) in height and wooded, but has no prominent marks. D Light-buoy (special) is moored 5½ miles SSW of Long Island. Thence:

6 SE of Great Spoon Island (15 miles WSW), the largest of a group of grassy islands that lie 2 miles off the E coast of Isle du Haut. Colt Ledge, which has a depth of 2·4 m (8 ft) over it and is marked by 2A Buoy (starboard hand) on its S side, lies 1½ miles SSW. Thence:

7 SE of Eastern Head (17 miles WSW), 39 m (129 ft) in height, the SE extremity of Isle au Haut (2.137).

Eastern Ear Ledge, awash, lies 7½ cables SE of this headland and is marked on its SE side by No 2 Buoy (starboard hand). Thence:

SE of Roaring Bull Ledge (18½ miles WSW), which dries 1·2 m (4 ft) and is marked on its S side by No 2 Light-buoy (starboard hand), and:

8   SE of Western Head (19 miles WSW), 54 m (176 ft) in height, at the S extremity of Isle au Haut.

Useful mark:

Baker Island Light (white stone tower, 13 m in height) (44°14′N 68°12′W).

(Directions continue for coastal passage at 2.127, for East Penobscot Bay at 2.139, and for West Penobscot Bay at 2.167).

Dyer Bay

Description and topography
2.34

1   Dyer Bay (44°25′N 67°55′W) affords good anchorage, but the dangers in it are unmarked and it is seldom used except by small local vessels.

2   Dyer Bay is entered 3¼ miles NW of Petit Manan Light (2.6) between Petit Manan Point and Dyer Point, 1¾ miles NW. Bonny Chess Ledge and The Castle, groups of rocks with passages between them, lie in the entrance to the bay.

Tidal streams in the entrance are strong but follow the direction of the channel except near Dyer Point where they set into Gouldsboro Bay (2.37).

3   **Channel.** The channel through Dyer Bay narrows to a width of 1½ cables between shoals which extend from Stanley Point on the W side, and Yellow Birch Head on the E side of the bay, 1 mile N of the entrance. Then for 1¼ miles it is 5 cables wide, reducing to 2 cables at the head of the bay abreast Sheep Island.

Fish weirs
2.35

1   **Caution** should be exercised as there are several fish weirs, which are covered at HW, in the bay.

Directions and anchorage
2.36

1   There should be no difficulty for a vessel to enter Dyer Bay by day with good visibility, but no vessel with a draught of over 2·4 m (8 ft) should attempt to enter at LW unless the mariner has local knowledge.

Vessels entering the bay should pass about 1½ cables E of The Castle (2.34) and proceed up Dyer Bay in mid-channel.

2   **Anchorage** should be selected near the middle of the bay, not less than 1¼ miles above The Castle, in depths of 6 to 13 m (19 to 42 ft), but not more than 2½ cables above Sheep Island (3 miles N of the entrance).

Gouldsboro Bay

Description and topography
2.37

1   Gouldsboro Bay, (44°25′N 67°57′W) which provides good anchorage, is entered 4 miles NW of Petit Manan Light (2.6) between Dyer Point (2.34) and Youngs Point, 1¼ miles SW.

2   The bay is also the approach route to the villages of Gouldsboro and Steuben, which lie at the head of the bay 6¼ and 6½ miles, respectively, above the entrance. Steuben can be reached at HW by vessels with a draught of 2·4 m (8 ft).

3   Sally Islands are a chain of islands and rocks that lie across the entrance to Gouldsboro Bay. Eastern Way and Western Passage are the two navigable channels leading through the Sally Islands into the bay. These passages are not easy to identify when approaching from the W.

Ice
2.38

1   Ice obstructs navigation in Gouldsboro Bay from December to March and in severe winters the bay is completely closed.

Directions
2.39

1   **Eastern Way** leads between Eastern Island and Bald Rock, 3 cables W. The passage is 1½ cables wide with depths of over 5·5 m (18 ft) and ¾ cable wide with depths of over 13·7 m (45 ft). Depths of 5·2 m (17 ft) extend up to 1¼ cables from the islands on either side of the channel. Vessels should pass midway between Eastern Island and Bald Rock.

2   **Caution.** The tidal streams set strongly across this channel with the flood tide setting NE and the ebb SW.

2.40

1   **Western Passage** leads between Sally Island and Sheep Island (4 cables W) at the W end of the Sally Islands. The passage has a least depth of 4·9 m (16 ft) and is ½ cable wide. Vessels should pass close along the E side of Sheep Island and W of the drying ledges that extend 2½ cables W of Sally Island.

2   **Tidal streams** follow the channel at a maximum rate of between 2 and 3 kn.

Caution. This passage should not be attempted without local knowledge.

2.41

1   **Useful mark:**

Point Francis (high and wooded) (44°27′N 67°59′W). This point which is 3¼ miles above Youngs Point, can clearly be seen from the entrance of the bay.

Berths
2.42

1   **Anchorage** can be obtained anywhere between the entrance and Port Francis, not less than 2½ cables from the shore.

Pier. There are small piers at Dolly Head on the E side of the bay 1¼ miles NNE of Point Francis, on the opposite side of the bay.

Corea Harbor

Description and topography
2.43

1   Corea Harbor (44°24′N 67°58′W) is a well sheltered cove which lies 4½ cables SW of Youngs Point (2.37) inside Western Island and Outer Bar Island, the W two islands of the Sally Islands (2.37).

Corea, a fishing village, stands at the head of the harbour.

Depths
2.44

1   The anchorage in the harbour has a controlling depth of 2 m (6 ft), with lesser depths along the N edges.

Ice
2.45

1   Ice usually obstructs the harbour from December to March, but fishing vessels can continue to operate from the entrance piers during that period.

Landmark
2.46

1 Church spire (44°24′·0N 67°58′·7W), standing NW of the head of the harbour.

Directions
2.47

1 From a position S of Western Island (2.43) an unmarked channel leads N and then NE, passing (with positions relative to W end of Western Island):

  W of a rock which dries 1·8 m (6 ft) (2½ cables SE). No 2 Buoy (starboard hand) is moored 1 cable ESE of the rock. Thence:

  W of Western Island (wooded), thence:

  NW of a rock awash (reported 1979) (¾ cable NW).

  Thence along the NE side of the entrance into the harbour. Low water is the best time to enter the harbour.

2.48

1 **Anchorage** is available in the centre of the harbour.

  Moorings, which are controlled by the Harbour Master, are available.

  Wharves. Two lobster wharves with pontoons have reported depths alongside of 1·8 to 2·4 m. Other wharves dry at LW.

  Supplies: fuel.

Prospect Harbor

Description and topography
2.49

1 Prospect Harbor, 4½ miles NNE of Schoodic Island (2.33), is entered between Cranberry Point (44°23′N 67°59′W), 1½ miles SW of Youngs Point, and Spruce Point, 2½ miles farther SW. The outer harbour has ample depth and affords anchorage for large vessels, but is exposed to S and SE winds. It is easily entered through the channels that lead on either side of the dangers off the entrance, but it is seldom used.

2 Prospect Harbor Point, 1½ miles NW of Cranberry Point, divides the head of the harbour into two coves, Inner Harbor, the W, with the village of Prospect Harbor at its head, and Sand Cove, N.

  The approaches to Prospect Harbor are obstructed by a group of rocky patches.

3 **Ice** seldom obstructs the harbour.

Directions
2.50

1 **From east.** From a position SE of Cranberry Point the E approach to Prospect Harbor leads NW, within the white sector (317°–323°) of Prospect Harbor Point Light (white conical tower, 12 m in height) (44°24′N 68°01′W), passing (with positions relative to Cranberry Point (44°23′N 67°59′W)):

  SW of Moulton Ledge (2¼ miles SE) (2.33), thence:

2 NE of Little Black Ledge (1 mile SSE) and Big Black Ledge (1 mile SSW), which are awash and 1·5 m (5 ft) in height, respectively, thence:

  SW of Cranberry Point. 2CP Buoy (starboard hand) is moored 3 cables S of this point.

  Thence into the outer harbour.

2.51

1 **From south.** From a position E of Spruce Point the S approach to Prospect Harbor leads N, within the white sector (348°–356°) of Prospect Harbor Point Light, passing (with positions relative to Prospect Point (44°23′N 68°01′W)):

2 E of the entrance to Bunkers Harbor (1 mile SSW) (2.55), and:

  W of No 2 Buoy (starboard hand) (1 mile SE) marking the SW edge of Old Woman, which dries 1·5 m (5 ft), thence:

  E of Prospect Point.

  Thence into the outer harbour.

2.52

1 **Useful marks** (with positions relative to Prospect Point):

  Church spire (1 mile WNW) at the head of Birch Harbor (2.55).

  Prospect Harbor Point Light (1¼ miles N) (2.50).

Small harbours
2.53

1 **Inner Harbor,** entered between Prospect Harbor Point and Clark Point (4 cables SW), has depths of 3·7 to 11 m (12 to 36 ft) just inside its entrance and is sheltered from all but SE winds. Small local vessels use the harbour.

  The head and NE side of the harbour are obstructed by ledges; those extending from Clark Point on the SW shore are marked by No 3 Buoy and No 5 Beacon (both port hand).

2 **Anchorage** may be obtained in depths of 4 to 10 m (13 to 33 ft), soft bottom, in the SW part of the harbour.

  Pier with depths alongside of 3·7 m is situated at the cannery at Clark Point.

  Supplies are available at the village of Prospect Harbor, at the head of the inlet.

2.54

1 **Sand Cove,** NE of Inner Harbor, has depths of 7·3 to 11 m (24 to 36 ft) in its outer part, but is seldom used.

2.55

1 **Bunkers Harbor and Birch Harbor** are two shallow coves lying on the W side of the harbour between Prospect Point and Spruce Point. Both these coves are obstructed by reefs and their entrance channels are unmarked. Each harbour has a fishing village at its head.

2 Bunkers Harbor is obstructed by Bunkers Ledge on the S side of its entrance. The E end of this ledge is marked by No 1 Buoy (port hand). The harbour has a pier with a pontoon and a dredged anchorage, each providing a berth with a depth of 1·8 m (6 ft).

Schoodic Harbor

Description
2.56

1 Schoodic Harbor (44°21′N 68°02′W), the entrance of which lies between Spruce Point (2.49) and Schoodic Point (2.63), has ample depth, but is exposed to the sea and is considerably obstructed by reefs. It is rarely used as an anchorage.

FRENCHMAN BAY AND ADJACENT WATERS

General information

Charts 4746, 2492 (see 1.17)

Description and topography
2.57

1 Frenchman Bay, centre about 44°25′N 68°11′W, lies between the Schoodic Peninsula and the E side of Mount Desert Island. From its entrance between Schoodic Point (2.63) and Baker Island (2.63), the bay is 12 miles long and 4 miles wide to its head, which is divided into several arms. It is rocky, but the water is deep and generally free from dangers except near its shores.

2   The bay is divided halfway up by The Porcupines, a group of islands which extend across the bay and have two good channels leading between them to the upper part of the bay.

3   Cadillac Mountain, 466 m (1530 ft) in height, the summit of Mount Desert Island, is the highest point on the coast of Maine and in clear weather is visible between 35 and 45 miles. However it should be noted that there are several peaks on the island of nearly the same elevation, making it difficult to identify individual peaks.

Recommended routes
2.58

1   Deep-draught vessels, high-speed ferries and other commercial vessels transiting through Frenchman Bay are requested to follow recommended routes as shown on the charts. These routes have been established to provide safe passage for increased commercial traffic and to prevent the loss of fishing gear placed in the approaches to, and within, Frenchman Bay.

Pilotage
2.59

1   Pilotage is compulsory for all foreign vessels and US vessels under register in foreign trade, with a draught of 2·7 m (9 ft) or more, for navigation in Frenchman Bay. The pilot boards about 1½ miles S or 2 miles SE of FB Light-buoy (2.63). See *Admiralty List of Radio Signals Volume 6(5)* for details.

Natural conditions
2.60

1   **Local magnetic anomaly**. The normal magnetic variation has been observed to decrease by as much as 1°, N of a line joining Bar Harbor (2.69) to Winter Harbor (2.65). In the vicinity of Jordan Island (2.73) an anomaly of 3° has been observed.

2   **Ice**. During mild winters Frenchman Bay is usually clear of ice to Skillings River, but the bays and rivers opening into the N part of the bay are frozen over. Winter Harbor is reported to be always clear of ice.

Fog. It is reported that during foggy weather Frenchman Bay usually clears of fog during the day, although it may remain thick outside the harbour entrance.

Directions

Principal marks
2.61

1   **Major lights:**
Mount Desert Rock Light (43°58′N 68°08′W) (2.32).
Great Duck Island Light (44°09′N 68°15′W) (2.32).
Egg Rock Light (44°21′N 68°08′W) (2.64).

Other aids to navigation
2.62

1   **Racon:**
FB Light-buoy (44°19′N 68°07′W).
See *Admiralty List of Radio Signals Volume 2* for details.

Approach
2.63

1   **South-east approach**. From position 44°15′N 67°56′W the recommended track leads WNW to FB Light-buoy (44°19′N 68°07′W), passing (with positions relative to Egg Rock Light (2.64)):

2   SW of Schoodic Point (4 miles ESE), the S point of Little Moose Island which lies 1 mile S of Schoodic Head (134 m (440 ft) in height), the most prominent mark on the E side of Frenchman Bay, thence:
SW of Big Moose Island (3½ miles ESE), on the NE side of which stands a prominent water tower, thence:
To a position close NE of FB Light-buoy.

3   **South approach**. From position 44°03′N 68°09′W the recommended track leads N to FB Light-buoy (preferred channel to port) (44°19′N 68°07′W), passing (with positions relative to Egg Rock Light):

4   E of Baker Island (7 miles SSW), which is mostly wooded, but with grass on its NW end and has several houses on it. The island is surrounded by above and below-water ledges and should be given a berth of at least 4 cables. A light (2.33) stands on the island. Thence:

5   E of East Bunker Ledge (5½ miles SW) (2.82), which lies in the entrance to Southwest Harbor (2.85), thence:
E of Otter Point (3½ miles SW). Otter Cliff Ledge, which dries 1·8 m (6 ft), lies 2 cables E of the point and is marked by No 1 Buoy (port hand).

6   Thence to a position close W of FB Light-buoy.

Entrance and inner part
2.64

1   From a position in the vicinity of FB Light-buoy the recommended track through the entrance and into the inner part of Frenchman Bay leads generally WNW then NW, passing (with positions relative to Egg Rock Light (44°21′N 68°08′W)):

2   ENE of Old Whale Ledge (1¾ miles SW), which is awash and lies 1¾ cables offshore between Great Head and Schooner Head with its E side marked by No 3 Light-buoy (port hand). Thence:
WSW of No 4 Buoy (starboard hand) (1 mile SSW), thence:

3   WSW of Egg Rock Light. The light stands on Egg Rock, a low and mostly bare island from which drying ledges extend 1 cable NE and 4 cables SW. Thence:

4   ENE of The Thrumcap (1¾ miles WNW), which is round and rocky with a clump of trees in the centre, thence:
SW of Ironbound Island (2 miles N), 44 m (143 ft) in height, which is the largest island in Frenchman Bay and is thickly wooded with high vertical cliffs, thence:

5   NE of Bald Porcupine Island (2¾ miles NW), 57 m (186 ft) in height, with bare rocky slopes. A breakwater, which dries, extends SW from the island for 1¼ cables, its extremity being marked by a light-beacon (white diamond, orange border, marked   DANGER   SUBMERGED BREAKWATER). The island and the breakwater form the S side of Bar Harbor (2.69). Thence two routes lead into the inner harbour.

6   **West route** leads NW between Sheep Porcupine Island (3¾ miles NW) and Burnt Porcupine Island, 5 cables ENE. This channel, the W side of which is marked by No 7 Buoy (port hand), is deep and clear of dangers.

East route leads NE between Long Porcupine Island (3¼ miles NNW) and Ironbound Island.

Anchorages and harbours
within Frenchman Bay

Winter Harbor

2.65

1   Winter Harbor (44°22′N 68°05′W), situated on the E side of Frenchman Bay, is a much frequented harbour of refuge and provides good anchorage and holding ground in depths of 9 to 16 m (29 to 52 ft). It is comparatively free from dangers, and although open S, a heavy sea never enters.

2.66

1   **Entrances.** The main entrance lies 2 miles NW of Schoodic Point, between Turtle Island and Mark Island on the W and the Schoodic Peninsula on the E. This entrance is deep, and clear of dangers. The harbour can also be entered from N along the W side of Grindstone Neck, a promontory which forms the W side of the N part of the harbour. This entrance should not be used without local knowledge.

2.67

1   **Directions.** From a position S of Mark Island the route through the main entrance leads N, passing E of MI Light-buoy (preferred channel to starboard), that is moored 2 cables SSE of Mark Island, and thence E of Grindstone Point to the head of the harbour, which is divided into three coves.

2   **Useful marks** (with positions relative to Mark Island):
> White tower (disused lighthouse) standing on Mark Island.
> Cupola (1½ miles NNW). Grey house with glass roof on the E side of the harbour.
> Spire (2 miles N) in the town of Winter Harbor.

2.68

1   **Winter Harbor**, a small town, stands at the head of Henry Cove, the E cove. Supplies and small repairs are available.

    Anchorage. Best anchorage is available in Sand Cove, the W cove.

Bar Harbor

2.69

1   **Function.** Bar Harbor (44°24′N 68°12′W) is situated on the W side of Frenchman Bay, 4 miles within the entrance. It is a port of entry, summer resort and yachting centre. The harbour is also visited by cruise liners.

2   The harbour is bounded on the W and N by the coast of Mount Desert Island, Bar Island, 52 m (170 ft) in height and wooded, and Sheep Porcupine Island (2.64). On the S it is bounded by Bald Porcupine Island and a breakwater (2.64).

3   **Swell.** Although the breakwater affords some shelter, a swell sets into the harbour with SE winds and vessels should not attempt to ride out a gale from that direction.

    Ice. Port operations are not affected by ice.

2.70

1   **Directions**. The harbour is normally entered from the E between Bald Porcupine Island and Sheep Porcupine Island, through the main entrance, which is clear of dangers.

2   There is also a channel, ¾ cable wide with a depth of 11·3 m (37 ft), leading into the harbour from the S, between the SW breakwater and the W shore. This channel should be used with caution as in calm weather at HW, there may be no indication of the breakwater except for the

light-beacon marking its SW end. This channel should only be used with local knowledge.

2.71

1   **A Anchorage**, with depths of 9 to 31 m (30 ft to 17 fm), is situated 6 cables SE of the E end of Bar Island.

    B Anchorage, with depths of 14 to 55 m (46 ft to 30 fm), soft mud, is situated 4 cables N of Bar Island.

    Municipal Pier, situated on the N side of the town, has a reported depth of 3 m at its head. There are other wharves and landing stages with less water.

2   **Ferry terminal**, situated 1 mile NW of the town, is used by many cruise vessels and ferries.

    Traffic. In 2005 the port was used by 2 vessels with a total deadweight 25 198 tonnes.

2.72

1   **Repairs:** minor repairs.

    Other facilities: hospital.

    Supplies: fuel; water; provisions and stores.

Stave Island Harbor

2.73

1   Stave Island Harbor (44°25′N 68°08′W), which is on the E side of Frenchman Bay 5 miles within the entrance, is an excellent harbour of refuge.

    The harbour is bounded on the E by the mainland, the S by Jordan Island and the W by Stave Island. Both these islands are linked to the mainland by bars.

2   South Gouldsboro is a village on the NE shore of the harbour and Summer Harbor is a cove with a settlement on the SE shore.

    Ice usually obstructs the harbour from December to March.

2.74

1   **Directions.** The route into the harbour leads ENE between Yellow Island, wooded with yellowish rocks, which lies off the NW point of Jordan Island, and the S end of Stave Island. The entrance is clear of charted dangers.

2.75

1   **Anchorage**, which is sheltered from all but SW winds, may be found in the harbour in depths of 6 to 11 m (20 to 36 ft), soft bottom.

    Pier with depth alongside of 1 m is situated at South Gouldsboro.

Sullivan Harbor

2.76

1   Sullivan Harbor is situated in the N part of Frenchman Bay, 8 miles within its entrance. It is entered between Bean Point (44°28′N 68°12′W) and Hancock Point, the SE extremity of Crabtree Neck, 1½ miles WSW.

    The harbour extends 9 miles N and has a least depth of 7·6 m (25 ft) as far as Sullivan Falls, 3 miles NNW of Bean Point. Navigation above Sullivan Falls should not be attempted without local knowledge.

    Ice obstructs navigation in Taunton Bay and Sullivan Harbor from January to March.

2.77

1   **Sorrento Harbor** lies on the E side of the entrance to Sullivan Harbor on the S side of the promontory extending W from the SW end of Waukeag Neck. On the S side the harbour is bounded by Preble Island and Dram Island.

2   The harbour contains a small anchorage used by pleasure craft and has two entrances.

Skillings River
2.78
1 Skillings River (44°29′N 68°16′W) is situated in the NW part of Frenchman Bay. It is entered between Hancock Point and Meadow Point, 1¾ miles W. The river narrows to a width of 2 cables abreast Pecks Point, 1¾ miles NW of Hancock Point, above which is a narrow, winding, unmarked channel much obstructed by dangers. **Local knowledge** is necessary to navigate beyond Pecks Point.

2 **Anchorage,** for vessels wishing to enter the river, may be obtained in depths of 9 to 13 m (29 to 42 ft), 1½ miles above Hancock Point.

Eastern Bay
2.79
1 Eastern Bay is situated at the head of Frenchman Bay, 9 miles from the entrance. It is entered between Sand Point (44°26′N 68°16′W) and Meadow Point, 1 mile N. The bay is generally clear of dangers, except for Googins Ledge lying off the N side of the bay. This ledge dries and its S edge is marked by No 14 Buoy (starboard hand).

2 Eastern Bay leads into Mount Desert Narrows, which in turn leads through a narrow, difficult, unmarked channel into Blue Hill Bay (2.91). This channel, which is crossed by a fixed bridge with a vertical clearance of 7·6 m (25 ft), can be used at HW by craft with a draught of 2·7 m (9 ft).
2.80
1 **Anchorage** is available for deep-draught vessels. A good berth is S of Googins Ledge, in depths of 13 to 14 m (42 to 46 ft), 3 cables from the shore off Salsbury Cove. Another berth may be found in depths of 11 to 16 m (36 to 53 ft) W of Googins Ledge.

Southwest Harbor and adjacent waters

Description
2.81
1 The waters on the W side of the approaches to Frenchman Bay, W of a line joining Baker Island (44°15′N 68°12′W) (2.63) and East Point 3 miles NNW, contain a number of harbours and coves, of which the most important is Southwest Harbor (2.85), which is much used as a harbour of refuge. These waters are the approaches to several important villages and summer resorts, and are frequented by fishing boats and pleasure craft.

2 **Approaches.** Eastern Way, with a least depth of 12·2 m (40 ft), is the main approach to Southwest Harbor. It is well marked and the recommended route for deep-draught vessels. Small vessels may approach Southwest Harbor through Gilley Thorofare (2.83), the channel S of Sutton Island, or through Western Way (2.84).

Directions for Southwest Harbor
2.82
1 **Eastern Way.** From a position N of Baker Island the main route to Southwest Harbor leads generally W through a well marked channel, passing (with positions relative to East Point (44°17′N 68°14′W)):

2 N of Lewis Rock (5 cables SE), which has a depth of 1·8 m (6 ft) over it and lies 2 cables NNW of East Bunker Ledge, which is partly above-water and has a stone beacon standing near its SW end. 3A Buoy (port hand) marks the NW side of Lewis Rock. Thence:

3 S of No 4 Light-buoy (starboard hand) (3 cables SE), which marks a rocky ledge extending SE from East Point, thence:

S of Bowden Ledge (4 cables SW), with a depth of 0·6 m (2 ft) and marked by No 6 Buoy (starboard hand), thence:

4 N of Sutton Island (1½ miles SW), a wooded island with the summer resort of Sutton standing at its W end. The ferry pier, with a depth alongside of 1·8 m, is on the S shore. And:

S of Long Pond Shoal (9 cables WSW), with a least depth of 1·5 m (5 ft) at its W end. No 8 Buoy (starboard hand) marks the S side of the shoal. Thence:

5 S of Bear Island (1½ miles WSW), 24 m (80 ft) in height and partly wooded. No 10 Light-buoy (starboard hand) is moored ¾ cable S of the island and a light (white tower, 30 m in height) is exhibited from the island. Thence:

S of Eastern Point (2½ miles WSW), the SE extremity of Greening Island (2.85). No 6 Buoy (starboard hand) is moored 1 cable S of the point.

2.83
1 **Passage south of Sutton Island.** From a position S of East Bunker Ledge (44°17′N 68°13′W), Gilley Thorofare, the passage S of Sutton Island, which has a depth of 4·9 m (16 ft) leads WSW, passing (with positions relative to East Bunker Ledge):

2 S of Old Tom (5 cables SW), a patch with a depth of 7·3 m (24 ft) over it, thence:

Between Spurling Rock (1¾ miles SW) and the S side of Sutton Island. The rock, which has a depth of 2·1 m (7 ft) over it, is marked by No 2 Light-buoy.

Thence W through waters clear of charted dangers to Southwest Harbor.
2.84
1 **Western Way,** which leads between the W side of Great Cranberry Island and Mount Desert Island, has a least depth of 4 m (13 ft) over the bar at its N end and is marked by light-buoys and buoys. Unmarked patches with depths of 3 and 3·7 m (10 and 12 ft) lie close to the fairway.

2 This passage is frequently used by small vessels approaching Southwest Harbor and Frenchman Bay from the W in calm weather, but should not be used by vessels with a draught of more than 3 m (10 ft) without local knowledge.

Southwest Harbor
2.85
1 Southwest Harbor, which is entered between the SE extremity of Greening Island, which is low and wooded, and Kings Point, 6 cables SSW, is the most important harbour on the S side of Mount Desert Island. It provides well sheltered anchorage in depths of 2 to 15 m (6 to 49 ft). The village of Southwest Harbor lies on the N side of the head of the harbour.

Ice does not usually restrict the harbour, but in very severe winters has been known to extend as far as the Cranberry Islands but is carried out to sea from Somes Sound on the ebb tide.

2 **Anchorage** is available in depths of 10 to 15 m (33 to 49 ft) midway between Greening Island and the S shore. Smaller vessels can anchor farther in and depths decrease gradually to 4 m (13 ft) at a distance of ½ cable from the rock, marked by a beacon, at the head of the harbour.

3 **Alongside berths.** A number of berths, including the Coast Guard wharf, with depths alongside of 1 to 5 m, are situated on the N and S shore of the harbour.

2.86

1   **Repairs.** Patent slip available to vessels, of up to 30 m in length, is situated at a boat building yard on the N shore.

2   **Rescue.** A Coast Guard station (44°16′·5N 68°18′·7W) is situated at the S end of Clark Point.

Other anchorages and harbours
2.87

1   **Seal Harbor**, on the N side of Eastern Way, between East Point and Crowninshield Point (44°17′N 68°15′W), 3½ cables E, provides anchorage for small vessels in depths of 5 m (16 ft), but is exposed to SE winds. No 1 Buoy (port hand) marks the E side of a ledge, partly above-water, that extends 2 cables E from the W side of the entrance.

2   The village of Seal Harbor, consisting of hotels and houses, is situated around the cove. Its main wharf, with a depth alongside of 2·7 m, is situated on the E side of the Harbor. Fuel and water are available.

    Bracy Cove, 6 cables W of Seal Harbor, is unsuitable for anchoring as the bottom is rocky and the cove is open SE.

2.88

1   **Cranberry Harbor** (44°16′N 68°15′W) is situated between Little Cranberry Island and Great Cranberry Island, both of which are low and wooded, and provides anchorage in depths of 4 to 6 m (13 to 20 ft) in the middle of the harbour SW of Hadlock Cove.

2   **Caution.** An unmarked obstruction, shown on the US chart, with a swept depth of 1·8 m (6 ft) over it, lies in the approaches.

    Piers. Three piers with pontoons are situated at Hadlock Cove. The ferry pier has a depth alongside of 2·7 m.

    Repairs. Three patent slips at Hadlock Cove are available for craft of up to 15 m in length.

2.89

1   **Northeast Harbor**, an important yachting centre, is entered W of Bear Island (44°17′N 68°16′W).

    The harbour is reported to be free of ice in the average winter, but to freeze out as far as Bear Island in severe winters.

2   A rock, which dries 0·9 m (3 ft), lies in the middle of the entrance to the harbour. Nos 1 and 2 buoys (lateral) mark the E and W side of this rock. The best passage into the harbour leads W of the rock.

    The head of the harbour is shallow, but there is anchorage for small vessels in depths of 4 to 9 m (14 to 28 ft) in the lower part of the harbour.

3   Piers, with depths alongside of 1·8 to 2·4 m, are situated on the W shore of the harbour.

    Supplies: fuel; water and provisions.

2.90

1   **Somes Sound**, a narrow rocky inlet, is entered to the N of Greening Island (44°17′N 68°18′W), between Manchester Point and Fernald Point. It extends 4½ miles N to Somes Harbor.

    The entrance, where the navigable channel is only ¾ cable wide, has a least depth of 6·1 m (20 ft). Middle Rock, with a depth of 2·7 m (9 ft) over it and marked by No 5 Light-buoy (port hand), lies in the W side of the entrance.

2   Anchorage is available within Somes Sound in depths of 16 to 22 m (52 ft to 12 fm), but the sound is little used. Heavy squalls occasionally blow down from the mountains.

BLUE HILL BAY AND ADJACENT WATERS

General information

Chart 2492 (see 1.17)

Description and topography
2.91

1   The following paragraphs describe Blue Hill Bay and its adjacent waters, including Jericho Bay (2.109).

    Blue Hill Bay lies between Mount Desert Island on the E, and the mainland with a chain of islands and shoals which extend SE from Naskeag Point (44°14′N 68°32′W) on the W.

2   The bay is entered between Bass Harbor Head (44°13′N 68°20′W), the S end of Mount Desert Island, and North Point, the N end of Swans Island, 4 miles SW, and extends 18 miles N.

3   A group of islands lies in the entrance to the bay and other islands lie within the bay. The channels between these islands are mostly deep and clear and important dangers are marked.

    The bay is frequented by a few coasters, fishing vessels and pleasure craft.

Ice
2.92

1   Ice will prevent navigation in bays at the head of Blue Hill Bay during winter months.

Approach and entrance channels
2.93

1   Blue Hill Bay may be entered from E across Bass Harbor Bar (44°13′N 68°20′W) (2.99), from the S through Eastern Passage (44°10′N 68°23′W) (2.95), from the SW through Southwest Approach (44°06′N 68°24′W) (2.100) and the W from Jericho Bay through Casco Passage (44°12′N 68°28′W) (2.101).

    Vessels of deep draught can only enter the bay through Eastern Passage.

Directions
Principal marks
2.94

1   **Landmark:**
        Blue Hill (44°26′N 68°35′W), a rounded peak that appears blue from a distance. A conspicuous lookout tower stands on the summit.

    Major light:
        Great Duck Island Light (44°09′N 68°15′W) (2.32).

Eastern Passage
2.95

1   From a position SW of Great Duck Island Light (44°09′N 68°15′W) the route through Eastern Passage into Blue Hill Bay leads NW, passing (with positions relative to Bass Harbor Head Light (44°13′N 68°20′W)):

        NE of Richs Head (44°06′N 68°20′W), the SE extremity of Long Island (2.33), thence:

        SW of The Drums (4¾ miles SSE), a dangerous ledge awash, which is marked on its SE side by D Buoy (preferred channel to starboard), thence:

2   NE of Northeast Ledge (5 miles S), with a depth of 4 m (13 ft) over it. LI Light-buoy (safe water) is moored 3 cables NNW of the ledge. Thence:

        SW of Green Islands (3¾ miles S), two rocky islets with grassy summits. Otter Ledge, awash, lies 1 mile SW of the W islet and two patches, each with a depth of 7 m (23 ft) over them lie 2 and 4 cables, respectively, E of the ledge. Thence:

3   SW of Black Island (3 miles S), 48 m (157 ft) in height and wooded. A marine farm lies on the NW side of the island. Thence:

NE of East Point, Swans Island (4¼ miles SSW). This island is the largest of the islands in the approaches to Blue Hill Bay and has permanent inhabitants, who are mainly fishermen. Thence:

4   SW of Placentia Island (2 miles SW), which is 41 m (135 ft) in height and wooded except at its E end, thence:

NE of Staple Ledge (3¼ miles SW), which dries. This ledge, which lies nearly in mid–channel, is marked on its NE side by No 1 Buoy (port hand).

2.96

1   From a position NW of Placentia Island the route continues NNW and then NW, passing:

ENE of Ship and Barges Ledge (4 miles W), which dries 1·8 m (6 ft). The ledge is marked at its S end by SB Beacon, and No 3 Buoy (port hand) is moored off the E side of the ledge. Thence:

2   NE of Ship Island and Trumpet Island (4½ miles WNW), the S islands of a chain of islands which lie in the centre of Blue Hill Bay. Ship Island is high and Trumpet Island is low. Thence:

3   NE of Bar Island and Tinker Island (5½ and 7 miles NW, respectively). Bar Island is high and grassy and Tinker Island is partly wooded. No 5 Buoy (port hand) is moored at the edge of foul ground that extends 3 cables NE from Bar Island, and Nos 6 and 8 Buoys (starboard hand) mark the N and W limits of Cow and Calf Ledge which extends from the NW end of Tinker Island. A channel, the centre of which is marked by T1 Buoy (safe water) and with a depth of 5·2 m (17 ft), crosses the shoal ground between Bar Island and Trumpet Island.

4   Thence most vessels proceeding to the N part of the bay follow the route between Tinker Island and Hardwood Island and thence between Long Island and Bartlett Island. Small vessels sometimes use the more protected passage between Moose Island and Hardwood Island.

2.97

1   **Useful mark:**

Bass Harbor Head Light (white tower and dwelling) (44°13′N 68°20′W).

Other entrance channels

General
2.98

1   As most of the vessels navigating Blue Hill Bay do not exceed 2·7 m (9 ft) in draught, the bay is usually entered through one of the inshore channels described as follows.

Bass Harbor Bar
2.99

1   The entrance across Bass Harbor Bar (44°13′N 68°20′W) is used by small vessels entering Blue Hill Bay from the E. Vessels with a draught of not more than 2·7 m (9 ft) frequently use this passage; in smooth seas vessels with a draught of 5·5 m (18 ft) sometimes use this passage at HW.

2   **Directions.** From a position NE of Great Gott Island (44°12′N 68°20′W), the route across the bar leads 1¾ cables S of Bass Harbor Head Light (2.97), through a narrow channel which had a mid–channel controlling depth

of 4·3 m (14 ft) (1992). The centre of the channel is marked at each end by a buoy (safe water).

3   **Caution.** The channel should be navigated with caution because in heavy weather breakers extend right across it and with strong winds against the tidal stream conditions dangerous to small vessels can build up.

Southwest Approach
2.100

1   Southwest Approach (44°06′N 68°24′W) may be used by vessels entering Blue Hill Bay from the W.

2   **Directions.** From a position SSW of Southwest Point, Long Island (44°06′N 68°22′W), the approach leads N between Long Island and Johns Island, passing between J Buoy (preferred channel to port) marking Johns Island Sunken Ledge and No 2 Buoy (starboard hand) marking Beach Ledge, and thence between Sister Islands and Red Point, the SE point of Swans Island. This part of the route passes over patches with swept depths of 7·3 and 4·6 m (24 and 15 ft). From a position NW of the Sister Islands, the route then leads NE to join Eastern Passage (2.95).

Casco Passage
2.101

1   Casco Passage connects Jericho Bay with Blue Hill Bay through a channel, N of Swans Island, between Orono Island (44°11′N 68°28′W) and Black Island (5 cables N). This passage divides into two branches in its W part, the N part continuing as Casco Passage and the S part as York Passage.

Both channels are well marked, and buoyed as for a passage proceeding from E to W.

2   Casco Passage is the straighter and recommended passage with a least width of ½ cable and a depth of 4 m (13 ft) in the fairway, but rocks lie on both sides of it.

York Narrows, with a width of ½ cable and a depth of 4 m (13 ft), has dangerous rocks on either side of it and is not recommended.

Tidal streams in Casco Passage set E with a rising tide and W with a falling tide.

Local knowledge is required.

Pond Island Passage
2.102

1   Pond Island Passage leads into the N part of Jericho Bay, N of Pond Island (44°13′N 68°29′W).

The passage, which is marked by buoys, has a least depth of 5·8 m (19 ft) in the fairway, but shoal patches lie close by.

Local knowledge is required.

Anchorages and harbours

Bass Harbor
2.103

1   **Position and function.** Bass Harbor (44°14′N 68°21′W), which is entered between Bass Harbor Head and Lopaus Head (1 mile WNW) on the E side of the entrance to Blue Hill Bay, is an important fishing village and is sometimes used as an anchorage by coastal traffic.

Limiting conditions. The outer anchorage is exposed to the S.

2   **Directions.** The outer harbour can be entered passing either side of Weaver Ledge, which lies 3 cables E of Lopaus Point. This ledge dries 1 m (3 ft) and is marked by Nos 1 and 2 Buoys (lateral) at its SE and NW extremities.

The villages of Bass Harbor (E side) and Bernard (W side), at the head of the inner harbour, are reached by a buoyed channel, which has a depth of 3 m (10ft).

3   **Anchorage** may be obtained in depths of 9 to 14 m (30 to 46 ft) in the outer harbour between Weaver Ledge and the entrance to the channel.

Wharves, with depths alongside of 2·1 and 3 m, exist in Bass Harbor. There are also fish wharves, with depths alongside of 1·8 m, at Bernard.

Repairs: minor repairs.

Supplies: fuel; water and provisions.

Mackerel Cove
2.104

1   **Position.** Mackerel Cove, which is entered between North Point (44°11′N 68°26′W) and Crow Island, 6 cables WSW, on the W side of the entrance to Blue Hill Bay is a good anchorage.

The village of Atlantic stands at the head of the cove.

2   **Directions.** Although there are several dangers in the cove, it is easy to enter from N during the day. To enter the bay vessels should pass W of No 1 Light-buoy (port hand) that marks the ledge extending NW from North Point, and E of No 2 Buoy (starboard hand) that marks the ledge close E of Crow Island. Care must be taken to avoid a patch with a depth of 3·4 m (11 ft) over it that lies 7 cables SSW of North Point. This patch is marked by No 3 Buoy (port hand) on its W side. Below-water rocks lie in the approach to the ferry pier 5 cables S of North Point and a reported below-water rock (position approximate) lies mid-way between Nos 2 and 3 Buoys.

3   **Useful mark.** Church tower (1¼ miles SSE of North Point) situated in the village of Atlantic.

Anchorage may be obtained, clear of a cable area, between No 3 Buoy and the buoy E of Crow Island, in depths of 7 to 10 m (24 to 32 ft), or between No 3 Buoy and a drying ledge (3 cables SW).

Ferry pier is situated 5 cables S of North Point.

Western Bay
2.105

1   **Position.** Western Bay is entered between North Point, Bartlett Island (44°23′N 68°25′W) and Oak Point, 1¼ miles N.

2   **Topography.** The bay forms part of the channel which separates Mount Desert Island from the mainland and leads into Mount Desert Narrows (2.79). Alley Island, the largest in the bay, lies 1¾ miles ENE of Oak Point. Foul ground extends 2½ cables SE from the island, which is connected to the NW side of the bay by a drying ridge.

3   **Anchorage** may be obtained by vessels of all sizes in depths of 13 to 19 m (42 to 62 ft) SW of Alley Island, but the broken rocky ground which extends 4 cables SE of Oak Point should be avoided.

There is also anchorage in depths of 6 to 12 m (20 to 39 ft) SE and E of Alley Island, avoiding the foul ground extending from the island.

Union River Bay
2.106

1   **Position.** Union River Bay is entered between Oak Point (44°24′N 68°25′W) and High Head on Newbury Neck, 1½ miles SW.

2   **Topography.** The bay extends 5½ miles N to Weymouth Point (44°29′N 68°26′W) and is almost free of dangers except near its head where it divides into two arms; Patten Bay, the W arm which leads to the village of Surry; and

Union River, the N arm, which leads to the city of Ellsworth, 3½ miles N of Weymouth Point.

Tupper Ledge, partly awash and marked on its S side by TL Buoy (preferred channel to starboard) lies 6 cables S of Weymouth Point in the entrance to Union River.

3   **Anchorage.** Good anchorage may be obtained in depths of 6 to 12 m (19 to 39 ft) in mid-channel, 1 mile NW of Tupper Ledge.

Landing stage with a depth alongside of 1·5 m is situated in Contention Cove 1¾ miles WNW of Tupper Ledge.

4   **Union River**, which should only be entered with local knowledge, flows into the arm of Union River Bay, E of Weymouth Point. The river is about 1 mile wide at the entrance but reduces to ½ cable in width 1¼ miles above the entrance. In 2003 the controlling depth was 1·4 m (4·5 ft) to Black Point, about 3½ miles above the entrance. Between Black Point and Ellsworth the controlling depth (2003) was 1·2 to 1·4 m (4 to 4·5 ft).

5   **Ice** usually closes the river from December to April.

Morgan Bay
2.107

1   **Position.** Morgan Bay is entered between Darling Island, (44°24′N 68°31′W), wooded, and the SW shore of Newbury Neck, 1¾ miles ESE. The bay extends 3 miles N from its entrance.

Topography. The inner part of Morgan Bay is obstructed by Jed Islands, which lie on a shallow bank which extends 1 mile W from Newbury Neck.

2   **Directions.** From a position E of No 8 Buoy (starboard hand) that marks the SE side of Darling Ledge, awash, (3 cables SE from Darling Island) and W of No 2 Buoy (starboard hand), which marks the rock 5½ cables SSW of Jed Island, the route into the bay leads N and NE through a narrow channel. This channel, with a least depth of 7 m (23 ft), passes W of Conary Nub, a rock with a clump of scrub on it, that lies 4½ cables W of Jed Islands and 2 cables from Conary Point, on the W shore. The channel E of Conary Nub should only be used with local knowledge.

3   **Useful mark.** Spire (1 mile N of Darling Island) in the village of East Blue Hill.

Anchorage. Good anchorage may be obtained in depths of 2 to 11 m (7 to 36 ft) N of Seal Ledge and Black Rock, two dangers that lie 3 and 5 cables, respectively, NE of Conary Nub.

4   **Alongside berths** are available on the shore W of Darling Island and in McHeard Cove at East Blue Hill.

Repairs: slip for vessels 33 m in length.

Supplies: fuel and water.

Blue Hill Harbor
2.108

1   **Position.** The outer part of Blue Hill Harbor is entered between Woods Point (44°24′N 68°32′W) and Stills Point, 1¾ miles SSW.

2   **Topography.** Blue Hill Harbor consists of an outer and inner harbour. The inner harbour is entered between Sculpin Point, 1¼ miles W of Woods Point, and Parker Point, 2 cables SW, and extends 1¼ miles WNW to the village of Blue Hill. Middle Ground, with rocks awash, lies off the entrance to the inner harbour and Nos 1 and 2 Buoys (port hand) mark the E side of the ground.

3   **Directions for entering the inner harbour.** Vessels can enter the inner harbour on either side of Middle Ground, but the N side is easier and safer. After passing along the N side of Middle Ground the entrance channel, which S of

Sculpin Point is only 15 m (49 ft) wide with a depth of 5·8 m (19 ft), leads between Nos 5 and 6 Buoys (lateral) and into the anchorage.

4 **Local knowledge** is necessary to enter the harbour with vessels with a draught of more than 3·7 m (12 ft).

Ice. In severe winters the harbour is usually closed between December and April but during mild winters is relatively free of ice.

5 **Anchorage**, protected from N and W, may be obtained in depths of 7 to 15 m (23 to 49 ft) in the middle of the outer harbour. In the inner harbour secure anchorage may be obtained in depths of 3 to 8 m (10 to 26 ft), 1 to 3 cables above Sculpin Point, and also in depths of 4 to 8 m (13 to 26 ft) about 6 cables WNW of that point.

6 **Facilities:** hospital.
Supplies: fuel and provisions.

Jericho Bay

Description
2.109

1 Jericho Bay comprises the area, 3 miles wide, between Swans Island and Marshall Island (44°07′N 68°30′W) on the E, and Isle au Haut (2.137) and Deer Isle on the W. It is obstructed by numerous islands and shoals.

The upper portion of the bay provides inshore navigation for local vessels between Blue Hill Bay on the E and Penobscot Bay (2.119) on the W. The lower part of the bay is little used except by local fishermen and yachts.

2 Neither the bay nor its approaches should be entered without local knowledge and therefore only an outline description of this area is given as follows.

Passages and channels
2.110

1 **South-east approach** to Jericho Bay leads from S of Johns Island Sunken Ledge (44°06′N 68°25′W), between Brimstone Island and Green Island and then between Marshall Island and Swans Island passing through Toothacher Bay. This passage, which is marked by buoys (lateral) enters Jericho Bay N of Halibut Rocks Light (red and white chequered diamond on framework tower) (44°08′N 68°32′W).

2 **South approach.** Two entrance channels, for which local knowledge is required, lead into Jericho Bay from S between the dangers which lie between Marshall Island and Isle au Haut. Though these channels are the most direct route from to the bay from the S, many dangers are unmarked and consequently the recommended channel is that from the SE through Toothacher Bay.

Passages to Blue Hill Bay. See 2.101 and 2.102.
2.111

1 **Merchant Row**, which is the S of the inner channels between Jericho Bay and E Penobscot Bay, leads through the islands and shoals lying between Deer Isle (2.109) and Isle au Haut, 4 miles SSE. The channel is entered between Southern Mark Island, lying 2¾ miles W of Long Point, the N extremity of Marshall Island, and Southern Mark Island Ledge (44°08′N 68°35′W).

2 This channel is used by vessels of moderate draught at all times of the year, and in winter is used by other vessels when Deer Island Thorofare is blocked by ice. Merchant Row is not quite so direct as Deer Island Thorofare, but the channel is wider and deeper. There are numerous dangers on both sides of the channel, but the principal ones are marked by buoys and beacons.

The channel can easily be followed, by day, by those with local knowledge.
2.112

1 **Deer Island Thorofare** is a narrow channel along the S side of Deer Isle, between it and the numerous islands S. It is entered from the E, either S of Whaleback Ledge (44°09′N 68°33′W) or between Long Ledge (44°11′N 68°33′W) and Potato Ledge, 3 cables SSW.

2 The passage, which connects Jericho Bay and East Penobscot Bay and is used by vessels proceeding coastwise, is marked by buoys and beacons. It has a least width of ½ cable and a least depth of 4·3 m (14 ft) at its W end between Moose Island (44°09′N 68°41′W) and Crotch Island.

3 Vessels of up to 5·5 m (18 ft) draught are reported to have used the passage but many unmarked dangers, with depths of 2·7 to 4·3 m (9 to 14 ft) over them, lie close to the channel.

The channel should not be attempted without local knowledge.

4 This channel is occasionally closed by ice which is soon broken up by icebreakers. During severe winters solid ice has formed between Stonington (2.116) and Isle au Haut.

Eggemoggin Reach
2.113

1 Eggemoggin Reach is the channel between the Deer Isles and the mainland N, which connects the head of Jericho Bay with Penobscot Bay, near its head. There are several villages along its shores.

The reach is 11 miles long and has a least width of 4 cables near Byard Point (44°18′N 68°41′W). The Deer Island — Sedgwick Bridge, with a vertical clearance of 25·9 m (85 ft) for 30·5 m (100 ft) either side of the centreline, spans the reach near this point, narrowing the channel to 1¾ cables.

2 The main channel through the reach is generally broad and has sufficient depth for deep-draught vessels, however the channel is narrow in places and the bottom irregular and its navigation needs care.

The channel is entered from the E about 1 mile SW of Mahoney Island (44°13′N 68°31′W), a position 2 miles SW and WNW of the W ends of Pond Island Passage and Casco Passage, respectively.

3 The channel is marked with beacons and buoys (lateral), as for a vessel entering from the E. The principal dangers are buoyed and can easily be avoided by day in clear weather.

Anchorages and harbours
2.114

1 **Burnt Coat Harbor**, on the S side of Swans Island, is entered from Toothacher Bay (2.110) between Harbor Island (44°08′N 68°26′W) on the SE and Hockamock Head on the NW. The fairway in the entrance has a least width of ¼ cable, with a depth of 6·4 m (21 ft). Burnt Coat Harbor Light stands on Hockamock Head. A prominent tower is situated on the E side of the harbour, 1 mile N of the lighthouse.

2 Anchorage, small but well sheltered, can be obtained E of the lighthouse, in an area 2½ cables wide with depths of 6 to 10 m (20 to 33 ft), soft bottom, or in the channel farther N in depths of 4 to 7 m (13 to 23 ft). These anchorages are much used by local fishing vessels and yachts.

3 Swans Island is a village on the W side of the harbour, and Minturn is a settlement on the E side. Both have

wharves with depths alongside of about 1·5 m. Fuel and provisions may be obtained in both places.

2.115

1 **Southeast Harbor** (44°11′N 68°36′W), which lies NW of the E end of Deer Island Thorofare between Stinson Neck and Whitmore Neck provides the best anchorage in the vicinity of this thoroughfare. Anchorage may be obtained in depths of 6 to 12 m (20 to 39 ft). Boat Rock, with a depth of 1·8 m (6 ft) over it and marked on its SE side by a buoy (preferred channel to port), lies 9 cables SE of the entrance.

2 The harbour is seldom closed by ice.

2.116

1 **Stonington** (44°09′N 68°40′W) is a town on the N shore of Deer Island Thorofare, NE of Crotch Island.

2 **Wharf.** There is a cannery wharf, with depths alongside of 2·1 m, extending from Staple Point in the centre of the town. There are several wharves with depths alongside of 1·5 to 3·0 m, either side of Staple Point.

Supplies: fuel and provisions.

3 **Allen Cove**, situated on the E side of Moose Island (44°09′N 68°41′W), 1 mile W of Staple Point, is protected by a breakwater. A shipyard, with several piers and patent slips, for vessels up to 250 tonnes, is situated on the SE side of Moose Island. General hull and engine repairs can be carried out at the shipyard.

2.117

1 **Eggemoggin Reach** (2.113). Vessels can anchor anywhere within the reach, clear of a cable area crossing the reach about 1 mile SE of Byard Point, where the depth is suitable and the bottom soft. Small vessels can anchor in the coves described as follows, all of which are on the N side of the reach (with positions relative to Byard Point (44°18′N 68°41′W)):

2 **Center Harbor** (5 miles ESE) is a small cove situated on the N side of Chatto Island. The harbour is approached from W, passing N of

Torrey Ledge, which is marked by No 12 Buoy (starboard hand).

There is good anchorage off the W side of Chatto Island in depths of 7 m (23 ft), soft bottom.

3 The town of Brooklin stands on the N side of the harbour, where there is a wharf with a depth of 1·8 m alongside and a patent slip for craft up to 15 m in length.

Benjamin River (2½ miles ESE) lies close NW of Cape Carter. The entrance channel has a least depth of 5·8 m (19 ft), but is obstructed by shoals and ledges and is only ½ cable wide.

4 West Brooklin, a village with a prominent church spire, stands on the E side of the river near the entrance. A wharf with a depth alongside of 2·4 m is situated about 5 cables above the river entrance.

5 **Billings Cove** entered close E of Byard Point at the N end of the suspension bridge, provides anchorage in a depth of about 8 m (25 ft) in the middle of the cove just inside the entrance.

Sargentville, a village, situated on the E shore of the cove, has a wharf with a depth alongside of 2·4 m.

2.118

1 **Bucks Harbor** (3 miles NW) is an excellent anchorage and is often used by small vessels. Harbor Island, in the middle of the harbour, has a channel either side of it. The best anchorage is in depths of 8 to 11 m (26 to 36 ft) W and NW of the island.

South Brooksville, a village at the head of the harbour has two wharves with depths alongside of 3·7 m.

Supplies: fuel, water and provisions.

2 **Orcutt Harbor** (4 miles NW) is entered W of Condon Point. It has good anchorage in the middle of the harbour in depths of 4 to 16 m (13 to 52 ft), just above a wooded islet on the W side near the entrance. A rock, with a depth of 1·5 m (5 ft) over it lies 1 cable S of the islet.

PENOBSCOT BAY AND APPROACHES

GENERAL INFORMATION

Chart 2486
Description

2.119

1 The entrance to Penobscot Bay lies between Western Head (44°00′N 68°39′W) (2.33), the S point of Isle au Haut, and Whitehead Island, 20 miles W. This bay is the largest of the many indentations on the coast of Maine, and extends 28 miles inland to the mouth of the Penobscot River. There are several towns on the bank of the Penobscot River and the city of Bangor is situated 20 miles upstream at the head of navigation.

2 A chain of islands, of which the largest are Vinalhaven Island, North Haven Island and Islesboro Island divides the bay into two parts, East Penobscot Bay (2.136) and West Penobscot Bay (2.162). The S part of East Penobscot Bay is known as Isle au Haut Bay.

A number of islands and dangers lie in the S and SW approaches to Penobscot Bay. These are well marked by lights, buoys and beacons.

Logs

2.120

1 With high tides many logs from the Belfast area are adrift in the bay and are a danger to small vessels.

Pilotage

2.121

1 Pilotage is compulsory for all foreign vessels and US vessels under register in foreign trade, with a draught of 2·7 m (9 ft) or over, entering or leaving any harbour within the waters of Penobscot Bay or River, N of a line joining Western Head, Matinicus Rock Light (2.127) and Marshall Point Light (43°55′N 69°16′W).

Notice of ETA. 48, 24 and 12 hours.

2 **Pilots board as follows:**

Vessels from the E. Two miles E of WP Light-buoy (43°56′N 68°53′W) (2.168).

Vessels from the W. In the vicinity of 14M Light-buoy, about 2½ miles WSW of Monhegan Island Light (43°46′N 69°19′W).

3 About 5 cables S of WP Light-buoy (43°56′N 68°53′W). This position is for tug and barge units bound to and from Canadian ports, but can also be used by other vessels with prior arrangement.

For Penobscot River. About 2 miles SSE of the town wharf at Searsport (2.199).

See *Admiralty List of Radio Signals Volume 6(5)* for details.

Tugs
2.122

1 Tugs are available at Belfast (2.194) and 24 hours advance notice is required. Large vessels require the services of a tug for docking at Searsport (2.199) and for the river ports a tug usually accompanies the vessel upriver. Tugs meet vessels bound for Searsport 1½ miles SSE of the harbour and for the river ports, off Fort Point (44°28′N 68°49′W).

Under-keel clearances
2.123

1 The US Coast Guard recommends the following minimum under-keel clearances for vessels navigating in Penobscot Bay and River:

(a) A minimum of 0·9 m (3 ft) when transiting S of Turtle Head (2.171).

(b) A minimum of 0·6 m (2 ft) when transiting Penobscot River N of Turtle Head.

(c) A minimum of 0·3 m (1 ft) at all berthing areas.

Ice
2.124

1 In winter many of the harbours are obstructed by ice, but Penobscot River usually remains open with assistance of ice breakers. The inner channels are only occasionally obstructed by ice.

ISLE AU HAUT TO MONHEGAN ISLAND

General information

Chart 2486
Description
2.125

1 The following paragraphs describe the coastal passage between Western Head (44°00′N 68°39′W) (2.33), the S point of Isle au Haut, and Monhegan Island, 34 miles SW.

Traffic regulations
2.126

1 **Danger zone.** Seal Island (2.128) lies within a danger zone used by naval aircraft as a bombing target area. See Appendix VI for details.

Directions
(continued from 2.33)

Principal marks
2.127

1 **Landmarks:**
Monhegan Island (43°46′N 69°19′W). The island is 50 m (165 ft) in height with a rocky coast and high bluffs in places. A light stands in the centre of the island.

2 **Major lights:**
Matinicus Rock Light (43°47′N 68°51′W).
Two Bush Island Light (43°58′N 69°04′W) (2.167).
Monhegan Island Light - as above.

Isle au Haut to Monhegan Island
2.128

1 From a position SE of Western Head (44°00′N 68°39′W) the coastal passage leads SW, passing (with positions relative to Matinicus Rock Light (43°47′N 68°51′W)):

2 SE of Seal Island (8 miles NE), which is 23 m (77 ft) in height, bare and rocky, in the entrance to Penobscot Bay (2.119). Three Fathom Ledge with a swept depth of 4·9 m (16 ft) over it, and marked by DTF Light-buoy (isolated danger) close E, lies 1½ miles ENE of the NE end of Seal Island, and Malcolm Ledge, which dries 2·7 m (9 ft) at its N end, lies 1½ miles SW of the SW end of the island. A target with a radar reflector is moored 4 cables SE of the island (see 2.126). Thence:

3 SE of Wooden Ball Island (5 miles NNE), which is rocky with grass on its summit and has a prominent knoll, 19 m in height at its E end. 2WB Light-buoy (starboard hand) is moored 5 cables SW of the island. Thence:

4 SE of Matinicus Rock, which is 17 m in height and is the outermost danger in the S approaches to Penobscot Bay. A light (2.127) stands on the S end of the rock. Thence:

SE of Monhegan Island (20 miles W) (2.127).
(Directions continue for coastal passage at 3.11, and for West Penobscot Bay at 2.169).

APPROACHES TO PENOBSCOT BAY

General information

Chart 2486
General information
2.129

1 The outlying islands and dangers in the approaches to Penobscot Bay extend from Three Fathom Ledge (2.128) (43°54′N 68°42′W) to Monhegan Island (2.127) and its surrounding dangers, 28 miles WSW.

There is no secure harbour in any of these outlying islands.

2 There are settlements on the E side of Matinicus Island (43°52′N 68°54′W) (2.134), on the NW side of Ragged Island (43°50′N 68°54′W) (2.132) and on the W side of Monhegan Island (2.135).

Approach channels
2.130

1 The E part of the bay may be entered between Isle au Haut and Vinalhaven Island.

The main approach route for entering the W part of the bay from the S is through Two Bush Channel (43°57′N 69°04′W) (2.163). Muscle Ridge Channel (44°00′N 69°06′W) (2.172) also leads into the bay, but its use requires local knowledge.

2 There are other channels between the islands, which are mostly deep and have been well surveyed. However they have much broken ground with irregular soundings, and such areas should be avoided.

Deep draught vessels
2.131

1 There are recommended routes for deep draught vessels in Penobscot Bay. The route for vessels approaching from the W is described at 2.169, and for vessels approaching from the E at 2.168.

2 Deep draught vessels entering and departing Penobscot Bay and River are requested to remain within the recommended routes; two-way traffic is possible within all parts of the routes. Other vessels, while not excluded, should exercise caution in these areas and monitor VHF channels 16 or 13 for information concerning vessels transiting.

Anchorages and harbours

Ragged Island
2.132

1   **Criehaven Harbor** (43°50′N 68°54′W) is situated on the NW side of Ragged Island, an island which is 36 m in height and partly wooded. The harbour does not provide shelter in NW winds.

Layout and berths. A breakwater extends N from the S entrance point of the harbour. There is a depth of 1·5 m along the inner side of the breakwater. Other wharves in the harbour dry out.

2   **Supplies:** fuel; limited supply of provisions and water.
2.133

Seal Cove is situated on the E side of the island and is sheltered from NW winds.

Anchorage, clear of the cable area that runs through the cove, is available to small vessels up to 30 m in length, in depths of 21 m (69 ft), sand and shell.

Local knowledge is necessary.

Matinicus Island
2.134

1   **Matinicus Harbor** (43°52′N 68°53′W) is situated on the E side of Matinicus Island.

This island is mostly wooded and has a prominent mast, 30 m (100 ft) in height and visible from all directions, standing near its centre.

2   The harbour is protected by a breakwater which extends ¾ cable from the N side. No 2 Light (red triangle on framework tower) is exhibited from the outer part of the breakwater. Harbor Ledge, with a depth of 1·2 m (4 ft), lies off the entrance to the harbour and is marked on its S side by a buoy (preferred channel to port).

3   **Berths.** The village of Matinicus stands at the head of the harbour and has a pier with a depth alongside of 0·3 m.

A ferry sails to Rockland (2.177) on the mainland.

Anchorage. Small vessels can anchor in the outer harbour in depths of 2 to 8 m (6 to 26 ft), but this anchorage is exposed to NE winds.

Supplies: fuel; limited supply of provisions and water.

Monhegan Island
2.135

1   **Monhegan Harbor** (43°46′N 69°19′W), used principally by fishermen and yachtsmen, lies on the W side of Monhegan Island (2.127). It is situated in the channel, the N end of which is almost closed by a grass-covered islet, that lies between Monhegan Island and Manana Island.

2   **Berths.** Anchorage is available in depths of 4 to 7 m (13 to 26 ft), but the harbour is narrow, with poor holding ground and is exposed to the S.

The village of Monhegan stands on the E side of the harbour, where there is a pier with depths of 3·7 m alongside.

A ferry sails to Port Clyde (3.16) on the mainland.

3   **Supplies:** fuel; limited supply of provisions and water.

EAST PENOBSCOT BAY

General information

Chart 2486
Description
2.136

1   **East Penobscot Bay** is entered from the S between Western Head (44°00′N 68°39′W) (2.33) and Brimstone Island (5 miles W) and is the part of Penobscot Bay which lies E of Vinalhaven (2.119), North Haven (2.119) and Islesboro Island (2.119). The S part of the bay, known as Isle au Haut Bay lies between Isle au Haut and Vinalhaven Island. The N part of the bay is separated from the remainder of the bay by a group of islands that stretch NE from North Haven Island to the W entrance of Eggemoggin Reach.

2   The recommended route for deep draught vessels proceeding to the N part of the bay lies W of Vinalhaven and North Haven Islands and is described at 2.168 and 2.169.

The islands in East Penobscot Bay have numerous coves and small harbours, but few of these are suitable as anchorages, some on account of their depth and others owing to the numerous dangers which obstruct their entrances.

Topography
2.137

1   **Isle au Haut**, which forms the E shore of Isle au Haut Bay, is a prominent landmark 166 m in height, wooded, and the highest land in the vicinity. The island is surrounded by numerous dangers and should be approached with caution. There are no good anchorages on its coast except Isle au Haut Thorofare (2.143).

Traffic routes
2.138

1   The principal traffic through East Penobscot Bay is in an E-W direction through the inside passages, but there is a clear channel, in which the principal dangers are marked, through the bay from the sea to its head.

Directions
(continued from 2.33)

Principal marks
2.139

1   **Major light:**
Fort Point Light (44°28′N 68°49′W) (2.226).

Isle au Haut Bay
2.140

1   From a position S of Western Head (44°00′N 68°39′W) the route from sea into Isle au Haut Bay leads NNW in depths of over 9·1 m (30 ft), passing (with positions relative to Saddleback Ledge Light (44°01′N 68°44′W)):

2   WSW of Western Ear (3 miles ESE), a wooded islet, close S of Western Head. Western Ear Ledge and The Washers, groups of rocks that dry, lie 2 cables S and 8 cables WNW, respectively, of the island. No 2 Buoy (starboard hand) is moored 8 cables W of Western Ear. Thence:

3   ENE of Saddleback Ledge Light (grey conical tower, 13 m in height), standing on a small rocky islet, thence:

WSW of The Brandies (2 miles ENE), a group of rocks, the highest of which dries 2·4 m (8 ft).

Attention is drawn to a patch, with a depth of 9·1 m (30 ft), which lies 6 cables SW. No 4 Buoy (starboard hand) is moored 3 cables W of The Brandies. Thence:

4   WSW of Isle au Haut Light (4½ miles NE), which stands on Robinson Point, the S entrance point to Isle au Haut Thorofare (2.143). The red sector of this light covers The Brandies and the 9·1 m (30 ft) patch 6 cables SW. Thence:

5   WSW of Kimball Head (4½ miles NE). Kimball Rock and a number of patches with depths of less than 9·1 m (30 ft) lie between 5 cables and 1¼ miles SW of the headland. And:

ENE of Calderwood Point (3¾ miles NW), the E point of Vinalhaven Island. F Light-buoy (special) is moored 2¼ miles NE of Calderwood Point. Thence:

6   WSW of The Brown Cow (6½ miles N), a rock 0·9 m (3 ft) in height, which is the W danger at the W entrance of Merchant Row (2.111). 2BC Buoy (starboard hand) is moored 6 cables SSW of the rock.

Thence into the inner part of East Penobscot Bay.

Inner part of East Penobscot Bay
2.141

1   From the vicinity of The Brown Cow (44°07′N 68°44′W) the main route through the inner part of East Penobscot Bay leads generally N and then NW, passing (with positions relative to Dunham Point (44°13′N 68°44′W)):

2   W of Stinson Point (3 miles S). Sellers Rock, which partly dries, lies 3 cables W of the point and a patch with a depth of 5·5 m (18 ft) lies 4 cables farther WSW. No 2 Buoy (starboard hand) is moored 2 cables WSW of the rock.

3   Between Hardhead Island (1 mile W), a bare island, 23 m (76 ft) in height, and Eagle Island, which is 45 m in height and wooded. Eagle Island Light (1½ miles WSW) stands on the NE point of Eagle Island and 3A Buoy (port hand) is moored 2 cables off the point. Thence:

4   SW of Middle Rock (1½ miles WNW), which has a depth of 3 m (10 ft) over it and is marked on its W side by No 4 Buoy (starboard hand). Thence:

Between Bradbury Island (1½ miles NW) and Butter Island (2 miles W). The channel between Bradbury Island and Pickering Island, wooded, 1½ miles NNE, is much obstructed and should not be used without local knowledge. Thence:

5   NE of Beach Island (4½ miles NW), thence:

SW of Green Ledge Light No 4 (red triangle on framework tower, 5 m in height) (6 miles NW) which stands on Green Ledge, a grassy islet which is the W of a group of islands in the W entrance to Eggemoggin Reach (2.113). No 2 Buoy (starboard hand) is moored 3 cables SW.

6   Thence the route leads N into the N part of East Penobscot Bay, which lies between Cape Rosier, an extension of the mainland on the E side of the bay, and Islesboro Island on the W.

Useful mark:

7   Deer Island Thorofare Light (5 miles SSE) which stands on Mark Island (2.145) and lies at the W entrance to Deer Island Thorofare.

East Penobscot Bay deep draught route
(continued from 2.168 and 2.169)
2.142

1   From a position E of Monroe Island (44°05′N 69°02′W) the recommended route for deep draught vessels to the head of Penobscot Bay passing E of Islesboro Island initially leads N, then NE, passing (with positions relative to Owls Head Light (44°05′·6N 69°02′·6W)):

2   NW of PB Light-buoy (safe water) (2 miles ENE), thence:

SE of McIntosh Ledge (5¼ miles NE), a rock awash at low water. No 1 Buoy (port hand) is moored close E.

3   The route then continues NNE, passing (with positions relative to Hewes Point (44°18′·2N 68°53′·2W)):

ESE of No 3 Buoy (port hand) (7¾ miles SSW), thence:

ESE of Pendleton Point (4¾ miles SSW), the S point of Islesboro Island, thence:

ESE of Hewes Point, thence:

4   ESE of No 9 Buoy (port hand) (3 miles NNE), which marks the E side of Islesboro Ledge, a rock with a depth of 2·4 m (8 ft) over it.

Thence the track continues N, passing:

W of Dice Head (5½ miles NNE) (2.159) thence:

Through an oil transfer area (44°25′·0N 68°50·7W) as shown on the chart.

5   Thence to a position at the entrance to Penobscot River.

Side channels

Isle au Haut Thorofare
2.143

1   Isle au Haut Thorofare, which is entered from the W between Robinson Point (44°04′N 68°39′W) (2.140) and Marsh Cove Head, 3 cables NW, separates Kimball Island from Isle au Haut.

A dredged channel, marked by buoys, leads across the ledges at the NE end of the passage. This channel is 23 m (75 ft) wide.

Local knowledge is required to navigate this passage.

2   **Useful marks** (with positions relative to Robinson Point):

Isle au Haut Light (on Robinson Point) (2.140).

Spire (9 cables NE) in village of Isle au Haut.

West entrance Merchant Row
2.144

1   The W entrance of Merchant Row (2.111) is entered S of The Brown Cow (44°07′N 68°44′W) (2.140) and between Scraggy Island and Farrel Island, both of which are wooded, on the N, and Sparrow Island, which is grassy, on the S.

West entrance Deer Island Thorofare
2.145

1   The W entrance of Deer Island Thorofare (2.112) is entered N of The Brown Cow (44°07′N 68°44′W) and between West Mark Island Ledge (44°08′·3N 68°43′·1W), which is marked by No 2 Buoy (starboard hand), and Mark Island (44°08′·1N 68°42′·1W) on which stands Deer Island Thorofare Light.

Fox Islands Thorofare
2.146

1 Fox Islands Thorofare, leading from East Penobscot Bay to West Penobscot Bay, between Vinalhaven Island and North Haven Island, is one of the chain of inshore passages that commences at Bass Harbor (2.103) and ends at Whitehead Island (43°59′N 69°07′W).

The thoroughfare, which is 7 miles long, is entered from East Penobscot Bay between Bluff Head (44°06′N 68°48′W) and Babbidge Island, 2¼ miles N.

2 The thoroughfare has a least depth of 5·2 m (17 ft) and a least width of ½ cable between Iron Point (44°08′N 68°52′W) and Zeke Point. These narrows and the principal dangers are marked by buoys and beacons. It is sometimes closed by ice in winter.

3 Tidal streams are usually not strong and meet at Iron Point, the stream setting through either entrance with a rising tide.

At LW the thoroughfare is seldom used by vessels exceeding 4·3 m draught and should not be attempted without local knowledge.

4 **Caution** is necessary during strong winds from E and W as they may considerably increase the rate of the tide.

Useful mark:

> Goose Rocks Light (white conical tower, with black round base) (44°08′N 68°50′W), standing inside the E entrance.

North of North Haven Island
2.147

1 There is a passage for small vessels N of North Haven Island, with a least depth of 7·6 m (25 ft), which is used in winter when Fox Islands Thorofare is closed by ice. **Local knowledge** is required.

2 **Directions.** From a position 4 cables N of Bald Island (44°11′N 68°47′W) the route leads W, passing N of Grass Ledge and Oak Island, both grassy, and S of Spoon Ledge, 4·6 m (15 ft) in height with grassy summit.

Anchorages and harbours in south part of East Penobscot Bay

Moores Harbor
2.148

1 Moores Harbor (44°03N 68°39′W), which lies 2½ miles N of Western Head, is obstructed by many dangers, both in the harbour and its approach, and is an unsafe anchorage.

Isle au Haut and Lookout
2.149

1 Isle au Haut and Lookout (44°05′N 68°38′W) are villages at the NE end of Isle au Haut Thorofare (2.143). Both villages have wharves, with depths alongside of 1·8 and 2·8 m, respectively, which are approached by buoyed channels.

Supplies: fuel and limited provisions are available at Isle au Haut.

Carver Cove
2.150

1 Carver Cove (44°07′N 68°50′W) lies on the S side of the E entrance to Fox Islands Thorofare (2.146) and may be approached from either side of Widow Island (44°08′N 68°50′W).

Anchorage may be obtained 5 cables from the head of the cove in depths of 5 to 6 m (16 to 20 ft), good holding ground. The shores of the cove should be given a berth of 1½ cables.

Kent Cove
2.151

1 Kent Cove is entered W of Goose Rocks Light (44°08′N 68°50′W) (2.146) at the E end of Fox Islands Thorofare.

Good anchorage for small vessels may be obtained in depths of 5 to 7 m (15 to 24 ft), good holding ground.

Waterman Cove
2.152

1 Waterman Cove, separated from Kent Cove by Fish Point (44°08′N 68°51′W), and 9 cables W of Goose Rocks Light, is a good anchorage for small vessels with depths of 5 m (18 ft) at its entrance. The cove shoals to 1·2 m (4 ft) near its head.

North Haven
2.153

1 North Haven is a village on the N shore of Fox Islands Thorofare, 7 cables W of Iron Point (44°08′N 68°52′W) (2.146). It is an important yachting centre.

Shoals, with depths of 0·6 and 2·4 m (2 and 8 ft), marked by buoys, lie off the village.

Berths. The town wharf has a depth alongside of 3·7 m. There are several other wharves.

2 **Repairs:** patent slip; small repairs.

Supplies: fuel and provisions.

Southwest Harbor
2.154

1 Southwest Harbor is entered 1½ miles N of Stinson Point (44°10′N 68°43′W) and lies within Sheephead Island and Sheephead Island Ledge.

Anchorage is available in depths of 6 to 9 m (20 to 29 ft), but is seldom used as it is open SW.

The village of Sunset is situated at the head of the harbour.

Useful mark: Church spire in village.
2.155

1 **Sylvester Cove** is entered 8 cables SE of Dunham Point (44°13′N 68°44′W). A reef that partly dries lies on the S side of the entrance, and its extremity is marked by No 2 Buoy (starboard hand).

Berth. A wharf, used by ferries, with a depth alongside of 2·7 m, stands on the N side of the harbour.

Northwest Harbor
2.156

1 Northwest Harbor is entered between Heart Island (44°15′N 68°42′W), 18 m (60 ft) in height and partly wooded, and Gull Ledge, 7 cables SW. A rocky spit, which partly dries, extends 2½ cables NW from the S entrance point and is marked at its outer end by No 2 Buoy (starboard hand).

The harbour is closed by ice during January and February.

2 **Good anchorage** may be obtained by small vessels in mid-channel, in the outer part of the harbour, with depths of 4 to 5 m (13 to 16 ft). There is also good anchorage, in depths of 6 to 9 m (20 to 30 ft), between Gull Ledge and Heart Island.

The village of Deer Isle is situated near the head of the harbour, and has two small wharves that dry.

Anchorages and harbours in north part of East Penobscot Bay

WEST PENOBSCOT BAY AND ENTRANCES

General information

Islesboro Harbor
2.157
1   Islesboro Harbor is entered N of Hewes Point (44°18′N 68°53′W). Hewes Ledge, awash, lies 2½ cables N of Hewes Point and is marked on its N end by No 1 Buoy (port hand) and its S end by No 2 Buoy (starboard hand).

2   **Anchorage** with good shelter from the W, is available in depths of 9 to 13 m (30 to 43 ft), rocky bottom.

The village of Islesboro stands on the S side of the harbour.

Sabbathday Harbor
2.158
1   Sabbathday Harbor is entered 2 miles N of Hewes Point (44°18′N 68°53′W). A dangerous rock, with a depth of less than 1·8 m (6 ft) over it, lies ¾ cable SSE of the W entrance point.

Anchorage is available for small vessels in depths of 2 to 6 m (7 to 20 ft). **Local knowledge** is necessary.

2   The village of North Islesboro stands on the W side of the harbour.

Castine Harbor
2.159
1   Castine Harbor is entered between Dice Head (44°23′N 68°49′W) and Nautilus Island, 7 cables SE, at the mouth of the Bagaduce River. The town of Castine, which is an important summer resort, stands on the N bank of the river about 1 mile from its mouth.

Ice. The Bagaduce River is usually free of ice at Castine and for some distance above but in very severe winters it is entirely closed.

2   **Directions.** From a position S of Dice Head Light (red and white chequered diamond on framework tower) (44°23′N 68°49′W), the track into the harbour leads NE passing:

> Either side of CH Buoy (safe water) which is moored 4 cables SSE of Dice Head, thence:
>
> SE of a buoy (port hand) that marks foul ground extending from the N side of the entrance.

2.160
1   **Alongside berths.** The wharf of the Maine Marine Academy, at the W end of the waterfront, has a depth alongside of 7·9 m. There are other wharves with depths alongside of 3 and 3·7 m.

Repairs: minor repairs.

Other facilities: hospital.

Supplies: fuel and water.

Smith Cove
2.161
1   Smith Cove is entered between Hospital Island and Henry Point (44°23′N 68°47′W), 1½ miles SE of the town of Castine.

Anchorage is available in depths of 6 to 18 m (19 to 58 ft), soft bottom and well sheltered.

General information

Charts 2490, 2486 (see 1.17)
Description
2.162
1   West Penobscot Bay is that part of Penobscot Bay that lies W of Vinalhaven Island, North Haven Island and Islesboro Island.

Entrance routes
2.163
1   From E the seaward entrance to West Penobscot Bay is clear of the islands and shoals which front the S and W sides of Vinalhaven Island. This entrance is suitable for deep-draught vessels (see 2.131).

2   From W the entrance for deep-draught vessels is through Two Bush Channel, a deep and well marked channel, which is entered E of Two Bush Island (43°58′N 69°04′W). Muscle Ridge Channel also leads into West Penobscot Bay from W, passing E of Whitehead Island (43°59′N 69°08′W), but local knowledge is required for its use.

3   For vessels of moderate draught the entrance from East Penobscot Bay is either through Fox Islands Thorofare (2.146), or through the passage between the islands N of North Haven Island (2.147).

Pilotage
2.164
1   See 2.121 for pilotage to ports in West Penobscot Bay.

Oil transfer anchorage areas
2.165
1   Two oil transfer anchorage areas, as shown on the chart, have been established at the head of Penobscot Bay, (with positions relative to Turtle Head (44°24′N 68°53′W)):

Centred 2 miles NW, with diameter of 2 miles.

Centred 2 miles NE, with diameter of 1 mile.

Naval trial course
2.166
1   A naval trial course, running course of 000½°-180½° and 5 miles in length, is established in the S part of W Penobscot Bay. The ends of this course are marked by PA Light-buoy (44°01′N 69°00′W) and PB Light-buoy (44°06′N 69°00′W).

Vessels must keep clear of the course while trials are in progress.

Directions
(continued from 2.33)

Principal marks
2.167
1   **Landmark:**

Monhegan Island (43°46′N 69°19′W) (2.127).

Major lights:

Matinicus Rock Light (43°47′N 68°51′W) (2.127).

Monhegan Island Light (43°46′N 69°19′W) (2.127).

2   Two Bush Island Light (43°58′N 69°04′W).
Owls Head Light (white tower) (44°06′N 69°03′W).
Rockland Breakwater Head Light (44°06′N 69°05′W)
    (2.179).
Fort Point Light (44°28′N 68°49′W) (2.226).

Entering from east
2.168

1   From a position S of Western Head (44°00′N 68°39′W)
the recommended route for deep draught vessels (2.131)
from E into West Penobscot Bay leads initially W, passing
(with positions relative to Heron Neck Light (44°02′N
68°52′W)):
Either side of PBA Light-buoy (safe water) (43°56′N
    68°40′W), thence:
2   N of Three Fathom Ledge (43°54′N 68°42′W)
    (2.128), marked on its E side by DTF Light-buoy
    (isolated danger), thence:
N of Seal Island (43°53′N 68°44′W) (2.128), thence;
S of Snippershan Ledge (43°57′N 68°45′W), with a
    depth of 11 m (36 ft) over it, thence:
3   S of Bay Ledge (3½ miles S) which has a depth of
    0·9 m (3 ft) over it and is marked close SW by
    DBL Buoy (isolated danger), thence:
S of WP Light-buoy (safe water) (5¾ miles SSW).
Thence the track leads NW, passing:
SW of a 9·1 m (30 ft) patch that lies 5 cables SSW of
    Perry Ledge (3 miles WSW), thence:
4   NE of Junken Ledge (6 miles WSW), with a least
    depth of 5·8 m (19 ft) over it. This ledge is marked
    by DJ Buoy (isolated danger). Thence:
NE of PA Light-buoy (safe water) (6¼ miles W).
Thence the track leads N to a position E of Monroe
Island (8 miles WNW).
5   An alternative recommended deep draught route leads
initially NE from a position 1 mile SW of Wooden Ball
Island (43°51′N 68°49′W) (2.128), passing (with positions
relative to Matinicus Rock Light (43°47′N 68°51′W)):
NW of 2WB Light-buoy (3½ miles NNE), thence:
NW of Wooden Ball Island, thence:
SE of Greens Ledge (5 miles N).
6   The route then leads NW passing:
NE of Zephyr Rock (43°53′·8N 69°51′·8W), marked
    on its NE side by No 5 Light-buoy, thence:
To a position SW of No WP Buoy (43°55′·8N
68°53′·1W), where it joins the recommended route
described above.
7   **Useful mark:**
Heron Neck Light (44°02′N 68°52′W).
*(Directions for West Penobscot Bay continue at 2.170;
directions for East Penobscot Bay continue at 2.142)*

Entering from south and west
(continued from 2.128)
2.169

1   From the vicinity of 14M Light-buoy (starboard hand)
(43°45′N 69°22′W), which is moored 2½ miles WSW of
Monhegan Island Light, the main route from S and W
leads NE, and then generally ENE through Two Bush
Channel (2.163), passing (with positions relative to Two
Bush Island Light (43°58′N 69°04′W)):
2   NW of the dangers lying off the NW side of
    Monhegan Island (15 miles SW) (2.127).
    No 5 Light-buoy (port hand) is moored 2 cables
    NW of Duck Rocks, the outermost of these
    dangers. Thence:

SE of 2OM Light-buoy (starboard hand) (13 miles
    SW). The recommended route for deep draught
    vessels (2.131) is entered 1 mile SE of this buoy.
    Thence:
3   SE of Burnt Island (11 miles SW). This island, which
    forms part of the Georges Islands, is 47 m (156 ft)
    in height and wooded. A prominent Coast Guard
    lookout tower stands on its summit.
    2OM Light-buoy (starboard hand) marks Old Man
    Ledge and 2OC Buoy (starboard hand) marks Old
    Cilly Ledge, two dangers on the NW side of the
    channel, that lie 2 miles SSW and NE,
    respectively, of Burnt Island. Thence:
4   NW of the dangers lying W of Metinic Island
    (5 miles SSW). This island is partly wooded and
    24 m in height. No 3 Buoy and MI buoy,
    respectively, mark Roaring Bull and Metinic Island
    Ledge, two dangers on the SE side of the channel,
    that lie 3 miles W and 2¼ miles NW, respectively,
    of the S point of Metinic Island. Thence:
5   SE of Mosquito Island (7 miles SW), a wooded island
    24 m (78 ft) in height. No 2 Buoy (starboard hand)
    is moored 2 cables S of the island. Thence:
NW of MP Light-buoy (safe water) (5½ miles SW),
    marking the SW approach to Two Bush Channel,
    thence:
6   NW of No 4 Buoy (starboard hand) (4 miles SW),
    marking a rocky shoal with a least depth of 11·0 m
    (36 ft), thence:
Between 5TB Light-buoy (port hand) (1¼ miles
    SSW) and No 6 Buoy (starboard hand) moored
    6 cables ESE, thence:
7   SSE of Two Bush Island Light, thence:
SSE of No 7 Buoy (port hand) (2 miles ENE).
The route then leads N, passing (with positions relative
to Two Bush Island Light):
W of TBI Light-buoy (safe water) (3 miles E),
    thence:
W of Junken Ledge (4 miles ENE) (2.168), thence:
8   Between PA Light-buoy (safe water) (4½ miles NE)
    and No 9 Buoy (port hand) (4½ miles NNE),
    which marks a 7 m (23 ft) shoal that lies 1 mile SE
    of Fisherman Island, thence:
W of F Light-buoy (special) (6½ miles NNE), thence:
9   To a position E of Monroe Island (7 miles NNE).
    No 11 Light-buoy (port hand) is moored 3 cables
    E of the island.
Useful mark:
Browns Head Light (44°07′N 68°55′W) (2.176).
(Directions continue for East Penobscot Bay at 2.142)

To the head of Penobscot Bay
(continued from 2.168)
2.170

1   **Monroe Island to Seven Hundred Acre Island.** From a
position E of Monroe Island (44°05′N 69°02′W) the
recommended route for deep draught vessels passing W of
Islesboro Island to the head of Penobscot Bay leads N then
NNE, through the S part of West Penobscot Bay, passing
(with positions relative to The Graves (44°11′N 69°02′W)):
2   E of Owls Head (5½ miles S), a prominent headland
    that forms the S entrance point of Rockland
    Harbor (2.177). A light (2.167) stands on the
    headland. Thence:
3   E of Beauchamp Point (1½ miles SW), which is
    prominent. Indian Island and Lowell Rock, which
    form the E entrance point to Rockport Harbor

(2.184), lie close S of Beauchamp Point. A tower (disused lighthouse) stands on the former and Lowell Rock Light No 2 (2.185) stands on the latter. Thence:

4   W of Mark Island (2½ miles E), which is high, rounded and prominent. This island lies 7¾ cables N of Robinson Rock, which is 7 m in height and grassy. The limit of the dangers that extend S from Robinson Rock is marked by No 12 Buoy (starboard hand). Thence:

5   E of The Graves, a reef partly above-water, with a large drying area; No 13 Light-buoy (port hand) is moored close E. Thence:

E of Curtis Island Light (1¼ miles NNW) (2.190), which stands on Curtis Island. The island and light, situated on the S side of the entrance to Camden Harbor (2.188), are prominent. Thence:

6   ENE of Moxy Reef (2 miles N), with a depth of 6·1 m (20 ft) over it, thence:

ENE of Dillingham Ledge (2¾ miles N), marked by No 1 Buoy (port hand), thence:

WNW of Seven Hundred Acre Island (5 miles NNE).

2.171

1   **Seven Hundred Acre Island to the head of the bay.** From a position WNW of the N point of Seven Hundred Acre Island (44°16′N 68°57′W), the route to the head of West Penobscot Bay leads NNE, passing (with positions relative to Great Spruce Head (44°19′N 68°57′W)):

2   WNW of Grindel Point Light (2½ miles S), standing on the N entrance point to the N entrance of Gilkey Harbor (2.214). Thence:

ESE of Spruce Head (2 miles SSW), the NE entrance point of Ducktrap Harbor (2.215), thence:

ESE of Great Spruce Head, a bold headland. Thence:

3   WNW of Marshall Point (4 miles NE), which is marked by prominent yellowish bluffs. No 11 Light-buoy (safe water) is moored 7 cables NW of the headland.

The route then leads generally NE passing:

4   NW of Turtle Head, a wooded and prominent headland that is joined to Islesboro Island by a low, narrow wooded neck.

Thence as necessary to the ports at the head of West Penobscot Bay or to the mouth of the Penobscot River.

(Directions continue for Penobscot River at 2.226; directions for Belfast are given at 2.196)

Other entrance and side channels

Muscle Ridge Channel
2.172

1   **Description.** Muscle Ridge Channel leads W of the group of islands and rocks lying on the NW side of Two Bush Channel. It is entered from seaward close S of Whitehead Island (43°59′N 69°08′W).

The channel is much used in clear weather in daylight as it is sheltered and provides good anchorage.

2   **Depths.** The channel has a least depth of 7·9 m (26 ft) in the fairway, but shoal depths of 4 to 6·7 m (13 ft to 22 ft) are close by.

2.173

1   **Directions.** From a position S of Whitehead Island the channel leads NE for 5 miles, passing between dangers that are well marked by beacons and buoys as shown on the chart.

Useful mark:

Whitehead Island Light (43°59′N 69°08′W).

2   **Local knowledge.** The dangers are well marked, however the channel is narrow in places and should not be used without local knowledge.

Fisherman Island Passage
2.174

1   **Description.** Fisherman Island Passage, with depths of 6·7 m to 8·2 m (22 to 27 ft), leads between Fisherman Island (44°02′N 69°02′W) and Sheep Island (1¼ miles NNW), from the N end of Muscle Ridge Channel into West Penobscot Bay. The channel, which is about 2½ cables wide between the shoals extending from the two islands, is marked by buoys.

Owls Head Bay
2.175

1   **Description.** Owls Head Bay is a channel that leads between Sheep Island (44°04′N 69°03′W) and Monroe Island on the E, and the mainland on the W. It is an alternative route to Fisherman Island Passage, leading into West Penobscot Bay.

2   **Width and depths.** The channel is buoyed but is very narrow off the W side of Sheep Island, being only 76 m (250 ft) wide between the 9·1 m (30 ft) depth contours, and with a depth of 11·6 m (38 ft) in the fairway.

Anchorage, clear of the cable areas that cross the N and S entrances, may be obtained in the bay in depths of 12 to 22 m (39 ft to 12 fm).

West entrance to Fox Islands Thorofare
2.176

1   Fox Islands Thorofare is entered from the W between Crockett Point (44°06′N 68°55′W) and Stand-in Point, 1¼ miles NW. The entrance is considerably restricted by numerous off-lying dangers.

2   **Directions.** From the vicinity of FT Light-buoy (safe water) (44°05′N 68°57′W), the white sector (050-061°) of Browns Head Light (44°07′N 68°55′W) leads through the dangers in the W entrance to Fox Islands Thorofare. The channel is marked by buoys and beacons.

3   **Useful marks** (with positions relative to Browns Head Light):

Beacon (1½ miles SW), a grey stone column standing on Fiddler Ledge.

Sugar Loaves (3 cables NW), a ledge of prominent rocks 9 m (30 ft) in height.

Rockland Harbor

General information
2.177

1   **Position and function.** Rockland Harbor, which is situated on the W side of West Penobscot Bay, is entered between Owls Head (44°06′N 69°03′W) (2.170) and Jameson Point.

Rockland Harbor is one of the most important harbours in Penobscot Bay and is a port of entry.

The city of Rockland has trade in fish and petroleum products and a number of light industries.

Limiting conditions and arrival information
2.178

1   **Project depths.** Main approach channel 5·5 m (18 ft). Three branch channels, each with a turning basin, to N, W and SW part of waterfront, 4·3 m (14 ft).

Deepest berth. Main pier, 4·3 m.

Tidal levels. Mean spring range about 3·4 m; mean neap range about 2·5 m. See information in *Admiralty Tide Tables.*

2 **Weather.** The harbour is exposed to E winds and NE winds raise a heavy sea in the SW part of the harbour.
Pilots and tugs. See 2.121 and 2.122.

Principal marks
2.179

1 **Landmarks:**
  Rockland Breakwater Head Light (44°06'·2N 69°04'·7W).
  Radio Tower (44°06'·4N 69°06'·5W), which is lit at night.
  Knox County Airport Light (44°03'·6N 69°05'·4W).
  Major light:
  Rockland Breakwater Head Light — as above.

Directions
2.180

1 From a position N of Owls Head Light the track leads W passing S of Breakwater Head Light, giving the breakwater a berth of at least ½ cable, and thence between anchorage areas A and B towards No 2 Buoy (starboard hand) which is moored 3 cables W of the entrance to the dredged channel.

Berths
2.181

1 **Anchorages** (the limits of which are shown on the US chart):
  Area A. In the S part of the harbour with depths of 6 to 15 m (20 to 50 ft). For vessels over 20 m in length.
  Area B. In the N part of the harbour with depths of 6 to 12 m (20 to 40 ft). For vessels over 20 m in length.
2 Area C. In W part of harbour with depths of 4 to 6 m (13 to 20 ft). For small commercial and pleasure craft up to 20 m in length.
  A channel, 2½ cables wide, is left between Areas A and B. No vessel may anchor in the channel or within 1½ cables of any wharf without permission.
2.182

1 **Alongside berths:**
  Ferry terminal. Length 85 m. Reported depth alongside of 3·4 m.
  Other wharves. Reported depths alongside of 1·8 to 4·3 m.

Port services
2.183

1 **Repairs** to small vessels may be carried out at a shipyard at Atlantic Point in the SW part of the harbour. A slipway can handle vessels up to length 68 m, beam 12·2 m, displacement 1200 tonnes and draught 4·8 m.
  Other facilities: hospital.
  Supplies: fuel; provisions and water.
  Rescue. Coast Guard station on E side of Crockett Point (44°06'·4N 69°06'·3W).

Rockport Harbor

General information
2.184

1 **Position.** Rockport Harbor is entered between Lowell Rock (44°10'N 69°04'W) and the coast W. It is a good anchorage for all classes of vessels and is sheltered from all but S winds.

The entrance to the harbour is deep and clear, with the exception of Porterfield Ledge, which lies 6 cables S of Lowell Rock. It is 7 cables wide at the entrance and narrows to 1 cable at its head and is easy of access.
Rockport is a town at the head of the harbour.

Directions
2.185

1 Vessels may enter Rockport Harbor on either side of Porterfield Ledge Beacon, giving the ledge a berth of at least ¾ cable.
  Useful marks (with positions relative to Lowell Rock):
  Porterfield Ledge Beacon (6 cables S) which stands on a ledge that dries several feet.
2 Lowell Rock Light No 2 (red triangle on post).
  Tower (1½ cables NNW), which stands on Indian Island.
  Clock Tower (1½ miles NNW).

Anchorage
2.186

1 Anchorage may be obtained for deep-draught vessels between the entrance and 1 mile from the head of the harbour in depths of 13 to 19 m (42 to 63 ft), soft bottom. Smaller vessels can anchor nearer the head of the harbour.
2.187

1 **Repairs:** boatyard for minor repairs on W side of harbour.
  Supplies: fuel; provisions and stores.

Camden Harbor

General information
2.188

1 **Position and function.** Camden Harbor is entered between Curtis Island (44°12'N 69°03'W) and Northeast Ledge (3 cables NE), which extends 3 cables SSE from Northeast Point.
  The town of Camden, situated at the head of the inner harbour in an inlet off the W side of the bay, is a yachting centre.

Ice
2.189

1 Ice sometimes forms in the harbour from January to March, but is not dangerous for vessels in the outer harbour and is usually cleared by W winds.

Directions
2.190

1 From a position N of The Graves (44°11'N 69°02'W) the track into the harbour leads NW, passing:
  Between Curtis Island and Nos 2 and 4 Buoys (starboard hand) which mark the NE side of the channel, thence:
  Between No 7 Buoy (port hand) off Dillingham Point and No 6 Buoy (starboard hand) marking the SE side of Inner Ledges, thence to the anchorage in the outer harbour.
2 **Useful marks** (with positions relative to Curtis Island Light):
  Curtis Island Light (44°12'N 69°03'W).
  Northeast Point Light No 2 (red triangle on white framework tower and small white house) (4½ cables NNE).
  Mount Battie (1½ miles NW). The summit, which is marked by a small stone memorial tower, shows as a ridge from the offing.

Anchorage
2.191

1 Anchorage may be obtained in the outer harbour in depths of 4 to 10 m (13 to 33 ft), soft bottom. The anchorage area is NE of a line joining Eaton Point (44°12'·5N 69°03'·4W) and the buoy 4 cables SE.

Inner harbour
2.192

1 The inner harbour, which is entered between Eaton Point and the shore 1 cable SW, has depths of about 2·4 to 3·0 m (7¾ to 10 ft) in the middle and 1·4 to 1·8 m (4½ to 6 ft) along the E and W shores with lesser depths towards the shore. It is chiefly used by small commercial vessels and pleasure craft.

Port services
2.193

1 **Repairs:** boatyard where minor repairs can be carried out. The largest slip in the inner harbour can accommodate craft up to 33 m in length.
Other facilities: hospital.
Supplies: fuel; provisions and stores.

Belfast Harbor

General information
2.194

1 **Position.** Belfast Harbor is situated at the head of Belfast Bay, which is entered between Browns Head (44°23'N 68°59'W) and Moose Point, 3 miles NNE. Passagassawakeag River flows into the head of the bay.
The city of Belfast, which in 2005 had an estimated population of 6872, stands on the SW side of the river.
Belfast is a port of entry.

Limiting conditions and arrival information
2.195

1 **Deepest berth.** Marshall Wharf. See 2.197.
Channel depth. There is a least depth of 4·3 m (14 ft) in the channel to Belfast.
Tidal levels. Mean spring range about 3·5 m; mean neap range about 2·5 m. See information in *Admiralty Tide Tables.*
Ice obstructs navigation in the river and bay in severe winters. The bay has been frozen as far as Islesboro Island.
Pilotage and tugs. See 2.121 and 2.122.

Directions
2.196

1 From a position NE of Browns Head (2.194), the approach leads NW passing SW of Steets Ledge (44°25'N 68°58'W), an extensive shoal, with a least depth of 0·3 m (1 ft) over it. No 2 Light-buoy (starboard hand) is moored close S of the ledge and a disused lighthouse stands on the ledge. Thence the approach leads to the anchorage and river mouth.

Berths
2.197

1 **Good anchorage** is available in depths of 6 to 8 m (20 to 26 ft) W of Steets Ledge and also in mid-channel in the river 5 cables W of Paterson Point. Small vessels may anchor ½ cable off the wharves, abreast the town, in depths of 3 to 7 m (10 to 22 ft).

2 **Alongside berths.** Deepest berth is Marshall Wharf, owned by a towage company, with a reported depth alongside of 4·6 m. There are two other berths with depths alongside of 2·4 to 3 m.

Port services
2.198

1 **Repairs:** boatyard with 12 m patent slip for hull repairs.
Other facilities: hospital.
Supplies: fuel; provisions and stores.

Searsport Harbor

General information
2.199

1 **Position.** Searsport Harbor and Long Cove (2.201) lie at the head of a bay which is entered between Moose Point (44°26'N 68°57'W) and the S end of Sears Island.
Searsport Harbor provides good anchorage for all classes of vessels. The town of Searsport stands at the head of the harbour.

2 **Function.** The port handles mainly petroleum products, potatoes, general and dry bulk cargoes.
The commercial development of the port is situated on the SE side of Mack Point and the W shore of Sears Island at the entrance to Long Cove, 1½ miles ESE of the town.
Traffic. In 2005 the port was used by 17 vessels with a total deadweight 683 348 tonnes.
Port Authority. Maine Port Authority, State House Station, Augusta, ME 04333.

Limiting conditions and arrival information
2.200

1 **Deepest and longest berth.** Maine Port Authority Dry Cargo Pier. See 2.202.
Maximum size of vessel handled. 80 000 dwt, length 228 m, beam 32 m.

2 **Approach channel depth.** In 2005 the controlling depth in the dredged approach channel and turning basin was 10·4 m (34 ft) except for shoaling to 10·3 m (33·8 ft) in the NE corner and 9·4 m (31 ft) in the NW corner.
Pilotage and tugs. See 2.121 and 2.122.
Customs and quarantine officers for Searsport are stationed at Belfast.

Anchorages
2.201

1 **Searsport Harbor.** Good anchorage sheltered from N winds, is provided for all classes of vessels in depths of 5 to 10 m (18 to 32 ft), within 1 mile S of Mack Point.
Long Cove, which is entered E of Mack Point, is mostly shoal but provides good anchorage just inside the entrance, in depths of 7 m (24 ft).

Alongside berths
2.202

1 Two commercial piers extend SSE from the SE corner of Mack Point.
Largest berth (Maine Port Authority Dry Cargo Pier). Length 244 m. Depths alongside: East side 12·8 m; West side 9·7 m.

Port services:
2.203

1 **Facilities:** hospital in Belfast; oily waste disposal.
Supplies: fuel; water and provisions.
Communications: Nearest airport Bangor (40 km).

Anchorages and harbours in the entrances to West Penobscot Bay

Carvers Harbor
2.204

1   Carvers Harbor, the entrance to which lies on the S side of Vinalhaven Island, 1½ miles NE of Heron Neck Light (44°02′N 68°52′W) (2.168), affords secure anchorage for small vessels, but local knowledge is required. The village of Vinalhaven stands at the head of the harbour.

Ice seldom closes the harbour.

2   **Approaches.** The harbour may be approached:

From the E through the buoyed channel between Vinalhaven Island and the islands S of it.

From the S in the buoyed channel between Colt Ledge, 1¼ miles SE of Heron Neck Light, and Arey Ledges on the E and The Breakers on the W.

From the SW in the white sector of Heron Neck Light.

From the NW through The Reach.

3   **Useful marks** (with positions relative to Heron Neck Light):

Heron Neck Light (44°02′N 68°52′W) (2.168).

Carvers Harbor Light No 2 (red triangle on post) (1 mile ENE).

Water tower (1¾ miles NE).

2.205

1   **Anchorages.** The best anchorage for small vessels lies on the E and SE side of the harbour. The W side is used for commercial craft and fishing vessels. In 2003 the harbour had depths of 3 m (11 ft) in the centre and about 2 to 3 m (8 to 10 ft) along the N and S sides.

Alongside berths. Small wharves in Vinalhaven with depths alongside of 2 to 3 m.

Repairs: minor repairs.

Supplies: fuel; water and provisions.

Tenants Harbor
2.206

1   Tenants Harbor, which is entered between Southern Island (43°58′N 69°11′W) and Northern Island, 2½ cables N, is an excellent anchorage, easy of access. It is much used by small vessels as a harbour of refuge.

Ice frequently obstructs the harbour in February and in extremely cold periods it may be frozen as far as Southern Island.

2   The village of Tenants Harbor stands on the N side of the bay. A tower (disused lighthouse) stands on the E end of Southern Island and No 1 Light-buoy (port hand) is moored 1 cable E of the island.

3   **Anchorage.** Depths gradually shoal from 10 m (33 ft) in the entrance to 4 m (13 ft) 9 cables farther in. Anchorage may be obtained in depths of 9 to 5 m (30 to 16 ft) between 1 and 6 cables W of a line joining the W ends of Southern and Northern Islands.

4   **Alongside berths.** Landing stages with depths alongside of 2·1 to 2·4 m are situated at the village.

Repairs: minor repairs.

Supplies: fuel; water and provisions.

Seal Harbor
2.207

1   Seal Harbor (44°00′N 69°07′W) lies on the NW side of the S part of Muscle Ridge Channel (2.172). It was formerly much used as an anchorage by coasters. The outer part has depths of 5 to 12 m (15 to 39 ft). The principal

dangers in the entrance are buoyed. The harbour is easily entered in daytime.

Dix Island Harbor
2.208

1   Dix Island Harbor (44°00′N 69°04′W) is an anchorage off the SE side of Muscle Ridge Channel. The harbour is entered from SW through a narrow channel leading between the ledges N of Hewett Island.

Local knowledge is required to use this anchorage.

Anchorages and harbours in the south part of West Penobscot Bay

Hurricane Sound
2.209

1   Hurricane Sound (44°03′N 68°53′W), between the W coast of Vinalhaven Island and the islands about 1 mile offshore, is deep but little used except by local vessels as there are no good anchorages in it. Several buoyed channels lead into the sound, but are narrow and obstructed and should not be used without local knowledge.

Southern Harbor
2.210

1   Southern Harbor, which is situated at the W end of Fox Islands Thorofare, is entered between Dumpling Islands (44°08′N 68°54′W) and Amesbury Point, 5 cables WNW.

Good anchorage is available in the middle of the harbour in depths of 6 to 7 m (20 to 23 ft), soft bottom.

Bartlett Harbor
2.211

1   Bartlett Harbor, 2 miles NNE of Stand-in Point (44°07′N 68°57′W), is a small cove that provides good anchorage in depths of 11 to 15 m (36 to 50 ft), sheltered from all but W and N winds.

Caution. A rock with a depth of 2·7 m (9 ft) over it, and steep-to, lies in the middle of the entrance.

Pulpit Harbor
2.212

1   Pulpit Harbor, 2 miles NE of Bartlett Harbor and 2½ miles SW of Webster Head, the partly wooded headland at the N end of North Haven Island, provides secure anchorage to small vessels of up to 4 m (13 ft) draught. **Local knowledge** is required.

2   Pulpit Rock, 3 m in height and pointed, stands nearly ½ cable within the outer end of a reef that extends from the W entrance point. The entrance channel, which lies E of Pulpit Rock, is over ½ cable wide.

Caution. A patch with a depth of 4·3 m (14 ft) over it, lies in mid-channel just within the entrance. It has deeper water on its W side.

3   **Anchorage** is obtainable in the widest part of the harbour in depths of 5 to 10 m (16 to 33 ft).

Owls Head Harbor
2.213

1   Owls Head Harbor is situated close SW of Dodge Point (44°05′N 69°03′W) at the N end of Owls Head Bay (2.175).

Anchorage is available for small vessels in the entrance to the harbour in depths of 3 to 7 m (9 to 24 ft), and in the middle of the harbour in a depth of 1·8 m (6 ft).

Local knowledge is required.

Anchorages and harbours in north part of West Penobscot Bay

Gilkey Harbor
2.214

1   Gilkey Harbor (44°15′N 68°56′W) lies between the W side of the S end of Islesboro Island and Seven Hundred Acre Island. The harbour provides secure anchorage and in summer is much frequented by yachts. **Local knowledge** is required.

Ice frequently closes the harbour in winter.

2   **Entrances.** The main entrance to the harbour is from the SW between Job Island (44°13′N 68°57′W) and Ensign Islands, 6 cables NW. This entrance, which is partly buoyed, is easy to enter and has a least depth of 8·2 m (27 ft) in mid-channel. The N entrance between Grindel Point (44°17′N 68°56′W) to the N and Warren Island and Spruce Island to the S is narrow and also partly buoyed.

3   **Anchorage,** clear of the charted cable areas, is available in depths of 7 to 18 m (23 to 59 ft), with good holding ground.

Repairs: minor repairs in Cradle Cove on the W side.

Supplies: fuel, water and provisions are available in the village of Dark Harbor on the E side of the anchorage and fuel and water in Cradle Cove.

Ducktrap Harbor
2.215

1   Ducktrap Harbor is an open bay, which is entered between Frohock Point (44°17′N 69°00′W) and Spruce Head (1½ miles NE).

Haddock Ledge, with a depth of 1 m (3 ft) over it, lies in the middle of the harbour and is the only off-lying danger. It is marked on its S side by No 2 Buoy (starboard hand). Other dangers can be avoided by giving the shores of the bay a berth of 2½ cables.

2   **Anchorage,** sheltered from N and W winds, is available in depths of 9 to 13 m (30 to 43 ft) with soft bottom in places, at a distance of 2½ cables off the N shore.

Alongside berth. A ferry pier and landing stage, with reported depths of 1 m alongside, are situated at the village of Lincolnville.

Seal Harbor
2.216

1   Seal Harbor (44°19′N 68°55′W) on the W side of Islesboro Island, provides good anchorage, sheltered from all but SW winds. The harbour is easy of access and used by vessels as a night anchorage.

Main entrance is from SW between Flat Island, a bird sanctuary which is grassy, and the shore of Islesboro Island. This entrance is deep and clear of dangers. Other entrances should not be used without local knowledge.

2   **Anchorage,** with plenty of swinging room, is available for deep-draught vessels 5 cables E of Flat Island in depths of 16 to 18 m (53 to 59 ft). Anchorage may also be obtained in depths of 14 to 17 m (46 to 56 ft) in the middle of the harbour 2½ cables off the SE shore. Attention is drawn to the foul ground that extends 2 cables S from the N shore.

Turtle Head Cove
2.217

1   Turtle Head Cove is entered between Marshall Point (44°23′N 68°54′W) and Turtle Head, 1¼ miles NE.

Dangers. The E and S shores should not be approached within 1½ and 2½ cables respectively, and in the W half of the cove foul ground extends 4 cables from the S shore.

2   **Anchorage.** The cove provides good anchorage in depths of 5 to 11 m (16 to 36 ft) sheltered from S and E winds in its E part. The anchorage has a clear width of 3½ cables and is in the E part of the cove.

Stockton Harbor
2.218

1   Stockton Harbor is entered between the SE extremity of Sears Island (44°26′N 68°53′W) and Squaw Point, 1¼ miles NE, the S extremity of Cape Jellison.

Entrance channel is marked by buoys (lateral).

Anchorage. It is a secure harbour for vessels up to 6·7 m draught, and is easy of access.

2   **Berth.** An offshore platform with dolphins and mooring buoys is situated 7 cables SSE of Kidder Point, It has 61 m of berthing space with a reported depth alongside of 10·1 m and handles chemical cargoes. It was reported (2006) that the platform was no longer being used.

PENOBSCOT RIVER

General information

Chart 2486 (see 1.17)

Description
2.219

1   The mouth of Penobscot River, which flows into the head of Penobscot Bay, lies between Fort Point (44°28′N 68°49′W) and Wilson Point, 1 mile SE.

The river forms the approach to the towns of Bucksport (2.229) and Winterport (2.234), and the cities of Brewer (2.239) and Bangor (2.239), the latter two being situated at the head of navigation, 24 miles from the river mouth.

2   **Local knowledge.** There is considerable trade to Bangor, but the river should not be entered without local knowledge.

Depths
2.220

1   Controlling depths in marked channel:
Fort Point to Bucksport: 9·4 m (31 ft) (1998).
Bucksport to Winterport: 5·8 m (19 ft) (1997).
Winterport to South Brewer: 4·6 m (15 ft) (1993).
South Brewer to Bangor: 1·5 m (5 ft) (1993).

Logs
2.221

1   At HW springs, many logs floating down river may be a hazard to small vessels.

Pilotage and tugs
2.222

1   See 2.121 and 2.122.

Arrival anchorages
2.223

1   The usual anchorage for smaller vessels waiting at the river entrance is N of Fort Point on either side of the channel. Anchorage in the river is not advised because vessels tend to drag anchor on strong ebb tides.

2   Larger vessels usually anchor S of Fort Point or off Searsport (2.201).

An alternative anchorage, which is frequently used by smaller vessels, is in Fort Point Cove, in depths of 2 to 7 m (5 to 23 ft).

Vertical clearance
2.224

1   **Bridges.** There are two bridges spanning the Penobscot River between Fort Point and Bangor, which are situated:

One mile S of Bucksport with a vertical clearance of 41·1 m (135 ft).

One mile S of Bangor with a vertical clearance of 22·5 m (74 ft).

2   **Overhead power cables.** Power cables span the river 5 cables NW of Fort Knox (44°34′N 68°48′W) and 5 cables N of Oak Point (44°40′N 68°49′W). The vertical clearance of these power cables is 44·2 m (145 ft) and 48·5 m (159 ft), respectively.

Natural conditions
2.225

1   **Tidal streams** between Odom Ledge (3 miles N of Fort Point) and Orrington (5 miles below Bangor) often reach a rate of 3 kn during the outgoing ebb stream, which may be occasionally increased to 5 kn at maximum spring tides.

2   **Ice** impedes, but seldom prevents, navigation above Winterport for nearly five months of the year, beginning in December. During extreme winters the river may be closed at its mouth. The most difficult place below Winterport is abreast Fort Knox, opposite Bucksport, where ice jams may occur. If this point can be passed, it is normally possible to reach Winterport.

3   The river is kept free of ice to immediately upstream of the I-395 Veterans Remembrance Bridge by a US Coast Guard icebreaker. However, the US Coast Guard has suggested that future ice breaking operations may be limited or terminated altogether due to declining commercial traffic entering the Bangor-Brewer area in recent years.

4   **Freshets** occur in the river during March and April and are sometimes dangerous to vessels.

Directions
(continued from 2.171)

Principal marks
2.226

1   **Major light:**
Fort Point Light (44°28′N 68°49′W).

Penobscot Bay to Bucksport
2.227

1   From a position WNW of Turtle Head (2.171) the track leads generally NE for 5 miles, passing (with positions relative to Fort Point Light):
SE of No 1 Light-buoy (port hand) (4 miles SW) marking a 7 m (23 ft) patch 6 cables S of Sears Island (2.199), thence:
SE of Squaw Point (2¼ miles WSW) (2.218).

2   Thence the channel up river leads generally N for 6 miles, passing (with positions relative to Fort Point Light):
Between Fort Point Ledge and Fort Point. Fort Point Ledge, which dries 1·5 m (5 ft), has No 2 Light-beacon (red triangle on post on stone monument) near its N end. No 1 Buoy (port hand) is moored off Fort Point. Thence:

3   E of Sandy Point (1¾ miles N). Buoys (lateral), which mark the main channel, are moored off this point (see Caution). Thence:
W of Odom Ledge (3 miles N), which partly dries. 6A Beacon (red triangular daymark, stone base) stands on the ledge and No 6 Light-buoy (starboard hand) marks its SW side (see Caution). Thence:

4   Between the towers marking the ends of the road bridge (2.224), 3 cables S of Fort Knox (6 miles N). See 2.225.

Caution. Deep-draught vessels should proceed with caution between Fort Point and Bucksport as there are mid-channel depths of 9·4 m (31 ft), 5 cables E of Sandy Point, and of 10·1 m (33 ft), 2½ cables SW of Odom Ledge.

Bucksport to Bangor
2.228

1   The river channel from Bucksport to Bangor, which is buoyed as far as 3 miles below Bangor, can best be seen on the chart.

Cautions. The channel is crooked and narrow in places and frequent changes occur.

The most difficult sections are off Lawrence and Luce Coves, 1 mile NW of Bucksport, where depths are liable to change, and off Frankfort Flats, 2 miles farther upstream, where there are sharp bends.

2   Navigation at night is extremely dangerous due to the lack of lighted aids to navigation.

Large vessels require the assistance of a tug to navigate the turns.

At times of maximum out-going tidal stream, buoys are occasionally pulled under.

Bucksport

General information
2.229

1   **Position and function.** Bucksport (44°34′N 68°48′W), which is situated 6 miles from the mouth of the Penobscot River, stands on the E bank of the river.

Bucksport is a railway terminal. Paper production and oil distribution are its main industries. The town has a customs station. The port handles petroleum and paper products.

Traffic. In 2005 the port was used by 1 vessel with a total deadweight 47 236 tonnes.

Limiting conditions and arrival information
2.230

1   **Deepest and longest berth.** See 2.232.
Largest vessel. Length 213 m, draught 10·36 m (34 ft).
Approach channel depth. See 2.220.
Pilots and tugs. See 2.121 and 2.122.

Directions
2.231

1   See 2.227.

Alongside berths
2.232

1   **Tanker berth** 213 m in length, depth alongside of 10·7 m.
Paper mill has berths with depths alongside of 1·5 to 7·3 m.

Port services
2.233

1   **Supplies**: fuel; water and provisions.
Communications: Nearest airport Bangor (30 km).

Winterport

General information and limiting conditions
2.234

1   **Position.** Winterport (44°38′N 68°51′W), which is situated about 12 miles above the mouth of Penobscot River, stands on the W side of the river.

Function. The port handles fresh and frozen foods.
Deepest berth. See 2.237.

2   **Approach channel depth.** See 2.220.
Largest vessel handled. Length 150 m, draught 7·45 m.

Arrival information
2.235
1   **Pilots and tugs.** See 2.121 and 2.122.

Directions
2.236
1   See 2.228.

Alongside berth
2.237
1   A floating barge, 82 m in length, with depths alongside of 7·6 m is moored 90 m offshore, 3 cables S of the town.

Port services
2.238
1   **Repairs:** boatyard for minor repairs.
Other facilities: nearest hospital 20 km.
Supplies: fuel; water and provisions.
Communications: nearest airport at Bangor, 20 km.

Bangor

General information
2.239
1   **Position and function.** Bangor (44°48′N 68°46′W), which is situated at the head of navigation, stands on the W bank of the Penobscot River. The city of Brewer stands on the E bank opposite Bangor, and South Brewer is 1 mile S.

Bangor, which in 2005 had an estimated population of 31 074, is an important city. The port handles mainly oil cargoes.

Limiting conditions and arrival information
2.240
1   **Deepest berth.** See 2.242.
Tidal levels. Mean spring range about 4·5 m; mean neap range about 3·3 m. See information in *Admiralty Tide Tables.*
Approach channel depth. See 2.220.
Vertical clearance. See 2.224.
Pilots and tugs. See 2.121 and 2.122.

Directions
2.241
1   See 2.228.

Alongside berths
2.242
1   **East Hampden.** Oil wharf 1½ miles S of Bangor.
South Brewer. Paper mill wharf 1 mile S of Bangor with depths alongside of 3·9 to 4·5 m.
Brewer. Oil wharves for small tankers.
Bangor. Number of wharves with depths alongside of 2·1 to 4·2 m.

Port services
2.243
1   **Facilities:** hospitals; oily waste disposal.
Supplies: fuel; water and stores.
Communications: nearest airport 3 km.

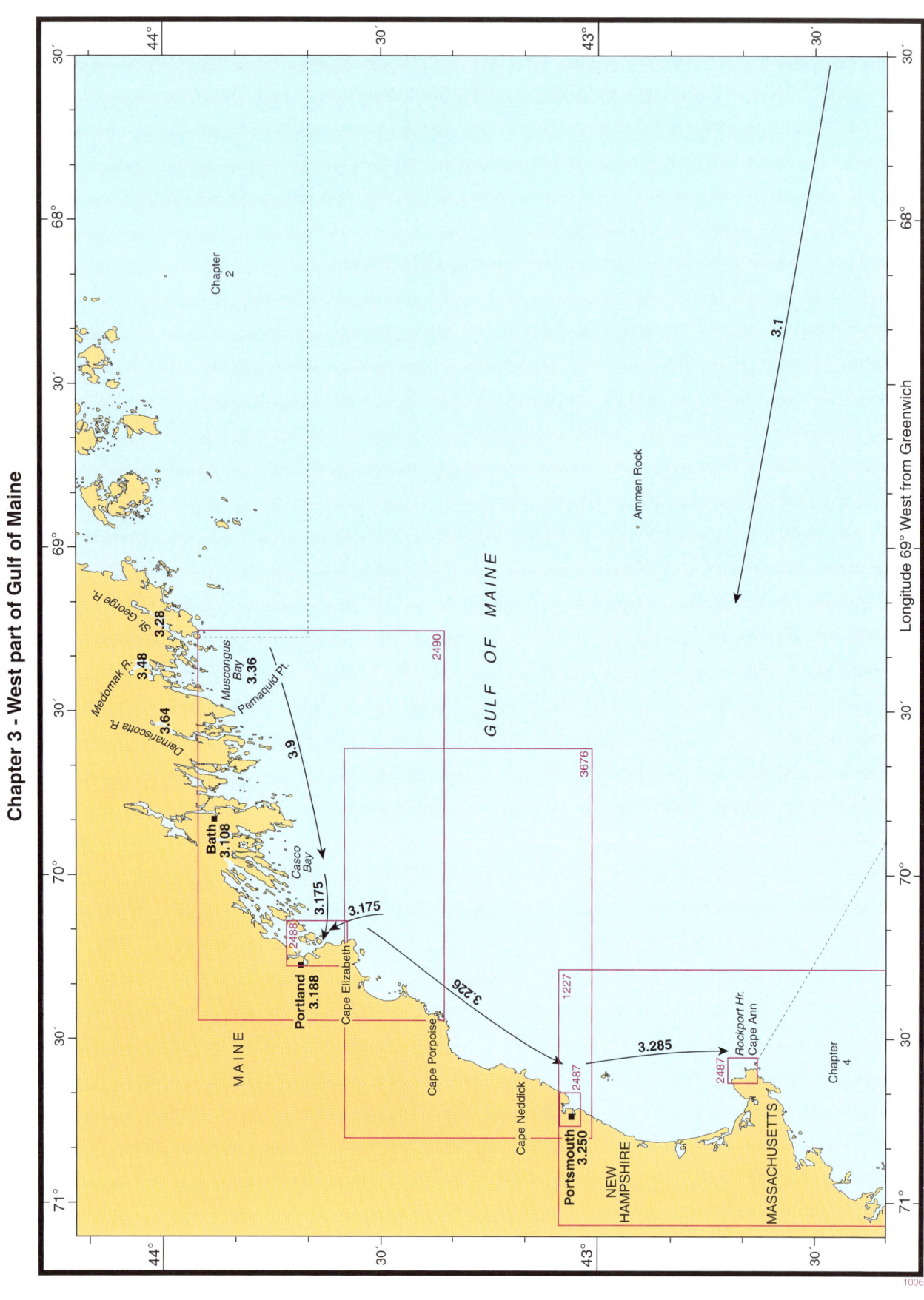

Chapter 3 - West part of Gulf of Maine

Chapter 2

Longitude 69° West from Greenwich

GULF OF MAINE

Ammen Rock

3.1

St. George R. **3.28**
Medomak R. **3.48**
Damariscotta R. **3.64**
Muscongus Bay **3.36**
Pemaquid Pt.
3.9

2490

3676

Bath **3.108**

Casco Bay

3.175
3.175

MAINE

Portland **3.188**
Cape Elizabeth

2488

1227

3.226

Cape Porpoise

Cape Neddick

2487

3.285

Rockport Hr.
Cape Ann

2487

Chapter 4

Portsmouth **3.250**

NEW
HAMPSHIRE

MASSACHUSETTS

1006

CHAPTER 3

WEST PART OF GULF OF MAINE

GENERAL INFORMATION

OFFSHORE APPROACH
TO GULF OF MAINE

General information

Chart 2492
Outlying banks
3.1

1 The Gulf of Maine is entered between the SW end of Nova Scotia (43°30′N 66°00′W) (See *Nova Scotia and Bay of Fundy Pilot*) and Cape Cod (4.63), about 200 miles WSW.

2 **Georges Bank.** The W part of the entrance to the Gulf of Maine is obstructed by Georges Bank, which lies between 80 miles ESE and 120 miles E of Cape Cod. This extensive bank has depths of less than 91 m (50 fm) and the bottom is of sand, with shells and pebbles in places.

3 The two principal dangers on Georges Bank are Georges Shoal (3.5) and Cultivator Shoal (3.5), which lie in the middle part of an area 100 miles in extent, on the NW part of the bank. These shoals have irregular depths of less than 37 m (20 fm) and are dangerous to navigation.

On the NE side of Georges Bank there is a deep channel about 25 miles wide in which there are depths of over 180 m (100 fm).

4 **Other outlying banks.** There are several other outlying banks in the central part of the Gulf of Maine, but of these Ammen Rock on Cashes Ledge is the only danger.

Cashes Ledge (42°53′N 68°57′W) is a bank with depths of 25·6 m (14 fm) over it in places. Ammen Rock (3.5) lies near the centre of the bank.

5 **Fippennies Ledge** (42°47′N 69°18′W) has a least known depth of 68 m (37 fm) over it.

Jeffreys Bank (43°22′N 68°44′W) has a depth of 64 m (35 fm) over it.

Platts Bank (43°09′N 69°37′W) has a least known depth of 53 m (29 fm) over it.

Unexploded Ordnance
3.2

1 A number of areas where there are reports of unexploded ordnance exist in the Gulf of Maine, as shown on the chart.

Ship Reporting System
3.3

1 A mandatory ship reporting system for the protection of the Northern right whale is established to the E of Cape Ann and Cape Cod (4.63). For further information see 4.7, Appendix VIII and *Admiralty List of Radio Signals Volume 6(5)*.

Tidal streams
3.4

1 Tidal streams over Georges Bank and its vicinity are rotary, and there is no slack water. The maximum rate over Georges Bank is 2 kn.

Details of tidal streams in the Gulf of Maine are given on the charts.

Directions
3.5

1 From the vicinity of 42°25′N 67°35′W the offshore approach route to the ports in the W part of the Gulf of Maine leads generally W, passing (with positions relative to Highland Light, Cape Cod (42°02′N 70°04′W)):

2 N of Georges Shoal (41°40′N 67°40′W). This shoal has a least depth of 2·7 m (9 ft) over it and the submerged remains of a tower lie on the N part of the shoal. From its centre, shoals and patches, with depths of 18·3 m (60 ft) or less extend for between 15 and 25 miles. A shoal with a depth of 9·4 m (31 ft) over it lies 15 miles NE of the shallowest part of Georges Shoal. Thence:

3 N of Cultivator Shoal (90 miles ESE). This shoal has a least depth of 6·7 m (22 ft) over it near its N end, with patches with depths of less than 18·3 m (60 ft) extending between 4 miles N and 46 miles SSW from the shallowest part. Thence:

4 S of Ammen Rock (72 miles NE). In heavy weather the sea breaks over this shoal.

Thence proceed as necessary through waters clear of charted dangers to the approaches to the ports of Portland (3.188), Portsmouth (3.250) and Boston (4.76).

5 **Caution.** The whole area covered by Georges Bank, within depths of 37 m (20 fm), has an extremely broken bottom in which all the shoalest spots may not have been found. The S and W sides of Georges Bank should not be approached in depths of less than 55 m (30 fm). On the SE side of the bank depths decrease gradually and soundings can be of considerable value, but on the NW side of the bank depths decrease abruptly. The area should be avoided.

(Directions continue for approaches to Portland at 3.182, for Portsmouth at 3.273, for Boston at 4.69)

MONHEGAN ISLAND TO CAPE ELIZABETH

GENERAL INFORMATION

Chart 2490
Description
3.6

1   The coast between Monhegan Island (43°46′N 69°19′W) and Cape Elizabeth (40 miles WSW) is rocky and much indented by numerous bays and rivers, many of which are excellent harbours. The approaches to these bays and rivers are obstructed by numerous islands and dangers.

2   The W part of this stretch of the coast consists of Casco Bay, which is entered between Cape Small (43°42′N 69°51′W) and Cape Elizabeth, 18 miles WSW.

Inside Passage
3.7

1   Inside Passage from Boothbay Harbor to Bath is about 11 miles long and leads through the islands between Boothbay Harbor (3.78) and Kennebec River (3.99). The channel is very narrow in places, has strong tidal currents and is much obstructed by rocks and shoals. Most dangers are marked.

    Local knowledge is required for the navigation of this passage by vessels with a draught of more than 2 m.

2   **Route.** The passage leads through Townsend Gut (3.79), across Sheepscot River, through Goose Rock Passage (3.90), Knubble Bay (3.90), Hockomock Bay (3.90), Sasanoa River (3.90) and thence into the Kennebec River opposite the city of Bath.

Regulations
3.8

1   **Navigation Rules for US Inland Waters** apply to the greater part of the inland waters of Casco Bay. The limits of the waters to which these rules apply are given in each section. See 1.47 and Appendix VII for further information.

COASTAL PASSAGE BETWEEN MONHEGAN ISLAND AND APPROACHES TO PORTLAND

General information

Chart 2490
Description
3.9

1   The following paragraphs describe the coastal passage between Monhegan Island (43°46′N 69°19′W) and the approaches to Portland, 30 miles WSW.

Traffic regulations
3.10

1   **Danger zone.** An area SE of Cape Small, centred approximately on 43°40′N 69°48′W, as shown on the chart, is used by naval aircraft for mining practice.

    For details see Appendix VI.

2   **Restricted area.** A naval sonobuoy test area, 1 mile in radius, is situated 8 miles SSE of Pemaquid Point (43°50′N 69°31′W), as shown on the chart. Vessels are requested to keep clear when sonobuoys are being dropped. The area is connected to the shore by submarine cables.

    For details see Appendix VI.

Directions
(continued from 2.128)

Principal marks
3.11

1   **Landmark:**
    Monhegan Island (43°46′N 69°19′W) (2.127).
    Major lights:
    Monhegan Island Light (43°46′N 69°19′W) (2.127).
    Burnt Island Light (43°50′N 69°39′W).

2   Seguin Island Light (43°43′N 69°46′W), standing on the summit of Seguin Island, which is grassy and 44 m (144 ft) in height.
    Halfway Rock Light (white tower and dwelling, 23 m in height) (43°39′N 70°02′W).

3   Portland Head Light (43°37′N 70°12′W) (3.182).
    Cape Elizabeth Light (43°34′N 70°12′W) (3.182).

Other aids to navigation
3.12

1   **Racon:**
    P Light-buoy (43°32′N 70°06′W) (3.187).
    See *Admiralty List of Radio Signals Volume 2* for details.
3.13

1   From a position about 10 miles SE of Monhegan Island (43°46′N 69°19′W) the coastal passage to the approaches to Portland leads W for about 37 miles, passing (with positions relative to Seguin Island Light (43°43′N 69°46′W)):

2   S of Monhegan Island (19 miles E) (2.127), thence:
    S of Pemaquid Point (13 miles NE) (3.39), the W entrance point to Muscongus Bay (3.36), thence:
    S of Poor Shoal (6½ miles E) (3.76), 6½ cables SE of Bantam Rock (3.76), awash, which is marked by No 2 Light-buoy (starboard hand), thence:

3   S of Mile Ledge (1 mile S), marked by 20ML Light-buoy (3.102), thence:
    S of Seguin SSW Ledge (2½ miles SSW), thence:
    S of Fuller Rock Light (red and white chequered diamond on white framework tower) (3¼ miles W), thence:

4   S of Temple Ledge (5½ miles WSW), thence:
    S of Lumbo Ledge (7¾ miles WSW). 2Q Light-buoy (starboard hand) marks the SW part of the ledge. Thence:

5   S of a shoal (12½ miles WSW) with a depth of 10·7 m (35 ft) over it, 3 cables SSW of Halfway Rock Light (3.11). Deep-draught vessels should not pass N of Halfway Rock.

    Useful marks:
    Pemaquid Point Light (43°50′N 69°30′W) (3.39).
    The Cuckolds Light (43°47′N 69°39′W) (3.76).
    (Directions continue for approaches to Portland at 3.182, and for coastal passage at 3.228)

INSHORE WATERS BETWEEN MOSQUITO ISLAND AND GEORGES ISLANDS

General information

Charts 2492, 2486, 2490 (see 1.17)
Description
3.14

1   The inshore waters between Mosquito Island (43°55′N 69°13′W) (2.169) and Georges Islands (5 miles SW) consist

of Port Clyde and adjacent waters, the approaches to Saint George River, and Saint George River.

Traffic regulations
3.15

1 **Navigation Rules for US Inland Waters** do not apply to any of the waters described in this section.

Port Clyde and adjacent waters

General information
3.16

1 **Position and function.** Port Clyde (43°55′N 69°16′W) is a small but excellent harbour between Marshall Point and the SE side of Hupper Island, 2½ cables W. The port is used as a harbour of refuge by fishermen and coasters and is the mainland terminal of the ferry service to Monhegan Island.

Local knowledge is required.

2 **Approaches.** The main approach channel is from the E. See 3.18.

The harbour can also be entered through the N entrance, 7 cables N of Marshall Point. The N entrance is obstructed by a bar and Raspberry Island lies on this bar. There is a narrow passage with a depth of 1·5 m (5 ft) on either side of the island, but both are difficult to navigate and should not be attempted without local knowledge.

3 South-east approach channel is unmarked and there are shoals close to it.

Limiting conditions
3.17

1 **Maximum size of vessel handled.** Draught 3·7 m (12 ft) through the E entrance.

Ice rarely interferes with navigation except in very severe winters and even then usually only lasts for a short time.

Directions for approach from east
3.18

1 From a position close S of No 2 Buoy (starboard hand), moored 2 cables S of Mosquito Island (43°55′N 69°13′W) (2.169), the E approach channel to Port Clyde leads, (with positions relative to Marshall Point (43°55′N 69°16′W)):

NE of Barter Shoal (1½ miles ESE) and a 5·5 m (19 ft) patch 3 cables NW, thence:

2 NE of Hay Ledge (1¼ miles ESE), 4·6 m in height, thence:

N of The Brothers (1 mile ESE), 5·6 m in height, thence:

Between Nos 4 and 5 Buoys (starboard and port hand) (8 cables E), marking, respectively, the SE side of Mosquito Ledge and the N end of Gunning Rocks, thence:

3 S of No 6 Buoy (starboard hand) (2 cables SE), marking Marshall Ledge, thence:

Close W of a 5·5 m (18 ft) patch situated mid-channel in the harbour entrance, thence:

Through the entrance into the S part of the harbour.

4 **Useful mark:**

Marshall Point Light (white tower) (43°55′N 69°16′W).

(Directions for approach to Saint George River continue at 3.22)

Berths
3.19

1 **Anchorage** may be obtained, with good holding ground with a width of 1 to 1½ cables, in the channel between Marshall Point and the bar, in depths of 7 to 11 m (23 to 35 ft). Attention is drawn to a cable area, shown on the US chart, which extends across the harbour N of the ferry wharf.

2 **Alongside berths.** The ferry wharf lies 5 cables N of Marshall Point on the E shore of the harbour. The town landing stage with depths alongside of 1·5 to 3 m, lies close N of the ferry and there are several other wharves in the harbour with depths alongside of 1·8 to 5·4 m.

Supplies: fuel; water and stores.

Approaches to Saint George River
Description and topography
3.20

1 The approaches to Saint George River are obstructed by Georges Islands and by numerous dangers. Between these islands and dangers several channels lead to the river. The most important of these dangers are marked by buoys and beacons.

2 **Georges Islands** extend 5 miles S from Caldwell Island (43°56′N 69°18′W) to Allen Island. The larger islands are generally wooded, the smaller are grassy and rocky. Many dangers fringe these islands and some navigable channels lead between them.

Main approach channels
3.21

1 There are two main approach channels:

From the east by the E approach to Port Clyde (3.18) and thence between Hupper Island and the Georges Islands to pass E of Caldwell Island.

From the south-west coming from the E part of Muscongus Bay, passing NW of Franklin Island (43°53′N 69°23′W) (3.39) and thence NW of Caldwell Island.

Directions
(continued from 3.18)
3.22

1 **East approach.** From a position S of the entrance to Port Clyde the E approach to the entrance to the Saint George River continues SW and then N around the S and W side of Hupper Island, passing (with positions relative to Marshall Point (43°55′N 69°16′W)):

NW of No 7 Buoy (port hand) (4 cables SW) which marks the N edge of the dangers extending N from Hart Island, thence:

2 S of No 8 Buoy (starboard hand) (9 cables SW) which marks two shoals, 1·8 m (6 ft) and 3·7 m (12 ft) in depth, that lie off the S side of Hupper Island, thence:

W of No 2 Buoy (starboard hand) (1 mile W) which marks Kelp Ledges. A 2·7 m (9 ft) patch lies 1 cable NW of the N end of the ledge. Thence:

Clear of Murray Ledge (1¼ miles NW), with a depth of 4·5 m (15 ft) over it, thence:

3 Clear of Channel Rock (1½ miles NW), with a depth of 1·5 m (5 ft) over it and with DCR Buoy (isolated danger) marking its W side, thence:

Into the entrance to Saint George River.

Useful mark:

No 10 Beacon (1½ miles WSW), standing on Old Horse Ledge.

(Directions continue at 3.32)

3.23

1 **South approach.** See 3.41.

Other channels
3.24

1 **Davis Strait** (43°53′N 69°19′W), which leads between Davis Island, grassy, and the islets extending SE from Thompson Island, is a narrow channel that forms part of the inshore route used by many vessels with a draught not exceeding 3·7 m.

2 Griffin Ledge, with a depth of 3 m (10 ft), lies in mid-channel, and is marked on its SE side by No 12 Buoy (starboard hand). The channel SE of the buoy is 68 m wide.

Local knowledge is required.

(Directions for inshore route continue at 3.45)

3.25

1 **Davis Strait to Hupper Island.** A channel leads NE from Davis Strait to Hupper Island passing NW of Gig Rock and The Sisters. Both these dangers are marked by Nos 11 and 9 Buoys (port hand), respectively, on their NW sides. The channel then passes SE of Old Horse Ledge (3.22).

Anchorages
3.26

1 **Caldwell Island.** Anchorage is available for deep-draught vessels E of Caldwell Island (43°56′N 69°18′W) in depths of 10 to 16 m (33 to 53 ft), soft bottom.

3.27

1 **Hupper Island.** In S winds anchorage is available for small vessels N of Hupper Island and E of Blubber Island (43°56′N 69°16′W), in depths of 6 to 7 m (20 to 23 ft).

Saint George River

Chart 2492 (see 1.17)
Description
3.28

1 From its entrance, close N of Caldwell Island (43°56′N 69°18′W), Saint George River extends 10 miles NE to the town of Thomaston, above which it is shallow and of no navigational importance.

Depths
3.29

1 There are depths of 6·7 to 24 m (22 ft to 13 fm) as far as Broad Cove, 5 miles above the entrance. After this the depth gradually decreases and the channel narrows and passes between extensive flats, which dry. The channel has a least depth of 6·7 m (22 ft) to within 1 mile below Thomaston.

2 Thence a narrow channel, dredged to a depth of 4·9 m (16 ft) leads toward the wharf. In 1984 the controlling depth to the bend at Thomaston was 3·3 m (11 ft).

Vertical clearance
3.30

1 A fixed bridge with a vertical clearance of 1·5 m (5 ft) crosses the river above the wharf at Thomaston.

Ice
3.31

1 Ice closes the river in severe winters from December to March. In ordinary winters the river is not normally entirely closed for more than a month, though ice sufficient to interfere with navigation may be encountered at any time for a period of three months.

Directions
(continued from 3.22 and 3.41)
3.32

1 From a position NE of Caldwell Island the passage up Saint George River leads NE, passing (with positions relative to Bailey Point (44°00′N 69°15′W)):

Between Nos 4 and 5 Buoys (starboard and port hand) (3½ miles SW), that are moored off Howard Point and Pleasant Point, respectively, thence:

2 SE of No 7 Buoy (port hand) (2 miles SW), which marks the dangers off Stones Point, the SW entrance point to Maple Juice Cove (3.34), thence:

Through the middle of the Narrows (1½ miles SW), taking care to avoid two rocks with depths of 6·7 m and 7 m (22 and 23 ft), which are situated, respectively, 1¼ miles and 8 cables SSW of Bailey Point, thence:

3 SE of No 9 Buoy (port hand) (3 cables ESE), marking Bailey Ledge which has a rock awash near its outer end. Bailey Ledge lies off Bailey Point, the SW entrance point to Broad Cove (3.29). There is a marine farm, marked by buoys, in the centre of Broad Cove. Thence:

Between Watts Point (1 mile E) and Bradford Point (8 cables NE).

4 From NNE of Watts Point the passage leads through a channel between the mud flats, which is marked by buoys (lateral). The safest time to make this passage is at LW when the flats are uncovered or when the tide is rising.

Anchorages on east side
3.33

1 **Deep Cove**, just N of Hupper Point (43°56′N 69°16′W), provides good anchorage, with soft bottom, in depths of 6 to 13 m (21 to 43 ft). A patch, with a depth of 3·7 m (12 ft) over it, lies in the N part of the cove.

Turkey Cove, S of Turkey Point (43°58′N 69°16′W), provides good anchorage in its entrance in depths of 5 to 8 m (15 to 27 ft), soft bottom.

2 **Otis Cove** (43°59′N 69°14′W) provides anchorage off its entrance in depths of 6 to 8 m (20 to 27 ft), soft bottom.

Anchorage on west side
3.34

1 **Maple Juice Cove** (43°59′N 69°17′W), which is entered between Henderson Ledge and Burton Point, 3 cables N, provides anchorage in depths of 4 to 7 m (13 to 24 ft). No 7 Buoy (port hand) marks Henderson Ledge.

Thomaston
3.35

1 Thomaston (44°04′N 69°11′W) is not a commercial port but has a public wharf with a depth alongside of 4·6 m.

Repairs: Slipway and a number of boatyards where repairs can be effected.

Supplies: fuel; water and limited stores.

MUSCONGUS BAY

General information

Charts 2490, 2492 (see 1.17)
Description
3.36

1 Muscongus Bay lies between Georges Islands (43°52′N 69°19′W) (3.20) and Pemaquid Neck, a wooded peninsula lying 7 miles W. It forms the approach to Meduncook River (3.44), Medomak River (3.48), and Muscongus Sound (3.47).

2 The bay is frequented by many local fishing boats and yachts, but is obstructed by numerous islands and ledges, and is seldom entered by vessels seeking shelter in heavy weather as Tenants Harbor (2.206) and Port Clyde (3.16) to the E, and Boothbay Harbor (3.78) to the W, are easier to enter and more convenient.

Many of the dangers in the bay are buoyed.

Traffic regulations
3.37
1 **Navigation Rules for US Inland Waters** do not apply to any of the waters described in this section.

Approaches to Muscongus bay

Principal mark
3.38
1 **Major Light:**

Monhegan Island Light (43°46′N 69°19′W) (2.127).

Directions
3.39
1 Muscongus Bay is approached from the S between Monhegan Island (43°46′N 69°19′W) and Pemaquid Point, 10 miles WNW. Moser Ledge, which has a least depth of 4·6 m (15 ft) over it and is marked on its NW side by DM Buoy (isolated danger), lies in the middle of the entrance 3¾ miles ESE of Pemaquid Point. Depths are irregular 1 mile S of the ledge.

2 **Useful marks:**

Franklin Island Light (white tower) (43°53′N 69°22′W) standing on the NW side of Franklin Island.

Pemaquid Point Light (white conical tower) (43°50′N 69°30′W).

3 **Unexploded ordnance** is reported (1961) to lie in an area, 1 mile radius, centred 3 miles SSE of Pemaquid Point. A similar sized area used for the naval testing of sonobuoys lies 5 miles farther S. See 3.10.

Rivers and channels in the east part of Muscongus Bay
3.40
1 There are three deep, but mostly unmarked, channels that lead in a N direction through the E part of Muscongus Bay and into Saint George River.

West of Georges Islands
3.41
1 From a position W of 2OM Light-buoy moored 3 cables S of Old Man Ledge (43°50′N 69°19′W) the E channel leads N and then NE, passing (with positions relative to The Kegs (43°53′·5N 69°20′·6W)):

Between Allen Island and Little Egg Rock (2¼ miles SSE and S), thence:

2 E of Seal Ledges (1¼ miles S), which dry 0·9 m (3 ft). No 13 Buoy (port hand) is moored on the N side of the ledges. Thence:

Between Thompson Rock (7 cables ENE), with a depth of 3·4 m (11 ft) over it and The Kegs, awash and marked by TK beacon, thence:

3 Between Jenks Ledge (2 miles NNE), awash at LW and marked on its W side by 2JL Buoy (starboard hand), and Otter Island (2 miles N). A number of dangers lie off the E side of Otter Island. Thence:

Between Goose Rock and Goose Rock Ledge (2¾ miles NE). The SE side of the ledge is marked by No 1 Buoy (port hand). Thence:

4 Between the N point of Caldwell Island and Gay Cove Ledge (3½ miles NE). The SE side of the ledge is marked by No 3 Buoy (port hand).

Thence to the entrance of Saint George River.

(Directions continue at 3.32)

Old Hump Channel
3.42
1 From a position W of Shark Island (43°51′N 69°21′W) Old Hump Channel leads generally NNE, passing (with positions relative to Shark Island):

ESE of Eastern Egg Rock (1½ miles NW), which has No 15 Beacon on its N point and No 14 Buoy (starboard hand) marking the SE side of Egg Rock North Ledge, 2 cables NNE, thence:

2 WNW of Old Hump Ledge (2 miles N), above water. A rock, with a depth of 4·3 m (14 ft) over it, lies 3½ cables S. Thence:

WNW of The Kegs (3 miles N) (3.41) and:

ESE of Gangway Ledge (3 miles N), a bare above-water rock lying at the N end of the dangers extending N from Eastern Egg Rock.

(Directions continue as in 3.41)

Between Franklin Island and Crane Island
3.43
1 From a position W of Eastern Egg Rock (43°52′N 69°23′W) (3.42), the channel between Franklin Island and Crane Island leads NNE to the W of the dangers extending N from Eastern Egg Rock, passing (with positions relative to Franklin Island (43°53′N 69°22′W)):

2 Between Franklin Island and Crane Island (5 cables NW), thence:

SSE of Harbor Island (1 mile NNW), 22 m in height and almost connected to Crane Island and Hall Island at LW.

Between Gangway Ledge (1 mile NE) and Hall Island (1 mile N).

(Directions continue as in 3.41)

Meduncook River
3.44
1 Meduncook River (43°57′N 69°19′W) is entered 5 cables W of the W entrance to Georges River between Gay Island and Morse Island, 3 cables W. The estuary forms an approach to Friendship Harbor (3.51).

Anchorage. See 3.50.

2 The river extends 3 miles NNE from its entrance. It has a narrow channel and is obstructed by numerous unmarked dangers.

Local knowledge is required for its navigation.

Inshore route
(continued from 3.24)
3.45
1 The inshore route, suitable for vessels with a draught of not more than 3·7 m (12 ft), leads WSW from Davis Strait, passing (with positions relative to Seal Ledges (43°52′·4N 69°20′·5W)):

N of No 13 Buoy (port hand), which marks the N side of Seal Ledges (3.41), thence:

2 S of Old Hump Ledge (7 cables WNW) (3.42). A rock, with a depth of 4·3 m (14 ft) over it, lies 3½ cables S. Thence:

Between Eastern Egg Rock (3.42) and Egg Rock North Ledge (3.42), the SE side of which is marked by No 14 Buoy (port hand).

3 Thence the route continues WSW to pass S of Pemaquid Point.

Rivers and channels in the west part of Muscongus Bay

Approaches to Friendship Harbor and Medomak River
3.46

1   From a position SW of Eastern Egg Rock (43°51′·5N 69°22′·9W) the approach route to Friendship Harbor (3.51) and Medomak River (3.48) leads generally NNE, passing (with positions relative to Franklin Island Light (43°53′N 69°22′W)):

ESE of Western Egg Rock (2 miles WSW), 8 m (25 ft) in height and grassy. A shoal, with a depth of 1·2 m (4 ft) over it, which is marked by No 1 Buoy (port hand), lies 3 cables ENE. Thence:

2   ESE of Devils Elbow and Devils Back (1½ miles W), two rocks which dry 0·3 m (1 ft) and 2·4 m (8 ft), respectively. No 3 Buoy (port hand) is moored close SE of Devils Back, thence:

WNW of Harbor Island Rock (1¼ miles NW) with a depth of 2·4 m (8 ft) over it, thence:

3   SE of the 4·6 (15 ft) patch lying 3 cables E of Wreck Island (1½ miles NW) and SE of a patch with a swept depth of 2·7 m (9 ft), 5 cables NE of this island. The latter patch has a charted depth of 5·8 m (19 ft) on Chart BA 2490. Wreck Island is 15 m (48 ft) in height and wooded. Thence:

4   Between Black Island (2 miles N) and Jones Garden Island (2¼ miles NNW), thence:

E of Gull Rock (4 miles N), two rocks close together, if bound for Friendship Harbor (3.51), or:

W of Gull Rock if bound up Medomak River (3.48).

Muscongus Sound
3.47

1   Muscongus Sound is situated on the W side of Muscongus Bay between Louds Island and Hog Island on the E and the mainland on the W.

The S entrance, which is entered between the S point of Louds Island and Browns Head (43°54′N 69°28′W), is obstructed by dangers, but the most important of these are buoyed.

2   The N entrance to the sound leads through Lower Narrows, a narrow passage between Hog Island and Hockomock Point. There is no safe passage between Louds Island and Hog Island.

Directions. From a position about 1 mile W of Haddock Island the route through Muscongus Sound leads generally N, passing (with positions relative to Browns Head):

3   W of Webber Sunken Ledge (1 mile SE), Browns Head Ledge (4 cables SE) and Bar Island Ledge (5 cables NE), all of which are marked by buoys (starboard hand), thence:

E of Poland South Ledge and Poland North Ledge (1½ miles N). The ledges are marked by Nos 7 and 9 Buoys (port hand) on their E and S side, respectively. Thence:

4   E of No 11 Buoy (port hand) marking the S side of Halftide Ledge (4¼ miles N), thence:

Through Lower Narrows (5 miles NNE) which is marked by Nos 13 and 15 Buoys (port hand) and has a depth of 4 m (13 ft).

Medomak River
3.48

1   Medomak River flows into Muscongus Bay between Martin Point (43°58′N 69°22′W) and Hockomock Point, 2½ miles WNW.

Local knowledge is necessary to enter the river owing to the numerous unmarked dangers, narrow winding channels and the strong tidal streams.

2   The lower part of the river is divided by islands into two channels. The E entrance channel, which is 9 cables wide between Martin Point and Cow Island, divides into two passages at its upper end, 2 miles N of Martin Point. One passage leads along the E and N sides of Hungry Island and the other through Flying Passage between Hungry Island and Bremen Long Island. Both passages are very narrow in places and unmarked rocks are situated in the fairway and at its sides.

3   The W entrance channel, Hockomock Channel, with a least depth of 6·1 m (20 ft), leads between Bremen Long Island and the mainland NW. It is the preferred channel, but it is narrow in places and the tidal streams are strong.
3.49

1   Both entrance channels unite N of Bremen Long Island, from the N end of which a reef extends 4 cables N.

For 5 miles above the entrance, the channel up the river has a least depth of 6·1 m (20 ft) and some of the dangers are marked, but unmarked dangers lie close to the fairway. For the next 2½ miles, to within 1½ miles of Waldoboro (44°06′N 69°22′W), the channel leads through flats which are almost dry at LW and depths decrease gradually to 1·5 m (5 ft).

2   **Tidal streams** are reported to be strong in the narrow passage off Locust Island, 4 miles S of Waldoboro.

Ice closes the river from December to April.

Anchorages and harbours in Muscongus Bay

Estuary of Meduncook River
3.50

1   Good anchorage may be obtained in the entrance in depths of 3 to 9 m (10 to 30 ft).

Friendship Harbor
3.51

1   Friendship Harbor (43°58′N 69°20′W) lies between Friendship Long Island and Garrison Island on the S and the S side of Jameson Point on the N.

The harbour has two entrances. The E, which is buoyed, leads from the estuary of Meduncook River (3.44) between Garrison Island and Friendship Long Island. The W entrance leads NE from between the SW end of Friendship Long Island and Martin Point, 1 mile N.

2   **Useful mark.** Spire (43°59′N 69°20′W).

Anchorage, in depths of 6 to 9 m (21 to 28 ft), is available in the harbour and is much used by fishing vessels and small craft.

Ice seldom closes the harbour.

Dangers. Ledges extend from the N and S shore of the harbour. Their outer edges are marked by beacons and buoys.

Friendship
3.52

1   Friendship is a town on the N shore of Friendship Harbor.

Alongside berths. There are several piers and wharves, with depths alongside of 0·6 to 3·7 m, on the N side of the harbour along Jameson Point. Caution is necessary when approaching the stone town pier in the N part of the harbour due to below–water rocks in the vicinity.

2   **Repairs:** minor repairs.

Supplies: fuel; water and provisions.

3.53

1   Hatchet Cove between Martin Point (43°59′N 69°20′W) and Jameson Point, 1 mile ENE, is shallow and obstructed by islands and rocks. It is not suitable as an anchorage.

New Harbor
3.54

1   New Harbor (43°52′N 69°29′W), situated on the W shore of Muscongus Bay, is a cove which is used as an anchorage by small craft only, and though open to E is well sheltered.

Long Cove
3.55

1   Long Cove (43°53′N 69°29′W), 5 cables N of New Harbor, is open S, but provides good anchorage in winds from other directions, in depths of 4 to 16 m (14 to 53 ft).

Round Pond
3.56

1   Round Pond (43°56′N 69°27′W), a small landlocked harbour, is situated on the W shore of Muscongus Sound, 2¼ miles N of Browns Head. The village of Round Pond stands on the N shore of the harbour.

2   **Anchorage** may be obtained for small vessels in depths of 3 to 5 m (10 to 17 ft). The best anchorage is in the middle of the harbour.

Berths with depths alongside of 0·9 to 1·8 m are situated in the harbour.

Repairs: patent slip for craft up to 14 m (45 ft) long.
Supplies: fuel and limited supplies.

North of Poland North Ledge
3.57

1   **Anchorage** is available in Muscongus Sound between Poland North Ledge (3.47) and Muscongus Harbor in depths decreasing gradually from 15 to 7 m (49 to 23 ft).

Muscongus Harbor
3.58

1   Muscongus Harbor (43°58′N 69°27′W) is a small cove on the W side of Muscongus Sound.

Broad Cove
3.59

1   Broad Cove (44°02′N 69°24′W) on the W side of Medomak River is sometimes used by fishermen. The channel into the cove is unmarked.

Waldoboro
3.60

1   Waldoboro (44°06′N 69°22′W) is at the head of navigation on Medomak River. There is no commercial water-borne traffic from the town. There are two wharves, both in a poor state of repair and with little water alongside.
Supplies: fuel, provisions and stores.

INSHORE WATERS BETWEEN PEMAQUID POINT AND CAPE NEWAGEN

General information

Chart 2490, 2492 (see 1.17)
Description
3.61

1   The inshore waters between Pemaquid Point (43°50′N 69°31′W) and Cape Newagen (7 miles WSW) consist of Johns Bay and adjacent waters, Damariscotta River and approaches, and Booth Bay and adjacent waters.

Traffic regulations
3.62

1   **Navigation Rules for US Inland Waters** do not apply to any of the waters described in this section.

Johns Bay and adjacent waters
General information
3.63

1   Johns Bay is entered between Pemaquid Point (43°50′N 69°31′W) and Thrumcap Island, 1½ miles WSW. It extends 2 miles N between Pemaquid Neck and Rutherford Island, to Johns Island. Pemaquid River (43°53′N 69°31′W) and Johns River (43°53′N 69°33′W) flow into the head of the bay.

2   There is no commercial traffic and the bay is only used as an anchorage by fishermen and yachtsmen as, except near the head of the bay and in the coves, the holding ground is poor. Port Clyde (3.16), and Boothbay Harbor (3.78), are at all times preferable anchorages.

Damariscotta River and approaches
General information
3.64

1   **Damariscotta River** is entered between Thrumcap Island (43°49′N 69°33′W) and the S end of Linekin Neck. The main entrance channel lies W of Inner Heron Island (3.68), which is situated 6 cables NW of Thrumcap Island. From its entrance the river leads N for 14 miles to the towns of Damariscotta and Newcastle (3.74), situated, respectively, on either side of the river at the head of navigation.

2   **Approaches.** A group of islands and dangers, extending 5 miles S from Linekin Neck, lie in the S and W approaches to Damariscotta River.

Topography. The channel of the river is narrow and in many places further contracted by islands and shoals.

3   **Depths.** There is a least depth of 6·1 m (20 ft) in the channel for a distance of 11 miles. Above this point the depth decreases gradually to 3 m (10 ft).

Pilotage is compulsory for all foreign vessels and for US vessels under registry with a draft of 2·7 m (9 ft) or more and may be obtained from the fishermen at South Bristol (3.70) or East Boothbay (3.71).

4   **Local knowledge** is required to navigate above The Narrows (3.68), 4½ miles above the entrance.

Natural conditions
3.65

1   **Tidal streams** are strong.
Ice. The river is closed by ice for a distance of 4 miles below Damariscotta from January to March.

Directions for south approach
3.66

1   From the vicinity of 43°44′N 69°32′W the S approach to the mouth of Damariscotta River leads generally N, passing (with positions relative to Pumpkin Island (43°45′N 69°35′W)):

E of Outer Pumpkin Island Ledge (1¼ miles S), thence:

2   E of Southeast Breaker (7½ cables SE), thence:
E of Pumpkin Island. A shoal, with a swept depth of 3 m (10 ft), lies 5 cables E of the island. Thence:
E of Outer Heron Island Ledge (1¼ miles NE), the E side of which is marked by No 1 Buoy (port

hand). Outer Heron Island, which is wooded, lies
1 mile WNW of the ledge. Thence:

3   E of White Islands Ledge (2¾ miles NNE). White
Islands, two high, rounded and prominent
landmarks, lie 7½ cables WSW of the ledge.

Directions for west approach
3.67

1   From a position about 3 cables W of Fisherman Island
(43°48′N 69°36′W) the W approach to Damariscotta River
leads NE and ENE through Fisherman Island Passage,
passing (with positions relative to Ram Island Light
(43°48′N 69°36′W)):

    NW of Ram Island, grassy. Ram Island Light stands
on the NW side of the island. Thence:

2   SE of Gangway Ledge (3 cables NW), the S side of
which is marked by No 4 Buoy (starboard hand),
thence:

    NNW of No 3 Buoy (port hand) (2 cables NE), which
marks the limit of a shoal extending N from the N
point of Fisherman Island. Thence:

3   NNW of No 1 Buoy (port hand) (6 cables E) which
marks the N end of The Hypocrites, two low, bare,
above-water rocks, lying on a reef. Thence:

    NNW of HL Light-buoy (safe water) (9 cables ENE).

    Useful mark:

    Large stone house standing on the highest part of the
N end of Fisherman Island.

4   **Local knowledge** is required for this passage, which
may only be used by vessels with a draught not exceeding
5·5 m (18 ft).

Directions for river
3.68

1   From a position SW of Thrumcap Island (43°49′N
69°33′W) the channel up the Damariscotta River leads
generally N, passing (with positions relative to Fort Island
(43°53′·5N 69°35′·1W)):

    W of Inner Heron Island (4 miles S), which is thickly
wooded. No 2 Buoy (starboard hand) marks Inner
Heron Ledge which lies 3 cables SW of the island.
Thence:

2   W of Foster Point (3 miles SSE), the SW point of
Rutherford Island. FP Buoy (preferred channel to
port) is moored 1¼ cables S of the point at the
outer edge of a ledge. Thence:

    E of Farnham Point (2¼ miles SSE), opposite the
village of South Bristol (3.70), thence:

3   SW of Jones Point (1½ miles SSE), which is opposite
the village of East Boothbay (3.71). Shoals with a
dredged depth of 6·4 m (21 ft) and 4 m (13 ft) lie
on the W side of the channel opposite this point.
Thence:

    E of Western Ledge (5 cables S), awash. The ledge is
marked on its S side by No 11 Buoy (port hand).
Thence:

4   SE of Fort Island which contracts The Narrows to
½ cable.

    Above The Narrows, the channel, though marked by
beacons and buoys, should not be attempted without local
knowledge. The final 2 miles below Damariscotta are
bordered by mudflats.

Inner Heron Island
3.69

1   **Berths** with depths alongside of 3·7 m are situated on
the NE side of Inner Heron Island (43°50′N 69°34′W).
Vessels approaching the berths should avoid the reef, which

dries 1·5 m (5 ft) and extends N from the island, the limit
of which is marked by No 4 Buoy (starboard hand).

South Bristol
3.70

1   South Bristol (43°52′N 69°34′W) is a village on the S
side of The Gut.

    Alongside berth. The town wharf, with a depth
alongside of 0·9 m, lies close W of the bridge.

    Shipyard on the N side of the Gut, W of the bridge,
which can build ships up to 45 m in length, has a pier
which is reported to have depths alongside of 1·5 to 3·6 m.

    Supplies: fuel; water and stores.

East Boothbay
3.71

1   East Boothbay (43°52′N 69°35′W) is a village 5 cables
N of Farnham Point (3.68). The large buildings of three
boatyards, where small craft are built, are prominent.

    Anchorage is available in depths of 2 m (7 ft) close off
the village.

2   **Alongside berths.** There are three wharves in use with
depths alongside of 3 m.

    Repairs: patent slips are available for craft up to 30 m
in length. Hull and engine repairs can be effected.

    Supplies: fuel; water and stores.

Meadow Cove
3.72

1   **Anchorage** is available in Meadow Cove (43°52′·5N
69°35′·3W) NW of Montgomery Point in depths of 9 to
15 m (30 to 48 ft). This anchorage is normally used by
vessels bound up river above The Narrows, while awaiting
favourable weather, the tide or a pilot (3.64).

Above The Narrows
3.73

1   **Anchorage** may be obtained anywhere in the channel
above The Narrows (43°53′N 69°35′W) where the depth
and bottom are suitable.

Damariscotta and Newcastle
3.74

1   Damariscotta (44°02′N 69°32′W) on the E bank and
Newcastle on the W bank are connected by a fixed bridge
with a clearance of 1·5 m. There is little traffic to these
towns by water except for small craft and fishing vessels.

2   **Alongside berths.** The town landing stage, with a depth
alongside of 2·4 m, extends from the E bank just below the
bridge.

    Anchorage may be obtained in depths of 3 m (10 ft) off
the landings.

    Supplies: fuel; water and provisions.

Booth Bay and adjacent waters
Description
3.75

1   **Booth Bay** lies between Linekin Neck and Fisherman
Island (43°48′N 69°36′W) on the E and Southport Island
on the W. Cape Newagen, the SE extremity of Southport
Island, lies 2¾ miles SW of the S point of Linekin Neck.

2   **Squirrel Island** (3.76) is situated in the middle of the
bay with a deep channel on either side. N of the island the
bay divides into Linekin Bay (3.77) to the NE and
Boothbay Harbor (3.78) to the NW.

    Approaches. Islands and dangerous rocks extend
5½ miles SSW from Linekin Neck. For a description of the
islands and dangers forming the E part of this group see
3.66.

Directions
3.76

1   **Approach from east.** Booth Bay is approached from the E through Fisherman Island Passage (43°48′N 69°36′W) (3.67).

  Approach from south. From a position SW of Bantam Rock (43°44′N 69°38′W) the approach route into Booth Bay leads generally NNE, passing (with positions relative to The Cuckolds (43°47′N 69°39′W)):

2   WNW of Bantam Rock (3 miles SSE), awash. No 2 BR Light-buoy (starboard hand) marks the SW side of the rock. Poor Shoal, with a depth of 10 m (33 ft) over it, lies 6½ cables SE of Bantam Rock. Thence:

    WNW of Damariscove Island (1¾ miles ESE), which is bare and nearly divided in the middle. Shoal patches with depths of 2·7 to 7·3 m (9 to 24 ft) lie up to 5 cables off the W coast of the island. Thence:

3   ESE of The Cuckolds, two bare islets 3 to 4 m in height. The Cuckolds Light (white 8-sided tower on dwelling, 15 m in height) stands on the E islet. IC Buoy (port hand) is moored 4 cables S of the lighthouse. Thence:

4   Between Squirrel Island (43°48′N 69°38′W), wooded with many large houses visible on it, and Wylie Rock (6 cables SE), thence:

    Follow the E coast of Squirrel Island until abreast the N point.

5   Thence NE to the entrance of Linekin Bay or NW to the entrance of Boothbay Harbor (3.78).

  Useful marks:

    Two towers (43°45′N 69°37′W), standing on the S end of Damariscove Island.

    Burnt Island Light (43°49′·5N 69°38′·5W) (3.11).

Linekin Bay
3.77

1   **Description.** Linekin Bay, the NE arm of Booth Bay, is entered between Negro Island and Spruce Point (43°50′N 69°37′W), 5 cables NW.

  The entrance is obstructed by Spruce Point Ledges, awash, the SE and NW extremities of which are marked by Nos 1 and 2 Buoys (port and starboard hand, respectively).

2   **Entrance channels.** The best and deeper channel passes between Negro Island and Spruce Point Ledges.

  A narrow passage leads between Spruce Point Ledge and the reef extending S from Spruce Point, which point should be given a berth of ½ cable. **Local knowledge** is required to navigate this passage.

3   **Dangers.** The inner part of the bay is obstructed by a number of dangers. The principal dangers are (with positions relative to Cabbage Island, wooded with a house in its centre, (43°50′·5N 69°36′·4W)):

    Tibbits Ledge (5 cables SE), which has a depth of 2·4 m (8 ft) over it and is marked on its SW side by No 2 Buoy (starboard hand).

4   Holbrook Ledge (3 cables E), which dries 0·9 m (3 ft), lies nearly in mid-channel and is marked on its NW side by No 4 Buoy (starboard hand).

    Seal Rock (5 cables NNE), awash, lies on a shoal, the E side of which is marked by No 5 Buoy (port hand). The channel between the rock and the shoal extending from the shore W should not be navigated without local knowledge.

5   Perch Island (8 cables NE), marked by No 6 Buoy (starboard hand), and Fish Hawk Islet (8 cables N),

both of which have several trees on them, lie at the head of the bay. There are numerous unmarked rocks at the head of the bay.

6   **Anchorage** is available in depths of 12 to 23 m (40 ft to 13 fm) in the lower part of the bay and in depths of 9 to 11 m (30 to 36 ft) in the upper part of the bay clear of a cable area, shown on the chart, extending across the bay E of Cabbage Island.

Boothbay Harbor
3.78

1   **Description.** Boothbay Harbor (43°50′N 69°38′W), the NW arm of Booth Bay, is one of the best anchorages on the coast of Maine, being well sheltered with good holding ground. It is entered between Spruce Point (43°50′N 69°37′W) and Burnt Island, (8 cables WSW) and extends N for 1¾ miles to the town of Boothbay Harbor.

2   Mouse Island, wooded, lies on the W side of the harbour, 1½ cables N of Burnt Island.

  Tumbler Island, low and wooded with a house and flagstaff on it, lies 7½ cables NW of Spruce Point. The passage between the island and the shore E is encumbered with rocks and should not be attempted without local knowledge.

3   McFarland Island lies close off the town of Boothbay Harbor, 7 cables NNE of Tumbler Island. No 9 Light-buoy (port hand) marks the S end of a shoal that surrounds the island.

  Ice sometimes obstructs navigation during severe winters above Tumbler Island, during February and March. In normal winters the harbour is free of ice as far as the footbridge.

4   **Pilotage** is compulsory and is available at any time. Boarding location depends on sea conditions. Tugs are available. Advance notice of 48 hours is required for services of pilot and tug. See *Admiralty List of Radio Signals Volume 6(5)* for details.

3.79

1   **Entrance channel from south.** The main entrance channel leads NNW from between Burnt Island and No 6 Buoy (starboard hand) which marks a 2·7 m (9 ft) shoal 2½ cables W of Spruce Point. It then leads NNE passing WNW of No 8 Light-buoy (starboard hand) which lies 1 cable WNW of Tumbler Island, and thence into the inner harbour.

2   **Townsend Gut**, the SE entrance of which lies 3 cables NW of Mouse Island, is a narrow and winding channel that leads into Boothbay Harbor from Sheepscot River (3.84).

  As part of the Inside Passage (3.7), used by small vessels between Boothbay Harbor and Bath (3.108), it leads from Boothbay Harbor between Southport Island and the mainland N, into Ebenecook Harbor (3.94).

3   A drawbridge with an open span 16 m wide crosses the channel 5 cables within the SE entrance.

  Local knowledge is necessary.

  Useful mark:

    Tower on McKown Point (43°50′·6N 69°38′·4W).

3.80

1   **Anchorage** is best obtained between Tumbler Island and the head of the harbour clear of a pipeline area, shown on the US chart, extending NNW from McKown Point to the opposite shore. There are depths of 13 to 7 m (42 to 24 ft), good holding ground, in the outer harbour between N of Tumbler Island and McKown Point, 5 cables NW, and depths of 7 to 2 m (24 to 6 ft) in the inner harbour SE of McFarland Island (43°50′N 69°38′W).

2   **Alongside berths** are available as follows:

Mouse Island. N and E side with depths alongside of 3·7 m.

McFarland Island. Several wharves on the E side.

3   Boothbay Harbor town. There are a number of wharves on the NE side of the harbour with depths alongside of 1·2 to 4·6 m.

3.81

1   **Repairs:** Several shipyards are situated along the waterfront. Hull and engine repairs are available.

Other facilities: hospital.

Supplies: fuel; water and provisions.

Rescue. A Coast Guard station (43°50′·6N 69°38′·5W) is situated ½ cable SW of the NE tip of McKown Point.

INSHORE WATERS BETWEEN CAPE NEWAGEN AND CAPE SMALL

General information

Charts 2490, 2492 (see 1.17)

Description

3.82

1   The inshore waters between Cape Newagen (43°47′N 69°39′W) and Cape Small (10 miles SW) consist of Sheepscot River and approaches, Kennebec River and approaches, and the port of Bath.

Traffic regulations

3.83

1   **Navigation Rules for US Inland Waters.** The Navigation Rules for US Inland Waters do not apply to any of the waters described in this section.

Danger zone. For information on a danger zone SE of Cape Small see 3.10.

Sheepscot River and approaches

Description

3.84

1   **Sheepscot River** is the approach to several small villages and the city of Wiscasset (3.98). The river is entered between The Cuckolds (43°47′N 69°39′W) (3.76) and Griffith Head, 3 miles W.

Approach. Sheepscot Bay, lying between the S point of Damariscove Island (43°45′N 69°37′W) and Salter Island, 6 miles W, forms the approach to Sheepscot River.

2   **Depths.** The channel in Sheepscot River is deep and the principal dangers are marked, depths however are irregular and many rocks and ledges rise abruptly from deep water.

The channel has a depth of over 9·1 m (30 ft) as far as Wiscasset.

3   **Pilotage** is compulsory and is normally available during daylight hours only. The pilot boarding location varies according to sea conditions. See 3.78 for further details.

4   **Under-keel clearances.** The US Coast Guard recommends a minimum under-keel clearance of 0·6 m (2 ft) for vessels transiting the Sheepscot River N of 2SR Light-buoy (3.87) and of 0·3 m (1 ft) at all berthing areas.

Measured distance

3.85

1   Off the W side of Barters Island (43°53′N 69°41′W) there is a measured distance.

N Marks: Beacons in line bearing 105¾°.

S Marks: Beacons in line bearing 105¾°.

Distance: 1 mile.

Running track: 015¾°/195¾°.

Natural conditions

3.86

1   **Tidal streams** generally follow the direction of the channel, their strength being considerable in the narrow parts.

Ice does not generally interfere with navigation below Wiscasset, but above the town the river is usually closed in winter.

Directions

3.87

1   **Sheepscot Bay.** From a position in the vicinity of 43°43′N 69°42′W the route through Sheepscot Bay leads N to the entrance of Sheepscot River, passing (with positions relative to The Cuckolds Light (43°47′N 69°39′W)):

E of Tom Rock (4 miles SW), awash, lying at the SE end of a shoal. 2TR Buoy (starboard hand) is moored SW of the rock. Thence:

2   E of The Sisters (4 miles SW), three small above-water rocks, lying at the NW end of the same shoal. 4S Buoy (starboard hand) lies 2 cables NW of The Sisters. Thence:

E of The Black Rocks (3¼ miles WSW), a group of rocks consisting of two above-water rocks, 3 and 5 m (10 and 15 ft) in height, in its N part, and several rocks awash and below-water in its S part. And:

3   W of 2SR Light-buoy (starboard hand) (2 miles SW), which marks the W side of two shoals with swept depths of 12·2 m (40 ft), thence:

W of The Cuckolds (3.76) upon which stands The Cuckolds Light (3.76) and:

E of Griffith Head Ledge (2½ miles W), the SE side of which is marked by No 3 Buoy (port hand).

3.88

1   **Lower Sheepscot River.** From a position W of Lower Mark Island (43°47′·6N 69°40′·6W), high, wooded and prominent, the channel in Sheepscot River leads N, passing (with positions relative to Hendricks Head (43°49′·3N 69°41′·4W)):

2   W of Cat Ledges (1¼ miles SSE), a group of rocks partly above-water. A shoal, with a swept depth of 5·8 m (19 ft), which is marked by 4CL Buoy (starboard hand), lies 4 cables SW of the ledge. Thence:

E of a line of shoals with depths of 6·1 to 10·7 m (20 to 35 ft), which lie between Griffith Head Ledge and Bull Ledge, 3 miles N, and:

3   E of Wood Island (1½ miles SW), thence:

W of Hendricks Head Light. The dangers off Southport Island on the E side of the channel between Lower Mark Island and Cedarbush Island are covered by the red sector of this light. And:

E of Five Islands (8 cables WSW), thence:

4   E of No 9 Buoy (port hand) (7 cables NNW) which marks the S end of Bull Ledge. Thence between the ledge and:

W of Dogfish Head (9 cables NNE), rocky and grass-covered with a low neck behind, which forms the S entrance point to Ebenecook Harbor (3.94), thence:

5   W of Green Islands (1¼ miles NNE), wooded group, situated on the N side of the entrance to Ebenecook Harbor, thence:

W of No 10 Buoy (starboard hand) marking the S end of Harding Ledge (1¾ miles), which has a depth of 1·5 m (5 ft) over it, and:

6   E of Middle Mark Island (1½ miles NNW), 4 m (12 ft) in height, round and bare, lying on a reef that extends 1 cable N and S of it, thence:

E of Middle Ledge (2 miles NNW), with a charted depth of 2·4 m (8 ft) over it, although less has been reported. No 13 Buoy (port hand) marks the N end of the ledge and the approach to Goose Rock Passage (3.90).

7   **Caution** With an out-going tide there is a strong set W near Bull Ledge and a strong set E near Middle Ledge, but the sets are not noticeable on a rising tide.

3.89

1   **Upper Sheepscot River.** From a position SW of Isle of Springs (43°52′N 69°41′W), a wooded island with a high tank on its summit, the channel leads N and then NNE, passing (with positions relative to Cross Point (43°55′·6N 69°40′·3W)):

2   E of Clous Ledge (4¼ miles SSW), which dries and is marked by No 15 beacon (port hand), and:

W of Powderhorn Island (4¼ miles S), 7 m (25 ft) in height and grassy. No 16 Light-buoy (starboard hand) marks Powderhorn Ledge 1½ cables N of the island. Thence:

3   E of Fourfoot Rock (4 miles SSW), with a depth of 1·2 m (4 ft) over it. No 17 Buoy (port hand) is moored 1 cable SE of the rock. Thence:

W of Ram Islands (3¾ miles S). A rocky patch with a depth of 7·3 m (24 ft) over it lies 1 cable W of Ram Islands. Thence:

4   Between Upper Mark Island (3½ miles SSW) and No 18 Buoy (starboard hand) marking a ledge, 5 cables NE, thence:

Between Hodgdon Ledge (3 miles SSW), the S end of which is marked by No 19 Buoy (port hand), and No 20 Buoy (starboard hand) marking the S end of Stover Ledge, which extends from the S part of Barters Island, thence:

5   W of the beacons marking the measured distance (1 and 2 miles SSW) (3.85), thence:

Between Cross Point and the shore of Westport Island, close N of Fowle Point. Cross River flows into the E side of Sheepscot River at Cross Point and CP Light-buoy (preferred channel to port) is moored at the junction.

6   Thence the channel leads between the N part of Westport Island and the mainland E to the head of navigation at Wiscasset.

Side channels
3.90

1   **Goose Rock Passage**, which forms part of the Inside Passage (3.7), is entered between the N side of MacMahan Island (43°51′N 69°42′W) and Whittum Island, 3 cables N, which is wooded.

2   Clous Ledge and Middle Ledge, which lie in the approaches, are marked by No 15 Beacon and No 13 Buoy (port hand), respectively, and a shoal which extends from the N point of MacMahan Island is marked by No 1 Beacon (port hand).

3   The passage is marked by No 5 Light (green square on framework tower on caisson) on the S shore of the W end of the passage, and by Nos 3 and 4 Buoys (lateral) at the N entrance to Little Sheepscot River.

Ice usually closes the passage for about 2 months but it has been known for it to remain open in mild winters.

Knubble Bay, part of the Inside Passage, leads N from the W end of Goose Rock Passage into Hockomock Bay.

4   **Lower Hell Gate.** The NW entrance to this bay is narrow, being only 1 cable wide at its narrowest point and its passage should only be attempted at slack water as tidal streams of up to 9 kn have been observed in the vicinity.

Hockomock Bay. A channel marked by buoys (lateral) leads through Hockomock Bay into Sasanoa River.

5   **Sasanoa River** is entered between Mill Point (43°53′N 69°46′W) and Hockomock Point, 1 cable N. The channel, which is marked by buoys (lateral) and beacons, is very narrow. It passes through Upper Hell Gate, ¼ cable wide, 9 cables NW of Mill Point.

A bridge, with a vertical clearance of 15·5 m, crosses the W end of the river at its junction with Kennebec River.

3.91

1   **Back River**, which is entered between Sawyer Island (43°52′N 69°41′W) and the S part of Barters Island, is a channel that separates this island from the mainland E. It is shallow, narrow and unmarked for most of its length and only suitable for small craft.

Cape Harbor
3.92

1   Cape Harbor (43°47′N 69°40′W) is a channel that leads between Cape Island and Newagen Point. It is used by small craft and fishing boats.

Cozy Harbor and Hendricks Harbor
3.93

1   Cozy Harbor (43°49′N 69°41′W) and Hendricks Harbor lie between Pratts Island and Hendricks Head.

Cozy Harbor is used as an anchorage by small craft and Hendricks Harbor is shoal and foul.

Ebenecook Harbor
3.94

1   Ebenecook Harbor (43°50′N 69°41′W) is situated between Green Islands, Boston Island, high and partly wooded, and Spectacle Islands on the W, and the N part of Southport Island on the E.

This is the first large anchorage for vessels entering the river.

2   **Entrances.** The harbour is entered from Sheepscot River between Dogfish Head (3.88) and the S point of Green Islands. The W end of Townsend Gut (3.79), part of the Inside Passage (3.7), enters the NE part of the Ebenecook Harbor at Cameron Point.

3   **Anchorage** is available near the middle of the harbour in depths of 7 to 11 m (23 to 36 ft), soft bottom. The S side of the harbour divides into three arms, the entrances of which provide good anchorage in depths of 4 to 7 m (13 to 23 ft). Attention is drawn to a cable area, shown on the US chart, situated in the E arm.

Sawyer Island
3.95

1   **Anchorage** is available in the channel, which is part of the Inside Passage, leading from Ebenecook Harbor between Sawyer Island (43°52′N 69°41′W) and Isle of Springs (3.89).

Barters Island
3.96

1   **Anchorage** is available in depths of 22 m (12 fm) or less in the channel off Barters Island above Stover Ledge (43°53′N 69°41′W).

Colby Cove
3.97

1   **Anchorage** is available in depths of 15 to 18 m (48 to 60 ft) in Colby Cove (43°58′N 69°40′W), on the W side of the river 2½ miles S of Wiscasset.

Wiscasset
3.98

1   Wiscasset is situated on the W side of Sheepscot River, 14 miles above the entrance. The wharves are in ruins and there is virtually no commercial traffic.

    Anchorage is available S and SW of the town wharves in depths of 8 to 15 m (26 to 49 ft), mud.

2   **Alongside berths.** Pier at Birch Point, 5 cables SW of Wiscasset, for servicing a power station. The berth has a depth alongside of 10 m for a length of 230 m but it was reported (2006) that it was closed to traffic.

    Town landing, with depth of 4·6 m alongside, is situated S of the ruined wharves.

3   **Repairs:** patent slip for craft up to 12 m in length.

    Other facilities: oily waste disposal.

    Supplies: fuel; water; provisions and stores.

Kennebec River and approaches

General information
3.99

1   **Kennebec River** is entered between Salter Island (43°45′N 69°45′W) and Pond Island (3.104), 7 cables SW. It is the approach to the cities of Bath (3.108), Richmond and Augusta; there is little commercial traffic beyond Bath. Small craft can reach Augusta, the head of navigation on the Kennebec River, which is about 44 miles above the river entrance.

2   **Approaches.** There are two entrance channels which lead E and W, respectively, of Seguin Island (3.102). The E channel (3.102) is generally used by vessels of over 5·5 m (18 ft) draught.

3   **Project depth** from the mouth of the river to a point 6 cables above the bridge at Bath is 8·2 m (27 ft), thence 5·2 m (17 ft) to Gardiner and 3·4 m (11 ft) to Augusta. For the latest controlling depths the charts and port authority should be consulted.

4   **Dangers.** The principal dangers in Kennebec River are marked, but the channel is narrow in places.

    Pilotage is compulsory; pilots usually board near White Ledge Light-buoy No 1 (43°43′·8N 69°44′·9W). See *Admiralty List of Radio Signals Volume 6(5)* for details.

    Local knowledge is required.

5   **Traffic regulations:**

    Danger zone. An area used by naval aircraft as a practice mining range lies SW of Seguin Island (3.103). See Appendix VI for details.

    Restricted area. An area surrounding the shipyard at Bath is a restricted area under the control of the United States Navy. See Appendix VI for definitions and general regulations covering restricted areas.

3.100

1   **Local magnetic anomaly**, increasing the variation by up to as much as 8°, exists in the vicinity of Ellingwood Rock (43°43′N 69°46′W), for 1 mile in all directions.

2   **Tidal streams** have considerable strength at the entrance to Kennebec River and in the narrow parts of the river.

Between the entrance and Bath the average maximum rate is from 2 to 3 kn and a rate of 6 kn may occur on the out-going stream.

    Freshets occur in March and April and also after heavy rains in the autumn, but are not dangerous to shipping unless accompanied by ice.

3   **Ice** usually closes the river above Bath from December to April. Below Bath vessels are rarely delayed by ice and icebreakers clear the channel if necessary.

    Drift ice coming down the river generally follows the W shore.

3.101

1   **Landmark:**

    Seguin Island Light (43°43′N 69°46′W) (3.11).

    Major Light:

    Seguin Island Light — as above.

Directions
3.102

1   **South-east approach to Kennebec River.** From a position E of Seguin Island the route through the SE approaches to Kennebec River leads NW, passing (with positions relative to Seguin Island Light (43°43′N 69°46′W)):

    NE of 20ML Light-buoy (starboard hand) (1 mile S), which marks the S side of Mile Ledge, thence:

2   NE of Seguin Island, thence:

    SW of Tom Rock and The Sisters (2½ miles NE). 2TR Buoy (starboard hand) marks the SW side of a shoal close S of Tom Rock and 4S Buoy (starboard hand) lies 2 cables NW of The Sisters. Two shoals with swept depths of 8·2 and 15·2 m (37 and 50 ft), respectively, lie 3 cables SW of Tom Rock. Thence:

3   NE of Seguin Ledges (port hand) (9 cables N), 2 m (5 ft) in height. Ellingwood Rock (3.103) lies 5 cables SW of these ledges. Thence:

    NE of No 1 Light-buoy (port hand) (1¼ miles NNE) marking White Ledge, a shoal with a depth of 3·4 m (11 ft) over it, thence:

4   NE of a 4·9 m (16 ft) patch (1½ miles N) marked by KR Buoy (preferred channel to starboard), thence:

    SW of Whaleback Rock (2 miles N), 2 m (8 ft) in height, high and bare.

3.103

1   **South-west approach to Kennebec River.** From a position SE of Cape Small (43°42′N 69°51′W) the route through the SW approaches to Kennebec River leads NE, through a danger zone (see 3.99), passing (with positions relative to Seguin Island Light (43°43′N 69°46′W)):

    SE of Halibut Rocks (2¾ miles W), with depths of 7·3 m (24 ft) over them, thence:

2   NW of Camel Ground (1 mile SW), with a swept depth of 7 m (23 ft), and over which the sea breaks in heavy weather, thence:

    Between Ellingwood Rock (6 cables N), 5 m in height and bare, and Jacknife Ledge with a depth of 2·4 m (8 ft) over it. No 1 Buoy (port hand) marks the SE side of the ledge. Thence:

3   Between Seguin Ledges (3.102) (1 mile N) and No 3 Buoy (port hand) that is moored on the outer part of Pond Island Shoal, 5 cables NW. Vessels should not pass between this buoy and Pond Island (3.104), which lies 6 cables farther NW. Thence:

    NW of White Ledge (1¼ miles NNE) (3.102). Thence as directed for SE approaches, passing clear of the

4·9 m (16 ft) patch (2½ cables NW of White Ledge) marked by KR Buoy.

3.104

1 **Kennebec River**. From a position SE of Pond Island Light (white tower) (43°44′N 69°46′W), a light which is intensified up and down the river, the channel to Bath leads generally NNW, passing (with positions relative to Squirrel Point Light (43°49′N 69°48′W)):

2 Between Pond Island (4¾ miles SSE), 9 m in height and grassy, and No 4 Buoy (starboard hand) which lies 3 cables E, marking the S limit of a spit extending 3 cables S from Stage Island, thence:

Between South Sugarloaf (4½ miles SSE), high, rounded, bare and rocky, and No 5 Buoy (port hand), which is moored off Popham Beach, 2 cables W, thence:

3 SW of North Sugarloaf (4 miles SSE), high, rounded, bare and rocky, and No 6 Buoy (starboard hand) moored ¾ cable W, which marks the S side of a shoal with a least depth of 5·2 m (17 ft) over it. The fairway is only ½ cable wide at this point and is the narrowest part of the channel below Bath. Thence:

4 SW of Gilbert Head (3¾ miles SSE), high and wooded. A prominent white house stands on the head and is a good mark in hazy weather. And:

NE of Hunnewell Point (3¾ miles SSE). Fort Popham, a disused stone fort, stands on the point. Fort Popham Light (post), which is intensified up and down the river, stands on a parapet of the fort. Thence:

5 W of Shag Rock (3¼ miles SSE), 1 m in height. No 8 Light-buoy (starboard hand) lies close W of the rock. Thence:

E of Cox Head (3 miles SSE), 43 m in height and wooded, thence:

6 Between Nos 11 and 12 Buoys (lateral) (2½ miles SSE), which mark, respectively, a shoal off the N side of Dix Island, and the S limit of Perkins Island Ledge that extends 4 cables SSW from Perkins Island. The E limit of the white sector (018°–038°) of Perkins Island Light leads clear of the ledge. Thence:

7 Between Perkins Island (2 miles S), bare on the S end and wooded at the N end, and No 13 Buoy (port hand) which lies 1 cable W, marking the SE side of a patch with a depth of 1·5 m (5 ft) over it, thence:

8 E of Parker Head (1¾ miles SSE), which is a prominent headland, and Parker Flats, which lie NNW. The white sector, astern, of Perkins Island Light (172°–188°) and the white sector of Squirrel Point Light (321°–324°) lead clear of these flats. Thence:

9 E of Seal Rocks (5 cables SSE), which dry 1·5 m (5 ft) and are marked by No 17 Buoy (port hand), thence:

W of Squirrel Point, on which stands Squirrel Point Light.

Useful mark:

Church spire (43°49′N 69°49′W). A good leading mark for the reach between Bald Head and Squirrel Point.

3.105

1 From a position W of Squirrel Point the channel continues generally N, passing (with positions relative to Squirrel Point Light (43°49′N 69°48′W)):

E of Pettis Rocks (9 cables N), which are bare at the top and marked by No 23 Light (green square on framework tower) at the S end, thence:

2 E of Ram Island (1¼ miles N), low and bushy with a ledge extending E, which is marked by No 25 Light (green square on framework tower and small white house).

Caution. This is a dangerous part of the river and vessels inbound, after passing the S end of Lee Island (43°50′N 69°48′W), 39 m in height and wooded, should keep close to the E side of the river to keep clear of the shoals extending from Pettis Rocks and Ram Island.

3.106

1 From a position W of Green Point (43°50′N 69°48′W) the channel continues N, passing (with positions relative to Green Point):

W of Bluff Head (1 mile N) where the river narrows to a width of 1 cable.

2 **Doubling Point Leading Lights:**

Front light (2¾ miles N).

Rear light (215 m from front light).

From a position W of Bluff Head (43°51′N 69°48′W) the alignment (359°) of these lights leads N through the upper part of the reach between Bluff Head and the turn into Fiddler Reach, passing (with positions relative to Bluff Head):

3 Close E of patches (1¼ miles N) with depths of 8·8 and 8·2 m (29 and 27 ft) over them, and:

Close W of a patch with a depth of 8·8 m (29 ft) over it.

After passing through Fiddler Reach and rounding Doubling Point (2¾ miles NNW), the track leads N to the port of Bath.

4 **Useful mark:**

Doubling Point Light (2 miles NNW).

Side channels

3.107

1 **Sasanoa River**, which is part of the Inside Passage (3.7), enters Kennebec River opposite Bath. See 3.90.

Bath

3.108

1 **General information.** Bath (43°54′N 69°49′W), a city which in 2005 had an estimated population of 9257, stands on the W side of the Kennebec River, 12 miles above the entrance.

It is a port of entry and shipbuilding facility for the US Navy, but there is little water-borne traffic except for barges and vessels for repair at the shipyard.

2 **Depths and maximum size of vessel.** Channel is dredged to depth of 8·2 m (27 ft) and vessels with a draught of up to 9·1 m can be accepted at a suitable tide.

Vertical clearance. A combined road and rail drawbridge crosses the river between Bath and Woolwich (3.109). Vertical clearances of 41·1 m (135 ft), when open, and 3 m (10 ft) when closed. A road bridge close N of the drawbridge has a fixed span with a clearance of 21·3 m (70 ft).

3 **Tidal levels.** Mean spring range about 2·1 m; mean neap range about 1·5 m. See information in *Admiralty Tide Tables*.

Ice. See 3.100.

Pilotage. See 3.99.

4 **Anchorage** may be obtained off Bath more than 1 cable S of the bridge. For precise limits of anchorage port regulations should be consulted.

Alongside berths. Pier 213 m in length extends SE from the S end of the repair yard. Depth alongside its N side reported to be 9·1 m. Dry dock alongside its S side. Town landing with depth alongside of 4·6 m is situated on the W side just above the bridge.

5   **Repairs.** Shipyard situated on the W side of the river just below the bridge. Shipbuilding and repairs carried out.
Other facilities: hospital.
Supplies: fuel; provisions and stores.

Anchorages and harbours
3.109

1   **No 1 Light-buoy** (43°44′N 69°45′W). Large vessels awaiting a pilot may anchor in the vicinity of this light-buoy in depths of 15 to 20 m (49 to 66 ft).
Bay Point (43°45′N 69°46′W) is a village on the point of that name. There is a wharf, with a depth alongside of 1·2 m at the village.

2   **Perkins Island Ledge** (43°47′N 69°47′W). Anchorage is available, in depths of 11 to 15 m (36 to 49 ft), on the E side of the channel S of No 12 Buoy which marks the S edge of this ledge.
Parker Flats (43°48′N 69°47′W). Anchorage is available, in depths of 7 to 11 m (23 to 36 ft), on the W side of the channel off Parker Flats, clear of the cable area crossing the channel close N of Parker Head.

3   **Above Parker Flats** vessels anchor wherever they can find suitable depths and good holding ground, keeping out of the strength of the tidal streams, clear of the cable area, shown on the US chart, crossing the channel W of Squirrel Point.
Woolwich (43°55′N 69°48′W), standing on the N side of the W entrance of the Sasanoa River, has a pier with a depth alongside of 6·7 m.
A bridge, with a vertical clearance of 15·2 m (50 ft), crosses the river between Sasanoa Point and Preble Point.

EASTERN PART OF CASCO BAY

General information

Chart 2490 (see 1.17)
Description
3.110

1   Casco Bay, which is entered between Cape Small (43°42′N 69°51′W) and Cape Elizabeth, 18 miles WSW, is divided by Harpswell Neck and Halfway Rock.
The E part of the bay is encumbered with islets and above and below-water rocks, with narrow but deep channels leading up to 10 miles N.

2   There are a number of anchorages in this area which are suitable for small vessels, but are of little importance. There are several villages, but no towns in this part of Casco Bay.

Traffic regulations
3.111

1   **Navigation Rules for US Inland Waters.** The limit of the waters to which these rules apply is a line joining Bald Head (43°42′N 69°51′W), SE point of Ragged Island (43°44′N 69°56′W), S point of Jaquish Island (43°43′N 70°00′W) and Little Mark Island (43°43′N 70°02′W). See 1.47 and Appendix VII for further information.

Natural conditions
3.112

1   **Tidal streams** in Casco Bay are not strong, but in the bay and across its entrance, there is a perceptible N set with a rising tide and a S set with a falling tide.
Ice forms in considerable quantities at the heads of the numerous sounds, bays and river in the E part of Casco Bay, but the principal anchorages are usable throughout the year.

Outer approaches to east part of Casco Bay

Topography
3.113

1   Cape Small, the E entrance point of Casco Bay, is wooded. Small Point (43°42′N 69°50′W) is its S extremity and Bald Head, a bare round knob, is at the SW extremity. Fuller Rock, low and bare, lies 4 cables SSE of Small Point; a light (3.13) stands on the rock.
3.114

1   Broken ground lies S and W of Cape Small on which are (with positions relative to Small Point):
Buttonmold Ledges (3 cables SW).
Bill Wallace Ground (5 cables SW).
Bald Head Ledge (7½ cables WSW), the S side of which is marked by 2BH Light-buoy (starboard hand) and upon which there is an obstruction.

2   Temple Ledge (2 miles SW).
Lumbo Ledge (4 miles WSW).
Halfway Rock (9 miles WSW), a low islet on which stands Halfway Rock Light (3.11).

Approaches to New Meadows River

Description
3.115

1   The approaches to New Meadows River, which lie between Bald Head (43°42′N 69°51′W) and Ragged Island (3.123), 4 miles WNW, are obstructed by numerous islands and dangers, the positions of which are best seen on the US charts.
Local knowledge is required to navigate in the approaches to New Meadows River.

Directions
3.116

1   **From south.** From a position about 5 cables SW of Bald Head (43°42′N 69°51′W) the approach leads NNW and N, passing (with positions relative to Bald Head):
Between Spoonbowl Ledge (6 cables NNW) and the patches lying within 7 cables E and NE of East Brown Cow (1½ miles W), thence:

2   WSW of Gooseberry Island Ledge (9 cables NNW), awash, the NW side of which is marked by No 2 Buoy (starboard hand), thence:
ENE of Wyman Ledge (1½ miles NW), marked by No 3 Buoy (port hand), thence:

3   W of No 4 Light-buoy (starboard hand) (1½ miles NW), 4 cables SW of the S extremity of Wood Island, a partly wooded island, thence:
Between Carrying Place Head (2½ miles NNW) and No 7 Buoy (port hand) moored at the S end of Jamison Ledge, 5 cables W, which dries at its S end; thence clear of shoals NNW of Jamison Ledge to the mouth of the New Meadows River.
3.117

1   **From south-west.** From a position in the vicinity of WB Light-buoy (safe water) (43°43′N 69°55′W) the

approach leads NNE, passing (with positions relative to Mark Island (43°43′N 69°54′W)):

Between Mark Island Ledge (4 cables SW), marked on its W side by No 2 Buoy (starboard hand), and White Bull, 8 cables W, a high, bare, rounded island, thence:

2   NW of Mark Island, high and thickly wooded, thence:

SE of Sisters Ground (1¼ miles NW), a shoal that lies 5 cables SE of The Sisters, two rocks above-water, the E of which is 1·8 m (6 ft) in height, thence:

3   Between Flag Island (1¾ miles N), high and thickly wooded, and Long Ledge, 4 cables NW, two grassy islets 3 and 4 m (10 and 12 ft) in height, thence:

4   Between Goudy Ledge (2¾ miles N), marked by a beacon, and North Jenny Ledge, 5 cables W, which is marked on its S side by No 2 Buoy (starboard hand), thence:

SE of Rogue Island (3 miles N), low with scattered trees; thence into the river entrance.

Minor channels
3.118

1   **North Jenny Ledge.** A protected route, used by small craft, leads NE from SE of Jenny Island (43°46′N 69°55′W) and North Jenny Ledge between Goudy Ledge and Rogue Island.

2   **Gurnet Strait.** New Meadows River can be entered by small craft 5 miles above its entrance through Gurnet Strait (3.131).

Local knowledge is required to navigate these channels.

Minor anchorages and harbours
3.119

1   **Small Point Harbor** (43°44′N 69°52′W), entered either side of Wood Island (3.116), is used by local fishermen and small craft.

Carrying Place Cove and Fish House Cove, lying either side of West Point, provide anchorage for small craft.

New Meadows River

Description
3.120

1   **New Meadows River** is entered between Bear Island (43°47′N 69°53′W) and Fort Point, 3 cables W. No 1 Light-buoy (port hand) is moored off Fort Point.

2   The river extends N for 8½ miles to road and railway bridges and a dam at the head of navigation. There is a deep water channel from the river entrance for about 5 miles; above this the depths gradually decrease and the channel has a least depth of 3·7 m (12 ft) to within 5 cables of the bridges. The principal dangers are marked.

3   Thence the channel is winding and unmarked and has a depth of 2·1 m (7 ft) to the villages of New Meadows and Harding.

The river is seldom used except by local fishing boats and small pleasure craft.

Local knowledge is required.

Anchorages and harbors
3.121

1   **Cundys Harbor** lies on the W side of the river, 1 mile above its entrance. Cedar Ledges, partly above-water, extend from the W side of the river on the N side of the

entrance. No 3 Buoy (port hand) marks the S end of the ledges.

2   Anchorage is available for small vessels in depths of 7 to 9 m (22 to 31 ft).

The village of Cundys Harbor is situated on the W side of the harbour. Wharves, with depths alongside of 2·1 to 3 m, are situated at the fish factories.

3   **The Basin** is a cove on the E side of the river, 1 mile N of Bear Island. It has a very narrow entrance and is only used by small craft. Sheep Island Ledge, awash, and marked by No 5 Buoy (port hand) on its E side lies in the fairway 6 cables WSW of the entrance.

4   **Winnegance Bay** (43°49′N 69°52′W) is entered between Birch Point and Basin Point, 1 mile SSE. Foul ground with Bushy Islet and Hen Islet on it, extends 3 cables from the SE side of the bay. Beacon (red triangular-shaped daymark) stands on Hen Island Ledge, which dries 0·6 m (2 ft), at the SW end of the foul ground, 3 cables N of Basin Point. A dangerous wreck, the position of which is doubtful, lies 1½ cables WNW of Hen Island Ledge.

5   Anchorage is available in the NW side of the bay in depths of 5 to 7 m (16 to 23 ft).

Bragdon Rock (43°51′·0N 69°53′·5W), which has a beacon on it, marks the entrance to two long narrow inlets separated by the peninsula of Rich Hill.

Quahog Bay and adjacent waters

Description
3.122

1   Quahog Bay (43°47′N 69°56′W) (3.124) lies on the S side of Sebascodegan Island.

The approaches from S lead between two chains of islands that extend S from either entrance point. The approach from E or W is by the buoyed channel leading across the entrance of the bay, between the waters off the E side of Bailey Island and the entrance to New Meadows River.

2   Ridley Cove (3.125) and Gun Point Cove (3.126) lie to the E and W of Quahog Bay, respectively.

Directions
3.123

1   From a position SW of Bold Dick, a rock which dries 2·1 m (7 ft) (43°42′·8N 69°56′·6W), a S approach route leads NNE, passing (with positions relative to Gun Point (43°46′N 69°57′W)):

2   Between Saddleback Ledge (3 miles S), which dries 1·5 m (5 ft), and No 3 Light-buoy (port hand) which marks the S edge of the shoal ground surrounding Round Rock, 5 cables WNW, thence:

Between Ragged Island (2¼ miles S) and Middle Ground Rock, 6 cables W, which dries 0·6 m (2 ft), thence:

3   WNW of Blacksnake Ledge (1¾ miles SSE), which dries. A rock, with a swept depth of 4·6 m (15 ft), lies 3 cables W of the N extremity of this ledge. Thence:

WNW of Yellow Rock (1¼ miles SSE), thence:

ESE of Cedar Ledges (9 cables S), bare and partly above-water with a height of 0·6 m, thence:

4   WNW of Two Bush Island (1 mile SSE), grassy, thence:

WNW of Elm Islands (9 cables SE), which stand on a reef and are separated by a narrow channel from the S end of Yarmouth Ledges. No 6 Buoy (starboard hand) marks the N side of the channel.

Quahog Bay

3.124

1 Quahog Bay is entered between Yarmouth Ledges (43°46′N 69°56′W), which extend S from Yarmouth Island, and the S extremity of Sebascodegan Island, 2½ cables SE of Gun Point. It is a narrow arm extending 4 miles NNE. Good anchorage is available for small vessels.

Local knowledge is required.

Ridley Cove

3.125

1 Ridley Cove, situated 7½ cables W of the entrance to New Meadows River, is entered between West Cundy Point (43°46′N 69°54′W), which has a prominent white house on it, and Flash Island, 4 cables WNW.

Foul ground extends 5 cables SSW and 1 mile SW from the E and W entrance points of the cove.

2 A narrow obstructed passage leads from the N part of the cove, N of Yarmouth Island into Quahog Bay.

Anchorage, exposed to S and SW winds, is available in depths of 7 to 11 m (23 to 37 ft) in the cove.

Local knowledge is necessary.

Gun Point Cove

3.126

1 Gun Point Cove (43°46′N 69°57′W) is a narrow and unimportant inlet that extends 2 miles NNE between the S part of Sebascodegan Island and Orrs Island, W of it.

Lowell Cove

3.127

1 Lowell Cove (43°45′N 69°59′W), used as an anchorage by local fishermen, is situated at the S end of Orrs Island.

Merriconeag Sound and Harpswell Sound

Description

3.128

1 **Merriconeag Sound,** which is entered between Jaquish Island (43°43′N 70°00′W) and Haskell Island, 1 mile W, extends with Harpswell Sound 10 miles NNW. Although of little commercial importance, they afford good anchorage, with good holding ground, for deep-draught vessels.

2 **Dangers.** The principal dangers are marked for the first 4 miles above the entrance, but above this the channel is narrow and flats extend in places to a considerable distance from the shore.

Depths. The fairway of the approach channel, which lies on the E side of the channel, has been swept to a depth of 12·8 m (42 ft).

3 **Local knowledge** is necessary to proceed beyond Stover Point (43°45′N 70°00′W) (3.130).

Directions

3.129

1 **Approaches.** From a position NNW of Halfway Rock (43°39′N 70°02′W) (3.114) the fairway of the approach channel into Merriconeag Sound leads NNE, passing (with positions relative to Little Mark Island (43°42′·6N 70°01′·9W)):

2 Close WNW of Drunkers Ledges (1¼ miles S), two rocky ledges, 3 cables apart. The NW ledge dries 0·9 m (3 ft) and is marked by No 4 Buoy (starboard hand). Eastern Drunkers Ledge, which has a depth of 1·2 m (4 ft) over it, and over which the sea breaks in rough weather, is marked by No 2 Buoy (starboard hand). Thence:

3 WNW of No 6 buoy (starboard hand) (6 cables SE), moored close N of Mark Island Ledge which has a depth of 1·2 m (4 ft) over it, and:

ESE of Whale Rock, which lies 4 cables SW and is 2 m in height, thence:

ESE of Little Mark Island, 11 m in height and grassy. A light (black and white square stone pyramid) stands on the island. Thence:

4 WNW of No 8 Light-buoy (starboard hand) (7 cables ENE) moored 1 cable SW of Turnip Island Ledge which dries 0·6 m (2 ft). Turnip Island, grassy and 5 m in height with a stone cairn, lies 2 cables ENE of the ledge.

5 **Swept depths.** The charted depths of 8·5 m (28 ft), 6 cables N of Halfway Rock; of 9·8 m (32 ft), 5 cables NW of Drunkers Ledge; and 7 m (23 ft), 6 cables W of Mark Island Ledge, have been swept to depths of 7·3, 9·1 and 6·1 m (24, 30 and 20 ft) respectively.

6 **Useful Marks:**

Two observation towers and a house (43°43′·1N 70°00′·2W), standing on the S end of Bailey Island.

3.130

1 **Merriconeag Sound.** From a position between Turnip Island and Great Mark Island (43°43′N 70°02′W), 7 m in height and grassy, the channel through Merriconeag Sound and Harpswell Sound leads NNE, passing (with positions relative to Stover Point (43°45′N 70°00′W)):

2 WNW of Abner Point (2 miles S), the N entrance point to Mackerel Cove. No 1 Light-buoy (port hand) is moored off the point. Thence:

ESE of Pinkham Island (Ram Island) (1½ miles SW), grassy with a white house on it. No 2 Buoy (starboard hand) marks the outer end of a reef that extends 3 cables SSW from the island. Thence:

3 ESE of No 9 Buoy (port hand) (1 mile SSW), which marks Interval Shoal, thence:

ESE of Stover Point. No 13 buoy (port hand) is moored at the outer end of a reef that extends 2 cables NE from the point.

Thence into Harpswell Sound.

Side channels

3.131

1 **To Broad Sound.** A narrow buoyed channel suitable for small craft, which is entered between Little Mark Island and Great Mark Island (43°43′N 70°02′W), leads W to Broad Sound (3.139).

2 **To Potts Harbor.** A narrow winding channel, with a depth of 4·3 m (14 ft) and only suitable for small craft, leads S of Pinkham Island and Potts Point (43°44′N 70°02′W) into Potts Harbor (3.141).

3 **Gurnet Strait** (43°51′·5N 69°54′·9W) is a narrow channel with a least depth of about 1·8 m (6 ft), suitable for small craft, that leads from the N end of Long Reach into Long Meadow River round the N end of Sebascodegan Island.

Anchorages and small harbours

3.132

1 **Mackerel Cove,** used as an anchorage by small craft, is entered N of the SW end of Bailey Island (43°43′N 70°00′W). No 1 Light-buoy (port hand) is moored off Abner Point (3.130), the N entrance point to the cove.

Harpswell Harbor is entered between Stover Point (43°45′N 70°00′W) and the S end of Merriman Ledges, 1 mile NNE. These ledges dry in the centre and are marked by Nos 17 and 15 Buoys (port hand) at the N and S ends.

A rock, with a swept depth of 4 m (13 ft), lies 2½ cables S of No 15 Buoy.

2   Anchorage is available in depths of 5 to 11 m (18 to 36 ft), with depths decreasing gradually to the head of the harbour. Harpswell Harbor is a special anchorage (1.49).

WESTERN PART OF CASCO BAY

General information

Chart 2490 (see 1.17)
Description
3.133

1   The W part of Casco Bay, between Harpswell Neck and Halfway Rock (43°39′N 70°02′W) on the E and the port of Portland on the W, contains numerous sounds, bays and rivers, separated by islands lying in a NE-SW direction.

2   There are broad channels into this part of the bay, through Broad Sound (3.139), Luckse Sound (3.157) and Hussey Sound (3.164) and secure anchorage can be found for vessels of any draught. The bay is frequented by small inter-island ferries, many small craft and some fishing vessels.

Traffic regulations
3.134

1   **Navigation Rules for US Inland Waters.** The limit of the waters to which these rules applies is a line joining Little Mark Island (43°43′N 70°02′W), NE and SW extremity of Jewell Island (43°41′N 70°05′W), Outer Green Island (43°39′N 70°07′W), Ram Island Ledge (43°38′N 70°11′W) and Portland Head (43°37′·4N 70°12′·5W). See 1.47 and Appendix VII for further information.

Natural conditions
3.135

1   **Tidal streams.** See 3.112 for details of tidal streams in Casco Bay.

    Ice forms in considerable quantities at the heads of the numerous sounds, bays and river in the W part of Casco Bay, but the principal anchorages are usable throughout the year.

Special anchorages
3.136

1   Potts Harbor (3.141), Staples Cove (3.151) and Diamond Island Pass (3.166) are designated special anchorages (1.49).

Inshore channel
3.137

1   An inshore channel, used by inter-island ferries, yachts and fishing craft, extends from the S point of Great Chebeague Island (43°42′N 70°08′W) around either side of Bangs Island (43°44′N 70°06′W), across Broad Sound and through Potts Harbor (3.141) to Merriconeag Sound (3.128).

Principal marks
3.138

1   **Landmarks:**
      Stone tower (43°49′·1N 70°06′·8W).
      Tank (43°47′·6N 70°11′·9W).
      Two chimneys (43°45′·1N 70°09′·4W) stand close to the power plant on Birch Point (3.174), the SW point of Cousins Island.

Broad Sound

Description
3.139

1   **Broad Sound** is entered SW of Eagle Island (43°43′N 70°03′W) (3.140) and extends 4½ miles NNW from its entrance and is generally about 5 cables wide. Channels lead from the sound to Potts Harbor, Middle Bay and other waters in the N part of Casco Bay.

    Depths. The fairway of the channel is swept to a depth of 12·8 m (42 ft).

2   **Anchorage** may be obtained in the upper part of the sound in suitable depths under the lee of islands.

Directions
3.140

1   From a position S of Eagle Island (43°43′N 70°03′W) the fairway leads NNW and N, passing (with positions relative to Whaleboat Island Light (43°44′·5N 70°03′·7W)):

    Clear of BS Buoy (safe water) (2¾ miles S), moored 6 cables E of West Brown Cow, a grassy islet 11 m (36 ft) in height. Foul ground extends 5 cables NE from this islet. Thence:

2   Between Nos 1 and 2 Buoys (lateral) (2 miles S) that mark the entrance to the sound and lie SW of Eagle Island, which is 20 m (64 ft) in height, prominent and wooded and with a house on its NE side, thence:

3   ENE of the N ends of Bates Island and Ministerial Island (1¾ miles SSW), both grassy and 9 m (29 ft) and 7 m in height, respectively. These islands are opposite the entrance to Potts Harbor (3.141). Thence:

    Clear of a light-buoy (special) (1 mile S), thence:

4   W of WS Buoy (preferred channel to starboard) (3 cables SSW), thence:

    Between the S extremity of Whaleboat Island (3.144) and the N extremity of Stockman Island. A light (red and white chequered diamond on white square framework tower) stands on the S end of Whaleboat Island. Thence:

5   WSW of No 6 Buoy (starboard hand) (7½ cables NW), moored close W of Whaleboat Ledge which has a depth of 1·8 m (6 ft) over it, thence:

    E of Chebeague Point (1¾ miles NW), with a house and a chimney on it. This point is on the W side of the N entrance to Luckse Sound (3.157). Thence:

6   E of Upper Green Islets (2 miles NNW). Green Island Ledge, marked by No 10 Buoy (starboard hand) on its SW side, lies 2 cables SW of the S islet.

Potts Harbor
3.141

1   Potts Harbor (43°44′N 70°02′W), which indents the SW end of Harpswell Neck, lies between Potts Point and Basin Point (9 cables WNW).

    Directions. From a position 1 mile SW of Basin Point (43°44′·3N 70°02′·6W) the main entrance channel into the harbour leads ENE and NE, passing (with positions relative to Basin Point):

2   Clear of a rock (8 cables SSW) with a depth of 0·9 m (3 ft) over it, marked on its SW side by No 4 Buoy (starboard hand), thence:

    Between Upper Flag Island (7½ cables S), 18 m (59 ft) in height and grassy, and Little Birch Island, which lies 5 cables NW. No 6 Buoy

3 (starboard hand) marks a ledge extending 1 cable S from Little Birch Island. Thence:

SE of Horse Island (2½ cables SSW), 7 m in height and grassy, and thence into the anchorage.

The harbour can also be entered from Merriconeag Sound, S of Potts Point.

Anchorage is available in depths of 7 to 10 m (24 to 33 ft). The harbour is designated a special anchorage.

4 **Town wharf**, with a reported depth alongside of 1·8 m, is situated near the village of South Harpswell, about 4 cables N of Potts Point on the E shore of the harbour. There are other landings in the harbour with depths alongside of 1·5 to 1·8 m.

Middle Bay

Description
3.142

1 **Middle Bay** is entered on the E side of Broad Sound, between Basin Point (43°44'·3N 70°02'·6W) and Little Whaleboat Island, 11 m (35 ft) in height and wooded, which lies 1¾ miles NNW. The bay extends NE for 9 miles, its E shore being formed by Harpswell Neck, and its W side by Lower Goose Island, Upper Goose Island, Birch Island and White Island. Shelter Island lies in mid-channel, abreast Upper Goose Island, 2½ miles NE of Whaleboat Island.

2 Middle Bay affords good anchorage, but is seldom used.

Local knowledge is necessary to proceed above the S end of Birch Island (43°49'N 70°01'W), where only some of the dangers are buoyed.

Measured distance
3.143

1 Off the W side of Whaleboat Island there is a measured distance.

Marks: Beacons in line bearing 128°.
Distance: 5946 ft.
Running track: 038°/218°.

Entrance
3.144

1 There is a deep channel on either side of Whaleboat Island (43°45'N 70°03'W). This island is wooded at its N end and grassy at its S end. Both channels are marked by buoys (lateral).

Anchorages and alongside berths
3.145

1 **Anchorage.** An extensive anchorage with depths of 14 to 18 m (46 to 59 ft) lies above Whaleboat Island.

Alongside berths. A disused T-shaped pier of a former naval fuel depot, with a reported depth alongside of 11 m, extends from the W side of Harpswell Neck, 2½ miles NNE of Basin Point.

Merepoint Bay and Maquoit Bay

Approaches
3.146

1 Merepoint Bay and Maquoit Bay can be approached from Middle Bay through the passages S or N of Goose Islands. They can also be approached from the head of Broad Sound passing NW of the foul ground extending W from Little Whaleboat Island and then between Lower Goose Island (43°48'N 70°02'W) and French Island, 19 m (62 ft) in height and wooded, and Little French Islands.

This channel has been swept to a depth of 9·1 m (30 ft) in its lower part and 6·7 m (22 ft) in its upper part.

Merepoint Bay
3.147

1 Merepoint Bay is entered between Birch Island (43°49'N 70°01'W) and Mere Point, the SW point of Merepoint Neck, and extends 2 miles NE between Birch Island and White Island on the SE and Merepoint Neck on the NW. The bay is shallow and obstructed by flats in its N part.

2 Merepoint is a village on the neck at which there are several landing stages.

Maquoit Bay
3.148

1 Maquoit Bay is entered between Mere Point (43°49'N 70°02'W) and Sister Island, 12 m (41 ft) in height and wooded, 6 cables SW. The bay is obstructed by flats, with depths of less than 1·2 m (4 ft) over them, through which two narrow channels with least depths of 5·8 m (19 ft) lead for 1¼ miles from its entrance.

2 **Ice.** The bay can be covered by ice about 50 cm thick.

Harraseeket River

Approach and entrance
3.149

1 Harraseeket River is approached between Bustins Island (43°48'N 70°04'W), high with numerous cottages on it, and Moshier Island, 28 m (91 ft) in height and wooded, 1 mile SW.

2 It is entered between Moore Point and Stockbridge Point, 1¼ miles WNW of Buskins Island. The entrance is narrow, being obstructed by Pound of Tea Islet. Except for a dangerous rock, with a depth of 0·6 m (2 ft) over it, that lies in mid-channel ½ cable S of the islet, the fairway has a depth of 7 m (23 ft).

3 The principal dangers in the approach and entrance are buoyed.

Local knowledge is necessary.

Directions
3.150

1 From a position off the E side of Moshier Island the channel leads N and NW, passing (with positions relative to Crab Island (43°48'N 70°06'W)):

NE of No 1 Buoy (port hand) (4 cables SE), which marks Moshier Ledge, thence:

2 W of Little Bustins Island, (6 cables E), 5 m in height with a house and clump of trees in the centre, thence:

NE of Crab Island, thence through the harbour entrance.

Useful mark:

Stone turreted tower (43°49'N 70°07'W), standing on high ground at South Freeport.

Berths
3.151

1 **Anchorage** is available in Staples Cove between Stockbridge Point and South Freeport. This berth is designated a special anchorage.

Alongside berths. Town wharf at South Freeport with a reported depth alongside of 4·6 m.

Royal River

General description
3.152

1 Royal River is entered between Fogg Point and Parker Point. It is a narrow winding stream, which can only be navigated by small craft, and leads to the town of Yarmouth (43°48′N 70°12′W) on the S side of the river, 2½ miles above the entrance.

Approaches to Luckse Sound and Hussey Sound

Description
3.153

1   The approaches to the entrances of Luckse Sound (3.157) and Hussey Sound (3.164) lie between a ridge, on which there is a chain of islets and shoals lying between Jewell Island (3.154) and Outer Green Island (3.185) (43°39′·0N 70°07′·5W) on the E; and Long Island and Peaks Island (3.164) on the W.

2   Within 2¼ miles of the entrances of the sounds there are several islands and dangers that are common to the approach of both sounds.

Directions
3.154

1   From a position in the vicinity of No 2 Light-buoy (starboard hand) (43°39′N 70°09′W) the approach routes to Luckse Sound and Hussey Sound lead NE and N, passing (with positions relative to Outer Green Island (43°39′·0N 70°07′·4W)):

> WNW of Outer Green Island (3.185). Junk of Pork, a high rock surrounded by above-water rocks, lies 1½ cables SE. Thence:

2   Either side of The Hussey (1 mile WNW), a rock with a depth of 2·7 m (9 ft) over it, which is marked by No 4 Buoy (starboard hand) on its S side.

> When proceeding to Luckse Sound:
> WNW of Inner Green Island (1¼ miles NE), 5 m (15 ft) in height and grassy, and:
> ESE of Vaill Island (2 miles NW).

3   **Useful mark:**

> Stone tower (2 miles NE) which stands on the S end of Jewell Island, an island which is 32 m (104 ft) in height and partly wooded.

> *(Directions continue for Luckse Sound at 3.159, and for Hussey Sound at 3.165)*

Green Island Passage
3.155

1   Green Island Passage (43°39′N 70°07′W) leads between Outer Green Island and Green Island Reef. The passage is marked by Nos 3 and 2 Buoys (lateral) which lie, respectively, off Johnson Rock, at the N end of the bank surrounding Outer Green Island, and off the S side of Green Island Reef.

2   The passage, which is used by small vessels, is 2 cables wide and has a depth of 11·3 m (37 ft).

Local knowledge is necessary.

Jewell Island
3.156

1   **Pier** is situated on the W side of the island about 7 cables N of the S end of the island. There are depths of 6·7 m at the head of the pier.

Luckse Sound

Description
3.157

1   Luckse Sound, which extends 4 miles NE from its entrance (43°41′N 70°08′W) to its junction with Broad Sound (3.139), is entered between the SW point of Cliff Island and Vaill Island, 1½ miles WSW.

2   The sound is bounded by Cliff Island and Stave Island on the SE and by Long Island and Great Chebeague Island on the NW. The sound is divided by Hope Island, Sand Island, Bangs Island and Stockman Island (3.140).

Depths
3.158

1   The channel E of Hope Island and Sand Island has been swept to a depth of 12·8 m (42 ft) as far as the vicinity of Bangs Island, and thence the channel SE of that island has been swept to a depth of 7·6 m (25 ft) and the channel to the N of it to a least depth of 6·1 m (20 ft).

Directions
(continued from 3.154)
3.159

1   From a position ESE of Vaill Island (43°41′N 70°09′W) the swept channel through Luckse Sound leads NE, passing (with positions relative to SW point of Cliff Island (43°41′N 70°07′W)):

> SE of Obeds Rock (1¼ miles W), thence:

2   NW of No 6 Buoy (starboard hand) (5 cable SW), which marks the SW extremity of Johns Ledge, a shoal that extends SW from Cliff Island, thence:

> SE of Stepping Stones (1 mile NW), two islets, thence:
> Clear of a dangerous wreck (1 mile N), and:

3   SE of Hope Island (1 mile NNW), 27 m (90 ft) in height and wooded, except at its SW end where there is a large house, chimney and flagstaff. No 2 Light-buoy (starboard hand) is moored 2 cables SW of its S extremity and Rogues Island, 5 m in height and grassy, lies off its NE side. Thence:

> SE of Sand Island (2 miles NNE), low and grassy.

3.160

1   The swept channel then divides and leads both SE and W of Bangs Island (3 miles NNE), 20 m (66 ft) in height and grassy.

The channel SE of Bangs Island leads NE, passing (with positions relative to Sand Island):

2   NW of Stave Island (1 mile ENE), sparsely wooded with a house on its N point. No 8 Buoy (starboard hand) marks the NE limit of Stave Island Ledge which extends 3 cables NE from the island. Thence:

> SE of Stockman Island (1½ miles NE) (3.140).

Thence into Broad Sound (3.139).

3   The channel W of Bangs Island leads N, passing (with positions relative to Sand Island):

> E of Crow Island (1 mile N), 5 m in height, grassy with a house on it, thence:
> E of No 5 Buoy (port hand) (1 mile N), thence:

4   W of Goose Nest (1½ miles NNE), a grassy islet 1 m in height, thence:

> W of No 8 Buoy (starboard hand), which lies close NW of Goose Nest Ledge (2 miles NNE). The ledge dries 2·1 m.

Thence into Broad Sound.

Other channels
3.161

1   **North-west of Hope Island and Sand Island.** A channel leads between Hope Island and Sand Island to the SE, and Great Chebeague Island, to the NW.

A shoal, 4 m (13 ft) in depth, obstructs the NE entrance to this channel, leaving only a narrow passage, ½ cable wide, between it and the shore bank of Great Chebeague Island.

2   **Between Hope Island and Sand Island.** A passage, marked by Nos 1 and 2 Buoys (lateral), leads between Hope and Sand Island.

Cliff Island
3.162

1   **State Pier**, with a depth alongside of 6·7 m at its head, and a pontoon berth, are situated on the W side of Cliff Island 7 cables from the S end of the island (43°41′N 70°07′W).

Chandler Cove
3.163

1   Chandler Cove (43°43′N 70°08′W) is situated between the NE end of Long Island and the S end of Great Chebeague Island. Little Chebeague Island, 16 m (52 ft) in height and wooded, forms the W side of the cove and is connected at LW with Indian Point, a sandspit with a house on it.

2   **Approach.** Chandler Cove can be entered either from Luckse Sound between Long Island and Deer Point, or from between Long Island and Little Chebeague Island. Both entrances are buoyed but the E entrance is preferred, being less obstructed.

3   **Directions for E entrance.** From a position SSW of Hope Island (3.159) the track leads N, passing (with positions relative to Deer Point (43°42′·5N 70°07′·7W)):

E of Stepping Stones (9 cables SSW) (3.159), thence:
W of No 2 Light-buoy (starboard hand) (6½ cables S), thence:
E of the NE extremity of Long Island (4½ cables SW), thence:

4   W of No 2 Light-buoy (starboard hand) (1¾ cables SW) marking a rock with a depth of 3·6 m (11 ft) over it, thence:
E of Crow Island (3 cables W); thence into the cove.
The approach to the W entrance to Chandler Cove is described at 3.171.

5   **Anchorage** is available in depths of 9 to 18 m (30 to 60 ft) clear of the cable areas, as shown on the chart.
State pier and landing stage are situated on the NE side of the cove, 5 cables N of Deer Point. The pier, from which a ferry plies to Portland, has depths alongside of 4·6 m.

Hussey Sound

Chart 2488
Description
3.164

1   Hussey Sound, which extends 2 miles N from its entrance (43°40′N 70°10′W) into the W part of Casco Bay, is entered between Overset Island, situated close S of Jerry Point, the S point of Long Island, and the E extremity of Peaks Island, 7 cables SSW.

2   The sound is bounded on the E by Long Island and on the W by Peaks Island, Great Diamond Island and Cow Island (3.165).
Depths. The channel through the sound is swept to a depth of 12·2 m (40 ft).

3   **Under-keel clearances.** For recommended minimum under-keel clearances in Hussey Sound see 3.180.

Directions
(continued from 3.154)
3.165

1   From a position in the vicinity of No 2 Light-buoy (starboard hand) (43°39′N 70°09′W) the channel through Hussey Sound leads NW and N, passing (with positions relative to Jerry Point (43°40′·6N 70°10′·1W)):
Between Nos 3 and No 4 Light-buoys (lateral) (6 cables S). An obstruction, the position of which is approximate, was reported (1966) to lie close NW of No 3 buoy. Thence:

2   SW of No 6 Light-buoy (starboard hand) (4 cables SW), which marks the SW side of Soldier Ledge, a shoal with a depth of 12·2 m (40 ft) over it. A dangerous wreck, the position of which is approximate, lies on the S side of the shoal. Q Light-buoy (special) is moored close S of the wreck. Thence:

3   E of No 7 Light-buoy (port hand) (5 cables W), which lies 1 cable E of Pumpkin Nob, an islet, thence:
W of College Islet (3 cables NW), which lies on foul ground extending 2 cables from the SW side of Long Island, thence:

4   E of Crow Island Light No 9 (green square on framework tower, 4 m in height) (1 mile NW), which stands on the S end of Crow Island, thence:
W of No 10 Light-buoy (starboard hand) (1 mile N), which marks the outer end of a ledge that extends 2 cables NNW from Ponce Landing, thence:
E of Cow Island (1¼ miles NW), 17 m in height.

Diamond Island Pass
3.166

1   Diamond Island Pass separates Peaks Island from Great Diamond Island and Little Diamond Island. It is buoyed at either end and has a least depth of 4·9 m (16 ft).
The pass is much used by small vessels.

Diamond Cove
3.167

1   Diamond Cove (43°41′N 70°11′W), which is situated on the NE side of Great Diamond Island, can be entered on either side of Crow Island (3.165).

South-west part of Casco Bay

Charts 2490, 2488 (see 1.17)
Description
3.168

1   Between the N end of Hussey Sound and Cousins Island (43°45′N 70°09′W), 3½ miles NNE, there is a large area, suitable for anchorage, bounded on the E by Long Island and Chebeague Island, and on the W by Clapboard Island and Sturdivant Island, situated respectively 1¼ and 2½ miles N of Cow Island (43°42′N 70°11′W).

2   The S half of the area is almost clear of dangers with depths of 13 to 24 m (43 ft to 13 fm); the N half is obstructed by Basket Island and adjacent ledges, but there is still a considerable area with depths of 7 to 14 m (23 to 46 ft).

Transhipment Area
3.169

1   An oil transfer area, the limits of which are shown on the charts, is situated NE of Cow Island.

Transfer of liquid cargo between tankers takes place regularly in this area. Vessels engaged in these operations may be at anchor or otherwise unable to manoeuvre, and should be given a wide berth.

Naval anchorage area
3.170
1   A naval anchorage extends N from Great Diamond Island to the S end of Cousins Island, and between Cow Island and Clapboard Island on the E and the mainland on the W.

The position of berths in this anchorage are shown on US charts.

South-west approach to Chandler Cove
3.171
1   From a position NW of Mariner Ledge (43°42′N 70°10′W), the N limit of which is marked by No 9 Buoy (port hand), the SW approach channel to Chandler Cove (3.163), which is marked by buoys, leads NE into the cove. The channel passes SE of Channel Rocks, which have a depth 2·7 m (9 ft) over them and are buoyed on their S side.

Other channels
3.172
1   From a position N of Great Diamond Island a channel, which is marked and swept, leads generally NNE, passing (with positions relative to Basket Island (43°44′N 70°10′W)):

2   Either side of Cow Island Ledge (43°42′·2N 70°11′·2W), to a position NE of Clapboard Island, wooded. A light (red and white chequered diamond on post on red caisson), stands on the ledge. The ledge, which dries at its S end, is marked on its NE side by CIL Buoy (preferred channel to starboard).

3   Thence either:

Clear of Upper Clapboard Island Ledge (5 cables WSW), which is marked on its E side by No 3 Light-buoy (port hand), thence:

Between Basket Island, wooded, and Sturdivant Island. No 4 Light-buoy (starboard hand) marks the shoal water NW of Basket Island, thence:

4   N of Upper Basket Ledge (5 cables NE), marked by a beacon, to a position S of Spruce Point (1 mile NE), the S extremity of Cousins Island.

or an alternative route leads:

SE of Lower Basket Ledge (5 cables ESE), marked at its E end by No 15 Beacon (port hand), thence:

SE of Spruce Point (1 mile NE), the S extremity of Cousins Island, thence:

5   SE of Doyle Point (1½ miles NE), thence:

Between No 18 Light-buoy (starboard hand) (2¼ miles NE) which lies 1 cable NNW of the N end of a shoal spit that extends N from Great Chebeague Island, and the SE shore of Littlejohn Island that lies 1 cable NW.

Thence into Broad Sound (3.139).
3.173
1   From a position N of Great Diamond Island a channel, marked by buoys and beacons, leads generally N along the W shore of Casco Bay, passing (with positions relative to Basket Island (43°44′N 70°10′W)):

2   W of Lower Clapboard Island Ledge and Jones Ledge (2 miles SW), both of which lie on the edge of the foul ground that lies SW of Clapboard Island and are marked by Nos 12 and 14 Buoys (starboard hand), thence:

3   E of Prince Point Ledge and York Ledge (1¾ miles WSW), both of which lie on the coastal bank and are marked on their E sides by Nos 15 and 17 Buoys (port hand); York Ledge is also marked on its W side by YL Beacon. Thence:

4   Between Underwood Ledge (1¼ miles W) which is marked by No 19 Buoy (port hand), and No 20 Buoy (starboard hand) which marks the edge of the shoal ground SW of Sturdivant Island.

Thence the track leads NE, passing:

NW of Sturdivant Island, 16 m (51 ft) in height and partly wooded, thence:

5   SE of The Nubbin (1½ miles NNW), an islet 3 m (10 ft) in height; foul ground extends 1½ cables SW of the islet. Thence:

NW of Sandy Point Ledges (2 miles NNE), the SW edge of which is marked by No 22 Buoy, and after which the channel becomes shallow, winding and unmarked.

Birch Point
3.174
1   **Birch Point** (43°45′·0N 70°09′·5W), the SW point of Cousins Island, has a large green painted power plant, with two prominent chimneys, on its N side. A T-shaped pier, situated at the plant, has berthage for vessels of up to 217 m in length and a draught of 10 m. In 1979 depths alongside of 10 m were reported.

2   Vessels usually secure starboard side to and require the assistance of tugs and pilot, both of which are available at Portland.

APPROACHES TO PORTLAND

General information

Charts 2490, 3676, 2488
Description
3.175
1   The approaches to Portland lie S of Halfway Rock (43°39′N 70°02′W) and E of Cape Elizabeth (9 miles SW).

A line of dangerous shoals lies in the approaches to Portland, extending 7½ miles SW from East Cod Ledge (43°36′N 70°02′W) to Old Anthony Rock, marked by No 2 Light-buoy (starboard hand), at the SW end of West Cod Ledge. The bottom is very irregular in the vicinity.

Pilotage
3.176
1   Pilots for Portland are embarked in the vicinity of P Light-buoy (43°31′·6N 70°05′·5W). See 3.202.

Traffic regulations
3.177
1   **Traffic separation schemes.** Two TSSs lead from ESE and SSE to the approaches to Portland, as shown on the chart.

Both schemes are IMO-adopted and Rule 10 of the *International Regulations for Preventing Collisions at Sea (1972)* applies.

2 **Precautionary Area.** A Precautionary Area has been established at the inshore ends of the TSSs, as shown on the chart. Traffic within the Precautionary Area may consist of vessels operating between Portland and one of the established lanes. Mariners are advised to exercise extreme care when navigating within this area. The centre of this area is marked by P Light-buoy (43°31'·6N 70°05'·5W).

Unexploded ordnance
3.178

1 Unexploded depth charges were reported (1982) to lie in an area, 6 miles in diameter, which covers the E part of the Precautionary Area. The limits of this area are shown on the charts.

Spoil ground
3.179

1 Spoil ground marked by two light-buoys (special) lies in the NE part of the Precautionary Area, 3½ miles NE of P Light-buoy.

Under-keel clearances
3.180

1 The US Coast Guard recommends the following minimum under-keel clearances for vessels navigating in the Port of Portland:
(a) A minimum of 0·9 m (3 ft) when transiting N of a line drawn between Portland Head Light (3.182) and Ram Island Ledge Light (1 mile NE), to No 5 Light-buoy (43°39'·5N 70°14'·1W).
(b) A minimum of 0·6 m (2 ft) when transiting Fore River SW of No 5 Light-buoy.
(c) A minimum of 0·6 m (2 ft) when transiting via Hussey Sound, NW of a line between Nos 3 and No 4 Light-buoys (3.165).
(d) A minimum of 0·3 m (1 ft) at all berthing areas.

Natural conditions
3.181

1 **Tidal streams** in the vicinity of P Light-buoy average less than ¼ kn at strength. The in-going stream sets 335° and the out-going stream 140°.

Current. Since the tidal streams are weak, currents of 1 kn or more only occur with strong winds. See also tidal stream tables on chart.

Directions
(continued from 3.5 and 3.13)

Principal marks
3.182

1 **Major lights:**
Halfway Rock Light (43°39'N 70°02'W) (3.11).

Cape Elizabeth Light (white conical tower, 20 m in height) (43°34'N 70°12'W). A disused lighthouse stands 1½ cables SW.
Portland Head Light (43°37'N 70°12'W).

Other aids to navigation
3.183

1 **Racon:**
P Light-buoy (43°32'N 70°06'W) (3.187).
See *Admiralty List of Radio Signals Volume 2* for details.

General
3.184

1 If approaching the outer dangers to Portland in thick weather, which is comparatively frequent on this coast, vessels need to exercise the utmost caution.

They should not attempt to close the land if relying on soundings only, owing to the uneven nature of the bottom, and should keep in depths of over 90 m (50 fm) until the fog lifts.

From east
3.185

1 From a position S of Halfway Rock, the coastal passage continues W in the white sector (274¼-275¾°) of Portland Head Directional Light, passing (with positions relative to Halfway Rock Light (43°39'N 70°02'W)):
N of 1EC Light-buoy (port hand) (2¾ miles S), marking the N end of East Cod Ledge (3.175), thence:
2 N of Bulwark Shoal (3½ miles SSW), the SE side of which is marked by BS Buoy (preferred channel to port), thence:
S of a 10·4 m (34 ft) patch (3 miles SW), which lies 2 miles N of Bache Rock, thence:
3 S of Junk of Pork (3.154) 1½ cables SE of Outer Green Island (3¾ miles W), grassy, which lies on the E side to the approaches to Luckse Sound (3.157) and Hussey Sound (3.164), thence:
N of No 1 Light-buoy (port hand) (6 miles WSW), which marks the outer end of the entrance channel.

From east south-east and south south-east
3.186

1 **Traffic separation schemes.** From the vicinity of positions 43°25'N 69°30'W and 43°08'N 69°53'W at the seaward of the ends of the TSS in the approaches to Portland, the ESE and SSE inbound traffic routes lead WNW and NNW, respectively, through waters clear of charted dangers to the centre of the Precautionary Area.
3.187

1 **Within Precautionary Area.** From the vicinity of P Light-buoy (safe water) (43°32'N 70°06'W) the approach route leads NW and N, passing (with positions relative to Cape Elizabeth Light (43°34'N 70°12'W)):
NE of East Hue and Cry (3 miles SE), a shoal that is marked on its E by No 1 Light-buoy (port hand). West Hue and Cry lies 8 cables WSW. Thence:
2 Through the channel between Corwin Rock and West Cod Ledge Rock (3 miles E), the limits of which are marked by Nos 3 and 4 Light-buoys (lateral), respectively. 4WC Buoy (starboard hand) lies at the S end of West Cod Ledge Rock. Alden Rock,

which is marked by No 4 Buoy (starboard hand), lies 8 cables SW of Corwin Rock.

3   The track then alters N, passing:
    E of Mitchell Rock (1¼ miles ENE), thence:
    E of No 5 Buoy (port hand) (1½ miles NE) which marks the SE side of Broad Cove Rock, that lies on foul ground extending 1 mile offshore S of Broad Cove. Thence:
    E of No 1 Light-buoy (port hand) (3½ miles NNE).

*(Directions continue for Portland Harbor at 3.208.
Directions for approaches to Luckse Sound
and Hussey Sound are given at 3.154)*

PORTLAND HARBOR

General information

Chart 2488 (see 1.17)
Position
3.188

1   Portland (43°39′N 70°14′W) is situated in the NW part of Gulf of Maine and stands on the N side of the entrance to the Fore River. The city of South Portland stands on the S side of the river.

Function
3.189

1   Portland, which in 2005 had an estimated population of 63 889, is the most important port on the coast of Maine. It is a port of entry.

The ice-free harbour offers secure anchorage to deep-draught vessels in all weathers.

2   The main products handled are petroleum, wood pulp, paper, seafood products and general cargo.

It is the Atlantic terminus of pipeline shipments of petroleum products to Canada.

Port limits
3.190

1   The harbour consists of the area W of Cushing, Peaks, House and Great and Little Diamonds Islands, from the entrance at Portland Head to the entrance of Fore River at Fish Point (43°40′·0N 70°14′·3W).

Entry
3.191

1   The main entrance channel, which is buoyed, passes between Portland Head (43°37′·4N 70°12′·5W) and Cushing Island, 7 cables N.

Traffic
3.192

1   **Traffic.** In 2005 the port was used by 221 vessels with a total deadweight 27 697 956 tonnes.

Port Authority
3.193

1   City of Portland Department of Transportation and Waterfront, 40 Commercial St, Suite 100, Portland, ME 04101.
    Internet. www.portofportlandmaine.org

Limiting conditions

Controlling depths
3.194

1   **Project depths. From the sea to Fort Gorges** (43°39′·8N 70°13′·3W): 13·7 m (45 ft).
    Inner Harbor and Fore River between Fish Point (3.190) and the combined road and rail bridge (43°38′·5N 70°17′·0W)*:* 10·7 m (35 ft).
    For the latest controlling depths the charts and port authority should be consulted.

South Portland from SW (3.188)
(Original dated 1990)

(Photograph - Joseph R Melanson of www.skypic.com)

Vertical clearance
3.195
1   **Casco Bay Bridge** has a bascule span with a vertical clearance of 16·8 m (55 ft).

  Combined road and rail bridge has a vertical clearance of 3 m (10 ft).

Deepest and longest berth
3.196
1   Portland Pipeline Pier No 2.

Tidal levels
3.197
1   Mean spring range about 3·1 m; mean neap range about 2·3 m. See information in *Admiralty Tide Tables*.

Maximum size of vessel handled
3.198
1   **Largest vessel.** Draught 13·5 m; 124 000 dwt; length 277 m.

Ice
3.199
1   Ice seldom obstructs navigation and when it does it is only for a limited time. Tugs keep a clear channel to the wharves.

Arrival information

Vessel traffic service
3.200
1   Vessel traffic service scheme is in operation for the control of shipping. See *Admiralty List of Radio Signals Volume 6(5)* for details.

Notice of ETA required
3.201
1   48 and 24 hours notice is required.

Pilotage
3.202
1   **Pilotage**, which is available 24 hours, is compulsory for all foreign vessels, and for US vessels engaged in the foreign trade with a draught of over 2·7 m (9 ft).

  Pilots embark in the vicinity of P Light-buoy (43°32′N 70°06′W).

Tugs
3.203
1   **Tugs** meet vessels off Spring Point (43°39′·0N 70°13′·5W). Large vessels normally use them.

Traffic regulations
3.204
1   **Safety and security zones:**

    A safety and security zone extending 1 mile ahead, 5 cables astern and 1000 yards on either side is established around any LPG vessel.

  Entry into or movement within these zones is prohibited unless previously authorized by the Captain of the Port (COTP).

2   **Security zone:**

    A security zone of 100 yards radius is established around any passenger vessel at anchor or alongside. A security zone extending 200 yards ahead, 100 yards on either side and 100 yards astern is established around any passenger vessel that is underway.

3   Entry into or movement within this zone is prohibited unless previously authorized by the Captain of the Port (COTP).

  See Appendix V for definitions and general regulations covering safety and security zones.

Regulations concerning entry
3.205
1   **Speed limit** within Portland Harbor is 5 kn. There are also restrictions on the wake produced by vessels in the harbour. The port authority should be consulted for further details.

Harbour
General layout
3.206
1   Portland Harbor has an outer and inner harbour.

  Outer harbour comprises the area W of Cushing, Peaks, House, Great Diamond and Little Diamond Islands from the entrance at Portland Head to the entrance of Fore River at Fish Point. The outer harbour includes the three deep water anchorages (3.212) Portland Pipe Line Pier No 2 (3.214).

International Ferry Terminal

Spring Point Ledge Light   *Floating Dock*

Portland Harbour from E (3.206)
(Original dated 1991)

(Photograph - E.A. Arts Council)

2   **Fore River,** the inner part, which extends from the Casco Bay Bridge to the head of navigation at the combined road and rail bridge (3.194), 1¼ miles farther upstream.

Natural conditions
3.207
1   **Tidal streams** within the harbour have a rate of about ½ kn.

Caution. Strong cross currents tend to set vessels on to the S side of the Casco Bay Bridge.

Climate information. See 1.152 and 1.153.

Directions
(continued from 3.187)

Principal marks
3.208
1   **Landmarks:**

Tower (43°36′·9N 70°12′·7W), constructed of stone.
Tower (43°38′·6N 70°11′·7W) standing on NE part of Cushing Island.
Tower (43°38′·5N 70°12′·0W) standing in centre of Cushing Island.

2   Tower (43°39′·9N 70°14′·9W). An old observatory tower which resembles a lighthouse.

Major Light:

Portland Head Light (43°37′·4N 70°12′·5W) (3.182).

Main entrance channel
3.209
1   From the vicinity of 43°37′N 70°09′W the white sector (274·3°–275·8°) of Portland Head Light (43°37′·4N 70°12′·5W) leads W on a course of 275°, passing (with positions relative to Portland Head Light):

N of No 1 Light-buoy (port hand) (2 miles E), thence:

2   S of No 2 Light-buoy (starboard hand) (1½ miles E), marking the S side of Witch Rock, a shoal, thence:

Close N of No 3 Light-buoy (port hand) (1 mile E), which lies 3 cables NNE of Jordan Reef. The S side of this shoal is marked by No 10 Buoy (starboard hand). Thence:

3   S of Ram Island Ledge Light (light-grey conical granite tower) (1 mile ENE). The ledge upon which this light stands extends 2½ cables S from Ram Island, and is awash in places. Thence:

N of D Light-buoy (isolated danger) (4 cables ESE) which lies on the S side of a shoal with a depth of 9·5 m (31 ft).

3.210
1   From a position about 2 cables E of Portland Head Light, the white sector (331°–337°) of Spring Point Ledge Light leads NNW for about 1½ miles, passing (with positions relative to Spring Point (43°39′·0N 70°13′·5W)):

2   ENE of No 11 Light-buoy (port hand) (1½ miles SSE), thence:

WSW of No 12 Light-buoy (starboard hand) (1¼ miles SSE), lying 2 cables off the S end of Cushing Island, which is mostly grassy, thence:

Clear of PH Light-buoy (safe water) (7 cables SSE), thence:

3   Between Spring Point, on which there are a number of prominent buildings, and Fort Scammel Point Light No 2 (red triangle on tower) (5 cables E), which stands on Fort Scammel Point, the S end of House Island. This island can be identified by the prominent Fort Scammel on its SW part and a flagstaff on the summit of its NE part. Thence:

4   NE of Spring Point Ledge Light (1½ cables NNE), thence:

NE of No 3 Light-buoy (port hand) (5 cables NNW), and:

5   SW of Fort Gorges (8 cables N), a prominent grey stone structure on Diamond Island Ledge. A light-beacon (red and white chequered diamond on framework tower) stands on the W edge of this ledge. Thence to the entrance to the Inner Harbour.

Other entrance channels
3.211
1   **Whitehead Passage** (43°39′N 70°12′W), which is sometimes used by small vessels, is entered NW of White Head and leads W with a depth of about 7·3 m (24 ft) between Cushing Island and Peaks Island. The principal dangers are marked, but the channel, which is obstructed by Trotts Rock, is narrow and should only be used with local knowledge.

2   **Diamond Island Pass.** See 3.166.

West of Great Diamond Island. From a position SE of The Brothers (43°42′N 70°13′W) a channel with a least charted depth of 6 m (20 ft) and marked by buoys, leads S passing W of Great Diamond Island and Little Diamond Island and into Diamond Island Roads (3.212).

Local knowledge is necessary.

Berths

Anchorages
3.212
1   Secure anchorage for any vessel is available at all times in Portland Harbor. Anchorages, which are shown on the chart, are as follows (with positions relative to Fish Point (43°40′N 70°14′W)):

A. (5 cables E). General anchorage in depths of 7 to 18 m (23 to 59 ft). Soft mud and fair holding.

2   B. (1¼ miles ESE). Diamond Island Roads. General anchorage and quarantine anchorage in depths of 7 to 14 m (23 to 46 ft). These roads are especially intended for tankers and deep-draught vessels entering at night for temporary anchorage before berthing the next day. An obstruction lies in the SE quarter of the anchorage, as shown on the chart,

3   C. (1¾ miles ESE). Temporary anchorage for small vessels in depths of 4 to 15 m (13 to 49 ft).

D. (1½ miles E and 1 mile SSW). Anchorages for small craft.

Alongside berths
3.213
1   Deep water berths include seven petroleum terminals, one general cargo terminal and one international ferry terminal. The oil terminals are on the S side of the river at South Portland and the general cargo terminal and the ferry terminal are on the N side of Fore River at Portland.

3.214

1   Tanker terminals on the S side of the Fore River are as follows:

   Portland Pipe Line Pier No 2 (43°39'·3N 70°13'·7W); two berths, 277 m in length with dolphins, with a depth alongside of 14·6 m. This is the terminal for the crude oil pipeline to Montreal in Canada and handles tankers up to 124 000 dwt.

2   Gulf Oil Terminal (43°39'·2N 70°14'·4W); 219 m in length with depths alongside of 8·5 to 9·7 m.

   Portland Pipe Line Pier No 1 (43°39'·1N 70°14'·5W); two berths, 259 m berthing space with a depth alongside of 10·3 m.

   Motiva Terminal (43°38'·5N 70°15'·8W); two berths, 274 m in length with a depth alongside of 11·8 m.

3   Cargill Energy Terminal (43°38'·2N 70°16'·6W); 207 m in length with a depth alongside of 11·5 m.

   Mobil Terminal (43°38'·3N 70°16'·9W); 183 m in length with a depth alongside of 10·7 m.

   Sprague Energy Terminal (43°38'·5N 70°17'·9W); 183 m in length with a depth alongside of 10·9 m.

3.215

1   Terminals on the N side of the Fore River are as follows:

   Maine State Pier (43°39'·4N 70°14'·9W); 85 m in length with a depth alongside of 10·6 m.

2   International Marine Terminal (43°38'·8N 70°15'·4W); 237 m in length with depths alongside of 10·3 m.

   Merrill's Marine Terminal (43°38'·4N 70°16'·9W); 274 m in length with depths alongside of 10·6 m.

Port services

Repairs
3.216

1   Repair yard situated 6 cables SW of Fish Point, including part of State Pier.

   Dry dock for vessels up to 80 000 tonnes. Length 257 m, width 42 m, depth over sill 14·3 m.

   Berths. Two repair berths, with total length of 487 m, with depths alongside of 11·3 m.

Other facilities
3.217

1   Hospitals; oily waste disposal.

Supplies
3.218

1   Fuel at the tanker berths or by barge; fresh water at most piers; provisions and stores.

Communications
3.219

1   Portland International Jetport 8 km.

Rescue
3.220

1   A Coast Guard station (43°38'·7N 70°14'·9W) is situated in South Portland on the S bank of the Fore River.

CAPE ELIZABETH TO CAPE ANN

GENERAL INFORMATION

Charts 3676, 1227
Ports
3.221

1   Portsmouth Harbor (43°04'N 70°45'W) (3.250) is the only harbour on this stretch of the coast suitable for deep-draught vessels.

   There are a number of smaller harbours between Cape Elizabeth and Portsmouth that provide shelter for smaller vessels.

Regulations
3.222

1   **Navigation Rules for US Inland Waters** on this stretch of the coast only apply to the harbour waters of Portsmouth and Annisquam (43°40'N 70°41'W). See 3.269 and 3.301.

Outlying danger and banks
3.223

1   See 3.1.

Tidal streams
3.224

1   On the coast of Maine, E of Portland, the in-going stream sets E and is stronger than the out-going stream, that sets W.

Submarine submerged transit lanes
3.225

1   A lane used by submerged submarines runs SE from off Portsmouth Harbor and thence SSE to the N end of Great South Channel (41°00'N 69°00'W). See 1.14.

COASTAL PASSAGE BETWEEN CAPE ELIZABETH AND PORTSMOUTH

General information

Chart 3676
Description
3.226

1   The coast between Cape Elizabeth (43°34'N 70°12'W) and Portsmouth, 40 miles SSW, is less indented than that farther N and the outlying dangers are fewer. This stretch of the coast is more thickly populated and there are many summer resorts marked by prominent buildings.

Traffic regulations
3.227

1   **A safety zone** with a radius of 5 cables, centred on a wreck (43°06'·2N 70°27'·2W), has been established 7 cables SE of Southeast Shoal. Fishing and anchoring are prohibited within the area. See 3.229 and Appendix V for further details.

2   **A security zone** into which entry is prohibited, as shown on the chart, lies to the SE of Cape Arundel

(43°20′N 70°28′W). For a general description of security zones see Appendix V.

Directions
(continued from 3.13)

Principal marks
3.228

1   **Landmarks:**
Water Tower (43°33′N 70°21′W) which stands on Blue Point Hill.
Tank (43°26′N 70°23′W) which stands on a high framework tower 2½ miles WSW of Wood Island Light.
Tank (43°22′N 70°27′W) which stands behind Cape Porpoise.
Mount Agamenticus (43°13′N 70°42′W) which has a tower on its summit and is the highest and S of three peaks on a ridge.

2   **Major lights:**
Cape Elizabeth Light (43°34′N 70°12′W) (3.182).
Wood Island Light (white conical tower and dwelling) (43°27′N 70°20′W).
Boon Island Light (grey conical tower and dwelling, 41 m in height) (43°07′N 70°29′W).

3.229

1   From the vicinity of P Light-buoy (43°32′N 70°06′W), 5 miles ESE of Cape Elizabeth, the coastal route leads SSW, passing (with positions relative to Cape Island (43°22′N 70°25′W)):
ESE of East Hue and Cry (3.187), West Hue and Cry, Alden Rock (3.187) and Old Anthony Rock (3.175), four rocks that lie between 2 and 3 miles SW of Cape Elizabeth, thence:

2   ESE of Richmond Island (43°33′N 70°14′W) (3.230), thence:
ESE of Wood Island Light (7 miles NE) (3.228) which stands on Wood Island at the S entrance point to Saco Bay (3.235), thence:

3   ESE of Cape Island. Goat Island Light stands on the SW side of Goat Island, 4 cables SW. Thence:
ESE of ADA Light-buoy (special) (4 miles SSW), thence:

4   ESE of two patches (6 miles S) with depths of 9·8 and 10·4 m (32 and 34 ft) over them, thence:
ESE of B Light-buoy (special) (11 miles S). Thence:
ESE of Bald Head Cliff (11 miles SW), a prominent headland on which stand two prominent white buildings, thence:

5   ESE of Boon Island Ledge (43°08′N 70°25′W), awash. No 22A Light-buoy (starboard hand) is moored SE of the ledge. No attempt should be made to pass between Boon Island Ledge and Boon Island because of the shoal, with a depth of 4·9 m (16 ft) that lies between them. Thence:

6   ESE of Southeast Shoal (43°07′N 70°28′W), which lies 8 cables SE of Boon Island, a low rocky islet on which stands a light (3.228). A number of lighted mooring buoys mark the wreck of MV *Empire Knight* which lies 7 cables SE of the shoal (see 3.227). US naval vessels may be operating with submarines in this area. Sanders Ledge, Pollock Rock, and a shoal with a depth of 7·6 m (25 ft) lie S and W and within 1½ miles of Boon Island.

(Directions for the coastal route continue at 3.286)

7   Thence the track continues WSW to the approaches to Portsmouth, passing (with positions relative to Duck Island (43°00′N 70°36′W)):
Clear of an obstruction (3½ miles NE), the position of which is approximate, thence:

8   SSE of 24YL Light-buoy (starboard hand) (4¼ miles NNE). This buoy is moored SE of York Ledge and E of Murray Rock, two dangers marked by buoys YL (preferred channel to port), and 2MR (starboard hand), respectively), which lie 2½ miles off the coast. Vessels should pass well to seaward of 24YL Light-buoy to avoid the broken ground lying inshore of it. Thence:

9   Clear of two shoal patches (2¼ miles NNE and 2¼ miles NW) with depths of 10·6 m (35 ft) and 10·4 m (34 ft), respectively, thence:
NNW of Duck Island (3.287).
Thence the track continues WSW to a position W of Duck Island.

10   **Useful mark:**
Cape Neddick Light (3.247).
(Directions for Portsmouth Harbor continue at 3.273)

Anchorages and harbours
Seal Cove
3.230

1   Seal Cove (43°33′N 70°14′W), used as an anchorage by small craft, is entered between High Head, the SW point of Cape Elizabeth and East Point, the NE point of Richmond Island. The cove is much encumbered by rocks of which The Sisters, awash and Seal Rock, which dries 1·2 m (4 ft), lie in its central part.

Richmond Island Harbor
3.231

1   Richmond Island Harbor (43°33′N 70°15′W) is often used as an anchorage by small craft.

Spurwink River
3.232

1   Spurwink River (43°34′N 70°16′W), a shallow unimportant stream, flows into the sea 1½ miles NW of Richmond Island. It is only suitable for small craft to enter at half tide.

Prouts Neck
3.233

1   Prouts Neck (43°32′N 70°19′W), which is partly wooded and marked by numerous houses, lies 3 miles WSW of Richmond Island. Shooting Rock, a reef, partly above-water extends 7 cables E from the beach on the E side of Prouts Neck.
Useful marks (with positions relative to SW point of Prouts Neck):

2   Tower (3½ cables E).
Water tower (2 cables ENE).
Water tower (2 miles NW) (3.228).

Scarborough River
3.234

1   Scarborough River (Scarboro River) (43°33′N 70°21′W) is entered NW of Prouts Neck. It is accessible only to small craft from half tide.

Saco Bay
3.235

1   Saco Bay is entered between Prouts Neck (43°32′N 70°19′W) and Wood Island, 4 miles SSW. Stratton Island and Bluff Island, grass-covered and surrounded by ledges, lie 1 mile S of Prouts Neck.

In the N part of the bay, Bar Ledge and Little River Rock lie 1 and 1½ miles WSW, respectively, of Prouts Neck and in the S part Eagle Island lies 2 miles NW of Wood Island.

2   **Old Orchard Beach** (43°31′N 70°23′W) lies in the central part of Saco Bay between Scarborough River and Saco River. There are several large hotels and a pier at Old Orchard Beach.

Saco River
3.236

1   Saco River (43°27′N 70°20′W), with its entrance in the S end of Saco Bay 2 miles W of Wood Island Light, is the approach to the cities of Biddeford on the S bank and Saco on the N bank. The cities are the head of navigation, but there is no commercial traffic on the river and the wharves are no longer in good repair.

Ice closes the river from January to April.

Chart 3676 (see 1.17)
Wood Island Harbor
3.237

1   **Description.** Wood Island Harbor (43°27′N 70°21′W), an anchorage suitable for small and medium sized vessels, is situated between Wood Island, Negro Island and Stage Island on the N and Fletcher Neck on the S. The village of Biddeford Pool stands on Fletcher Neck.

2   The islands on the N side of the harbour are low; Wood Island, 12 m (38 ft) in height, which has a few trees on it, is the highest. Fletcher Neck, 15 m (49 ft) in height, may best be distinguished by the many large houses standing on it and the tank (3.228) standing at the inner end of the neck.

3   **Local knowledge** is necessary.

Cable area, 2 cables in width, extends SW from the W end of Wood Island to the N part of Fletcher Neck.
3.238

1   **Approaches.** Wood Island Harbor can be approached from the N between Negro Island and Stage Island or from the E between Wood Island and Gooseberry Island.

Directions for north approach. From the vicinity of SA Buoy (safe water) (43°27′·9N 70°20′·3W) the approach leads SW and SSW, passing:

2   Between Negro Island Ledge and Ram Island Ledge, which are marked, respectively, on their N and E side by Nos 1 and 2 Buoys (lateral), thence:

Between Negro Island and a buoy (preferred channel to starboard), which marks the ledges extending from the NE extremity of Stage Island; thence into the anchorage.

3   **Directions for east approach.** From a position E of Wood Island Light the approach leads SW and W, passing:

Between the E end of Wood Island and the 3 m (10 ft) shoal that lies 2 cables SE and thence to the anchorage.

Alternatively, from a position SE of Wood Island Light the approach leads NW, passing:

4   Between Dansbury Reef (5 cables SSE of Wood Island Light), the S side of which is marked by No 2 Buoy (starboard hand) and Washman Rock, 2 cables SW, which is marked by 3A Buoy. An unmarked channel, 2 cables wide, leads between Dansbury Reef and the 3 m (10 ft) shoal lying to the N. Thence:

5   E of Gooseberry Island, thence into the anchorage.
Useful marks:
Wood Island Light (E extremity of Wood Island) (3.228).
Monument (NE side of Stage Island) (43°27′·4N 70°21′·1W).
3.239

1   **Anchorage** is available in the following parts of Wood Island Harbor:
South of Wood Island, E of the cable area, in depths of 5 to 11 m (16 to 36 ft).
Between Negro Island and Stage Island, in depths of 5 to 7 m (16 to 23 ft).
South-west part of the harbour, in depths of 2 to 5 m (6 to 18 ft).

Between Fletcher Neck and Cape Porpoise
3.240

1   **Goosefare Bay,** only used by small fishing and pleasure craft, is entered between Timber Island (43°24′N 70°24′W) and Stage Island, 1½ miles SSW.

Stage Island Harbor (43°22′N 70°25′W), which is used by small craft only, is a small area that lies within Stage Island and Cape Island (3.241).

Cape Porpoise Harbor
3.241

1   Cape Porpoise Harbor (43°22′N 70°25′W) lies in a group of islands and rocks which extend 1 mile from the coast. Cape Island is the E of this group.

The harbour is a good anchorage for fishing and pleasure craft, and is often used as a harbour of refuge.

Turbats Creek
3.242

1   Turbats Creek, which is only used by small craft, lies 7½ cables WSW of Goat Island Light.

Kennebunk River
3.243

1   Kennebunk River, the entrance of which is fronted by several reefs and shoals, is entered 6 cables NW of Cape Arundel (43°20′·4N 70°28′·0W) and is the approach to the popular summer resort and yachting centre of Kennebunkport.

Between Kennebunk River and Cape Neddick
3.244

1   **Mousam River** (43°21′N 70°31′W), suitable for small craft, is entered W of Great Hill, a prominent yellow bluff with houses standing on it.
3.245

1   **Wells Harbor** (43°19′N 70°34′W), which is used by local fishermen and pleasure craft, is entered between Drakes Islands Beach which extends 1¼ miles NE to the shallow Little River, and Wells Beach which extends 2 miles S. A foul area, with rocks awash, extends 7½ cables offshore from Drakes Island Beach.
3.246

1   **Perkins Cove** (43°14′N 70°35′W) at the mouth of Josias River, 7½ cables SSE of Ogunquit River entrance, is small but landlocked and is much used by small craft.
3.247

1   **Cape Neddick Harbor** (43°10′N 70°36′W), which is used by small craft, lies 1¼ miles NNW of Cape Neddick Light which stands on Cape Neddick Nubble, a rock close

off the E extremity of the cape. It is entered between Weare Point and Barn Point.

York Harbor

3.248

1   York Harbor (43°08′N 70°38′W), the lower part of York River, is entered between East Point, 2¼ miles SW of Cape Neddick and Western Point, 6 cables SW.

Function. The harbour is used by numerous fishing boats and pleasure craft and forms the approaches to the town and resort of York Harbor, which is situated on the N side of the river, 5 cables NW of Western Point.

Brave Boat Harbor

3.249

1   Brave Boat Harbor (43°06′N 70°39′W) which mostly dries out, is used by local small craft.

PORTSMOUTH HARBOR

General information

Charts 3676, 1227, 2487 plan of Portsmouth Harbor (see 1.17)

Position

3.250

1   Portsmouth Harbor (43°04′N 70°45′W) is situated on the W side of the Gulf of Maine and is formed by the mouth of the Piscataqua River.

Function

3.251

1   The city of Portsmouth, which in 2005 had an estimated population of 20 674, is a port of entry. It stands on the S bank of Piscataqua River, 3 miles above the entrance. The town of Kittery stands on the N bank opposite Portsmouth.

2   The port, which is the only harbour of refuge available for vessels of deep draught between Portland and Gloucester (4.15), handles petroleum products, gypsum, frozen fish, fish products and salt.

A United States Naval Base is situated in the harbour (3.270).

Entry

3.252

1   The harbour is approached from either side of the Isles of Shoals (3.288) and entered between Whaleback Light (43°03′·5N 70°41′·8W), 5 cables SW of Gerrish Island and Jaffrey Point (3.275), the SE extremity of New Castle Island (3.275).

Traffic

3.253

1   **Traffic.** In 2005 the port was used by 67 vessels with a total deadweight 4 396 677 tonnes.

Port Authority

3.254

1   New Hampshire State Port Authority, 555 Market Street PO Box 506, Portsmouth, NH 03801.

Internet. www.portofnh.com

Limiting conditions

Controlling depths

3.255

1   **From entrance to Memorial Highway Bridge.** Marked channel, 10·7 m (35 ft).

Memorial Highway Bridge to upper turning basin. Controlling depth 8·2 m (27 ft) in the dredged channel, thence 10 m (33 ft) in the basin situated 3½ miles above the bridge.

For the latest controlling depths the charts and port authority should be consulted.

Gulf of Maine – Portsmouth Outer Harbour from SE (3.252)

(Original dated 2005)

(Photograph – David M Walker – Reproduced by permission of Marblehead Sail & Power Squadron. United States Power Squadrons)

Under-keel clearances
3.256
1 The US Coast Guard recommends the following under-keel clearances for vessels in the Port of Portsmouth:
(a) A minimum of 0·9 m (3 ft) when transiting inside 2KR Buoy (43°03′N 70°42′W).
(b) A minimum of 0·3 m (1 ft) at all berthing areas.

Vertical clearance
3.257
1 **Memorial Highway Bridge.** A lift span bridge with a vertical clearance of 5·8 m (19 ft) when closed and 45·7 m (150 ft) when open.
Sara Long Bridge. A lift span bridge with a vertical clearance of 3 m (10 ft) when closed and 41·1 m (135 ft) when open.
2 **Interstate Route 95 Bridge.** A fixed bridge with a vertical clearance of 40·8 m (134 ft).
Span bridge operators monitor VHF.

Horizontal clearance
3.258
1 **Memorial Highway Bridge.** Horizontal clearance 79 m.
Sara Long Bridge. Horizontal clearance 61 m.

Deepest and longest berth
3.259
1 **Deepest:**
Storage Tank Development Corp. Dock (3.279).
Longest:
Newington Terminal Wharf (3.279).

Tidal levels
3.260
1 Mean spring range about 2·8 m; mean neap range about 2 m. See information in *Admiralty Tide Tables.*

Maximum size of vessel handled
3.261
1 **Largest vessel.** 45 000 dwt. Tankers up to 213 m in length, draught 10·7 m.

Ice
3.262
1 Portsmouth Harbor has never been frozen over.

Arrival information

Vessel traffic service
3.263
1 Vessel traffic service scheme is in operation for the control of shipping. See *Admiralty List of Radio Signals Volume 6(5)* for details. Positions of reporting points are shown on the chart.

Notice of ETA required
3.264
1 24 hours notice is required.

Outer anchorages
3.265
1 Anchorage for medium sized vessels is on the E and N side of the channel between Wood Island (43°03′·8N 70°41′·9W) and Clarks Island (1½ miles NW), in depths of 5 to 22 m (18 ft to 12 fm), but there is only room for one medium sized vessel N of Fort Point (3.275). With S winds the best anchorage is above Fort Point on the S side of the channel in depths of 15 to 18 m (49 to 58 ft), clay.

2 **Caution.** Deep draught vessels should not pass N of Kitts Rocks (43°03′·2N 70°41′·5W) without a pilot owing to the strong tidal streams and eddies off Fort Point (43°04′·3N 70°42′·6W). Whilst awaiting a pilot or tide, vessels should anchor between Kitts Rocks and Gunboat Shoal (2 miles SSW).
Cable areas, the limits of which are marked on the chart, lie either side of the approaches to Portsmouth.

Pilotage
3.266
1 **Pilotage**, which is available 24 hours a day, is compulsory for all foreign vessels and US vessels engaged in foreign trade.
Pilots embark 1 mile SSE of 2KR Light-buoy (43°03′N 70°42′W). See *Admiralty List of Radio Signals Volume 6(5)* for details.

Tugs
3.267
1 **Tugs**, which are also used as pilot boats, are available and two or more are normally required by larger vessels.

Mooring master
3.268
1 **Mooring master.** When the range of tide at HW and LW Boston is 3·66 m (12 ft) or greater, vessels having a draught greater than 9·75 m (32 ft) are recommended to obtain the services of a mooring master when moored on the Piscataqua River if LOA meets the following criteria:
Portsmouth-Schiller terminal: 189·28 m (621 ft)
Sprague Avery Lane terminal: 197·51 m (648 ft)
Sprague River Road terminal: 201·47 m (661 ft).
2 Intention to obtain the services of a mooring master must be included in the 24-hour notice of ETA. Vessels meeting the criteria, that do not obtain the services of a mooring master, must obtain permission from the US Coast Guard Captain of the Port, Portsmouth.

Traffic regulations
3.269
1 **The Navigation Rules for US Inland Waters** apply within a line drawn SW from the tower (43°04′·0N 70°41′·2W) on the S point of Gerrish Island, to Whaleback Light, thence Jaffrey Point Light 2A and thence Frost Point (43°03′·2N 70°43′·2W). See 1.47 and Appendix VII for further information.
2 **Regulated navigation area.** A regulated navigation area has been established NW of Seavey Island in the vicinity of the Portsmouth Naval Dockyard. A speed limit of 4½ kn is in force in this area.
See Appendix V for definitions and general regulations covering regulated navigation areas.
3 **Safety and security zones.** A safety and security zone extending 1 mile ahead, 5 cables astern and 1000 yards on either side is established around any LPG vessel.
A safety and security zone, radius 500 yards, is established around any LPG vessel moored at Newington on the Piscataqua River.
4 Entry into or movement within these zones is prohibited unless previously authorized by the Captain of the Port (COTP).
See Appendix V for definitions and general regulations covering safety and security zones.
5 **Restricted areas.** Restricted areas, into which entry is prohibited, have been established, as shown on the chart, at the E end of Seavey Island between Clarks Island and Jamaica Island, 2 cables N, and on the SW and NW sides

of Seavey Island. See Appendix VI for definition and details of restricted areas.

Harbour

General layout
3.270

1   Portsmouth Harbor has an outer harbour in the entrance to the Piscataqua River, in which are situated the outer anchorages for deep draught vessels, a number of anchorages for smaller vessels and a few minor jetties.

The United States Naval Base is situated on Seavey Island (43°04′·8N 70°44′·0W) at the inner end of the outer harbour.

2   The commercial harbour is upstream of Memorial Highway Bridge (43°04′·8N 70°45′·2W), which crosses Badgers Island. The majority of berths lie on the S bank of the river, above the second and third bridges, which lie 5 cables and 1 mile, respectively, above the Memorial Highway Bridge. There are two dredged turning basins in this stretch of the river.

Hazards
3.271

1   Owing to the very strong tides on the Piscataqua River and its tributaries vessels moving along a berth must only do so during periods of slack water. It is extremely dangerous to attempt to shift a vessel at any other time and it should not be attempted. Masters should be particularly vigilant in tending to their vessel's moorings.

2   The strong tidal streams in the narrow channel make passage through the bridges difficult and large vessels generally require two tugs and pass through at HW.
See also 3.268 and 3.272.

Tidal streams
3.272

1   Tidal streams in Portsmouth Harbor are strong and require special care. The rates of tidal streams are given in the tables on the chart.

Directions
(continued from 3.5 and 3.229)

Principal marks
3.273

1   **Landmarks:**
     Tower (43°04′·0N 70°41′·2W) standing at the S end of Gerrish Island.
     Cupola (43°03′·8N 70°41′·9W) on white buildings on Wood Island.
     Cupola (43°03′·6N 70°43′·6W) on hotel at the SW end of New Castle Island.

2   Square tower (43°04′·6N 70°43′·9W) on the SE part of Seavey Island.

Gangway Rk

Portsmouth Inner Harbour from ESE (3.270)
(Original dated 2005)

(Photograph - David M Walker - Reproduced by permission of Marblehead Sail & Power Squadron. United States Power Squadrons)

Major light:

Whaleback Light (grey conical granite tower, 23 m in height) (43°03'·5N 70°41'·8W).

Approach

3.274

1   From a position W of Duck Island (3.287) (43°00'N 70°36'W) the approach to Portsmouth Harbor leads NW passing NE of No 1 Light-buoy (port hand), which marks the NE side of Gunboat Shoal (43°01'N 70°42'W).

Vessels approaching from the S should pass at least 5 cables W of the Isles of Shoals.

2   **Useful mark:**

Round tower (square daymark painted with red and white triangles) (43°02'N 70°43'W).

Entrance

3.275

1   **Leading lights:**

Front light (red rectangle, white stripe, on framework tower) (43°04'·9N 70°42'·5W).

Rear light (similar structure) (140 m from front light).

2   From the vicinity of the pilot boarding position, 1 mile SSE of 2KR Light-buoy (43°03'·0N 70°41'·5W), the alignment (352¾°) of these lights leads N, passing (with positions relative to Fort Point (43°04'·3N 70°42'·6W)):

E of Odiornes Point (1¾ miles S), thence:

W of Kitts Rocks (1½ miles SE), marked on their S side by 2KR Light-buoy (starboard hand), thence:

3   E of Jaffrey Point (9 cables SSW), the SE extremity of New Castle Island and N entrance point to Little Harbor. No 4 Light-beacon (red triangle on framework tower) stands on the end of a submerged breakwater that extends SSW from the point. Thence:

4   W of Whaleback Light (1 mile SE) (3.273), standing on Whaleback Reef, thence:

W of Wood Island (7 cables SE) (3.265). A building with a cupola stands on the island and No 2 Light-buoy (starboard hand) is moored 2 cables SW. Thence:

5   E of Stielman Rocks (3 cables S) which stand on the outer edge of the shore bank. No 3A Beacon (port hand) stands on the W side of the rocks and No 3 Buoy (port hand) marks their outer edge. Thence:

6   E of Fort Point, the NE point of New Castle Island. Portsmouth Fort Point Light (white conical tower) stands on the SE end of the point. A Coast Guard station and lookout tower also stand on the point.

3.276

1   **Leading lights:**

Front light (red rectangle, white stripe on conical tower) (43°04'·4N 70°44'·5W).

Rear light (similar structure) (78 m from front light).

From a position NNE of Fort Point the alignment (266°) of these lights on Pierces Island leads W, passing (with positions relative to Fort Point):

2   N of No 5 Light-buoy (port hand) (2 cables NW), which lies 2 cables NE of Salamander Point, thence:

S of No 8 Light-beacon (red triangle on sectional spindle) (7 cables WNW), which stands on the S side of Clarks Island, thence:

3   S of No 10 Light-beacon (red triangle on framework tower) (1¼ miles WNW), which stands on Henderson Point.,

Thence the track continues upstream, the river channel being marked by buoys and light-buoys (lateral).

Berths

Anchorages

3.277

1   There are no anchorages for deep-draught vessels upstream of Clarks Island.

Alongside berths

3.278

1   Deep water berths include one general cargo and container terminal, two bulk cargo terminals and four petroleum terminals. All deep water berths are situated on the S side of the Piscataqua River between the Memorial Highway Bridge and Dover Point, 4 miles farther upstream.

3.279

1   A summary of the main terminals is given as follows (with positions relative to Memorial Highway Bridge):

Granite State Minerals Dock (3 cables upstream).

91 m in length with a depth alongside of 9·8 m.

Handles salt, dry bulk cargoes and heavy lift items.

New Hampshire State Port Authority Marine Terminal (4½ cables upstream).

2   176 m in length with a depth alongside of 10·7 m.

Handles containers, scrap metal and general cargo.

National Gypsum Co Wharf (9 cables upstream).

91 m in length with a depth alongside of 10·4 m.

Bulk handling of gypsum and petroleum products.

Simplex Wire and Cable Co Wharf (2¼ miles upstream).

3   210 m in length, with dolphins, with a depth alongside of 9·1 m.

Specialist berth for handling wire and cable.

Oil terminals (1¾ to 3½ miles upstream).

76 to 237 m in length, with dolphins, with depths alongside of 9·7 to 11·6 m.

Four terminals, one of which, Newington Dock, is owned by the US Government.

Port services

Repairs

3.280

1   There are no major repair facilities for commercial vessels.

Other facilities

3.281

1   Hospitals, oily waste disposal.

Supplies

3.282

1   Fuel available at oil terminals; water; provisions and stores.

Communications

3.283

1   Nearest airport 3 km.

Rescue

3.284

1   A Coast Guard station is situated on Fort Point (43°04'·3N 70°42'·6W) at the NE extremity of New Castle Island.

PORTSMOUTH HARBOR TO CAPE ANN

General information

Chart 1227
Description
3.285

1   Between the entrance to Portsmouth Harbor (43°02′N 70°41′W) and the E extremity of Cape Ann, 25 miles SSE, the coast is composed mainly of sandy beaches.

The Merrimack River enters the bay 15 miles SSW of Portsmouth Harbor and N of its mouth the beaches are separated by reefs extending 5 cables offshore.

2   There are a number of summer resorts and small harbours on this stretch of the coast, the latter being used by fishing vessels and small craft.

Isles of Shoals (3.288), a group of islands, lie between 5 and 7 miles SE of the entrance to Portsmouth Harbor.

3   **Cape Ann** (42°38′N 70°39′W) is an island separated from the mainland by the Annisquam River. It is rocky and broken, rising to its greatest height at Pool Hill. The E end of the cape is comparatively low and off its NE and E sides are several islands and dangers. The cape is covered with numerous summer residences.

4   **Local magnetic anomaly** increases the variation by as much as 3° in the vicinity of Cape Ann.

Ship Reporting System. A mandatory ship reporting system for the protection of the Northern right whale is established to the S and E of Cape Ann. See 3.3.

5   **Rescue.** A Coast Guard station (42°49′N 70°52′W) is situated on the S bank of the Merrimack River about 6 cables within the entrance.

No-Discharge Zone (NDZ). All the coastal waters of New Hampshire, from Portsmouth to Hampton Harbor, extending out 3 miles off shore and including the Isle of Shoals, have been designated as a NDZ. See 1.44.

Directions
(continued from 3.229)

Principal marks
3.286

1   **Major Lights:**
    Whaleback Light (43°04′N 70°42′W) (3.273).
    Isles of Shoals Light (42°58′N 70°37′W), which stands on White Island at S end of Isles of Shoals.
    Cape Ann Light (42°38′N 70°35′W), which stands on the E side of Thacher Island.

Portsmouth Harbor to Cape Ann
3.287

1   From a position ESE of Southeast Shoal (3.229) the coastal passage leads S to Cape Ann, passing (with positions relative to Isle of Shoals Light (42°58′N 70°37′W)):

2   E of Duck Island (2½ miles NNE), the N island of the Isles of Shoals (3.288). This island is 5 m in height and surrounded by reefs and shoals. The Isles of Shoals may be seen from a distance of 10 miles on a clear day, the houses being prominent. Thence:

    E of Smuttynose Island (1¼ miles NE), thence:

3   E of Cedar Island Ledge and Anderson Ledge (1 mile ENE and ESE, respectively), both of which dry 1·2 m (4 ft). Cedar Island Ledge is marked by DC Buoy (isolated danger), and Anderson Ledge is

marked by No 2 Buoy (starboard hand). A fish trap area, marked by buoys, lies 1¾ miles SW of Anderson Ledge. Vessels passing to the E of the islands should give them a berth of 1½ miles, to clear these ledges. Thence:

4   E of The Salvages (42°40′N 70°34′W) consisting of two reefs connected by a ridge. No 1 Light-buoy (port hand) is moored 5 cables NE of Dry Salvages, the E reef. Thence:

    E of Thacher Island (42°38′N 70°35′W) which lies 5 cables E of Emerson Point, the E point of Cape Ann. Londoner, a shoal marked by a beacon, lies 4 cables ESE of Cape Ann Light.

5   **Caution.** Trawlers and other vessels conducting bottom operations within a 6¾ mile radius seaward of Isle of Shoals Light should exercise caution because of Jet Assist Take-Off racks and other debris on the seabed associated with the naval bombing range centred on Shag Rock (3.289).

6   **Useful marks:**
    Isles of Shoals Light (42°58′N 70°37′W) (3.286).
    Plum Island Light (white conical tower) (42°49′N 70°49′W).
    Thacher Island Light (grey stone conical tower) (42°38′·4N 70°34′·4W).
    Cape Ann Light (42°38′N 70°35′W) (3.286).
    (Directions continue at 4.12)

Isles of Shoals

Description
3.288

1   Isles of Shoals (42°59′N 70°37′W) is a group of seven islands and a number of rocks and ledges which lie SE of the entrance to Portsmouth Harbor. The islands are occupied in summer by fishermen and visitors, but only a few residents inhabit the islands in winter. A ferry service operates between Star Island and Portsmouth Harbor.

Traffic regulations
3.289

1   **Danger zone.** An area of radius 2½ cables, centred on Shag Rock (43°00′·2N 70°36′·2W), lies to the E of Duck Island (3.287). The zone is used for naval aircraft bombing practice. For details see Appendix VI.

Channels
3.290

1   **Between Appledore Island and Duck Island.** The channel separating Appledore Island, 21 m in height and the largest island of the group, from Duck Island (3.287) has irregular depths; rocky patches with depths of 7·6 m and 8·2 m (25 to 27 ft) lie in the channel.
3.291

1   Gosport Harbor lies between Malaga Island, joined to Smuttynose Island by a breakwater, and the N side of Star Island. It is protected from the E by Cedar Island and the breakwaters that connect this island to Smuttynose Island and Star Island. The harbour offers good protection from all but W winds.

2   **Anchorage** is available for small coasters in depths of 6 to 15 m (20 to 49 ft).

Stone pier, length 60 m with depths alongside of 3·7 m, extends from the village of Gosport, at the N point of Star Island.

Approaches to Portsmouth - Isles of Shoals from SSW (3.288)

(Original dated 1990)

(Photograph - Joseph R Melanson of www.skypic.com)

Useful marks
3.292
1   (With positions relative to Isles of Shoals Light (42°58′·0N 70°37′·4W)):
> Tower (1¼ miles NNE) standing on Appledore Island.
> Cupola (1¼ miles NNE) of an old Coast Guard station, 1 cable E of the tower.

2   White hotel and flagstaff (7 cables NE) on N part of Star Island.
> Monument (7 cables NE), 12 m in height, standing 1 cable SSE of the hotel flagstaff.
> Isles of Shoals Light (3.286) standing on S part of White Island.

Sandy Bay

Chart 2487 plan of Rockport Harbor
Description
3.293
1   Sandy Bay lies between Andrews Point (42°41′N 70°37′W), 5 cables SE of Halibut Point and Straitsmouth Island, low and grassy, lying 2 miles SE.

2   **Breakwater.** The S part of the bay is protected by a partially completed breakwater, which extends N and NW for 1 mile from Avery Ledge. In 1979 the breakwater was awash except for a length of 1½ cables near the centre, where it was above-water, and about 2 cables at either end

that are submerged at LW. No 3 Light-buoy (port hand) and No 2 Light-buoy (starboard hand), respectively, mark the NW and S ends of the breakwater.

Arrival information
3.294
1   **Entrance.** The main entrance to the bay, which is deep and clear, lies between Andrews Point and No 3 Light-buoy. There is a narrow passage, with a least depth of 6·7 m (22 ft) leading into the bay at the S end of the breakwater, but this should not be used without local knowledge.

2   **Dangers.** A bank with rocks on it, two of which are awash, lies on the W side of Sandy Bay. The S rock, Dodge Rock, is marked by No 2 Beacon. Ninefoot Rock, which is marked by No 3 Buoy (port hand), lies 3 cables NW of Gap Head, the S entrance point to the bay.

3   **Useful marks** (with positions relative to Andrews Point):
> Chimney (6 cables S) at the head of Pigeon Cove.
> Tank (1 mile SSW) on Pigeon Hill.
> Straitsmouth Island Light (white round tower) (2 miles SE).

4   **Anchorage.** The depths within the bay are from 10 to 26 m (33 ft to 14 fm) and it is sometimes used as an anchorage. It is however exposed to N and NE winds. It has been reported that in good weather vessels up to 46 m

in length anchor in the cove S of Sandy Bay Ledge (42°39′·9N 70°37′·2W).

Rockport Harbor
3.295

1   Rockport Harbor (42°40′N 70°37′W), at the SW end of Sandy Bay, is used by small craft and is reported to be secure in all weathers. The town of Rockport lies to the S of the harbour.

Anchorages and harbours

Chart 1227 (see 1.17)
Rye Harbor
3.296

1   Rye Harbor (43°00′N 70°45′W), which lies 1 mile SSW of Concord Point, is a small cove used by fishing and pleasure craft.

Hampton Harbor
3.297

1   Hampton Harbor (42°54′N 70°49′W) and Hampton River form a shallow inlet that is entered 4 miles SSW of Little Boars Head, yellow bluff with building on it, and 1½ miles SSW of Great Boars Head.

   The harbour is used principally as an anchorage for fishing vessels and pleasure craft.

Merrimack River
3.298

1   Merrimack River is the largest river in the E part of Massachusetts and forms the approach to the cities of Newburyport (42°49′N 70°53′W) and Haverhill. It is navigable by coasters with a draught of 3·7 m (12 ft) to Newburyport but the river is seldom entered for refuge and has virtually no commercial traffic.

2   **Local knowledge** is necessary and pilotage is compulsory for all foreign vessels.

   Approach and entrance. The entrance lies 4½ miles S of Hampton Harbor and 2¾ miles S of Breaking Rocks, the E side of this shoal being marked by No 2 buoy (starboard hand).

3   A breakwater extends from each entrance point, the outer ends being 98 m apart. No 4 Light (red triangle on framework tower) stands at the head of the N breakwater and No 2 Light-buoy (starboard hand) is moored 4 cables E of this light.

   At HW the S breakwater may be difficult to distinguish, particularly at night, as its outer end will be awash.

4   The entrance is obstructed by a shifting bar which is dangerous to cross in heavy weather. A bar guide light and visual warning signal, situated at the N end of Plum Island on the S side of the entrance, is operated by the Coast Guard to warn of conditions on the bar.

   Tidal streams are strong in the river, with the outgoing stream flowing at a rate of up to 3 kn.

5   **Ice** occasionally obstructs navigation as far as the first bridge at Newburyport. W winds carry drift ice out to sea whilst winds from other directions allow the flood tide to prevent drift ice leaving the river.

   Above the bridges at Newburyport the river is normally closed by ice from January to March.

3.299

1   **Channel.** A buoyed channel leads over the bar to Newburyport and thence upstream to Haverhill. It is well marked and easy to follow as far as Newburyport, but is then narrow and winding.

2   **Depths.** In 1998-2001 the channel over the bar had a controlling depth of 2·1 m (7 ft) and the channel to the road bridge at Newburyport had a controlling depth of 2·3 m (7·5 ft). For the latest depths the charts and the harbour authorities should be consulted.

3   **Vertical clearance.** Road and rail bridges cross the river at Newburyport with a vertical clearance of 10·7 m (35 ft) when open and clearance of 4 m when closed. The channel leads through the N opening span of each bridge.

4   **Alongside berths.** There are a number of landings with depths alongside of 2·4 to 5·5 m at the Newburyport waterfront. A town landing is situated on the N bank, E of the bridges.

   Port services: hospital; fuel; water and provisions.

5   **Rescue.** A Coast Guard station is situated on the S bank of the river, 6 cables within the entrance.

Ipswich Bay and adjacent waters
3.300

1   **Plum Island Sound**, entered between the S end of Plum Island and Castle Neck (42°41′N 70°45′W), is frequented by small craft.

   Ipswich River, which flows into the S end of Plum Island Sound S of Little Neck (42°41′·7N 70°47′·8W), is frequented by small craft.

2   **Essex Bay**, the estuary to Essex River, entered between Castle Neck (42°41′N 70°44′W) and Coffins Beach in the S part of Ipswich Bay, is used by local fishermen and pleasure craft.

Chart 1227 (see 1.17)
Annisquam River and Blynman Canal
3.301

1   Annisquam River, which is entered between Wigwam Point (42°40′N 70°41′W) and Farm Point, 6 cables SW, and the Blynman Canal at its S end, provide a thoroughfare for small craft proceeding from Ipswich Bay to Gloucester Harbor (4.15).

2   **Local magnetic anomaly** of about 3° has been observed in the vicinity of Annisquam, a village on the E side of the river just within its N end.

Hodgkins Cove
3.302

1   Hodgkins Cove (42°40′·2N 70°40′·2W) is entered close E of Davis Neck. There are unmarked dangers in the entrance and a channel 21 m wide leads to a long stone pier on the E side, which has depths alongside of 3·7 m at its outer end.

Folly Cove
3.303

1   Folly Cove (42°41′·3N 70°38′·5W) is entered close SE of Folly Point. There is a wharf on the E side with a depth alongside of 4·9 m. A rock, with a depth of 0·9 m (3 ft) over it, lies ½ cable W of the wharf.

71°　30′　70°　30′　69°

Gulf of Maine

2487

Cape Ann

Gloucester Harbor ■
4.15

2487

2427

Salem ■
4.41

30′

Lynn ■
4.60

1516

Massachusetts Bay

Boston ■
4.76

1528

4.62

42°

1227

3096

4.128

4.151
Provincetown ■

4.149

Plymouth ■　**4.136**
4.142

4.145

Cape Cod Bay

Wellfleet ■
4.159

MASSACHUSETTS

4.149

Cape Cod Canal
(Chapter 5)

Cape Cod

Barnstable ■
4.160

2891

4.62

30′

Martha's Vineyard

Nantucket I.

Chapter 5

Nantucket Shoals

41°

2456

2489

Longitude 70° West from Greenwich

CHAPTER 4

MASSACHUSETTS BAY, BOSTON HARBOR AND APPROACHES

GENERAL INFORMATION

Chart 2492
Scope of chapter
4.1

1   The area covered by this chapter includes:

    Massachusetts Bay, including Cape Cod Bay and the entrance to Cape Cod Canal (41°47′N 70°29′W).

    The port of Boston and its seaward approach from the S end of Nantucket Shoals (40°35′N 69°00′W).

    The inshore waters on the E side of Nantucket Sound and Cape Cod.

Pilotage
4.2

1   Pilotage is compulsory for merchant vessels with a draught of 2·1 m (7 ft) or over entering all ports in Massachusetts Bay. Arrangements for pilots should be made 24 hours in advance.

Regulations
4.3

1   **Navigation Rules for US Inland Waters** apply to the waters of the ports of Gloucester, Salem and Boston and the Cape Cod Canal. The limits of the waters to which these rules apply are given in each section. See 1.47 and Appendix VII for further information.

Submarine pipeline
4.4

1   **Gas pipeline.** A gas pipeline extends from Danvers River (4.50) to North Weymouth (42°14′·8N 70°57′·8W) passing through Beverley Channel (4.50), Salem Sound (4.28), Marblehead Channel (4.39), Childrens Island Channel (4.40), Black Rock Channel (4.104), Nantasket Roads (4.110), and Weymouth Fore River (4.118).

    Caution. See 1.39.

Stellwagen Bank National Marine Sanctuary
4.5

1   The Stellwagen Bank National Marine Sanctuary consists of an area of about 638 sq nautical miles situated in the approaches to Massachusetts Bay (42°25′N 70°20′W). The limits of the area surround Stellwagen Bank, Tillies Bank to the NE of Stellwagen Bank, and portions of Jeffreys Ledge to the N of Stellwagen Bank. This area also includes parts of the TSS off Cape Cod.

2   For information on Marine Sanctuaries see 1.45.

Designated Critical Habitat
4.6

1   Designated critical habitats have been established for the Northern right whale (*Eubalaena glacialis*) as follows:

    Cape Cod Bay, Massachusetts. The area bounded by 42°04′·8N 70°10′W; 42°12′N 70°15′W; 42°12′N 70°30′W; 41°46′·8N 70°30′W and on the S and E by the shoreline of Cape Cod.

2   Great South Channel. The area bounded by 41°40′N 69°45′W; 41°00′N 69°05′W; 41°38′N 68°13′W; and 42°10′N 68°31′W.

    The designated critical habitats delineate the only known areas where these whales calve.

3   Northern right whales are the most endangered large whale species in the world with only about 300 in existence. These slow-moving animals are vulnerable to collisions as they can be difficult to spot, often do not move out of the way of approaching ships, and mate, rest, feed and nurse their young on the surface.

4   It is recommended that the following measures be taken to reduce the risk of collision when operating in the critical habitat:

    As soon as possible, prior to entry, check USCG Broadcast Notice to Mariners, NAVTEX, Coast Pilot, local pilots and other sources for recent right whale sighting reports.

5   Keep a good lookout for whales during daylight hours.

    Attempt to avoid passage through the area by remaining offshore and minimize the distance travelled through the area when entering or leaving port. Try to avoid night time transits.

6   When and where possible ships should proceed at a maximum speed of 14 kn.

    If a right whale is reported within 20 nautical miles of a vessel's position, post a lookout, exercise caution and proceed at a safe speed, bearing in mind that reduced speed may minimize the risk of collision.

7   Do not assume right whales will move out of your way. They are generally slow moving and seldom travel faster than 5 to 6 kn. Consistent with safe navigation, manoeuvre around observed right whales or the positions of recently reported sightings.

8   Any whale accidentally struck, any dead whale, or any whale observed entangled in fishing gear should be reported immediately to the USCG on VHF channel 16 noting the precise location, date, and time of the accident or sighting. In the event of a strike or sighting, amplifying information such as the speed of the vessel, size of the vessel, water depth, wind speed and direction, description of the impact, fate of the whale, species and size should be reported if known.

9   Right whales can occur anywhere along the E coast of the USA. Therefore, mariners are urged to exercise prudent seamanship with regard to right whales at all times when transiting the E coast of the USA.

    For regulations affecting approach and avoidance of right whales, see Appendix VIII.

North-east Northern right whale Mandatory Ship Reporting (MSR) System
4.7

1   A mandatory ship reporting system (MSR) (WHALESNORTH) covering Cape Cod Bay, Massachusetts Bay and the Great South Channel E and SE of Massachusetts has been established for the protection of the Northern right whale. The system is in operation all year

round and the area is bounded by the following co-ordinates:

2   Point on Cape Ann (42°39'·2N 70°35'·8W).
       42°45'·0N 70°13'·0W.
       42°10'·0N 68°31'·0W.
       41°00'·0N 68°31'·0W.
       41°00'·0N 69°17'·0W.
       42°05'·0N 70°02'·0W.
       42°04'·0N 70°07'·7W.

3   Thence along the Massachusetts shoreline of Cape Cod

and Massachusetts Bay to a point on Cape Ann (42°39'·2N 70°35'·8W).

See *Admiralty List of Radio Signals Volume 6(5)* for details.

Tidal streams
4.8

1   Tidal streams in Massachusetts Bay are generally weak except in the narrow entrances to the rivers and harbours. See Tidal Stream tables on the charts.

NORTH PART OF MASSACHUSETTS BAY

COASTAL PASSAGE BETWEEN CAPE ANN AND BOSTON HARBOR

General information

Chart 1227
Description
4.9

1   Between Cape Ann (42°38'N 70°36'W) and Boston Harbor, 24 miles SW, the coast is rocky and generally bold with many dangers extending up to 3 miles offshore.

Ship Reporting System
4.10

1   For details of a mandatory reporting system for the Northern right whale see 4.7 and *Admiralty List of Radio Signals Volume 6(5)*.

Local magnetic anomaly
4.11

1   The normal magnetic variation has sometimes been increased by 3° in the vicinity of Cape Ann and Gloucester Harbor.

Directions
(continued from 3.287)

Principal marks
4.12

1   **Major lights:**
       Cape Ann Light (42°38'N 70°35'W) (3.286).
       Eastern Point Light (42°35'N 70°40'W) (4.19).
       Bakers Island Light (42°32'N 70°47'W) (4.36).

Other aids to navigation
4.13

1   **Racon:**
       B Light buoy (safe water) (42°23'N 70°47'W).
       See *Admiralty List of Radio Signals Volume 2* for details.

Cape Ann to Boston Harbor
4.14

1   From a position about 2½ miles E of Thacher Island the coastal route to Boston Harbor leads SW, passing (with positions relative to Bakers Island (42°32'N 70°47'W)):

SE of Thacher Island (13 miles ENE) (3.287), thence:
SE of a dangerous wreck (8½ miles ENE), thence:
NW of ODAS A Light–buoy (special) (10 miles E), thence:

2   SE of Burnham Rocks and Saturday Night Ledge (5 miles E). These rocky patches lie in the approaches to Salem Sound (4.28). Thence:
SE of No 1 Light–buoy (port hand) (2½ miles SE), which marks the extremity of the shoal water that extends 2 miles SE from Bakers Island (4.38), thence:

3   SE of No 4 Light–buoy (starboard hand) (5 miles SSW) moored E of Great Pig Rocks (4.54), the SE dangers of the foul ground that extends SE from the shore between Marblehead Neck (4.51) and Grass Head, 3 miles SW, thence:
Clear of B Light–buoy (safe water) in the centre of the Precautionary Area (4.66).

(Directions for Boston Harbor continue at 4.95)

Gloucester Harbor

Charts 1227, 2487 plan of Gloucester Harbor
General information
4.15

1   **Position.** Gloucester Harbor (42°36'N 70°40'W) is situated on the S side of Cape Ann. The city of Gloucester, which is of great historical interest, covers the greater part of Cape Ann.

Function. Gloucester Harbor is one of the most important fishing ports in the United States. It is also a port of entry and an important harbour of refuge. In 2005 Gloucester had an estimated population of 30 713.

Its principal industries are connected with fishing and fish products.

2   **Port limits.** Inner Harbor consists of the waters within a line joining Fort Point (4.23) (42°36'·5N 70°39'·9W) and Black Rock (4.23), 1½ cables SE.

Port Authority. Gloucester Port Authority, 19 Harbor Loop, Gloucester, MA 01930, USA.

Limiting conditions
4.16

1   **Depths.** The main entrance channel to the outer harbour, which leads between shoals extending from Round Rock Shoal (4.20) and Mussel Point, has depths of 11·6 to 15·9 m (38 to 52 ft).

The dredged Entrance Channel to Inner Harbor has a mid–channel controlling depth of 6·1 m (20 ft) (2004). There are mid–channel controlling depths of 3·8 to 5·5 m

(12·5 to 18 ft) (2004) in various access channels within Inner Harbor.

2   For the latest controlling depths the charts and port authority should be consulted.

Deepest berth. See 4.26.

Tidal levels. Mean range of tide about 2·7 m.

Largest vessel. Length 152 m, draught 7·3 m.

Ice seldom extends outside Tenpound Island at the entrance to Inner Harbor and the movement of boats normally keeps Inner Harbor open.

3   **Weather.** During heavy SE gales the sea at times breaks nearly the whole distance across the entrance. Strangers should enter by the deepest channel W of Round Rock Shoal, where there is reported to be a space known not to break.

Arrival information

4.17

1   **Port operations.** Speed limit of 5 kn is enforced in Inner Harbor.

Notice of ETA. 24 hours.

Outer anchorages. See 4.24.

Pilotage. See 4.2. The pilot normally embarks in the vicinity of No 2 Light–buoy (starboard hand), which is situated 1 mile SE of the harbour entrance.

2   **Tugs.** The nearest tugs are stationed at Boston and the pilot boat normally acts in this capacity for vessels up to 6000 gt.

3   **Traffic regulations.** Navigation Rules for US Inland Waters apply within a line joining the W end of the harbour breakwater and a point on the shore below the stone building with twin towers, 2 cables WSW of Mussel Point (4.18). See 1.47 and Appendix VII for further information.

Harbour

4.18

1   **General layout.** Gloucester Harbor consists of an outer harbour and an inner harbour.

The outer harbour, which extends 1½ miles N, is entered between Eastern Point (42°35′N 70°40′W) and Mussel Point, 1 mile WNW. The harbour is partially protected by a breakwater which extends 4 cables WNW from Eastern Point. There are a number of coves within the harbour.

2   Inner Harbor is entered from the NE part of the outer harbour. Within the harbour, Harbor Cove lies to the NW of the entrance and Smith Cove is entered on the SE side. An anchorage, alongside berths and port facilities are situated in Inner Harbor.

3   **Measured distance.** Off the W side of the entrance to Gloucester Harbor there is a measured distance.

N marks: Beacons (white tripods) on Dolliver Neck (4.22) in line bearing 295°.

4   **S marks:** Beacon (white tripod) on the shore and a painted mark on Norman's Woe Rock (4.20), the latter being sometimes difficult to distinguish from guano. No 3 Buoy (port hand) is moored on this transit.

Distance: 1 mile.

Running track: 025°/205°.

5   **Tidal streams** set directly in and out of the outer harbour and their rates are comparatively small. In the entrance to Inner Harbor the tidal streams are stronger, especially with the out–going stream.

Gloucester Inner Harbour from SSE (4.18)

(Original dated 2005)

(Photograph – David M. Walker – Reproduced by permission of Marblehead Sail & Power Squadron, United States Power Squadrons)

Principal marks
4.19

1 **Landmarks:**

Square tower (42°36'·8N 70°40'·6W).

Spire (42°36'·8N 70°40'·0W).

Major light:

Eastern Point Light (white conical tower and dwelling, 11 m in height) (42°35'N 70°40'W).

Directions
4.20

1 **Main entrance.** From the vicinity of the pilot boarding position (42°34'N 70°40'W) the route to the entrance of Gloucester Harbor leads NW, passing (with positions relative to Eastern Point Light):

2 SW of Eastern Point Light, keeping clear of a dangerous wreck which lies 5 cables SSW of Eastern Point, thence:

SW of Gloucester Breakwater Light (white tower on brown square framework tower, 11 m in height) (4 cables WNW), which stands at the head of the breakwater that extends WNW from Eastern Point, thence:

3 Between Norman's Woe Rock (1¼ miles W), a rounded rocky islet 14 m in height; and RR Light–buoy (preferred channel to port) (7 cables W), moored off the SW edge of Round Rock Shoal (6 cables WNW). Thence:

Between Round Rock Shoal and Mussel Point (4.18), the W entrance point to Gloucester Harbor.

4 Thence the track leads into the outer harbour.

Useful mark:

Twin towers on stone building (42°35'N 70°42'W).

Caution. Owing to the irregular depths and many dangers in Gloucester Harbor and its approaches, careful navigation is necessary, particularly in thick weather.

4.21

1 **Dog Bar Channel** (42°35'·0N 70°40'·5W) leads between Dog Bar, on which the breakwater is built, and Round Rock Shoal. It has a least depth of 5·2 m (17 ft) and a width of 160 m. The channel is marked on its E side by 2DB Buoy (starboard hand), and on its W side by 1DB Buoy (port hand) at the NE edge of Round Rock Shoal.

2 During SE gales the sea at times breaks nearly the whole distance across the entrance and local knowledge is required to navigate this channel.

4.22

1 **Outer harbour.** From the harbour entrance the track through the outer harbour leads NNE, passing (with positions relative to Tenpound Island Light (42°36'N 70°40'W)):

ESE of Dolliver Neck (1 mile SW), on which stand the beacons of the N end of the measured mile (4.18), thence:

2 Between No 7 Light–buoy (port hand) (5 cables WSW), which marks the E side of Prairie Ledge, a danger that lies in the outer part of Freshwater Cove, and No 6 Buoy (starboard hand) (4 cables SW) which marks a 4·9 m (16 ft) patch, thence:

WNW of Tenpound Island Ledge (3 cables SW), thence:

3 WNW of Tenpound Island Light, which stands on the W end of Tenpound Island. Mayflower Ledge lies 1½ cables SW of the light and is marked by No 8 Buoy (starboard hand).

Thence the track leads into Inner Harbor.

4 **Useful mark:**

Square tower (42°36'·8N 70°40'·6W).

4.23

1 **Inner Harbor.** The Entrance Channel to Inner Harbour leads NE passing between Fort Point (42°36'·5N 70°39'·9W) and Rocky Neck, which is high and partly wooded. The entrance is marked by No 11 Light–buoy (port hand); Babson Ledge, which is marked by No 9 Buoy (port hand), lies 1 cable W of No 11 Light–buoy.

2 Within the entrance the Entrance Channel divides into North Channel and South Channel which lead, either side of the Gloucester State Fish Pier, to the head of the harbour. Channels are marked by port and starboard hand buoys.

Leaving harbour. Vessels leaving Inner Harbor on the out–going stream should keep to the NW side of the channel when passing between Fort Point and No 12 Beacon on Black Rock.

Anchorages in the outer harbour
4.24

1 **Southeast Harbor** (42°35'·8N 70°39'·5W), which provides the best anchorage for vessels seeking shelter or bound for Inner Harbor, lies on the E side of the outer harbour between Black Bess Point, 5 cables N of Eastern Point, and Tenpound Island.

This cove, also known locally as Pancake Ground, provides good anchorage in depths of about 7 to 9 m (23 to 30 ft), soft mud and clay.

2 **Western Harbor** (42°36'·5N 70°40'·5W) lies at the S entrance to the Blynman Canal between Fort Point and Stage Head. This cove provides good anchorage in depths of 7 to 9 m (23 to 30 ft), soft mud and clay. The shore should be given a berth of 1½ cables.

Tidal streams at the entrance to the Blynman Canal average over 3 kn in strength.

Berths in Inner Harbor
4.25

1 **Anchorages.** A dredged anchorage, which is shown on the chart, is situated 1½ cables SW of the head of the State Fish Pier. In 2004 it had depths of 4 to 5 m (14 to 16 ft).

4.26

1 **Alongside berths.** There are many wharves within the Inner Harbor, most of which are used by the fishing industry. The principal wharves are (with positions relative to Fort Point (42°36'·5N 70°39'·9W)):

Gloucester State Fish Pier. NW side (7 cables NE). 305 m in length with reported depth alongside of 7·3 m.

2 Rogers Street Wharf (4 cables NE). 91 m in length with reported depth alongside of 7·6 m.

Rowe Square Wharf (4½ cables NE). 137 m in length with reported depth alongside of 6·7 m.

East Main Street Wharf (4 cables E). 110 m in length with reported depth alongside of 6·4 m.

Port services
4.27

1 **Repairs.** There are shipyards on Rocky Neck where repairs can be carried out. Repair berth has a length 82 m; reported depth alongside of 4·6 to 4·9 m.

Patent slip is available capable of handling craft of up to 44 m in length and up to 600 gt.

2 **Other facilities:** hospital; oily waste disposal.

Supplies: fuel; water; provisions and stores.

Rescue. A Coast Guard station is situated on the E side of Harbor Cove.

SALEM SOUND AND ADJACENT WATERS

General information

Charts 1227, 2427
Description
4.28

1 Salem Sound and the harbours of Manchester (42°34′N 70°47′W), Beverly (42°33′N 70°53′W), Salem (42°31′N 70°52′W) and Marblehead (42°30′N 70°51′W) lie in a large irregular indentation in the NW part of Massachusetts Bay. This indentation is entered between Gales Point (42°33′·6N 70°46′·8W) to the N and Marblehead Neck, 4 miles SW. The area is obstructed by numerous islands and rocks, above and below–water, through which several channels lead to the various harbours.

2 Outside this indentation the coast between Gloucester Harbor and Gales Point is indented by several shallow and unimportant coves and is fronted by numerous islands and rocks, above and below–water, which extend up to 1 mile offshore.

Channel depths
4.29

1 In 2002 the dredged section of Salem Channel, the N most important and deepest channel, had controlling depths of 9 m (29½ ft) in the channel and 8·2 m (27 ft) in the turning basin.

Childrens Island Channel, the middle channel, has depths of 7·9 m (26 ft).

2 In Marblehead Channel, the SW channel, all dangers in the fairway of less than 5·5 m (18 ft) are marked.

For the latest controlling depths the charts and port authorities should be consulted.

Pilotage and tugs
4.30

1 **Pilotage** to the ports in this area is compulsory for all foreign vessels, and all US vessels under register in the foreign trade which draw over 2·1 m.

The pilot, provided by Gloucester (4.17), normally embarks in the vicinity of No 2 Light–buoy (42°34′N 70°40′W) S of Eastern Point (4.18).

2 **Tugs** from Boston, for vessels entering Salem, normally join vessels off No 16 Light–buoy (42°32′·2N 70°51′·2W).

Local knowledge
4.31

1 Local knowledge is required to navigate all channels except for Salem Channel.

Traffic regulations
4.32

1 **Navigation Rules for US Inland Waters** apply inshore of lines joining Gales Point (42°33′·6N 70°46′·7W) to Marblehead Light (42°30′·3N 70°50′·0W), as shown on the chart. See 1.47 and Appendix VII for further information.

Safety and security zone. A safety and security zone surrounds Salem Terminal Wharf (4.46).

Submarine pipeline
4.33

1 **Gas pipeline.** A gas pipeline, as shown on the chart, is laid through Salem Sound and its approaches. See 4.4.

Special anchorages
4.34

1 Special anchorages, the positions of which are shown on the chart, are established in Beverly Harbor (4.50), Salem Harbor (4.41) and Marblehead Harbor (4.51). See 1.49.

Natural conditions
4.35

1 **Tidal streams** are weak in Salem and Marblehead Harbors, but have considerable rates in Beverly Harbor, where they set across the channel in places.

2 **Ice** does not seriously effect the harbours in this area except during unusually severe winters when it may extend as far out as Great Haste (42°32′·1N 70°50′·5W) and very occasionally as far as Eagle Island (42°31′·5N 70°48′·8W). Of the ports in the area Marblehead Harbor is the least likely to be obstructed by ice.

3 **Fog** presents a problem all the year round, being worst during the late spring and early summer.

Directions

Principal marks
4.36

1 **Landmarks:**
Tower (27 m (90 ft) in elevation) (42°33′·7N 70°46′·4W), on Gales Point.
Spire (tallest) (42°32′·9N 70°52′·7W). Rear mark of Salem Channel entrance transit.
Spire (42°33′·0N 70°52′·7W).
Radio tower (42°31′·1N 70°51′·7W).

2 Chimney (42°31′·0N 70°53′·2W).
Water tower (42°30′·6N 70°51′·4W).
Water tower (conical top) (42°30′·1N 70°51′·9W).
Major Lights:
Eastern Point Light (42°34′·8N 70°39′·9W) (4.19).
Bakers Island Light (white conical tower) (42°32′·2N 70°47′·2W).

Eastern Point to Salem Channel
4.37

1 From the vicinity of the pilot boarding position S of No 2 Light–buoy (42°34′N 70°40′W), SE of the entrance to Gloucester Harbor, the route to the entrance of Salem Channel (Main Ship Channel) leads generally WSW, passing (with positions relative to Bakers Island Light (42°32′N 70°47′W)):
NNW of Kettle Island Ledge (4 miles E), thence:

2 SSE of Kettle Island (3¼ miles NE), partly wooded, which lies in the entrance to Magnolia Harbor (4.48), and:
Clear, depending on draught, of Middle Ground (3½ miles ENE), thence:
SSE of Great Egg Rock (2¾ miles NE), bare, thence:

3 NNW of the foul ground which extends SE from Bakers Island to Newcomb Ledge, marked on its N side by Nos 3, 5 and 7 Buoys (port hand) (2 miles, 1¼ miles and 5 cables, respectively, ESE). In this area are Southeast Breakers, Middle Breakers and Searle Rock, all of which break in heavy weather. No 1 Light–buoy (port hand) lies 5 cables farther SE of this foul ground. And:

4 SSE of No 6 Buoy (starboard hand) (1¼ miles NE), which marks the S edge of a bank on which lie Gales Ledge and Pilgrim Ledge. A rock, with a depth of 11 m (36 ft) over it, lies 2 cables SE of the buoy.

5 **Caution.** In view of the irregular depths in the approaches to the harbours of Beverly, Salem and

Marblehead and of the islands and rocks, above and below–water, on either side of the channels, caution is necessary for their navigation at all times; in thick weather local knowledge is necessary. Without local knowledge approach should only be made by Salem Channel.

(Directions continue for Eagle Island Channel at 4.40)

Salem Channel

4.38

1   **Leading lights:**

Front light (white pyramidal tower) (42°32'·8N 70°51'·4W), standing on Hospital Point.

Rear light (1 mile from front light) (light on tallest of two church spires; see 4.36).

2   The alignment (276¼°) of these lights leads W from S of No 6 Buoy, passing (with positions relative to Bakers Island Light (42°32'·2N 70°47'·2W)):

S of Whaleback (7 cables N), a dangerous rock awash, just outside the entrance to Manchester Bay, on which stands No 8 Beacon (red daymark), thence:

3   N of No 9 Light–buoy (port hand) (2 cables NNW) which marks Powers Rock, a danger that lies at the N end of shoal water extending from Bakers Island. This island, which is prominent, is 30 m in height, with numerous houses standing on it. Thence:

4   N of SE Buoy (preferred channel to starboard) (5 cables WNW), which lies in the N entrance to Eagle Island Channel (4.40), thence:

S of No 10 Light–buoy (starboard hand) (7½ cables WNW) which lies at the SW end of the shoal ground extending from Little Misery Island, which lies close S of Great Misery Island. A rock with a depth of 10·1 m (33 ft) over it lies ½ cable WSW of the light–buoy. Thence:

5   N of No 11 Light–buoy (port hand) (1 mile WNW), which lies on the N side of the shoal ground surrounding Bowditch Ledge. This ledge is marked by a beacon (red and white diamond daymark on conical granite monument, 9 m (30 ft) in height). Thence:

S of No 12 Light–buoy (starboard hand) (1½ miles WNW), which lies on the S side of John Ledge. Thence into Salem Sound.

(Directions for Salem Harbor continue at 4.45)

Marblehead Channel

4.39

1   From a position SW of Halfway Rock, (42°30'·1N 70°46'·5W), high, bare and resembling a sugar loaf, the route through Marblehead Channel leads WNW, NW and then N, passing (with positions relative to Marblehead Light (42°30'N 70°50'W)):

2   NNE of Tinkers Ledge (1¾ miles SE) and, depending on draught, clear of a number of other unmarked shoals with depths of 4·3 to 7·3 m (14 to 24 ft), which extend up to 9 cables E of Marblehead Neck. These shoals break in E gales. Thence:

3   Clear of FR Light–buoy (preferred channel to port) (7 cables E), which marks Fifteen Foot Rock, thence:

NE of Marblehead Rock (4 cables ESE), which is high and bare, and:

SW of Childrens Island (9 cables NE), which is bare with several houses near its centre, thence:

4   NE of Marblehead Light (brown square framework tower, black top, 32 m in height), standing on the N point of Marblehead Neck. Nos 1 and 1MH Buoys (both port hand) mark the shoal ground off this point. Thence:

E of the entrance to Marblehead Harbor (4.51) and W of No 2 Buoy (starboard hand) (6 cables NE), which marks Archer Rock lying to the W of Childrens Island, thence:

5   E of Chappel Ledge (9 cables NNE), marked on its E side by No 3 Light–buoy (port hand), which lies on the N side of the entrance to South Channel (4.40), and:

W of the entrance to Eagle Island Channel (4.40), marked by No 4 Light–buoy (starboard hand), thence:

6   Between No 5 Buoy (port hand) (1¼ miles N) and No 6 Buoy (starboard hand) (1½ miles NNE). These buoys mark, respectively, the E side of the shoal water upon which lie Coney Island and Coney Ledge, and the W side of Eagle Bar. Thence into Salem Sound, keeping clear of an obstruction, the position of which is approximate, and a wreck, with a depth of 9·8 m (32 ft) over it, (both 2 miles NNE).

Other Channels

(continued from 4.37)

4.40

1   **Eagle Island Channel**, which is buoyed and sheltered, leads SW from the entrance to Salem Channel to Marblehead Channel at the entrance to Marblehead Harbor, passing (with positions relative to Bakers Island Light (42°32'N 70°47'W)):

2   Between Bakers Island and Hardy Rocks (6 cables W). HR Beacon (red and white daymark) stands on Hardy Rocks. Thence:

Between Nos 5 and 6 Buoys (lateral) (9 cables SW), which mark the channel between Pope Head, a rugged rock, and Cutthroat Shoal which lies on the N part of Eagle Bar, thence:

3   Between Brimbles (1¼ miles SW), a rock awash marked by a beacon, and Eagle Island, a rocky island covered in grass, thence into Marblehead Channel.

This channel is used by craft bound for Marblehead Harbor from the NE. Local knowledge is required.

4   **Childrens Island Channel** is entered from W of Halfway Rock (42°30'N 70°47'W) (4.39) and leads NW between Satan Rock (42°30'·6N 70°48'·1W), above–water and marked by No 6 Beacon, and Childrens Island (4.39). The channel then leads between Brimbles and No 7 Buoy (port hand), which marks Martin Rock, into Marblehead Channel SW of Eagle Island.

Local knowledge is required.

5   **South Channel**, which is winding and in places less than ½ cable wide, leads W along the NW side of the peninsula which separates Marblehead Harbor from Salem Harbor.

Local knowledge is required.

Salem Harbor

General information

4.41

1   **Position.** Salem Harbor (42°31'N 70°52'W) lies SW of Salem Sound. The city of Salem lies on the W side of the harbour.

Function. Salem is a port of entry and its chief water–borne trade is in coal and petroleum. In 2005 Salem had an estimated population of 41 756.

2   **Approach and entry.** Salem Harbor is approached by a dredged channel from the SW part of Salem Sound and entered between Naugus Head (42°31′N 70°52′W) and Winter Island on the E side of Salem Neck.

Traffic. In 2005 the port was used by 2 vessels with a total deadweight 101 551 tonnes.

Port Authority. New England Power Company.

Limiting Conditions
4.42

1   **Depths.** Dredged channel controlling depth (2002) 9 m (29½ ft), thence 8·2 m (27 ft) in the turning basin. For the latest controlling depths the charts and port authority should be consulted.

Deepest berth. See 4.46.

2   **Tidal levels.** Mean spring range about 2·9 m; mean neap range about 2·1 m. See information in *Admiralty Tide Tables.*

Maximum size of vessel handled. Length 213 m, draught 10·4 m.

3   **Ice.** The head of Salem Harbor on the flats is usually closed by ice every winter during January and February, but ice formations rarely extend beyond Salem Terminal Wharf except in very severe winters.

N and NW winds enhance local ice formation. S and SW winds can carry light ice formations out to sea and E winds break up ice within the harbour and its approaches.

Natural conditions. See 4.35.

Arrival information
4.43

1   **Port operations.** Speed limit of 5 kn within the harbour limits.

Notice of ETA. 24 hours.

2   **Outer anchorages.** Good anchorage may be obtained in depths of 6 to 15 m (20 to 50 ft) in Salem Sound, clear of a gas pipeline, NE of a line drawn between Curtis Point (42°32′·9N 70°50′·7W) and the NE extremity of Eagle Island (2 miles SE).

Submarine pipeline. A gas pipeline is laid through Salem Sound. See 1.39 and 4.4.

3   **Pilotage.** See 4.30.

Tugs. See 4.30.

Traffic regulations. A safety and security zone surrounds Salem Terminal Wharf (4.46). See Appendix V for general rules covering safety and security zones.

Time of berthing. Daylight hours with a rising tide.

Harbour
4.44

1   **General layout.** Berths are situated on the NW side of the harbour. Large vessels berth at the power station at the end of the dredged channel.

The head of Salem Harbor is shallow.

Tidal streams. See 4.35.

Directions
(continued from 4.38)
4.45

1   From Salem Sound the entrance channel to Salem Harbor leads SW, passing (with positions relative to Naugus Head (42°31′N 70°52′W)):

NW of Nos 13 and 15 Light–buoys (port hand) (1½ miles NE), the latter marking Haste Shoal, thence:

2   SE of No 16 Light–buoy (starboard hand) (1 mile NNE), which lies at the entrance to the dredged channel, thence:

Between two pairs of buoys and light–buoys that mark the channel, and into the harbour.

3   **Useful marks:**

Fort Pickering Light (white conical tower, concrete base) (4 cables NNW), which stands on the SE point of Winter Island.

Five chimneys (42°31′·5N 70°52′·6W).

Salem from ENE (4.44)
(Original dated 2005)

(Photograph – Reproduced by permission of Marblehead Sail & Power Squadron, United States Power Squadrons)

Berths
4.46
1   **Alongside berth.** Salem Terminal Wharf (6 cables W of Naugus Head). 250 m in length, with dolphins, with a depth alongside of 10·4 m. Used to supply fuel to the power station.

Other wharves are in ruins or in various stages of disrepair or disuse.

Port services
4.47
1   **Facilities:** oily waste disposal.
Supplies: fuel; water; provisions and stores.

Anchorages and harbours

Magnolia Harbor
4.48
1   **General information.** Magnolia Harbor (42°34'·5N 70°43'·2W), the largest cove between Gloucester and Gales Point (4.28), lies 2½ miles W of Eastern Point and is used by small craft.

Manchester Harbor
4.49
1   **General information.** Manchester Harbor (42°34'·1N 70°46'·5W) is principally a yachting centre with a small amount of commercial fishing. It is approached through the Manchester Channel, a buoyed and dredged channel, leading from the NE part of Manchester Bay.

Beverly Harbor
4.50
1   **General information.** Beverly Harbor (42°32'·5N 70°52'·0W) is N of Salem Neck and lies at the W end of Salem Sound. It is formed by the confluence of the North River, Danvers River and Bass River which flow into the head of the harbour from S, W and N respectively.

2   The harbour is entered between Juniper Point (42°32'N 70°52'W), the NE extremity of Salem Neck, and Hospital Point, 8 cables NNE. Beverly Channel, which is buoyed, leads from the entrance to the inner harbour.

A gas pipeline is laid through Danvers River and Beverly Harbor (see 4.4).

The city of Beverly stands on the N side of the harbour.
Local knowledge is required.

Marblehead Harbor
4.51
1   **General information.** Marblehead Harbor (42°30'N 70°51'W), 1 mile long and 3½ cables wide, lies to the SE of the Marblehead Peninsula and is formed by Marblehead Neck, high and rocky, and Back Beach, a narrow ridge with a causeway connecting the neck with the mainland. It is entered between the N end of Marblehead Neck and Fort Sewall, 4 cables WNW.

2   Marblehead on the W and Marblehead Neck on the E are both important resorts, and the harbour is a very important yachting centre.

3   **Ice** rarely interferes with navigation in the harbour. However the winter of 2004 was the coldest in over 100 years leading to extensive ice formation. The harbour is used as a refuge when Gloucester, Salem or Lynn Harbors are ice-bound.

INSHORE WATERS BETWEEN MARBLEHEAD NECK AND BROAD SOUND

General information
Chart 1227 (see 1.17)
Extent of area
4.52
1   The area covered by this section includes:
     The foul ground between Marblehead Neck (42°30'N 70°50'W) and Phillips Point, 3 miles SW.
     Nahant Bay.
     North part of Broad Sound including Lynn Harbor.

Principal marks
4.53
1   **Landmarks:**
     Water Tower (conical top) (42°30'N 70°52'W) (Chart 2427).
     Water tower (42°28'·7N 70°54'·6W).
     Cupola (42°28'·2N 70°54'·6W) on a school in Swampscott.
     Spire (42°28'N 70°55'W).
     Spire (42°28'·1N 70°56'·5W).
2   Observatory (42°28'N 70°57'W).
     Two concrete observation towers (42°25'·0N 70°54'·6W).
     Concrete observation tower (42°25'N 70°56'W).
   Major light:
     Bakers Island Light (42°32'N 70°47'W) (4.36).

Marblehead Neck to Phillips Point
Charts 1227, 2427
Description
4.54
1   Between Marblehead Neck (4.51) and Phillips Point (4.56) foul ground with islets and rocks, above and below–water, extends 2½ miles S and SW of Flying Point, the S extremity of Marblehead Neck.

The outer edge of this area is marked by No 4 Light–buoy, which lies on the E side of Outer Breakers and Great Pig Rocks, which lie 1¾ miles S of Flying Point.

2   Tinkers Island and Ram Islet, high and grassy, lie 5 cables SE and 1 mile SW, respectively, of Flying Point; Roaring Bull, Little Pig Rocks and Sammy Rock lie, respectively, 6 cables SSE and 7 cables and 1¼ miles SW of Flying Point. Roaring Bull is marked by No 2 Beacon and Sammy Rock by No 6 Buoy (starboard hand).

Channels
4.55
1   A number of channels lead through the dangers in this area. Some of these dangers are buoyed, but local knowledge is required to navigate in this area.

Nahant Bay
Chart 1227
General information
4.56
1   Nahant Bay is entered between Phillips Point (42°28'N 70°54'W) and East Point, the E extremity of Nahant, a peninsula 2½ miles S.

Phillips Point is 15 m in height and rocky with houses along its shores. Dread Ledge, a rocky ledge which dries, extends 2½ cables S from Phillips Point and is marked by a beacon (starboard hand).

2 Nahant is 24 m in height with bluff seaward faces and on it stands the town of Nahant, a summer resort. Little Nahant, a high grassy head lies on the E side of Long Beach, a strip of sand that connects it to the mainland. Egg Rock, a bird sanctuary, lies 8 cables NNE of East Point.

Berths
4.57

1 **Anchorage.** The bay, which is largely clear of dangers, is exposed to S and E winds and is seldom used except for temporary anchorage which may be obtained in depths of 6 to 11 m (18 to 36 ft).

2 The usual anchorage is off Swampscott on the N shore SW or W of Lincoln House Point, a promontory which extends from the N shore 6 cables W of Phillips Point. A dangerous below–water rock, marked by No 2 Buoy (starboard hand) moored close S, lies ½ cable S of Lincoln House Point and rocks, with depths over them of 4·9 and 5·5 m (16 and 18 ft), lie 2 cables S and 3½ cables SSW, respectively, of the point.

Broad Sound

General information
4.58

1 Broad Sound is entered between East Point (42°25′N 70°54′W) and Deer Island, 5 miles SSW, and leads to Nahant Harbor on its NE side, to Lynn at its N end, to summer resorts on its W side and the N entrance to Boston Harbor at its S end.

2 The W side of the sound is very shallow with below–water and drying rocks extending up to 7½ cables offshore in places.

Dangers. Flip Rock, marked by FR buoy (preferred channel to port) and Nahant Rock, marked by C1 Buoy (port hand), lie 9 cables SSE and 8 cables SW of Bass Point, the SW point of Nahant.

3 **Safety and security zones.** Within Broad Sound a safety and security zone of 500 yards radius has been established around any LNG vessel at anchor in the area, as shown on the chart.

Entry into these zones is prohibited unless previously authorized by the Captain of the Port (COTP).

4 See Appendix V for further information, definitions and general rules covering safety and security zones.

Nahant Harbor
4.59

1 Nahant Harbor is a cove on the S side of Nahant.

Approaches. Shag Rocks, 4 cables SW of East Point, lie in the E approaches to the cove. No 2 Light–buoy (starboard hand) marks the limit of the shoal that extends S from the rocks.

2 **Directions.** From a position SW of Shag Rocks the track into the harbour leads between Joe Beach Ledge and The Spindle, which are marked, respectively, by DJB and DBR Buoys (both isolated danger). Shoal water lies between The Spindle and the W entrance point of the harbour, 3½ cables NW.

3 **Berths.** The town wharf, on the E side of the harbour near its head, has a depth alongside of 1·8 m. The Boston pilot boat lands and picks up pilots at this wharf.

Temporary anchorage, in depths of 6 to 7 m (18 to 24 ft), may be obtained off the town wharf.

Lynn Harbor
4.60

1 **General information.** Lynn Harbor is entered between Bass Point (42°25′N 70°57′W) and Revere Beach, 2 miles W. The harbour is encumbered with shoal ground and drying mud and sand flats, through which a channel leads to the industrial city of Lynn which, in 2005, had an estimated population of 88 792.

2 **Local knowledge** is required as the channels in the harbour are narrow and winding.

Controlling depths. In 1997 the mid–channel controlling depth in the dredged channel to the turning basin was 5·2 m (17 ft), thence depths of 4·3 to 4·8 m (14 to 16 ft) were available in the basin. For the latest depths the charts and port authority should be consulted.

Pilots may be obtained from the Boston pilot boat (4.89).

3 **Main approach channel,** which is dredged, is entered 7½ cables WNW of Bass Point, 1 mile N of Nahant Rock (4.58), and leads to a turning basin at the head of Lynn Harbor. The entrance to the channel is marked by No 2 Light–buoy (starboard hand) and thence by light–beacons and buoys.

An extension of the main approach channel leads SW from the turning basin to the power station. In 1985 this channel had a controlling depth of 3 m (10 ft).

4 **Other channels.** Western Channel, which is entered 1 mile W of Bass Point, leads N into Saugus River which flows into the NW part of the harbour at the Point of Pines. In 2000 this channel had a controlling depth of 2·1 m (7 ft).
4.61

1 **Anchorage** is available W of Bass Point, clear of a pipeline area shown on the chart, in depths of 9 to 2 m (30 to 5 ft).

Facilities: hospital; oily waste disposal.
Supplies: fuel; provisions; stores.

BOSTON HARBOR AND APPROACHES

APPROACHES TO BOSTON HARBOR

General information

Charts 2492, 2489, 3096, 1227
Synopsis
4.62

1 The area covered by this section includes:
The outer approaches to Boston Harbor from the S end of Nantucket Shoals (40°35′N 69°00′W) to the entrance of Massachusetts Bay, N of Race Point (42°04′N 70°15′W).

The inner approaches to Boston Harbor from the entrance of Massachusetts Bay to B Light–buoy (safe water) (42°23′N 70°47′W) in Boston Bay.

2 The inshore waters on the E side of Cape Cod, N of Monomoy Island (41°35′N 70°00′W) (5.30) but excluding the channels between Nantucket Shoals and leading into Nantucket Sound (41°30′N 70°10′W) (5.19) which are described in Chapter 5.

Description
4.63

1   The outer approaches to Boston Harbor lead from SE of Nantucket Island (41°16′N 70°05′W), between Nantucket Shoals and Georges Bank (3.1), some 45 miles ENE, thence off the E and N side of Cape Cod into Massachusetts Bay.

2   **Nantucket Shoals** (5.19) is the name given to the numerous shoals that lie E and S of Nantucket Island. The shoals extend 24 miles E and 44 miles SE from Sankaty Head (41°17′N 69°58′W) (5.21), the E extremity of Nantucket Island.

The shoals are liable to shift and their depths vary from 0·9 to 9·1 m (3 to 30 ft).

3   **Cape Cod,** a long peninsula extending 30 miles E and 25 miles N, forms the E extremity of Massachusetts. The S portion of the cape between Cape Cod Canal and Chatham is known as the Upper Cape. This region is wooded and has numerous towns and villages. The N extension of the peninsula, which is sometimes called Hook of the Cape, forms the Lower Cape. It is well settled and is composed almost entirely of sand, with high sandhills and low level plains.

Designated Critical Habitat
4.64

1   A designated critical habitat has been established for the Northern right whale (*Eubalaena glacialis*) in Great South Channel. For details see 4.6.

Ship Reporting System
4.65

1   A mandatory ship reporting system is established for the protection of the Northern right whale. For details see 4.7 and *Admiralty List of Radio Signals Volume 6(5)*.

Traffic regulations
4.66

1   **Navigation Rules for US Inland Waters** do not apply to any of the waters described in this section.

Traffic separation scheme for the approaches to Boston leads NNW and WNW from the outer Precautionary Area. This TSS is IMO–adopted and Rule 10 of the *International Regulations for Preventing Collisions at Sea (1972)* applies. The two traffic lanes are separated by a 1 mile wide separation zone. This zone is marked by light–buoys.

2   **Area to be avoided**, the limits of which are shown on the chart, is established around Nantucket Shoals. See 5.5.

Precautionary Areas. An outer Precautionary Area, centred 40°35′N 69°00′W, and with a radius of about 15 miles, has been established SE of Nantucket Island. Traffic separation schemes for New York and Boston originate from the W and N sectors, respectively, of this area.

3   An inner Precautionary Area, centred 42°23′N 70°47′W, which is marked by B Light–buoy (safe water), and with a radius of five miles, has been established in the final approaches to Boston Harbor.

Mariners should navigate with particular care within these areas.

4   **Safety and security zones.** A safety and security zone extending 2 miles ahead, 1 mile astern and 500 yards on each side has been established around any LNG vessel while underway.

Entry into these zones is prohibited unless previously authorized by the Captain of the Port (COTP).

5   For information concerning LNG vessels at anchor in Broad Sound see 4.58 and see Appendix V for further information, definitions and general rules covering safety and security zones.

Rescue
4.67

1   **Cape Cod Coast Guard Air Station** (41°37′·5N 70°31′·5W) is situated on Cape Cod at Otis Air Force Base.

Coast Guard station (41°40′N 69°57′W) is situated near Chatham Light (4.69).

Natural conditions
4.68

1   **Tidal streams** off the N and E side of Cape Cod are comparatively weak, averaging not more than ½ to 1 kn in strength and running approximately parallel to the coast, but the time of strength alters rapidly with position.

2   Off Nauset Beach Light (41°52′N 69°57′W) the N–going stream attains its highest rate about 4¼ hours before HW Boston, off Chatham (41°40′N 69°58′W) the same rate is reached about 5½ hours before HW Boston.

3   Off Race Point (42°04′N 70°15′W) the tidal streams have a rate of about 2 kn in strength. The in–going stream sets S and the out–going stream N. Tide rips occur during heavy weather when wind and stream are opposed.

See Tidal Stream table on Chart 2492 for tidal streams between Georges Bank and Nantucket Shoal.

Ice. See 1.121.

Directions
(continued from 3.5 and 5.8)

Principal marks
4.69

1   **Landmarks:**

    Cupola (41°50′·6N 69°56′·9W), part of buildings of ruined Coast Guard station.

    Radar domes (42°02′N 70°03′W).

    Pilgrim Monument (42°03′N 70°11′W) (4.153).

    Race Point Lighthouse (white tower, 12 m in height) (42°04′N 70°15′W).

2   **Major lights:**

    Sankaty Head Light (41°17′N 69°58′W) (5.21).

    Chatham Light (white conical tower, 15 m in height) (41°40′N 69°57′W).

    Nauset Beach Light (white conical tower, red top, 15 m in height) (41°52′N 69°57′W).

3   Highland Light (Cape Cod Light) (42°02′N 70°04′W), which stands on a bluff.

    Race Point Light — as above.

    Boston Light (42°20′N 70°53′W) (4.95).

Other aids to navigation
4.70

1   **Racons:**

    B Light–buoy (safe water) (42°23′N 70°47′W).

    NC Light–buoy (safe water) (42°23′N 70°54′W).

See *Admiralty List of Radio Signals Volume 2* for details.

From south-east
4.71

1   From the Precautionary Area (centred 40°35′N 69°00′W) the outer approaches to Boston lead NNW for 90 miles through a TSS, the centre of which is marked at 30 mile intervals by light–buoys (special), passing (with positions relative to Highland Light (42°02′N 70°04′W)):

2   ENE of Asia Rip, Phelps Bank, Middle Rip and Fishing Rip (66 to 82 miles SSE), banks which form the SE part of Nantucket Shoal, thence:

ENE of Davis Bank (55 miles SSE), the E part of Nantucket Shoal, thence:

3   ENE of Nauset Beach Light (12 miles SSE) (4.69). A building with a cupola stands 1 mile S. Thence:

ENE of Highland Light (4.69). A stone crenellated tower, a red brick chimney and three radar domes stand on a ridge 5 cables S of the light.

From east
4.72

1   From a position NE of Highland Light the outer approaches to Boston lead WNW for 35 miles, through a TSS to the Precautionary Area in Boston Bay at the entrance to Boston Harbor, passing (with positions relative to Race Point (42°04′N 70°15′W)):

NNE of Race Point Light (4.69). An aero light stands 1½ miles NE. Thence:

2   NNE of BE Light–buoy (special) (11 miles N) moored on the Stellwagen Bank in the separation zone of the TSS.

Thence into the Precautionary Area in Boston Bay, the E limit of which is marked by BF Light–buoy (special).

(Directions for Boston Harbor continue at 4.95 and 4.101)

Inshore waters between Chatham and Race Point

Charts 2489, 3096
General information
4.73

1   **Topography.** From Chatham (41°40′N 60°57′W), at the SE extremity of Cape Cod, to Race Point 30 miles NNW, the shore of the E and N coast of the cape consists of sand dunes which are high in places. The highest stretch of the coast, which has elevations of 45 m (150 ft), lies between Nauset Beach Light (41°52′N 69°57′W) and Highland Light, 12 miles NNW.

2   There are no sheltered anchorages along this stretch of the coast, but there are breaks in the coast that lead to Chatham Harbor and Nauset Harbor, both of which harbours can only be used by small craft.

Chatham Harbor
4.74

1   Chatham Harbor (41°40′N 69°57′W) lies between the S part of Nauset Beach, a low narrow sandy beach covered with small hillocks, and the higher land behind it. The harbour is used by small craft.

Nauset Harbor
4.75

1   Nauset Harbor (41°48′N 70°57′W), entered 3¾ miles S of Nauset Beach Light, and the area offshore of the harbour is extremely dangerous for any vessel larger than a small craft.

BOSTON HARBOR AND FINAL APPROACHES

General information

Charts 1516, 1528
Position
4.76

1   Boston Harbor (42°22′N 71°02′W) lies at the head of Boston Bay on the W side of Massachusetts Bay.

Function
4.77

1   Boston is the largest seaport in New England and the most important port on the E coast of the United States N of New York.

The city of Boston is the capital of the state of Massachusetts and is a port of entry.

Population. In 2005 Boston had an estimated population of 559 034.

Port limits
4.78

1   Boston Harbor includes all tidal waters which lie within a line joining the S point of Deer Island and Point Allerton, 3¾ miles SE.

Final approaches and entrance channels
4.79

1   Numerous dangers extend up to 4 miles off the entrance to the harbour. A number of channels lead between these dangers.

Boston North Channel (4.97), entered 2 miles W of The Graves (42°22′N 70°52′W), is the main entrance channel used by deep–draught vessels visiting the port of Boston.

2   **Boston South Channel** (4.98), entered 1½ miles WSW of The Graves, is rarely used by deep–draught vessels.

Hypocrite Channel (4.99), entered 1¼ miles SW of the Graves, has several unmarked dangers. Local knowledge is required for its navigation and its use by large vessels is not recommended.

3   **South entrance channel** (4.101), entered 2¾ miles S of The Graves, is used by deep–draught vessels and leads to Nantasket Roads (4.110) and the port facilities in the S part of Boston Harbor.

Traffic
4.80

Traffic. In 2005 the port was used by 171 vessels with a total deadweight 14 398 948 tonnes.

Port Authority
4.81

1 Massachusetts Port Authority, One Harborside Drive, Suite 200S, East Boston, MA 02128-2909.
Internet. www.massport.com

Limiting conditions

Controlling depths
4.82

1 Boston North Channel (4.97) has a project depth of 12·2 m (40 ft) in the E part and 10·7 m (35 ft) in the W part.
Boston South Channel (4.98) has a project depth of 9·1 m (30 ft).
Boston Main Channel (4.100) has a project depth of 12·2 m (40 ft). The NE half of the channel from President Roads to Commonwealth Pier No 5 (4.114) and the SW half of the channel just NW of Commonwealth Pier No 5 to the Charles River (4.123) has a project depth of 10·7 m (35 ft).

2 South entrance channel (4.101) and channel to Weymouth Fore River (4.102) have a project depth of 10·7 m (35 ft).
For the latest depths the charts and port authority should be consulted.

Vertical clearance
4.83

1 Tobin Memorial Bridge (42°23′N 71°03′W), a fixed bridge which crosses the entrance to the Mystic River, has a vertical clearance of 41·1 m (135 ft).

2 Two lifting bridges cross the lower part of the Chelsea River, the Andrew P. McArdle Bridge at the entrance and the Chelsea Street Bridge, 8 cables upstream. The former has a vertical clearance of 6·1 m (20 ft) when closed and the latter has a vertical clearance of 2·7 m (9 ft) when closed and 25·3 m (83 ft) when open.

Deepest and longest berths
4.84

1 See 4.113.

Tidal levels
4.85

1 Mean spring range about 3·1 m; mean neap range about 2·3 m. See information in *Admiralty Tide Tables.*

Ice
4.86

1 **Ice.** The channels of Boston Harbor are navigable throughout the year and ice rarely forms in the main channels. Occasionally during severe winters the greater part of the harbour is frozen, but shipping keeps the main channels open. The Charles, Mystic and Chelsea Rivers and the minor passages in the harbour are sometimes frozen during severe winters. When ice is prevalent the buoys may be displaced or even carried away.

Arrival information

Vessel traffic service
4.87

1 Vessel traffic service scheme is in operation for the control of shipping; see *Admiralty List of Radio Signals Volume 6(5)* for details. Positions of reporting points are shown on the chart.

Notice of ETA
4.88

1 See *Admiralty List of Radio Signals Volume 6(5)* for details.

Pilotage
4.89

1 **Pilotage** is compulsory for all foreign vessels and for US vessels under register in the foreign trade. Pilots should be contacted 2 hours in advance.
Pilots for Boston and Quincy board 1½ miles E of BG Light–buoy (safe water) (42°23′·4N 70°51′·5W). The pilot boats have black hulls and orange superstructure with the word "PILOT" on the side.

Tugs
4.90

1 **Tugs** are available and normally meet vessels off Anchorage area No 1 (42°21′N 71°02′W) or No 2 (42°20′N 70°58′W).

Traffic regulations
4.91

1 **Navigation Rules for US Inland Waters** apply within a line joining the easternmost tower at Nahant (42°25′·4N 70°54′·6W) to B Light–buoy, thence to the E radio tower at Hull (42°16′·7N 70°52′·5W). See 1.47 and Appendix VII for further information.

2 **Safety and security zones.** Numerous safety and security zones have been established within Boston Harbor and its approaches. See Appendix V for further information, definitions and general rules covering safety and security zones.

Quarantine
4.92

1 Quarantine is enforced in accordance with the regulations of the US Public Health Service.
Quarantine anchorage. See 4.108.

Boston Harbour from SE (4.93)

(Original dated 2001)

(Photograph – Joseph R Melanson of www.skypic.com)

Harbour

General layout
4.93

1 The main port facilities and berths for deep water vessels are situated in the NW part of Boston Harbor on Boston Main Channel (4.100) in South Boston, East Boston and Charlestown, and on the Chelsea and Mystic Rivers.

2 Deep water berths, which are approached by two marked channels from Nantasket Roads (4.110), are also available on the Weymouth Fore River (4.102) and in Town River Bay (4.113) in the SW part of the harbour.

Dorchester Bay (4.107) and Quincy Bay indent the W part of the harbour, and Hingham Bay and Hull Bay indent the SE part of the harbour. These bays are only used by small craft.

Natural conditions
4.94

1 **Tidal streams.** See tables on charts.
Fog is prevalent throughout the year.
Climate information. See 1.154.

Directions for entrance channels
(continued from 3.5, 4.14 and 4.72)

Principal marks
4.95

1 **Landmarks:**
Water tower (42°22′N 70°58′W), red, white and blue in colour, standing on Winthrop Head.
Tank (42°21′·3N 70°57′·6W) standing on Deer Island.
Chimney (42°20′·9N 70°57′·5W) standing on Deer Island.

Great Brewster (42°20′N 70°54′W), an island with a bluff at its N end.

2 Water tower (42°19′·3N 70°57′·9W) standing on Long Island.
Control tower (42°21′·9N 71°01′·1W) of Logan International Airport.
Dome (State House) (42°21′·5N 71°03′·8W).

3 Tower (42°18′·5N 70°53′·1W), which is turreted, standing on Point Allerton.
Tank (42°17′·4N 70°52′·8W) standing on Strawberry Hill.
Radio towers (42°16′·7N 70°52′·5W) on central part of Nantasket Beach.

4 Flagstaff (42°15′·0N 70°56′·5W) standing on Weymouth Great Hill.

Major lights:
Boston Light (white conical tower, 27 m in height) (42°19′·7N 70°53′·4W).
The Graves Light (light-grey conical granite tower, 34 m in height) (42°21′·9N 70°52′·2W).

Other aids to navigation
4.96

1 **Racons:**
B Light–buoy (safe water) (42°23′N 70°47′W).
NC Light–buoy (safe water) (42°23′N 70°54′W).
See *Admiralty List of Radio Signals Volume 2* for details.

Boston North Channel
4.97

1 From the vicinity of B Light–buoy (safe water) (42°23′N 70°47′W) the route into Boston Harbor through Boston North Channel leads W and then SW, passing (with positions relative to Green Island (42°21′·1N 70°53′·5W)):

Tanks   *Water tower*

Boston Harbor – Appr. to N Channel – Deer Island from NE (4.97)

(Original dated 2003)

(Photograph - Crown Copyright)

2   Between BG Light–buoy (safe water) (2¾ miles NE) and No 5 Light–buoy (port hand) (2 miles NE). The latter light–buoy marks the extremity of shoal water that extends 8 cables NE from The Graves. Thence:

Head, the shoal water that extends N from Lovell Island (4.103), thence:

SSE of PR Light–buoy (preferred channel to starboard) at the S end of Boston North Channel. Thence into Boston Main Channel.

N of The Graves (1¼ miles NE), a group of above and below–water rocks, upon which stands a light (4.95). Thence:

3   Clear of NC Light–buoy (safe water) (1½ miles NNW), at the entrance to Boston North Channel, thence:

Into the dredged channel (1½ miles NW), which is marked by light–buoys (lateral), thence:

4   Between Deer Island Light (red round tower, black round base) (3 miles WSW), standing 3 cables S of the S point of Deer Island, and Long Island Head. Long Island Head Light (white round tower) stands on the N point of Long Island.

Thence into Boston Main Channel (4.100).

(Directions for Boston Main Channel
continue at 4.100)

Hypocrite Channel
4.99

1   From a position S of The Graves (42°22′N 70°52′W) the track through Hypocrite Channel leads SW into the SW part of Boston South Channel, passing (with positions relative to Green Island (42°21′·1N 70°53′·5W)):

SE of Roaring Bulls (5 cables ENE), a group of rocks that partly dry, thence:

2   NW of Outer Brewster (1 mile SE). Another island, Middle Brewster, lies 5 cables WSW. Thence:

Between Green Island and Little Calf Island (4 cables SSW), thence:

SE of No 2 Buoy (starboard hand) (6 cables SW), which marks Halftide Rock, thence:

3   SE and S of Aldridge Ledge (1 mile WSW), thence:

Between No 9 Light–buoy (port hand) (1¼ miles WSW), and No 11 Buoy (port hand) (1½ miles WSW) which marks Ram Head Flats. Thence into Boston South Channel.

Boston South Channel
4.98

1   From a position E of NC Light–buoy (42°22′·5N 70°54′·3W) the route through Boston South Channel leads SW and WSW, passing (with positions relative to Green Island (42°21′·1N 70°53′·5W)):

NW of No 1 Buoy (port hand) (7 cables NNW), thence:

2   NW of No 3 Buoy (port hand) (6 cables WNW), which marks Commissioners Ledge, thence:

Between Nos 5 and 6 Light-buoys (lateral) (8 cables W), No 5 Light-buoy marks Devils Back. Thence:

NW of No 7 Buoy (port hand) (1 mile WSW), which marks Aldridge Ledge, thence:

3   Between Nos 9 and 10 Light–buoys (lateral) (1¼ miles WSW). These light–buoys mark the bend in the channel and its junction with Hypocrite Channel. Thence:

4   NNW of Nos 11 and 13 Buoys (port hand) (1½ and 2 miles WSW), which mark the N side of Ram

Boston Main Channel
(continued from 4.97)
4.100

1   Boston Main Channel, leads W, NW and then N, to the mouths of the Chelsea and Mystic Rivers (42°23′N 70°03′W), passing:

Along the S side of President Roads (4.108), thence:

Through a buoyed channel marked with light–buoys (lateral) passing N of Spectacle Island and S of Governors Island Flats, thence:

2   Between Castle Island which is connected to South Boston by filled land and Governors Island, a low lying peninsula at the S end of Logan International Airport, thence:

Between Boston and Charlestown, and East Boston, thence:

3   Clear of an obstruction (reported 2005) (42°22′·8N 71°02′·7W).

Water tower   *Long Island Bridge*

Long Island   *No 17 buoy*

Boston Inner Harbor – President Roads from ENE (4.98)
(Original dated 2003)

(Photograph – Crown Copyright)

Fort Independence

Castle Island   *Monument*

Boston – Inner Harbour – Fort Independence from ESE (4.98)
(Original dated 2003)

(Photograph – Crown Copyright)

Head of Approach   *Control tower*
Light Lane Jetty   **E Boston – Inner Harbour from S (4.98)**
(Original dated 2003)

(Photograph – Crown Copyright)

South entrance channel

(continued from 4.72)

4.101

1   From a position S of B Light–buoy (safe water) (42°23′N 70°47′W) the South entrance channel leads WSW to Nantasket Roads (4.110), passing (with positions relative to Point Allerton (42°18′·6N 70°53′·0W)):

    SE of No 2 Light–buoy (starboard hand) (3 miles NE), which lies 2 cables SE of Three and One–Half Fathoms Ledge, thence:

2   NW of No 1 Light–buoy (port hand) (2½ miles ENE), which marks the N side of Thieves Ledge, and:

    SE of No 6 Buoy (starboard hand) (1½ miles NNE) which marks Boston Ledge, thence:

3   N of Point Allerton, a headland that is backed by a hill with many buildings and a conspicuous tower on it. No 3 Light–buoy (port hand) lies 5 cables N of the point and 3 cables E of the entrance to the dredged channel.

4   The dredged part of South entrance channel, which is marked by light–buoys and buoys (lateral), leads W, then WSW, for 2 miles, passing:

    S of the shoals that lie between Little Brewster Island (1 mile NNW) and Georges Island (2 miles WNW). Boston Light (4.95) stands on Little Brewster Island. And:

5   N of the coast running W between Point Allerton and Windmill Point (1¾ miles W). Shoals and rocks extend 3 cables N from this coast.

    Thence into Nantasket Roads.

Nantasket Roads to Weymouth Fore River

4.102

1   From the E end of Nantasket Roads a channel marked by light–beacons, light–buoys and buoys, leads S and SE to the port facilities in Weymouth Fore River (42°15N 70°58′W), passing (with positions relative to Prince Head (42°17′·1N 70°56′·3W)):

2   Through Hull Gut (1¼ miles NNE), which leads between Windmill Point and the NE extremity of Peddocks Island. WP Light–beacon (red and white chequered diamond on grey framework tower) stands on Windmill Point. Thence:

3   Between Prince Head and Sheep Island (6 cables ESE). HR Light–beacon (red and white chequered diamond on grey framework tower on pile structure), marking the SE side of Harrys Rock, stands 3 cables NE of Prince Head. Thence:

4   WNW of Grape Island (1 mile SE), thence:

    SE of No 16 Light–beacon (red triangular framework tower on pile structure) (1 mile S).

    Thence into the entrance of Weymouth Fore River.

Other channels

The Narrows

4.103

1   The Narrows (42°19′·5N 70°56′·0W) is a well marked channel that leads NW from the inner end of the South entrance channel to President Roads. It is bounded on the NE by Great Brewster Spit and Lovell Island and on the SW by Georges Island and Gallops Island.

    Depths. The channel has a controlling depth of about 7·9 m (26 ft); however there are shoals of considerably lesser depth along the edges.

2   **Directions.** Because of strong currents and sharp turns it is necessary to navigate the ship by eye through the channel and care must be taken to prevent the ship being set off course by cross currents sweeping in and out of Black Rock Channel (4.104) and the channel between Gallops Island and Georges Island.

Black Rock Channel

4.104

1   Black Rock Channel (42°20′N 70°55′W) leads SW from Hypocrite Channel (4.99) to The Narrows between Great Brewster Spit on the SE and Ram Head Flats and Lovell Island on the NW.

    Local knowledge is necessary and the channel is only used by local small craft.

Nubble Channel

4.105

1   Nubble Channel (42°20′N 70°57′W), marked by buoys (lateral), leads NNW from Nantasket Roads to President Roads between Gallops Island and Long Island.

    Depths. There is a least depth of about 4·3 m (14 ft) in the channel.

Sculpin Ledge Channel

4.106

1   Sculpin Ledge Channel (42°19′N 70°59′W) leads SW between Long Island and Spectacle Island. Sculpin Ledge lies in the S part of the channel. A fish haven, with a depth of 4·3 m (14 feet) over it, lies in the channel, about 3 cables WNW of the conspicuous water tower on Long Island.

2   From the S part of Sculpin Channel a channel leads SE between West Head, the SW extremity of Long Island and Moon Head, passing under Long Island Viaduct, which has a vertical clearance of 15·5 m (51 ft).

    Depths. Channels have sufficient depth to permit the navigation of vessels with a draught of 2·4 m (8 ft).

3   **Directions.** When navigating Sculpin Ledge Channel vessels should keep to the Long Island side of the channel, keeping clear of the fish haven described above, and round the SW extremity of this island at a distance of 1½ cables before passing under the channel span of Long Island Viaduct.

    A patch with a swept depth of 1·5 m (5 ft) lies on the SE side of the viaduct.

Dorchester Bay Channel

4.107

1   A channel, used by small craft, leads through Dorchester Bay. This bay is filled with extensive flats, large areas of which nearly dry at LW and rise abruptly from the channel.

Main anchorages

President Roads

4.108

1   General Anchorage No 2 (42°20′N 70°58′W), the limits of which are shown on the chart, lies on the N side of Boston Main Channel between Deer Island and Governor Island Flats. It is the principal anchorage in Boston Harbor.

2   **Anchorage** is available in depths of 8 to 20 m (26 to 64 ft), good holding ground.

    Quarantine anchorage. The N part of the area is used as a quarantine anchorage.

    Explosives anchorage. The Captain of the Port may authorise this area to be used as an explosives anchorage, in which case vessels may have to move at short notice.

Long Island Anchorage
4.109

1   General Anchorage No 3 (42°19′N 70°57′W), the limits of which are shown on the chart, lies between Gallops Island and Georges Island on the E and Long Island on the W.

Anchorage is available in depths of up to 10 m (34 ft), good holding ground. The anchorage is sheltered from E winds.

Berths in this anchorage are allocated by the Captain of the Port.

Nantasket Roads
4.110

1   Explosive anchorages No 5 (42°18′N 70°57′W), the limits of which are shown on the chart, is situated SW of Georges Island (42°19′N 70°56′W) at the inshore end of the South entrance channel.

2   **Good anchorage** may be obtained in depths of up to 15 m (49 ft), clear of a submarine gas pipeline (4.4), and SE of a line drawn between the S extremity (42°19′·0N 70°55′·7W) of Georges Island (4.101) and 4P Light–beacon (red triangle on grey framework tower on pile structure) (2 miles SW).

Castle Island Anchorage
4.111

1   General Anchorage No 4 for small vessels (42°20′N 71°01′W), the limits of which are shown on the chart, lies in the approach to Dorchester Bay.

Anchorage is generally available in depths of 2 m (7 ft), but there is deeper water in its S part.

Inner Harbor
4.112

1   **Anchorage** in the inner harbour is only permitted in anchorage area No 1 on the N side of Boston Main Channel, 1 mile NW of Governors Island (42°20′·0N 71°00′·5W). This anchorage has depths of 8 to 10 m (26 to 33 ft).

2   **Caution.** A tunnel crosses Boston Main Channel from a position 1 cable E of Pier 5 (42°21′·0N 71°02′·0W), passing between anchorage areas No 1. Three other tunnels cross the channel about 1 mile farther NW, as shown on the chart. Anchoring is prohibited within an area extending 1 cable each side of the tunnels.

Alongside berths

Chart 1528
General
4.113

1   The port of Boston has over 100 piers and wharves. The majority of deep–draught berths are situated on Boston Main Channel in South Boston, East Boston and Charlestown and on the Mystic River and Chelsea River. There are also deep–draught berths on Weymouth Fore River and Town River Bay in the S part of the harbour.

2   Container traffic is handled at the Conley Container Terminal in South Boston and most of the deep water oil and bulk terminals are on the Chelsea and Mystic Rivers.

All of the large general cargo terminals are owned or leased by the Massachusetts Port Authority.

A summary of the principal terminals in the various complexes are given as follows.

South Boston
4.114

1   Main berths (with positions relative to Fort Independence (42°20′·3N 71°00′·7W)):

Paul W. Conley Marine Terminal (1 cable N to 5 cables NW). Container terminal with 4 berths. Nos 11–12 with a combined length of 622 m with a depth alongside of 13·7 m are the largest.

Coastal Oil New England (7½ cables WNW). One berth 213 m in length, with dolphins, with a depth alongside of 11·6 m. It was reported (2006) that this berth was closed.

2   **Boston Marine Industrial Marine Park** (7 cables NW). Nine berths. Berths 1 and 2; length 294 m with a depth alongside of 10·7 m. Black Falcon Cruise Terminal, a passenger terminal for cruise vessels, situated at berths 7 to 9 with a combined length of 640 m with a depth alongside of 10·7 m is the largest. Berths 1 to 3 handle bulk cement.

A safety and security zone surrounds the passenger terminal.

3   **Massport Marine Terminal Wharf** (9 cables NW). 244 m in length with a depth alongside of 10·7 m. US Government vessels only.

Commonwealth Pier No 5 (1½ miles NW). SE and NW side; 366 m in length with a depth alongside of 10·1 to 11·6 m. Passenger terminal for cruise vessels.

Charlestown
4.115

1   Main berths (with positions relative to S end (42°23′·0N 71°02′·9W) of Mystic River–Tobin Memorial Bridge):

Mystic Pier No 1 (2 cables SSE); S side: length 273 m. N side: 205 m with depths alongside both sides of 10·7 m.

Mystic Pier Nos 48–50 (1 cable SSE). Three berths; No 48, 171 m in length with a depth alongside of 7·6 m is the largest. It was reported (2006) that these berths were closed.

Mystic River
4.116

1   Berths on N bank (with positions relative to S end (42°23′·0N 71°02′·9W) of Mystic River–Tobin Memorial Bridge):

Chelsea Terminal Wharf (2 cables ENE); 171 m in length with a depth alongside of 10·7 m handling petroleum products.

2   Everett Terminal Wharf (4½ cables WNW). Three berths handling petroleum products; berths 3 and 4 with a combined berthing space of 290 m with depths alongside of 10·6 to 12·2 m are the largest.

LNG Terminal (6½ cables WNW); 305 m of berthing space with a depth alongside of 10·9 m. A safety and security zone of 366 m (400 yards) radius surrounds any LNG vessel at this berth.

3   Scrap Metal Wharf (7½ cables WNW); 250 m of berthing space, with dolphins, with a depth alongside of 12·2 m.

Berths on S bank (with positions relative to S end (42°23′·0N 71°02′·9W) of Mystic River–Tobin Memorial Bridge):

4   Gypsum Wharf (½ cable W); 150 m in length with a depth alongside of 8·2 m.

Boston Autoport (formerly Moran Container Terminal) (2 cables W); 335 m in length with a depth alongside of 12·2 m. Vehicle import/export terminal.

5   Cement Terminal (5 cables W); 186 m in length with a depth alongside of 9·4 m.

Medford Street Terminal (6 cables W); 138 m in length with a depth alongside of 10·7 m.

Chelsea River
4.117

1 Berths on N Bank (with positions relative to Chelsea Street Bridge (42°23'·2N 71°01'·4W)):

Coastal Oil New England Terminal (5 cables W); handling petroleum products, with 192 m of berthing space with depths alongside of 5·5 to 7·3 m.

2 Gulf Oil Terminal (5 cables NNE); handling petroleum products, with 216 m of berthing space with a depth alongside of 11·0 m.

Berths on S Bank (with positions relative to Chelsea Street Bridge (42°23'·2N 71°01'·4W):

3 Conoco/Phillips Terminal (1 cable SW); handling petroleum products, with 183 m of berthing space with a depth alongside of 11·6 m.

Four terminals (8 cables NNE); handling petroleum products, with berthing lengths 168 to 183 m with depths alongside of 3·0 to 11·3 m.

Chart 1516
Weymouth Fore River and Town River Bay
4.118

1 There are two deep–draught facilities on Weymouth Fore River and two on Town River Bay.

Largest berth on Town River. Sprague Energy Terminal Wharf (42°15'·2N 70°59'·2W), 213 m of berthing space, with dolphins, with a depth alongside of 10·7 m.

2 **Largest berth on Weymouth Fore River.** Citgo Petroleum Corp., Braintree Terminal Wharf (42°14'·2N 70°58'·1W), 213 m of berthing space, with dolphins, with a depth alongside of 11·6 m.

Port services

Repairs
4.119

1 Facilities are available for carrying out all types of hull and engine repair to vessels of all sizes. The largest repair facility is located in South Boston.

2 **Docking facilities.** There are several dry docks and marine railways available in the port. South Boston yard has two dry docks, the largest of which has a length of 358 m, width of 38·7 m and depth over the sill of 10·9 m. A patent slip in the port can handle vessels up to 55 m in length and 1000 tonnes.

Other facilities
4.120

1 Deratting; hospitals; oily waste disposal.

Supplies
4.121

1 Fuel; fresh water; provisions and stores.

Communications
4.122

1 Logan International Airport in East Boston.

Rescue
4.123

1 **Coast Guard District Office** and Marine Safety Office are situated at Boston. See 1.65.

Coast Guard stations are situated on the S side of the mouth of the Charles River (42°22'·1N 71°03'·2W) and in Hull Bay about 4 cables E of Windmill Point (42°18'·8'N 70°55'·3W).

SOUTH PART OF MASSACHUSETTS BAY

GENERAL INFORMATION

Chart 3096
Extent of area
4.124

1 The S part of Massachusetts Bay consists of the coastal waters between Strawberry Point (42°15'N 70°46'W) and Gurnet Point (42°00'N 70°36'W) and the waters of Cape Cod Bay.

Cape Cod Bay
4.125

1 Cape Cod Bay, which forms the main part of the S part of Massachusetts Bay, is entered between Gurnet Point (42°00'N 70°36'W) and Race Point (42°04'N 70°15'W), 16 miles ENE. The bay is bounded on the E and S by the peninsula of Cape Cod (4.63) and on the W by the mainland of Massachusetts.

2 **Ice.** Plymouth, Barnstable and Wellfleet, and other shallow harbours in Cape Cod Bay are usually closed to navigation during a part of every winter. Instances are on record of this ice, and the ice which forms in the shallower parts of the bay in severe winters, being driven by winds out into the bay, where it masses into heavy fields or belts, sometimes 3 m (10 ft) or more in thickness, rendering navigation of parts of the bay unsafe or impracticable at times.

3 The movement of the ice depends largely on the winds, the tidal streams having little or no apparent effect. N winds drive the ice down to the S end of the bay.

Designated Critical Habitat
4.126

1 Except for a narrow area along the W side, almost all of Cape Cod Bay lies within the federally designated critical habitat for Northern right whales. For further details see 4.6 and Appendix VIII.

Ship Reporting System
4.127

1 A mandatory ship reporting system is established for the protection of the Northern right whale. See 4.7 and *Admiralty List of Radio Signals Volume 6(5)* for details.

STRAWBERRY POINT TO GURNET POINT

Chart 3096
Description
4.128

1 Between Strawberry Point (42°15'N 70°46'W) and Gurnet Point (4.124), 17 miles SSE, the coast is generally low–lying and marshy and the harbours at the mouth of the rivers flowing into this stretch of the coast, are shallow and only available to small craft.

2 **Stellwagen Ledges**, which front the coast between Strawberry Point and Cedar Point, consist of numerous rocks and below–water ledges. The outer ledges, mostly

3   unmarked, lie over 1 mile offshore and have depths of 2·1 to 5·5 m (7 to 18 ft) over them, with surrounding deep water.

3   The coast between Scituate Harbor (42°12′N 70°43′W) and Green Harbor, 8 miles SSE, is fronted by several shoals with depths of 9·1 m (30 ft), which extend up to 4½ miles offshore.

Rescue
4.129
1   **Coast Guard** station is situated on the S side of Scituate Harbor (42°12′N 70°43′W).

Directions

Principal marks
4.130
1   **Landmark:**
    White tower (42°12′N 70°43′W).
  Major lights:
    Gurnet Point Light (42°00′N 70°36′W) (4.139).
    Race Point Light (42°04′N 70°15′W) (4.69).

Approaches to Cape Cod Bay
4.131
1   From the central part of Massachusetts Bay (42°15′N 70°30′W) the route into Cape Cod Bay leads S, passing (with positions relative to Gurnet Point (42°00′N 70°36′W)):

2   E of No 21 Light–buoy (port hand) (42°16′·6N 70°42′·4W), which marks a dangerous wreck and a 6·4 m (21 ft) patch at the outer limit of the foul ground that extends 4 miles NE from Strawberry Point. Vessels should not approach within 3 miles E of the coast between Strawberry Point and Cedar Point, 4 miles SE. Thence:

3   E of No 6 Light–buoy (5½ miles N). Deep–draught vessels entering Cape Cod Bay from the N should keep E of the meridian of 70°30′W to avoid the irregular ground extending from the shore between Cedar Point and Green Harbor. Thence:

4   W of Race Point (42°04′N 70°15′W) (4.73), thence: Clear of a dangerous wreck (3 miles E), thence: E of Gurnet Point, and thence into Cape Cod Bay.

  Caution is necessary when navigating in the vicinity of Race Point, especially at night and in low visibility by day, owing to the numerous fishing vessels which operate in the vicinity.

  (Directions for Plymouth Bay continue at 4.140, and for the N approach to Cape Cod Canal at 4.147)

Anchorages and harbours

Chart 1516
Cohasset Harbor
4.132
1   Cohasset Harbor (42°15′N 70°47′W), which is shallow, is situated on the W side of Scituate Neck and is entered between Gull Island, 1½ cables N of Strawberry Point and Brush Islet, 1 mile E.

  The harbour is used by numerous yachts and fishing craft.

2   **Ice** usually closes the harbour for about 2 months in the winter.

  Anchorage may be obtained in the outer harbour 5 cables W of Strawberry Point, in depths of 2 to 3 m (6 to 11 ft).

Chart 3096
Scituate Harbor
4.133
1   Scituate Harbor (42°12′N 70°43′W) is entered between Cedar Point and First Cliff and is only suitable for small craft.

New Inlet
4.134
1   New Inlet (42°10′N 70°43′W), which is entered on the N side of Fourth Cliff and 5 cables S of Third Cliff, both prominent yellow bluffs, is the approach to North River and South River. A prominent tower stands on Fourth Cliff.

  The harbour is only suitable for small craft.

Green Harbor River
4.135
1   Green Harbor River (42°05′N 70°39′W), is entered W of Blackmans Point, 8 cables S of Brant Rock. The harbour is only suitable for small craft.

WEST SIDE OF CAPE COD BAY

Chart 3096
Description
4.136
1   The W side of Cape Cod Bay lies between Gurnet Point (42°00′N 70°36′W), the S extremity of Duxbury Beach, a low sandy tongue; and the N entrance to the Cape Cod Canal, 14 miles SSE.

  The N part of this stretch of coast as far S as Manomet Point (41°56′N 70°32′W) is indented by Duxbury Bay and Plymouth Bay.

2   The S part, as far as Peaked Cliff, 7 miles S, consists of a line of bluffs backed by wooded hills. Two dangers lie off this stretch of the coast; Mary Ann Rocks, two rocks which dry about 1·5 m, lie 6 cables E of Manomet Point and Stellwagen Rock, unmarked and with a depth of 2·1 m (7 ft) over it, lies 2 miles SE of that point. Mary Ann Rocks are covered by the red sector (323°–352°) of Gurnet Point Light. No 12 Light–buoy (starboard hand) is moored 1 mile to seaward of Mary Ann Rocks; a dangerous wreck, the position of which is approximate, lies 2 cables S of the light–buoy.

Principal marks
4.137
1   **Landmarks:**
    Monument (42°00′·8N 70°40′·9W).
    Manomet Hill (41°56N 70°36′W) (4.147).

Water tower (41°53′N 70°32′W) standing on Indian Hill.

Water tower (41°48′N 70°32′W) standing on Sagamore Beach 4 miles S of Centre Hill Point.

2   **Major Lights:**
Gurnet Point Light (42°00′N 70°36′W) (4.139).
Cape Cod Canal Breakwater Head Light (41°47′N 70°29′W) (4.147).

Plymouth Bay

Chart 3096 (see 1.17)
General information
4.138

1   **Description.** Plymouth Bay, the approach to Plymouth Harbor (4.142), Duxbury Bay (4.143) and Kingston Bay (4.144), is entered between Gurnet Point (42°00′N 70°36′W) and Rocky Point, 3¼ miles SSE.

2   The bay is bounded on the N by Saquish Neck connecting Gurnet Point to Saquish Head, a bare hill, 18 m in height, which lies 1¾ miles WSW. On the W the bay is bounded by Plymouth Beach, a narrow neck that extends 2½ miles NW from the mainland. The bay is divided by Browns Bank, which partly dries and extends 2½ miles NE from Plymouth Beach.

3   **Depths.** In 2004 the channel through Plymouth Bay had a controlling depth of 3·7 m (12¼ ft) to the SE side of the anchorage basin. For the latest controlling depths the charts and port authority should be consulted.

Traffic regulations. A safety and security zone, close inshore, surrounds the Pilgrim Nuclear Power Plant (41°57′N 70°35′W).

For details see Appendix V.

4   **Tidal streams** between Gurnet Point and Duxbury Pier Light attain a rate of 1½ kn. They generally follow the direction of the channel, but the out–going stream sets S and E across Browns Bank and the in–going stream sets N and W inside Saquish Head and sweeps strongly round Duxbury Pier Light.

Local knowledge is necessary.

Principal marks
4.139

1   **Landmarks:**
Gurnet Point Light (white 8–sided pyramidal tower on dwelling, 12 m in height) (42°00′N 70°36′W).
Standish Monument (42°01′N 70°41′W), which stands on Captains Hill, 61 m in height, on the peninsula between Duxbury Bay and Kingston Bay.

2   Tower (41°58′N 70°43′W) standing on Monks Hill.
Manomet Hill (41°56N 70°36′W) (4.147).
Flagstaff (41°56′N 70°35′W), 1 mile NE of Manomet Hill.

Major light:
Gurnet Point Light — as above.

Directions
(continued from 4.131)
4.140

1   From a position about 1 mile ESE of Gurnet Point a buoyed channel leads 3 miles in a generally WSW direction through Plymouth Bay, passing between the shoals that front Gurnet Point and Saquish Neck to the N and Browns Bank to the S.

2   The entrance to the channel, which is marked by No 2 Buoy (starboard hand) and No 1 Light–buoy (port hand), is 4 cables SE of Gurnet Point.

At the W end of the channel the track passes S of Duxbury Pier Light (brown conical tower, white top) (41°59′·2N 70°38′·9E), which stands at the junction of the three channels leading to Duxbury Bay, Kingston Bay and Plymouth Harbor.

Anchorage
4.141

1   Temporary anchorage may be obtained, during S winds, in depths of 6 to 10 m (20 to 33 ft), sand, in Warren Cove in the S part of Plymouth Bay.

Anchorage may also be obtained, when waiting for favourable tide or weather, in depths of 7 m (22 ft) on the N side of the approach channel SE of Saquish Head.

2   **Cowyard** (42°00′N 70°39′W) provides the best anchorage in the area. See 4.143.

Plymouth
4.142

1   **General information.** Plymouth Harbor (41°58′N 70°40′W) is entered between the N end of Plymouth Beach and High Cliff, 1¼ miles W. The port of Plymouth stands on the SW side of the harbour and in 2005 had an estimated population of 54 923. It is a port of entry but is mainly used by fishing vessels and pleasure craft.

2   **Ice** often closes Plymouth Harbor from early January to late February. W winds tend to carry the ice out in fields; N winds sometimes bring in ice, but S winds carry it out.
For effect of ice on anchorages, see 4.143.

3   **Directions.** From a position W of Duxbury Pier Light (41°59′N 70°39′W) the white sector (195½°-199½°) of No 12 Light–beacon (red triangle on red framework tower, black round base) (41°58′·8N 70°39′·4W) leads through the N part of the channel.

4   **Anchorage.** In 2004 the anchorage basin in Plymouth had depths of 1 to 2 m (5 to 8 ft) in it. See also 4.141 and 4.143.

Berths. Two berths, the largest has a depth alongside of 3·6 m.

Facilities: hospital.

Supplies: fuel; water and stores.

Duxbury Bay
4.143

1   **General information.** Duxbury Bay is bounded on the NE by Duxbury Beach, on the SE by Saquish Neck (42°00′N 70°38′W) and on the W by the mainland. It is composed of sand and mud flats, mostly drying, through which several channels wind.

The town of Duxbury lies in the NW part of the bay.

2   **Anchorage** is available in depths of 6 to 11 m (20 to 36 ft) in Cowyard, a stretch of water that lies between Duxbury Pier Light and Clarks island, 1 mile N. This is the best anchorage for vessels waiting to enter Plymouth.

Caution. It is not a safe anchorage when there is ice in the harbour and in these conditions vessels should anchor S or E of Saquish Head.

Kingston Bay
4.144

1   **General information.** Kingston Bay is entered between High Cliff (41°59′N 70°41′W) and Goose Point, the W point of Duxbury Bay, 1½ miles N. The bay has numerous flats and has little importance as a harbour.

Local knowledge is advised.

GURNET POINT TO EAST ENTRANCE TO CAPE COD CANAL

General information

Charts 3096, 2891
Extent of area
4.145

1   This section describes the N approach to the E entrance of the Cape Cod Canal. Cape Cod Canal itself is described in Chapter 5.

Description
4.146

1   The E entrance to Cape Cod Canal (41°47′N 70°29′W) is situated in the SW part of Cape Cod Bay. The entrance is protected on its N side by a breakwater, with a light (4.147) at its seaward extremity, which extends 3½ cables ENE from the shore, and on its S side by a short breakwater which extends parallel to the N breakwater.

2   **Approach** to the entrance is marked by CC Light–buoy (safe water) moored 2½ miles NNE of the entrance.

Pilots meet vessels ESE of CC Light–buoy (41°49′N 70°28′W). See *Admiralty List of Radio Signals Volume 6(5)* for details.

Directions
(continued from 4.131)

Principal marks
4.147

1   **Landmarks:**
Manomet Hill (41°56N 70°36W). Thickly wooded.
Chimney (41°46′·2N 70°30′·6W) of a power station, standing 1 cable SW of Cape Cod Canal front leading light.

2   **Major lights:**
Race Point Light (42°04′N 70°15′W) (4.69).
Gurnet Point Light (42°00′N 70°36′W) (4.139).
Cape Cod Canal Breakwater Head Light (red round tower) (41°47′N 70°29′W).

4.148

1   From a position E of Gurnet Point (42°00′N 70°36′W) in the entrance to Cape Cod Bay, the N approach to the E entrance of Cape Cod Canal leads S, passing (with positions relative to Breakwater Head Light (41°46′·8N 70°29′·4W)):
E of a dangerous wreck (41°56′·3N 70°29′·5W), thence:

2   Clear of a dangerous wreck (8¾ miles NNE), the position of which is approximate, and:
E of No 12 Light–buoy (starboard hand) (8½ miles N), marking Mary Ann Rocks (4.136), thence:
E of Stellwagen Rock (7 miles NNW) (4.136), thence:
Clear of CC Light–buoy (safe water) (2½ miles NE), thence:

3   NW of No 1 Light–buoy (port hand) (1 mile ENE), which marks the limit of an extension of the shore bank.

Cape Cod Canal – East Entrance (4.146)

(Original dated 2002)

(Photograph – Robert P. David – Reproduced by permission of Cape Cod Sail & Power Squadron, United States Power Squadrons)

Thence the alignment (245°) of leading lights:

Front light (red rectangle, white stripe on framework tower) (1 mile WSW).

Rear light (similar structure) (244 m from front light) leads through the canal entrance between the breakwaters, passing:

4   NNW of No 3 Light–buoy (port hand) (3 cables E), thence:

SSE of Breakwater Head Light (4.147) standing at the head of the N breakwater.

(Directions for Cape Cod Canal from W are given at 5.175)

EAST AND SOUTH SIDE OF CAPE COD BAY

General information

Chart 3096 (see 1.17)
Description
4.149

1   The E and S sides of Cape Cod Bay lie between Race Point (42°04′N 70°15′W) and the entrance to the Cape Cod Canal, 21 miles SW.

The bay is bounded on its E and S side by the peninsula of Cape Cod which is composed almost entirely of sand, with high bare sandhills and low, nearly level plains. The peninsula is well populated.

Ice
4.150

1   For general details of ice conditions in Cape Cod Bay, see 4.125.

Provincetown Harbor and approaches

General information
4.151

1   **Provincetown Harbor**, formed by the bend in the N end of the Hook of Cape Cod, lies between Long Point (42°02′N 70°10′W), the NE end of the hook, and the coast 2 miles NE.

The harbour is one of the best on the Atlantic coast of the United States, having a large anchorage area with excellent holding ground; coasters and fishing vessels shelter in it from gales from any direction.

2   The town of Provincetown, on the NW side of the harbour, is the site of the first landing of the *Mayflower* and is the base of numerous fishing, lobster and pleasure boats.

Ice
4.152

1   Ice forms in Provincetown Harbor in severe winters only, and then only for short periods. Instances are on record of fields of heavy ice from the shallow harbours of Cape Cod Bay being driven N by the wind into the harbour, closing it to navigation for a few days. Such conditions are rare and usually the harbour is not obstructed by ice.

Principal marks
4.153

1   **Landmarks:**

Race Point Light (42°04′N 70°15′W) (4.69).

Pilgrim Monument (42°03′N 70°11′W). A stone tower, 77 m in height, from which red obstruction lights are exhibited.

2   Radar domes (42°02′N 70°03′W) at North Truro.

Spire (42°00′N 70°03′W) of a large church at Truro.

Major light:

Race Point Light — as above.

Provincetown from SSW (4.151)
(Original dated 2004)

(Photograph - Joseph R Melanson of www.skypic.com)

Directions
4.154

1 **Approach from north-west.** From a position W of Race Point, the approach to Provincetown Harbor leads SE, passing (with positions relative to Wood End Light (42°01'·2N 70°11'·6W)):

SW of Wood End Light (white square tower, 12 m in height), thence:

SW of No 1 Light–buoy (port hand) (9 cables S), which is moored close SSW of a dangerous wreck, the position of which is approximate.

2 Thence the approach leads NE through waters clear of charted dangers, passing:

SE of No 3 Light–buoy (port hand) (1½ miles ENE), which marks the limit of a bank extending E from Long Point. A light (white square tower) stands on the point.

Thence to the anchorages and the inner harbour.

3 **Cautions.** Shipping should keep a sharp lookout when navigating in the vicinity of Race Point, especially during the hours of darkness and low visibility, because of the numerous fishing craft that operate in the area.

A 2·4 m (8 ft) shoal is reported 1 cable S of the head of the town pier. Mariners are advised to exercise caution when operating in this area.

Anchorage
4.155

1 Excellent anchorage is available SE and E of Long Point in depths of up to 18 m (60 ft).

Anchorage is prohibited in the approach fairway, 90 m (300 ft) wide, which leads NW from a point 3 cables E of Long Point to the piers at Provincetown, and within 90 m (300 ft) of the piers.

Alongside berths
4.156

1 **Town pier,** known as MacMillan Wharf, extends 400 m SE from the waterfront in the NW part of the harbour and has a depth alongside of 4 m at its head.

Berths at this pier are allocated by the Harbour Master, whose office is at the end of the pier.

Breakwater, 4 cables long and parallel to the shore, lies 1½ cables off the town pier. Nos 4 and 5 Light–beacons (red triangle and green square, respectively, on framework towers) stand at the W and E ends, respectively, of the breakwater.

Supplies
4.157

1 Provisions and stores can be obtained in the town.

Rescue
4.158

1 **Rescue.** Coast Guard station is situated on the SW side of the harbour about 4 cables SW of the town pier.

Anchorages and harbours

Wellfleet Harbor
4.159

1 **General information.** Wellfleet Harbor is entered between Jeremy Point (41°53'N 70°04'W), the S point of Great Island which forms the W side of Wellfleet Harbor, and the mainland 2½ miles E.

The harbour is almost filled with shallow flats, between which is a buoyed channel, dredged in its N part, leading into the inner harbour.

2 The harbour, which is protected by a breakwater, is only used by small fishing craft and yachts.

The town of Wellfleet stands at the head of the harbour.

Ice usually closes the harbour for part of each winter.

3 **Restricted area,** centred on a dangerous wreck (41°50'N 70°03'W) which is used as an aerial bombing target, lies to the S of the approaches to Wellfleet. No vessel may enter within a radius of 5 cables of the wreck, which has DJ Light–buoy (isolated danger) moored 3 cables W. For details see Appendix VI.

4 **Anchorage** can be obtained in the outer harbour NE of Smalley Bar in depths of 4 to 6 m (12 to 21 ft), but is somewhat exposed to W winds.

In N gales anchorage is possible on the lee side of Billingsgate Shoal (41°51'·2N 70°07'·8W) in depths of 4 to 13 m (12 to 42 ft).

Barnstable Harbor
4.160

1 Barnstable Harbor is entered 10½ miles E of the entrance to Cape Cod Canal (5.165), between Beach Point (41°44'N 70°17'W), the E extremity of Sandy Beach, and the coast 1¼ miles E.

The harbour is the approach to the town of Barnstable, situated 1¾ miles SW of Beach Point, and is used by local fishing craft and yachts.

Ice generally obstructs the harbour during part of the winter.

Pamet Harbor
4.161

1 Pamet Harbor (41°59'N 70°05'W) at the mouth of the Pamet River, which leads E to Truro, is a small harbour used by small craft and a few fishermen.

Rock Harbor
4.162

1 Rock Harbor (41°48'N 70°00'W), 8 miles S of Wellfleet and 7 miles ENE of Sesuit Harbor is only used by small craft. Shoal ground extends up to 3 miles off this stretch of the coast and the shorebank dries for 1 mile offshore. Billingsgate Shoal (4.159) lies 6 miles NW of the harbour.

Sesuit Harbor
4.163

1 Sesuit Harbor (41°45'N 70°09'W), used only by small craft, lies 5 miles E of the entrance to Barnstable Harbor at the mouth of a creek leading to the village of East Dennis.

Scorton Harbor
4.164

1 Scorton Harbor (41°45'N 70°26'W), 3 miles ESE of the entrance to Cape Cod Canal, is surrounded by sandhills and backed by cultivated land. Scorton Ledge lies 7½ cables NNE of the entrance.

The narrow entrance to the harbour dries, but small fishing boats sometimes enter at half tide. There are no wharves or facilities.

Sandwich Harbor
4.165

1 Sandwich Harbor (41°46'N 70°28'W), 1 mile SE of the entrance to Cape Cod Canal, is the approach to the town of Sandwich. The harbour is only suitable for small craft and has no facilities.

Chapter 5 - Nantucket Shoals to Providence

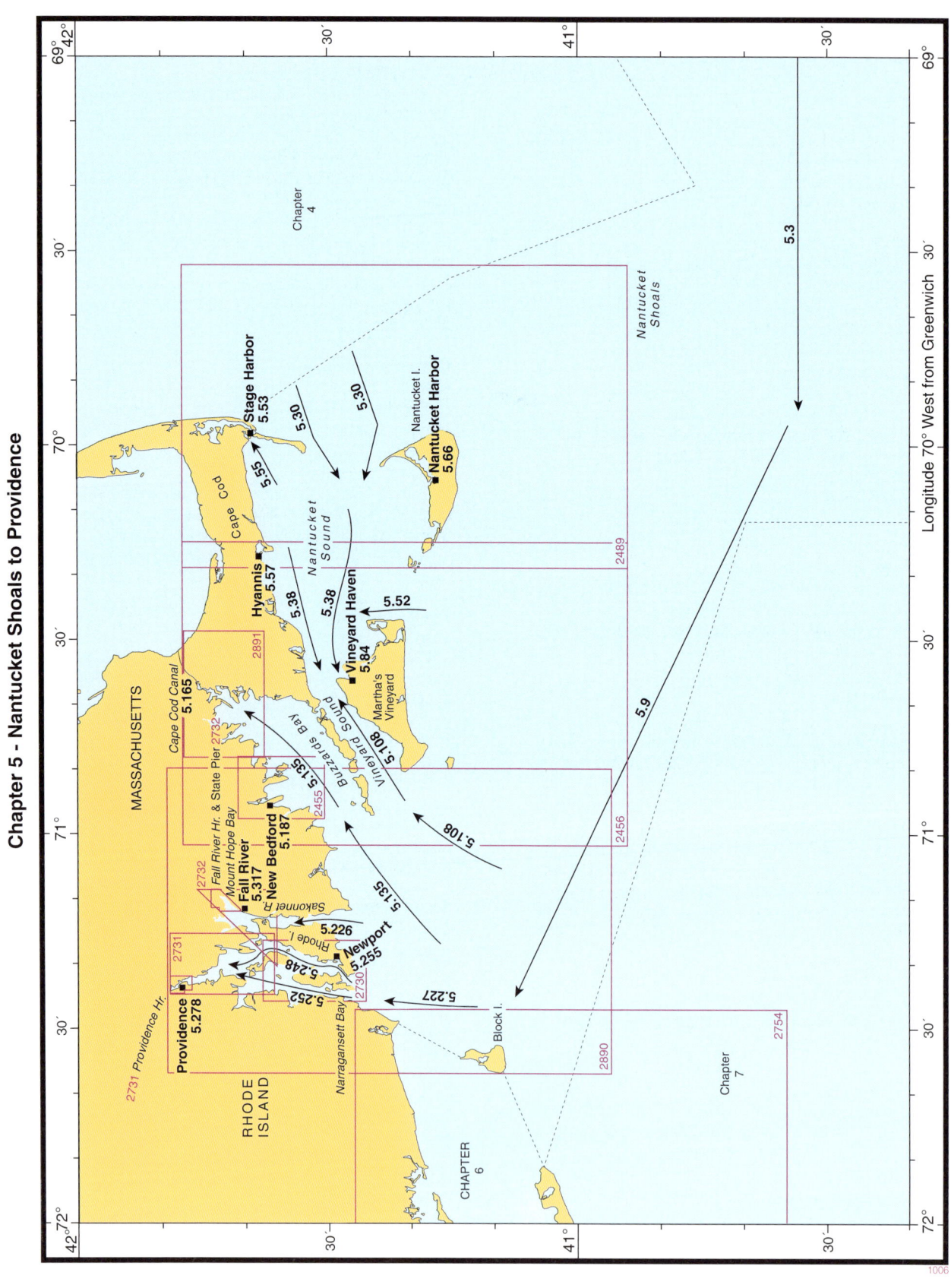

CHAPTER 5

NANTUCKET SHOALS TO PROVIDENCE

GENERAL INFORMATION

Chart 2860
Scope of the chapter
5.1

1   The area covered by this chapter includes:
Outer approaches to ports S of Cape Cod.
Rhode Island Sound (41°15′N 71°10′W) (5.9).
Nantucket Shoals (41°00′N 69°40′W) (5.19).
Nantucket Sound (41°30′N 70°16′W) (5.38).
Vineyard Sound (41°26′N 70°45′W) (5.108)
Buzzards Bay (41°30′N 70°50′W) (5.135).
Narragansett Bay (41°35′N 71°20′W) (5.216).

Recommended routes
5.2

1   Recommended routes for deep-draught vessels, tugs and barges, as shown on the charts, have been established in Buzzards Bay and Narragansett Bay. Pleasure craft, fishing vessels and other small vessels should exercise caution in and around these routes and should monitor VHF channels for information concerning vessels transiting these routes.

NANTUCKET SHOALS TO RHODE ISLAND SOUND

SEAWARD APPROACH TO NANTUCKET SHOALS

General information

Charts 2670, 2492
Routes
5.3

1   Transatlantic routes from Europe, which terminate in the vicinity of Nantucket Shoals, are described in *Ocean Passages for the World.*

Underwater topography
5.4

1   The edge of the continental shelf, situated 30 to 50 miles to seaward of Georges Bank (3.1) and Nantucket Shoals (5.19), is indented by several submarine gorges or canyons.
Lydonia Canyon lies 50 miles S of Georges Shoal and Atlantis Canyon lies 85 miles S of Nantucket Island (41°16′N 70°05′W). Between these two canyons, from E to W, lie Gilbert Canyon, Oceanographer Canyon, Welker Canyon, Hydrographer Canyon and Veatch Canyon.

2   By echo sounding along the charted 180 m (100 fm) depth contour in this area, a vessel's position can be verified with some accuracy when crossing these canyons.

Traffic regulations
5.5

1   **Precautionary Area**, centred 40°35′N 69°00′W, has been established SE of Nantucket Shoals.
Traffic separation scheme which forms part of the Precautionary Area leads W from the W side of this area. Another TSS leads NNW from the N side of the Precautionary Area. Both schemes are IMO adopted and Rule 10 of the *International Regulations for Preventing Collisions at Sea (1972)* applies.

2   **Area to be Avoided.** Because of the great danger of stranding, and for reasons of environmental protection, all vessels carrying dangerous cargoes of oil or hazardous materials, and all other vessels of more than 1000 gt, should avoid the area of Nantucket Shoals.
The limits of the area are shown on the chart.

Tidal streams
5.6

1   See tidal stream tables on charts.

Directions

Other aids to navigation
5.7

1   **Racon:**
N Light-buoy (40°30′·3N 69°15′·1W).
See *Admiralty List of Radio Signals Volume 2* for details.

Directions
5.8

1   From the vicinity of position 40°30′N 67°35′W the seaward approach to Nantucket Shoals leads generally W, passing (with positions relative to N Light-buoy (40°30′·3N 69°15′·1W)):
S of Little Georges Shoals (58 miles NE), the SW part of Georges Bank (3.1), thence:
Through the Precautionary Area (11 miles E), thence:
(Directions continue for approaches to Boston at 4.69)

2   North of N Light–buoy (special) to the W end of the TSS. ODAS light–buoy 44008 (special) is moored 8 miles W of N Light–buoy.
Caution. When passing Georges Bank continuous sounding is essential for safety owing to the irregularity of the depths.
(Directions continue for Rhode Island Sound at 5.13, and for New York at 7.13)

SEAWARD APPROACH FROM NANTUCKET SHOALS TO RHODE ISLAND SOUND

General information

Charts 2860, 2890
Description
5.9

1   The seaward approach to Rhode Island Sound, the area of water lying between Block Island (41°11′N 71°35′W) (5.227) and Martha's Vineyard, 35 miles ENE, leads through waters clear of charted dangers, between 40 and 50 miles SW of Nantucket Island (5.16) and Martha's Vineyard (5.17).
Climate information. See 1.154.

Traffic regulations
5.10

1 **Precautionary Area**, centred 41°06′N 71°23′W with a radius of about 5 miles, has been established SE of Block Island. Traffic separation schemes for Narragansett Bay (5.228) and Buzzard Bay (5.138) originate from the N and NE sectors, respectively, of this area.

Mariners are advised to exercise extreme caution when navigating within this area.

Submarine exercise areas and transit lanes
5.11

1 Submarines, both surfaced and dived, exercise frequently in the area between the meridians of 69°30′W and 72°15′W in the approaches to New York and Rhode Island Sound. See *Admiralty Annual Notice to Mariners No 8.*

2 **Lanes** used by submerged submarines run S from Block Island for 80 miles and thence run E. Positions of these lanes are shown on charts of the US Ocean National Survey, and the times that the lanes are used are published in local Notice to Mariners. When the lanes are in use by submarines, ships should not tow submerged objects in them.

Unexploded ordnance
5.12

1 Unexploded ordnance, the positions of which are shown on the chart, exists in this area.

Directions
(continued from 5.8)

Principal marks
5.13

1 **Major lights:**
Gay Head Light (41°21′N 70°50′W) (5.114).
Block Island South–east Light (41°09′N 71°33′W) (5.230).
Montauk Point Light (41°04′N 71°51′W) (6.13).

Other aids to navigation
5.14

1 **Racon:**
'A' Light–buoy in the centre (41°06′N 71°23′W) of the Precautionary Area.
See *Admiralty List of Radio Signals Volume 2* for details.

Directions
5.15

1 From the vicinity of the W end of the TSS (40°30′N 70°15′W) S of Nantucket Shoals the approaches to Rhode Island Sound lead NW for about 60 miles to the Precautionary Area SE of Block Island.
(Directions continue for Buzzards Bay at 5.144 and for approaches to Narragansett Bay at 5.230
Directions for inshore route off S coast of Long Island given at 7.21, for Vineyard Sound at 5.114 and for Block Island Sound at 6.13)

South shores of Nantucket Island and Martha's Vineyard

Charts 2489, 2456
Nantucket Island
5.16

1 The S coast of Nantucket Island has no harbours and is only frequented by local fishermen. Old Man Shoal extends

6 miles SSW from the SE part of the island and Miacomet Rip extends 1¼ miles offshore from midway along the island.

Fishing stakes, which may be submerged, are likely to be met within the areas adjacent to the coast, as indicated on the charts.

2 **Useful marks:**
Aero Light (41°15′·4N 70°03′·8W) and dome (2 cables WSW) at Nantucket Memorial Airport.
Radio tower (41°15′N 70°08′W).

Martha's Vineyard
5.17

1 The S coast of Martha's Vineyard, for 13 miles W from Wasque Point (41°21′N 70°27′W), is low and backed by ponds.
Useful marks:
Wasque Shoal Light (metal tripod with mast) (41°19′·5N 70°33′·6W), S of Edgartown Great Pond.
Water tower (41°23′N 70°31′W) at Edgartown.
Aero Light (41°23′N 70°37′W) at Martha's Vineyard Airport.

Muskeget Channel
5.18

1 Muskeget Channel leads E of Wasque Point into Nantucket Sound. See 5.50.

NANTUCKET SHOALS

General information

Charts 2489, 2456
Description
5.19

1 Nantucket Shoals is the name given to the numerous shoals which lie E and S of Nantucket Island. The shoals extend 24 miles E, 41 miles SE and 29 miles S from Sankaty Head Light (41°17′N 69°58′W) (5.21).

The shoals are liable to shift and their depths vary from 0·9 to 9·1 m (3 to 30 ft), with channels of depths of 18·3 m (60 ft) or more between those farthest offshore.

Tidal streams
5.20

1 Tidal streams over Nantucket Shoals and their vicinity are rotary, and there is no slack water. They have a maximum rate of 2½ kn, but vary from place to place and can reach a velocity of 5 kn around the sides of shoals.

Principal marks
5.21

1 **Major light:**
Sankaty Head Light (white tower, red band, 21 m in height) (41°17′N 69°58′W) standing on Sankaty Head, a high bluff.

Caution
5.22

1 **Nantucket Shoals** should be entirely avoided by deep–draught vessels on account of the treacherous currents.

Local knowledge is necessary for shallow–draught vessels to navigate the channels which pass through the various shoals.

NANTUCKET SOUND AND VINEYARD SOUND

GENERAL INFORMATION

Charts 2489, 2456

Description
5.23
1　Nantucket Sound (41°30′N 70°16′W) and Vineyard Sound (41°26′N 70°45′W) (5.108) lie between the S coast of Cape Cod and Elizabeth Islands (5.108) on the N, and Nantucket Island and Martha's Vineyard, with their off–lying islands and shoals, to the S.

Route
5.24
1　The sounds are a thoroughfare for numerous coasters and pleasure craft, this route being more direct for vessels bound along the coast than the route outside Nantucket Shoals.

Depths
5.25
1　Vessels of 7·3 m (24 ft) draught can pass through the sounds, and with good local knowledge a depth of 9·1 m (30 ft) can be obtained through them.

Hazards
5.26
1　**Concentration of traffic.** Caution is necessary in the navigation of Nantucket and Vineyard Sounds, owing to the large number of vessels which are often encountered in the narrow parts of the channels.

2　**Adverse natural conditions.** Caution is necessary in the navigation of Nantucket and Vineyard Sounds, owing to the numerous shoals, strong tidal streams and thick fog at certain seasons. In some places the tidal stream sets directly on the shoals. Most of the shoals are steep–to and the depths are very irregular, so soundings alone cannot be depended upon for warning of too close an approach to danger.

Pilotage
5.27
1　Pilotage is compulsory in Nantucket Sound and Vineyard Sound for all vessels of 350 gt or more and tows with barges carrying 6000 barrels or more of petroleum cargoes.

　　Pilots board in the vicinity of 41°23′N 71°21′W, 4 miles SSE of the entrance to Narragansett Bay (5.216), or 5 cables ESE of CC Light–buoy (41°49′N 70°28′W), off the E entrance to the Cape Cod Canal.

Natural conditions
5.28
1　**Tidal streams.** See Tidal Stream tables on the charts.

　　Ice interferes little with navigation in the sounds in mild winters. In severe winters pack ice accumulates, but powered vessels can normally force their way through it. During NW winds, which prevail in winter, the passage along the N shore of Nantucket Sound will be clear when other parts of the sound are unsafe.

2　**Local weather.** Fog is liable to occur in the sounds at any time but is more frequent from April to October than during the remainder of the year. It occurs more frequently with E and S winds; NW winds clears it away, SW winds are usually accompanied by haze.

Aids to navigation
5.29
1　Aids to navigation are coloured and numbered for a passage through the sounds from E to W.

EAST APPROACHES TO NANTUCKET SOUND

General information

Chart 2489

Description
5.30
1　Nantucket Sound is entered between Monomoy Point (41°33′N 70°00′W), the S extremity of Monomoy Island, and Great Point (9¼ miles S), low, sandy and the termination of a long beach extending N from Nantucket Island.

Route
5.31
1　The E entrance to Nantucket Sound passes through Monomoy Shoals, numerous and detached, which extend 6 miles E and 14 miles SE from Monomoy Point. These shoals are subject to change in depth and position.

　　Two principal channels lead into Nantucket Sound from E.

2　**Pollock Rip Channel** (41°33′N 69°53′W) (5.36) and Butler Hole (5.36), which lead through the N part of Monomoy Shoals, form the most direct route for vessels from N of Cape Cod to Nantucket Sound.

　　Local knowledge is advisable.

3　**Great Round Shoal Channel** (5.37) is entered 10 miles SE of Pollock Rip Channel and passes between Monomoy Shoals and Nantucket Shoals. It is used by many large fishing vessels.

Depths
5.32
1　**Pollock Rip Channel** has a least charted depth of 6·7 m (22 ft).

　　Great Round Shoal Channel. The buoyed channel has a controlling depth of 8·2 m (27 ft), but is subject to change.

Tidal streams
5.33
1　**Pollock Rip Channel.** At its E entrance the NE–going stream sets about 055° and the SW–going stream 225°, or at an angle of about 20° to axis of the channel, at a rate of 2 kn at springs and 1¼ kn at neaps. See also Tidal Stream table on chart.

2　At No 8 Light–buoy (41°32′·8N 69°58′·9W) the strength of the NE and SW streams set, respectively, in an 035° and 225° direction, with average rates of 2 and 1¾ kn. The strength of the NE stream occurs about 5 hours before, and that of the SW stream about 1 hour after, HW at Boston.

3　Off S end of Handkerchief Shoal, the strength of the E and W streams set, respectively, about 080° and 250°, at an average rate of about 2¼ kn. The strength of the E stream occurs about 4¼ hours before, and that of the W stream about 2 hours after, HW at Boston.

　　Great Round Shoal Channel. See Tidal Stream tables on chart.

Anchorage
5.34
1　Anchoring is prohibited in or near the fairways of the Pollock Rip Channel and Butler Hole and also near any of the aids to navigation, as local vessels navigate from buoy to buoy in poor visibility.

　　Areas where anchoring is permitted are shown on the chart:

2   East of Monomoy Island within the pecked line leading from the shore 1 mile NE of Chatham (41°40′N 69°57′W) to the SE part of Monomoy Island.

East and SE of the pecked line leading from 41°40′N 69°48′W to No 17 Light–buoy (23 miles SW) and thence SSE to the N shore of Nantucket Island at 41°19′N 70°05′W.

Directions

Principal marks
5.35

1   **Landmark:**
Tower (41°34′N 70°00′W), a disused lighthouse, stands 1 mile NE of Monomoy Point.
Major lights:
Chatham Light (41°40′N 69°57′W) (4.69).
Sankaty Head Light (41°17′N 69°58′W) (5.21).

Pollock Rip Channel and Butler Hole
5.36

1   From the vicinity of 41°34′N 69°51′W, Pollock Rip Channel and the channel through Butler Hole lead WSW and SW, passing (with positions relative to the disused lighthouse (5.35)):
SSE of a dangerous wreck, the position of which is approximate (5½ miles ENE), thence:

2   SSE of No 4 Light–buoy (starboard hand) (3¾ miles E), moored between the NW end of Broken Part of Pollock Rip and the SE end of Bearse Shoal, thence:
NNW of No 5 Buoy (port hand) (2¾ miles ESE), which lies on the N side of Pollock Rip, thence:

3   SSE of Nos 6 and 8 Light–buoys (starboard hand) (2 miles ESE and 1 mile SE), which mark the S side of Bearse Shoal.
Thence into Butler Hole, passing:
NW of No 9 Light–Buoy (port hand) (1½ miles S), thence:

4   SE of No 10 Light–buoy (starboard hand) (1¾ miles SSW), which marks the SE side of Shovelful Shoal. An obstruction and a dangerous wreck, the position of which is approximate, lie between this shoal and Monomoy Point. Thence:

5   NW of No 11 Buoy (port hand) (3 miles S), which marks the W end of Stone Horse Shoal, thence:
SE of Nos 12 and 14 Buoys (starboard hand) (4¼ and 6 miles SW), which mark the SE side of Handkerchief Shoal. An isolated shoal patch, with a depth of 4·3 m (14 ft) over it, lies about 7 cables W of No 14 Buoy.
Thence into Nantucket Sound.

6   **Cautions.** Small craft and fishing vessels should avoid the area during thick or foggy weather, since large vessels may be encountered in this channel.
Owing to the distance of Monomoy Shoals from land and the strong tidal streams that set over them, navigation through them in thick or foggy weather is hazardous.

7   Attention is drawn to the dangerous wrecks which are in the vicinity of the channel.
The channel is liable to change frequently and the buoys are moved as necessary.
Local knowledge. Due to the numerous shoals existing in the channel, mariners should seek local knowledge before entering Pollock Rip Channel or Butler Hole.

(Directions continue at 5.46)

Great Round Shoal Channel
5.37

1   From the vicinity of 41°26′N 69°43′W Great Round Shoal Channel leads W, passing (with positions relative to Great Point (41°24′N 70°03′W)):
Between light–buoys (lateral) (14 to 8 miles E), which, on the S, mark the N limits of Rose and Crown Shoal and McBlair Shoal, and, on the N, the S limits of Orion Shoal and Great Round Shoal, thence:

2   N of a dangerous wreck (position approximate), (6¾ miles E) lying on the S side of the channel, thence:
Between No 10 Light-buoy (starboard hand) (6½ miles E) and No 9 Buoy (port hand) (6 miles E), a dangerous wreck lies 4 cables WNW of No 9 Buoy.

3   Thence the track leads NW, passing:
NE of No 11 Buoy and No 13 Light–buoy (both port hand) (4 miles NE), which mark the NW limit of Point Rip.
Thence the track leads W into Nantucket Sound, passing:
N of No 15 Light–buoy (port hand).

4   **Caution.** The channel is subject to frequent change and the buoys are moved as necessary.
Useful mark:
Great Point Light (white tower, 21 m in height) (41°23′N 70°03′W).

(Directions continue at 5.46)

NANTUCKET SOUND

General information

Charts 2489, 2456
Description
5.38

1   Nantucket Sound lies between the S coast of Cape Cod to the N and Nantucket Island and part of Martha's Vineyard to the S. It has a length of 28 miles between its E entrances on the N side of Nantucket Shoals and its W entrance at the NE entrance to Vineyard Sound. The sound is between 6 and 22 miles wide.

2   **Shoals.** There are numerous shoals in the sound with well marked channels between. Unlike the shoals in the E approach and entrance, those in the sound are stable.

Routes
5.39

1   Two well marked channels lead between the shoals in Nantucket Sound to the NE end of Vineyard Sound.
Main Channel leads through the centre of the sound S of Horseshoe Shoal (41°30′N 70°20′W). This channel is used by most vessels passing through the sound.

2   **North Channel** leads along the N side of the sound and is entered either side of Bishop and Clerks (41°34′N 70°15′W) and passes N of Horseshoe Shoal (5.47) and L'Hommedieu Shoal (5.49). This channel is used mostly by vessels bound to places on the N side of Nantucket Sound and by vessels passing through that sound during N winds or in winter, when the prevailing NW winds keep the N shore clear of ice.

3   **Caution.** Passage of this channel should not be attempted at night or without local knowledge.
Both channels unite N of West Chop (41°29′N 70°36′W).

No-discharge zones
5.40

1   Numerous No-discharge zones (NDZs) have been established throughout Nantucket Sound. See 1.44.

Depths
5.41

1   **Main Channel** has a least depth of 9·4 m (31 ft), but the draught of vessels using this channel seldom exceeds 7·3 m (24 ft).

    North Channel has a least depth of about 4·9 m (16 ft), but should not be used by vessels drawing more than 4·3 m (14 ft).

Pilotage
5.42

1   See 5.27.

Anchorage
5.43

1   Anchoring is prohibited in or near the fairway of Main Channel and also near any of the aids to navigation, as local vessels navigate from buoy to buoy in poor visibility.

    Areas where anchoring is permitted are shown on the chart:

2   In the N part of Nantucket Sound N of the pecked line leading from Monomoy Point (41°33′N 70°00′W) to No 18 Light–buoy on the S part of Half Moon Shoal (41°28′N 70°14′W), thence to Nobska Point (41°31′N 70°39′W).

3   In the S part of Nantucket Sound W and S of the pecked line leading NW from the N shore of Nantucket Island at 41°18′N 70°06′W to No 21 Light–buoy (41°27′N 70°18′W), thence to Oak Bluffs (41°27′N 70°33′W).

4   In a triangular area centred 2 miles N of Cape Poge (41°25′N 70°27′W). Squash Meadow, marked by buoys lies at the W end of this area.

Fish traps
5.44

1   Numerous fish traps are located in Nantucket Sound, particularly along the S shore of Cape Cod, as indicated on the charts. These areas may be marked by private lights.

Rescue
5.45

1   **Coast Guard** station is situated on Brant Point (41°17′·4N 70°05′·5W) on the W side of the entrance to Nantucket Harbor.

Directions
(continued from 5.36 and 5.37)

Principal marks
5.46

1   **Landmarks:**

    Tower (41°37′N 70°16′W). A disused lighthouse standing on the S extremity of Point Gammon, wooded.

    Water tank (41°37′·4N 70°26′·5W) on W side of Cotuit Bay. A second prominent water tank stands 4 cables N.

2   Spire (41°17′N 70°06′W) in Nantucket (5.66).

    Church tower (41°23′·4N 70°30′·9W) in Edgartown.

    Dome (41°27′·4N 70°33′·6W) in Oak Bluffs.

    Cupola (41°27′·4N 70°34′·0W) in Oak Bluffs.

Major lights:

    Chatham Light (41°40′N 69°57′W) (4.69).

    Barnstable Airport Light (41°40′N 70°17′W).

Main Channel
5.47

1   From the vicinity of No 17 Light–buoy (41°27′N 70°11′W) Main Channel is entered between Halfmoon Shoal and Tuckernuck Shoal, and leads W, passing (with positions relative to Cape Poge Light (41°25′N 70°27′W)):

    S of No 18 Light–buoy (starboard hand) (41°27′N 70°14′W), which marks the S side of Halfmoon Shoal, thence:

2   Between Nos 20 and 21 Light–buoys (lateral) (7¾ miles ENE), which mark the S side of Horseshoe Shoal and the N side of Cross Rip Shoal, respectively, thence:

    Clear of a wreck with a least depth of 18·3 m (60 ft) over it (7 miles ENE), thence:

3   S of MT Light (monopole metal tower on pile supported platform marked MT) (7 miles ENE), thence:

    Clear of NS Light–buoy (safe water) (3½ miles NE), which is moored 2 miles ENE of the entrance to Muskeget Channel (5.50), thence:

    N of No 21A Light–buoy (port hand) (2¼ miles NE), thence:

4   S of 20WR Light–buoy (starboard hand) (2½ miles NNE), a wreck with a least depth of 12·2 m (40 ft) over it lies 2 cables ESE, and:

    N of Cape Poge, a bare precipitous bluff which is the N extremity of Chappaquiddick Island. Cape Poge Light (white conical tower) stands on this headland.

5   Thence the track leads WNW, passing:

    SSW of No 22 Light–buoy (starboard hand) (3½ miles NNW), which marks the S side of Hedge Fence. The red sector of Nobska Point Light (263°-289°) (5.104) covers Hedge Fence and the patches W of it bordering the N side of the channel. Thence:

6   NNE of East Chop and West Chop (6 and 8 miles WNW, respectively), the entrance points to Vineyard Haven (5.84). Both these headlands terminate in a high wooded bluff and are prominent from the sound. Lights stand on each headland. NW Light–buoy (safe water) lies in mid–channel in the approaches to Vineyard Haven.

7   **Useful marks:**

    East Chop Light (41°28′N 70°34′W) (5.89).

    West Chop Light (41°29′N 70°36′W) (5.89).

North Channel
5.48

1   North Channel is entered from E, either S or N of Bishop and Clerks, a shoal awash in the middle, the central part of which is marked by a light (white and red round tower) (41°34′·4N 70°15′·0W).

    South entrance. From a position SSE of Bishop and Clerks the S entrance channel leads NW, passing (with positions relative to Bishop and Clerks Light):

2   Between No 2 Light–buoy (starboard hand) (1¼ miles SSE) and Broken Ground, thence:

    SW of Bishop and Clerks Light, thence:

    S of No 4 Buoy (starboard hand) (7 cables W), which marks the W side of Bishop and Clerks.

    North entrance. From a position E of Bishop and Clerks the N entrance channel leads W, passing (with positions relative to Point Gammon (41°36′N 70°16′W)):

3 N of No 1 Light–buoy (port hand) (2¼ miles SE),
marking the NE side of Bishop and Clerks, thence:
N of Bishop and Clerks Light (2¼ miles SSE),
thence:
S of a wreck (1 mile S), with a depth of 5·2 m (17 ft)
over it, lying close S of Hallets Rock at the edge
of shoal ground extending S from Point Gammon.
Thence:

4 S of HH Light–buoy (safe water) (1¼ miles SW),
which marks the approach to Hyannis Harbor
(5.57), thence:
Across West Southwest Ledge, thence:
SE of No 2 Buoy (port hand) (2½ miles SW) and
thence join the S entrance channel.

5.49

1 From a position W of Broken Ground (5.48) North
Channel continues W, passing (with positions relative to
Succonnesset Point (41°33′N 70°29′W)):
N of No 5 Light–buoy (port hand) (6 miles E) which
lies on the N side of Horseshoe Shoal, thence:

2 Between No 7 Buoy (port hand) and No 8 Light–buoy
(starboard hand) (4 miles E), which mark,
respectively, the NW side of Horseshoe Shoal and
the E end of Wreck Shoal, thence:
NNW of No 9 Buoy (port hand) (3¼ miles ESE),
which marks the N side of Eldridge Shoal, thence:
S of No 10 Light–buoy (starboard hand) (2¼ miles
ESE), moored S of two patches that lie S of
Succonnesset Shoal, thence:
S of a 4·7 m (15 ft) shoal (2 miles SE), thence:

3 N of a buoy (preferred channel to starboard)
(1½ miles SSE), which marks the NE limit of
L'Hommedieu Shoal. The red sector (263°-289°)
of Nobska Point Light (5.104) covers
L'Hommedieu Shoal with the exception of the N
extremity of a shoal spit that extends from the
middle of the N side of the shoal. Thence:

4 S of the coastal bank which extends up to 6 cables
offshore between Succonnesset Point and Falmouth
Harbor (6 miles W) (5.104). The limits of the bank
are marked by light–buoys and a buoy (starboard
hand). Thence:
N of Nos 13 and 15 Buoys (port hand) (2¼ miles
SW and 4½ miles WSW). No 15 Buoy marks the
W end of L'Hommedieu Shoal. Thence:

5 N of No 17 Buoy (6¼ miles WSW), which marks the
W end of some shoals that extend W from
L'Hommedieu Shoal.
Vineyard Sound can be entered W of No 15 Buoy or
No 17 Buoy, or clear of the W–most shoal (7 miles WSW),
which has a least depth of 4 m (13 ft) and the N side of
which is marked by a buoy (preferred channel to port).

Muskeget Channel

Chart 2456
Description
5.50

1 Muskeget Channel is an opening 6 miles wide that leads
into the S part of Nantucket Sound between the dangerous
shoals that extend SW, W and NW of Muskeget Island
(41°20′N 70°18′W), and Chappaquiddick Island.

Buoyage. The channel is marked by buoys and a
light–buoy.

2 **Local knowledge** is required to navigate this channel
due to the very strong tidal streams and shifting shoals that
make navigation dangerous.

Tidal streams
5.51

1 Tidal streams are strong having an average rate of
3¾ kn on the in–going stream and 3¼ kn on the out–going
stream. A rate of 5 kn is reached in the channel at times.
See Tide table on chart.

Directions
5.52

1 From the vicinity of MC Light–buoy (safe water)
(41°15′N 70°26′W) the channel leads N, passing (with
positions relative to Wasque Point (41°21′N 70°27′W)):
Clear of a dangerous wreck (4¾ miles S), thence:
E of No 1 Buoy (port hand) (3½ miles S), thence:
W of No 2 Light–buoy (starboard hand) (2 miles SE),
which marks Mutton Shoal, thence:

2 E of No 3 Buoy (port hand) (1½ miles SE), marking
the E side of Wasque Shoal, which is steep–to,
thence:
E of No 5 Buoy (port hand) (1½ miles NNE), which
marks the coastal bank that extends from the E
side of Chappaquiddick, thence:

3 W of No 4 Buoy (starboard hand) (2½ miles NE),
which marks the S extremity of Hawes Shoal,
thence:
W of No 6 Buoy (starboard hand) (5 miles NNE),
which marks the NW extremity of Hawes Shoal
and the N entrance to the channel.
Thence into Nantucket Sound.
(Directions for Main Channel are given at 5.46)

Chatham Roads

Chart 2489 (see 1.17)
General information
5.53

1 Chatham Roads (41°38′N 70°02′W) are situated at the
NE end of Nantucket Sound between Common Flat, which
extends 1½ miles NW from the N part of Monomoy Island,
and the shoal ground extending S from the N shore at
Harwich Port (2½ miles NW).

2 The roads are the approach to Stage Harbor and the
summer resort of Chatham.
Ice closes the harbour for short periods each winter.
Climate information. See 1.156.

Principal marks
5.54

1 **Landmarks:**
Radio Tower (41°40′·2N 70°01′·5W) at Mill Creek.
Stage Harbor Light (tower) (41°39′·5N 69°59′·1W) at
SW end of Harding Beach.

2 Domes (41°39′·4N 69°57′·6W) of National Weather
Service installation on Morris Island.
Chatham Light (41°40′N 69°57′W) (4.69).
Major light:
Chatham Light — as above.

Directions
5.55

1 From a position S of Kill Pond Bar (41°38′N 70°08′W),
a shoal with depths of 1·2 to 5·5 m (4 to 18 ft) over it

which lies NW of the entrance to Chatham Roads, the alignment (063°) of Stage Harbor Light and Chatham Light leads to SH Light–buoy (safe water) 8 cables WSW of Stage Harbor Light.

Anchorage
5.56

1 **Anchorage** may be obtained in Chatham Roads for vessels up 5·5 m (18 ft) draught in depths of 6 to 9 m (21 to 30 ft), soft bottom.

Caution. In SW gales this anchorage is insecure for small vessels.

Hyannis Harbor and adjacent waters

Charts 2489, 2456 (see 1.17)
General information
5.57

1 **Hyannis Harbor** (41°37′N 70°17′W), on the N side of Nantucket Sound, is entered between Point Gammon (5.46) and Hyannis Point, 2½ miles WNW. Lewis Bay, with depths of 0·6 to 3·6 m (2 to 12 ft), extends NE from Hyannis Harbor and has the summer resort of Hyannis in its NW corner. A dredged channel leads from Hyannis Harbor to Lewis Bay.

2 Hyannis Harbor, which is protected by a breakwater extending 5 cables SE from Hyannis Port on the W side of the harbour, is used as a harbour of refuge by coasters and pleasure craft drawing less than 4·3 m (14 ft).

Depths
5.58

1 Depths in the approach channel to Hyannis Harbor are 4 to 4·9 m (13 to 16 ft).

Controlling depths (2004) of the dredged channel leading from Hyannis Harbor to Lewis Bay and thence to the anchorage basin (5.64) N of Harbor Bluff, were 3·2 m (10·5 ft) to the anchorage basin, 3 to 4 m (9·6 to 13 ft) in the basin and 3·2 m (10·5 ft) to the town wharf.

Ice
5.59

1 Ice seldom interferes with the movement of vessels in Hyannis Harbor during normal winters. During severe winters or persistent SW winds the harbour may be temporarily closed to navigation and during very severe winters it has been closed by ice for up to 3 months.

Speed limit
5.60

1 Speed limit of 5 kn is in force in the channel leading to Hyannis Port Yacht Club and in Lewis Bay, N of Harbor Bluff (5.63).

Principal marks
5.61

1 **Landmarks:**
No 4A Beacon (starboard hand) (41°37′N 70°17′W), standing on Great Rock (5.62).
Tower (41°36′·6N 70°16′·0W) (5.46).
Tower (41°38′N 70°18′W).
Tower (41°37′·8N 70°18′·4W).
Major light:
Barnstable Airport Light (41°40′N 70°17′W).

Directions
5.62

1 **Hyannis Harbor.** From a position S of Point Gammon the approach to Hyannis Harbor leads S and W of that point, passing (with positions relative to tower on Point Gammon (41°37′N 70°16′W)):

2 S of No 2 Light–buoy (starboard hand) (5 cables S), which marks Gazelle Rock. Hallets Rock and a dangerous wreck lie 1 and 1¼ miles, respectively, S of the tower on Point Gammon. Thence:
Clear of HH Light–buoy (safe water) (1¼ miles SW), thence:

3 W of No 4 Light–buoy (starboard hand) (1¼ miles WNW), marking a rock, and No 4A Beacon (5.62) (1 mile WNW) standing on Great Rock, thence:
E of Hyannis Harbor Breakwater Head Light (black and white chequered diamond shaped daymark on black framework tower) (1½ miles NW).
Thence into Hyannis Harbor.
5.63

1 **Lewis Bay.** From a position E of Hyannis Harbor Breakwater Head Light the entrance channel, which is dredged and marked by light–buoys and buoys, passes (with positions relative to Breakwater Head Light):
NW of No 6 Light–buoy (starboard hand) (3 cables SE), which marks the entrance to the channel, thence:

2 Between Dunbar Point (1 mile ENE) and the W extremity of Egg Island, the entrance points of Lewis Bay, thence:
NE of Harbor Bluff (1½ miles NE).
Thence to the town wharf at Hyannis.

Berths
5.64

1 **Anchorage** is available in Hyannis Harbor N of the breakwater in depths of 5 to 6 m (15 to 20 ft). A dangerous wreck lies 3½ cables N of the Breakwater Light.

Port services
5.65

1 **Repairs:** patent slip for craft up to 43 m.
Other facilities: hospital at Hyannis.
Supplies: fuel; water and stores.

Nantucket Harbor

Chart 2489 (see 1.17)
General information
5.66

1 **Nantucket Harbor** (41°17′N 70°05′W) is situated on the N side of Nantucket Island, in the SE part of Nantucket Sound.

Nantucket, which is situated on the W side of the harbour, is the main town on the island and its principal industry is fishing. Coastal tankers bring petroleum cargoes from New York and it is also the terminal for the cargo and ferry service that is maintained between Nantucket Island and the mainland.

2 **Entrance.** Nantucket Harbor is approached by a dredged channel which leads between two breakwaters extending across shallow flats that extend one mile offshore. The harbour is entered between Brant Point and Coatue Point, the SW end of Coatue Beach, 4 cables N.

At half tide the E breakwater is almost entirely below–water and the W breakwater partially so.

Local knowledge is required to enter the harbour.

Depths
5.67

1 Controlling depth (2005) of the dredged channel was 4·6 m (15 ft) to No 9 Buoy thence 3·3 m (10¾ ft) to Brant Point.

Weather
5.68
1 **Fog** is frequent, particularly in the spring and summer.

Ice. Except in severe winters, ice of local formation seldom closes the harbour, however the harbour is frequently closed by drift ice from the sound during N winds.

Speed limit
5.69
1 Speed limit of 5 kn is in force in the harbour.

Principal marks
5.70
1 **Landmarks:**
> Spire (41°17′·0N 70°06′·0W).
> Water tower (41°17′·3N 70°08′·0W).

Directions
5.71
1 **Leading lights:**
> Front light (red rectangle, white stripe, on white framework tower) (41°17′·4N 70°05′·6W).
> Rear light (similar structure) (73 m from front light).

2 From the vicinity of NB Light–buoy (safe water) (41°19′N 70°06′W) the alignment (162°) of these lights leads SSE to the harbour entrance, passing between pairs of buoys and light–buoys (lateral) which mark the edge of the dredged channel.

3 **Useful marks:**
> East Breakwater Head No 3 Light (green square on framework tower) (41°19′N 70°06′W).
> Brant Point Light (white round tower) (41°17′N 70°06′W).

Anchorage
5.72
1 Anchorage is available in depths of 2 to 5 m (6 to 17 ft) off the S and SW sides of Brant Point or in depths of 4 to 5 m (12 to 17 ft) in the general anchorage S of Brant Point.

In general the bottom is good holding ground. In NE winds anchorage may be dangerous off the wharves and safer anchorage may be obtained in Head of the Harbor, 4 miles NE of Brant Point, in depths of 2 to 8 m (6 to 23 ft).

Alongside berths
5.73
1 **Ferry pier** with depths alongside of 4·3 m extends from the W shore 3½ cables SW of Brant Point.

Port services
5.74
1 **Facilities:** health clinic.
Supplies: fuel; water and stores.

Edgartown Harbor and adjacent waters

Chart 2456 (see 1.17)
General information
5.75
1 **Edgartown Harbor** (41°24′N 70°29′W) is formed by the channel between Chappaquiddick Island and Martha's Vineyard. It is divided into an outer and inner harbour.

2 The outer harbour is used primarily as a harbour of refuge in winds from all directions, except N, and as a night anchorage. The inner harbour provides a good anchorage for small vessels.

Edgartown, on the W side of the inner harbour, is a fishing town and summer resort and is much frequented by small craft during the summer.

3 **Cape Poge Bay**, a shallow lagoon in the N part of Chappaquiddick Island, is entered from the E side of Edgartown outer harbour. The unmarked entrance is mainly used by local pleasure and fishing craft.

Depths
5.76
1 In 1986 there was a controlling depth of 4·9 m (16 ft) in the channel from the outer harbour to off the town.

Pilots and tugs
5.77
1 There are no pilots. Fishing vessels will assist as tugs in an emergency.

Natural conditions
5.78
1 **Tidal streams.** The in–going and out–going tidal streams in the narrow part of the channel have a double period. Near the middle of each period there is a slack period preceded and followed by a period of maximum rate. The average rate is about 1 kn and a maximum rate of 3 kn has been reported.

2 **Ice.** It is reported that the harbour is normally closed by ice during January and February, except for the ferry channel that is kept open. Strong tidal streams normally keep the inner harbour open.

Fog is prevalent in the summer and at times appears without warning.

Principal marks
5.79
1 **Landmarks:**
> Edgartown Light (white conical tower) (41°23′·5N 70°30′·2W).
> Church tower (41°23′·4N 70°30′·9W) standing in Edgartown.
> Water tower (41°22′·7N 70°31′·2W).

Directions
5.80
1 From the vicinity of 41°26′N 70°29′W the buoyed channel through the outer harbour leads S through waters free from dangers and has depths of 6·1 to 11·3 m (20 to 37 ft) until No 8 Buoy is reached at the S end of the harbour. The channel then leads W to the wharves at the town.

Anchorages
5.81
1 **Outer harbour.** Anchorage is available in E gales W of Cape Poge on the E side of the harbour, and in W and S gales in the S part of the harbour 4 cables E or ESE of Edgartown Light.

2 **Inner harbour.** Anchorage is available 5 cables SE of the town, S of Middle Ground Shoal, in depths of 7 to 9 m (24 to 30 ft), clay.

Vessels should not anchor in the channel abreast the town where the bottom is hard, the channel narrow, the tidal stream strong and where there are cable areas and a ferry route.

Alongside berths
5.82
1 **Town wharf** has a depth alongside of 7·6 m. Other wharves have general depths alongside of 3·4 m.

Port services
5.83
1   **Facilities:** health clinic.
   Supplies: fuel; water and stores.

Vineyard Haven and adjacent waters

General information
5.84
1   **Vineyard Haven** (41°28′N 70°35′W) is situated on the N side of Martha's Vineyard. This haven, which is easy of access, is the most important harbour of refuge between Provincetown (4.151) and Narragansett Bay (5.216). It is exposed to NE gales, but vessels with good tackle can ride out most gales.

2   **Vineyard Haven Town** is situated on the W side of the head of the haven. It is the ferry terminal for services to the mainland. The ferry slip is protected by a detached breakwater which extends SE from the shore N of the town.

3   **Lagoon Pond**, which is only used by local craft, extends 2 miles SSW from the SE part of Vineyard Haven.

Depths
5.85
1   Depths in the haven are sufficient for the largest vessels passing through Nantucket and Vineyard Sound, ranging from 12·2 to 4·6 m (40 to 15 ft) between the entrance and the head of the harbour.
   Dredged channel from SE of the breakwater to the ferry wharf has a controlling depth of 4·9 m (16 ft).

Pilots and tugs
5.86
1   Pilots are not available. Tug, equipped for salvage, is stationed in the harbour.

Natural conditions
5.87
1   **Tidal streams** in Vineyard Haven are weak.
   Ice. Both fast ice and pack ice obstruct, and at times, entirely close the harbour during severe winters. Strong N winds drive pack ice into the harbour and endanger vessels at anchor.

Principal marks
5.88
1   **Landmarks:**
   Cupola (41°27′·4N 70°34′·0W) in Oak Bluffs.
   Water tower (41°26′·4N 70°34′·9W).
   Tank (41°26′·7N 70°36′·8W).

Directions
5.89
1   From the vicinity of NW Light–buoy (41°29′N 70°34′W) the track leads SSW into Vineyard Haven passing between East Chop Light (white tower) (41°28′N 70°34′W) and West Chop Light (white conical tower) (1½ miles WNW), which stand, respectively, on East Chop (5.47) and West Chop (5.47).

2   Vessels proceeding to the head of the haven pass between No 7 Light–beacon (green square on post) and No 6 Buoy (starboard hand) which mark the edge of the shoal water on either side of the haven.
   Caution. Care should be taken during the W–going stream not to approach West Chop too closely, as this stream sets on the shoal ground extending N and E from the point.

3   **Useful marks:**
   Breakwater Head Light No 10 (red triangle on post) (41°27′·5N 70°35′·8W).
   Ferry slip light (on roof of shed) (41°27′N 70°36′W).

Anchorage
5.90
1   Anchorage may be obtained anywhere according to draught clear of the cable area shown on the chart, shallow-draught vessels favouring the W shore. A good berth is NE of No 6 Buoy in depths of 6 to 7 m (20 to 23 ft). The anchorage is very crowded in bad weather and the principal danger in NE gales is from vessels with poor ground tackle that are liable to drag.

Alongside berths
5.91
1   **Ferry wharf** at the head of the channel has a reported depth alongside of 7·3 m at its outer face.
   Town wharf lies 1 cable N of the ferry wharf.

Port services
5.92
1   **Facilities:** hospital.
   Supplies: fuel; water and stores.

Anchorages and harbours

Chart 2489 (see 1.17)
Saquatucket Harbor
5.93
1   Saquatucket Harbor (41°40′N 70°04′W) at the mouth of the Andrews River is only used by small craft.

Wychmere Harbor
5.94
1   Wychmere Harbor (41°40′N 70°04′W), which lies 2½ cables W of Saquatucket Harbor and 5 cables E of the village of Harwich Port, is entered between two jetties and is used by fishing and pleasure craft.

Allen Harbor
5.95
1   Allen Harbor (41°40′N 70°06′W), used by small craft, lies 1 mile W of Wychmere Harbor and has a narrow entrance between two breakwaters leading into Doanes Creek.

Herring River
5.96
1   Herring River (41°39′N 70°07′W), used by small craft, is entered between two small jetties.

Bass River
5.97
1   Bass River (41°39′N 70°12′W), used by small craft, is entered between two jetties.

Chart 2456 (see 1.17)
Centerville Harbor
5.98
1   Centerville Harbor (41°38′N 70°21′W), which lies between Hyannis Point (5.57) and Osterville Point, 3 miles WSW, is an open bay the approach to which is obstructed by numerous rocks and shoals which extend nearly 2½ miles offshore.

2   **Depths** of 3 m (10 ft) can be found in the natural channel leading to the anchorage.
   Although good anchorage can be obtained, it is seldom used for shelter as it is exposed to the S and the shoals off

the harbour do not break the sea sufficiently to make it a safe anchorage.

Ice sometimes closes the anchorage in winter.

Local knowledge is required to enter the anchorage, except in clear weather during daylight.

3 **Directions.** From a position S of Hodges Rock (41°35′·4N 70°19′·0W), a buoyed channel with depths of 3 m (10 ft) leads NW into Centerville Harbor, passing (with positions relative to Hodges Rock):

SW of Hodges Rock, marked on its S side by No 2 Buoy (starboard hand), thence:

NE of Gallatin Rock (9 cables WNW), marked by No 3 Buoy (port hand) on its SE side, thence:

4 Between Bearse Rock (1 mile NW) and Channel Rock (1¼ miles NW) which are marked, respectively, by No 4 Buoy (starboard hand) and a buoy (preferred channel to starboard); thence:

SW of Gannet Ledge, marked by No 6 Buoy (starboard hand).

Thence into Centerville Harbor.

5 **Useful mark.** Water tank (41°39′·5N 70°21′·2W).

Anchorage, with depths of 5 to 6 m (15 to 21 ft), is available about 5 cables offshore, taking care to avoid Spindle Rock, which is marked on its S side by No 8 Buoy (starboard hand).

West Bay
5.99
1 West Bay (41°37′N 70°24′W), used by small craft, is entered between two breakwaters 46 m apart and is the approach to the village of Osterville.

Ice closes the bay for about two months each year.

Cotuit Anchorage
5.100
1 Cotuit Anchorage (41°36′N 70°25′W) is an anchorage for small craft and is seldom used, except by local vessels, as it is exposed to the S.

Waquoit Bay
5.101
1 Waquoit Bay (41°34′N 70°31′W), used by small craft, is entered between two breakwaters, 2¼ miles WSW of Succonnesset Point.

Eel Pond
5.102
1 Eel Pond (41°33′N 70°33′W), used by small craft, is entered between breakwaters.

Green Pond
5.103
1 Green Pond (41°33′N 70°34′W), used by small craft, is entered between breakwaters.

Falmouth Harbor
5.104
1 Falmouth Harbor is the open roadstead extending from 1 to 3 miles ENE of Nobska Point (41°31′N 70°39′W), a bluff headland. It affords a lee in N winds and in S winds the sea is partly broken by L'Hommedieu Shoal.

This anchorage is frequently used by vessels with good ground tackle where a gale can be rode out in comparative safety, and the crowded conditions of Vineyard Haven in such weather can be avoided.

2 **Directions.** The anchorage can be entered by passing E of No 18 Buoy (starboard hand) which lies 3 cables ENE of Nobska Point Light (white tower, floodlit) or W of No 17 Buoy (port hand), which lies 2 miles E of this light. Vessels should keep clear of the shoal area, the N side of which is marked by a buoy (preferred channel to port), that extends W from L'Hommcdieu Shoal.

3 **Useful mark:**

High green water tower (41°33′·1N 70°38′·4W).

Anchorage. I Anchorage is situated 8 cables offshore in depths of 7 to 11 m (24 to 36 ft). Smaller vessels can anchor closer inshore in depths of 5 to 6 m (15 to 18 ft). Holding ground is good and depths decrease gradually towards the shore.

Falmouth Inner Harbor
5.105
1 Falmouth Inner Harbor (41°33′N 70°37′W) is a dredged basin which is entered between two breakwaters. The harbour lies W of Falmouth Heights, a prominent yellow bluff on the summit of which is a large hotel and many houses. No 1 Light (green square on white framework tower) stands on the W breakwater.

2 **Approach** is marked by No 16 Light–buoy (starboard hand) which lies 5 cables S of the entrance.

Depths. In 2004 the controlling depth in the entrance channel was 2·2 m (7·1 ft). In 2004 the controlling depth in the inner harbour was 1·9 m (6·2 ft), except for shoaling to 1·1 m (3·7 ft) in the NW part.

Ferry operates to Oak Bluffs (5.107) in summer.

Sengekontacket Pond
5.106
1 Sengekontacket Pond (41°25′N 70°34′W), on the NE side of Martha's Vineyard has two entrances that are subject to shoaling. The lagoon is used by local and fishing craft.

Oak Bluffs Harbor
5.107
1 Oak Bluffs Harbor (41°27′·6N 70°33′·6W) is a landlocked basin which is entered between two breakwaters. It is frequented by pleasure craft and some fishing vessels.

VINEYARD SOUND AND SOUTH-WEST APPROACHES

General information

Charts 2890, 2456
Description
5.108
1 Vineyard Sound (41°26′N 70°45′W) is bounded on the NW by the Elizabeth Islands extending 14 miles SW from the SW end of Cape Cod. The principal of these islands are Cuttyhunk Island, Nashawena Island, Pasque Island, Naushon Island and Nonamesset Island (5.118). The islands

are from 30 to 50 m high and their coasts are generally low bluffs separated by narrow passages forming harbours and means of communication between Vineyard Sound and Buzzards Bay (5.135).

2   The SE side of Vineyard Sound is bounded by the NW shore of Martha's Vineyard. This coast is rugged and generally inaccessible.

To the W, Vineyard Sound joins Rhode Island Sound on a line joining Cuttyhunk Island (41°25′N 70°56′W) and Gay Head (5½ miles SE) and to the E it joins Nantucket Sound on a line joining Nobska Point (41°31′N 70°39′W) (5.104) and West Chop (3 miles SE).

3   The channel through the sound is well marked and generally free of dangers.

South-west approach to Vineyard Sound is made from the E part of Rhode Island Sound. Nomans Land, an island situated 5 miles S of Gay Head, lies on the E side of these approaches. The island is prominent and rocky with many hills, the highest of which is over 30 m high. The shore is mainly clay and gravel cliffs.

Scientific Test Area
5.109
1   A Scientific Test Area, the position of which is marked by four light–buoys (special), lies 10 miles WSW of Gay Head. Numerous surface and subsurface buoys may lie within this area.

Pilotage
5.110
1   See 5.27.

Traffic regulations
5.111
1   **Navigation Rules for US Inland Waters** apply to the waters that lie inshore of lines joining:
> The S entrance points of Canapitsit Channel (41°25′N 70°54′W).
> Fox Point (41°26′N 70°51′W), the E point of Nashawena Island, and the S tangent of Naushon Island, 2¾ miles ENE.

2   Tarpaulin Cove Light (41°28′N 70°46′W) and Nobska Point Light, 5½ miles NE.
See 1.47 and Appendix VII for further information.

Prohibited area. A danger area surrounds Nomans Land, the limits of which are shown on the chart. Vessels should not enter this area. For details see Appendix VI.

3   **Prohibited anchorage.** Anchoring is prohibited in the fairway. The limits of the general areas where anchoring is permitted are shown on the chart.

Rescue
5.112
1   **Coast Guard** stations are situated near Menemsha Light (41°21′N 70°46′W) at the W end of Martha's Vineyard, and at Woods Hole (41°31′N 70°40′W).

Tidal streams
5.113
1   See Tidal Stream tables on the chart.

Directions

Principal marks
5.114
1   **Landmarks:**
> Buzzards Bay Entrance Light (41°24′N 71°02′W) (5.144).

Monument (41°24′·9N 70°56′·9W), 15 m in height, standing at the W end of Cuttyhunk Island.

2   **Major lights:**
> Gay Head Light (red brick tower, 16 m in height) (41°21′N 70°50′W).
> Buzzards Bay Entrance Light (41°24′N 71°02′W) (5.144).

Other aids to navigation
5.115
1   **Racon:**
> Buzzards Bay Entrance Light (41°24′N 71°02′W).
> See *Admiralty List of Radio Signals Volume 2* for details.

South-west approaches
5.116
1   From a position in the vicinity of 41°10′N 71°00′W, in the W part of Rhode Island Sound, the SW approach to Vineyard Sound leads generally NNE, passing (with positions relative to Gay Head (41°21′N 70°50′W)):

2   WNW of a dangerous wreck (12 miles S), the position of which is approximate, thence:
> WNW of Southwest Shoal (8 miles S), which lies on the SW side of the Prohibited Area surrounding Nomans Land. The S limit of this Prohibited Area is marked by No 2 Light–buoy (starboard hand). Thence:
> ESE of the Scientific Test Area (41°16′N 71°02′W) (5.109).

3   Thence to the entrance to Vineyard Sound, which lies between Gay Head and Cuttyhunk Island (6 miles NW). Deep–draught vessels should steer to pass at least 3½ miles S of the SW end of Cuttyhunk Island.

Vineyard Sound
5.117
1   From a position at least 3½ miles S of the SW end of Cuttyhunk Island, in the entrance to Vineyard Sound, the track leads generally NE through the sound, passing (with positions relative to Gay Head (41°21′N 70°50′W)):

2   SE of the shoals, marked by No 32 Light–buoy (starboard hand), with a least depth of 8·2 m (27 ft), that extend up to 3 miles S of Sow and Pigs Reef (6 miles WNW), which partly dries and extends 1½ miles SW from Cuttyhunk Island. The SW extremity of this reef is marked by No 36 Light–buoy (starboard hand) and its S side by No 34 Buoy (starboard hand). And:

3   NW of a dangerous wreck (3½ miles W), thence:
> NW of Devils Bridge which extends 1 mile NW from Gay Head and is marked by No 31 Light–buoy (port hand), thence:
> SE of No 30 Light–buoy (starboard hand) (3 miles N), moored 8 cables S of an 8·5 m (28 ft) patch, thence:

4   NW of No 29 Light–buoy (port hand) (4½ miles NNE), which marks the W extremity of Lucas Shoal, a narrow shifting ridge which lies on the SE side of the channel, thence:
> NW of Middle Ground (12 miles NE), the NE part of the ridge. The SW end of Middle Ground is marked by No 27 Light–buoy (port hand).

5   Thence the channel leads E into the W part of Nantucket Sound.

Useful mark:
    Tarpaulin Cove Light (white tower with small white building) (41°28′N 70°45′W).
(Directions for Main Channel through Nantucket Sound are given at 5.46, and for North Channel at 5.48)

Woods Hole

Chart 2456 (see 1.17)
General information
5.118

1   **Description.** Woods Hole (41°31′N 70°40′W) lies between the SW end of Cape Cod and Nonamesset Island and provides a narrow and intricate passage between Vineyard Sound and Buzzards Bay.

2   **General layout.** Woods Hole includes Great Harbor (5.126) and Little Harbor (5.127) in the E part, and Hadley Harbor in the W part. The two parts of Woods Hole are connected by Woods Hole Passage, which has a dredged section. Its E part also forms the approach to the town of Woods Hole on the NE shore of Great Harbor.

3   The main E-W part of Woods Hole Passage, which is known as The Strait, has two spur channels at either end. The S spur at the E end is known as Broadway, and the N spur at the W end is known as Branch.

   Woods Hole Town is a busy commercial centre and ferry terminal for traffic to Nantucket Island and Martha's Vineyard. During the summer it is a busy holiday resort.

4   **Local knowledge** is necessary to navigate this channel except at slack water.

No-discharge zones
5.119

1   Numerous No-discharge zones (NDZs) have been established in the vicinity of Woods Hole. See 1.44.

Controlling depths
5.120

1   In 1989 the controlling depths were 4 m (13 ft) in The Strait (5.118), 3·4 m (11 ft) in Broadway and 3·6 m (12 ft) in Branch. For the latest controlling depths the charts and port authority should be consulted.

Traffic regulations
5.121

1   **Navigation Rules for US Inland Waters.** See 5.111.

Natural conditions
5.122

1   **Tidal streams** through Woods Hole are so strong that passage is difficult and dangerous. Buoys marking the channel are sometimes towed under by the strong tidal stream.

2   Tidal streams in the passage turn W at about ½ an hour before HW Boston and to the E about 4¾ hours after HW Boston. At the E entrance the maximum rate of the streams is about 1½ kn and at the W entrance 1 kn, but at the narrowest part of the passage the rate is about 4 kn at springs. Both the rate of the streams and the time of slack water are affected by strong winds.

3   **Ice.** Strong tidal streams normally keep Great Harbor clear of ice. Drift ice is brought through from Buzzards Bay, but seldom interferes with navigation, except in unusually severe winters, when it may close the W entrance to Woods Hole.

Principal marks
5.123

1   **Landmarks** (with positions relative to Nobska Point):
    Nobska Point (41°31′N 70°39′W) (5.104).
    Water tower (2¼ miles NNE).
    Dome (9 cables NW) of Woods Hole Oceanographic Institution.

Woods Hole from NE (5.118)
(Original dated 2003)

(Photograph - Joseph R Melanson of www.skypic.com)

Directions

5.124

1   **Great Harbor Leading Lights:**

Front light (red rectangle, white stripe, on tower) (41°31′·5N 70°40′·5W).

Rear light (similar structure) (339 m from front light).

2   From a position SW of Nobska Point (41°31′N 70°39′W), in the vicinity of No 2 Light–buoy (starboard hand), the alignment (344°) of these lights leads NNW through the S entrance to Woods Hole, passing (with positions relative to Juniper Point Light No 6A (red triangle on framework tower, concrete base) (41°31′N 70°40′W)):

ENE of Nonamesset Shoal (5 cables SSW), which is marked by No 1 Buoy (port hand), and:

3   WSW of Great Ledge (3 cables S), marked by Nos 4 and 4A Buoys (starboard hand), thence:

Between No 5 Light–buoy (port hand) (2 cables SW) and Juniper Point. No 6 Buoy (starboard hand) marks the foul ground to the S of this point.

Thence into Great Harbor (5.126).

5.125

1   **Woods Hole Passage.** From a position W of Juniper Point the dredged channel, marked by buoys (lateral), leads generally WNW through Broadway, The Strait and Branch, passing (with positions relative to Juniper Point (41°31′N 70°40′W)):

NE of Mink Point (4 cables W), the NE point of Nonamesset Island, which lies 1 cable SW of the entrance to Broadway, thence:

2   SSE of Penzance Point (7 cables WNW), the S extremity of Penzance Island, which lies on the NW side of Great Harbor. Thence:

SSW of No 10 Light–buoy (starboard hand), which is moored at the W end of the dredged channel.

Thence the passage leads N into Buzzards Bay.

3   **Useful mark:**

Woods Hole Passage Light (red and white chequered diamond on dolphin) (41°31′·3N 70°40′·3W) is a directional light, and is exhibited along the 077°/257° axis of The Strait.

Great Harbor

5.126

1   Great Harbor lies on the NE side of Woods Hole N of the entrance from Vineyard Sound. There are several wharves and piers on the E side of the harbour.

2   **Anchorage** is available in the N part of the harbour in depths of 6 to 19 m (19 to 62 ft). The holding ground at the head of the harbour is poor, but good anchorage can be obtained in depths of 9 to 11 m (29 to 36 ft) about 1 cable NW of the National Marine Fisheries Service wharf.

3   **Alongside berths.** Depths alongside the various berths vary from 3·4 to 9·1 m. The principal berths are (with positions relative to Juniper Point Light No 6A):

Ferry Pier (4 cables NNW).

Oceanographic Institute wharf (4½ cables NNW).

Marine Biology Laboratory wharf (5 cables NNW).

4   National Marine Fisheries Service wharf (6 cables NNW).

Town Pier (6½ cables NNW).

Little Harbor

5.127

1   Little Harbor is the E cove in Woods Hole and is separated from Great Harbor by Juniper Point. Woods Hole Coast Guard station is on the W side of the harbour.

Entrance. The harbour is entered from Vineyard Sound by a narrow dredged channel, which is entered E of No 1 Light–buoy (port hand) 5½ cables SE of Juniper Point Light No 6A.

2   **Controlling depths** in 2001 were 4·9 m (16 ft) in the channel and 4·6 m (15 ft) in the basin on the W side of the harbour.

Speed limit of 5½ kn is enforced in the harbour.

Hadley Harbor

5.128

1   Hadley Harbor (41°31′N 70°42′W) approached through a narrow winding channel, suitable only for small craft, is situated in the W part of Woods Hole between Nonamesset Island and Uncatena Island.

Other channels

Charts 2456, 2890 (see 1.17)

Between Nomans Land and Martha's Vineyard

5.129

1   The passage between Nomans Land (41°15′N 70°49′W) and Squibnocket Point, 3 miles NNE, the S point of Martha's Vineyard, is obstructed by below–water rocks of which Old Man and Lone Rock lie in mid–channel.

2   **Channel.** A buoyed channel, suitable for small vessels by day, leads through this passage N of these rocks and S of the shoal ground extending S and SW from Squibnocket Point. No 1 Light–buoy (port hand) marks the E end of the channel.

Quicks Hole

5.130

1   Quicks Hole (41°27′N 70°51′W) leads between the E end of Nashawena Island and Pasque Island (5.108).

It is the only passage from Vineyard Sound to Buzzards Bay, through the Elizabeth Islands, that does not require local knowledge and is available to vessels with a draught of more than 3 m (10 ft). The passage is much used by vessels in tow, especially with W and S winds, to avoid the heavy sea in the entrance to Vineyard Sound.

2   The channel through this passage is nearly straight and has a width of 2 cables and is marked by light–buoys and buoys as for vessels proceeding N.

Depths are generally 9·1 m (30 ft) or more, but there are patches of 4·9 to 8·2 m (16 to 27 ft).

3   **Largest vessel.** Owing to the irregular depths the passage should not be attempted by vessels drawing more than 6·4 m (21 ft) unless local knowledge is available.

Tidal streams attain a rate of about 2½ kn and set N with the W–going stream in Vineyard Sound and S with the E–going stream. Strong winds affect the regularity of the tidal streams.

4   **Directions.** From a position NE of No 1 Light–buoy (41°25′·8N 70°50′·4W), which marks the S entrance, the channel leads generally N, passing (with positions relative to North Point (41°27′·0N 70°51′·4W)):

E of a dangerous wreck (7 cables SE), thence:

W of No 2 Light–buoy (starboard hand) (6 cables SE), marking shoal ground that extends 2½ cables W from Pasque Island, thence:

5   E of No 3 Buoy (port hand) (4 cables SE) which marks Felix Ledge, a patch with a depth of 4·9 m (16 ft) over it, thence:

E of Lone Rock (7 cables N), which is marked on its S side by a light–buoy (preferred channel to starboard).

Thence into Buzzards Bay.

Robinsons Hole
5.131

1   Robinsons Hole (41°27′N 70°48′W) is a narrow passage from Vineyard Sound to Buzzards Bay, leading between the E end of Pasque Island and the SW end of Naushon Island.

This passage is buoyed, being marked for craft proceeding NW and is sometimes used by local craft, but it is encumbered by rocks and the tidal streams are strong so that the buoys often tow under.

Other anchorages and harbours

Chart 2456 (see 1.17)
Menemsha Bight
5.132

1   Menemsha Bight (41°21′N 70°47′W) is situated near the W end of Martha's Vineyard.

Anchorage is available which provides shelter for vessels of any size from S and E winds, in depths of 8 to 18 m (25 to 60 ft) in good holding ground. The shores of the bight should be given a berth of 3 cables.

Menemsha Creek
5.133

1   Menemsha Creek is entered on the E side of Menemsha Bight through a dredged channel leading into a basin just inside the entrance, thence S to Menemsha Pond, 7½ cables above the entrance. The village of Menemsha stands on the E side of the basin.

2   **Entrance** to the creek is protected by two stone jetties. No 1 Buoy (port hand) lies in the approach to the entrance and the outer end of the E jetty is marked by No 3 Light–beacon (green square on framework tower).

Tidal streams through the entrance have a velocity of 3 kn or more. Slack water is reported to occur 45 minutes after local HW and LW.

3   **Depths.** In 1992 the controlling depth was 3 m (10 ft) to Menemsha Basin and thence 0·5 m (1½ ft) to Menemsha Pond. There are depths of 1·7 to 3 m (5½ to 10 ft) in the NW part of the basin and 1·1 to 1·5 m (3½ to 5 ft) in the SE part. For the latest controlling depths the charts should be consulted.

4   **Berths.** Moorings and alongside berths are available in the basin and anchorage may be obtained in Menemsha Pond, the S part of which has depths of 5·5 m (18 ft).

Tarpaulin Cove
5.134

1   Tarpaulin Cove (41°29′N 70°45′W) lies on the NW side of Vineyard Sound. It provides shelter from N and W winds and is frequently used. Tarpaulin Cove Light (5.117) stands on the S entrance point.

2   **Marks and dangers.** No 1 Buoy (port hand) is moored 2 cables NE of the light off the shore bank and a buoy (preferred channel to starboard) which is moored 3 cables N of the light, marks a rock with a depth of 2·4 m (8 ft) over it. The N shore of the cove should be given a berth of 1 cable and the W and SW shores a berth of more than 1½ cables.

3   **Navigation Rules for US Inland Waters.** See 5.111.

Anchorage is available in the cove in depths of 4 to 6 m (14 to 18 ft), good holding ground, with Tarpaulin Cove Light bearing between 189° and 212°. Large vessels should anchor farther out in depths of 11 m (36 ft) or more.

BUZZARDS BAY, CAPE COD CANAL AND NEW BEDFORD HARBOR

BUZZARDS BAY AND APPROACHES

General Information

Charts 2890, 2456
Description
5.135

1   **Buzzards Bay**, entered between Cuttyhunk Island (41°25′N 70°56′W) and Gooseberry Neck, 5½ miles NW, extends 24 miles NE. Besides this main entrance the bay may also be entered from Vineyard Sound through Woods Hole (5.118) and Quicks Hole (5.130). The bay forms the approach to the port of New Bedford and the W entrance of the Cape Cod Canal.

2   The shores are generally low, rocky and indented by many bays and rivers. Large boulders are a prominent feature and in some places they extend a considerable distance offshore rendering a close approach to the land dangerous.

Approach. The main entrance to the bay is approached from Rhode Island Sound.

3   **Entrance.** The main entrance has a clear width of 4¼ miles between Sow and Pigs Reef, which extends SW from Cuttyhunk Island, and Hen and Chickens which lies S of Gooseberry Neck.

Caution see 5.149.

No–discharge zone (NDZ). The whole of Buzzards Bay has been designated as a NDZ. See 1.44.

Depths
5.136

1   Depths in Buzzards Bay, especially in its entrance and approach, are irregular with boulder reefs in places. There are shoals in the entrance, with depths of 5·2 to 10·7 m (17 to 35 ft) over which the sea breaks in heavy SW gales.

2   The main channel, which leads up the bay to the entrance of the dredged channel leading to Cape Cod Canal, has a least depth of 8·5 m (28 ft). The head of the bay is encumbered with shoals.

Pilotage
5.137

1   Pilotage is compulsory in Buzzards Bay for all vessels of 350 gt or more and tows with barges carrying 6000 barrels or more of petroleum cargoes.

Pilots board:
In the vicinity of 41°23′N 71°21′W, 4 miles SSE of the entrance to Narragansett Bay (5.216), or:
2   In the vicinity of 41°17′N 71°30′W, 4 miles E of the NE entrance to Block Island Sound (6.6), or:
5 cables ESE of CC Light–buoy (41°49′N 70°28′W), off the E entrance to the Cape Cod Canal.

Traffic regulations
5.138

1   **Navigation Rules for US Inland Waters** apply to all waters lying within a line joining the extremity of Cuttyhunk Island (41°25′N 70°57′W) and the tower on Gooseberry Neck, 5¾ miles NW. See 1.47 and Appendix VII for further information.

Precautionary Area. See 5.10.

2   **Traffic separation scheme** for the approaches to Buzzards Bay leads NE from the Precautionary Area. This TSS is IMO–adopted and Rule 10 of the *International Regulations for Preventing Collisions at Sea (1972)* applies. The two traffic lanes are separated by a 1 mile wide separation zone. This TSS is not marked by buoys.

3   **Speed limits.** A speed limit of 4½ kn is enforced in many of the small harbours within Buzzards Bay.

Recommended routes
5.139
1   Recommended routes for deep-draught vessels, tugs and barges, as shown on the charts, have been established in Buzzards Bay. See 5.2.

Anchorages
5.140
1   General anchorage areas L and M, as shown on the chart, lie in the central part of Buzzards Bay, SE and NW, respectively, of the Recommended route (5.139).

Cable area
5.141
1   Cable areas, the limits of which are shown on the chart, are situated in the main entrance to Buzzards Bay between Cuttyhunk Island and Gooseberry Neck.

Rescue
5.142
1   **Cape Cod Coast Guard Air Station.** See 4.67.

Natural conditions
5.143
1   **Ice.** The head of Buzzards Bay and the harbours in its vicinity are generally closed to navigation during the winter months.

2   The approaches to the harbours on the E side are rendered dangerous by pack ice which, in exceptionally severe winters, extends across the bay and joins local ice on the W shore, thus forming an impassable barrier for a short while. Ice forms more rapidly with the wind from between N and W. Under ordinary circumstances a NE wind, lasting for two days, will clear the bay of ice. S winds diminish the extent and weaken the strength of the pack ice.

3   **Tidal streams** are strong in the passages between Vineyard Sound and Buzzards Bay.

At a position about 2 miles SSE of the S extremity of Gooseberry Neck, the tidal stream is rotary, turning clockwise. The maximum stream sets 065° and 215° at an average rate of ½ kn at about 4¾ hours before and ½ hour after HW at Boston.

The average rate of tidal streams in Buzzards Bay is less than ½ kn.

Directions
(continued from 5.15)

Principal marks
5.144
1   **Landmarks:**
Buzzards Bay Entrance Light (tower on red square on 3 red piles with large tube, with name on sides) (41°24′N 71°02′W).
Monument (41°24′·9N 70°56′·9W) (5.114).
2   Watch tower (41°29′N 71°02′W) standing on Gooseberry Neck.

Twin cupolas (41°34′N 70°39′W) on a hotel standing on Hamlin Point.
Radar dome (41°32′N 70°56′W) standing on Round Hill Point.
3   **Major lights:**
Buzzards Bay Entrance Light — see above.
Gay Head Light (41°21′N 70°50′W) (5.114).
Cleveland East Ledge Light (white round tower and dwelling, red caisson) (41°38′N 70°42′W).

Other aids to navigation
5.145
1   **Racons:**
Buzzards Bay Entrance Light (41°24′N 71°02′W).
Cleveland East Ledge Light (41°38′N 70°42′W).
See *Admiralty List of Radio Signals Volume 2* for details.

Approaches
5.146
1   From within the Precautionary Area, centred 41°06′N 71°23′W, the approach to the main entrance to Buzzards Bay leads NE for 20 miles through a TSS, passing:
NW of Browns Ledge (41°20′N 71°06′W) and an unnamed bank, with a depth of 9·8 m (32 ft) over it, which lies 2 miles farther NE.

Entrance
5.147
1   From the NE end of the TSS the track through the entrance to Buzzards Bay leads NE, passing (with positions relative to Buzzards Bay Entrance Light (41°24′N 71°02′W):
NW of Buzzards Bay Entrance Light (5.144), thence:
2   SE of a 6·7 m (22 ft) shoal (2 miles N), marked by No 1 Light–buoy (port hand), thence:
NW of No 2 Light–buoy (starboard hand) (2½ miles NNE), thence:
NW of Coxens Ledge (4 miles NE), the W extremity of which is marked by No 4 Light–buoy (starboard hand), thence:
3   Between Mishaum Ledge and a 7 m (23 ft) shoal (6 miles NE), which are marked, respectively, by No 5 Light–buoy (port hand) and No 6 Light–buoy (starboard hand).
Thence into Buzzards Bay.
5.148
1   An alternative route, which is suitable for vessels with a draught not exceeding 4·9 m (16 ft), leads ENE from the vicinity of 41°27′N 71°05′W, passing (with positions relative to Buzzards Bay Entrance Light (41°24′N 71°02′W)):
2   Between Old Cock and No 3 Light–buoy (port hand) (3½ miles N). Old Cock is marked by a pipe and No 1 Buoy (port hand) which is moored on its S side. Thence:
Between Nos 5 and 6 Light–buoys (6 miles NE).
5.149
1   **Caution.** Owing to the irregularity in depths, it is necessary to proceed with caution when crossing areas where the vessel's maximum draught is within 1·8 m (6 ft), of the charted depth. When drawing more than 4·9 m (16 ft) the irregular depths in the approach and entrance should be avoided.

Within Buzzards Bay
5.150
1   From within the entrance to Buzzards Bay (41°28′N 70°57′W) the route continues to lead NE, passing (with reference to Round Hill Point (41°32′N 70°56′W)):

2   Between Wilkes Ledge (2 miles SSE), marked on its SE side by No 7 Light-buoy (port hand), and a shoal with a depth of 8·8 m (29 ft) (4 miles SE), marked on its NW side by No 8 Light-buoy (starboard hand). Thence:

3   Either side of BB Light-buoy (safe water) (4½ miles ESE), which lies at the entrance to the buoyed channel leading to New Bedford (5.190), thence:

SE of a shoal with a depth of 9·1 m (30 ft) (7 miles E), marked on its SE side by No 9 Light-buoy (port hand), thence:

4   NW of a shoal with a depth of 7·0 m (23 ft) (9½ miles ENE) marked on its N side by No 10 Light-buoy (port hand). A dangerous wreck lies a farther 1 mile ENE. Thence:

NW of No 2 Light-buoy (11 miles ENE).

Thence to the W entrance to the Cape Cod Canal (5.165) (11½ miles ENE).

(Directions continue for Cape Cod Canal at 5.175. Directions for New Bedford Harbor are given at 5.206)

Anchorages and harbours

Chart 2456 (see 1.17)
Cuttyhunk Harbor
5.151

1   Cuttyhunk Harbor (41°26′N 70°55′W) is formed by the bay between the E end of Cuttyhunk Island and the W end of Nashawena Island and is protected from the N by Penikese Island and Gull Island together with the shoal ground surrounding them. It is exposed to NE winds.

Function. The harbour, sometimes used for shelter by coasters and fishing vessels, forms the approach to Cuttyhunk Pond (5.152) and the village of Cuttyhunk (5.152).

2   **Approach and depths.** The harbour is normally entered from Buzzards Bay. Vessels approaching from NW should not have a draught of more than 3 m (10 ft). The approach from NE is deeper. The principal dangers are buoyed.

Local knowledge. The harbour is foul round its shores and entry should not be attempted without local knowledge except in daytime with clear weather.

3   **Cable areas** exist in the NW passage and in the centre of the harbour.

Ice is carried into the harbour with N winds and closes it for short periods in severe winters.

Anchorage, in depths of 3 to 7 m (10 to 24 ft), can be obtained clear of the cable area and the foul ground that extends up to 2½ cables offshore.

Cuttyhunk Pond
5.152

1   Cuttyhunk Pond is entered on the SW side of Cuttyhunk Harbor through a narrow dredged channel. The village of Cuttyhunk lies on the SW side of Cuttyhunk Pond. The entrance is protected by two jetties, the N, above–water, being marked at its end by No 8 Light–beacon (red triangle on grey framework tower, concrete base) and the S, which dries, being marked by No 9 Buoy (port hand).

2   **Depths.** In 2003 the entrance channel had a controlling depth of 2·2 m (7·3 ft), thence 2·7 m (9 ft) in the channel to the turning basin, which had depths of 2·1 to 3 m (7 to 10 ft).

Quisset Harbor
5.153

1   Quisset Harbor (41°32′N 70°40′W), on the E side of Buzzards Bay, is entered 1½ miles NE of the N entrance to Woods Hole and is used by small pleasure craft.

Chart 2455
Apponaganset Bay
5.154

1   Apponaganset Bay (41°34′N 70°56′W) is entered S of Padanaram Breakwater off Ricketsons Point about 2½ miles NNW of Dumpling Rocks Light (5.208). No 8 Light (red triangle on grey framework tower) stands at the head of the breakwater.

The bay is used by pleasure craft and a few fishing vessels in summer, but is insecure in SE gales.

2   **Local knowledge** is required to enter Apponaganset Bay at night or during thick weather owing to the dangers in the approach.

Anchorage can be obtained in the bay in depths of 4 to 6 m (13 to 20 ft), sticky bottom, between the entrance and 3½ cables NW of the breakwater light–beacon. Care should be taken to avoid Dartmouth Rock, with a depth of 1·2 m (4 ft) over it, which lies on the E side of the bay.

Clarks Cove
5.155

1   Clarks Cove (41°36′N 70°55′W) is entered between Ricketsons Point and Clarks Point, the W entrance point to New Bedford Harbor (5.187), and provides anchorage in depths of 4 to 7 m (13 to 23 ft), but it is exposed to S winds and seldom used.

Charts 2455, 2456 (see 1.17)
Nasketucket Bay
5.156

1   Nasketucket Bay (41°36′N 70°49′W), on the W side of Buzzards Bay, is entered between West Island and Cormorant Rock. The outer part of the bay is sometimes used as an anchorage in SW winds, but N and W of West Island is much obstructed by foul ground.

Charts 2456, 2455, 2891
Mattapoisett Harbor
5.157

1   Mattapoisett Harbor (41°38′N 70°48′W), on the W side of Buzzards Bay, is entered between the SE extremity of Mattapoisett Neck, and Strawberry Point and Angelica Point. The harbour is the approach to the town of Mattapoisett and is much frequented by yachts in the summer.

Chart 2456 (see 1.17)
West Falmouth Harbor
5.158

1   West Falmouth Harbor, on the E side of Buzzards Bay, is entered immediately N of Chappaquoit Point (41°36′N 70°39′W). A prominent tower stands on Chappaquoit Point. The harbour is used only by small craft.

Chart 2891
Wild Harbor
5.159

1   Wild Harbor, a cove on the E side of Buzzards Bay, is entered between the W end of Nyes Neck (41°38′N 70°39′W), on which stands a prominent tower, and Crow Point, 3 cables SE. No 1 Light–buoy (port hand) marks the N side of the entrance.

The shores of the harbour are foul and its E part is shoal.

2   **Anchorage**, sheltered from N and E winds, is available just inside the entrance in depths of 4 to 6 m (13 to 20 ft).

Megansett Harbor
5.160

1   Megansett Harbor (41°39′N 70°39′W), on the E side of Buzzards Bay, is entered between Nyes Neck and Scraggy Neck, 1 mile N, and leads to the towns of North Falmouth, Megansett and Cataumet, situated respectively, on the SE, E and NE shores of the harbour. Cataumet Rock, marked by No 4 Buoy (port hand), lies on the S side of the entrance.

2   **Channel**, marked by buoys and with a least depth of 2·4 m (8 ft) leads into the harbour.

Anchorage in depths of 3 to 7 m (10 to 22 ft) is available between 2 and 5 cables W of the breakwater at Megansett.

Pocasset Harbor and Red Brook Harbor
5.161

1   Pocasset Harbor and Red Brook Harbor, on the E side of Buzzards Bay, are situated between Scraggy Neck (41°40′N 70°39′W) and Wings Neck, 1 mile N. They have a common entrance between Southwest Ledge, which extends 8 cables W from Scraggy Neck, and Wings Neck, 8 cables NNE. The NW side of Southwest Ledge is marked by No 10 Buoy (starboard hand). The two harbours are separated by Bassetts Island and are only used by small craft.

2   **Entrance**. Irregular depths of 5·2 to 5·8 m (17 to 19 ft) extend across the entrance, and Eustis Rock marked by ER Buoy (preferred channel to starboard) lies about 2 cables off the N side of Scraggy Neck.

Anchorage is available, to vessels drawing up to 4·3 m (14 ft), in the entrance in depths of 6 to 9 m (20 to 30 ft) about 2½ cables W of Eustis Rock.

Sippican Harbor
5.162

1   Sippican Harbor (41°42′N 70°45′W), on the W side of Buzzards Bay, is entered between Converse Point (41°40′N 70°45′W) and Bird Island, 1¼ miles ESE. The harbour forms the approach to the town of Marion, which stands on its W shore, and is much used by yachts and pleasure craft.

Ice usually closes Sippican Harbor for about a month or more each winter.

Wings Cove
5.163

1   Wings Cove is entered S of Great Hill Point (41°42′N 70°43′W), 2 miles N of Bird Island. It provides shelter from W winds in depths of 2 to 5 m (7 to 16 ft).

Wareham River
5.164

1   Wareham River, flowing into the NW side of the head of Buzzards Bay, is entered between Cromeset Point (41°43′N 70°43′W) and Long Beach Point, 5 cables NE. The river is the approach to the town of Wareham, at the head of navigation, 2 miles above the entrance.

CAPE COD CANAL
AND ADJACENT WATERS

General information

Chart 2891
Description
5.165

1   Cape Cod Canal is a deep–draught sea–level waterway connecting Buzzards Bay and Cape Cod Bay. The waterway is 15 miles long from its W entrance at Cleveland East Ledge Light (41°38′N 70°42′W) to deep water in Cape Cod Bay.

2   The canal shortens the distance between points N and S of Cape Cod by 50 to 150 miles and provides an inside passage to avoid Nantucket Shoals.

Cape Cod Canal - West Entrance (5.165)
(Original dated 2002)

(Photograph - Robert P. David - Reproduced by permission of Cape Cod Sail & Power Squadron, United States Power Squadrons)

The canal is maintained by the Federal Government as a free waterway.

Depths
5.166

1   The project depth for the canal is 9·76 m (32 ft). For the latest controlling depths the charts and port authority should be consulted.

Maximum size of vessel
5.167

1   Length: 251·6 m   (825 ft).
       Draught: 9·76 m   (32 ft).
       Beam: 38·1 m   (125 ft).

Tidal levels
5.168

1   **Tidal levels.** At the Buzzards Bay entrance to the Cape Cod Canal, the mean spring range is about 1·3 m; mean neap range about 0·8 m. At the Cape Cod Bay entrance the mean spring range is about 2·9 m; mean neap range about 2·1 m. See information in Admiralty Tide Tables.

Canal effect
5.169

1   Mariners are warned to be on the alert for the effects of passing through the restricted waters of a canal. These effects may cause the vessel to take a sudden sheer.

Pilotage and tugs
5.170

1   **Pilots** board:
       Off the E entrance (41°47′N 70°29′W) 5 cables ESE of CC Light–buoy, or:
       In the vicinity of 41°23′N 71°21′W, 4 miles SSE of the entrance to Narragansett Bay (5.216), or:

2   In the vicinity of 41°17′N 71°30′W, 4 miles E of the NE entrance to Block Island Sound (6.6).
    Pilots services are generally arranged in advance by ship's agents or directly by shipping companies.
    See *Admiralty List of Radio Signals Volume 6(5)* for details.
    Tugs of up to 2200 hp are based at the village of Buzzards Bay (41°45′N 70°37′W).

Traffic regulations
5.171

1   For regulations governing the use, administration and navigation of Cape Cod Canal, see Appendix IX.
    Navigation Rules for US Inland Waters apply W of a line drawn from Canal Breakwater Light 4 (41°46′·8N 70°29′·3W) S to the shoreline. See 5.138, 1.47 and Appendix VII for further information.

2   **Traffic lights**, red, green and yellow in colour, are situated:
       At the SW end of Wings Neck (41°41′N 70°40′W) governing the W entrance of Hog Island Channel.
       On the S side of the E canal entrance (41°46′·5N 70°29′·8W).

3   At the Canal Electric Terminal Basin (41°46′·3N 70°30′·2W) on the S side of the canal at Sandwich. These traffic lights only apply to vessels using this terminal.
    Traffic signals apply to all vessels over 20 m (65 ft) in length wishing to transit the canal. For detailed information of signals see Appendix IX.

Vertical clearance
5.172

1   **Bridges** cross the Cape Cod Canal as follows:
       Rail bridge at Buzzards Bay (41°44′·6N 70°36′·8W) with vertical lift span. Vertical clearance when opened 41 m (135 ft). Span is normally in raised position.

2   State Route 25/28 road bridge at Bourne (41°44′·8N 70°35′·4W). Fixed span with vertical clearance of 41 m (135 ft).
       US 6/State Route 3 road bridge at Sagamore (41°46′·6N 70°32′·6W). Fixed span with vertical clearance of 41 m (135 ft).

3   **Overhead power cables.** The vertical clearance of overhead power cables is 48·8 m (160 ft).

Rescue
5.173

1   **Coast Guard** station is situated on the S side of the canal 3 cables from the E entrance.

Natural conditions
5.174

1   **Tidal streams.** The large differences in range and timing of the tide between Buzzards Bay and Cape Cod Bay cause strong tidal streams in the canal. Tides may lower the canal level 0·6 m below MLW or even more if attended by heavy offshore winds. Under ordinary conditions the E–going tidal stream has a rate of 4 kn and the W–going tidal stream a rate of 4½ kn.

2   **Ice.** The canal itself has never been closed by ice, but occasionally Buzzards Bay and Cape Cod Bay become so congested with ice that navigation through the canal is prevented.
    Fog is said to be less dense over Cape Cod Canal than outside, but at times a water vapour rises from the canal to such an extent that traffic has to be suspended.

Directions
(continued from 5.150)

Principal marks
5.175

1   **Landmarks:**
       Cleveland East Ledge Light (41°38′N 70°42′W) (5.144).
       Tower (41°38′N 70°39′W) standing on Nyes Neck.
       Water tower (41°42′·6N 70°43′·3W) standing on Great Hill.
       Rail and road bridges crossing canal. See 5.172.

2   **Major lights:**
       Cleveland East Ledge Light — as above.
       Cape Cod Canal Breakwater Head Light (41°47′N 70°29′W) (4.147).

Other aids to navigation
5.176

1   **Racon:**
       Cleveland East Ledge Light.
    See *Admiralty List of Radio Signals Volume 2* for details.

Cleveland Ledge Channel
5.177

1   **Leading light–beacons:**
       Front light (red rectangle, white stripe, on white tower) (41°41′·6N 70°40′·5W).
       Rear light (similar daymark on white framework tower) (1·6 miles from front light).

2   The alignment (015°) of these lights leads NNE for 3 miles through Cleveland Ledge Channel, passing between Nos 3 and 4 Light–buoys (lateral).

Hog Island Channel
5.178
1   From the vicinity of No 1 Light–buoy (port hand) (41°41′N 70°41′W) at the N end of Cleveland Ledge Channel, Hog Island Channel leads NE for about 4 miles between pairs of light–buoys (lateral) and light–beacons, passing (with positions relative to Burgess Point (41°44′N 70°39′W)):

SE of Stony Point Dike (2 miles SW) which is 1·5 m high, thence:

2   Between Cedar Island Point (7 cables SSW) and the W extremity of Mashnee Island (7 cables SSE) (5.184), thence:

Between Hog Neck (5.185) (3 cables SSE) and Hog Island (5 cables ESE).
Thence into Canal Land Cut.

Canal Land Cut
5.179
1   From the vicinity of Taylor Point (41°44′N 70°37′W) Canal Land Cut leads generally ENE for 7 miles through the isthmus connecting Cape Cod to the mainland, to Cape Cod Bay.

*(Directions for E entrance to
Cape Cod Canal are given at 4.147)*

Berths

Anchorage areas
5.180
1   Anchorage areas C and D have been established on the W and E side, respectively, of the N part of Cleveland Ledge Channel (5.177). The limits of these areas are shown on the chart.

Mooring basins
5.181
1   Mooring basins, with mooring dolphins, are situated at both ends of Canal Land Cut. The basin at the W end, where shoaling was reported (1979), is on the E side of Hog Island Channel abreast Hog Island (41°44′N 70°38′W). The basin at the E end is on the N side of the canal, 5 cables within the entrance.

Wharves
5.182
1   **State Pier** at Taylors Point (41°44′N 70°37′W), site of Massachusetts Maritime Academy. 182 m in length with a depth alongside of 7·6 m. In 1981 shoaling to 3 m (10 ft) was reported off the pier. Vessels should not attempt to go alongside except at slack water. Passing vessels should proceed slowly.
2   **Oil berth** 1¼ miles WSW of Cape Cod Canal Breakwater Head Light No 6 (41°47′N 70°29′W). Mooring platform 228 m in length with a depth alongside of 12·2 m. Vessels over 50 000 tonnes moor at HW during daylight hours. Vessels under 50 000 tonnes moor at slack water day or night.

Adjacent waters

Pocasset River
5.183
1   Pocasset River (41°42′N 70°37′W), used only by small craft, is approached from Buzzards Bay through the buoyed

channel leading to Phinneys Harbor (5.184). It is entered from the N side of Wings Neck through a privately dredged channel that leads S between two breakwaters to a road bridge 4 cables above the entrance.

Phinneys Harbor
5.184
1   Phinneys Harbor (41°43′N 70°37′W), situated between Mashnee Island and Tobys Island forms the approach to the village of Monument Beach. Back River flows into the NE corner of the harbour.
2   **Approaches.** The harbour is approached from Buzzards Bay by a buoyed channel which leads along the N side of Wings Neck to close E of No 7 Light–beacon (green square on pile), thence N to the harbour where the channel with a least depth of 3 m (10 ft) leads NE to the anchorage. Rocks situated 2½ cables off the S part of the E side of the harbour are buoyed.
3   **Anchorage** can be obtained in the middle of the harbour in depths of 4 to 5 m (13 to 17 ft) and off the public pier in depths of 2 m (8 ft).
Public pier in the SE corner of the harbour has depths alongside of 2·4 to 3 m.

Onset Bay
5.185
1   Onset Bay (41°44′N 70°39′W) lies on the NW side of Hog Island Channel between Hog Neck and Sias Point. It forms the approach to the village of Onset.
Approach. Onset Bay is entered between Hog Neck the E extremity of Great Neck and Sias Point, 7 cables NNE. A dredged channel, marked by buoys, leads from between Hog Neck and No 21 Light–beacon (green square on framework tower) along the S side of the bay to a turning basin off the village.
2   **Depths.** In 1995 depths were 4 m (14 ft) in the channel and 4 to 4·6 m (13 to 15 ft) in the basin.
Special anchorage is situated in the N part of Onset Bay between Wickets Island, high and wooded, and the mainland NE, with depths of 2 to 4 m (7 to 13 ft). There are additional anchorages at the head of the channel with depths of 2 m (6 to 8 ft).
3   **Wharf.** The public wharf at Onset has a depth alongside of 4·3 m.

Buttermilk Bay
5.186
1   Buttermilk Bay (41°45′N 70°37′W), situated NE of Long Neck, has depths of 0·3 m to 2·1 m (1 to 7 ft) and is only suitable for small craft.

NEW BEDFORD AND APPROACHES

General information
Chart 2455
Position
5.187
1   **New Bedford** (41°38′N 70°55′W) stands on the W bank of the Acushnet River at the head of New Bedford Harbor. Fairhaven stands on the opposite bank of the river.

Function
5.188
1   New Bedford, which in 2005 had an estimated population of 93 102, is a manufacturing city. Principal imports include general cargo and frozen fish.
New Bedford is a port of entry.

Port limits
5.189

1   New Bedford Harbor, the tidal estuary of Acushnet River, includes all the tidal waters N of a line joining Clarks Point (41°35′N 70°54′W) and Wilbur Point, the S extremity of Sconticut Neck, 2 miles ESE.

Approach and entry
5.190

1   New Bedford Harbor is approached through the bay lying between Round Hill Point (41°32′N 70°56′W) and Wilbur Point, 4 miles NE and the shoals lying off them. The bay is much obstructed by ledges and shoals, between which there are a number of channels leading to the dredged entrance channel.

Traffic
5.191

1   In 2005 the port was used by 1 vessel with a deadweight 6232 tonnes.

Port Authority
5.192

1   Harbor Development Commission, 106 Co-op Wharf, New Bedford MA 02740.
      Internet: www.ci.new-bedford.ma.us

Limiting conditions

Controlling depth
5.193

1   The project depth is 9·1 m (30 ft) in the main channel leading from Buzzards Bay to the turning basin above the New Bedford - Fairhaven Bridge. For the latest controlling depths the charts and port authority should be consulted.

Deepest and longest berths
5.194

1   **Deepest:** Maritime Terminal Wharf (5.211).
      Longest: South Terminal Wharf (5.211).

Tidal levels
5.195

1   Mean spring range about 1·3 m; mean neap range about 0·8 m. See information in *Admiralty Tide Tables*.

Ice
5.196

1   The channels and anchorage area are usually navigable throughout the year, although in prolonged periods of extreme cold weather the harbour as well as all of Buzzards Bay may be closed to navigation because of ice. Such conditions are infrequent and of short duration.

Local weather
5.197

1   The prevailing winds during the winter are from N to W, and during the summer, from S to SW.
      Fog. Thick fog is reported to close in quickly with little warning in New Bedford Harbor.

Arrival information

Outer anchorages
5.198

1   Outer anchorage is available in depths of 6 to 9 m (20 to 30 ft) in a position 7 cables S of Clarks Point.

Pilotage
5.199

1   **Pilotage** is compulsory for all vessels of 350 gt or more and is generally arranged for in advance by ships agents. 24 hours notice is required. See *Admiralty List of Radio Signals Volume 6(5)* for details.
      Pilots board:
         5 cables ESE of CC Light–buoy (41°49′N 70°28′W), off the E entrance to the Cape Cod Canal, or:
2   In the vicinity of 41°23′N 71°21′W, 4 miles SSE of the entrance to Narragansett Bay (5.216).

Tugs
5.200

1   **Tugs.** Ocean going vessels normally require assistance from tugs when berthing. Tugs up to 2200 hp are available at New Bedford.

Traffic regulations
5.201

1   **Navigation Rules for US Inland Waters.** See 5.138.

Harbour

General layout
5.202

1   New Bedford Harbor is divided into an outer and inner harbour. The outer harbour consists of the area S of the hurricane barrier at Palmer Island (41°37′·5N 70°54′·6W) and the inner harbour consists of the area N of the barrier to a short distance above New Bedford–Fairhaven Bridge.
2   The inner harbour is divided by Fish Island and Popes Island, which are connected by causeways to the W and E shore, respectively, 1 mile above the barrier. A swing bridge (5.204) connects the two islands.

Hurricane barrier
5.203

1   A hurricane barrier extends from the W shore, over Palmer Island to Fort Phoenix on the E.
      Hurricane barrier traffic lights are displayed on a house on the W side of the entrance and adjacent to the old fort at Clarks Point (5.189).
2   The 46 m (150 ft) opening is kept in the open position during fair weather but is closed during periods of high winds, high tides or when a hurricane is expected.
      Lights mark the E and W side of the opening.

Vertical clearance
5.204

1   Swing Bridge connects Fish Island and Popes Island providing a double opening, each with a vertical clearance of 1·8 m (6 ft) when closed.
      Two road bridges with fixed spans about 1 mile above the swing bridge. Vertical clearance 2·4 m (8 ft).

Horizontal clearance
5.205

1   The swing bridge connecting Fish Island and Popes Island has a horizontal clearance of 29 m.

Directions

Principal marks
5.206

1   **Landmark:**

Radar dome (41°32′N 70°56′W) standing on Round Hill Point.

Outer harbour
5.207

1   **Main channel.** From the vicinity of BB Light–buoy (41°31′N 70°50′W) the approach channel leads NNW for about 4 miles, passing (with positions relative to Wilbur Point (41°35′N 70°51′W)):

Between Nos 1 and 2 Light–buoys (lateral) (3¼ miles S), thence:

2   ENE of Negro Ledge (2 miles SSW) which is marked on its E side by No 3 Buoy (port hand). Hursell Rock lies 2½ cables WSW. Thence:

Between Nos 4 and No 5 Light–buoys (starboard and port hand) (1½ miles SSW), thence:

3   WSW of Mosher Ledge (1 mile S), thence:

Between Brooklyn Rock and Henrietta Rock (1¼ miles and 1 mile SW), which are marked, respectively, by No 7 Light–buoy (port hand) and No 6 Light–buoy (starboard hand).

Thence through the dredged channel, which is marked by pairs of light–buoys, to the hurricane barrier.

4   **Useful marks** (with positions relative to Fort Phoenix (41°37′·5N 70°54′·1W)):

Fort (2 miles S) standing on Clarks Point.

Fort Phoenix.

Radio tower (1 mile NNW) on W side of Popes Island.

Charts 2456, 2455
5.208

1   **Alternative routes.** There are a number of alternative routes with least depths of 6·7 m (21 ft) that lead from Buzzards Bay to New Bedford Harbor W of the main channel. However they are not as well marked as the main channel and unmarked shoals with depths of 2·7 to 5·5 m (9 to 18 ft) lie near the track.

2   **From south-west.** From a position S of No 5 Light–buoy which is moored to the SE of Mishaum Ledge (5.147), a route leads NNE, passing (with positions relative to Dumpling Rocks No 7 Light (41°32′N 70°55′W)):

ESE of Salters Point Rock (1 mile SW), marked on its SE side by No 1 Buoy (port hand), thence:

3   WNW of No 2 Buoy (starboard hand) (6½ cables S), marking a 4·9 m (16 ft) patch, thence:

WNW of The Sandspit (6 cables SE), the W end of which is marked by No 4 Light–buoy (starboard hand), and:

4   ESE of the shoal water that extends S from Dumpling Rocks No 7 Light (green square on framework tower). The outer limit of the shoal is marked by No 5 Buoy (port hand). Thence:

WNW of No 8 Light–buoy (starboard hand) (7 cables E), marking a 5·5 m (18 ft) patch, thence:

5   ESE of Middle Ledge (1¼ miles NNE). AB Light–buoy (preferred channel to port) is moored 3 cables SSW of this ledge, thence:

6   ESE of Inez Rock (1½ miles NNE), which is marked by No 11 Buoy (port hand), thence:

WNW of Decatur Rock (2 miles NE), which is marked by No 10 Buoy (starboard hand), thence:

WNW of North Ledge (2½ miles NE), marked on its NW side by No 12 Buoy (starboard hand), thence:

ESE of Clarks Point (5.189).

Thence the track continues NNE to join the main route near Butler Flats Light (white conical tower, black round base) (41°36′N 70°54′W).

7   **From south.** From a position SE of Wilkes Ledge (41°30′·5N 70°54′·5W), which is marked on its SE side by No 7 Light–buoy (port hand), a route leads N passing W of Great Ledge, marked on its W side by No 8A Buoy (starboard hand) and E of the 5·5 m (18 ft) patch, marked by No 8 Light–buoy. The route then joins the approach from the SW in the vicinity of Decatur Rock.

Cautions
5.209

1   Vessels should not attempt to enter New Bedford except in clear weather when aids to navigation are visible, unless local knowledge is available.

Vessels should proceed with caution where the under–keel depth is less than 1·8 to 2·4 m (6 to 8 ft), because of the broken nature of the bottom.

Berths

Chart 2455
Anchorages
5.210

1   **Outer harbour.** General anchorage areas A and B, as shown on the chart, lie E and W, respectively, of the dredged channel S and SE of the hurricane barrier. No vessel should anchor outside these areas except in cases of great emergency.

Inner harbour. Vessels may anchor in the two dredged anchorage areas on either side of the channel in depths of 7 to 9 m (23 to 30 ft).

Alongside berths
5.211

1   The main alongside berths, which lie on the W side of the inner harbour, are given as follows (with positions relative to Fort Phoenix (41°37′·5N 70°54′·1W)):

South Terminal Wharf (6 cables W); 490 m in length with a depth alongside of 9·1 m. Refrigerated storage and seafood products.

2   **Global Companies Petroleum Terminal** (8 cables WNW); N side 225 m in length, with dolphins, with a depth alongside of 9·1 m. Petroleum products.

State Pier (1 mile NW); N side 236 m in length, S side 183 m in length, face 137 m in length, with depths alongside of 7·6 to 9·1 m. General cargo, ferry and cruise ship terminal.

3   **Maritime Terminal Wharf** (1¼ miles NW); 183 m in length with a depth alongside of 9·4 m. General cargo, frozen food and fish.

Bridge Terminal Wharf (NE side of Fish Island (41°38′·3N 70°55′·2W); 137 m in length with a depth alongside of 8·5 m. Receipt of frozen food.

4   **Two wharves** (NW of Fish Island); 177 and 305 m in length with depths alongside of 7·6 to 9·1 m. Frozen foods and general cargo.

Port services

Repairs
5.212

1   Largest patent slip in area is capable of handling vessels of up to 100 m in length.

Other facilities
5.213

   Hospitals; oily waste disposal.

Supplies
5.214

1   Fuel; water ex wharf and by barge to vessels at anchor; provisions and stores.

Communications
5.215

1   Nearest airport 6 km.

NARRAGANSETT BAY AND ADJACENT WATERS

GENERAL INFORMATION

Chart 2890
Description
5.216

1   **Narragansett Bay** (41°35′N 71°20′W) and the adjacent waters of Sakonnet River (5.226) and Westport Harbor (5.225) open on the N side of Rhode Island Sound, between Buzzards Bay and Block Island Sound. Narragansett Bay forms the approach to the cities of Newport (5.255), Providence (5.277), Taunton (5.308) and Fall River (5.316).

Pilotage
5.217

1   Pilotage is compulsory for all foreign vessels and US vessels under register when entering and departing from Narragansett Bay and all ports in the State of Rhode Island.

   Pilots embark in the vicinity of 41°23′N 71°21′W, S of a line extending from Point Judith (41°21′N 71°29′W) to Sakonnet Point, 14 miles ENE.

   Pilot boats have either black or grey hulls with white superstructures and the word "PILOT" on the side.

   Pilot services are normally arranged 24 hours in advance through ship's agents or directly by shipping companies.

2   Pilots for US registered vessels in coastwise trade board off Point Judith. The pilot boats have a blue hull with white superstructure and maintain a listening watch on VHF 2 hours before a vessel's ETA.

Recommended routes
5.218

1   Recommended routes for deep-draught vessels, tugs and barges, as shown on the charts, have been established in Narragansett Bay. See 5.2.

Security Broadcast System
5.219

1   A compulsory system is in force, to be used by vessels to report movements within Narragansett Bay. See *Admiralty List of Radio Signals Volume 6(5)* for details.

No-discharge zones
5.220

1   Numerous No-discharge zones (NDZs) have been established throughout Narragansett Bay. See 1.44.

BUZZARDS BAY TO NARRAGANSETT BAY

General information

Chart 2890 (see 1.17)
Description
5.221

1   Between Gooseberry Neck (41°29′N 71°02′W) and Brenton Point, the E entrance point to Narragansett Bay, 14½ miles W, lie the entrances to Westport Harbor (5.225) and Sakonnet River (5.226). Foul ground extends up to 1½ miles offshore, in places, along this stretch of the coast.

Fish traps
5.222

1   The limits of areas where fish traps may be found in the coastal waters between Gooseberry Neck and Brenton Point are shown on the chart.

Principal marks
5.223

1   **Landmarks:**
     Buzzards Bay Entrance Light (41°24′N 71°02′W) (5.144).
     Tower (41°29′N 71°02′W) standing on Gooseberry Neck.
     Church tower (41°29′·5N 71°16′·5W) standing 7 cables N of Easton Point on the S side of Rhode Island.

2   **Major light:**
     Buzzards Bay Entrance Light (41°24′N 71°02′W) (5.144).
     Beavertail Light (41°27′N 71°24′W) (5.230).

Other aids to navigation
5.224

1   **Racon:**
     Buzzards Bay Entrance Light (41°24′N 71°02′W).
   See *Admiralty List of Radio Signals Volume 2* for details.

Anchorages and harbours

Westport River
5.225

1   **General information.** Westport River, with Westport Harbor (41°31′N 71°05′W) close within its entrance, flows into the head of a bight which extends from Gooseberry Neck to Warren Point. The river is used by fishing and pleasure craft.

2   Numerous dangers encumber the bight, of which Pinetree Ground, Kibby Ground, Twomile Ledge and Twomile Rock, marked by No 3 Beacon, lie in the approaches to Westport River. Foul ground also extends 7 cables SW and W from Gooseberry Neck and is marked by No 6 Buoy (starboard hand).

3   **Local knowledge** is required to enter the harbour.

Sakonnet River
5.226

1   **General information.** Sakonnet River lies between the mainland and the E shore of Rhode Island and is entered between Sakonnet Point (41°27′N 71°12′W) and Sachuest Point 2½ miles WNW.

The river, which is little used except by fishing vessels and small local craft, extends 12 miles N to Mount Hope Bay (5.303).

2   **Navigation Rules for US Inland** waters apply to all waters within a line joining Sakonnet Harbor Breakwater Light No 2 (red triangle on framework tower, concrete base (41°28′·0N 71°11′·7W) and a position on the S part of Sachuest Point at position 41°28′·5N 71°14′·8W. See 1.47 and Appendix VII for further information.

Ice. The river N of Fogland Point (41°34′N 71°13′W) is normally closed by ice for short periods each winter.

3   **Anchorage** for vessels drawing up to 5·2 m (17 ft) can be obtained in mid–river just below High Hill Point (41°33′N 71°13′W), clear of the restricted areas shown on the chart, in depths of 6 to 8 m (20 to 26 ft). Although open S, a heavy sea seldom reaches as far as this anchorage.

Local knowledge is required to navigate above High Hill Point.

APPROACHES TO NARRAGANSETT BAY

General information

Charts 2890, 2730
Description
5.227

1   Narragansett Bay is approached between Block Island (41°11′N 71°35′W) and Sakonnet Point, 22 miles NE.

Block Island (41°11′N 71°35′W) is hilly, the highest point being Beacon Hill, 61 m (200 ft) high. The island is nearly divided in two in its central part by Great Salt Pond (6.22); Old Harbor (5.233) lies on the E coast opposite Great Salt Pond.

2   The coast of Block Island is mostly fringed with boulders and should be given a berth of at least 5 cables.

Traffic regulations
5.228

1   **Navigation Rules for US Inland Waters** apply to all waters in Narragansett Bay lying within an E–W line drawn through Beavertail Point (41°27′N 71°24′W) between Brenton Point and the Boston Neck shoreline. See 1.47 and Appendix VII for further information.

2   **Traffic separation scheme** leads N from the Precautionary Area (5.10) in Rhode Island Sound. This TSS is IMO–adopted and Rule 10 of the *International Regulations for Preventing Collisions at Sea (1972)* applies. The two traffic lanes are separated by a 2 mile wide zone. This zone is a restricted area.

3   **Safety zones.** A safety zone, centred on 41°25′N 71°23′W with a radius of 1 mile, has been established for high interest vessels while at anchor in the waters of Rhode Island Sound. High interest vessels include barges or ships carrying LNG, LPG, chlorine, anhydrous ammonia or any other cargo deemed to be of high interest.

A moving safety zone has been established 2 miles ahead, 1 mile astern and 1000 yards either side of high interest vessels transiting Narragansett Bay or the Providence and Taunton Rivers.

For definition and general regulations concerning safety zones see Appendix V.

4   **Restricted area** situated between the traffic lanes of the TSS is a Torpedo Range and is closed to shipping during torpedo firing. Another restricted area, which is used for naval mine–hunting exercises, is marked on the chart E of the northbound traffic lane. See Appendix VI.

Rescue
5.229

1   **Coast Guard** station is situated on Point Judith (41°22′N 71°29′W) near the light.

Directions
(continued from 5.15)

Principal marks
5.230

1   **Major lights:**
    Block Island South–east Light (red brick 8-sided pyramidal tower on dwelling, 20 m in height) (41°09′N 71°33′W), standing on Southeast Point.
    Point Judith Light (white 8–sided tower, brown top, 16 m in height) (41°22′N 71°29′W).
2   Beavertail Light (square granite tower, white dwelling) (41°27′N 71°24′W).

Other aids to navigation
5.231

1   **Racons:**
    'A' Light–buoy (41°06′N 71°23′W).
    NB Light–buoy (41°23′N 71°23′W).
    See *Admiralty List of Radio Signals Volume 2* for details.

Directions
5.232

1   From within the Precautionary Area, centred 41°06′N 71°23′W the approach route to Narragansett Bay leads N through the TSS to the vicinity of the pilot boarding position, passing E of NB Light–buoy (41°23′N 71°23′W), at the N end of the TSS.

(Directions continue at 5.246)

Old Harbor
General information
5.233

1   Old Harbor (41°11′N 71°33′W), often used as a harbour of refuge, is situated 1 mile NW of Old Harbor Point and is formed by two breakwaters. No 3 Light (green square on white framework tower on base) stands at the head of the E breakwater.

Depths
5.234

1   In 2006 controlling depths were 2·6 m (8·4 ft) in the entrance channel, thence 2·6 to 4·6 m (8·4 to 15 ft) in the anchorage basin. The inner harbour has depths of 2·6 to 4·6 m (8·4 to 15 ft).

Berths
5.235

1   The ferry wharf is situated in the SW part of the harbour.

Anchorage is available in the inner harbour, but the E side of the harbour is kept clear for the ferry.

Port services
5.236

1   **Limited repairs** can be effected.
Supplies: fuel; provisions and stores.

NARRAGANSETT BAY

General information

Charts 2890, 2730, 2731, 2732
Description
5.237

1 Narragansett Bay is entered between Brenton Point (41°27′N 71°21′W), the SW extremity of Rhode Island, and Point Judith Neck, 6 miles SW. The bay is 18 miles in length from its entrance to the mouth of the Providence River (5.277).

2 Rhode Island forms the E shore of the bay. Conanicut Island and Prudence Island, together with several smaller islands, lie in the bay and divide the entrance and the lower part of the bay into East Passage and West Passage, which unite 3 miles below the entrance to Providence River. Bristol Neck (5.267), extending 5 miles S from the head of the bay, divides the head into two arms: Mount Hope Bay (5.303), the NE arm into which Taunton River (5.303) flows; and the N arm, the approach to Providence River.

Entrances
5.238

1 **East Passage**, which is the principal passage into Narragansett Bay, is entered between Brenton Point and Beavertail Point, the S extremity of Beaver Neck. The passage is the deeper and most direct route to the ports of Newport, Bristol, Fall River and Providence.

2 **West Passage** is entered between Beavertail Point and Boston Neck, 2 miles W. This passage is the approach to Dutch Island Harbor (5.271), Wickford Harbor (5.272) and Greenwich Bay (5.276). Vessels may also go to Providence by West Passage, but the route through East Passage is generally used.

Depths
5.239

1 **East Passage** has depths of 18·3 m (60 ft) in the buoyed channel, for 10 miles from the entrance to where the channel divides E of Prudence Island. For depths beyond this point see 5.282 and 5.305.

2 **West Passage** has depths suitable for vessels drawing up to 8·5 m (28 ft) as far as Dutch Island Harbor, and for vessels drawing 5·8 m (19 ft) as far as Providence River by way of a narrow channel NW of Patience Island (41°39′N 71°22′W).

Fish traps
5.240

1 Fish trap areas, in which below–water piling may exist, fringe some of the shores of Narragansett Bay.

Pilotage
5.241

1 See 5.217.

Traffic regulations
5.242

1 **Navigation Rules for US Inland Waters.** See 5.228. **Security Broadcast System.** See 5.219. Reporting positions are shown on the chart.

2 **Regulated navigation area.** A regulated navigation area has been established between NB Light-buoy (41°23′N 71°23′W) and Fox Point (41°49′N 71°24′W) with restrictions applying between Conimicut Light (41°43′·0N 71°20′·7W) and Fuller Rock Light (41°47′·6N 71°22′·8W).

For definition and general regulations concerning regulated navigation areas see Appendix V.

3 **Safety zone.** See 5.228.
Restricted areas. A restricted area about 6 miles in length, the limits of which are shown on the chart, is situated between Gould Island (41°32′N 71°21′W) and a position NE of Hope Island (41°36′N 71°22′W). See Appendix VI.

4 A restricted area, the limits of which are shown on the chart, surrounds Coddington Cove (41°32′N 71°19′W) (5.265) and Coasters Harbor Island (41°30′·6N 71°19′·6W). See Appendix VI.

A restricted area, the limits of which are shown on the chart, surrounds Explosives Anchorage X–1 (centred 41°33′·3N 71°30′·0W), NNE of Gould Island.

Vertical clearance
5.243

1 **Narragansett Bay Bridge** spans East Passage, 4 miles above its entrance, between Taylor Point on Conanicut Island and Rhode Island, ESE. The central span has a vertical clearance of 59 m (194 ft).

2 **Jamestown-North Kingston Bridges**. A pair of bridges, ¾ cable apart, span West Passage, 5 miles above its entrance, between Conanicut Island and the mainland W. Vertical clearances 41·2 m (135 ft) and 40·9 m (134 ft).

Rescue
5.244

1 **Coast Guard** station is situated on W shore of Newport Neck near Castle Hill Light (41°28′N 71°22′W).

Natural conditions
5.245

1 **Tidal streams**. Over the greater part of Narragansett Bay, the maximum rate of flood and ebb streams is about ½ kn in the wider channels and 1½ kn in the narrower parts. For further details see Tidal Stream tables.

2 **Ice.** Navigation in Narragansett Bay is sometimes impeded by floating ice, and in severe winters by pack or field ice. The ice breaking up in Providence River and Mount Hope Bay, is set by NE winds down the bay through East Passage and sometimes, for a short period, blocks this passage abreast Fort Adams at the S entrance to Newport Harbor. The passages are rarely closed for any length of time below Gould Island (41°32′N 71°21′W) in East Passage, and Dutch Island (41°30′N 71°24′W) in West Passage.

Directions
(continued from 5.232)

Principal marks
5.246

1 **Landmarks for East Passage:**
Radar tower (41°27′·3N 71°23′·8W).
Cupola (41°28′·5N 71°22′·5W).
Church tower (41°29′·6N 71°19′·2W) in Newport.
Three spires (41°29′·1N 71°18′·7W) in Newport.
Tower (41°30′·5N 71°19′·8W) on SW part of Coasters Harbor Island.

2 Two Cupolas (41°30′·4N 71°19′·7W) of Naval War College.
Hog Island Shoal Lighthouse (white conical tower, black round base) (41°37′·9N 71°16′·4W).
Old Light House (white tower and dwelling) (41°43′·5N 71°20′·3W) standing on Nayatt Point.

3 **Landmarks for West Passage:**
Radar tower — as above.
Spire (41°29′·5N 71°25′·5W).

Tower (41°29'·8N 71°24'·3W) at S end of Dutch Island.

Disused old lighthouse (41°31'·8N 71°24'·3W) close N of the Jamestown - Kingston Bridges.

4 **Major lights:**

Beavertail Light (41°27'N 71°24'W) (5.230).

Other aids to navigation
5.247

1 **Racon:**

NB Light-buoy (41°23'N 71°23'W).

See *Admiralty List of Radio Signals Volume 2* for details.

East Passage
5.248

1 **Entrance.** From the vicinity of the pilot boarding position (41°23'N 71°21'W) the track through the entrance leads generally NE between the S part of Conanicut Island and Newport Neck, the S part of Rhode Island, passing (with positions relative to Castle Hill Light (41°27'·7N 71°21'·8W)):

2 SE of Beavertail Light (5.230) (1¾ miles WSW) standing on Beavertail Point, the S extremity of Beaver Neck, thence:

NW of Castle Hill Light (conical granite tower, white top) standing on Castle Hill, the W point of Rhode Island, thence:

3 SE of Kettle Bottom Rock (7½ cables NW), marked on its SE side by No 7 Light–buoy (port hand), thence:

SE of No 9 Light–buoy (port hand) moored 2 cables SE of Bull Point (1 mile NNE), a rugged headland fronted by above and below–water rocks. Thence:

4 SE of The Dumplings (1¼ miles NNE), a group of rocks that extend N from Bull Point. No 11 Light–buoy (port hand) is moored 2 cables NE of these rocks. Thence:

NW of Fort Adams (1½ miles NE) on the N point of Newport Neck, the S entrance point to Newport Harbor. Fort Adams Light No 2 (red triangle on white framework tower) stands at the entrance to a boat camber on the N side of the point.

5.249

1 **Fort Adams to Halfway Rock.** From a position NW of Fort Adams, East Passage continues N and NNE through the outer harbour of Newport (5.255) to a position ENE of Halfway Rock (41°34'N 71°20'W), passing (with positions relative to Gould Island Light (41°31'·8N 71°20'·6W)):

2 W of Rose Island (2 miles S), in the central part of the outer harbour of Newport (5.255). Rose Island Light (white dwelling) stands on the SW point of the island and No 12 Light–buoy (starboard hand) lies 1 cable SW of this point. Thence:

3 Through the central span of Narragansett Bay Bridge (1½ miles S), see 5.243, thence:

WNW of Bishop Rock Shoal (9 cables SSE), marked on its W side by No 14 Light–buoy (starboard hand), thence:

4 ESE of Gould Island, a US naval reservation which is flat and sparsely wooded. A light (red and white chequered diamond on framework tower) stands at the S end of the island. A small boat harbour at the N end of the island is protected by moles. Thence:

5 WNW of No 18 Breakwater Light (red triangle on red framework tower) (9 cables ENE), at the head of the breakwater protecting Coddington Cove (5.265), thence:

ESE of Halfway Rock (2 miles NNE), marked by a beacon (red and white).

5.250

1 **Halfway Rock to Hog Island.** From a position ESE of Halfway Rock, East Passage continues NNE between Prudence Island and Rhode Island to the vicinity of Hog Island (41°38'·5N 71°17'·0W) (5.267), passing (with positions relative to Sandy Point Light (41°36'·4N 71°18'·2W)):

2 ESE of Fiske Rock (2½ miles SSW), the N end of which is marked by a buoy (preferred channel to starboard), thence:

ESE of WR 21 Light-buoy (2 miles SSW), marking a wreck with a depth of 11 m (36 ft) over it, thence:

3 WNW of No 24 Light–buoy (starboard hand) (9 cables S), which lies 1½ cables NW of a bank, with swept depths of 4·9 m (16 ft), and 5 cables NNW of Dyer Island. Thence:

Between Nos 25 and 26 Light–buoys (lateral) (4 cables SSE), which mark the start of the entrance channel leading to Providence River, thence:

Rose Island

East Passage – Castle Hill Lt, No 6 Buoy and Newport Bridge from SSW (5.248)

(Original dated 2003)

(Photograph - Olivia Pearson)

4   ESE of Sandy Point, on which stands Sandy Point
Light (white 8–sided tower), thence:

Either side of SP Light–buoy (preferred channel to
port) (7 cables NNE), which marks the S side of
the area where the channels to Providence River
and Mount Hope Bay divide.

(Directions for Mount Hope Bay continue at 5.311)

Hog Island to Providence River entrance
5.251

1   From the vicinity of SP Light–buoy (41°36′·9N
71°17′·6W) the entrance channel to the mouth of
Providence River, which is marked by light–buoys (lateral),
leads generally NNW, passing (with positions relative to
North Point, Popasquash Neck (41°41′N 71°18′W)):

2   WSW of Southwest Point (2¾ miles SSE), the SW
extremity of Hog Island (5.267). Shoal water
extends 5 cables SW from this point. Thence:

WSW of Popasquash Point (2 miles S), which forms
the N entrance point to the SW approach to Bristol
Harbor (5.267), thence:

3   E of Ohio Ledge (1 mile W), the SE part of a larger
shoal area, which is marked on its SE side by a
buoy (preferred channel to starboard), thence:

Through Rumstick Neck Reach, the final leg of the
entrance channel, and thence into the Providence
River.

(Directions for Providence River continue at 5.295)

West Passage
(continued from 5.232)
5.252

1   **Entrance.** From the vicinity of the pilot boarding
position (41°23′N 71°21′W) the track through the entrance
leads generally N between Conanicut Island and Boston
Neck, passing (with positions relative to the tower on S
end of Dutch Island (41°29′·8N 71°24′·3W) (5.271)):

2   Between Whale Rock (3 miles SSW), which is
marked by No 3 Light–buoy (port hand) off its E
side, and Beavertail Point. Thence:

E of Jones Ledge (2¼ miles SSW). No 5 Buoy (port
hand) lies 1½ cables E of the ledge. Thence:

W of a dangerous wreck (1¼ miles S) (reported
2004), the position of which is approximate,
thence:

3   W of WR 6 Light–buoy (6 cables S), thence:

Between South Ferry (7½ cables WSW), a point with
an old pier and several dolphins and piles in its
vicinity, and Beaverhead (4 cables SE), a rocky
bluff at the S entrance to Dutch Island Harbor,
thence:

4   W of Dutch Island, thence:

Through the central span of Jamestown–North
Kingstown Bridge (2 miles N). See 5.243.

5.253

1   **Jamestown–North Kingston Bridges to abreast Pine
Hill Point**. From a position N of the bridge West Passage
leads N, passing (with positions relative to Conanicut Point
(41°34′·4N 71°22′·3W)):

E of Halfway Ledge (2 miles SW) lying 5 cables E of
Fox Island, which is low lying with a few trees on
it, thence:

Between Conanicut Point and a 3 m (10 ft) shoal
marked by a buoy (preferred channel to port)
(1¼ miles WNW), thence:

2   W of a shoal with boiler awash (1¼ miles N) lying
4 cables SW of Hope Island, on which are low
grassy hills with a few trees. No 2 Light–buoy
(starboard hand) marks the SW side of the shoal.

Thence to a position abreast Pine Hill Point (41°37′·9N
71°20′·8W).

5.254

1   **Head of West Passage.** From N of a line joining Pine
Hill Point to Calf Pasture Point 2½ miles W, the channel
leads N and then NE through the shoals that encumber the
head of West Passage to Providence River, passing (with
positions relative to Warwick Point Light (white conical
tower) (41°40′·0N 71°22′·7W)):

2   E of No 5 Buoy (port hand) (2 miles S), at the
entrance to the channel, thence:

W of No 6 Buoy (starboard hand) (1¾ miles S),
marking the E side of the channel, thence:

3   Between the shoal water that extends from Northwest
Point (6 cables SE) on Patience Island and
Southeast Ledge (2 cables SE). No 8 Light–buoy
marks the W limit of the shoal water that extends
from Northwest Point.

Thence the track leads NE, passing:

NW of Providence Point (1½ miles E), the N
extremity of Prudence Island, thence:

NW of a buoy (preferred channel to port) (1½ miles
ENE), which marks the shoals extending N from
Providence Point.

Thence the track leads SE and then E, passing about
6 cables S of Ohio Ledge, to join the entrance channel
leading to Providence River.

Newport Harbor

Chart 2730
General information
5.255

1   **Position.** Newport Harbor (41°29′N 71°20′W) is situated
in the N side of Newport Neck, the SW part of Rhode
Island.

Function. Newport Harbor is an important harbour of
refuge, much used by coasters and yachts. It is a port of
entry.

2   The town of Newport, which in 2005 had an estimated
population of 25 340, lies on the E side of the harbour and
is one of the principal summer resorts on the US Atlantic
coast. It is also a naval base.

Traffic. In 2005 the port was used by 10 vessels with a
total deadweight 198 794 tonnes.

Limiting conditions
5.256

1   **Depths.** Outer harbour: see 5.239. Inner harbour: 4 to
5·5 m (13 to 18 ft).

Vertical clearance. A bridge, with a vertical clearance
of 4·3 m (14 ft), joins Goat Island to the mainland across
the N entrance to the inner harbour.

Deepest berth. See 5.261.

2   **Tidal levels.** Mean spring range about 1·2 m; mean neap
range about 0·8 m. See information in *Admiralty Tide
Tables.*

Ice may interfere with navigation for short periods
during severe winters. Vessels and tugs keep ice well
broken up in the main channel through the inner harbour.

3   **Weather.** Prevailing winds are SW in the summer and
NW in the winter. The heaviest gales are usually from the
NW and NE.

Arrival information
5.257

1   **Speed limit** of 4½ kn is in force in the inner harbour.
Outer anchorages. See 5.260.
Pilotage. See 5.217.
Tugs may be obtained from Providence.

Harbour
5.258

1   **General layout.** Newport Harbor, which is divided into an inner and outer harbour, lies between Fort Adams (41°29′N 71°20′W) and Gould Island, 3 miles N.

2   The outer harbour consists of that part of East Passage between The Dumplings (5.248) and Gould Island. It includes the passage, obstructed by Gull Rocks and Tracey Ledge, that passes between Rose Island and Coasters Harbor Island. The outer harbour contains a number of anchorages.

3   The inner harbour, which lies between the E side of Goat Island and the waterfront of Newport has two entrances. The S entrance is between the S end of Goat Island and Ida Lewis Rock, 3 cables S, and the N entrance leads between Goat Island and Rose Island. The inner harbour contains anchorages for small craft and a number of alongside berths.

4   **Tidal streams.** In the S entrance off Bull Point (41°28′·8N 71°21′·3W) the tidal streams are irregular; at strength the in–going stream may reach 1¼ kn and the out–going stream 1½ kn. N of Bull Point rates seldom exceed 1 kn and in the inner harbour are usually less than ½ kn.

5   **Landmarks:**
    Church tower (41°29′·6N 71°19′·2W) in Newport.
    Three spires (41°29′·1N 71°18′·7W) in Newport.
    Tower (41°30′·5N 71°19′·8W) on SW part of Coasters Harbor Island.
    Two cupolas (41°30′·4N 71°19′·7W) of Naval War College.

Directions
(continued from 5.248)
5.259

1   **Outer harbour.** See 5.249.
    Inner harbour. The two entrances, N and S of Goat Island, are well marked. The harbour is easy to enter by day or night and the chart is the best guide. The bridge (5.258) across the N entrance limits the size of vessels that can enter the harbour from that direction.

Basins and berths
5.260

1   **Anchorages.** The following anchorage areas, the limits of which are shown on the chart, are established in Newport. No vessel, except in emergency, may anchor outside these areas.

Newport Harbour from SSW (5.258)
(Original dated 1990)

(Photograph – Joseph R Melanson of www.skypic.com)

Outer harbour:

2   **A.** West side of East Passage between Bull Point and NW of Gould Island. The part of this area N of Jamestown approach is for US Naval vessels only. The requirements of US Naval vessels have priority in the area S of this approach.

3   **C.** Five cables W of Coasters Harbor Island (41°30'·6N 71°19'·6W). US Naval requirements take precedence.

    D. Five cables W of Goat Island. US Naval requirements take precedence between 1 May and 1 October.

4   **E.** Two cables S of Coasters Harbor Island (41°30'·6N 71°19'·6W). US Naval requirements take precedence between 1 May and 1 October.

Inner harbour:

    No 1. In Brenton Cove (41°28'·5N 71°19'·9W) in the S part of the inner harbour.

5   **No 2.** In the central part of the inner harbour E of Goat Island.

    No 3. In the N entrance to the inner harbour N of the bridge connecting Goat Island to the mainland.

Anchorages Nos 1, 2 and 3 are special anchorages; see 1.49.

5.261

1 **Berths.** Alongside berths in the inner harbour consist of a city wharf and numerous private piers. The depths alongside the principal piers range between 2·1 and 5·5 m.

Port services
5.262

1 **Repairs.** Newport has a commercial shipyard specialising in repair, construction and conversion.

The largest patent slip can handle vessels up to 100 m in length and 6·6 m draught.

Other facilities: hospitals.

Supplies: fuel; water; provisions and stores.

Jamestown
5.263

1 Jamestown (41°29'·7N 71°22'·0W), on the E side of Conanicut Island, is situated at the head of an open bay which forms part of the outer harbour and lies between Bull Point and Taylor Point, 1¾ miles N.

East Passage — Other anchorages and harbours

Anchorage areas
5.264

1 The following anchorage areas, the limits of which are shown on the chart, are established in the East Passage N of Newport. No vessels, except in emergency, may anchor outside these areas:

    X-1. Explosives anchorage (41°33'N 71°20'W). Naval explosives and ammunition handling anchorage. See 5.242.

2   **B.** Naval and General Anchorage (41°33'N 71°19'W) between Coddington Cove and 1½ miles N of Coggeshall Point on the E side of East Passage.

    B-1. Naval and General Anchorage (41°34'·5N 71°19'·5W). Naval requirements have priority.

Coddington Cove
5.265

1 Coddington Cove (41°31'N 71°19'W) is entered between Coddington Point, close N of Newport, and the head of a

breakwater on which stands No 18 Light (5.249). The cove lies within a restricted area. See Appendix VI.

Berths. Two piers extend from the shore. The N side of the N pier is used by the US Navy, the S pier is used by a shipyard. There are numerous mooring buoys in the harbour.

Depths of 9·1 m are reported alongside both piers.

Melville
5.266

1 Melville (41°35'N 71°17'W) stands close S of Coggeshall Point. Weaver Cove lies S of Melville between Dyer Island and the shore.

A US Navy fuelling depot is situated at Melville.

2 **Approach** from the NW is through waters clear of charted dangers. The shoal water N and NE of Dyer Island (41°35'N 71°18'W) is marked by No 24 Light–buoy (starboard hand) and Nos 9, 7 and 5 Buoys (port hand). The shoal water S of Dyer Island is connected to Rhode Island by a bar with depths of 2·7 m to 5·2 m (9 to 17 ft) over it.

3 **Depths** alongside the fuel piers range from 12·2 to 13·7 m.

Chart 2731
Bristol Harbor
5.267

1 Bristol Harbor (41°40'N 71°17'W) lies between the S end of Bristol Neck and Popasquash Neck.

Bristol, which in 2005 had an estimated population of 24 658, stands on the E side of the harbour.

Approach. Bristol Harbor is entered between Bristol Point (41°38'·6N 71°15'·6W) and Popasquash Point, 1¾ miles WNW. Hog Island, low and wooded, lies in the entrance, with a natural channel on either side of it.

2 **Depths.** Both channels have depths of 5·8 to 7·6 m (19 to 25 ft). Bristol Harbor, in the N part of the cove, has depths of 4·6 to 5·2 m (15 to 17 ft).

Landmark:

    Hog Island Shoal Lighthouse (41°37'·9N 71°16'·4W) (5.246).

3 **Directions for west channel.** From the vicinity of No 2 Light–buoy, 8 cables W of Southwest Point (41°38'·2N 71°17'·1W), the W channel leads NNE, passing (with positions relative to Popasquash Point (41°39'·0N 71°18'·0W)):

    Clear of the shoal patches 5 cables SW and W of Southwest Point (1 mile SW), thence:

4   ESE of a light–buoy (preferred channel to port), (2 cables S), which marks the limit of the shoal water off Popasquash Point, thence:

    WNW of Castle Island (6½ cables ENE), No 2 Light (red triangle on framework tower) stands on the island, thence:

5   ESE of Usher Rocks (7 cables NNE), which lie 2 cables SE of Usher Point. No 3 Buoy (port hand) lies 1 cable E of the rocks.

Thence into Bristol Harbor.

Directions for the east channel. The chart is the best guide.

5.268

1 **Anchorage.** Anchorage area O, the limits of which are shown on the chart, extends from the W shore of Bristol Harbor. This area provides excellent anchorage in depths of 4·6 to 5·2 m (15 to 17 ft), soft bottom.

Wharves. There are depths alongside of 2·7 to 4 m at the wharves and piers at Bristol.

Chart 2731 (see 1.17)
Warren River
5.269

1   Warren River flows into the NE part of Narragansett Bay between Rumstick Point (41°42'·4N 71°18'·1W) and the shore of Bristol Neck, 5 cables E. The river is the approach to the towns of Warren and Barrington, and the Barrington River which flows into the Warren River opposite Warren.

2   **Depths.** Warren River, which is narrow and winding, has depths of about 2·7 m (9 ft) in the well buoyed channel to the lower wharves at Warren, and the same depth is in the Barrington River as far as the fixed bridge about 5 cables above the entrance.

3   **Anchorage.** An excellent anchorage may be found at the mouth of the Warren River in depths of 4 to 5 m (14 to 15 ft), mud, about 2 cables from the E shore.

    Useful mark. Allen Rock Light (green square on framework tower) stands on Allen Rock (41°42'·8N 71°17'·6W).

4   **Wharves.** Depths alongside of 2·1 to 6·1 m are reported at the major wharves at Warren.

    Repairs. There is a shipyard on the E side of the Warren River.

    Supplies: fuel; water; provisions and stores.

West Passage – Other anchorages and harbours

Chart 2730
Anchorage areas
5.270

1   The following anchorage areas, the limits of which are shown on the chart, are established in the S part of the West Passage. No vessels, except in emergency, may anchor outside these areas:

    H. General anchorage (41°28'·7N 71°24'·8W) on W side of entrance.

    I. General anchorage (41°28'·6N 71°24'·1W) on E side of entrance. A dangerous wreck (5.252) lies in this anchorage.

2   **J.** General anchorage (41°30'·2N 71°24'·9W) W of Dutch Island.

    K. General anchorage (41°29'·8N 71°23'·5W) in S part of Dutch Island Harbor (5.271).

    L. General anchorage (41°32'N 71°25'W) on the W side of West Passage between the N side of Dutch Island and Wickford (41°34'N 71°26'W) (Chart 2890).

3   **M.** General anchorage (41°30'·7N 71°23'·6W) in N part of Dutch Island Harbor and N of Dutch Island.

    N. General anchorage (41°34'N 71°23'W) SW of Conanicut Point.

Dutch Island Harbor
5.271

1   Dutch Island Harbor (41°30'N 71°23'W) lies off the W side of Conanicut Island, N of Beaverhead and E of Dutch Island.

    Approach. The harbour may be entered either S or N of Dutch Island. The S and principal entrance lies between Beaverhead and a tower (white square tower, disused lighthouse) on the S end of Dutch Island.

2   A light–buoy (preferred channel to port) marks the limit of a drying reef extending from the S point of Dutch Island, and No 2 Buoy (starboard hand) marks the limit of the shoal water extending N from Beaverhead.

    Depths. The S entrance may be used by vessels with a draught of up to 8·5 m (28 ft) and the N entrance by those drawing not more than 4·6 m (15 ft).

3   **Anchorage.** Area K and the S part of Area M (5.270) are situated in Dutch Island Harbor. Excellent anchorage in depths of 4 to 15 m (13 to 49 ft), sticky bottom, is available, but vessels with a draught of more than 5·5 m (18 ft) should give the E shore a berth of more than 4 cables.

Wickford Harbor
5.272

1   **Description.** Wickford Harbor (41°34'N 71°26'W), 4½ miles above Dutch Island Harbor, consists of an outer and inner harbour. It is mainly used by pleasure craft and fishing boats.

    Ice. The inner harbour is closed by ice in severe winters whist the outer harbour is usually open but with some drift ice.

Chart 2730
Quonset Point and Davisville Depot
5.273

1   Quonset Point (41°35'·3N 71°24'·3W) is marked by the elevated tanks and the conspicuous buildings of the Quonset Point Industrial Park. Davisville Depot is situated 1½ miles N.

    Approach. Both terminals are usually approached from East Passage, until N of Conanicut Point, thence through a buoyed dredged channel to a turning basin off Quonset Point from which a channel leads N to Davisville Depot.

2   **Depths:**
    Channel to turning basin of Quonset Point. 10·4 to 13·7 m (34 to 45 ft).
    Basin off Quonset Point: 10·1 to 10·7 m (33 to 35 ft) except for patches of 8·2 m (27 ft) and 9·1 m (30 ft).
    Channel to turning basin off Davisville Depot: Controlling depth (1965) 9·5 m (31 ft).

3   Basin off Davisville Depot: 8·2 m (27 ft).

    Berths. Pier at Quonset Point with a reported depth alongside of 9·1 m.

    Davisville Depot. Depths alongside of 8·8 m on the SW side of Pier 1 and in the basin between Pier 1 and 2.

Chart 2730 (see 1.17)
Allen Harbor
5.274

1   Allen Harbor (41°37'·4N 71°24'·8W) lies 2 miles N of Quonset Point and is used by small craft.

Chart 2890 (see 1.17)
Potowomut River
5.275

1   Potowomut River, entered 4 miles N of Quonset Point, is separated from Greenwich Bay by Potowomut Neck and is only used by small craft.

Charts 2731, 2890 (see 1.17)
Greenwich Bay
5.276

1   Greenwich Bay (41°40'N 71°24'W) is entered from the N part of West Passage between Sandy Point (41°39'·8N 71°24'·5W) and Warwick Point, 1½ miles NE. Round Rock lies in the entrance 8 cables SW of Warwick Point and is marked by No 1 Light–buoy (port hand) which lies 1 cable E.

2   There are general depths of 3 m (10 ft) and over within the bay.

Warwick Cove (41°41·5'N 71°23'·8W), Apponaug Cove (41°41'·5N 71°27'·0W) and Greenwich Cove (41°39'N 71°27'W) are small harbours, used by pleasure craft, situated within Greenwich Bay.

3   **Approach.** The bay is entered through a natural channel from a position S of Warwick Point.

Useful mark:

Warwick Point Light (5.254).

Local knowledge is necessary to enter the bay.

PROVIDENCE RIVER

General information

Chart 2731
Position
5.277

1   Providence River, which flows into the N arm of Narragansett Bay between Nayatt Point (41°44'N 71°20'W) and Conimicut Point, 1 mile WSW, is the approach to the city of Providence and the Seekonk River. The city of Providence lies at the head of navigation, 7 miles above the entrance and at the junction with Seekonk River.

Function
5.278

1   Providence, which in 2005 had an estimated population of 176 862, is a port of entry. The ports chief water-borne trade is in petroleum products, cement, lumber, scrap metal, general cargo and automobiles.

Port limits
5.279

1   The port area of Providence includes both sides of the navigable channel of the Providence River above Pomham Rocks (5.296), which lie 4 miles above the entrance.

Traffic
5.280

1   **Traffic.** In 2005 the port was used by 138 vessels with a total deadweight 7 882 313 tonnes.

Port Authority
5.281

1   Providence Port Authority, 35 Terminal Road, Suite 200, Providence, RI 02905.

Internet: www.provport.com

Limiting conditions

Depths
5.282

1   Project depth is 12·2 m (40 ft) in the main channel leading from just below Sandy Point Light (41°36'N 71°18'W) (5.250) (Chart 2730) to Fox Point (41°49'N 71°24'W) at the junction of the Providence River and Seekonk River. For the latest controlling depths the charts and port authority should be consulted.

Deepest and longest berth
5.283

1   No 6 Berth. See 5.299.

Tidal levels
5.284

1   Mean spring range about 1·6 m; mean neap range about 1·1 m. See information in *Admiralty Tide Tables.* Maximum range due to the effects of wind and other causes is 2·4 m.

Maximum size of vessel handled
5.285

1   Maximum length 274 m. Maximum draught 8·23 m.

Ice
5.286

1   The approach channel and the harbour are generally free of ice and navigable throughout the year. During severe winters, the harbour and lower part of Providence River are frozen over, but ice is usually broken up in the channels to the principal wharves by traffic in the harbour.

Local weather
5.287

1   **Climate information.** See 1.157.

Arrival information

Port operations
5.288

1   Security Broadcast System (See 5.219). A speed limit of 5 kn is in force in the harbour.

Traffic regulations
5.289

1   **Regulated navigation area.** The deep-draught channel between Conimicut Light (41°43'·0N 71°20'·7W) and Fuller Rock Light (5.297) is part of the Providence River, Providence, Rhode Island regulated navigation area.

For definition and general regulations concerning regulated navigation areas see Appendix V.

Outer anchorages
5.290

1   See 5.264.

Pilotage
5.291

1   **Pilotage.** See 5.217.

Tugs
5.292

1   **Tugs** are available 24 hours a day and are normally required for docking and undocking large vessels; 4 hours notice required.

Harbour

General layout
5.293

1   The piers and wharves of the port of Providence are along both sides of the Providence River between Pomham Rocks Light (41°46'·7N 71°22'·2W) (5.296) and Fox Point (2½ miles NW). The majority of berths are situated on the W bank.

Tidal streams
5.294

1   Tidal streams are weak in the approach channel and in the harbour except for the constricted part of Seekonk River.

Directions
(continued from 5.251)

Principal marks
5.295

1   **Landmarks:**

Old Light House (41°43'·5N 71°20'·3W) (5.246).
Spire (41°46'·0N 71°23'·5W) at Pawtuxet.
Gas tank (41°47'·8N 71°23'·8W).

Approach channel
5.296

1 From the mouth of the Providence River (41°43′N 71°21′W) the approach channel, marked by light–buoys (lateral), leads generally NNW through Conimicut Point Reach, Bullock Point Reach and Sabin Point Reach to the port of Providence, passing (with positions relative to Bullock Point (41°44′·7N 71°21′·5W)):

2 WSW of BP Light (red and white chequered diamond on framework tower) (5 cables SSW) which stands on a rock on the edge of a shoal extending SW from Bullock Point, thence:

3 Between Gaspee Point and Bullock Point, thence:
Between Pawtuxet Neck and Sabin Point (1¼ miles NNW). SP Beacon marks the extremity of the shoal extending SW from the point. Thence:
W of Pomham Rocks Light (white dwelling) (2 miles NNW) standing on the W side of Pomham Rocks.

Entrance channel
5.297

1 From a position W of Pomham Rocks Light the channel in the port area leads generally NNW through Fuller Rock Reach and Fox Point Reach to the junction of the Providence River and Seekonk River at Fox Point, passing (with positions relative to Kettle Point (41°47′·7N 71°22′·8W)):

2 ENE of Fields Point (6 cables S), thence:
WSW of Fuller Rock Light (red triangle on framework tower, granite base) (1 cable S), thence:
WSW of Kettle Point.
Thence to the vicinity of Fox Point.

Berths

Anchorages
5.298

1 Vessels anchor as directed by the Harbour Master on the edge of the channel between Fields Point and Fox Point. A few vessels may anchor E of Fox point in an area where part of Green Jacket Shoal has been removed.

Alongside berths
5.299

1 A summary of the principal alongside berths is given as follows with positions relative to Kettle Point (41°47′·7N 71°22′·8W).

East side of Providence River:
Mobil Oil Co. Wharf (9 cables SSE); 213 m berthing face with depths alongside of 6·1 to 11·6 m.

2 Amoco Oil Co. Wharf (1 cable NNW); 213 m in length, with dolphins, with a depth alongside of 11 m.
Wilkes–Barre Pier (1 mile NNW); 213 m in length, with dolphins, with a depth alongside of 12·2 m. Reclamation and construction of a new berth is taking place (2004) close SE of Wilkes–Barre Pier. This berth is planned to be 472 m in length with a depth alongside of 12·2 m.

3 **West side of Providence River:**
Municipal wharf (2½ cables WSW); Berths 1 to 6. Overall length 1058 m with depths alongside of 10·7 to 12·2 m. Berths 5 and 6: general and containerised cargo. Berths 1 to 4: general cargo and petroleum products including LPG.

4 New England Bituminous Wharf (3½ cables WNW); 117 m in length with a depth alongside of 9·1 m.

Lehigh Portland Cement and Lone Star Industries Wharves (5 cables NW); 107 and 64 m in length, respectively, with depths alongside of 6·1 and 8·5 to 9·1 m, respectively.

5 Algonquin LNG Wharf (6 cables WNW); 137 m in length with a depth alongside 7·6 m.
Texaco Harbor Junction Wharf (8 cables NW); S side 220 m berthing space with a depth alongside of 9·8 m; N side 183 m berthing space with a depth alongside of 7·6 m. Petroleum products.

6 (with positions relative to Fox Point (41°48′·9N 71°24′·0W):
State Pier (4 cables S); 36 m face with depths alongside of 9·4 to 11·3 m; N and S sides 182 m in length with depths alongside of 6·7 to 11·3 m. Bulk and general cargo; repair berth.

7 Northeast Petroleum Corp. Pier (2¾ cables S); 183 m in length with a depth alongside of 9·1 m.
C H Sprague & Son Co. Pier (2 cables SSW); 158 m in length, with platforms, with a depth alongside of 11·3 m. Petroleum products.

Port services

Repairs
5.300

1 There are no facilities for dry docking large vessels; the nearest such facilities are at Boston. Minor hull, machinery and electrical repairs can be carried out at Providence.

Other facilities
5.301

1 Hospitals; oily waste disposal.

Supplies
5.302

1 Fuel by barge or at tanker berths; water; provisions and stores.

MOUNT HOPE BAY, FALL RIVER HARBOR AND TAUNTON RIVER

General information

Chart 2732
Description
5.303

1 **Mount Hope Bay** (41°40′N 71°13′W), off the NE part of Narragansett Bay, is the approach to the city of Fall River (5.316) and Taunton River, which flows into its NE corner. Fall River Harbor (5.316) is situated at the mouth of the Taunton River. The bay is generally shallow with channels dredged through it.

Approaches
5.304

1 Mount Hope Bay can be approached from East Passage and entered between Bristol Point (41°38′·5N 71°15′·7W) and Musselbed Shoals Light (5.313), 4 cables S, or from Sakonnet River (5.226). The main approach is from East Passage (5.238) and the approach from Sakonnet River is little used.

Depths
5.305

1 The project depth in the main channel through Mount Hope Bay to about 9 cables above Brightman Street Bridge (5.308) is 10·7 m (35 ft).

Controlling depth (2004) in side channel leading to N entrance of Sakonnet River is 9·1 m (30 ft) and to North Tiverton (1998) (5.319) is 9·8 m (32 ft).

For the latest controlling depths the charts and port authority should be consulted.

Pilotage
5.306
1 See 5.217.

Traffic regulations
5.307
1 See 5.219. Vessels bound for Fall River Harbor should call Brightman Street Bridge (5.308) when entering Mount Hope Bay, if they need it opened.

Vertical and horizontal clearance
5.308
1 **Mount Hope Bridge** crosses the entrance to Mount Hope Bay between Bristol Point and Rhode Island. The bridge is a high level suspension bridge (5.308) with a vertical clearance of 41·1 m (135 ft).

Braga Bridge crosses the mouth of the Taunton River at Fall River. It is a fixed bridge with a vertical clearance of 41·1 m (135 ft).

2 **Brightman Street Bridge** crosses the Taunton River 1 mile upstream from Braga Bridge. The bridge has a bascule span with a horizontal clearance of 30 m and a vertical clearance of 8·2 m (27 ft) when closed. The bridge operator can be contacted on VHF. In 2006 a replacement bascule bridge, with a design clearance of 18·3 m (60 ft), was under construction about 2 cables upstream of the existing bridge.

3 **Between Fall River and Taunton** the river is crossed by three bridges. The road bridge at Berkley, 5 miles above Fall River, is a swing bridge with a vertical clearance of 2·1 m (7 ft) when closed and the road bridge at Taunton, 12½ miles upstream from Fall River, is a fixed bridge with a vertical clearance of 3·0 m (10 ft). The rail bridge 2 cables upstream of the road bridge has a vertical clearance of 2·7 m (9 ft).

4 **Overhead power cables,** with a vertical clearance of 44·2 m (145 ft). span the river 2½ cables below Brightman Street Bridge. Overhead power cables, with a vertical clearance of 19·8 m (65 ft), span the river at Taunton.

Fish traps
5.309
1 The limits of areas where fish traps may be found in the coastal waters of Mount Hope Bay are shown on the chart.

Natural conditions
5.310
1 **Tidal streams.** In Taunton River the tidal streams generally follow the direction of the channel and, except at bridges, do not hinder navigation. The out–going stream is normally stronger than the in–going.

2 **Ice.** The approach channels through Mount Hope Bay and the harbour are generally free from ice and navigable throughout the year. Taunton River is commonly closed from December to March. In severe winters the harbour and Mount Hope Bay are occasionally frozen over, but the channels to the principal wharves are kept open by vessels and tugs operating in the harbour.

3 **Weather.** The prevailing winds are NE except during the summer months when they are SW. The strongest gales are usually NW.

Directions
(continued from 5.250)

Principal marks
5.311
1 **Landmark:**
Towers of Mount Hope Bridge (41°38'·4N 71°15'·5W).

Other aids to navigation
5.312
1 **Racon:**
Mount Hope Bridge (41°38'·4N 71°15'·5W).
See *Admiralty List of Radio Signals Volume 2* for details.

Chart 2731
South-west approach to Mount Hope Bay
5.313
1 From a position S of Hog Island the main approach to Mount Hope Bay leads NE, passing (with positions relative to Hog Island Shoal Light (41°37'·9N 71°16'·4W)):
NW of Arnold Point (5 cables S), thence:
2 SE of Hog Island Shoal Light (5.246) standing on Hog Island Shoal. This shoal stands on the SE part of the bank that extends S from Hog Island. The SE limit of this bank is marked by No 3 Light–buoy (port hand). Thence:
3 NW of No 6 Buoy (starboard hand) (6½ cables ENE). Musselbed Shoals Light No 6A (red triangle on framework tower, stone base) stands close SE on Musselbed Shoals, a reef lying at the outer end of foul ground extending from Rhode Island. The white sector (049¼°–052¾°) of this light leads between the banks extending from Hog Island Shoal and Arnold Point.

Thence beneath Mount Hope Bridge (5.308) and into Mount Hope Bay.

Chart 2732, plan of Sandy Point to Fall River
Mount Hope Bay
5.314
1 **Main channel.** The main channel through Mount Hope Bay, which is marked by light–buoys and buoys (lateral), leads NE, passing (with positions relative to Mount Hope Point (41°40'·0N 71°14'·4W)):
SE of Mount Hope Point. Mount Hope, a prominent hill, stands 5 cables N of the point. Thence:
2 SE of Spar Island (1½ miles NE), small, low and in two parts, thence:
SE of Borden Flats Light (white conical tower, brown round base) (3¾ miles NE), which stands on the outer part of Borden Flats.

Thence beneath Braga Bridge (5.308) and into Fall River Harbor (5.316).

5.315
1 **Side channels.** From the vicinity of MH Light–buoy (preferred channel to port), 5 cables SSE of Mount Hope Point, a dredged side channel, marked with light–buoys and buoys, leads E for 1 mile passing N of Common Fence Point. The channel then divides, one branch leading S to the N end of Sakonnet River (5.226) and the other N to North Tiverton (5.319).

2 From a position in the main channel 3¼ miles NE of Mount Hope Point, the alignment (326°) of a pair of light beacons (piles) standing on the E side of Brayton Point, leads through a dredged channel, marked by light–buoys and buoys to a power station wharf. In 1998 this channel had a reported controlling depth of 10·4 m (34 ft).

Fall River Harbor

Chart 2732, plan of Fall River Harbor

General information

5.316

1   **Position.** The city of Fall River (41°41′N 71°10′W) is situated on the E shore of the mouth of Taunton River and the head of Mount Hope Bay. The harbour facilities of Fall River Harbor are along the Taunton and Sakonnet River and in Mount Hope Bay.

2   **Function.** Fall River, which in 2005 had an estimated population of 91 802, is a port of entry. It has a considerable coasting trade, and is an important manufacturing centre and distribution centre for oil products.

   Traffic. In 2005 the port was used by 2 vessels with a total deadweight 18 995 tonnes and in the same year Brayton Point (5.320) was used by 2 vessels with a total deadweight 163 790 tonnes.

   Port Authority. Fall River Port Authority, State Pier. Water Street, Fall River, MA 02721.

Limiting conditions

5.317

1   **Depths.** See 5.305.
   Largest berths. See 5.320.
   Ice. See 5.310.

Arrival information

5.318

1   **Port operations.** See 5.307.
   Pilotage. See 5.217.

   Anchorage is available either side of the dredged approach channel or anywhere in Mount Hope Bay where depth or bottom are suitable. The chart is the best guide. However, care should be taken not to anchor near the submarine cable area extending across Borden Flats (5.314) and into the main channel of the river.

   Tugs are available at Fall River and more powerful tugs are available at Providence for use at Fall River.

   Ice and local weather. See 5.310.

Harbour

5.319

1   **General layout.** The piers and wharves of Fall River Harbor are situated at:

   North Tiverton between the N entrance to the Sakonnet River (41°38′·9N 71°12′·7W) and the E side of Mount Hope Bay, 2 miles NNE.

   East side of Taunton River. Between Braga Bridge and the Turning Basin, 2 miles NNE.

2   West side of Taunton River. At Brayton Point (41°42′·5N 71°11′·5W) and on W bank of river abreast Turning Basin.

   Speed limit of 5 kn is in force in the channel off the piers and wharves.

Alongside berths

5.320

1   A summary of the principal alongside berths is given as follows:

   North Tiverton (with positions relative to Common Fence Point (41°39′·4N 71°13′·2W)):

      Texaco Tiverton Terminal (7 cables SE); 220 m in length, with dolphins, with a depth alongside of 10·7 m.

2   Northeast Petroleum Corp. Piers 1 and 2 (6 cables ESE); 213 m in length, with dolphins, with depths alongside of 9·8 to 10·4 m.

      Tiverton Terminal Pier (1½ miles NE); 242 m in length, with dolphins, with a depth alongside of 10·7 m. Petroleum products.

3   **East side of Taunton River** (with positions relative to State Pier (41°42′·3N 71°09′·9W)):

      Borden and Remington Corp. Wharf (2 cables SW); 116 m in length with a depth alongside of 8·5 m. Latex and caustic soda.

4   State Pier; NW face: 121 m in length with depths alongside of 5·5 to 10·7 m. SW side: 189 m in length with a depth alongside of 10·7 m. General and Ro–Ro cargo. Battleship *USS Massachusetts*, World War II memorial, and three other USN vessels, are berthed close N of State Pier.

5   Shell Oil Co. Wharf (2 miles NNE); 213 m in length, with dolphins, with a depth alongside of 9·1 m.

   West side of Taunton River (with positions relative to Borden Flats Light (41°42′·3N 71°10′·5W)):

      Brayton Point Station (7 cables WNW); 310 m in length with a depth alongside of 10·4 m. Receipt of coal and fuel oil for power station.

6   Montaup Electric Co. Wharf (2¼ miles NNE); 197 m in length with a depth alongside of 10·4 m. Receipt of coal and fuel oil for power station.

Port services

5.321

1   **Repairs.** Fall River has no dry docking or major repair facilities for deep-draught vessels. The nearest such facilities are at Boston (4.119).

   There are two small shipyards, one situated 6 cables above Braga Bridge on the W side and the other 9 cables below Braga Bridge, at Globe Wharf, on the E side. The N shipyard can handle craft up to 30 m in length and the S shipyard can handle steel craft of up to 250 tonnes and in 1981 had depths alongside of 6·7 to 7 m.

2   **Facilities:** oily waste disposal.
   Supplies: fuel; water; provisions and stores.

Chapter 6 - Block Island Sound and Long Island Sound

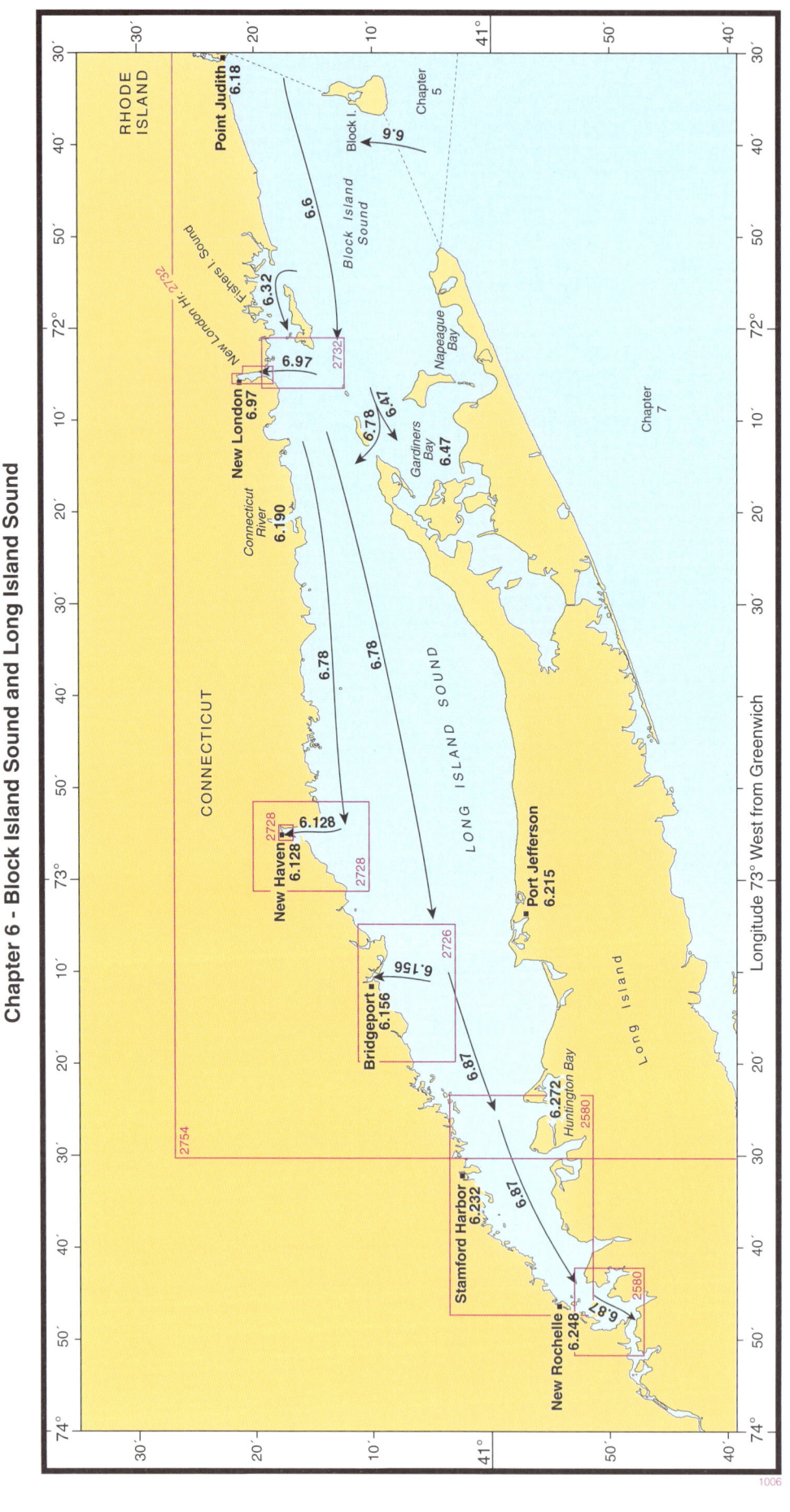

CHAPTER 6

BLOCK ISLAND SOUND AND LONG ISLAND SOUND

GENERAL INFORMATION

Charts 2754, 2580
Scope of the chapter
6.1

1   The area covered by this chapter includes:
> Block Island Sound (41°10′N 71°50′W) (6.6).
> Long Island Sound (41°05′N 72°45′W) (6.71).

Route
6.2

1   The waters of this chapter form a route that connects New York Harbor with Vineyard and Nantucket Sounds or Cape Cod Canal. This route is used extensively by coasting vessels drawing up to about 6 m (20 ft).

Hazards
6.3

1   **Small craft**, including commercial, fishing and pleasure boats, may be found in large numbers nearly all the year round in Block Island Sound and Long Island Sound.

    Tugs and barges on a long tow may also be encountered in these waters.

    Fish traps. The limits of areas where fish traps may be found in the coastal waters of Block Island Sound and Long Island Sound are shown on the chart.

Pilotage
6.4

1   Pilotage is compulsory for all foreign vessels in the waters covered by this chapter. Vessels bound from E for ports in Long Island Sound, may embark pilots in the following positions:
> Vicinity of 41°17′N 71°30′W.
> 3 miles S of Watch Hill Point (41°18′N 71°52′W).

2
> 7 miles S of Watch Hill Point (41°18′N 71°52′W).
> 3 miles E of MP Light-buoy (41°02′N 71°46′W).

    Vessels entering Long Island Sound from East River may embark pilots in a position 6 cables E of Execution Rocks (40°53′N 73°44′W) (6.95). See *Admiralty List of Radio Signals Volume 6(5)* for further information.

Regulations
6.5

1   **Navigation Rules for US Inland Waters** apply to all waters in Long Island Sound and to some of the inshore waters of Block Island Sound, Napeague Bay (41°03′N 72°03′W) and Gardiners Bay (41°07′N 72°12′W). See 1.47 and Appendix VII for further information.

2   **Regulated navigation area.** The whole of Block Island Sound and Long Island Sound lie within a regulated navigation area. For details, and definition and general regulations concerning regulated navigation areas see Appendix V.

BLOCK ISLAND SOUND AND ADJACENT WATERS

BLOCK ISLAND SOUND

General information

Charts 2890, 2754
Description
6.6

1   **Block Island Sound** is a deep navigable waterway forming the E approach to Long Island Sound (6.71), Fishers Island Sound (6.32) and Gardiners Bay (6.47).

2   Its E and S limits are defined by Point Judith (41°22′N 71°29′W), Block Island and the E end of Long Island; its N side by the mainland coast between Point Judith and Watch Hill Point, 17 miles W and thence by Fisher Island and a chain of islands leading WSW for 19 miles from Watch Hill Point to Orient Point (41°10′N 72°14′W); and its W side by Gardiners Island (41°06′N 72°06′W).

3   **No-discharge zone (NDZ).** All the waters W of a line joining Montauk Point (41°04′N 71°51′W) and Orient Point (18 miles WNW) have been designated as a NDZ. See 1.44.

Recommended routes
6.7

1   Recommended routes for deep draught vessels, tugs and barges, as shown on the charts, have been established in Block Island Sound. Pleasure craft, fishing vessels and other small vessels should exercise caution in and around these routes and should monitor VHF channels for information concerning vessels transiting these routes.

Entrances
6.8

1   Block Island Sound has two entrances from the Atlantic. The S entrance leads between Block Island and Montauk Point, a high sandy bluff, 12 miles WSW. The deepest passage in this entrance is just W of Southwest Ledge (41°07′N 71°40′W) and is 2 miles wide. The E entrance from Rhode Island Sound lies between the N part of Block Island and Point Judith, 9 miles NNE, and is used by vessels with a draught in excess of 11·5 m (38 ft) and those coming from the bays and sounds E of Long Island Sound. The Race (41°14′N 72°03′W) is the main entrance to Long Island Sound from Block Island Sound.

Pilotage
6.9

1   See 6.4.

Traffic regulations
6.10

1   Vessels with a draught in excess of 11·5 m (38 ft) are prohibited from using the S entrance (6.16), known locally as Montauk Channel. This channel should also not be used during periods of unfavourable weather, strong tidal streams, poor visibility, reduced under-keel clearance and heavy traffic.

2   **Restricted anchorage** for US submarines is situated 3 miles E of Gardiners Island (41°06′N 72°06′W). Its limits are shown on the chart.

Danger area. The area within 1½ cables of the ruin standing on Gardiners Point (6.49) is dangerous due to the existence of unexploded ordnance. Anchoring, fishing and trawling should not be carried out in this area.

The ruin itself, a former bombing target, is prohibited to the public.

Rescue
6.11

1   **Coast Guard** stations are situated at Point Judith (41°22′N 71°29′W) and W of Montauk Point in Montauk Harbor (41°04′N 71°56′W).

Natural conditions
6.12

1   **Tidal streams.** See Tidal Stream tables on the chart for the strength of tidal streams in the entrances to Block Island Sound.

Tidal levels. At Point Judith the mean spring range is about 1·1 m; mean neap range about 0·5 m. At Montauk Point the mean spring range is about 0·9 m; mean neap range about 0·4 m. See information in *Admiralty Tide Tables*.

2   **Ice.** Large quantities of ice usually pass through The Race during the out-going tide and during severe winters may cause some obstruction in Block Island Sound and around Montauk Point especially in February.

Fog is generally thickest with SE winds and its duration is usually from 4 to 12 hours. Periods of fog have been known to last for 4 to 6 days, with very short clear intervals.

Directions
(continued from 5.15)

Principal marks
6.13

1   **Landmark:**
   Tower (41°12′N 72°07′W) on Great Gull Island.

Major lights:
   Point Judith Light (41°22′N 71°29′W) (5.230).
   Block Island South-east Light (41°09′N 71°33′W) (5.230).
   Montauk Point Light (41°04′N 71°51′W).

2   Watch Hill Light (grey square granite tower, white dwelling) (41°18′N 71°52′W).
   Race Rock Light (granite tower and dwelling, 14 m in height) (41°15′N 72°03′W).
   Little Gull Island Light (grey granite tower, red dwelling) (41°12′N 72°06′W).
   Oyster Pond Reef Light (black conical tower, white band) (41°10′N 72°13′W).

Other aids to navigation
6.14

1   **Racons:**
   Southwest Ledge No 2 Light-buoy (41°06′N 71°40′W).
   MP Light-buoy (41°02′N 71°46′W).
   See *Admiralty List of Radio Signals Volume 2* for details.

East entrance
6.15

1   From a position SSE of Point Judith the route into Block Island Sound leads WSW, passing (with positions relative to Watch Hill Light (41°18′N 71°52′W)):

Montauk Point Light (6.13)
(Original dated 1999)

(Photograph - US Army Corps of Engineers)

2   SSE of No 2 Light-buoy (starboard hand) (17½ miles E) which marks a dangerous wreck lying approximately 4 cables NE, and shoal ground, consisting of numerous large boulders, extending SSE from Cape Judith. Thence:

SSE of Nebraska Shoal (13½ miles E), which is marked by 2NS Buoy (starboard hand) and lies 2½ miles WSW of Matunuck Reef, thence:

3   NNW of Block Island North Reef (14 miles ESE) which extends 2 miles NNE from Sandy Point, the N point of Block Island. 1BI Light-buoy (port hand) lies off the NW side of the reef. Thence:

SSE of Watch Hill Point, low and backed by Watch Hill, a high bare bluff. Watch Hill Light (6.13) stands on the point, thence:

4   NNW of an area in which numerous obstructions have been reported (9 miles S), thence:

NNW of Cerberus Shoal (9 miles SSW) on which the sea sometimes breaks. The NE side of this shoal is marked by No 9 Light-buoy (port hand).

Thence to the entrance of Long Island Sound or Gardiners Bay.

5   **Useful mark:**

Sandy Point Light (brown tower on grey dwelling, 16 m in height) (41°14′N 71°35′W) standing on the N end of Block Island.

(Directions for Gardiners Bay continue at 6.49 and for Long Island Sound at 6.81)

South entrance

6.16

1   From a position about 5 miles E of MP Light-buoy (safe water) (41°02′N 71°46′W) the track leads NNW, passing (with positions relative to Montauk Point Light (41°04′N 71°51′W)):

2   WSW of Southwest Ledge (9 miles ENE). This ledge, which breaks in heavy weather, is marked on its SW side by No 2 Light-buoy (starboard hand). Thence:

ENE of B Light-buoy (preferred channel to starboard) (6¾ miles ENE). A depth of 11·2 m (37 ft) lies close E of the buoy.

Thence into the central part of Block Island Sound.

3   **Caution.** See 6.10.

6.17

1   **Other channels.** A channel 1¼ miles wide with a least depth of 9·4 m (31 ft), rounds the SW end of Block Island at a distance of 1½ miles. The E side of this channel is marked by No 4 Light-buoy (starboard hand). It is inadvisable to use this passage in heavy weather.

2   Another channel leads between B Light-buoy and the broken shoal ground that extends from Montauk Point (41°04′N 71°46′W) (6.8). From a position E of Montauk Point this passage leads across the outer part of Endeavor Shoals, passing (with positions relative to Montauk Point):

3   ENE of No 1 Light-buoy (port hand) (4¼ miles ENE) and Great Eastern Rock (1½ miles E), thence:

ENE of Shagwong Rock (2½ miles WNW), which is marked on its E side by SR Light-buoy (preferred channel to starboard), thence:

4   ENE of Shagwong Reef (3½ miles NW), which is marked by 7SR Light-buoy (port hand). Washington Shoal lies between Shagwong Reef and Shagwong Rock. Thence:

Clear of Cerberus Shoal (7½ miles NW) (6.15).

Caution. Due to the presence of sandwaves and as the area is subject to continual change extra caution should be observed where the depths are less than 3 m (10 ft) greater than the draught of the vessel.

Point Judith Harbor of Refuge and Point Judith Pond

Chart 2890 (see 1.17)

General information

6.18

1   **Point Judith Harbor of Refuge** (41°22′N 71°30′W) lies on the W side of Point Judith.

The harbour is formed by a detached breakwater, which lies with its knuckle 1¼ miles WSW of Point Judith Light, and two shorter breakwaters extending from the coast. These breakwaters leave two entrances facing S on the E side and W on the W side, known locally as East Gap and West Gap, respectively. The harbour is easy of access for most vessels except with a heavy S sea.

2   **Lights** mark both entrances and the knuckle of the detached breakwater.

6.19

1   **Point Judith Pond** is a shallow tidal inlet used extensively by small fishing vessels and pleasure craft.

Limiting conditions

6.20

1   **Depths.** In 1981 the controlling depths in East Gap and West Gap were, 7·3 m (24 ft) and 5·5 m (18 ft), respectively.

Two shoals are situated in the central part of the Harbor of Refuge. The N shoal has depths of 4·3 to 5·5 m (14 to 18 ft) and the S shoal, which is marked by a buoy, has depths of 4·3 to 4·9 m (14 to 16 ft).

2   **Tidal stream** in the East Gap has a rate of ¾ kn. The tidal stream off the West Gap is rotary with a rate of ½ kn. Considerably stronger rates have been reported with the out-going tidal stream.

Berths

6.21

1   **Anchorage** is available in the area within the V-shaped detached breakwater, soft bottom. A good berth with depths of 7 to 9 m (22 to 30 ft) is on a line joining the two heads of this detached breakwater, keeping clear of an obstruction 1½ cables SE of the W head and a dangerous wreck, marked on its N side by No 5 Light-buoy (port hand), 2½ cables WSW of the E head. The breakwater should be given a berth of 1 cable to avoid broken and hard bottom.

Great Salt Pond

General information

6.22

1   Great Salt Pond (41°12′N 71°35′W) is entered on the W side of Block Island, 2 miles SSW of Sandy Point Light (6.15). It is the best harbour in Block Island Sound for vessels of 4·6 m (15 ft) draught or less.

Entrance. The entrance channel is dredged through a narrow strip of beach which forms the W side of Great Salt Pond.

2   **Local knowledge** is required to enter the harbour as the channel is subject to shoaling.

No-discharge zone (NDZ). The whole of Great Salt Pond has been designated as a NDZ. See 1.44.

Limiting conditions

6.23

1   **Depths.** In 2005 the mid-channel controlling depth of the entrance channel was 1·8 m (5·8 ft).

Tidal streams in the entrance have a maximum rate of less than ½ kn.

Directions
6.24

1 From the vicinity of No 2 Buoy (starboard hand), off the harbour entrance, the track leads through the entrance channel, which is buoyed. No 4 Light-beacon (red triangle on white round tower, red top) stands at the head of the breakwater which forms the SW side of the entrance.

Berths
6.25

1 **Anchorage.** The usual anchorage is near the SE end of the harbour off the ferry pier in depths of 5 to 14 m (16 to 46 ft), taking care to leave a fairway to the ferry pier. Anchorage is prohibited in the N and E part of the harbour, and cable and pipeline areas are situated in the W side of the harbour.

2 **Alongside berths.** The main pier, which is also the ferry pier, is reported to have depths of 6 m at its head.

A jetty with dolphins at its head lies 1 cable W of the main pier.

Fort Pond Bay

General information
6.26

1 Fort Pond Bay lies between Culloden Point (41°04′N 71°58′W) and Rocky Point, 1¾ miles SW. The bay is free of dangers, but flats with depths of 2·4 to 3·6 m (8 to 12 ft) extend from its E shore and shoaling is abrupt on its E and S sides.

The village of Montauk, the terminus of the Long Island Railroad, lies on the SE side of the bay.

Anchorage
6.27

1 **Anchorage** is available in depths of 12 to 15 m (40 to 50 ft), soft mud. It is exposed to N winds.

Napeague Bay

General information
6.28

1 Napeague Bay (41°04′N 72°02′W) is entered between Rocky Point and the S extremity of Gardiners Island. It is shallow in its W and SW part.

2 The bay forms the approach to Promised Land Channel, a buoyed passage that passes S of Gardiners Island and Cartwright Island, which lies 1¾ miles S of the S extremity of Gardiners Island, and thence into Gardiners Bay (6.47). The channel is marked by S Light-buoy (safe water) at its E entrance.

3 Napeague Harbor (41°01′N 72°03′W) and Promised Land (41°00′N 72°05′W) are used by pleasure craft and small craft.

Limiting conditions
6.29

1 **Depths.** Promised Land Channel has a centreline depth of about 4·3 m (14 ft), however the depth is continually changing due to the shifting shoals.

Tidal streams have a rate of about 1½ kn through all the channels between the shoals.

Local knowledge. It is not advisable for vessels drawing more than 3 m to make this passage unless local knowledge is available, and then only if the buoys are visible.

Minor harbours

Charts 2890, 2754 (see 1.17)
General information
6.30

1 The coast between Point Judith (41°22′N 71°29′W) and Watch Hill Point, 17½ miles WSW, is low and consists mainly of sandy beaches separated by rocky points with several summer resorts along this stretch of the coast.

2 Close behind it are a number of lagoons, the outlets of which may be closed at times.

Ninigret Pond entered through Charlestown Breachway, 7 miles W of Judith Point, Quonochontaug Pond entered through Quonochontaug Breachway, 10½ miles WSW of Point Judith, and Winnapaug Pond entered through Weekapaug Breachway, 12½ miles W of Point Judith, are only used by small local craft.

Montauk Harbor
6.31

1 Montauk Harbor (41°04′N 71°56′W), in the N part of Montauk Lake, is entered nearly 4 miles W of Montauk Point. It provides a good harbour for small craft, but local knowledge is required.

Star Island is situated just inside the entrance and is connected to the mainland by a causeway on its SW side.

2 **Rescue.** Coastguard station is situated at the N end of Star Island.

FISHERS ISLAND SOUND

General information

Chart 2754 (see 1.17)
Description
6.32

1 Fishers Island Sound is entered from E between Watch Hill Point (41°18′N 71°52′W) and East Point, 3 miles WSW and lies between Fishers Island and the mainland. It is used to some extent by shallow draught vessels, but it is obstructed by numerous shoals which are steep-to. The principal dangers are marked, but the entire area is encumbered by boulder patches.

2 The principal anchorages are on the N side of the sound, the harbours on the S side being suitable only for small craft.

Rescue. Coast Guard station is situated at the W end of Fishers Island in Silver Eel Pond (41°15′·4N 72°01′·9W). This station is manned during the summer months only.

Local knowledge is required for the navigation of the sound and harbours connected with it.

3 **No-discharge zone (NDZ).** Large areas of Fishers Island Sound have been designated as a NDZ. See 1.44.

Entrances
6.33

1 There are five passages between the reefs extending from Watch Hill Point to East Point, of which the E, Watch Hill Passage (6.37), is the only recommended passage.

2 The other passages, which are only partially buoyed and less frequently used are (with positions relative to Watch Hill Point), Sugar Reef Passage (9 cables SW), Catumb Passage (1¼ miles SW), Lords Passage (2¼ miles WSW) and Wicopesset Passage (2¾ miles WSW).

Depth. Watch Hill Passage has a least depth of 5·2 m (17 ft) between the reef that extends S from Watch Hill Point and a patch 1½ cables SW.

Traffic regulations

6.34

1   **Navigation Rules for US Inland Waters** apply inshore of a line joining Watch Hill Point Light and East Point on Fishers Island (3 miles WSW).

Regulated navigation area. See 6.5.

Natural conditions

6.35

1   **Tidal streams.** In the main channel through Fishers Island Sound, including Watch Hill Passage, slack water before the E-going and W-going stream, respectively, occurs ½ hour and 5¾ hours after HW at Boston. The strength of the stream occurs about 2½ hours after and 3¾ hours before HW at Boston.

2   In the main channel the maximum rate of the stream is about 2½ kn and in Watch Hill Passage is strong enough to tow spar buoys under water.

Ice. The tidal streams are of sufficient strength to prevent the formation of heavy local ice except in the shallow tributaries. The only ice likely to hinder navigation is that set in from Long Island Sound by wind and tidal stream.

Directions for through route

Principal marks

6.36

1   **Major light:**

Watch Hill Light (41°18′N 71°52′W) (6.13).

Watch Hill Passage to Latimer Reef

6.37

1   From a position 5 cables SE of Watch Hill Point the route through Fishers Island Sound leads NW through Watch Hill Passage and thence W to the vicinity of Latimer Reef, passing (with positions relative to Watch Hill Light):

2   Between WH Light-buoy (preferred channel to starboard) (3½ cables SSW) and No 2 Light-buoy (starboard hand) (2½ cables S). A dangerous wreck, the position of which is approximate, lies ½ cable ESE of No 2 Light-buoy (2½ cables S). Thence:

N of Sugar Reef (1 mile WSW), the N side of which is marked by No 5 Buoy (port hand), thence:

3   S of a dangerous wreck, the position of which is approximate (1 mile W), thence:

S of Napatree Point Ledge (1½ miles WSW), which is marked by No 6 Light-buoy (starboard hand) which lies 4 cables SSW of Napatree Point, thence:

N of Wicopesset Island (2½ miles WSW). Nos 9 and 11 Buoys (port hand) mark the edge of the shoal ground that extends N from this island. Thence:

4   Between Nos 12 and 13 Buoys (starboard and port hand, respectively) (3 miles W) that mark two rocks that lie 4½ and 7½ cables N of East Point. Thence:

S of Latimer Reef Light (white conical tower, brown band, on brown column, 15 m in height) (3½ miles W), which stands on the W end of Latimer Reef.

Latimer Reef to Seaflower Reef

6.38

1   From S of Latimer Reef the route through Fishers Island Sound continues W for 4½ miles to the W end of Fishers Island Sound, passing (with positions relative to North Dumpling Light (41°17′N 72°01′W)):

N of Youngs Rock (3¾ miles E), marked on its NW side by No 17 Buoy (port hand), thence:

2   N of East Clump (2½ miles ENE), the N side of which is marked by No 19 Buoy (port hand), thence:

S of Ram Island Reef (2¼ miles ENE), the S side of which is marked by No 20 Light-buoy (starboard hand), thence:

3   N of Middle Clump (2 miles ENE), the N side of which is marked by No 21 Buoy (port hand), thence:

S of Intrepid Rock (1 mile NE), DIR Buoy (isolated danger) marks the SE side of this rock, thence:

4   N of North Dumpling, a grassy islet. North Dumpling Light stands on the islet. The red sector of the light covers East Clump and the dangers W of it, except for the outer 4·6 m (15ft) patch, N of Middle Clump. Thence:

5   S of Seaflower Reef (6 cables NW) on which stands Seaflower Reef Light (green and white chequered diamond on framework tower), thence:

Through the approaches to New London Harbor.

(Directions for New London Harbor are given at 6.117, and for Long Island Sound at 6.81)

Stonington Harbor

General information

6.39

1   **Position.** Stonington Harbor (41°20′N 71°55′W) lies 3 miles NW of Watch Hill Point and is entered between Stonington Point and Wamphassuc Point. The town of Stonington lies on the E side of the inner harbour. The port is mainly used by fishing and pleasure craft.

2   **Breakwaters.** The entrance is protected by an outer breakwater with its NE end on Bartlett Reef, and a W breakwater that extends SE from close off Wamphassuc Point.

Approach. Stonington Harbor can be approached from SE or W. The SE approach is best, with fewer dangers.

3   **No-discharge zone (NDZ).** Stonington Harbor has been designated as a NDZ. See 1.44.

Depths

6.40

1   **Depths.** The controlling depth to the inner harbour is about 3·4 m (11 ft).

Directions

6.41

1   **South-east approach.** From a position E of Latimer Reef (6.37) the SE approach to Stonington Harbor leads NW and N, passing (with positions relative to Stonington Point (41°19·6′N 71°54′·3W)):

SW of No 2 Buoy (starboard hand) (1 mile S) at the SW end of Middle Ground, thence:

E of No 3 Buoy (port hand) (1 mile SSW) at the E end of Noyes Shoal, thence:

2   W of No 4 Light (red triangle on framework tower, hut, concrete base) (7 cables S) at the SW head of the outer breakwater, thence:

Between the head of the W breakwater (4 cables WSW) and Stonington Point. No 5 Light (green square on framework tower, concrete base) stands at the head of the breakwater.

Thence into the inner harbour.

6.42

1   **West approach.** From a position S of Ram Island Reef (41°18′N 71°58′W) the W approach to Stonington Harbor leads NE and E, passing (with positions relative to Wamphassuc Point (41°19'·7N 71°55'·3W)):

2   Between Eel Grass Ground (1¾ miles SW) and Ellis Reef (1¾ miles WSW). No 18 Buoy (starboard hand) is moored on the SW side of Eel Grass Ground and ER Beacon stands on Ellis Reef. Thence:

3   S of White Rock (8 cables WSW), above-water, thence:

        N of Noyes Rock, (5 cables WSW).

Thence into the inner harbour.

Berths
6.43

1   **Alongside berths.** The wharves have depths alongside of 2·1 to 3·6 m.

Anchorages and harbours

Mystic Harbor
6.44

1   **General information.** Mystic Harbor (41°20'N 71°59'W) is situated between Mason Island and the mainland. The harbour lies 2 miles W of Stonington Harbor. The town of Noank lies on the W side of the harbour and the town of Mystic lies on the E side of Mystic River, which flows into the head of the harbour.

  Ice usually closes the river during January and February.

2   The harbour is used by local fishing and pleasure craft.

Little Narragansett Bay
6.45

1   **General information.** Little Narragansett Bay (41°19'N 71°53'W) at the E end of Fishers Island Sound, is a shallow area enclosed by Napatree Beach on the S and by a long strip of sand, much of which is above water, extending SSE from Sandy Point, which lies 2¼ miles NW of Watch Hill Point.

2   The bay forms the approach to Pawcatuck River, which flows into the SE part of the bay, and Wequetequock Cove and Watch Hill Cove which lie on the N and S side of the bay, respectively. Pawcatuck River, Wequetequock Cove and Watch Hill Cove are only used by small craft.

  Ice generally closes the Pawcatuck River from January to March. Ice formations in Little Narragansett Bay are sometimes heavy enough to destroy structures exposed to them.

  Local knowledge is essential.

West Harbor
6.46

1   West Harbor (41°16'N 72°00'W) on the N side of Fishers Island, SE of North Dumpling Light (6.38), affords shelter from S winds.

GARDINERS BAY AND ADJACENT BAYS SOUTH-WEST

General information

Chart 2754 (see 1.17)

Description
6.47

1   Gardiners Bay lies at the W end of Block Island Sound, from which it is separated by Gardiners Island. It is formed by the forked E end of Long Island between Orient Point (41°10'N 72°14'W) and Hog Creek Point, 7 miles SSE,

with Gardiners Island on its E side and Shelter Island (6.57) across its head.

2   The bay affords excellent anchorage and is easily accessible, either by day or by night.

  It is the approach to Shelter Island Sound (6.57), the name given to the waters on the N, W and S sides of Shelter Island and to Little Peconic Bay (6.57) and Great Peconic Bay (6.70), which extend SW from that island.

3   **No-discharge zone (NDZ).** All the waters W of a line joining Montauk Point (41°04'N 71°51'W) and Orient Point (18 miles WNW) have been designated as a NDZ. See 1.44.

Entrances
6.48

1   **Main entrance** from Block Island Sound to Gardiners Bay lies between Gardiners Point (41°09'N 72°09'W) (6.49) and Pine Point (6.84), 2¾ miles WNW. The bay can also be entered through the narrow passage that leads through Promised Land Channel (6.28), S of Gardiners Island.

  Entrance from Long Island Sound is through Plum Gut (6.84) between Orient Point and Plum Island.

Directions
(continued from 6.15)

Main entrance
6.49

1   From a position NNE of Gardiners Island the track through the main entrance to Gardiners Bay leads WSW, passing (with positions relative to Orient Point (41°10'N 72°14'W)):

        SSE of Constellation Rock (5½ miles E), which is marked by No 2 Buoy (starboard hand), thence:

2   NNW of Gardiners Point (4¼ miles ESE) on which stand the ruins of a former bombing target (6.10). 1GI Light-buoy (port hand) is moored 5 cables NNW of Gardiners Point.

Thence into Gardiners Bay.

Other entrances
6.50

1   **South entrance.** See 6.28.

  Plum Gut. See 6.84.

Anchorages and harbours in Gardiners Bay

General
6.51

1   There is anchorage anywhere in Gardiners Bay according to draught.

Bostwick Bay
6.52

1   Bostwick Bay (41°07'N 72°09'W) is entered between Bostwick Point, the N extremity of Gardiners Island and Cherry Hill Point.

  Anchorage may be obtained in depths of 7 to 8 m (23 to 26 ft). This anchorage is excellent in E winds, but is exposed to W winds.

Cherry Harbor
6.53

1   Cherry Harbor (41°04'N 72°07'W) is entered between the S extremity of Gardiners Island and Crow Shoal, 3 miles WNW.

  Anchorage, clear of a cable area extending between Gardiners Island and Hog Tree Point (3 miles SW), may be obtained in depths of 7 to 8 m (23 to 26 ft), mud. The anchorage is sheltered from NE winds.

Acabonack Harbor

6.54

1   Acabonack Harbor (41°01′N 72°08′W), 2 miles SSE of Hog Creek Point, is only used by small craft.

Threemile Harbor

6.55

1   Threemile Harbor (41°02′N 72°12′W), on the S side of Gardiners Bay, is only used by small craft.

Coecles Harbor

6.56

1   Coecles Harbor (41°04′N 72°18′W), on the W side of Gardiners Bay, is only used by small craft.

Shelter Island Sound and Peconic Bays

General information

6.57

1   Shelter Island Sound is entered from the W side of Gardiners Bay through channels that run N and S of Shelter Island (41°04′N 72°19′W) and leads into Little Peconic Bay and Great Peconic Bay (6.70). Little Peconic Bay and Great Peconic Bay extend for about 15 miles to Riverhead at the head of navigation on Peconic River.

2   The town of Greenport (6.60) is situated on the NW side of the N channel and the town of Sag Harbor (6.61) on the S side of the S channel.

There are many summer resorts in the area which are much frequented by yachts and small craft in summer, but the waters are only suitable for vessels of shallow draught.

3   **Local knowledge** is necessary.

Navigation Rules for US Inland Waters apply to all the waters within this section. See 1.47 and Appendix VII for details.

Channel depths

6.58

1   **Depths.** There is a least charted depth of 6·7 m (22 ft) through the channel N of Shelter Island Sound and thence through Little Peconic Bay to Robins Island (6.70) (40°58′N 72°28′W), and about 4 m (13 ft) through the channel S of Shelter Island.

Between Little and Great Peconic Bay there is a controlling depth of 4 m (13 ft) across the bar.

Limiting conditions

6.59

1   **Tidal streams** have a rate of up to 1¾ kn in places where the channel is narrowed.

Ice obstructs navigation in coves and shallow harbours during January and February. In severe winters drift ice is reported to interfere with navigation for short periods and in the S arm of Shelter Island Sound the ice is heavy enough at times to destroy structures exposed to it.

Greenport Harbor

6.60

1   **General information.** Greenport Harbor (41°06′N 72°21′W) lies in the N channel of Shelter Island Sound. Greenport, an important town, lies on the W side of the harbour.

The NE side of the harbour is formed by a breakwater which extends 2½ cables SE from the shore. No 8A Light beacon (red triangle on framework tower) stands at the head of the breakwater.

2   **Wharves** with depths alongside of 2·1 to 6·4 m are situated between the entrance to Stirling Basin and Fanning Point, 1 mile SSW.

Repairs. There are several shipyards and patent slips at Greenport and repairs can be carried out.

Supplies: fuel; water; provisions and stores.

Sag Harbor

6.61

1   Sag Harbor (41°00′N 72°18′W) lies on the S side of the S channel of Shelter Sound, 2½ miles SW of Cedar Point. The town of Sag Harbor lies on the S side of the harbour.

The harbour is formed on the NE by a breakwater extending 5 cables NW from the shore. 3SH Light (green square on framework tower) stands at the head of the breakwater.

The approach to the harbour is obstructed by several dangers, but is well buoyed.

2   **Depths.** In 1974 the dredged channel into Sag Harbor had a controlling depth of 3 m (10 ft) in mid–channel through the entrance into the turning basin. In 1991 this channel was no longer being maintained.

Anchorage is available in depths of 2 m (7 ft) in the main anchorage area in the E part of the harbour.

Repairs. Repairs to hull and engines are available.

Supplies: fuel; water; provisions and stores.

6.62

1   **Sag Harbor Cove** is entered at the SW corner of the harbour through a channel with a depth of 2·4 m (8 ft).

The entrance is crossed by a fixed bridge with a vertical clearance of 6·4 m.

Other anchorages and harbours in the north part of Shelter Island Sound

6.63

1   **Orient Harbor** (41°08′N 72°19′W) lies on the N side of the entrance to the north channel to Shelter Island Sound. It is entered between Long Beach Point and Cleaves Point, 1½ miles W.

2   Excellent anchorage is available in depths of 6 m (20 ft) in the S part of the harbour and 5 m (16 ft) at its N end clear of the marine farms shown on the chart.

The village of Orient lies at the NE end of the harbour, where there is a pier with a depth of 2·5 m at its head.

6.64

1   **Dering Harbor** (41°05′N 72°21′W) on the NW side of Shelter Island, opposite Greenport, is a favourite anchorage for small craft.

6.65

1   **Southold Bay** (41°03′N 72°24′W) lies at the S end of the north channel. The town of Southold stands at the head of the bay.

Anchorage can be obtained in depths of 4 to 5 m (13 to 16 ft) between 2 and 4 cables ESE of the jetty at Southold clear of the marine farms shown on the chart.

Other anchorages and harbours in the south part of Shelter Island Sound

6.66

1   **Northwest Harbor** (41°02′N 72°15′W) lies on the E side of the entrance to the south part of Shelter Island Sound.

The harbour is strewn with boulders, over many of which there are depths of only 1·2 to 1·8 m (4 to 6 ft).

6.67

1   **Smith Cove** (41°03′N 72°19′W), a small bight on the S side of Shelter Island, is a good anchorage for small vessels in N winds.

    Anchorage is available in depths of 3 to 10 m (10 to 33 ft).

    A ferry operates between South Ferry, on the SW side of the cove, and North Haven Peninsula opposite.

6.68

1   **Noyack Bay** (41°01′N 72°21′W) lies between North Haven Peninsula and Jessup Neck, high and wooded, 2 miles WSW.

    Anchorage is available in depths of 7 to 10 m (23 to 33 ft), giving the shore a berth of 4 cables.

Anchorages and harbours in Little Peconic Bay
6.69

1   **Cutchogue Harbor** (41°00′N 72°28′W), at the NW end of Little Peconic Bay, provides anchorage for small vessels and is mainly used by local craft drawing up to 3 m (10 ft).

    The town of New Suffolk stands on the W side of the harbour and has a small basin with a depth of 2·8 m (8 ft).

Great Peconic Bay
6.70

1   Great Peconic Bay (40°57′N 72°30′W) is used mainly by local small craft. The bay is mainly clear, but shoals extend up to 2 miles from its shores except on the S side. The bay can also be entered from the S through the Shinnecock Canal (7.27).

LONG ISLAND SOUND

GENERAL INFORMATION

Charts 2754, 2580

Area covered
6.71

1   This section describes Long Island Sound, a deep navigable waterway lying between the shores of Connecticut and New York and the N coast of Long Island, which extends from Fishers Island (41°16′N 71°59′W) to Throgs Neck (7.44), 84 miles WSW.

Topography
6.72

1   The N shore of Long Island Sound is generally low and marshy on the coast, but rises to elevations of over 120 m at a distance of 3 miles inland. It is indented by numerous bays and rivers. The N coast of Long Island is generally bluff and rocky.

Hazards
6.73

1   **Spoil grounds.** There are numerous spoil grounds throughout Long Island Sound.

    Oyster grounds exist in shoal water in places in the sound and are usually marked by stakes and flags. Broken stakes, below-water, may exist in places; these may be dangerous to small craft.

Pilotage
6.74

1   See 6.4.

Submarine operating areas
6.75

1   Submarines operate in the approaches to New London Harbor and Connecticut River, and off the N shore of Long Island. As submarines may be operating submerged in these areas, vessels should proceed with caution. See 1.15.

Traffic regulations
6.76

1   **Navigation Rules for US Inland Waters.** See 6.5.

    Regulated navigation area. 6.5.

Natural conditions
6.77

1   **Tidal levels.** The time of tide is nearly simultaneous throughout Long Island Sound, but the range varies between about 1·0 m at the E end and about 2·6 m at the W end.

2   **Ice.** In ordinary winters the floating and pack ice in Long Island Sound, while impeding navigation, does not render it absolutely unsafe except in exceptionally severe winters, when only the most powerful vessels are able to proceed.

3   Pack ice, which is formed principally along the N shore, is forced under the influence of the prevailing NW winds across to the S side where it accumulates, massing into large fields, and remains until removed by S winds when it drifts back to the N shore.

4   In ordinary winters ice forms in the W end of the Sound as far E as Eatons Neck (40°56′N 73°23′W) and in exceptionally severe winters may extend to Falkner Island (41°13′N 72°39′W), 38 miles ENE. NE winds force the ice W, causing formations heavy enough to prevent the passage of all vessels until removed by W winds. These W winds, if of long enough duration, drive the ice through The Race into Block Island Sound and thence seaward.

5   **Fog.** Both the N and S shores are equally subject to fog, except that on spring and summer mornings, when there is little or no wind, fog will often hang along the Connecticut shore when it is clear offshore and to the S.

MAIN AND INSHORE PASSAGE THROUGH EAST PART OF LONG ISLAND SOUND

General information

Chart 2754

Description
6.78

1   **Main route.** A deep, well-marked channel leads through the E part of Long Island Sound.

    Inshore route. A well-marked inshore route leads along the N side of the E part of Long Island Sound between Hatchett Point (41°17′N 72°16′W) and Branford Reef (6.86), 25 miles W.

2   **East entrances.** The main entrance from the E is The Race (41°14′N 72°03′W) (6.83). The sound can also be entered through Plum Gut (6.84), 9 miles SW, and Fishers Island Sound (6.32).

Dangers
6.79

1   Several shoals of boulders exist in the sound but all dangers are well marked by light-structures, light-buoys and buoys.

    Caution. Vessels should navigate with caution where depths are irregular and less than 1·8 to 2·4 m (6 to 8 ft) greater than the draught.

Tidal streams
6.80

1 **The Race.** There are always strong rips and swirls in the wake of all broken ground except for ½ hour at slack water. The rips are exceptionally pronounced during heavy weather, especially when a strong wind opposes the tidal stream. See Tidal Stream table (Chart 2732) for further details.

2 **Plum Gut.** The maximum rate of the in-going stream is 3½ kn and of the out-going stream 4½ kn. It has been reported that a counter current develops during the in-going stream along the N shore of Plum Island.

Directions
(continued from 6.15)

Principal marks
6.81

1 **Landmark:**

Tower (41°12′N 72°07′W), standing on Great Gull Island.

Major lights:

Race Rock Light (41°15′N 72°03′W) (6.13).

Little Gull Island Light (41°12′N 72°06′W) (6.13).

2 Oyster Pond Reef Light (41°10′N 72°13′W) (6.13).

New London Ledge Light (41°18′N 72°05′W) (6.117).

New London Entrance Light (41°19′N 72°05′W) (6.117).

Stratford Point Light (41°09′N 73°06′W) (6.172).

3 Penfield Reef Light (41°07′N 73°13′W) (6.92).

Eatons Neck Light (40°57′N 73°24′W) (6.92).

Other aids to navigation
6.82

1 **Racons:**

No 11 Light-buoy, N of Valiant Rock (41°14′N 72°04′W).

TE (Twenty-Eight Foot Shoal) Light-buoy (41°09′N 72°30′W).

See *Admiralty List of Radio Signals Volume 2* for details.

Charts 2754, 2732 plan of Approaches to New London
East entrances
6.83

1 **The Race.** From a position SE of Race Point the main route into Long Island Sound, used by deep-draught vessels, leads NW, passing (with positions relative to Race Point (41°15′N 72°02′W)):

2 Between Race Rock (5 cables SW), on which stands Race Rock Light (6.13), and Valiant Rock (2 miles SW). No 11 Light-buoy (port hand) is moored on the N side of Valiant Rock, which is surrounded by heavy tide rips.

Thence into Long Island Sound.

(Directions for New London continue at 6.117)

Chart 2754 (see 1.17)
6.84

1 **Plum Gut.** From a position ESE of Pine Point (41°10′N 72°12′W) the route through Plum Gut leads WNW, passing (with positions relative to Pine Point):

2 SSW of Pine Point, the S point of Plum Island, thence:

NNE of Midway Shoal (6 cables WSW), which is marked on its N side by MS Buoy (preferred channel to starboard), thence:

SSW of a dangerous wreck (7½ cables WNW), and:

3 NNE of the NE extremity of Oyster Pond Reef (1 mile W), which extends 6 cables NE from Orient Point. Oyster Pond Reef Light (6.13) stands 2½ cables within the extremity of the reef. Thence:

SSW of Middle Ground (8 cables WNW), thence:

SSW of 2PG Light-buoy (starboard hand) (1 mile WNW).

4 Thence into Long Island Sound.

Local knowledge is required to navigate Plum Gut because of the rocks in the passage and the strong tidal streams that may be encountered.

Main route from east entrances to Stratford Shoal Middle Ground
6.85

1 From the vicinity of PI Light-buoy (safe water) (41°13′N 72°11′W) the main route for deep-draught vessels leads WSW for about 43 miles to the vicinity of Stratford Shoal Middle Ground, passing (with positions relative to Horton Point Light (41°05′N 72°27′W)):

Either side of CF Light-buoy (safe water) (7 miles NNE), thence:

2 NNW of Rocky Point (5 miles NE). The lookout tower of a disused coastguard station stands on the point. Thence:

SSE of Sixmile Reef (6½ miles NNW), the S side of which is marked by No 8C Light-buoy (starboard hand), thence:

3 NNW of Horton Point Light (white square tower, with dwelling), which stands on Horton Point, thence:

SSE of TE Light-buoy (preferred channel to port) (5 miles NW), which is moored on Twenty-Eight Foot Shoal, thence:

4 SSE of Falkner Island Light (white 8-sided tower, 14 m in height) (12 miles NW), which stands on Falkner Island, thence:

SSE of a light-buoy (special) (10 miles WNW), thence:

NNW of Riverhead Offshore Terminal (10½ miles WSW) (6.209), thence:

5 Either side of Stratford Shoal Middle Ground (30 miles W), which is marked on its N side by No 3 Buoy (port hand) and on its S side by No 2 Light-buoy (starboard hand). Stratford Shoal Middle Ground Light (grey 8-sided granite tower on dwelling) stands in the centre of the shoal. There is deep water N and S of Stratford Shoal, but vessels of deep draught normally use the channel S of the shoal.

Thence into the W part of Long Island Sound.

(Directions continue for W part of Long Island Sound at 6.92. Directions for approaches to Bridgeport are given at 6.172)

Chart 2754 (see 1.17)
Inshore route
6.86

1 From a position S of Hatchett Point (41°17′N 72°16′W) an inshore route leads W between Long Sand Shoal, Sixmile Reef and Falkner Island, and the N shore of Long Island Sound, passing (with positions relative to Hammonasset Point (41°15′N 72°33′W)):

S of Hatchett Reef (13 miles E), marked on its S side by No 6 Buoy (starboard hand), thence:

2 Between No 8 Light-buoy (starboard hand) (10 miles E) (6.193) and E Buoy, which lie in the approaches to Connecticut River (6.190), thence:

N of Long Sand Shoal, which extends WSW for 6 miles from E Buoy, and:

3   S of Cornfield Point Shoal (7 miles E), which lies 5 cables SSE of Cornfield Point and is marked by No 2 Light-buoy (starboard hand), and:

S of Hen and Chickens (6½ miles E), awash in places and buoyed at its E end, and:

S of Crane Reef (5½ miles E) marked on its S side by No 4 Buoy (starboard hand), thence:

4   N of W Light-buoy (4 miles ESE), which marks the W end of Long Sand Shoal, thence:

N of an area of shoal water (reported 1989), the N limit of which lies 1 mile SSE of the breakwater head, thence:

5   S of the shoal ground extending S from the head of Kelsey Point Breakwater (6.202), the S limit of which is marked by No 8 Buoy (1½ miles ESE), and:

S of Hammonasset Point, low and marshy with several wooded knolls, thence:

6   N of Kimberly Reef (4 miles WSW), marked on its S side by KR Light-buoy, and:

S of Charles Reef (3½ miles W), marked on its S side by No 14 Buoy (starboard hand). Madison Reef (6.204) lies 1 mile ENE. Thence:

7   N of the reef extending 4 cables N from Falkner Island (6 miles WSW). No 15 Light-buoy (port hand) marks the N extremity of this reef. Thence:

S of Chimney Corner Reef and Goose Rocks Shoals which lie off Sachem Head (7½ miles W) (6.204). These dangers are marked by No 20 Buoy and No 22 Light-buoy (both starboard hand), respectively. Thence:

8   S of The Thimbles (10 miles W) (6.205), a group of islands and shoals that extend 2 miles SW from Hoadley Point. Browns Reef and East Reef at the SW limit of The Thimbles are marked by No 26 Light-buoy (starboard hand). Thence:

9   S of Branford Reef Light (red and white chequered diamond on framework tower) (12 miles W), standing on Branford Reef.

Thence to the approaches to New Haven and the W part of Long Island Sound.

(Directions continue for approaches to New Haven at 6.146)

MAIN PASSAGE THROUGH WEST PART OF LONG ISLAND SOUND

General information

Charts 2754, 2580
Description
6.87

1   **Main route.** A deep well marked route leads through the W part of Long Island Sound from Stratford Shoal Middle Ground to Throgs Neck.

Dangers
6.88

1   See 6.79.

Submarine pipelines
6.89

1   A gas pipeline, as shown on the chart, is laid through Long Island Sound and East River from Northport Basin (6.271) to a position 2 cables NE of Hunts Point (7.67). **Caution.** See 1.39.

2   An oil pipeline, as shown on the chart, is laid across Long Island Sound from a position 2½ miles NE of Milford Point (6.195) to Northport Basin (6.271) (20 miles SW).

Tidal streams
6.90

1   See Tidal Stream tables on chart.

Rescue
6.91

1   **Coast Guard** station is situated near Eatons Neck Point (40°57′N 73°24′W) on the E side of the entrance to Huntington Bay.

Directions
(continued from 6.85)

Principal marks
6.92

1   **Major lights:**
Stratford Point Light (41°09′N 73°06′W) (6.172).
Penfield Reef Light (white tower on granite dwelling) (41°07′N 73°13′W).
Greens Ledge Light (brown conical tower, white top, black round base) (41°03′N 73°27′W).

2   Eatons Neck Light (white stone tower, 22 m in height) (40°57′N 73°24′W).
Great Captain Island Light (red and white chequered diamond on framework tower) (40°59′N 73°37′W).
Execution Rocks Light (white stone tower, brown band, granite dwelling) (40°53′N 73°44′W).

Other aids to navigation
6.93

1   **Racon:**
Execution Rocks Light — as above.
See *Admiralty List of Radio Signals Volume 2* for details.

Charts 2754, 2580
Stratford Shoal Middle Ground to Cable and Anchor Reef
6.94

1   From the vicinity of Stratford Shoal Middle Ground the route continues W for 15 miles to the vicinity of Cable and Anchor Reef, passing (with positions relative to Old Field Point Light (40°59′N 73°07′W)):
N of Old Field Point Light (black tower on granite house), which stands on Old Field Point, thence:

2   N of No 11B Light-buoy (port hand) (12½ miles W) which marks the limit of the shoal water that extends 3 miles N from Eatons Neck, which is wooded and 30 m high. Eatons Neck Light (6.92) stands on Eatons Neck Point (6.266). Thence:

3   S of Cable and Anchor Reef (14 miles W), the S part of which is marked by No 28C Light-buoy (starboard hand).

Chart 2580
Cable and Anchor Reef to Execution Rocks
6.95

1   From the vicinity of Cable and Anchor Reef the route through the W part of Long Island Sound continues WSW

for 16 miles to the vicinity of Execution Rocks, passing (with positions relative to Great Captain Island Light (40°59′N 73°37′W)):

2 Clear of a light-buoy (special) (8 miles E), thence:
Clear of WDA Light-buoy (special) (6½ miles E), which is moored near the centre of a spoil ground, thence:

3 NNW of Lloyd Point (6½ miles ESE), the N extremity of Lloyd Neck. Lloyd Neck is high and wooded. Shoal water, the N limit of which is marked by No 15 Light-buoy (port hand), extends 1 mile N from this headland. Thence:

4 SSE of No 32A Light-buoy (starboard hand) (3½ miles ESE), which marks the S side of a patch with a depth of 7·9 m (26 ft) over it, thence:
SSE of a light-buoy (special) (2½ miles SE), thence:

5 NNW of Matinecock Point (4¾ miles S). Shoal ground extending 5 cables NNW from this point is marked by No 21 Light-buoy (port hand). A fish haven is established 5 cables NE of Matinecock Point. Thence:

6 SSE of Execution Rocks (8 miles SW), passing through the channel that leads between these rocks and Sands Point, 8 cables SSE. The channel is marked on the SE side by Nos 23 and 25 Light-buoys (both port hand), which mark the shoal waters that extend from Manhasset Neck, and on the NW side by No 44A Light-buoy (starboard hand).

Execution Rocks to Throgs Neck
6.96

1 From a position S of Execution Rocks the main route through the W part of Long Island Sound continues SSW for 5 miles to Throgs Neck (7.44), at the E entrance of the East River, passing (with positions relative to Hewlett Point (40°50′N 73°45′W)):

2 WNW of Gangway Rock No 27A Light (green square on framework tower) (1¼ miles NNE), standing on Gangway Rock, which with No 27 Buoy (port hand) marks the limit of shoal water extending NW from Barker Point. Thence:

3 Between Hewlett Point and the S extremity of Hart Island (6.249), 8 cables WNW. The shoal ground off Hewlett Point is marked by No 29 Light-buoy (port hand); Hart Island No 46 Light (red triangle on framework tower, concrete base) stands on a rock lying off the S end of Hart Island. Thence:

4 WNW of Stepping Stones Light (red brick building, granite base, white band on SW side) (1¼ miles SW), which marks the NW end of reefs extending NW from the shore.

Thence to the E entrance of the East River (7.44) between Willets Point and Throgs Neck.

(Directions continue for East River at 7.55)

NEW LONDON HARBOR AND APPROACHES

General information

Chart 2732 (see 1.17)
Position
6.97

1 **New London Harbor** (41°21′N 72°05′W) is formed by the entrance to the Thames River which flows into the E

end of Long Island Sound between Avery Point (41°19′N 72°04′W) and Goshen Point (Chart 2754), 2¼ miles SW.

New London is a city situated on the W bank of the Thames River, 2½ miles above its mouth. The town of Groton stands on the E bank, opposite New London.

Function
6.98

1 New London Harbor is an important harbour of refuge where vessels of deep draught can find shelter in any weather and at all seasons. Waterborne commerce is chiefly in petroleum products, chemicals, coal, copper, lumber, seafood products and general cargo.

2 New London is a port of entry.
A US Naval Submarine Base is situated on the Thames River about 2 miles above New London.
In 2005 the estimated population of New London was 26 174.

Approach
6.99

1 New London Harbor is approached through the main entrance channel extending from deep water in Long Island Sound to deep water in the upper harbour.

6.100

1 **Caution.** Uncharted fishing and hunting devices and structures, some submerged, may exist in New London Harbour and its approaches, as noted on the chart. Mariners should proceed with caution.

Traffic
6.101

1 **Traffic.** In 2005 New London was used by 34 vessels with a total deadweight 1 173 422 tonnes and Groton was used by 3 vessels with a total deadweight 233 669 tonnes.

Port Authority
6.102

1 State of Connecticut Department of Transportation, Bureau of Aviation and Ports, State Pier, New London, CT 06320.

Limiting conditions

Depths
6.103

1 **US Navy project depths:**
Main channel entrance to Fort Trumbull (41°20′·6N 72°05′·7W): 12·2 m (40 ft).
Thence for 1 mile to State Pier No 1: 11·6 m (38 ft).
Thence to US Naval Submarine Base: 11 m (36 ft).

2 **Federal project depth:**
To waterfront channels N of Fort Trumbull and in Winthrop Cove: 7 m (23 ft).
For the latest controlling depths the charts and port authority should be consulted.

Vertical clearance
6.104

1 Two bridges cross the river between New London and Groton at Winthrop Point (41°21·7′N 72°05′·4W):
A bascule rail bridge with a vertical clearance of 9·1 m (30 ft) when closed. In 1998 it was reported that cross-currents of 1 to 2 kn may be encountered in the vicinity of this bridge.

2 A fixed double road bridge, with a vertical clearance of 41·1 m (135 ft), crosses the river close N of the rail bridge.
A fixed road bridge, with a vertical clearance of 22·9 m (75 ft), crosses the river about 8 miles above New London.

3   Overhead power cables, with a vertical clearance of 48·8 m (160 ft), span the river about 5 miles above New London.

Horizontal clearance
6.105

1   The bascule rail bridge (6.104) has a horizontal clearance of 46 m (151 ft). The double road bridge (6.104) has a horizontal clearance of 152·4 m (500 ft).
The fixed road bridge about 8 miles above New London has a horizontal clearance of 61 m (200 ft).

Deepest and longest berth
6.106

1   **Deepest berth:** Amerada Hess Corp. Wharf (6.122).
Longest berth: State Pier (6.122).

Tidal levels
6.107

1   Mean spring range about 0·9 m; mean neap range about 0·4 m. See information in *Admiralty Tide Tables.*

Maximum size of vessel handled
6.108

1   Bulk carrier 38 005 dwt; 10 m draught.

Arrival information

Port operations
6.109

1   Berthing and unberthing at Allyn Point (6.122) is in daylight hours only.

Notice of ETA required
6.110

1   See *Admiralty List of Radio Signals Volume 6(5)* for details.

Outer anchorages
6.111

1   The following anchorages are established in the approaches to New London Harbor (with positions relative to New London Ledge Light (41°18'·4N 72°04'·6W)):
C. General anchorage (5 cables WNW).
D. General anchorage (2½ miles SW) (Chart 2754).
2   E. General anchorage (1½ miles SSE).
F. Naval anchorage (2¼ miles SSE). Not to be used by other vessels without the permission of the Captain of the Port.
The limits of Areas C, E and F are shown on the chart.

Pilotage
6.112

1   **Pilots**, supplied by several different Pilot Associations, board in the following positions:
Vicinity of 41°17'N 71°30'W.
3 miles S of Watch Hill Point (41°18'N 71°52'W).
2   7 miles S of Watch Hill Point (41°18'N 71°52'W).
3 miles E of MP Light-buoy (41°02'N 71°46'W).
About 2 miles S of New London Ledge Light (6.111).
See also 6.4.

Tugs
6.113

1   **Tugs** are available. Vessels normally proceed to the upper harbour without assistance, although a tug may be required when entering with a head wind and contrary

current. Large vessels normally require tugs for docking and undocking.

Traffic regulations
6.114

1   **Security zones.** Zone A, as shown on the chart, encloses the area around the Electric Boat Corporation Shipyard on the E side of the river 1 mile below the bridges. Zone B, as shown on the chart, extends from 1½ to 2½ miles above the bridges and encloses the US Naval Base.
For definition and general regulations concerning security zones see Appendix V.
2   **Restricted area.** The area off the US Naval Submarine Base (6.115) is a restricted area. Passage through the area is normally allowed, subject to US Navy requirements.
For definition and general regulations concerning restricted areas see Appendix VI.

Harbour

General layout
6.115

1   The main harbour comprises the lower 3 miles of the Thames River from Long Island Sound to the bridges (6.104) at Winthrop Point joining New London and Groton.
2   The piers and wharves of New London Harbor are situated along both sides of the Thames River between a position 2 miles N of New London Ledge Light and the bridges 1½ miles farther N.
The upper harbour extends from the bridges to Norwich, the head of navigation, 11 miles N.
3   The US Naval Submarine Base is situated on the E side of the river between 1½ and 2½ miles above the bridges.

Natural conditions
6.116

1   **Tidal streams** follow the general direction of the channel and are usually not strong. During freshets, which usually occur in the spring, and when the river is high, a strong surface current sets out of the harbour even during the in-going stream.
See also Tidal Stream tables on chart.
2   **Ice** seldom forms below the naval station, 5 miles above the entrance. In extremely severe winters, however, pack ice from the sound, driven in by winds, has been known to extend about 1¾ miles above the entrance. Above the naval station ice obstructs navigation for about 2 months every winter.
3   Drift ice sometimes forms a dangerous obstruction in the approaches through Long Island Sound during severe winters, especially during February and March.

Directions
(continued from 6.83)

Principal marks
6.117

1   **Landmarks:**
Lighthouse (disused) (41°18'·9N 72°03'·8W), standing on Avery Point.
Chimney (41°19'·9N 72°04'·7W). Northernmost of five.
2   **Major lights:**
New London Ledge Light (red brick dwelling, square base) (41°18'·4N 72°04'·6W).
New London Entrance Light (white 8-sided pyramidal tower) (41°19'·0N 72°05'·4W).

Other aids to navigation
6.118
1 **Racon:**

Main channel span of road bridge (41°21'·8N 72°05'·3W).

See *Admiralty List of Radio Signals Volume 2* for details.

Approaches
6.119
1 From the vicinity of 41°16'N 72°05'W, NW of The Race, the route into New London Harbor leads N through the main entrance channel, passing (with positions relative to New London Ledge Light):

Between Nos 1 and 2 Light-buoys (lateral) (7 cables S) which mark the entrance to the main entrance channel, thence:

2 E of Sarah Ledge (8½ cables SW), marked on its SW side by SL Buoy (preferred channel to starboard). Sarah Ledge and the shoals W of it are covered by the red sector (000°-041°) of New London Entrance Light. Thence:

3 W of New London Ledge Light (6.117), which stands on the NW corner of New London Ledge and 3 cables W of Black Ledge, thence:

E of New London Entrance Light (8½ cables NW) (6.117), thence:

W of Eastern Point (8 cables N).

Thence into New London Harbor.

New London Harbor
6.120
1 From a position abreast Eastern Point the track leads N through the main entrance channel within the harbour to the bridges, 2½ miles N. The channel is marked by light-buoys (lateral). A direction light (354½°) is exhibited from the SE pier of the railway bridge (6.104).

From the bridges the channel continues N to the US Naval Submarine Base.

2 From the naval base a channel, with controlling depths (2003) of 24 ft leads to just below the berth at Allyn Point (6.121). Thence the channel to Norwich had controlling depths (2003) of 5·3 m (17·5 ft) with 4·0 m (13 ft) in the turning basin at Norwich. The channel is marked by light-beacons, light-buoys and buoys.

Berths

Anchorages
6.121
1 The following anchorages, the limits of which are shown on the chart, are established in New London Harbor (with positions relative to Fort Trumbull (41°20'·6N 72°05'·7W)):

A. For barges and small vessels drawing less than 3·6 m (12 feet) (4 cables NNE).

B. General anchorage (8 cables SSE).

Alongside berths
6.122
1 There are more than 30 wharves and piers. Most of these facilities are used as repair berths, and for mooring recreational craft, fishing vessels, barges, ferries and government vessels. Depths alongside these facilities range from 3 to 12 m.

Deep-draught facilities are described as follows:

2 Amerada Hess Corp. Wharf (41°20'·1N 72°04'·9W); T-head pier 292 m in length, with dolphins, with a depth alongside of 12·2 m. Receipt and shipment of petroleum products and receipt of molasses.

State Pier No 1 (41°21'·5N 72°05'·4W); E side: 311 m in length with a depth alongside of 10·4 to 11·6 m. W side: 305 m in length with a depth alongside of 7·0 to 8·2 m. General cargo.

3 Dow Chemicals Allyn Point Wharf (41°26'·5N 72°05'·1W); 228 m in length with a depth alongside of 9·1 m. Chemicals.

Port services

Repairs
6.123
1 A number of firms in New London carry out repair and salvage work.

Floating docks. The largest is situated 9 cables N of the bridges. Lift 10 000 tonnes; length 91 m, width 33·5 m.

Other facilities
6.124
1 **Degaussing range.** A degaussing range is situated in the main entrance channel 1½ miles within the entrance, 5 cables SE of Fort Trumbull (41°20'·6N 72°05'·7W).

Hospitals; oily waste disposal.

Supplies
6.125
1 Supplies of all kind are available. Fuel can be obtained from oil companies at 48 hours notice by road tanker. Water is available at most of the piers and wharves.

Communications
6.126
1 Nearest airport 4 km.

Rescue
6.127
1 **Coast Guard station** is situated at Fort Trumbull (41°21'N 72°06'W) on W side of channel.

NEW HAVEN HARBOR AND APPROACHES

General information
Chart 2728
Position
6.128
1 **New Haven Harbor** (41°15'N 72°55'W) is formed by a bay, situated on the N side of Long Island Sound about 70 miles from New York and 45 miles from the E entrance of Long Island Sound.

New Haven stands at the head of the harbour at the junction of Mill River and Quinnipiac River.

Function
6.129
1 New Haven Harbor is an important harbour of refuge. Waterborne commerce consists largely of petroleum products, scrap metal, lumber, cars, gypsum, paper and pulp products, steel products, chemicals, rock salt and general cargo.

New Haven, which in 2005 had an estimated population of 124 791, is an important manufacturing city and port of entry.

Port limits
6.130
1 The harbour comprises all the tidal waters lying N of the breakwaters constructed across the mouth of the bay and the navigable portions of West River, on the W side of the bay, and Mill River and Quinnipiac River, at the head of the bay.

Approach

6.131

1   New Haven Harbor is approached through the dredged entrance channel from the deep water of Long Island Sound.

Traffic

6.132

1   **Traffic.** In 2005 the port was used by 156 vessels with a total deadweight 7 450 575 tonnes.

Port authority

6.133

1   State of Connecticut Department of Transportation, Bureau of Aviation and Ports, State Pier, New London, CT 06320.

Limiting conditions

Depths

6.134

1   **Project depths:**

> Entrance channel from entrance to just below junction of Mill River and Quinnipiac River: 10·7 m (35 ft).
> Mill River Entrance Channel to 2½ cables above entrance: 3·7 m (12 ft).
> Quinnipiac River for 1 mile above entrance: decreasing from 6·7 m (22 ft) to 4·9 m (16 ft).

2   **Controlling depths:**

> Dredged channel to West River: mid-channel depth (1996) of 3 m (10 ft).
> For the latest controlling depths the charts and port authority should be consulted.

Vertical clearance

6.135

1   Two bridges cross the harbour above the principal port facilities, at the confluence of Mill River and Quinnipiac River:

> Tomlinson Bridge has a double bascule span with a vertical clearance of 4·0 m (13 ft) when closed and 18·9 m (62 ft) when open.

2   A fixed road bridge, close N of Tomlinson Bridge, has a vertical clearance of 18·3 m (60 ft).

A bascule bridge with a vertical clearance of 7·6 m (25 ft) crosses the Quinnipiac River and a swing bridge with a vertical clearance of 2·4 m (8 ft) crosses the Mill River.

3   An overhead power cable, with a vertical clearance of 27·7 m (91 ft), spans the channel just above the fixed road bridge.

Horizontal clearance

6.136

1   Tomlinson Bridge has a navigable width of 35·6 m (117 ft).

Fixed road bridge, close N of Tomlinson Bridge, has a navigable width of 86·3 m (283 ft).

Deepest and longest berth

6.137

1   **Deepest:** New Haven Terminal (6.150).
Longest: ARCO Wharf (6.150).

Tidal levels

6.138

1   Mean spring range about 2 m; mean neap range about 1 m. See information in *Admiralty Tide Tables.*

Maximum size of vessel handled

6.139

1   Draught 11·6 m subject to weather and tides. Vessels of 50 000 dwt, with part cargo, occasionally call, but should consult with port authority first.

Arrival information

Outer anchorages

6.140

1   Deep-draught vessels awaiting a berth can anchor about 1 mile S of NH Light-buoy (41°12′·1N 72°53′·8W), in good holding ground, clear of the charted cable area.

Pilotage

6.141

1   **Pilots** board in the following positions:

> Vicinity of 41°17′N 71°30′W.
> 3 miles S of Watch Hill Point (41°18′N 71°52′W).

2   7 miles S of Watch Hill Point (41°18′N 71°52′W).
3 miles E of MP Light-buoy (41°02′N 71°46′W).
In the vicinity, or 1 mile S, of NH Light-buoy (41°12′N 72°54′W).

3   See *Admiralty List of Radio Signals Volume 6(5)* for details.

Tugs

6.142

1   **Tugs** are available. Vessels normally proceed into the harbour without assistance. Large vessels normally require tugs for docking and undocking.

Arrangements for tug service should be made 24 hours in advance.

Traffic regulations

6.143

1   **Regulated navigation area**. There is a regulated navigation area, in which the movements of tugs and barges are restricted, in the waters surrounding the Tomlinson Bridge (6.135).

For definition and general regulations concerning regulated navigation areas see Appendix V.

Harbour

General layout

6.144

1   The outer harbour extends from the entrance to a line joining Sandy Point (41°16′·3N 72°55′·2W) and Fort Hale, 7 cables E. The main or inner harbour extends 2 miles farther N.

The deep-draught facilities lie along the N and E sides of the inner part of the harbour.

Natural conditions

6.145

1   **Tidal streams.** See Tidal Stream tables on chart.

Ice generally obstructs navigation to some extent for low powered vessels from December to March and sometimes extends to the mouth of the harbour. S winds force drift ice in from the sound and prevent local ice from leaving the harbour. Except in severe weather, powered vessels can always enter and leave the harbour without much difficulty.

Climate information. See 1.158.

Directions
(continued from 6.86)

Principal marks
6.146
1   **Landmarks:**

    Tower (disused lighthouse) (41°14′·9N 72°54′·2W) on Lighthouse Point.

    Chimney (41°17′·0N 72°54′·2W).

    Tank (41°18′·2N 72°54′·4W).

    Tower (41°18′·5N 72°55′·4W).

Entrance
6.147
1   **Leading lights:**

    Front light (white framework tower, concrete base) (41°15′·6N 72°56′·1W).

    Rear light (similar structure) (732 m from front light).

2   From the vicinity of NH Light-buoy (safe water) (41°12′·1N 72°53′·8W) the alignment (333½°) of these lights leads NNW through the dredged channel, marked by buoys and light-buoys (lateral), to the harbour entrance, passing (with positions relative to Lighthouse Point (41°14′·9N 72°54′·2W)):

3   SW of Southwest Ledge Light (white 8-sided dwelling, brown round base) (9 cables SSW) standing on the SW head of East Breakwater, and:

    NE of Luddington Rock Light (green and white chequered diamond on framework tower) (1¼ miles SW) standing on the NE head of Middle Breakwater.

    Thence into the outer harbour.

Harbour
6.148
1   From the breakwater entrance the dredged channel, marked by buoys and light-buoys (lateral), leads N through the outer harbour to the main harbour at the head of the bay.

    Useful mark:

    Sandy Point Breakwater Light (green and white chequered diamond on framework tower) (41°15′·7N 72°55′·1W).

Berths

Anchorages
6.149
1   There are no regulations prescribing the limits within which vessels may not anchor, except that the dredged channels must be kept clear.

2   Anchorage may be obtained, for vessels with a draught of up to 5·8 m (19 ft), within the outer harbour inside the West Breakwater and the SW part of Middle Breakwater. **Caution.** Mariners should be aware that water levels may drop significantly following a prolonged NW wind and should also avoid fish stakes in the area.

3   Anchorage is also available N of Southwest Ledge Light in depths of 5·5 to 6·1 m (18 to 20 ft), soft bottom. Care should be taken to avoid the ledges N of the E Breakwater.

Alongside Berths
6.150
1   The main deep-draught berths are described as follows (with positions relative to New Haven Long Wharf Light (41°17′·6N 72°54′·9W)):

    Exxon Co. Terminal Wharf (4½ cables SE); 213 m in length, with dolphins, with a depth alongside of 10·7 m, handling petroleum products.

2   New Haven Terminal (4 cables ESE) (3 berths); Scrap metal dock 195 m in length with a depth alongside of 10·7 m, handling scrap metal and lumber, and pier 198 m in length on each side, with depths alongside of 10·7 m on the N side and 11·9 m on the S side, handling general cargo, petroleum products, chemicals and metals.

3   ARCO Petroleum Products Co. Wharf (3½ cables E); 232 m in length, with dolphins, with a depth alongside of 10·7 m, handling petroleum products.

    Gateway Terminal Pier (4½ cables ENE) (3 berths); 229 m in length and handles 40 000 dwt tankers and 68 000 dwt dry cargo vessels with 11 m draught.

4   Gulf Refining and Marketing Co. Terminal (4¼ cables NE); 224 m in length, with dolphins, with a depth alongside of 10·7 m, handling petroleum products.

    Wyatt Terminal (9 cables NNW) (2 berths); 218 and 146 m in length with depths alongside of 11·6 and 9·1 m, handling petroleum products.

Port services

Repairs
6.151
1   New Haven has no facilities for making major repairs or for dry docking deep-draught vessels.

    Minor repair facilities are available.

Other facilities
6.152
1   Hospitals.

Supplies
6.153
1   Fuel alongside and by barge; water; provisions and stores.

Communications
6.154
1   Nearest airport 1 km.

Rescue
6.155
1   Coast Guard station is situated at Fort Hale (41°16′·3N 72°54′·2W). The station is approached by a channel with a reported depth of 3 m (10 ft).

BRIDGEPORT HARBOR AND APPROACHES

General information

Chart 2726
Position
6.156
1   Bridgeport Harbor (41°10′N 73°11′W) is situated on the N side of Long Island Sound at the head of the bight that

lies between Stratford Point (41°09′N 73°06′W) and Penfield Reef (6.182), 6 miles WSW. The harbour is 52 miles from New York.

2 The harbour consists of two widely separated areas. The main harbour and its branches serve the E and central parts of the city of Bridgeport, and Black Rock Harbor, 1½ miles W, serves the W part of the city. Black Rock Harbor is described at 6.180.

Function
6.157

1 Waterborne commerce consists largely of petroleum products, lumber, sand and gravel, building materials and scrap iron.

Bridgeport, which in 2005 had an estimated population of 139 008, is a port of entry.

Port limits
6.158

1 Bridgeport Harbor consists of both the main harbour at the mouth of the Pequonnock River and Black Rock Harbor on Cedar Creek, 2 miles WSW.

Approach
6.159

1 The main harbour is approached from the deep water of Long Island Sound through the main entrance channel, which is 2½ miles long.

Traffic
6.160

1 **Traffic.** In 2005 the port was used by 20 vessels with a total deadweight 2 523 925 tonnes.

Port authority
6.161

1 Bridgeport Port Authority, 330 Water Street, Bridgeport, CT06604

Internet. www.portofbridgeport.com

Limiting conditions

Depths
6.162

1 **Project depth** in the main entrance channel is 10·7 m (35 ft). For the latest controlling depths the charts and port authority should be consulted.

Vertical clearance
6.163

1 Connecticut Turnpike Bridge, a fixed bridge with a vertical clearance of 19·8 m (65 ft), crosses the river 7 cables above Tongue Point.

Five other bridges cross the upper reach of Pequonnock River, the first four of which are bascule bridges.

2 Bascule bridges cross the entrances to Johnsons Creek and Yellow Mill Channel, and the Connecticut Turnpike Bridge crosses Yellow Mill Channel with a vertical clearance of 12·2 m (40 ft).

Deepest and longest berth
6.164

1 Deepest berth: United Illuminating Co. Dock (6.175).

Tidal levels
6.165

1 Mean spring range about 2·2 m; mean neap range about 1·1 m. See information in *Admiralty Tide Tables.*

Maximum size of vessel handled
6.166

1 Vessels of 70 000 dwt and an overall length of 251 m call at the port.

Arrival information

Outer anchorages
6.167

1 Anchorage, which provides shelter from strong N winds, is available off the entrance. The holding ground is good.

Pilotage
6.168

1 **Pilots** board in the following positions:
Vicinity of 41°17′N 71°30′W.
3 miles S of Watch Hill Point (41°18′N 71°52′W).
2 7 miles S of Watch Hill Point (41°18′N 71°52′W).
3 miles E of MP Light-buoy (41°02′N 71°46′W).
In the vicinity, or about 1 mile S, of BH Light-buoy (41°06′N 73°12′W).
See *Admiralty List of Radio Signals Volume 6(5)* for details.

Tugs
6.169

Tugs are available from New Haven, Providence, Brooklyn or Staten Island with advance notice. Deep-draught vessels usually require tugs for mooring in Bridgeport Harbor.

Harbour

General layout
6.170

1 Bridgeport Harbor, which is protected by two breakwaters that extend from the entrance points of the mouth of the Pequonnock River, is formed by the lower part of the Pequonnock River and its tributaries, Johnsons Creek and Yellow Mill Channel.

2 The deep-draught facilities are S of Tongue Point (41°10′·0N 73°10′·7W) and on the E side of the harbour opposite Tongue Point.

Natural conditions
6.171

1 **Tidal streams.** See Tidal Stream table on chart.

Ice does not interfere seriously with navigation in the main harbour, although its branch channels are closed at times. Winds from the N and NW clear the harbour of drift ice and winds from SE through S to SW, force ice into the harbour. The ice, in severe weather, may cause the outer buoys to drift.

Directions

Principal marks
6.172

1 **Landmarks:**
Radio towers (41°09′·6N 73°09′·9W) standing on Pleasure Beach, the W entrance point to the harbour.
Chimney (41°10′·3N 73°11′·1W) with red and white bands.
2 White spire (41°10′·4N 73°11′·9W).
Tallest spire (41°10′·8N 73°11′·7W).
Major light:
Stratford Point Light (white conical tower, brown band) (41°09′·1N 73°06′·2W).

Bridgeport Harbor

6.173

1 From the vicinity of BH Light-buoy (safe water) (41°06'·2N 73°11'·7W) the entrance channel leads NNE for 3 miles between pairs of buoys and light-buoys (lateral) to the harbour entrance, passing (with positions relative to Tongue Point Light (41°10'·0N 73°10'·7W)):

2 Between Nos 12A and 13A Breakwater Head Lights (red triangle and green square on framework towers, respectively) (7 cables S), thence:

ESE of Tongue Point Light (black conical tower). Thence NW into Bridgeport Reach.

Berths

Anchorages

6.174

1 Anchorage is available in two areas within the breakwaters:

On the E side of the main channel, NW of Pleasure Beach (41°09'·7N 73°10'·2W), in depths of 6 to 12 m (21 to 39 ft).

2 On the W side of the channel, NW of Tongue Point, in depths of 5 to 9 m (17 to 28 ft). A rock with a depth of 3 m (10 ft) over it lies in the inshore part of this anchorage, 3½ cables NW of Tongue Point.

Alongside berths

6.175

1 The main deep-draught berths are described as follows (with positions relative to Tongue Point Light):

United Illuminating Co. Fuel Oil Dock (1½ cables SW); an offshore wharf 274 m in length, with dolphins, with depths alongside of 9·5 to 11·3 m, handling petroleum products.

2 Shell Oil Co. Dock (3½ cables E); 58 m face and 213 m in length with shore moorings, with a depth alongside of 10·7 m, handling petroleum products.

Cilco Terminal Co. Wharf (2¼ cables NE); 283 m in length with a depth alongside of 10 m, handling general cargo, lumber and steel products.

3 City recreational pier (4 cables ESE) at the NW end of Pleasure Beach has depths of 6 m at the end of the pier but it is seldom used for mooring vessels.

Port services

Repairs

6.176

1 Bridgeport has no facilities for making major repairs or dry docking deep-draught vessels.

Excellent minor repair facilities are available.

Other facilities

6.177

1 Hospitals.

Supplies

6.178

1 Fuel; water; provisions and stores.

Communications

6.179

1 Nearest airport 5 km.

Black Rock Harbor

General information

6.180

1 **Position.** Black Rock Harbor (41°09'N 73°13'W) is situated on the W side of Bridgeport, 2 miles SW of the entrance to Bridgeport Harbor.

2 **Approach and harbour.** The harbour is approached by a dredged channel which is entered S of Fayerweather Island (6.182) and leads N through Black Rock Harbor into Cedar Creek. At its head Cedar Creek divides into East Branch and West Branch. Ash Creek, approached by a dredged channel, is entered 8 cables W of Fayerweather Island.

Limiting conditions

6.181

1 **Depths.** The project depth in the dredged channel is 5·5 m (18 ft) from the entrance to the head of the project. For the latest controlling depths the charts and port authority should be consulted.

Ice usually closes the harbour during part of the winter.

Directions

6.182

1 From the vicinity of BH Light-buoy (safe water) (41°06'·2N 73°11'·7W) the outer approach to Black Rock Harbor leads NNW to the entrance of the dredged channel, passing (with positions relative to No 2A Light-beacon (41°08'·2N 73°13'·0W)):

2 ENE of Black Rock (1 mile S), marked by a beacon, and The Little Cows (8½ cables S), the outermost dangers of Penfield Reef, marked by LC Light-buoy (port hand). Penfield Reef Light (6.92) stands on the reef 4 cables SSW of these dangers. Thence:

3 WSW of No 2A Light-beacon (red triangle on framework tower), which marks the entrance to the dredged channel. This light-beacon stands 3 cables S of the S extremity of Fayerweather Island, on which stands a disused lighthouse.

4 Thence the dredged channel, marked by No 7 Light-beacon (green square on framework tower) and buoys (lateral), leads N and NE to the head of Cedar Creek.

Berths

6.183

1 **Anchorage** in depths of 5 to 7 m (16 to 23 ft), exposed to SE and NE winds may be found N of the bar which extends E to Black Rock (6.182).

Berths situated in East and West Branch have reported depths alongside of 2·4 to 5·5 m.

SMALL HARBOURS ON THE NORTH SIDE OF THE EAST PART OF LONG ISLAND SOUND

General information

Chart 2754 (see 1.17)

Scope

6.184

1 This section describes the smaller harbours and anchorages on the N side of the E part of Long Island Sound.

Niantic Bay and River

General information
6.185

1   **Position.** Niantic Bay (41°18′N 72°11′W) is entered between Goshen Point (41°18′N 72°07′W) and Black Point, 4¼ miles WSW.

Function. The bay affords good anchorage, sheltered from E, N and W winds.

2   **Approach.** The main approach is direct from Long Island Sound. The bay can also be approached from the E through Twotree Island Channel which passes between Bartlett Reef (6.188) and Twotree Island (6.188), and the coast. This channel should not be entered without local knowledge.

3   **Traffic regulations.** A safety and security zone, close inshore, surrounds the Dominion Millstone Nuclear Power Plant (41°18′N 72°10′W).

For definition and general regulations concerning safety and security zones see Appendix V.

Outer anchorage
6.186

1   A general anchorage, which extends 5 cables NW/SE and SW/NE, is centred 1 mile NE of Bartlett Reef Light (6.188) between Little Goshen Reef (41°17′·5N 72°06′·9W) and Bartlett Reef, 1 mile WSW.

Principal marks
6.187

1   **Landmark:**

Red and white chimney (41°18′·6N 72°10′·0W), 118 m (389 ft) in height, which is part of the nuclear power station standing on Millstone Point.

Directions
6.188

1   From a position SW of Bartlett Reef Light the track into Niantic Bay leads generally NNW, passing (with positions relative to Millstone Point (41°18′N 72°10′W)):

2   WSW of Bartlett Reef (1¾ miles SE), on the S end of which stands Bartlett Reef Light (red and white chequered diamond on framework tower). No 1 Buoy lies at the N end of the reef and No 4 Light-buoy (starboard hand) lies 1 mile S of the light. Thence:

3   WSW of Twotree Island (8 cables SE), small and bare, thence:

WSW of White Rock (5 cables WSW), an islet. No 6 Light-buoy (starboard hand) is moored 2 cables SSE of the rock. Thence:

4   Between Black Rock (6 cables NW) and Threefoot Rock (1½ miles W) marked, respectively, by No 8 Buoy (starboard hand) and No 7 Buoy (port hand).

Thence into Niantic Bay.

Anchorages
6.189

1   Niantic Bay affords anchorage in depths of 5 to 6 m (17 to 21 ft). Depths in the bay decrease gradually to the head of the bay.

Connecticut River

Chart 2754 (see 1.17)

General information
6.190

1   **Position.** Connecticut River flows into Long Island Sound between Griswold Point, 7 miles W of Niantic Bay and Lynde Point (41°16′N 72°21′W), 8 cables SW.

Function. The river is one of the largest and most important in New England. It is navigable as far as Hartford, the capital of Connecticut, which is situated 45 miles above the river entrance. Waterborne commerce on the river is mainly in petroleum products and chemicals.

2   **Approach and entry.** Long Sand Shoal (6.86) lies in the approaches to Connecticut River and the entrance is obstructed by Saybrook Outer Bar, which is of a shifting nature.

Limiting conditions
6.191

1   **Project depths** for the Connecticut River are 4·6 m (15 ft) in the entrance channel and in the cuts across the bars to Hartford. For the latest controlling depths the charts and port authority should be consulted.

2   **Vertical clearance.** A number of fixed and opening bridges cross the river between the river entrance and the port facilities at Hartford. They are listed as follows giving type, vertical clearance and positions relative to the river entrance:

3   Bascule rail bridge; 5·8 m (19 ft); (3 miles).

Fixed road bridge; 24·7 m (81 ft); (3½ miles).

Swing road bridge at East Haddam; 6·7 m (22 ft); (14½ miles).

Swing rail bridge at Middletown; 7·6 m (25 ft); (27¾ miles).

4   Fixed road bridge at Middletown; 27·1 m (89 ft); (28 miles).

Fixed road bridge at Wethersfield; 24·4 m (80 ft); (41¼ miles).

Charter Oak Bridge at Hartford, which is a fixed bridge; 21 m (69 ft); (44 miles).

5   **Tidal streams.** See Tidal Stream tables on chart.

Ice closes the river to navigation by wooden hulled boats for about two months every winter.

Arrival information
6.192

1   **Pilotage.** River pilot boards off Saybrook Point (41°17′N 72°21′W). 24 hours advance notice is requested.

Directions
6.193

1   **Connecticut River entrance.** From the vicinity of 41°14′N 72°18′W the route leads NW, passing (with positions relative to Lynde Point Light (41°16′N 72°21′W)):

Between the S extremity of Saybrook Outer Bar (2 miles SE), marked by No 8 Light-buoy (starboard hand), and the E end of Long Sand Shoal (2 miles SE), marked by E Buoy (preferred channel to port), thence:

2   Through the entrance channel between the breakwaters (5 cable S). Saybrook Breakwater Head Light (white conical tower, brown round base, 15 m in height) stands at the head of the W breakwater and No 2 Light-buoy (starboard hand) marks the E edge of the channel. Thence:

3   E of Lynde Point Light (white stone tower). No 5 Light-buoy (port hand) marks the edge of the channel. Thence:

Through the buoyed channel to the pilot boarding position off Saybrook Point (6.192) (8 cables NNW).

4 **Connecticut River.** From Saybrook Point to Hartford local knowledge is required.

Berths
6.194

1 **Anchorage.** There is a secure anchorage in depths of 5 to 9 m (16 to 30 ft) in the channel E and NE of Lynde Point Lighthouse. Farther up river anchorage can be obtained in wider parts of the river.

 Wharves. Connecticut River has more than twenty commercial piers and wharves, with depths alongside of 3·4 to 4·6 m, which are mainly used for the discharge of petroleum products from coastal tankers and barges.

2 The only commercial wharves at Hartford are those used for supplying fuel to the electric power company and gas company. These are situated on the W bank 2 cables below and 5 cables above Charter Oak Bridge, respectively.

Housatonic River

Charts 2754, 2726 (see 1.17)
General information
6.195

1 **Position.** Housatonic River flows into Long Island Sound between Milford Point (41°10′N 73°07′W) and Stratford Point, 1 mile S.

2 **Function.** The river, which is navigable for 11½ miles above its entrance, forms the approaches to the towns of Stratford, on the W bank, and Devon on the E bank. Waterborne commerce on the river is principally in shipments of aggregate, fuel oil to the power plant at Devon and seasonal commercial shell fishing.

3 **Approach and entry.** The river is entered through a dredged channel (6.198), marked by light-buoys and buoys, which is narrow and crooked with little depth on either side. **Local knowledge** is required.

Limiting conditions
6.196

1 **Project depths** for Housatonic River are 5·5 m (18 ft) from Long Island Sound to Culver Bar, 4½ miles upstream. Above this point the controlling depth (2005) is 0·7 m (2¼ ft). For the latest controlling depths the charts and port authority should be consulted.

2 **Vertical clearance.** Three bridges cross the river between the entrance and the town of Devon, 3½ miles upstream. They are listed as follows (with positions relative to the river entrance):

 Bascule road bridge; vertical clearance 9·8 m (32 ft); (3¼ miles).

 Fixed road bridge; vertical clearance 19·8 m (65 ft); (3½ miles).

 Bascule rail bridge; vertical clearance 5·8 m (19 ft); (3½ miles).

3 **Tidal streams** are strong, the out-going stream especially so when the river is high during freshets. At the entrance to the river there is a strong W set during the in-going stream and off Milford Point the tidal streams attain a rate of 1¼ kn.

 Ice closes the river above Stratford during the winter, and it sometimes extends to the entrance.

Pilots and tugs
6.197

1 Pilots and tugs can be obtained at New Haven.

Directions
6.198

1 **Entrance.** From a position SE of Stratford Point the route into Housatonic River leads NW to the entrance channel, passing (with positions relative to Stratford Point Light (41°09′N 73°06′W) (6.172)):

 NE of No 1 Light-buoy (port hand) (6½ cables ENE), which marks the beginning of the Entrance Channel, thence:

2 SW of No 2A Light-beacon (red triangle on framework tower) (7 cables NE) which stands at the end of the breakwater that extends 1 mile SE from Milford Point. The inner end of the breakwater is submerged at HW. Thence:

 Through the dredged channel that is marked by No 3 Light-buoy (port hand) and buoys (lateral), and light-beacons.

Berths
6.199

1 A berth at Stratford has a depth alongside of 2·7 m at its end.

Anchorages and harbours

Chart 2754 (see 1.17)
Between Black Point and Hatchett Point
6.200

1 The bay between Black Point (41°17′N 72°12′W) and Hatchett Point, 2½ miles W, is foul. The outer dangers consist of Blackboys, two drying rocks situated 7 cables W of Black Point, and Hatchett Reef, 1 mile S of Hatchett Point. These dangers are marked on their S sides by, respectively, Nos 2 and 6 Buoys (both starboard hand).

Westbrook Harbor
6.201

1 Westbrook Harbor (41°16′N 72°27′W) is the W part of the bight between Cornfield Point and Menunketesuck Island, 3½ miles W. The bight is obstructed by boulders and has not been properly examined.

2 **Anchorage,** which is entered between Crane Reef (6.86) and Menunketesuck Island, is seldom used, as the anchorage in Duck Island Roads (6.202) is better.

 Westbrook is at the head of the bight. There is a conspicuous spire in the town.

Duck Island Roads
6.202

1 Duck Island Roads (41°16′N 72°29′W), a harbour of refuge, is entered between Menunketesuck Island and Kelsey Point, 2 miles W. Patchogue River flows into the NE part of the harbour.

 Depths. Depths in the roads are between 2·4 and 8·2 m (8 and 27 ft). In 1998 the mid-channel controlling depth in the Patchogue River was about 2·3 m (7½ ft) to the head of the project.

2 **General layout.** The harbour is formed by two breakwaters which extend 1¾ cables N and 4½ cables W from Duck Island, a small islet with a chimney on it, that lies 1½ miles E of Kelsey Point. Further protection is provided by Kelsey Point Breakwater that extends 6½ cables S from Stone Island, situated 3¼ cables SW of Kelsey Point.

Anchorage may be obtained:

3   In the dredged anchorage enclosed by the breakwaters and extending N and W from Duck Island. Depths 1 to 2·4 m (3 to 8 ft) in the protected area and 2·4 to 4·6 m (8 to 15 ft) in the W end.

      In a small area N and NE of Duck Island North Breakwater Light (red and white chequered diamond on framework tower); this anchorage can be used in SW weather.

4   Between Duck Island West Breakwater Light (red triangle on framework tower) and the rocky patches, marked by No 8 Buoy (starboard hand), that lie 4 cables SSW of Kelsey Point Breakwater Light (green and white chequered diamond on framework tower). Depths 5·5 to 7·3 m (18 to 24 ft), sticky bottom. Exposed to winds S of E and W.

Clinton Harbor
6.203

1   Clinton Harbor (41°16′N 72°32′W), the bight W of Kelsey Point Breakwater (6.202), is entered between Kelsey Point (6.202) and Hammonasset Point and forms the entrance to Hammonasset River, which is used mainly by fishing and recreational craft.

Hammonasset Head to Sachem Head
6.204

1   Between Hammonasset Head (41°15′N 72°33′W) and Sachem Head, 7½ miles W, there is a broad bight sometimes used as an anchorage which is sheltered from N and NE winds. This anchorage has little to recommend it as there are boulders in the bight and it has not been thoroughly examined.

      Madison Reef obstructs the central part of the bight.

2   **Guilford Harbor** (41°16′N 72°40′W) is entered in the NW end of the bight, 2 miles NE of Sachem Head. It is only frequented by small craft.

Sachem Head to Branford Harbor
6.205

1   Between Sachem Head and the entrance to Branford Harbor (6.206), 5½ miles W, is a bight encumbered with numerous islands and rocks above and below-water.

2   **Joshua Cove** (41°15′N 72°43′W) is situated N of Uncas Point, the W extremity of Sachem Head. Though little used, it affords good anchorage in its entrance for small vessels in depths of 2 to 3 m (6 to 10 ft). The approach from SW is clear between Goose Rocks Shoals, which extend SW from Uncas Point, and Leetes Rocks, 6 cables NW.

3   **The Thimbles** are a group of islands extending over 2 miles SW from Hoadley Point (41°15′N 72°44′W) to East Reef (6.86). A buoyed passage with a depth of 4 m (13 ft) leads through the N part of The Thimbles.

      The whole area is suitable only for small pleasure craft.

Branford Harbor
6.206

1   **Position and function.** Branford Harbor (41°15′N 72°50′W) is a shallow cove mainly frequented by pleasure craft and the small local lobster fleet.

Milford Harbor
6.207

1   Milford Harbor (41°13′N 73°03′W) is principally used by pleasure craft and occasionally by fishing craft.

HARBOURS ON THE SOUTH SIDE OF THE EAST PART OF LONG ISLAND SOUND

General information

Chart 2754 (see 1.17)
Description
6.208

1   Between Orient Point (41°10′N 72°14′W) and Old Field Point (42 miles WSW) are situated Riverhead offshore oil terminal at Jacobs Point, and Port Jefferson Harbor. There are also a number of other small harbours used by pleasure craft.

Riverhead Offshore Terminal

General information
6.209

1   **Riverhead Offshore Terminal** (41°00′N 72°39′W) is situated 1 mile N of Jacobs Point. The terminal, which is used for the delivery and receipt of petroleum products, consists of a 30 m by 14 m steel platform with breasting and mooring dolphins.

      Traffic. In 2005 the port was used by 39 vessels with a total deadweight of 3 545 237 tonnes.

      Port Authority. Tosco Corporation Port Operations, 212 Sound Shore Road, Riverhead, NY11901.

Limiting conditions
6.210

1   **Deepest and longest berth.** NE side of the platform (6.213).

      Maximum size of vessel handled. 225 000 dwt; length 350 m; draught 18·9 m.

Arrival information
6.211

1   **Port operations**. See *Admiralty List of Radio Signals Volume 6(5)* for details.

      Pilotage is compulsory. The pilot serves as docking master and remains on board at standby while the vessel is at the platform. See 6.4.

2   **Tugs** are available from New Haven, Providence, Brooklyn or Staten Island on advance notice. Normally two or three tugs are used for docking and one or two tugs for undocking.

      Traffic regulations. A safety zone, with a radius of 2½ cables, surrounds the platform when an LPG vessel is moored there. For definition and general regulations concerning safety zones see Appendix V.

3   **Quarantine and customs.** New York City is the port of entry for Riverhead Terminal.

      Useful marks. Numerous light green oil tanks on Jacobs Point are prominent.

Berths
6.212

1   **Anchorage.** Vessels awaiting a berth at the platform normally anchor N of the platform; vessels of greater than 15 m draught may anchor in deeper water NW of the platform.

6.213

1   **Platform:**

NE side. Depth alongside 19·5 m. Maximum size of vessel: 225 000 dwt, length 350 m, draught 18·9 m.

SW side. Depth alongside 15·2 m. Maximum size of vessel: 42 000 dwt, length 183 m, draught 12·8 m.

2   **Wharf** (close E of Jacobs Point):

Barge pier. 243 m in length with a depth alongside of 4·9 m. Vessels with a draught greater than 3·6 m should exercise caution when approaching the pier and should try to arrive or depart at HW.

Port services

6.214

1   **Facilities:** hospital 11 km from the terminal; launch service available to ships at anchor and at the platform.

Supplies: fuel can be obtained from barges at the anchorage, fuelling of a vessel alongside the platform is not permitted; no fresh water at the terminal; supplies by launch.

Communications: nearest airport Islip MacArthur 64 km.

Port Jefferson Harbor

General information

6.215

1   Port Jefferson Harbor (40°58′N 73°05′W) is entered between two breakwaters 6 cables W of Mount Misery Point and 1¼ miles ESE of Old Field Point.

Port Jefferson is a town at the S end of the harbour. The principal industries of the port are the shipping of sand and gravel and the distribution of petroleum products.

2   **No-discharge zone (NDZ).** The whole of Port Jefferson has been designated as a NDZ. See 1.44.

Approach and entry. A dredged channel leads between the two breakwaters.

Limiting conditions

6.216

1   **Depths.** In 1990 the controlling depth in mid-channel was 7·9 m (26 ft) in the dredged channel to the berthing area off an oil wharf at the S end of the harbour.

Ice forms over the entire harbour and interrupts navigation in very cold weather, but does not endanger shipping in the harbour.

Arrival information

6.217

1   **Port operations.** Speed limits of 10 and 4 kn are enforced in the channel and off the berths, respectively.

Outer anchorage. Anchorage is available in depths of 25 to 30 m (14 to 16 fm) N of Mount Misery Shoal. Lighters from New York can be arranged.

2   **Pilotage** is compulsory. The pilot boards near PJ Light-buoy (40°59′·3N 73°06′·4W).

Tugs are available from New Haven, Providence, Brooklyn or Staten Island. Normally two tugs are used for docking and one for undocking.

Harbour

6.218

1   **Measured distance.** Off Old Field Beach on the W side of the harbour entrance there is a measured distance.

Limit marks: Two pairs of beacons; the front markers are orange posts and the rear markers are rectangles painted red with a black vertical stripe in the middle.

Length: 1 mile.

Running track: 121°-301°.

2   **Tidal streams.** In the channel between the jetties the in-going tidal stream has a rate of about 2½ kn.

Directions

6.219

1   **Leading lights:**

Front Light (red rectangle, white stripe, on pile) (40°56′·9N 73°04′·3W).

Port Jefferson from SE (6.218)
(Original dated 1993)

(Photograph - Joseph R Melanson of www.skypic.com)

Rear light (similar structure) (206 m from front light).

2 From the vicinity of PJ Light-buoy (safe water) (6.217) the alignment (146°) of these lights leads SE through the dredged channel, marked by light-buoys and buoys (lateral), to the head of the harbour, passing (with positions relative to East Breakwater Light (40°58'·4N 73°05'·5W)):

SW of Mount Misery Shoal (7 cables NNE), marked on its N side by No 11 Buoy, thence:

3 Between Nos 1 and 2 Light-buoys (lateral) (1 cable WNW), which mark the shoal water extending from the two entrance points, thence:

Between E Breakwater Light (green and white chequered diamond on framework tower), standing at the base of the E breakwater, and W Breakwater Light No 2A (red triangle on metal framework tower) standing at the head of the W breakwater.

4 Thence into the harbour.

Useful marks:

Old Field Point Light (40°58'·6N 73°07'·1W) (6.94).

Two chimneys of a power station (1½ miles SSE), on the SW side of the head of the harbour, are prominent.

Berths
6.220

1 **Anchorage** is available in the NE part of the harbour in depths of 5 m (16 ft), which provides excellent shelter from the N. Care must be taken to avoid shoal patches at the sides of this area.

2 **Alongside berths:**

Oil wharf (2 cables from head of harbour on W side), with a depth alongside of 8·8 m.

Powerplant wharf (1 cable NW of Oil wharf), with a depth alongside of 8·8 m.

Commercial wharves and piers at head of harbour with depths alongside of up to 8·8 m.

SMALL HARBOURS ON THE NORTH SIDE OF THE WEST PART OF LONG ISLAND SOUND

Norwalk Islands

Charts 2754, 2580 (see 1.17)
Description
6.221

1 Norwalk Islands, a group of islands, rocks and shoals, lie between 1 and 2 miles off the N coast of Long Island Sound in the approaches to Norwalk Harbor (6.224). The islands extend between Georges Rock (41°05'N 73°20'W), 1¼ miles E of Cockenoe Island and Greens Ledge Light (6.92), 1 mile WSW of Sheffield Island (41°03'N 73°25'W).

2 **Hazards.** The bottom is very irregular in the vicinity of the islands and vessels should proceed with caution when crossing shoal areas. The area is much obstructed by oyster stakes and spars which sometimes tow under and are a source of danger, especially to small vessels.

Cockenoe Harbor
6.222

1 Cockenoe Harbor, W of Cockenoe Island and N of Goose Island, is entered between Peck Ledge Light (white conical tower, brown band, black round base) (41°05'N 73°22'W) and No 4 Buoy (starboard hand). It is also an approach to Norwalk River (6.224).

Local knowledge is required to enter the harbour.

2 **Anchorage,** suitable for vessels of up to 2·7 m (9 ft) draught, is available. The best berth is in the deeper part of the harbour, in depths of 4 to 7 m (13 to 23 ft), N and NW of Peck Ledge Light. There are depths of only about 4 m (13 ft) in the entrance of the harbour.

Sheffield Island Harbor
6.223

1 Sheffield Island Harbor lies between Sheffield Island and Shea Island, and the mainland NW. The harbour forms the main approach to Norwalk Harbor and River and is entered between Greens Ledge Light and Long Neck Point, 1½ miles WSW.

Anchorage in depths of 4 to 6 m (13 to 20 ft) can be obtained NW of Sheffield Island.

Norwalk Harbor and River

Chart 2754 (see 1.17)
General information
6.224

1 Norwalk Harbor (41°05'N 73°24'W) is formed by the lower part of the Norwalk River, which flows into the N side of Long Island Sound between Calf Pasture Point and Mantresa Island, N of the Norwalk Islands.

2 The towns of East Norwalk and South Norwalk lie on the E and W side of the river, 1 and 1½ miles within the entrance, respectively. Norwalk, at the head of navigation, lies 2½ miles within the entrance.

South Norwalk is an important commercial and manufacturing city. Commercial traffic on the river is mainly in building materials, petroleum products and shell fishing.

3 **Approach and entry.** The main approach to Norwalk Harbor is from the SW by a dredged and marked entrance channel which leads NE from Sheffield Island Harbor.

Limiting conditions
6.225

1 **Depths.** The project depth is 3·6 m (12 ft) from Sheffield Island Harbor to the bascule road bridge at South Norwalk, thence 3 m (10 ft) to a basin at Norwalk.

Federal project provides for a depth of 1·8 m (6 ft) in the dredged channel leading W of Fitch Point, to the anchorage basin in East Norwalk.

2 East of Fitch Point a privately maintained channel, which in 1987 had a controlling depth of 2·4 m (8 ft), leads into Norwalk Cove.

For the latest controlling depths the charts and port authority should be consulted.

3 **Vertical clearance.** Three bridges and a power cable span the river between South Norwalk and Norwalk:

Road bascule bridge; with vertical clearance of 2·4 m (8 ft), 6 cables NW of Fitch Point.

Rail swing bridge; with a vertical clearance of 4·9 m (16 ft), close N of the road bridge.

4 Overhead power cable; with a vertical clearance of 61·9 m (203 ft), close N of the rail bridge.

Fixed road bridge at Oyster Shell Point; 5 cables N of rail bridge, with a vertical clearance of 18·3 m (60 ft).

5 **Ice.** The channel up to South Norwalk is navigable throughout the year, but above that the channel is normally closed for about 6 weeks each winter; the channel to East Norwalk is also closed for part of the winter.

Arrival information

6.226

1   **Pilotage.** Pilots who serve New London and New Haven also serve Norwalk.

Principal marks

6.227

1   **Landmark:**
Chimney (41°04'·3N 73°24'·7W) standing on Manresa Island, close NE of Keyser Point.
Major light:
Greens Ledge Light (41°02'·5N 73°26'·6W) (6.92).

Directions

6.228

1   From a position close NW of Greens Ledge Light the approaches to Norwalk Harbor and River lead NE through Sheffield Harbor, passing (with positions relative to Calf Pasture Point (41°05'N 73°24'W)):

2   NW of No 2A Light-buoy (starboard hand) (2¾ miles SW). A group of drying rocks lies on the inner part of Greens Ledge, 3½ cables E of this buoy. Thence:

SE of a shoal (2½ miles SW), with a depth of 3·4 m (11 ft) over it, the SE side of which is marked by No 1A Buoy (port hand), thence:

3   Between Noroton Point and the SW extremity of Sheffield Island (2½ miles SSW). A flagstaff and house with a cupola stand on Noroton Point and a disused lighthouse stands near the SW end of Sheffield Island. Thence:

4   Between No 2 Light-buoy (starboard hand) and No 3 Buoy (port hand) (1¾ miles SW) which mark the entrance to the channel.

Thence through the channel which is marked by light-buoys, light-beacons and buoys (lateral).

Berths

6.229

1   **Anchorages.** Apart from Cockenoe Harbor (6.222) and Sheffield Island Harbor (6.223), small vessels can anchor in depths of 2·4 to 2·7 m (8 to 9 ft) in the South Anchorage Basin. This basin lies on the E side of the channel, extending 2½ cables either side of the entrance to East Norwalk, 7 cables NW of Calf Pasture Point.

2   **Alongside berths** are available at wharves at South Norwalk, with depths alongside of 1·5 to 3 m, and at Norwalk, with depths alongside of 2·1 m.

Supplies

6.230

1   Fuel and stores.

Between Sheffield Island Harbor and Stamford Harbor

Chart 2580

General information

6.231

1   Between Wilson Point (41°04'N 73°26'W) and Shippan Point, 5½ miles SW, the coast is foul with many off-lying dangers up to 1 mile offshore. The coast is much indented by inlets and coves which provide shelter for small craft, but their approaches are encumbered with dangers and they should not be entered without local knowledge.

Stamford Harbor

Chart 2580 (see 1.17)

General information

6.232

1   **Stamford Harbor** (41°01'N 73°32'W), on the N side of Long Island Sound, 33 miles E of New York, comprises the bay N of a line from Shippan Point on the E, through Stamford Harbor Ledge Light, to the shore N of Greenwich Point, 2 miles WSW of Shippan Point. The entrance to the bay is protected by two detached breakwaters.

2   **Stamford** is a manufacturing city on a peninsula at the head of the harbour. Petroleum products, scrap metal, sand, gravel and crushed rock are the principal products handled in the harbour.

3   **Approach and entry.** The harbour is shoal and obstructed to a large extent by ledges and rocks. It is entered through a dredged entrance channel that leads N from between the two detached breakwaters, to a point about 1 mile above the entrance, at the junction with the dredged channels leading into East Branch and West Branch.

Limiting conditions

6.233

1   **Depths.** Project depths are as follows:
5·5 m (18 ft) to a point 5 cables below the junction of the two branches, thence:
4·6 m (15 ft) to the junction, thence:
4·6 m (15 ft) in the West Branch to the turning basin, 7 cables above the junction, and:

2   4·6 m (15 ft) in the East Branch to No 1 Light, 3½ cables above the junction, thence:
3·6 m (12 ft) to the head of the project, 7 cables above No 1 Light.

For the latest controlling depths the charts and port authority should be consulted.

3   **Tidal streams** in the harbour are weak and follow the direction of the channels.

Ice forms in the harbour most winters, but traffic usually keeps the channels clear. West Branch is usually navigable all the year, but East Branch is closed by ice for several weeks in severe winters.

Hurricane barrier

6.234

1   A hurricane barrier which constricts the East Branch to 27 m, is situated 4½ cables above the junction with West Branch. The barrier is kept open during fair weather, but will be closed on the approach of a storm or unusually high tides.

Directions

6.235

1   **Leading lights:**
Front Light (red rectangle, white stripe, on framework tower) (41°01'·8N 73°32'·3W).
Rear light (similar structure) (183 m from front light).
From a position about 1 mile SSW of Shippan Point the alignment (358°) of these lights leads N to the entrance and thence through the dredged channel, which is marked by buoys, to the junction of East and West Branch, passing (with positions relative to Shippan Point (41°01'N 73°32'W)):
Clear of a dangerous wreck (9 cables SSW), the position of which is approximate, thence:

W of The Cows (6 cables SSE), the S side of which is marked by No 32 Light-buoy (starboard hand), thence:

2   Between Nos 1 and 2 Buoys (lateral) (6 and 4 cables SW), which mark the shoal water lying either side the S end of the entrance channel, thence:

E of Harbor Ledge (6 cables WSW), on which stands a light (white conical tower, red round base), thence:

3   Between the ends of the detached breakwaters (3 cables WSW). No 3 Light (green square on tower) stands at the E end of the W breakwater, and No 4 Light (red triangle on framework tower) stands at the W end of E breakwater.

Berths
6.236
1   **Anchorage.** A dredged anchorage with depths of 4 to 5 m (12 to 18 ft) is situated 2½ cables N of the E end of the W breakwater just W of the alignment of the leading lights.

Commercial wharves, with depths alongside of 1·8 to 5·8 m, are situated along the East and West Branch.

Captain Harbor and adjacent waters

General information
6.237
1   Captain Harbor lies between Greenwich Point (41°00′N 73°34′W) and Manursing Island, 4½ miles WSW, and N of Great Captain Island and Little Captain Island.

2   The harbour provides shelter from all winds for small vessels. Captain Harbor also comprises the approaches to Port Chester Harbor (6.242), Greenwich Cove (6.259), Cos Cob Harbor (6.260), Indian Harbor (6.261) and Greenwich Harbor (6.262).

Entrances. Captain Harbor can be entered from the E or W.

Limiting conditions
6.238
1   **Largest vessel.** Vessels drawing up to 3·6 m (12 ft) can obtain shelter in Captain Harbor.

Tidal streams in the E entrance reach a rate ¾ kn.

Ice forms in the winter in all the coves and over the greater part of Captain Harbor. It sometimes extends outside Little and Great Captain Islands.

Principal marks
6.239
1   **Major Light:**

Great Captain Island Light (40°58′·9N 73°37′·4W) (6.92) standing at the E end of the island.

Directions
6.240
1   **East entrance.** The harbour is entered from the E between Flat Neck Point (41°00′N 73°35′W) and Hen and Chickens, a group of rocks, 1 mile WSW, that extend NE from Little Captain Island. This entrance, which is marked by No 1 Light-buoy and No 1A Buoy (port hand), and No 2 Buoy (starboard hand), is the clearer and better one for those without local knowledge.

2   **West entrance.** From a position SW of Great Captain Island the entrance route leads NNE, passing (with positions relative to Great Captain Island Light):

ESE of Bluefish Shoal (1¼ miles WSW), marked on its SE side by No 36 Buoy (starboard hand), thence:

3   WNW of a dangerous rock (6 cables SW), the E side of which is marked by No 2 Buoy (starboard hand), thence:

ESE of Fourfoot Rocks (9 cables WSW), marked on its S side by F Buoy, thence:

4   WNW of the W end of Great Captain Island (3 cables WSW), thence:

ESE of Jones Rocks (6 cables NW), the E side of which is marked by No 1 Buoy (port hand) and No 3 Light-beacon (green square on framework tower), and:

5   WNW of Cormorant Reef (5 cables NW), the NW extremity of which is marked by No 4 Buoy (starboard hand).

Caution. The harbour and its entrances are strewn with boulders. Mariners without local knowledge should proceed with caution, especially in shoaler water.

Anchorage
6.241
1   Anchorage is available in the deeper part of the harbour, 5 cables N of Great and Little Captain Islands, in depths of 5 to 9 m (15 to 30 ft), soft bottom. Vessels with a draught of 2·1 m (7 ft) or less may anchor on the flats.

Port Chester Harbor
6.242
1   Port Chester Harbor (40°59′N 73°40′W) lies at the mouth of Byram River, the lower part of which forms the boundary between the states of Connecticut and New York. The river leads to the towns of Port Chester and Byram, 1 mile upstream. Principal commerce is in building materials and petroleum products.

2   **Entrance.** The harbour is entered between the breakwater extending S from Byram Point, and the N part of Manursing Island. A dredged entrance channel, marked for 3 cables above the entrance, leads N through the harbour.

3   **Depths.** In 2005 controlling depths were 2·7 m (8¾ ft) in mid-channel to the fixed road bridge.

Maximum size of vessel handled. Vessels with a draught of up to 4·3 m (14 ft) can use the harbour.

Bridge. A fixed road bridge with a vertical clearance of 18·3 m (60 ft) crosses the river 8 cables above the entrance.
6.243
1   **Directions.** From a position SE of Byram Point the approach to Port Chester leads NW through waters obstructed by rocks, passing (with positions relative to Byram Point Breakwater Light (40°59′·1N 73°39′·4W)):

NE of Bluefish Shoal (9 cables SSE), thence:

SW of Fourfoot Rocks (7 cables ESE) (6.240), marked on its S side by F buoy, thence:

2   SW of Great Captain Rocks (3 cables ESE), marked on its SE side by No 2 Light-buoy (starboard hand), thence:

NE of Manursing Island Reef (1 cable SSE), marked on its NE side by No 3 Buoy (port hand), thence:

SW of Byram Point Breakwater Light (red triangle on framework tower), thence:

3   NE of No 5 Channel Light-beacon (green square on framework tower) (2 cables WNW).

Caution. The channel in Byram River is fairly well defined at LW, but those without local knowledge should take it on a rising tide and proceed with caution.

4　**Wharf.** There is an oil terminal with a reported depth alongside of 3·7 m at Fox Island, 6 cables above the entrance.

Supplies: fuel; water and stores.

Between Captain Harbor and Throgs Neck

General information
6.244

1　The N shore of Long Island Sound between Captain Harbor (41°00′N 73°37′W) and Throgs Neck (7.44), 11 miles SW, is similar in character to that E, being fringed by foul ground, islets and rocks, and there are numerous indentations in the coastline providing anchorage for small vessels.

2　**Local knowledge** is required for some of these harbours.

Speed limits of between 4 and 5 kn are in force in the harbours described as follows.

Mamaroneck Harbor
6.245

1　Mamaroneck Harbor (40°57′N 73°43′W) is an open bay, exposed to S winds, between Hen Island and Delancey Point, 1¼ miles SW. The important dangers in the bay are buoyed; these include Outer Steamboat Rock, near the channel entrance and Ship Rock, 5 cables SE.

The town of Mamaroneck stands on both sides of the inner part of the harbour.

2　Commercial traffic in the harbour is mainly barges carrying petroleum products.

No-discharge zone (NDZ). A NDZ has been established in Mamaroneck Harbor. See 1.44.

Channel. A dredged channel leads from the outer harbour in the bay to the inner harbour.

3　**Depths.** In 2005 the controlling depths in the dredged channel were 3·0 m (9·8 ft) in the entrance channel to the junction with the branch channels and thence 2·7 m (8·7 ft) in the N branch channel.

Anchorage. Depths in the outer harbour range from 2 to 4 m (7 to 12 ft).

Supplies: fuel; water and stores.

Larchmont Harbor
6.246

1　Larchmont Harbor (40°55′N 73°44′W) is entered between Edgewater Point and Umbrella Point, 5 cables SW. A breakwater, with No 2 Light (red triangle on framework tower) at its head, extends 2 cables SSE from Edgewater Point. In summer the harbour is full of mooring buoys for small craft.

2　**Entrance.** The entrance to the harbour is obstructed by Hen and Chickens Reef, Dauntless Rock and Umbrella Rock. Hen and Chickens Reef is marked by No 1 Light-buoy (port hand) and the limits of the other dangers are marked by buoys (lateral).

Channel. A buoyed channel leads into the harbour on either side of Hen and Chickens Reef.

3　**Depths.** The E channel, which is about 1½ cables wide, has a least depth of 4·6 m (15 ft).

Anchorage is available in depths of 4 m (12 ft) in the entrance to the harbour. Larger vessels anchor W of the breakwater in depths of 5 to 6 m (15 to 21 ft).

Echo Bay
6.247

1　Echo Bay (40°54′N 73°46′W), entered between Premium Point and Davenport Neck, 3 cables SW, is the principal approach to the city of New Rochelle, which is situated on the W shore of the bay.

2　**Approach.** Hicks Ledge, marked on its S side by HL Buoy (preferred channel to starboard), lies in the approaches to Echo Bay, 5 cables SE of its entrance. The entrance is marked by 3BR Light-buoy (port hand), off the S entrance point and No 4 Buoy (starboard hand), off Premium Point.

3　**Channel.** A dredged channel, marked by buoys, leads from the NW side of Echo Bay to a municipal wharf and turning basin at Beaufort Point, 3 cables within the entrance.

Depths. In 1985 the controlling depth was 2·6 m (8½ ft) in mid-channel and 2·0 to 2·1 m (6½ to 7 ft) in the basin.

4　**Anchorages.** Vessels can anchor in general anchorages on either side of the entrance, clear of a sewer outfall, in depths of 6 to 7 m (20 to 24 ft).

Supplies: fuel and water.

New Rochelle Harbor
6.248

1　New Rochelle Harbor (40°54′N 73°47′W) is a narrow channel situated between Davenport Neck and the mainland NW. The harbour leads to the S part of New Rochelle.

2　**Approach channels.** Two well marked channels lead to the harbour. From the N, the deeper channel leads between Davids Island and Davenport Neck. From the S a channel leads across the flats SW of Davids Island and thence between that island and Glen Island. The harbour is entered between Glen Island and Davenport Neck.

3　**Depths.** The S channel has a depth of 4 m (13 ft) and in 1990 the dredged channel in the harbour had a mid-channel controlling depth of 1·8 m (6 ft).

Anchorage is not recommended owing to congestion.

City Harbor
6.249

1　City Harbor, also known as Hart Island Roads (40°51′N 73°47′W), lies between Hart Island and City Island, 5 cables W.

The harbour is well sheltered from E and W winds. It is an important anchorage as a harbour of refuge for coasting vessels, and is also frequently used as a temporary anchorage.

2　**City Island** is largely built over and there are several shipyards on its E side. The island is connected to Rodman Neck, NW, by a bridge which has a vertical clearance of 3·6 m (12 ft).

Pilot. Pilots for New York are based at City Island. They board vessels off Execution Rocks (6.95).

3　**Ice** seldom interferes with navigation of powered vessels.

Useful marks (with positions relative to Hart Island Light (40°50′·7N 73°46′·0W)):

　　Chimney (4 cables NNW), on the S part of Hart Island.

4　　Hart Island No 46 Light (6.96) (red triangle on framework tower, concrete base), on extremity of reef extending from S end of Hart Island.

　　Spire (1¼ miles NW), on N part of City Island.

　　Spire (9 cables W), in the centre of City Island.

6.250

1　**Anchorages.** The usual anchorage for deep-draught vessels is SE of City Island, S of a line joining the S parts of City Island and Hart Island. Other general anchorages are situated between the W side of Hart Island and Rat Island, in the NW part of the harbour, and SW of Belden Point, the S end of City Island.

Minor anchorages and harbours

Chart 2726
Southport Harbor
6.251

1   Southport Harbor (41°08'N 73°17'W) is the lower part of Mill River, at the head of a bay between Pine Creek Point and Frost Point, 2 miles W. It is used mainly by pleasure craft.

Chart 2754 (see 1.17)
Saugatuck River
6.252

1   Saugatuck River lies with its entrance between Cedar Point (41°06'N 73°21'W) and Seymour Point, 8 cables WSW. The river is shallow, full of ledges and boulders and is used by barges carrying petroleum products, sand and gravel. It is also used by pleasure craft. The village of Saugatuck stands on the W side of the river 1½ miles above the entrance. The town of Westport, at the head of navigation, stands on the E bank 1½ miles above Saugatuck.

Chart 2580 (see 1.17)
Wilson Cove
6.253

1   Wilson Cove (41°04'N 73°26'W), which is entered on the W side of Wilson Point, is only used by small craft.

Fivemile River
6.254

1   Fivemile River is a narrow inlet entered 5 cables W of Noroton Point (41°03'N 73°26'W). It is chiefly used by fishing and pleasure craft.

Scott Cove
6.255

1   Scott Cove (41°03'N 73°28'W), which is entered W of the Fish Islands, is only used by small craft.

Goodwives River
6.256

1   Goodwives River, only used by small craft, is a small and shallow stream on the W side of Long Neck Point (6.223) (41°02'N 73°29'W).

Cove Harbor
6.257

1   Cove Harbor (41°03'N 73°30'W), situated 5 cables W of Goodwives River, is only used by small craft.

Westcott Cove
6.258

1   Westcott Cove (41°02'N 73°31'W), on the NE side of Shippan Point, is an anchorage for small craft.

Greenwich Cove
6.259

1   Greenwich Cove (41°01'N 73°35'W) opens into Captain Harbor N of Flat Neck Point. The cove is used by small local craft.

Cos Cob Harbor
6.260

1   Cos Cob Harbor (41°01'N 73°36'W), on the NE side of Captain Harbor, is entered through a dredged channel which leads N through the Mianus River for 1½ miles to the head of navigation at Mianus. It is used by small craft.

Indian Harbor
6.261

1   Indian Harbor (41°01'N 73°37'W), a narrow inlet about 1 mile W of Cos Cob Harbor, is an anchorage for small craft.

Greenwich Harbor
6.262

1   Greenwich Harbor (41°01'N 73°38'W) is situated 1½ miles N of Great Captain Island Light. Greenwich is at the head of the harbour.
Entrance. The harbour is entered through a dredged and marked entrance channel, 1¼ miles in length. This channel leads across the flats to two turning basins, one of which is at the head of the harbour and the other a short distance S, off the W side of the channel.

2   **Depths.** In 1981 the controlling depth in the channel was 2·4 m (8 ft) and the depths in the basins were between 0·6 and 1·8 m (2 and 6 ft).
Berths. Wharves lie on the E side of the harbour.

Rye Beach
6.263

1   Playland (40°58'N 73°40'W), a recreational centre at Rye Beach, is situated in the N part of a foul bight that lies between Manursing Island and Parsonage Point, 1½ miles SW. There is a small harbour, used by small craft, protected by breakwaters.

Milton Harbor
6.264

1   Milton Harbor (40°57'N 73°42'W) is entered between Milton Point and Hen Island, 3 cables W. The harbour provides shelter for small craft in the summer, but is open SW.

Eastchester Bay and Hutchinson River
6.265

1   Eastchester Bay (40°50'N 73°48'W) is situated between City Island and the mainland 1½ miles SW. Hutchinson River flows into the N end of the bay. The river should not be approached without local knowledge.

2   There are irregular depths in Eastchester Bay and the shores of the bay are fringed with boulders; there are many shoals and several wrecks. The shoals include Cuban Ledge in the centre of the bay, which is marked by a beacon, and on its SW side by No 2 Light-buoy (starboard hand). Caution is essential.

ANCHORAGES AND HARBOURS ON THE SOUTH SIDE OF THE WEST PART OF LONG ISLAND SOUND

Old Field Point to Eatons Neck Point

Chart 2754 (see 1.17)
General information
6.266

1   Between Old Field Point (40°59'N, 73°07'W) and Eatons Neck Point, a prominent wooded headland, 12½ miles W, there are a number of small harbours and anchorages.
Speed limit of 4½ kn is enforced in the harbours.

Smithtown Bay
6.267

1   Smithtown Bay is an open bight extending 7 miles WSW from Crane Neck Point. Rocky shoals extend 1 mile from the shore in places.

Anchorage is available in summer, in depths of 9 to 15 m (30 to 50 ft), sheltered from E winds, 1 miles S of Crane Neck Point.

Stony Brook Harbor
6.268

1   Stony Brook Harbor, a narrow shallow bay in the SE part of Smithtown Bay, is entered 2½ miles S of Crane Neck Point and is only used by small craft.

Nissequogue River
6.269

1   Nissequogue River (40°54′N 73°14′W), shoal and winding, is entered through a marked dredged channel 5 miles SW of Crane Neck Point and is only used by small craft.

Northport Offshore Terminal
6.270

1   Northport Offshore Terminal (40°57′N 73°20′W) for the receipt of oil, owned and operated by LILCO, is situated 2½ miles E of Eatons Neck Point. The terminal consists of a platform with off-lying mooring buoys. Lights are exhibited from each corner.

Traffic. In 2005 the port was used by 4 vessels with a total deadweight 331 397 tonnes.

2   **Pilotage** is compulsory. The pilot serves as docking master and remains on board at standby while the vessel is at the platform. See 6.4.

Tugs are available from New Haven, Providence, Brooklyn or Staten Island on advance notice.

Largest vessel. Length 251 m, draught 11·6 m (38 ft).

Northport Basin
6.271

1   Northport Basin (40°56′N 73°20′W) is a private harbour situated 3 miles SE of Eatons Neck Point. It is entered through a dredged channel between submerged breakwaters. No 1 Light-buoy (port hand) is moored close N of the entrance.

2   The four chimneys of the power station on the E side of the basin are prominent.

Depths. In 1977 the privately dredged channel had a controlling depth of 3·6 m (12 ft).

Huntington Bay and adjacent waters

Chart 2580 (see 1.17)
General information
6.272

1   Huntington Bay (40°57′N 73°26′W) lies between Eatons Neck Point and East Fort Point at the E end of Lloyd Neck (6.95), 2 miles SW. The bay is the approach to Northport Bay (6.273), Huntington Harbor (6.275) and Lloyd Harbor (6.276).

2   **Anchorage.** The bay is an excellent anchorage for large vessels, with shelter from all but N winds, in depths of 11 to 7 m (36 to 23 ft) for about 1 mile above its entrance. Anchorage can be selected according to draught and direction of wind. There is also anchorage for small vessels in depths of 11 to 5 m (36 to 16 ft), with shelter from NW winds, in the SW part of the bay.

3   **Measured distance.** Off the W side of Eatons Neck in the E part of the bay there is a measured distance.

        Limit marks: Two orange beacons situated 1¾ and 2¼ miles S of Eatons Neck Point.

        Length: Half a mile.

        Running track: 018°–198°.

4   **No-discharge zone (NDZ).** All the waters inside of a line joining East Beach (40°54′·9N 73°26′·1W) and West Beach (1¼ miles E) have been designated as a NDZ. See 1.44.

Northport Bay
6.273

1   Northport Bay (40°55′N 73°23′W) is entered from the SE part of Huntington Bay close S of the narrow tongue extending 1 mile S from the SW corner of Eatons Neck.

2   Centerport Harbor and Duck Island Harbor, shallow coves, are situated on the SW and N sides, respectively, of Northport Bay. Northport Harbor is situated on the E side of Little Neck at the SE end of Northport Bay. The village of Northport lies on the E side of the harbour.

Ice may close Northport Harbor for about two months during severe winters.

3   **Channels and depths:**

        Entrance to Northport Bay. A dredged channel with a depth of 3·6 m (12 ft) leads through the entrance to Northport Bay. No 1 Light-buoy (port hand) is moored at the outer end of the channel which is marked by buoys and a light-buoy.

6.274

1   **Anchorage,** which is well sheltered, can be obtained in the W part of Northport Bay in depths of 6 to 16 m (20 to 52 ft), and the E part of the bay in depths of 2 to 4 m (8 to 12 ft).

Huntington Harbor
6.275

1   Huntington Harbor (40°54′N 73°26′W) is entered from the S part of Huntington Bay through a narrow entrance which leads between the W end of East Neck and the E part of West Neck. The village of Huntington is at the head of the harbour.

2   **Channel,** which is marked by buoys and light-buoys, leads from outside the harbour entrance to the head of the harbour. The outer end of the channel is marked by Huntington Harbor Light (square concrete tower and dwelling) (40°54′·6N 73°25′·9W) and No 1 Light-buoy (port hand), 1 cable E. In 1991 a dangerous wreck was reported close to the channel 6 cables within the entrance.

3   **Depths.** There is a controlling depth of 2·4 m (8 ft) in the channel.

Tidal stream. The tidal stream in the entrance has an estimated rate of 2 kn.

Wharf at the head of the harbour is used by sand and gravel barges.

Lloyd Harbor
6.276

1   Lloyd Harbor (40°55′N 73°26′W), which lies between West Neck and Lloyd Neck, is a narrow arm extending W that is almost connected to Oyster Bay (6.277). The entrance is marked by Huntington Harbor Light (6.275) on the S side and by buoys.

Anchorage. Vessels can anchor close within the entrance in depths of 2 to 3 m (7 to 11 ft).

Oyster Bay and adjacent waters

General information and limiting conditions
6.277

1   The entrance to Oyster Bay (40°55′N 73°30′W) lies between NW Bluff on the W side of Lloyd Neck and Rocky Point, the N point of Centre Island. The bay is the approach to Cold Spring Harbor (6.278) and Oyster Bay Harbor (6.279) which are separated by Cove Neck.

2   Boulder reefs and shallow banks extend from the shores of the bay, especially at the entrance, where a bank extends almost across from the N part of Centre Island. The E end of this bank is marked by Cold Spring Harbor Light (red and white chequered diamond on framework tower on caisson).

3   **Largest vessel.** The bay S of Cold Spring Harbor Light offers a secure anchorage to vessels drawing up to 5·5 m (18 ft).

    Ice in severe winters may extend over the whole bay during part of January and February.

Cold Spring Harbor
6.278

1   Cold Spring Harbor (40°53′N 73°29′W), at the SE end of Oyster Bay is entered between Cooper Bluff and the W shore of West Neck, 1 mile E. The village of Cold Spring Harbor is on the E shore near the head of the harbour.

2   **Anchorage** is available in the bay, which has general depths of 4·3 to 5·2 m (14 to 17 ft), nearly to its head.

    Alongside berth. A tanker jetty, with a depth alongside of 4 m, is situated at the village.

    Supplies: fuel; water and limited stores.

Oyster Bay Harbor
6.279

1   Oyster Bay Harbor (40°53′N 73°31′W), the long winding arm that extends SW from Oyster Bay, is entered between Plum Point and No 5 Light-buoy (port hand), marking the limit of the bank that extends N from Cove Point. The village of Oyster Bay is situated on the S side of Oyster Bay Harbor.

2   **Depths and channels.** The harbour has depths of 18·3 m (60 ft) at the entrance, decreasing to 9·1 m (30 ft) off Moses Point, 1 mile SSW of Plum Point, where the channel narrows and is only suitable for vessels drawing less than 3 m (10 ft). The channel S of Centre Island between Moses Point and Brickyard Point, 6 cables W, is marked by buoys. Two channels, with depths of 2·7 m (9 ft) and 1·8 m (6 ft), lead SW and S, respectively, from the main channel to the wharves at Oyster Bay.

3   **Anchorages.** Good anchorage can be obtained SE and S of Moses Point in depths of 8 to 11 m (26 to 36 ft). Vessels of less than 2·1 m (7 ft) draught can anchor in West Harbor, W of Centre Island, in depths of about 2 m (6 to 8 ft). Anchorage is also available in Mill Neck Creek, situated on the S side of Oak Neck at the NW end of Oyster Bay Harbor, in depths of 1 to 5 m (3 to 16 ft). This berth is approached through a bascule bridge with a vertical clearance of 2·7 m.

4   **Wharves.** A wharf used by fishing vessels with reported depths alongside of about 3 m is situated at the village. There is a tanker berth about 1 cable farther S.

    Supplies: fuel; water; provisions and stores.

Hempstead Harbor

General information
6.280

1   Hempstead Harbor (40°51′N 73°40′W) is entered on the NE side of Manhasset Neck (6.95) between Matinecock Point (40°54′N 73°38′W) and Prospect Point, 4 miles SW. The harbour entrance then narrows to about 1 mile between the shore S of Weeks Point, 1¾ miles SW of Matinecock

Point, and Mott Point, 1¾ miles SW. The entrance is free of dangers as long as the shore is given a berth of 3 cables.

2   The harbour is divided into two by Bar Beach, a narrow tongue of land which extends nearly across the harbour, 2 miles SSE of Mott Point.

    Roslyn is a village at the head of the inner harbour.

3   The harbour is much used by vessels seeking shelter in any but strong N winds and provides excellent anchorage. Waterborne trade in the harbour is principally in sand, gravel, building materials and petroleum products, usually shipped in vessels with draughts of 1 to 3·7 m.

    Ice may stop navigation in severe winters for about six weeks during January and February.

4   **Useful mark:**

    Eight chimneys (40°49′·6N 73°38′·6W) at the power station at Glenwood Landing.

Anchorages
6.281

1   **Main anchorage.** Vessels drawing over 6 m (20 ft) should anchor in depths of 7 to 9 m (23 to 30 ft) between the entrance and a line joining Mott Point and Glen Cove Landing (6.282), 8 cables ENE. Vessels drawing 6 m (20 ft) or less will find good anchorage just inside that line in depths of 6 to 7 m (20 to 23 ft). Attention is drawn to the large submarine cable area that runs through Hempstead Harbor.

2   **Glen Cove Harbor**, S of the breakwater extending from the E shore 1 mile S of Weeks Point (40°53′N 73°39′W), provides anchorage in depths of 5 to 7 m (16 to 23 ft) in its outer half and 2 to 3 m (7 to 10 ft), closer inshore.

Landings
6.282

1   **Glen Cove Landing**, 1 mile S of Weekes Point, is protected by a breakwater extending 2½ cables from the shore. No 5 Light (green square on framework tower) stands at the head of the breakwater.

    Glenwood Landing is a village abreast Bar Beach. There are depths alongside of 2·4 to 3 m at the Glenwood Landing wharves.

Manhasset Bay

General information
6.283

1   Manhasset Bay (40°50′N 73°44′W) is entered on the SW side of Manhasset Neck between Barker Point, 1¾ miles SW of Prospect Point, and Hewlett Point, 1 mile farther SW.

    Port Washington is a village on the E side of the bay, 2 miles SE of Barker Point.

2   The bay affords excellent shelter for vessels drawing up to 3·7 m (12 ft) and is much frequented by small craft in the summer. Waterborne trade in the harbour is principally in petroleum products carried in vessels drawing 1·8 to 3 m (6 to 10 ft).

3   **Approach.** The bay is approached from SW of Gangway Rock No 27A Light (40°52′N 73°45′W) (6.96).

    Depths in the outer part of the bay range from 3·4 to 5·2 m (11 to 17 ft) and in the inner part, inside Plum Point, there are depths of 2·1 to 3·7 m (7 to 12 ft).

Anchorages
6.284

1   **General anchorage** is situated S of Barker Point and E of Hewlett Point.

Seaplane restricted area
6.285

1   A seaplane restricted area is established 5 cables E of Plum Point. Vessels shall not anchor or moor in the restricted area and vessels traversing the area shall pass directly through without unnecessary delay, and shall give seaplanes right of way at all times.

Channel
6.286

1   A buoyed channel, with a depth of 2·4 m (8 ft), leads E from No 1 Light-buoy (port hand), moored off Plum Point, to the wharves at Port Washington. Thence an unmarked channel leads along the E side of the bay to its N end, NE of Toms Point.

Wharves
6.287

1   Depths alongside the wharves are from 0·6 to 2·7 m.

Little Neck Bay

General information
6.288

1   Little Neck Bay (40°48′N 73°46′W) is entered SW of Great Neck, between Elm Point, 1½ miles SSW of Hewlett Point and Willets Point.

A small basin is situated at Kings Point, 3 cables SW of Elm Point. The US Merchant Marine Academy is situated on this headland.

2   **Depths.** The bay is shallow with depths of 3 to 3·7 m (10 to 12 ft) at its entrance, decreasing gradually to its head.

Anchorages
6.289

1   **General anchorage**, the position of which is shown on the chart, is situated at the entrance of the bay.

Alongside berths
6.290

1   In 1991 the basin at Kings Point had reported depths alongside of 3·6 to 4·3 m (12 to 14 ft).

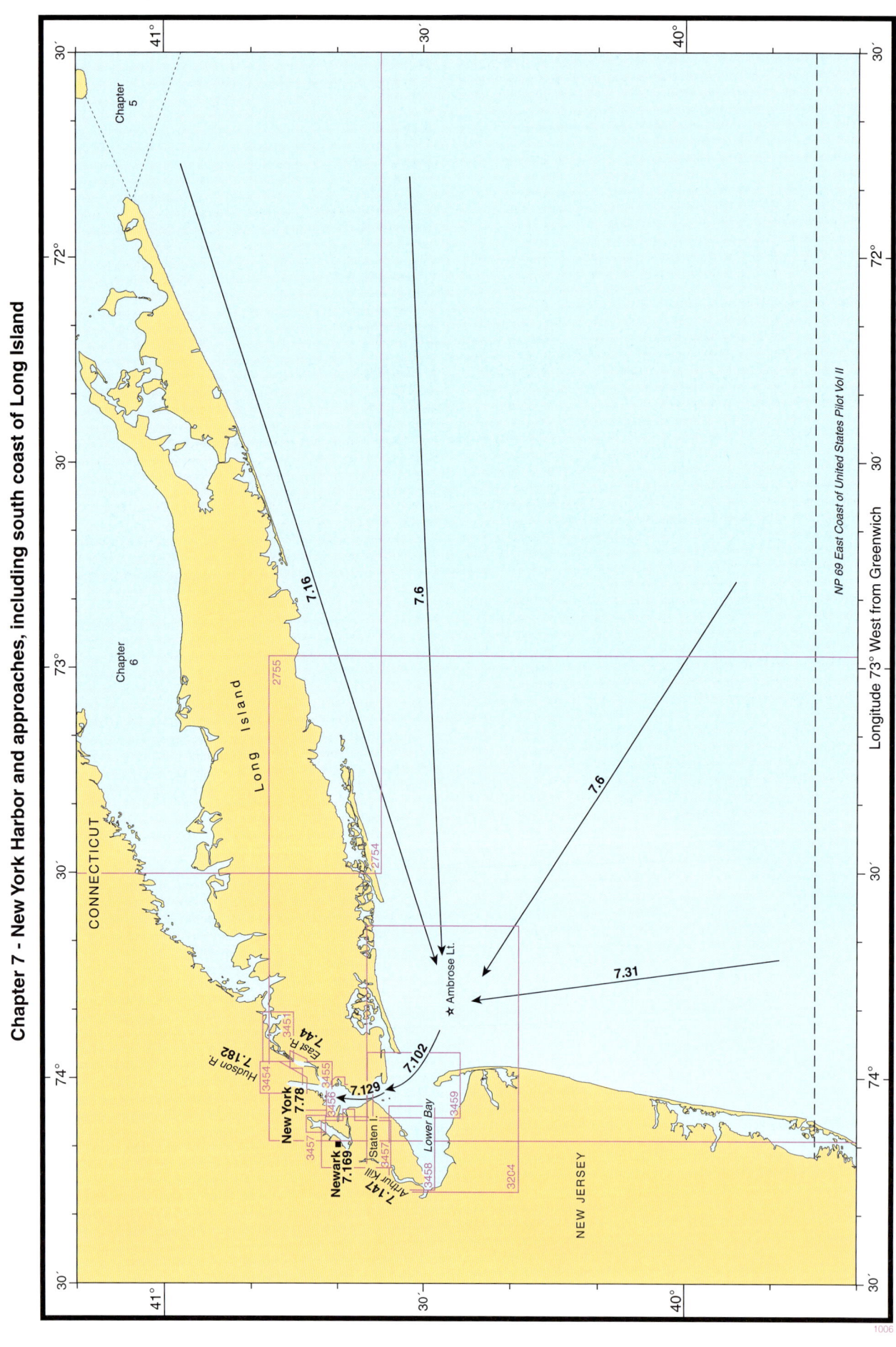

CHAPTER 7

NEW YORK HARBOR AND APPROACHES,
INCLUDING SOUTH COAST OF LONG ISLAND

GENERAL INFORMATION

Charts 2860, 2754, 2755
Scope of the chapter
7.1

1   The area covered by this chapter includes:
    The outer approach to New York Harbor from SW of
    Nantucket Shoals (40°30′N 70°15′W).

The S coast of Long Island (40°50′N 72°00′W).
The final approaches to New York Harbor including
    East River and New Jersey coastal waters N of
    Barnegat Inlet (39°46′N 73°45′W).
New York Harbor (40°41′N 74°02′W).

APPROACHES TO NEW YORK HARBOR

GENERAL INFORMATION

Charts 2860, 2754, 2755, 3204
Description
7.2

1   The approaches to New York Harbor from seaward are
generally along the S coast of Long Island or the E coast
of New Jersey, although the harbour is easily approached
from any direction between E and S.

2   During the approach the S shore of Long Island Sound
will be seen to the N and the sandy beaches of New Jersey
will be observed to the W. The Long Island shore is readily
identified by sandy hillocks and thickly settled beach
communities backed in places by low dark woods, and the
New Jersey shore is characterised by long sandy stretches
and many summer resort settlements.

Outer anchorages
7.3

1   It was reported (2006) that the Port of New York and
New Jersey had recommended that vessels awaiting a berth
should anchor offshore. It was also reported (2006) that
anchorage may be obtained ENE and NE of Ambrose Light
clear of charted dangers and hazards.

2   All vessels will limit the use of Stapleton (7.144), Bay
Ridge (7.144) and Gravesend Bay (7.119) anchorages to
lightering or loading, bunkering, receiving stores or parts,
repairs, Coast Guard inspections, crew changes, or
emergencies only.

3   On completion of these operations vessels will leave
these anchorages and anchor offshore to await a berth.

Pilotage
7.4

1   See 7.89.

Traffic regulations
7.5

1   **Traffic separation schemes.** Vessels approaching New
York from E, SE and S use different TSSs during the final
approach. The positions of the TSSs are shown on the
chart. These schemes are IMO–adopted and Rule 10 of the
*International Regulations for Preventing Collisions at Sea
(1972)* applies.

2   **Shipping Safety Fairway.** A Shipping Safety Fairway
has been established between the W end of the TSS S of
Nantucket Shoals and the E end of the TSS approaching
New York from the E. The position of this fairway, the use

of which is not mandatory, but is recommended, is shown
on the chart. See 1.48.

3   **Regulated navigation area.** All the coastal waters off
the S shore of Long Island lie within a regulated navigation
area that extends 12 miles offshore. For details, and
definition and general regulations concerning regulated
navigation areas see Appendix V.

4   **Safety and security zones.** The following areas are
safety and security zones:
    All waters within 100 yards of each moored or
        anchored US Coast Guard Cutter.
    All waters within 25 yards of each commercial
        waterfront facility that is capable of accepting
        barge, ferry or other commercial vessels.

5   All waters of the New York Marine Inspection Zone
        and Captain of the Port Zone within a 200 yard
        radius of any Liquefied Hazardous Gas (LHG)
        vessel or LHG facility.
    All waters within 25 yards of any bridge pier or
        abutments, overhead power cable tower, pier or
        tunnel ventilator south of the Troy, NY locks.

6   **Security zone.** An area between the Ambrose to Hudson
Canyon Traffic Lane and the Barnegat to Ambrose Traffic
Lane, extending 6 miles SSE from the Precautionary Area,
is a security zone.
    For definition and general regulations concerning safety
and security zones see Appendix V.

7   **Former mined area.** A former mined area, charted as a
danger area, the limits of which are shown on the chart, is
established in the S and SE part of the Precautionary Area.
See 7.11.
    For definition and general regulations concerning danger
areas see Appendix V.

8   **Precautionary Area.** The TSSs converge on a
Precautionary Area, with a radius of 7 miles, centred on
40°28′N 73°50′W.

EAST APPROACH TO
NEW YORK HARBOR

General information

Charts 2860, 2755, 3204
Route
7.6

1   The E approach to New York Harbor leads for about
160 miles from SW of Nantucket Shoals, along the S side
of Long Island, to the entrance of New York Harbor.

Underwater topography

7.7

1   Block Canyon and Hudson Canyon, 120 miles ESE and 90 miles SE of New York Harbor entrance, indent the edge of the continental shelf and can be of assistance in determining a vessels position when approaching New York Harbor from the E or SE. See also 5.4.

Submarine exercise area

7.8

1   Submarines excrcise at times between the meridians of 69°30′W and 72°15′W. A good lookout should be kept for them when passing through these waters. For details of submarine distress signals see 1.59.

Submarine submerged transit lanes

7.9

1   Lanes used by submerged submarines run S from Block Island (41°10′N 71°35′W) for 80 miles and thence run E. Positions of these lanes are shown on charts of the US Ocean National Survey, and the times that the lanes are used are published in local Notice to Mariners. When the lanes are in use by submarines, ships should not tow submerged objects in them.

Pilotage

7.10

1   See 7.48 and 7.89.

Traffic regulations

7.11

1   **Regulated navigation area.** See 7.5.

Security zone. See 7.5.

Former mined area. A former mined area charted as a danger area is centred 1½ miles SE of Ambrose Light (7.13). The area is open to unrestricted surface navigation, but all vessels are cautioned not to anchor, dredge, trawl, lay cables or to carry out similar types of operation owing to the residual danger of mines on the bottom.

Currents

7.12

1   The predominant current between Nantucket Shoals and New York Harbor is a branch of the Labrador Current which flows SW and is strongest in the winter.

Directions

(continued from 5.8)

Principal marks

7.13

1   **Landmarks:**

    Fire Island Light (40°38′N 73°13′W) (7.21).

    Water tower (40°36′N 73°31′W).

    Tank (40°36′N 73°36′W).

2   **Major lights:**

    Montauk Point Light (41°04′N 71°51′W) (6.13).

    Fire Island Light — as above.

    Ambrose Light (tower on red square with name on side) (40°27′N 73°48′W).

Other aids to navigation

7.14

1   **Racons:**

    NA Light-buoy (40°26′N 73°11′W).

    Ambrose Light (40°27′N 73°48′W).

    S Light-buoy (40°27′N 73°55′W) (7.109).

    Sandy Hook Channel Common Front Light (40°29′N 74°00′W) (7.109).

    HA Light-buoy (40°08′N 73°21′W).

2   See *Admiralty List of Radio Signals Volume 2* for details.

Approaches

7.15

1   **Approach from E.** From the vicinity of 40°33′N 70°15′W at the W end of the TSS S of Nantucket Shoals, the approach to New York Harbor leads W through the Shipping Safety Fairway (7.5) to the Precautionary Area in the entrance of New York Harbor, passing (with positions relative to Ambrose Light (40°27′N 73°48′W)):

2   N of NA Light-buoy (special) (28 miles E), which lies 5 miles within the separation zone between the two traffic lanes of the E TSS, thence:

    S of a dangerous wreck (14 miles ENE), thence:

    N of NB Light-buoy (special) (7 miles E), which marks the W end of the E TSS, and:

    S of a dangerous wreck (7 miles E).

3   Thence into the Precautionary Area.

Approach from SE from seaward is through the SE TSS passing NE of HA Light-Buoy (special) (28 miles SE) which lies within the separation zone between the two traffic lanes of the SE TSS.

Thence NW into the Precautionary Area.

(Directions continue for New York Harbor at 7.107)

SOUTH COAST OF LONG ISLAND

General information

Charts 2754, 2755

Description

7.16

1   The S coast of Long Island lies between Montauk Point (41°04′N 71°52′W) and Rockaway Point, at the entrance to New York Harbor, 100 miles WSW. From seaward this coast presents few prominent features.

Routes

7.17

1   **Inshore route.** A route, keeping clear of charted obstructions, leads about 2 to 3 miles offshore in depths of not less than 11 m (36 ft).

Traffic regulations

7.18

1   **Regulated navigation area.** See 7.5.

Fish traps and fish havens

7.19

1   **Fish traps** extend up to 1½ miles from the coast in places and the outer limits to the areas in which they are to be found are shown on the charts.

2   **Fish havens,** obstructions artificially placed to attract fish and usually marked by buoys, are situated near the mouths of inlets and their positions are shown on the charts. The least depth over these obstructions ranges between 12·2 and 15·2 m (40 and 50 ft), with the exception of one haven 4½ miles E of Rockaway Point, which has a least depth of 7·0 m (23 ft) over it.

Rescue

7.20

1   Coast Guard stations are situated at Montauk Point (41°04′·3N 71°56′·1W), Shinnecock (40°51′·0N 72°30′·3W), Moriches (40°47′·3N 72°45′·0W), Fire Island (40°37′·5N 73°15′·6W), Jones Beach (40°35′·4N 73°33′·4W) and Rockaway (40°34′·1N 73°53′·1W).

Directions
(continued from 5.15)

Principal marks
7.21

1 **Landmarks:**
   Fire Island Light (40°38′N 73°13′W).
   Water tower (40°36′N 73°30′W).
   Tank (40°36′N 73°36′W).

2 **Major lights:**
   Montauk Point Light (41°04′N 71°51′W) (6.13).
   Fire Island Light — as above.
   Ambrose Light (40°27′N 73°48′W) (7.13).
   Sandy Hook Light (40°28′N 74°00′W) (7.107).

Other aids to navigation
7.22

1 **Racon:**
   MP Light-buoy (safe water) (41°02′N 71°46′W).
   See *Admiralty List of Radio Signals Volume 2* for details.

Montauk Point to Rockaway Point
7.23

1   From a position in the vicinity of MP Light-buoy (safe water) (41°02′N 71°46′W) the inshore route along the S shore of Long Island leads WSW, passing (with positions relative to Shinnecock Light (40°51′N 72°29′W)):
   SSE of Montauk Shoal (31 miles ENE), which lies 2½ miles SSE of Montauk Point, thence:
   Clear of a dangerous wreck (28 miles ENE), thence:

2   NNW of a dangerous wreck (24 miles E), thence:
   SSE of Shinnecock Light (red framework tower) marking the entrance to Shinnecock Bay (7.27) and the approaches to Shinnecock Canal, which leads into Great Peconic Bay (6.70). SH Light-buoy (safe water) is moored 1½ miles S of the entrance. Thence:

3   SSE of a beacon (7 miles WSW), thence:
   SSE of E Breakwater Head No 2 Light (framework tower) (13½ miles WSW), which marks the entrance to Moriches Inlet (7.28). M Light-buoy (safe water) is moored about 1½ miles S of the entrance.

4   The route continues WSW, passing (with positions relative to Fire Island Light (40°38′N 73°13′W)):
   SSE of Fire Island Light (7.21), thence:
   SSE of Democrat Point (4 miles W), which forms the S side of the entrance to Fire Island Inlet (7.29), thence:
   SSE of a dangerous wreck (16½ miles WSW), thence:

5   SSE of JI Light-buoy (safe water) (18 miles WSW), which is moored 1½ miles S of the entrance to Jones Inlet (7.30), thence:
   S of ER Light-buoy (safe water) (26 miles W), close NNE of the outer limit of the Precautionary Area. This light-buoy is moored 1 mile SW of East Rockaway Inlet. Thence into the Precautionary Area.

(Directions continue at 7.107)

Jamaica Bay

Charts 2755, 3204 (see 1.17)
General information
7.24

1   Jamaica Bay (40°37′N 73°50′W) is on the S shore of Long Island and lies between Rockaway Beach on the S and Barren Island on the W. The bay is much obstructed by numerous marshy islands and shoals, with narrow channels between them. Commercial traffic in the bay consists of tankers, tugs and barges. The bay is extensively used by pleasure craft.

2   **Traffic regulations.** Safety and security zones have been established within approximately 100 and 200 yards of John F. Kennedy Airport.
   For definition and general regulations concerning safety and security zones see Appendix V.

3   **Vertical clearance.** A road bridge with a vertical lift span crosses Rockaway Inlet. The bridge has a vertical clearance of 17 m (55 ft) with the span down and 46·3 m (152 ft) when it is up.
   Rescue. Coast Guard station is situated on the N side of Rockaway Beach, 2½ miles E of Rockaway Point.

Limiting conditions
7.25

1   **Depths.** Rockaway Inlet entrance channel has mid-channel depths of about 4·6 m (15 ft) or more. Channels and basins in the bay have been dredged to project depths of 3·7 to 6·1 m (12 to 20 ft).
   Ice is a problem, mainly in the tributaries and basins, from early January to the middle of March.

Rockaway Inlet
7.26

1   Rockaway Inlet, the entrance to Jamaica Bay, lies between Rockaway Beach on the S, and the E part of Coney Island (7.108), known as Manhattan Beach, and Barren Island, on the N. The inlet is obstructed by a shifting sand bar, over which there is a buoyed channel (7.25).

2   The entrance is marked by No 2 Light-buoy (starboard hand), which lies 7 cables S of No 4 Rockaway Breakwater Light (red triangle on framework tower on piles). This light lies at the head of the breakwater extending from Rockaway Point at the W end of Rockaway Beach.

3   There are a number of wrecks and obstructions in the approaches to the inlet, the positions of which can best be seen on the chart.

Minor anchorages and harbours

Chart 2754 (see 1.17)
Shinnecock Bay
7.27

1   **General information.** Shinnecock Bay (40°52′N 72°28′W) is situated 30 miles WSW of Montauk Point and lies at the E end of the Long Island Intracoastal Waterway.
   Entrances. The bay is entered from the Atlantic through Shinnecock Inlet and from Great Peconic Bay (6.70) through Shinnecock Canal. Shinnecock Light (7.23) stands on the W side of the inlet.

2   **Caution.** Tidal streams through Shinnecock Inlet and Shinnecock Canal can be dangerous and the area is only used by small craft.

Moriches Bay
7.28

1   **General information.** Moriches Bay (40°47′N 72°44′W) is entered through Moriches Inlet, which lies 13 miles WSW of Shinnecock Inlet. Moriches Bay is connected to Shinnecock Bay by the Quogue Canal and Quantuck Canal which form part of the Long Island Intracoastal Canal.
   Caution. The entrance to Moriches Inlet between the breakwaters is subject to frequent change and attempts to navigate the inlet should not be made without recent local knowledge. The area is only used by small craft.

Charts 2754, 2755 (see 1.17)

Great South Bay

7.29

1   **General information.** Great South Bay extends from Bellport Bay (40°45'N 72°55'W) on the E to South Oyster Bay on the W and is about 20 miles long and 4 miles across at its widest part. The bay is separated from the Atlantic by Fire Island. Great South Beach, on which stand a number of resorts, forms the S shore of this island.

2   **Entrances.** The bay is entered from the Atlantic through Fire Island Inlet (40°38'N 73°18'W) and is connected to Moriches Bay by Narrow Bay, which forms part of the Long Island Intracoastal Waterway. It can also be entered from the W through Hempstead Bay (7.30).

3   **Caution.** Fire Island Inlet is subject to frequent change and buoys are moved accordingly. Mariners are warned to be beware of extreme tidal turbulence especially during times of tidal change. Navigation of the inlet is extremely difficult even with relatively calm seas, and for small craft it can be extremely dangerous. During heavy weather the entrance is usually obstructed by breakers.

4   **Ice** restricts navigation in the bay from early January to the middle of March, but endeavours are made to keep some of the channels clear.

Chart 2755 (see 1.17)

Hempstead Bay

7.30

1   **General information.** Hempstead Bay lies between the W end of Great South Bay and East Rockaway Inlet (40°35'N 73°45'W) and is separated from the Atlantic by Jones Beach and Long Beach. The bay has many areas of marshy ground and low-lying islands, separated by channels and inlets, which are marked by aids to navigation.

2   **Jones Inlet** (40°35'N 73°35'W) is the principal entrance to the inside passages and towns of Hempstead Bay.

    The bay is mainly used by fishing and pleasure craft.

SOUTH APPROACH TO NEW YORK HARBOR

General information

Chart 2755 (see 1.17)

Route

7.31

1   The final approach to New York Harbor from the S leads for about 40 miles along the New Jersey coast from the S end of the TSS W of Barnegat Inlet (39°46'N 74°06'W) (7.40) to the Precautionary Area in the entrance of New York Harbor.

Topography

7.32

1   The coast between Barnegat Inlet and Sandy Hook (7.102), 40 miles N, is low and sandy. For 20 miles N of Barnegat Inlet to Bay Head, the coast is formed by Island Beach which separates Barnegat Bay from the Atlantic. There is an almost continuous line of summer resorts between Bay Head (40°04'N 74°03'W) and Highlands Light, 20 miles N, the most prominent of which are Asbury Park and Long Branch, 11 and 6 miles S of Highlands Light, respectively.

Fish traps

7.33

1   Fish trap areas extend up to 1½ miles offshore between Sandy Hook and Barnegat Inlet.

Ice

7.34

1   Navigation is rarely hindered by ice along the New Jersey coast, but the inner waters are completely closed in severe winters.

Traffic regulations

7.35

1   Traffic separation scheme. See 7.5.
    Security zone. See 7.5.

Rescue

7.36

1   Coast Guard stations are situated at Barnegat (39°45'·5N 74°06'·4W), Manasquan Inlet (40°06'·2N 74°02'·2W), Shark River (40°11'·3N 74°00'·8W) and Sandy Hook (40°28'·2N 74°00'·8W).

Directions
(continued from East Coast of the United States Pilot, Volume II)

Principal marks

7.37

1   **Landmarks:**

    Disused lighthouse (abandoned) (39°46'N 74°06'W), standing on the S side of the entrance to Barnegat Inlet, consisting of a brick tower 49 m (161 ft) high, the lower part of which is white and the upper half dark red.

2   Water tower (40°04'N 74°03'W) at Bay Head.

    Highlands of Navesink (40°24'N 74°01'W), a high wooded ridge. Two brown towers stand in a cleared space at the SE end of the ridge.

    Radio Tower (40°24'N 74°03'W).

3   **Major lights:**

    Ambrose Light (40°27'N 73°48'W) (7.13).

    Sandy Hook Light (40°28'N 74°00'W) (7.107).

    Sandy Hook Point Light (40°28'·2N 74°01'·1W) (7.107) (Chart 3204).

Other aids to navigation

7.38

1   **Racon:**

    B Light-buoy (39°46'N 73°46'W).

    See *Admiralty List of Radio Signals Volume 2* for details.

Directions

7.39

1   From the vicinity of B Light-buoy (special) (39°46'N 73°46'W) which marks the S end of the separation zone of the S TSS, the coastal route leads N to the Precautionary Area centred on 40°28'N 73°50'W, through waters clear of charted dangers.

Inlets and inshore waters between Barnegat Inlet and Sandy Hook

Barnegat Inlet

7.40

1   **General information.** Barnegat Inlet (39°46'N 74°06'W) leads into Barnegat Bay and to the New Jersey Intracoastal Waterway (7.42). It is only used by small craft.

    Approaches. No 2 Light-buoy (starboard hand) lies 5 miles E and BI Light-buoy (safe water) lies 2 miles ESE of the entrance. A number of wrecks and obstructions, the positions of which are charted, lie in the approaches to the inlet.

Manasquan Inlet
7.41
1   **General information.** Manasquan Inlet (40°06′N 74°02′W) is the entrance to the Manasquan River and is the N entrance to the New Jersey Intracoastal Waterway (7.42). Manasquan River is connected to Metedeconk River at the N end of Barnegat Bay by Point Pleasant Canal, which forms part of the Intracoastal Waterway.

2   **Approaches.** 2M Light-buoy (starboard hand) lies 1 mile ESE of the entrance.

Pilotage is compulsory for foreign vessels and US vessels under register. It is available from the Sandy Hook Pilot Association; see *Admiralty List of Radio Signals Volume 6(5)* for details.

New Jersey Intracoastal Waterway
7.42
1   **General information.** New Jersey Intracoastal Waterway is a toll free passage for small craft, which leads from Manasquan Inlet, through Barnegat Bay and other bays, lagoons and thoroughfares for 118 statute miles to the entrance to Delaware Bay. It is described in *East Coast of the United States Pilot, Volume II.*

2   **Ice.** See 7.34.

Shark River Inlet
7.43
1   **General information.** Shark River Inlet (40°11′N 74°01′W) is the entrance to Shark River and lies 15 miles S of Sandy Hook. It is only used by small craft.

EAST RIVER

General information

Charts 2580, 3451, 3455
Description
7.44
1   East River is a 14 mile long tidal strait that connects Long Island Sound with Upper Bay (7.129) and separates the W end of Long Island from the New York mainland. Its E entrance is between Throgs Neck (40°48′N 73°48′W) and Willets Point, 7 cables SE, and its W entrance is between The Battery (40°42′N 74°01′W), at the S end of Manhattan Island, and Governors Island.

Depths
7.45
1   The project depth for the main channel is 10·7 m (35 ft) from Throgs Neck to the inactive New York Naval Shipyard, 2 miles from the W entrance, and thence 12·2 m (40 ft) to deep water in Upper Bay. For the latest controlling depths the charts and port authority should be consulted.

Governors Island from SW (7.44)
(Original dated 2004)

(Photograph - Airphoto - Jim Wark)

Tidal levels
7.46
1   **Mean tidal ranges** are:
>At Willets Point. 2·2 m.
>At Hell Gate. 1·6 m.
>At The Battery. 1·4 m.

Hazards
7.47
1   When proceeding through East River care should be taken to avoid fouling the dredgers and other equipment. Owing to the strength of the tidal streams and the crowded traffic the section of the river between Rikers Island (40°48′·5N 73°53′·0W) and the W entrance should not be attempted without local knowledge.

Pilotage and tugs
7.48
1   **Pilotage** is compulsory for all foreign vessels and US vessels under register. Vessels entering the Port of New York and New Jersey through Long Island Sound are boarded by the pilot for East River off Execution Rocks (40°53′N 73°44′W) (6.95). Arrangements are made 24 hours in advance through ship's agents and 24 hour and 6 hour ETAs are requested. 24 hour pilotage service is available on request.

2   Masters are requested at the time of boarding to proceed at a speed not exceeding 3 to 4 kn and provide a lee for the pilot boat.

Tugs are available from a number of towing companies. Vessels intending to employ a tug should do so before proceeding W of Rikers Island, 4 miles W of Willets Point.

Vessel traffic service
7.49
1   Vessel traffic service scheme with full radar surveillance is maintained for the control of shipping, for details, and list of reporting points, see *Admiralty List of Radio Signals Volume 6(5)* and Appendix III.

Traffic regulations
7.50
1   **Navigation Rules for US Inland Waters** apply to all waters covered in this section. See 1.47 and Appendix VII for further information.

Safety and security zones have been established within approximately 100 and 200 yards of La Guardia Airport.

2   **Security zones** are established in East River during the arrival or departure of dignitaries.

For definition and general regulations concerning safety and security zones see Appendix V.

Submarine pipelines
7.51
1   A gas pipeline, shown on the chart, is laid through Long Island Sound and East River from Northport Basin (6.271) to a position 2 cables NE of Hunts Point (7.67).

Caution. See 1.39.

Vertical clearance
7.52
1   The following fixed bridges cross East River (with positions relative to Whitestone Point (40°48′·0N 73°49′·2W)):
>Throgs Neck Bridge (1¼ miles E), with a vertical clearance of 46·3 m (152 ft) at centre of main span.

2   >Bronx-Whitestone Bridge (4 cables W), with a vertical clearance of 41·1 m (135 ft).

The following fixed bridges cross East River (with positions relative to Hallets Point (40°46′·7N 73°56′·1W)):
>Hell Gate Bridge (6 cables ENE), with a vertical clearance of 40·8 m (134 ft).

3   >Triborough Bridge (4 cables ENE), with a vertical clearance of 42·1 m (138 ft).

>Queensboro Bridge (1½ miles SW), with a vertical clearance of 39·9 m (131 ft) at the span crossing the main channel.

The following bridges cross East River (with positions relative to The Battery (40°42′N 74°01′W)):

4   >Williamsburg Bridge (2 miles ENE), with a vertical clearance of 40·5 m (133 ft).

>Manhattan Bridge (1·3 miles ENE), with a vertical clearance of 40·8 m (134 ft) and 35 m (115 ft) under a moving platform.

5   >Brooklyn Bridge (1 mile ENE), with a vertical clearance of 38·7 m (127 ft) and 33·5 m (110 ft) under moving platforms.

Rescue
7.53
1   A Coast Guard station is situated at Fort Totten on the E side of Little Bay (40°48′N 73°47′W).

Tidal streams
7.54
1   **Tidal streams.** In East River the tidal streams set E on a rising tide and W on a falling tide, which is the opposite direction to the tidal streams in Long Island Sound. The tidal streams generally follow the direction of the channel, but there are heavy swirls in Hell Gate and in the channels either side of Roosevelt Island (7.57 and 7.76).

2   See Tidal Stream tables on charts.

Directions
(continued from 6.96)

Throgs Neck to College Point
7.55
1   From between Throgs Neck (40°48′N 73°48′W) and Willets Point, on which stands Fort Totten, the channel through East River leads generally W to College Point, passing (with positions relative to Whitestone Point (40°48′·0N 73°49′·2W)):

2   >Beneath Throgs Neck Bridge (1¼ miles E), having passed at least 2 cables S of Fort Schuyler Light (black and white chequered diamond on framework tower) which stands at the head of Throgs Neck. No 48 Light-buoy (starboard hand) marks the shoal water off Throgs Neck. Thence:

3   >N of Whitestone Point Light (green square on black framework tower), standing on a small bluff, keeping to mid-channel. No 1A Buoy (port hand) is moored ½ cable N of the light and marks shoal water to the S. Thence:

Beneath Bronx-Whitestone Bridge (4 cables W), which extends SSE from Old Ferry Point to the Long Island shore opposite, thence:

4   N of College Point Reef (1½ miles W), which extends 2 cables NNE of College Point (7.68) and is marked by CP Light-beacon (green and white chequered diamond on framework tower), and:

N of No 3 Buoy (port hand) (1½ miles W).

College Point to Queensboro Bridge
7.56

1   From a position N of College Point Reef the channel through East River leads generally W and SW to Queensboro Bridge, passing (with positions relative to Lawrence Point (40°47'·4N 73°54'·6W)):

2   N of No 5 Light-buoy (port hand) (2 miles E). Vessels with a mast height of more than 38·1 m (125 ft) must keep more than ½ cable N of this buoy so as not to interfere with the glide path of La Guardia Airport (7.69). Thence:

3   Between the N shore of Rikers Island (1½ miles E), and Hunts Point (7.67) and Barretto Point on the N side of the river, thence:

N of North Brother Island (8 cables NE), the N side of which is marked by No 9 Light-beacon (green square on tower), or:

4   Through a channel between North Brother Island and South Brother Island, 1 cable S. This channel, with a controlling depth of about 7·6 m (25 ft), is marked on the N side by Nos 6 and 8 Buoys (starboard hand), and on the S side by two buoys and SB Beacon (green and white chequered diamond on framework tower). This channel is narrow and subject to strong currents and should not be used by vessels of limited manoeuvrability. Thence:

5   NW of LP Light-beacon (red and white chequered diamond on framework tower) (3 cables ENE), marking Lawrence Point Ledge. Lawrence Point, on which stands a power station, lies 3 cables WSW. Thence:

Beneath Hell Gate Bridge and Triborough Bridge (1 mile SW) and into Hell Gate.

6   **Caution.** The crooked channel, the strong tidal streams and the heavy traffic in Hell Gate make it necessary for the mariner to exercise particular caution when navigating this part of East River.

7   From the vicinity of Triborough Bridge, East River leads through Hell Gate and thence SW to Queensboro Bridge, passing (with positions relative to Gibbs Point (40°46'·1N 73°56'·4W)):

8   S of Holmes Rock and Hog Back (9 cables NNE) which lie close W of Negro Point, the S end of Wards Island. No 14 Light-beacon (red triangle on framework tower) marks Hog Back. Thence:

9   Between Mill Rock (7½ cables N), which is marked at N and S ends by Nos 1 and 16 Lights (green square on framework tower, white base and red triangle on tower, white base, respectively), and Hallets Point Light No 15 (green square on pile) (6 cables NNE), standing on Hallets Point, thence:

10   Between Horns Hook (5 cables NNW) and the grey stone tower (3 cables N) standing at the NE extremity of Roosevelt Island, thence:

Beneath the NW span of Queensboro Bridge (1 mile SW), which joins Roosevelt Island to Manhattan Island.

Queensboro Bridge to Brooklyn Bridge
7.57

1   From Queensboro Bridge the channel through East River leads SW to Upper Bay (7.129), passing (with positions relative to chimney (40°43'·6N 73°58'·4W) (Easternmost of four):

SE of 8FDR Light-buoy (1½ miles NNE), thence:

2   NW of Belmont Island (1¼ miles NNE), which lies 2½ cables SW of the S extremity of Roosevelt Island. Belmont Island Light No 17 (green square on framework tower, white base) stands on the S side of the island. Thence:

3   NW of B Light-buoy (preferred channel to starboard) (9 cables NNE), which is moored 3 cables SW of Belmont Island Light, and W of the entrance to Newtown Creek (7.77). At this position the main channel of East River crosses from the W side of the river to the E side. Depths of 7·3 m (24 ft) extend as much as 2 cables from the piers on the W side.

4   Thence the alignment (161°) of Poorhouse Flats Leading Lights (green rectangle, red stripe, on framework towers) (5 cables ESE), leads SSE through the best water (see caution), thence:

Beneath Williamsburg Bridge (8 cables S), Manhattan Bridge (1½ miles SW), and Brooklyn Bridge (1¾ miles SW) which cross the W part of East River. See 7.52.

Thence into Upper Bay.

5   **Caution.** Between Hunters Point (40°44'·3N 73°57'·7W) and Brooklyn Bridge shallow draught vessels normally keep to the W side of the channel whether N or S-bound, thereby reserving the E side of the channel for deep draught vessels. Vessels transiting East River should be aware of this practice and anticipate N-bound shallow draught vessels crossing from W to E in the vicinity of Newtown Creek and E to W in the vicinity of Corlears Hook (40°42'·7N 73°58'·6W).

(Directions are given for Hudson River at 7.135, and for Kill van Kull and Newark Bay at 7.166)

Harlem River

Chart 3451 (see 1.17)
General information
7.58

1   Harlem River, which joins East River in Hell Gate (40°47'N 73°56'W), extends about 7 miles N and connects with the Hudson River through Spuyten Duyvil Creek. The channel through Harlem River is narrow, tortuous, and only navigable by powered vessels. Traffic is heavy in the Harlem River.

Limiting conditions
7.59

1   **Depths.** In general there is a minimum depth of 4·3 m (14 ft) as far as the Hudson River, but care must be taken to avoid several isolated 3·4 to 4 m (11 to 13 ft) spots.

2   **Vertical clearance.** There are more than a dozen fixed and opening bridges over the Harlem River. The minimum vertical clearance under closed bridges is 7·3 m (24 ft) except for the rail swing bridge over the entrance from the Hudson River, where the clearance is only 1·5 m (5 ft). This rail bridge is kept open except for the passage of trains.

3   Vessels with heights too great to pass under the closed bridges should make the passage against the tidal stream.

Clearance under raised vertical lift spans and fixed bridges exceeds 30 m (100 ft).

7.60

1   **Tidal streams.** The tidal streams in Harlem River run S from Hudson River to East River while the E going current is running in Hell Gate. The velocity of the current is 2 kn or more in the narrower parts of the river.

Side channels, anchorages and harbours between Throgs Neck and Brooklyn Bridge

Charts 2580, 3451, 3455 (see 1.17)

Anchorage regulations

7.61

1   For recommendations regarding entry into certain anchorages within New York Harbor see 7.3.

2   The following regulations apply to the anchorages within East River and elsewhere within New York Harbor:

No vessel in excess of 244 m (800 ft) in length overall or 12·2 m (40 ft) draught may anchor unless it informs the Captain of the Port at least 48 hours prior to entering Ambrose Channel.

3   Except in cases of great emergency, no vessels shall be anchored in the navigable waters of the Port of New York outside the anchorage areas established, nor anchor in a cable or pipeline area shown on the chart.

Anchors of all vessels must be placed well within the anchorage areas so that no portion of the hull or rigging shall extend outside the boundaries of the anchorage area.

4   Any vessel anchoring under circumstances of great emergency outside the anchorage areas must be placed near the edge of the channel in such a position as not to interfere with the navigation of the channel.

No vessel shall be navigated within the limits of an anchorage at a speed exceeding 6 kn when in the vicinity of an anchored vessel.

5   Any vessel prohibited by these rules from anchoring in a specific anchorage because of the vessel's length or draught may anchor in the anchorage with permission from the Captain of the Port.

Little Bay

7.62

1   Little Bay lies on the S side of East River between Willets Point (40°47'·8N 73°46'·7W) and Cryders Point, 5 cables W. It is used as an anchorage by small craft.

Fort Schuyler

7.63

1   Fort Schuyler, which is used as a base for a nautical school, stands on the outer end of Throgs Neck. A wharf on the SW side of the fort has depths alongside of 7·6 m.

Between Throgs Neck and Old Ferry Point

7.64

1   The bight on the N side of East River between Throgs Neck and Old Ferry Point (40°48'·3N 73°49'·9W) affords anchorage, with good holding ground, in depths of 4·6 to 13·7 m (15 to 45 ft). The water shoals abruptly from depths of 5·5 m (18 ft) to depths of about 1·2 m (4 ft), 3 cables from the shore.

2   **Caution.** The gas pipeline (7.51), as shown on the chart, laid through East River passes very close to the S limit of this anchorage and mariners should bear this in mind when selecting an anchorage position. See 1.39.

Westchester Creek

7.65

1   Westchester Creek, on the N side of the East River, is entered through a dredged channel between Clason Point (40°48'·3N 73°50'·9W) and Old Ferry Point. The channel leads N for 2¼ miles to the town of Westchester and is buoyed for 1 mile above the entrance. Waterborne traffic is mainly in petroleum products, sand and gravel, and crushed rocks.

2   **Depths.** In 2003 there were mid-channel controlling depths of 1·6 m (5½ ft) to the bascule bridge, thence 3·4 m, (11 ft) to just below the head of the project.

Vertical clearance. Three fixed bridges and one bascule bridge cross the creek at Unionport, 1½ miles above the entrance. The fixed bridges have a least vertical clearance of 15·9 m (52 ft) and the bascule bridge a clearance of 4·3 m (14 ft).

Bronx River

7.66

1   Bronx River, on the N side of the East River, is entered through a dredged channel 1½ miles W of Old Ferry Point. The channel leads 2¼ miles NW to the head of navigation at East 172nd Street. Waterborne traffic on the river consists mainly of sand, gravel and crushed rock.

2   **Depths.** For the latest controlling depths the charts and port authority should be consulted.

Vertical clearance. Four bridges cross the river. The least vertical clearances are 5·5 m (18 ft) at the lower end and 2·4 m (8 ft) at the upper end.

Hunts Point

7.67

1   Hunts Point (40°48'·1N 73°52'·5W) is on the N side of East River opposite Flushing Bay.

A wharf, with reported depths alongside of 5·2 to 7·3 m alongside, extends 3 cables NE from the point.

2   **Caution.** The gas pipeline (7.51), as shown on the chart, laid through East River passes through this anchorage and mariners should bear this in mind when selecting an anchorage position. See 1.39.

College Point

7.68

1   The town of College Point lies to the S of the point (40°47'·6N 73°51'·2W) of the same name. The wharves on the W side of the town have depths alongside of up to 3 m.

Flushing Bay

7.69

1   Flushing Bay is entered between College Point (40°47'·6N 73°51'·2W), and Rikers Island and La Guardia Airport, 8 cables SW. Flushing Creek enters the head of the bay 2 miles SSE of its entrance.

Channel. A dredged channel, marked by buoys and light-buoys, leads SSE for 1¾ miles from within the entrance of the bay to a turning basin at the entrance to Flushing Creek.

2   **Traffic regulations.** Safety and security zones have been established within approximately 100 and 200 yards of La Guardia Airport.

For definition and general regulations concerning safety and security zones see Appendix V.

3   **Restricted area.** Part of the channel, 1¼ miles from the entrance and lying 91 m (300 ft) either side of the extension of the NW-SE runway of La Guardia Airport, is a restricted area in which vessels with a height of more than 10·7 m (35 ft) are prohibited when visibility is less than one mile.

4   **Ice** generally obstructs Flushing Bay and Flushing Creek during part of January and February.

  Depths. In 2005 the controlling depth in the bay channel was 3·0 m (9·8 ft) (4·3 m (14¼ ft) in mid-channel) to the turning basin thence 3·1 m (10¼ ft) in mid-channel as far as the first bridge in Flushing Creek. In 2005 the turning basin had controlling depths of 2·5 to 4·6 m (8¼ to 15 ft).

5   **Anchorages.** A general anchorage and a number of special anchorages are situated in Flushing Bay, the positions and limits of which are shown on the chart. See 1.49.

Rikers Island Anchorage
7.70

1   A general anchorage, which is frequently used and has depths of 6·4 to 12·2 m (21 to 40 ft), lies between the S side of the main channel and the flats off the N side of Rikers Island.

South Brother Island Channel and adjacent waters
7.71

1   **South Brother Island Channel**, marked by buoys and light-buoys, leads from the deep water E of North Brother Island (40°48′N 73°54′W), and along the W side of Rikers Island to a turning basin on the W side of Bowery Bay. Two terminals are situated close to the turning basin.

2   **Depths.** In 2001 the controlling depth of the South Brother Channel was 7·7 m (25·3 ft). The controlling depth in the turning basin was 10 m (33 ft).

3   **Vessel Mast Heights.** Vessels using the South Brother Channel should ballast prior to entry and are cautioned that mast heights in excess of 38 m (125 ft) may penetrate the glide path of the NW–SE runway of La Guardia Airport. If mast heights cannot be lowered below this height, the Air Traffic Control Tower should be contacted before entry into the channel or departure from the terminal.
7.72

1   **Rikers Island Channel** leads E from the turning basin along the S side of Rikers Island. Its E end is closed by a runway of La Guardia Airport and its lighted approach.

  Bowery Bay is a shallow bay lying to the S of Rikers Island Channel.
7.73

1   **Other channels.** Bowery Bay may be approached from the NW by a channel that passes between South Brother Island (40°47′·8N 73°53′·9W) and Lawrence Point Ledge, 3 cables SW. The channel is marked by No 2 Buoy (starboard hand) and by No 3 Light-beacon (green square on framework tower) which stands on South Brother Island Ledge.

2   **Vertical clearance.** A fixed bridge crosses Rikers Island Channel and Bowery Bay joining Rikers Island to the Borough of Queens, New York. The bridge has a vertical clearance over the channel of 15·9 m (52 ft) for a width of 38 m (125 ft).

Port Morris
7.74

1   Port Morris (40°48′·0N 73°54′·5W), on the N shore of East River, is a rail terminal for car ferries. There are also oil terminals.

Hallets Cove
7.75

1   Hallets Cove (40°46′·2N 73°56′·2W) is situated 2½ cables SE of the NE end of Roosevelt Island (7.56) and is the only recommended anchorage in East River, W of Rikers Island.

Channel east of Roosevelt Island
7.76

1   The channel E of Roosevelt Island is narrower than the main channel, which passes W of the island, and has a controlling depth of about 5·8 m (19 ft). The currents in this channel are strong (7.54).

  Vertical clearance. Two bridges cross this channel:

2   36th Avenue Lift Bridge; which has a vertical clearance of 12·2 m (40 ft) when closed and 30·2 m (99 ft) when open.

    Queensboro Bridge, E span; which is a fixed bridge with a vertical clearance of 40·5 m (133 ft).

Newtown Creek
7.77

1   Newtown Creek is entered on the E side of East River close S of Hunters Point (7.57). The creek extends 3¼ miles E and S and has several short tributaries or basins. English Kills forms the final 8 cables of the creek.

  Traffic is fairly heavy and consists mainly of petroleum products, sand, gravel and crushed rock.

2   **Depths.** The project depth is 7 m (23 ft) to Maspeth Creek, 2¼ miles from the East River, then 6·1 m (20 ft) for the next 7½ cables and then 3·6 m (12 ft) to the head of the project. For the latest controlling depths the charts and port authority should be consulted.

3   **Vertical clearance.** A number of fixed and bascule bridges, with a minimum vertical clearance of 25·3 m (83 ft) with the bascule bridges open, cross Newtown Creek and its tributaries.

NEW YORK HARBOR AND ADJACENT WATERS

GENERAL INFORMATION

Charts 2860, 2755
Scope of section
7.78

1   This section describes the waterways, anchorages and principal port facilities of:

    Lower Bay (7.102) and its entrance channels.

    The Narrows (7.129), Upper Bay (7.129) and Hudson River Channel (7.138).

2   Arthur Kill (7.147).

    Kill van Kull (7.161).

    Newark Bay (7.169).

  East River, the approach from Long Island Sound, is described at 7.44.

Position
7.79

1   New York Harbor (40°41′N 74°02′W) is situated at the mouth of the Hudson River between the W end of Long Island and the coast of New Jersey.

Function
7.80

1   New York Harbor, which is a spacious landlocked harbour, is the principal entrance by water to New York City and the surrounding New Jersey ports and is the site of the Port of New York and New Jersey.

The Port of New York and New Jersey is one of the great commercial centres of the world and the most important seaport on the E coast of the United States.

2   New York City, which in 2005 had an estimated population of 8 143 197, is the largest city in the United States.

The city is comprised of five boroughs, each of which is also a separate county: Manhattan on Manhattan Island; Bronx, lying NE of Manhattan and fronting Hudson River and East River; Brooklyn and Queens on Long Island and Richmond, which embraces the whole of Staten Island.

Traffic
7.81

1   In 2005 the port was used by 1606 vessels with a total deadweight 220 025 452 tonnes.

Port Authority
7.82

1   The Port Authority of New York and New Jersey serves as the joint state port development, operations and maintenance organisation. The Port Authority administers piers in Manhattan, Brooklyn, Hoboken, Port Newark and Port Elizabeth.

Address: 225 Park Avenue South, New York, NY 10003.
Internet: www.panynj.gov

2   The New York City Department of Ports and Terminals administers the piers along the New York waterfront within the city limits.

Limiting conditions

Controlling depth
7.83

1   The main channel from the sea to the deep water terminals in the Hudson River has a project depth of 13·7 m (45 ft). The depths of other channels are given in the appropriate section.

Tidal levels
7.84

1   At Sandy Hook and also at The Battery mean spring range about 1·6 m; mean neap range about 0·9 m. See information in *Admiralty Tide Tables.*

Ice
7.85

1   Navigation in New York Harbor is not restricted by ice. The main channels do not freeze over and any ice in the smaller waterways is well broken up by tugs and general traffic.

Fresh water ice in large floes is brought down during periods of thaw and occasionally there are large accumulations of ice at Spuyten Duyvil where the Harlem River joins the Hudson River. These conditions may obstruct low powered vessels and tows.

Arrival information

Vessel traffic service
7.86

1   Vessel traffic service scheme with full radar surveillance is maintained for the control of shipping, for details, and list of reporting points, see *Admiralty List of Radio Signals Volume 6(5)* and Appendix III.

Anchorage areas and regulations
7.87

1   The waters of New York Harbor, outside the channels, have been divided into a number of general anchorage areas, the limits of which are shown on the charts.
7.88

1   For recommendations and general regulations that apply to the anchorages within New York Harbor and adjacent waters see 7.3 and 7.61. Further specific details concerning these anchorage areas are given in the relevant sections.

Pilotage
7.89

1   Pilotage is compulsory for all foreign vessels and US vessels under register. Vessels entering Port of New York and New Jersey through Lower Bay are embarked in the triangular shaped cruising area W of Ambrose Light. The limits of this area are shown on the chart.

2   The pilot boats have a black hull and white superstructure, with the name "PILOT No 1" or "PILOT No 2" in yellow on each side, and fly a blue flag. Boarding is made from a smaller boat.

Pilots are arranged in advance by ship's agents. A 24 hour advance notice of ETA is requested with a 3 hour update.

3   Pilots for US registered vessels in coastwise trade board in the same area or 1½ miles SW of Ambrose Light. The pilot boats have a blue hull and white superstructure, with the word "PILOT" in blue on the front of the wheelhouse. They maintain a listening watch on VHF 1½ hours before a vessel's ETA.

4   For vessels entering New York Harbor from Long Island Sound through East River, see 7.48.

Traffic regulations
7.90

1   **Navigation Rules for US Inland Waters** apply to all waters within a line joining East Rockaway Inlet Light (40°35′N 73°45′W) and Sandy Hook Light (40°28′N 74°00′W), 13 miles SW. See 1.47 and Appendix VII for further information.

Times of entry
7.91

1   The following are recommended times of entry for starting from Ambrose Light in normal weather conditions.

Draught of vessel	Time after HW Sandy Hook
14·2 m (46½ ft)	½ hour
14 m (46 ft)	½ to 1 hour
13·9 m (45½ ft)	½ to 1½ hours
13·6 m (44½ ft)	½ to 2½ hours
13·3 m (43½ ft)	½ to 3½ hours
13 m (42½ ft)	½ to 5 hours
12·2 m (40 ft)	½ to 5 hours

2   All vessels in the above categories should pass through the Narrows before LW slack at the Narrows.

The recommended times listed above are guidelines only. Weather conditions, tides, and ship's capabilities must also be taken into consideration.

Harbour

Charts 3456, 3457, 3459, 3458
General layout
7.92

1   The main harbour is divided into Lower Bay (7.102) and Upper Bay (7.129) by The Narrows (7.129), a passage 6 cables wide. The entrance to Lower Bay is obstructed by an extensive bar, intersected by several channels, the principal of which is Ambrose Channel (7.108). From the inshore end of Ambrose Channel, the main channel leads through Lower Bay and The Narrows into Upper Bay and the mouth of the Hudson River.

2   Two channels, Arthur Kill (7.147) and Kill van Kull (7.161) which separate Staten Island from the New Jersey mainland, lead N from the W part of Lower Bay and W from Upper Bay, respectively, to Newark Bay (7.169).

East River (7.44), a channel leading from Long Island Sound, enters the NE part of Upper Bay.

Tidal streams
7.93

1   **Lower Bay.** The in-going stream generally sets parallel to the lower straight section of Ambrose Channel and tends to continue in that direction where the channel turns towards The Narrows, setting more or less diagonally across the upper straight section of Ambrose Channel.

2   **Upper Bay.** In the channel N of Governors Island the action of the tidal stream is very erratic and great care is necessary when navigating a large vessel. It is reported that the most dangerous conditions occur near the end of the in-going stream about 2½ hours after HW at Sandy Hook. At this time the tidal stream is setting N in the Hudson River and W from the East River.

3   The effect of the meeting of these two streams, known locally as *The Spider*, on a large vessel coming from S and turning E into East River, is to make her sheer to starboard towards the shoal ground off the N end of Governors Island. Coming from N in Hudson River the same effect tends to prevent a ship from turning and to cause her to overrun her course.

For detailed information see Tidal Stream tables on the charts.

Climate information
7.94

1   See 1.159 and 1.160.

Basins and berths

Waterfront facilities
7.95

1   The Port of New York and New Jersey has over 1100 waterfront facilities which are grouped into a number of terminals. Many of these facilities are privately owned and operated, and the remainder are owned or operated by railways serving the port, the Port Authority of New York and New Jersey, the city of New York, the States of New York and New Jersey, the Federal Government or other municipalities.

Terminals
7.96

1   **Passenger terminal.** The main passenger terminal is on the E side of the Hudson River above The Battery.

Container terminals are situated throughout the port, but principally at Elizabeth, Newark, Jersey City and Weehawken on the W side of the Hudson River. Other terminals are at Howland Hook, Staten Island and Brooklyn.

2   **General cargo terminals** are situated throughout the port, but principally along the E side of Upper Bay, on the East River and at Port Newark.

Oil terminals and other liquid cargo facilities are situated along Arthur Kill, on the Passaic and Hackensack Rivers and along Newtown Creek, Brooklyn.

Further details of the various terminals are given in the appropriate sections that follow.

Port services

Repairs
7.97

1   The Port of New York and New Jersey has extensive facilities for making all types of repairs to vessels.

Dry dock facilities. The main facilities are:

Brooklyn. Graving dock: length 332·8 m; width 43·6 m.

2   Brooklyn. Largest floating dock: lift 16 000 tonnes; length 176·8 m; width 30·5 m.

Staten Island. Largest floating dock: lift 8 000 tonnes; length 147·8 m; width 35·6 m.

Salvage. Several salvage companies perform all types of salvage work.

Other facilities
7.98

1   **Oily waste.** Facilities for the disposal of oily waste are available at many of the terminals in the Port of New York and New Jersey.

Deratting and issue of deratting exemption certificates. See 1.99.

Hospitals.

Supplies
7.99

1   Fuel alongside or by barge; fresh water; provisions and stores.

Communications
7.100

1   Three airports handling both domestic and international flights.

Rescue
7.101

1   Coast Guard stations are situated as follows:

Coast Guard Air Station Brooklyn, Floyd Bennett Airfield (40°35'·3N 73°53'·5W) on Barren Island.

E side of Sandy Hook Bay, 5 cables ESE of Sandy
Hook Point Light (40°28'·2N 74°01'·1W).
New York Coast Guard station (40°41'·5N 74°01'·0W)
on N side of Governors Island.

ENTRANCE CHANNELS AND LOWER BAY

General information

Chart 3204, 3459, 3458
Description
7.102

1   Lower Bay is the part of New York Harbor which is
entered between the N end of Sandy Hook and Rockaway
Point, 5¼ miles NE and extends W to Raritan River (7.116)
and N to The Narrows (7.129).

   Much of the Lower Bay is shoal, with depths of less
than 5·5 m (18 ft). A number of buoyed channels lead
through the bay.

Main channel depths
7.103

1   **Main entrance channels**. Lower Bay is entered from
the sea through two main channels:

   Ambrose Channel (7.108) is the most important
channel. This channel, which leads NW, then N,
towards The Narrows and Upper Bay, has a project
depth of 13·7 m (45 ft).

2   Sandy Hook Channel (7.109) is a secondary channel
which connects with Raritan Bay Channel and
other channels within the bay. It has a project
depth of 10·7 m (35 ft).

   Other main channels:

3   Raritan Bay Channel (7.110), which leads from the
inshore end of Sandy Hook Channel to the W part
of Lower Bay, has a project depth of 10·7 m
(35 ft).

4   Chapel Hill Channel (7.111), which leads N from the
E end of Raritan Bay Channel, has a project depth
of 9·1 m (30 ft).

   For the latest controlling depths the charts and port
authority should be consulted.

Measured distance
7.104

1   Off Atlantic Highlands (40°25'N 74°02'W) there is a
measured distance. The range markers are reported to be
difficult to identify.
   Length: 1 nautical mile.
   Running track: 110°–290°.

Fish trap areas
7.105

1   Several fish trap areas, the limits of which are shown on
the chart, are situated in Lower Bay. Mariners are warned
that numerous uncharted stakes and fishing structures, some
submerged, may be found in these areas.

Natural conditions
7.106

1   **Local magnetic anomaly.** Differences of as much as 5°
from the normal variation have been reported in Lower Bay
in the vicinity of 40°29'·6N 74°04'·2W on the N side of
Raritan Bay Channel.
   Tidal streams. See 7.93.

Directions for main channels
(continued from 7.15 and 7.23)

Principal marks
7.107

1   **Landmarks:**
   Highlands of Navesink (40°24'N 74°01'W) (7.37).
   Radio Tower (40°24'·2N 74°02'·6W).
   Tower (40°30'·5N 74°12'·8W).

2   **Major lights:**
   Ambrose Light (40°27'N 73°48'W) (7.13).
   Sandy Hook Light (40°27'·7N 74°00'·1W).
   Sandy Hook Point Light (black and white chequered
diamond on framework tower) (40°28'·2N
74°01'·1W).

3   Romer Shoal Light (white conical tower, brown top,
black round base) (40°30'·8N 74°00'·8W).
   West Bank Light (brown conical tower, black round
base) (40°32'·3N 74°02'·6W).
   Coney Island Light (white square framework tower)
(40°34'·6N 74°00'·7W).
   Staten Island Light (8-sided brick tower, grey base)
(40°34'·6N 74°08'·5W).

Ambrose Channel
7.108

1   **Leading lights:**
   Front light. West Bank Light (40°32'·3N 74°02'·6W)
(7.107).
   Rear light. Staten Island Light (7.107) (5 miles from
front light).

2   From the vicinity of Ambrose Light (40°27'N 73°48'W)
the alignment (297°) of these lights leads WNW through
the outer reach of Ambrose Channel, between East Bank
and Romer Shoal, passing (with positions relative to West
Bank Light):
   NNE of 'A' Light-buoy (safe water) (7½ miles ESE)
which marks the seaward entrance to the channel,
thence:

3   Between light-buoys (lateral) which mark the limits
of the channel, and:
   NNE of Romer Shoal Light (2 miles SE) (7.107).
   Thence the channel leads NNW passing:
   ENE of West Bank Light, thence:

4   ENE of Swinburne Island (1¾ miles N) and Hoffman
Island (2½ miles N) which lie on West Bank. Both
islands have houses on them. And:
   WSW of Norton Point (2¾ miles NNE), the W
extremity of Coney Island, on which stands Coney
Island Light (7.107).
   Thence through The Narrows (7.129).
   Caution. Numerous wrecks and obstructions lie in the
approaches to Ambrose Channel; the chart is the best
guide.

(Directions continue at 7.135)

Sandy Hook Channel
7.109

1   **East Leading Lights:**
   Common front light (green rectangle, black stripe on
SE face of framework tower, concrete base)
(40°29'·3N 73°59'·6W).
   Rear light (similar structure) (8½ cables from front
light).

2   From the vicinity of S Light-buoy (safe water)
(40°26'·5N 73°55'·0W) the alignment (308°) of these lights
leads NW for 3 miles through the E section of Sandy Hook
Channel, which is marked by light-buoys (lateral), to a

position between No 7 and No 8 Light-buoys (port and starboard hand respectively) where the channel turns WSW passing S of the front leading light.

3   **Main Leading Lights:**

    Common front light (red rectangle, white stripe on SW face of framework tower, concrete base) (40°29′·3N 73°59′·6W).

    Rear light (similar structure) (282 m from front light).

4   From a position NE of the N point of Sandy Hook the alignment (067½°), astern, of these lights leads WSW through the W reach of Sandy Hook Channel into Lower Bay, passing between Flynns Knoll (40°30′N 74°02′W) and the N shore of Sandy Hook. This reach is marked by light-buoys (lateral).

Charts 3459, 3458
Raritan Bay Channel
7.110

1   Raritan Bay Channel, which is dredged and marked by lights, light-buoys and buoys (lateral), consists of a number of reaches and bends that lead from the inshore end of Sandy Hook Channel to the S end of Arthur Kill (7.147), 11 miles W.

2   **Raritan Bay East Reach and West Reach.** From the vicinity of 40°28′·5N 74°02′·0W at the inshore end of Sandy Hook Channel, the E and W reaches of Raritan Bay Channel lead WNW to a position off Seguine Point (40°30′·6N 74°11′·8W) on the S shore of Staten Island.

3   **Useful marks:**

    Old Orchard Shoal Light (brown conical tower, white top, black round base) (40°30′·7N 74°05′·9W), which stands on the S part of Old Orchard Shoal (7.119).

No 20 Light-beacon (red triangle on framework tower) (40°30′·2N 74°09′·7W), standing on the N side of the channel.

4   **Seguine Point Bend.** Princes Bay Leading Lights:

    Front light (red rectangle, white stripe, on white framework tower) (40°30′·5N 74°12′·7W).

    Rear light (similar structure) (41 m from front light).

  From the W end of Raritan Bay West Reach the alignment (267°) of these lights leads W through Seguine Point Bend.

5   **Red Bank Reach and Ward Point Bend** lead SW, W and then NNW round the SW part of Staten Island, passing E of Anchorage No 44 (7.119), to the S end of Arthur Kill.

  Useful marks (with positions relative to Ward Point (40°30′N 74°15′W)):

6   No 42 Light-beacon (red triangle on square framework tower) (1¼ miles E) standing on the NW side of Red Bank Reach.

    No 52 Light-beacon (red triangle on framework tower with base) (7 cables SE).

    No 58 Light-beacon (red triangle on framework tower, red base) (2 cables S).

    (Directions continue for Arthur Kill at 7.151)

Chart 3459
Chapel Hill Channel
7.111

1   Chapel Hill Channel, which is marked by light-buoys and buoys (lateral), leads from the inshore end of Sandy Hook Channel to the N part of Ambrose Channel, passing to the W of Flynns Knoll and Romer Shoal.

  Useful mark:

    West Bank Light (40°32′·3N 74°02′·6W) (7.107).

Leonardo

Sandy Hook from NE (7.109)
(Original dated 2002)

(Photograph - Airphoto - Jim Wark)

Other channels

Chart 3459
False Hook Channel
7.112

1   False Hook Channel (40°28′N 73°59′W), which is not marked, leads close up the E side of Sandy Hook and joins Sandy Hook Channel close E of the N point of that promontory.

Depths. The channel has depths of 2·7 to over 6·1 m (9 to 20 ft).

Local knowledge is necessary.

Swash Channel
7.113

1   Swash Channel (40°30′N 74°00′W) is a natural buoyed passage between Ambrose Channel and Sandy Hook Channel.

Depths. The channel has a controlling depth of 5·5 m (18 ft) but care must be taken to avoid patches with least depths of 4 m (13 ft) near the edge of the channel, and charted obstructions within the channel.

2   **Directions.** The alignment (305°) of Swash Channel Front Leading Light (white tower) (40°33′·5N 74°06′·5W), on the shore of Staten Island, and Staten Island Light (7.107) leads WNW through the channel.

Fourteen Foot Channel
7.114

1   Fourteen Foot Channel (40°32′N 73°59′W) enters Lower Bay close N of Ambrose Channel.

The channel has a depth of about 4 m (13 ft) and is not marked.

Coney Island Channel
7.115

1   Coney Island Channel (40°34′N 73°59′W), marked by buoys and light–buoys (lateral), passes along the S shore of Coney Island and has a controlling depth (2002) of 3·6 m (11·7 ft) to Rockaway Inlet. In 1997, shoaling was reported in the S part of this channel.

It is mainly used by traffic going to Jamaica Bay and Coney Island.

Chart 2860 (see 1.17)
Raritan River
7.116

1   Raritan River flows into the W end of Raritan Bay between South Amboy (40°29′N 74°17′W) (7.126) and Ferry Point. The mouth of the river is approached from E through Great Beds Reach and South Amboy Reach and from the N through Raritan River Cutoff.

The river channel, which is well marked but very winding, extends 11 miles W from South Amboy to the city of New Brunswick. The principal commerce on the river is in coal, ore and petroleum products.

2   **Depths.** There is a project depth of 7·6 m (25 ft) from Raritan Bay to a point about 3 miles above the river entrance; thence 4·6 m (15 ft) for the next 2 miles to the junction with the Washington Canal; thence a controlling depth (1962) of about 2·7 m (9 ft) in mid-channel to New Brunswick.

3   **Vertical clearance** (with positions relative to Ferry Point):

Swing rail bridge (5 cables WSW). Vertical clearance 2·4 m (8 ft) when closed.

Fixed road bridge (1 mile WNW). Vertical clearance 32·3 m (106 ft).

Fixed road bridges (1½ miles WNW). Least vertical clearance 41·1 m (135 ft).

Ice. See 7.150.

US Naval Ammunition Depot — Leonardo

Charts 3204, 3459
General information
7.117

1   US Naval Ammunition Depot is situated at Leonardo (40°25′N 74°03′W) on the S shore of Sandy Hook Bay.

Approach. The depot is approached from the inshore end of Sandy Hook Channel through Terminal Channel and a turning basin, which are marked by buoys and light–buoys (lateral).

2   **Depths.** The channel and turning basin have a project depth of 10·7 m (35 ft). For the latest controlling depths the charts and port authority should be consulted.

Traffic regulations. The installations of the depot are surrounded by a restricted area and security zone, the limits of which are shown on the chart. In that section of the security zone comprising Terminal Channel, the following exceptional rules apply:

(1) No vessel shall anchor, stop, remain or drift without power at any time in the security zone.

(2) No vessel shall enter, cross, or otherwise navigate in the security zone when a public vessel, or any other vessel, that cannot safely navigate outside the Terminal Channel, is approaching or leaving the Naval Ammunition Depot Piers at Leonardo, New Jersey.

(3) Vessels may enter or cross the security zone, except as provided in paragraph 2 (above).

See Appendix V for definitions and general rules covering security zones and Appendix VI for definitions of restricted areas.

3   **Leading Lights.** The alignment (207½°) of two lights (red rectangle, white stripe, on pile) on the pier leads SSW through the centre of the channel.

Berths
7.118

1   Deep water berths are situated at the head of a pier extending 1½ miles NNE from the shore. This pier has two branches at its outer end. A dredged channel, with a least depth of about 3·4 m (11 ft), leads along the E side of the main pier to a berth halfway between the pierhead and the shore; this berth is used to load barges.

Anchorage areas

Charts 3204, 3459, 3458
General anchorages
7.119

1   The following general anchorage areas, the limits of which are shown on the charts, are established in Lower Bay. For recommendations and general regulations see 7.3 and 7.61.

2   **Anchorage No 25** is a naval anchorage in Gravesend Bay (40°35′N 74°01′W) (7.128) on the E side of the channel approaching The Narrows. Good anchorage is available in depths of 3 to 15 m (10 to 49 ft), clear of 2 wrecks, the positions of which are shown on the chart. When this anchorage is required by naval vessels, any commercial vessels therein must move when directed by the Captain of the Port.

3　In addition to the general regulations (7.61) the following specific regulations apply to Anchorage No 25:

No vessel may anchor unless it notifies the Captain of the Port when it anchors, of the vessel's name, length, draught and position in the anchorage.

Each vessel anchored must notify the Captain of the Port when it weighs anchor.

4　No vessel may conduct lightering operations unless it notifies the Captain of the Port before it begins lightering operations.

Each vessel lightering must notify the Captain of the Port at the termination of lightering.

No vessel may anchor unless it maintains a bridge watch, guards and answers Channel 16 FM, and maintains an accurate position plot.

5　If any vessel is so close to another that a collision is probable, each vessel must communicate with the other vessel and the Captain of the Port on Channel 16 FM and shall act to terminate the close proximity situation.

6　No vessel may anchor unless it maintains the capability to get underway within 30 minutes, except with the prior approval of the Captain of the Port.

7　No vessel may anchor in a "dead ship" status (propulsion or control unavailable for normal operations) without the prior approval of the Captain of the Port.

8　Each vessel in a "dead ship" status must engage an adequate number of tugs alongside during tide changes. A tug alongside may assume the Channel 16 FM radio guard for the vessel after it notifies the Captain of the Port.

9　**Anchorage No 26** is situated in Sandy Hook Bay, in the SE part of Lower Bay, S of a line joining Sandy Hook Point (40°28′N 74°01′W) and Point Comfort, 5 miles WSW. Sandy Hook Bay provides excellent anchorage in depths ranging from 9 m (30 ft) just inside Sandy Hook to 5 m (16 ft) in its S part. In 1983 shoaling to depths of 4·3 m (14 ft) was reported in the bay. A dangerous wreck lies 1¼ miles SSW of Sandy Hook Light (40°27′·7N 74°00′·1W).

10　Pleasure or commercial craft may not navigate or anchor within 750 yards of the Naval Ammunition Depot Pier at Leonardo (7.117).

See 7.120 and 7.117 for details of explosives anchorages, security zone and restricted area that lie within this general anchorage.

11　**Anchorage No 27** is divided into three parts. The E part, with depths of up to 17 m (57 ft), lies E of Sandy Hook; the other two parts, with depths of up to 19 m (62 ft), lie between the entrance channels and include Flynns Knoll and Romer Shoal, which have depths of 2·4 to 5·5 m (8 to 18 ft) and 1·2 to 5·2 m (4 to 17 ft), respectively, over them.

A pipeline area crosses this anchorage S of Romer Shoal and Flynns Knoll, and a submarine power cable area crosses the W part of the anchorage. For further information on submarine pipelines and cables see 1.38 and 1.39.

12　**Anchorage No 28**, with depths of up to 11 m (35 ft), lies in the central part of Lower Bay between the N side of No 26 Anchorage Area and Chapel Hill Channel, and the NW shore of the bay. Its W boundary leads NNW from Comfort Point (40°27′N 74°08′W). Old Orchard Shoal (40°31′N 74°07′W) and West Bank (7.108) lie within this anchorage.

13　A pipeline area, which is shown on the chart, crosses the S part of the anchorage. For further information on submarine pipelines see 1.39.

14　**Anchorage No 44**, with depths of about 11 m (36 ft), lies in the W part of Raritan Bay at the junction of Arthur Kill and Raritan River. The anchorage is restricted to deep draught vessels except that barges may anchor in the S part of the anchorage. No vessel shall occupy the deep draught part of the anchorage for more than 48 hours without the permission of the Captain of the Port.

15　**Anchorage No 46**, with depths of up to 11 m (35 ft), lies on the W side of Anchorage No 28 and N of Raritan Bay Channel.

Anchorage No 47, with depths of up to 7 m (24 ft), lies on the W side of Anchorage No 28 and on the S side of Raritan Channel. Raritan Bay lies within the anchorage. This bay is full of shoals with depths of between 2·1 and 5·5 m (7 and 18 ft).

Explosives anchorages
7.120

1　**Anchorages 49-F**, an emergency naval anchorage, with depths of 5 to 7 m (16 to 22 ft), **and 49-G**, a naval anchorage, with depths of 7 to 10 m (24 to 33 ft), the limits of which are shown on the chart, are situated within Anchorage No 26. They are reserved for vessels carrying explosives and may not be used as general anchorages.

No pleasure or commercial craft shall navigate or anchor within these areas when naval vessels, which are anchored in the area, display a red flag by day or a red light by night.

Anchorages and harbours

Chart 3459
Horseshoe Cove
7.121

1　Horseshoe Cove (40°26′N 74°00′W), on the E side of Sandy Hook Bay, is reported to provide satisfactory anchorage for small craft.

Chart 2755 (see 1.17)
Shrewsbury River and Navesink River
7.122

1　Shrewsbury River and Navesink River empty through a common entrance into the SE part of Sandy Hook Bay (40°25′N 73°59′W). and may be entered by small craft.

Ice. Navigation is generally suspended because of ice between December and March inclusive.

Chart 3459 (see 1.17)
Compton Creek
7.123

1　Compton Creek (40°26′N 74°05′W), 4 miles W of Sandy Hook, is used extensively as a harbour of refuge by small fishing craft.

Chart 3204 (see 1.17)
Keyport Harbor
7.124

1　Keyport Harbor (40°27′N 74°12′W), which is entered between Conaskonk Point and Matawan Point, is a shallow harbour on the S side of Raritan Bay, which is mostly used by local craft.

Cheesequake Creek and Stump Creek
7.125

1　Cheesequake Creek and Stump Creek (40°28′N 74°15′W) are situated on the S side of Raritan Bay and share a common entrance which is used by small craft. Within the entrance the creeks lead SW and SE, respectively.

Chart 2860 (see 1.17)
South Amboy
7.126

1   South Amboy (40°29′N 74°17′W) is a city on the S side of the entrance to the Raritan River (7.116). Main waterborne commerce at the port is the shipment of coal, petroleum products and building materials.

Berths. Depths alongside the wharves and piers range from 1·8 to 9·1 m.

Chart 3458
Great Kills Harbor
7.127

1   Great Kills Harbor (40°32′N 74°08′W), a shallow bight on the S side of Staten Island, is used as an anchorage by small craft.

Chart 3459
Gravesend Bay
7.128

1   Gravesend Bay (40°35′N 74°01′W) is situated in the N part of Lower Bay. It is entered N of Norton Point, the E end of Coney Island.

Approach. A buoyed channel, with a least depth of 3 m (10 ft), leads from deep water N of Coney Island to the docks in the E part of the bay.

THE NARROWS, UPPER BAY AND LOWER PART OF HUDSON RIVER

General information

Charts 3456, 3455, 3454
Description
7.129

1   **The Narrows**, connecting Lower Bay and Upper Bay, has a width of 6 cables at its narrowest part between the flats which extend from Fort Hamilton (40°37′N 74°02′W) on Long Island, and Fort Wadsworth on Staten Island.

2   **Upper Bay** is the part of New York Harbor situated between The Narrows and The Battery (7.44), 6 miles NNE. On the E side of the bay is the borough of Brooklyn and on the W side the city of Bayonne. Kill van Kull (7.161) is a waterway leading W from the N side of Staten Island, Hudson River flows into the head of the bay and East River is entered S of the Battery.

3   **Lower part of Hudson River** is the part of the river which lies between New York City waterfront as far as 7 miles above The Battery on the E side and the waterfronts of Jersey City, Hoboken, Weehawken and Edgewater on the New Jersey side of the river.

4   **No-discharge zone (NDZ).** All the waters of the Hudson River from the Battery to Troy (134 miles N) have been designated as a NDZ. See 1.44.

Depths
7.130

1   **Anchorage Channel** (7.137), which is an extension of Ambrose Channel and is the main channel through Upper Bay to The Battery, has a project depth of 13·7 m (45 ft).

Hudson River Channel (7.138), which continues N from The Battery for 5 miles to the limit of New York's major wharves at 59th Street, has a project depth of 13·7 m (45 ft).

New York Harbour from SSW (7.129)
(Original dated 2004)

(Photograph - Airphoto - Jim Wark)

2   **Hudson River Channel to Albany** (7.191). Except for a short stretch along the Weehawken-Edgemont waterfront, where it is 9·1 m (30 ft), the project depth is 9·8 m (32 ft) above the Hudson River Channel. See also 7.184.

For the latest controlling depths the charts and port authority should be consulted.

Traffic regulations
7.131

1   **Safety and security zones** have been established as follows:

> The area between the Global Marine Terminal (7.146) and the Military Ocean Terminal (1 cable SW), and the area surrounding the New York Passenger Ship Terminal (7.146).
> All waters within 150 yards of Liberty and Ellis Islands (7.137) and the bridge between Liberty State Park and Ellis Island.

For definition and general regulations concerning safety and security zones see Appendix V.

2   **Restricted Area.** An area where navigation is restricted, shown on the chart, lies to the E of Stapleton Naval Station (40°37′·7N 74°04′·4W). Navigation is prohibited within 183 m E of the pierhead and restricted to vessels transiting for the outer part of the area. Vessels at anchor in 23-A and 23-B anchorages (7.144) will be allowed to swing into the seaward part of the restricted area during tide changes. See Appendix VI.

3   **Regulated Navigation Area.** The S part of Pierhead Channel (7.142) is a Regulated Navigation Area. Movement in this area may be restricted during dredging operations and permission to enter or transit must be obtained from Vessel Traffic Services New York; see *Admiralty List of Radio Signals Volume 6(5)* and Appendix V for further information.

Vertical clearance
7.132

1   Verrazano-Narrows Bridge is a fixed suspension bridge that crosses The Narrows. The bridge has a vertical clearance of 65·5 m (215 ft) for the central 610 m. A travelling maintenance platform, when in operation, reduces the vertical clearance by 4·6 m (15 ft).

Fish traps
7.133

1   Fish traps are placed in the lower part of the Hudson River each spring, usually between the middle of March and the middle of May, in mid-channel between Manhattan and the Weehawken-Edgewater waterfront. The limits of these areas are shown on the chart.

Outer limits of the nets are usually marked by flags during the day and by lights at night.

2   **Caution** is advised when navigating in a fish trap area because broken off poles from previous traps may remain under the surface.

Tidal streams
7.134

1   See 7.93.

Directions

Principal marks
7.135

1   **Landmark:**

> Statue of Liberty (Torch) (40°41′·3N 74°02′·7W).

Hudson River - Verrazano-Narrows Bridge from SE (7.132)
(Original dated 2002)

(Photograph - Airphoto - Jim Wark)

Other aids to navigation
7.136
1 **Racon:**
  KV Light-buoy (40°39′N 74°04′W) (7.166).
  See *Admiralty List of Radio Signals Volume 2* for details.

Chart 3456
Anchorage Channel
7.137
1 From a position S of Verrazano-Narrows Bridge (40°36′·4N 74°02′·7W) Anchorage Channel leads NNW and then NNE from The Narrows to The Battery, 6 miles N, passing:

2 Between Fort Hamilton and Fort Wadsworth on either side of The Narrows, thence:
  ENE of the anchorages lying off the coast of Staten Island between Fort Wadsworth and Saint George (40°39′N 74°05′W), thence:

3 Between the anchorages lying off Bay Ridge Flats (40°39′·7N 74°01′·8W) on the E side of the channel and Jersey Flats (40°40′·0N 74°03′·5W) on the W side of the channel. The W limit of the anchorages lying off Bay Ridge Flats is marked by light-buoys (starboard hand). Robbins Reef Light (brown conical tower, white top, white base) (40°39′·4N 74°03′·9W) stands on the S part of Jersey Flats. Thence:

4 Between Governors Island (40°41′·3N 74°01′·1W) and Liberty Island, on which stands the Statue of Liberty (7.135). A light (red framework tower, white central column, on white hut) stands on the SW corner of Governors Island.

 Thence to a position at the entrance of the Hudson River between The Battery and Ellis Island.

Chart 3455, 3454
Hudson River Channel
7.138
1 From a position between The Battery (40°42′N 74°01′W) and Ellis Island the Hudson River Channel leads up the Hudson River for about 5½ miles to the vicinity of the New York City Passenger Ship Terminal on the E side and the Weehawken waterfront on the W side.

Other channels

Chart 3456
Bay Ridge Channel
7.139
1 Bay Ridge Channel (40°39′N 74°02′W) leads between Bay Ridge Flats and the wharves and piers of Bush Terminal in Brooklyn. The channel, the W side of which is marked by a buoy and light-buoys (port hand), has mid-channel depths generally of 10·7 to 12·2 m (35 to 40 ft), with lesser depths at the sides, and leads to Gowanus Bay (7.146) and the S end of Red Hook Channel.

Red Hook Channel
7.140
1 Red Hook Channel (40°40′N 74°01′W) leads between Gowanus Flats, the N part of Bay Ridge Flats, and the wharves and berths on the N side of Gowanus Bay. The channel, the W side of which is marked by light-buoys (port hand), has mid-channel depths generally of 10·7 to 12·2 m (35 to 40 ft), with lesser depths at the sides, and leads to the S end of Buttermilk Channel.

Chart 3455
Buttermilk Channel
7.141
1 Buttermilk Channel (40°41′N 74°01′W) leads between Governors Island and the wharves on the Brooklyn waterfront. The channel, which has mid-channel depths generally of 10·7 to 12·2 m (35 to 40 ft), with lesser depths at the sides, leads to the W end of East River (7.44).

 No 1 Light-buoy (port hand) marks a shoal extending from the SW end of Governors Island, and Nos 5 and 7 Buoys (port hand) mark shallow water off the E side of the island.

Chart 3456
Pierhead Channel
7.142
1 Pierhead Channel (40°40′N 74°04′N) leads NE, within Jersey Flats (7.137), from the E entrance to Kill van Kull (40°39′N 74°04′W) along the line of the terminals extending from the New Jersey shore, to a position 6 cables S of Liberty Island.

 The controlling depth of this channel is about 4·3 m (14 ft). A number of connecting channels lead from Pierhead Channel across Jersey Flats and to the terminals. All channels are marked by buoys and light-buoys.

 The S part of this channel is a Regulated Navigation Area. See 7.131.

Anchorage areas
Chart 3456, 3455, 3454
Regulations
7.143
1 For recommendations and general regulations applying to all anchorages see 7.3 and 7.61. For additional regulations applying to anchorages Nos 20A-G, 21A-C, 23A-B and 24 see 7.119.

General anchorages
7.144
1 The following general anchorage areas, the limits of which are shown on the charts, are established in Upper Bay and the lower part of the Hudson River:
  Anchorage No 24 is situated on the W side of Anchorage Channel close N of the Verrazano-Narrows Bridge.

2 **Anchorages No 23-A and B** are situated on the W side of Anchorage Channel N of Anchorage No 24.
  Anchorages No 21-A, B and C are situated on the E side of Anchorage Channel on Bay Ridge Flats and the waters to the W and SW of this shoal.

3 **Anchorages No 20-A through 20-G** are situated on the W side of Anchorage Channel between the entrance to Kill van Kull (40°39′N 74°04′W) and Ellis Island, 3 miles NNW.
  Anchorage No 19 is situated on the E side of the Hudson River between 1 and 6 miles above the Passenger Ship Terminal. See also 7.196.

Additional regulations
7.145
1 Unless otherwise authorised by the Captain of the Port the following regulations apply to particular anchorages.
  Anchorage No 24.
  No vessel may occupy this anchorage for more than 48 hours.

2 No vessel with a draught of more than 12·2 m (40 ft) may occupy this anchorage unless it anchors within 5 hours after the out-going current begins in The Narrows.

No vessel with a length overall of less than 243·8 m (800 ft), or with a draught of less than 12·2 m (40 ft), may occupy this anchorage.

Anchorage No 23-B.

No vessel may occupy this anchorage for more than 48 hours.

3 No vessel with a length of 204·2 m (670 ft) or less may occupy this anchorage.

No vessel with a draught of 12·2 m (40 ft) or more may occupy this anchorage unless it anchors within 5 hours after the out-going current begins in The Narrows.

See 7.131 for adjacent restricted area details.

4 **Anchorage No 23-A.**

No vessel may occupy this anchorage for more than 48 hours.

No vessel with a length of more than 204·2 m (670 ft) may occupy this anchorage.

No vessel with a draught of more than 12·2 m (40 ft) may occupy this anchorage unless it anchors within 5 hours after the out-going current begins in The Narrows.

5 See 7.131 for adjacent restricted area details.

Anchorage No 21-C.

No vessel with a draught of 10 m (33 ft) or less may occupy this anchorage.

Anchorage No 21-B.

No vessel with a draught of 3 m (10 ft) or less may occupy this anchorage.

6 **Anchorage No 20-G.**

Although this anchorage is designated a naval anchorage, commercial vessels may be permitted to occupy this anchorage temporarily, for about 24 hours. Upon notification of an anticipated naval arrival, any commercial vessel so anchored must leave the anchorage at its own expense.

7 **Anchorages Nos 20-F through 20-A.**

No vessel may occupy these anchorages for more than 72 hours.

Anchorage No 19.

No vessel may anchor in this anchorage without the permission of the Captain of the Port.

Each vessel shall report its position to the Captain of the Port immediately after anchoring.

8 No vessel may conduct lightering operations in this anchorage without the permission of the Captain of the Port.

When the use of this anchorage is required for naval vessels, the vessels anchored therein must move when the Captain of the Port directs them.

9 No vessel in excess of 244 m (800 ft) in overall length or 12·2 m (40 ft) draught may anchor unless it informs the Captain of the Port at least 48 hours prior to entering Ambrose Channel.

Terminals

Upper Bay and Lower Hudson River
7.146

1 A brief description of the principal terminals is given as follows:

South Brooklyn Marine Terminal on the S side of Gowanus Bay (40°40′N 74°01′W). Facilities available for handling container, general cargo and LASH freight. Eight berths, 2 of which are container berths. Depth alongside of up to 9·8 m.

2 Red Hook Container Terminal at the S end of Buttermilk Channel (40°41′N 74°01′W). Eight berths, 2 of which are container berths, 2 Ro-Ro berths and 4 container/general cargo berths. Depths alongside of 10·7 to 12·2 m.

3 Brooklyn Marine Terminal, between Brooklyn Bridge and the N end of Buttermilk Channel, extends for 3 km along the Brooklyn waterfront. Facilities available for handling general cargo. Berths mainly used are at Piers 6 to 8.

4 Global Marine Terminal on the W side of Upper Bay (40°40′N 74°04′W). A container terminal with 548 m of berthing space with a least depth alongside of 11·6 m.

Port Authority Auto Marine Terminal on the W side of Upper Bay at the SE end of Global Marine Terminal. Two berths with depths alongside of 9·8 m. The terminal specialises in handling the import and export of motor vehicles.

5 New York Passenger Ship Terminal (40°46′N 74°00′W) is situated on the E shore of the Hudson River on Manhattan Island, 4 miles above The Battery. The terminal, which handles over 800 000 passengers a year, has 5 berths.

ARTHUR KILL

General information

Charts 3458, 3457
Description
7.147

1 **Arthur Kill** is a narrow, winding waterway which separates Staten Island from the mainland of New Jersey, and leads in a general NNE direction for about 10 miles from its S entrance, at the W end of Lower Bay (40°30′N 74°15′W), to Elizabethport (7.160) at the W entrance of Newark Bay.

2 There is considerable traffic through Arthur Kill; the cities of Perth Amboy (7.154) and Tottenville stand either side of its S entrance. There are many oil terminals, oil refineries, large factories and storage facilities situated on its shores.

Depths
7.148

1 Project depth in Arthur Kill is 10·7 m (35 ft). For the latest controlling depths the charts and port authority should be consulted.

Vertical clearance
7.149

1 Two road bridges and one rail bridge cross Arthur Kill. **Outerbridge Crossing Bridge**, a fixed bridge 1¾ miles above the S entrance with a vertical clearance of 43·6 m (143 ft), connects Tottenville and Perth Amboy.

2 **Goethals Bridge,** a fixed road bridge with a vertical clearance of 41·8 m (137 ft) is at Elizabethport 1 mile from the N entrance.

A lift rail bridge, 1 cable above Goethals Bridge, has a vertical clearance of 9·5 m (31 ft) when closed and 41·1 m (135 ft) when open.

Ice
7.150

1   In ordinary winters ice does not seriously interfere with navigation in Raritan River or Arthur Kill, but in severe winters the ice sometimes prevents the movements of vessels for two weeks at a time when drift ice collects in Raritan Bay.

Directions
(continued from 7.110)
7.151

1   From the vicinity of Anchorage No 44 (7.119) a dredged channel leads N through Arthur Kill. This channel, which is entered between Ward Point (40°30′N 74°15′W) and Ferry Point is marked by leading lights, light-beacons, light-buoys and buoys.

Caution. Numerous sunken and visible wrecks are adjacent to both sides of the channel and caution is advised.

Anchorages

Anchorage No 42
7.152

1   Anchorage No 42 is established on the E side of Arthur Kill between Tottenville (40°31′N 74°15′W) and Port Socony, 1½ miles N, and between Port Socony and a point 1¼ miles NE.

2   A pipeline area, as shown on the chart, passes through the NE part of the anchorage. For further information on submarine pipelines see 1.39.

Anchorage No 41
7.153

1   Anchorage No 41 is established in the passage between Pralls Island (40°37′N 74°12′W) and Staten Island on the E side of Arthur Kill.

Harbours and terminals

Perth Amboy
7.154

1   Perth Amboy (40°30′N 74°16′W), which is a port of entry, is situated at the junction of the Raritan River and Arthur Kill.

Anchorage. Good anchorage in depths of 9 m (30 ft) is available abreast some of the wharves.

2   **Berths.** The principal wharves have depths alongside of 4·3 to 9·1 m. One tanker berth, 7·9 m.

Repairs. Several ship and boat repair yards are available.

Supplies: fuel; water and stores.

Port Socony
7.155

1   Port Socony (40°32′·6N 74°14′·9W), on the E side of Arthur Kill, is a bulk oil storage terminal.

Berths. In 1999 there were reported depths of 7·9 m alongside the S half of the dock, and from 4·6 to 6·4 m alongside the N half.

Port Reading
7.156

1   Port Reading (40°34′N 74°14′W), 4½ miles above Ward Point on the W side of Arthur Kill, has several oil storage facilities.

Berths. There are reported depths alongside of 5·5 to 9·1 m.

Fresh Kills
7.157

1   Fresh Kills (40°35′N 74°12′W) enters Arthur Kill from E, 5 miles N of Ward Point. It is being filled by the deposit of garbage and is closed to navigation.

Oil terminals between Fresh Kills and Goethals Bridge
7.158

1   There are a number of oil terminals between Fresh Kills and Goethals Bridge. The majority of them lie on the W side of Arthur Kill.

Berths at these terminals have depths alongside of 7·6 to 10·7 m.

Howland Hook Container Terminal
7.159

1   Howland Hook Container Terminal (40°38′·4N 74°11′·4W) is situated on Staten Island close N of Goethals Bridge. Ro-Ro facilities are available.

Berths. There is 760 m of berthing space with depths alongside of 10·7 to 12·2 m.

Elizabethport
7.160

1   Elizabethport (40°39′N 74°12′W), about 11 miles N of Ward Point, is the E part of the city of Elizabeth. It is at the N end of Arthur Kill at its junction with Newark Bay. The principal trade of the port is in petroleum products, building materials, chemicals and animal and vegetable oils.

Berths. Depths alongside the wharves range from 1 to 10 m.

KILL VAN KULL

General information

Charts 3457, 3456
Description
7.161

1   Kill van Kull (40°39′N 74°07′W) separates the S part of the city of Bayonne on the New Jersey mainland from the N part of Staten Island. It leads W from the W part of Upper Bay for about 3 miles to the entrance of Newark Bay and the N end of Arthur Kill.

2   Kill Van Kull is a major channel for petroleum and bulk cargo and has extensive through traffic and many factories on its shores. It forms the main approach to Newark Bay.

Depths
7.162

1   Project depth in Kill Van Kull is 13·7 m (45 ft) N of Shooters Island (40°38′·5N 74°09′·6W). The channel S of Shooters Island has a project depth of 9·1 m (30 ft). For the latest controlling depths the charts and port authority should be consulted.

Traffic regulations
7.163

1   **Regulated Navigation Area.** Kill Van Kull including its E entrance, Constable Hook Reach, and its W entrance, Bergen Point West Reach, is a Regulated Navigation Area when dredging operations are in progress. See 7.131 for entry requirements.

Vertical clearance
7.164

1   Bayonne Bridge, a fixed span bridge, crosses Kill Van Kull from close E of Bergen Point, the SW end of the city of Bayonne to the N shore of Staten Island. The bridge has a minimum vertical clearance of 42·1 m (138 ft) (46·0 m (151 ft) at the centre).

Tidal streams
7.165

1   The in-going tidal stream flows W and the out-going stream flows E. In 1991, tidal streams in Kill Van Kull were reported to deviate significantly from the official predictions.

Directions
7.166

1   **Constable Hook Leading Lights:**
     Front light (red rectangle, white stripe on framework tower) (40°39′·3N 74°05′·3W).
     Rear Light (similar structure) (120 m from front light).

2   From a position in Upper Bay, E of Saint George at the NE end of Staten Island and S of KV Light-buoy (preferred channel to port) (40°39′·0N 74°03′·9W), the alignment (290°) of these lights leads WNW through Constable Hook Reach to the entrance of the dredged channel which passes through Kill Van Kull. This channel, which is entered between Constable Hook at the SW end of Bayonne and Saint George, is marked by light-buoys (lateral) and leads to the entrance to Newark Bay.

3   **Caution.** Shoals, obstructions and numerous wrecks are on both sides of the channel. Numerous sunken and visible wrecks are in the channel S of Shooters Island.

(Directions for Newark Bay continue at 7.175)

Terminals and harbours

Oil terminals
7.167

1   Two oil terminals are situated on the N shore of Kill Van Kull.
     Exxon Bayonne Terminal, situated 1½ miles E of Bayonne Bridge, consists of a concrete pier 213 m in length. Vessels should arrive off the berth at slack water.

2   **Belcher Bayonne Terminal,** situated 1 mile E of Bayonne Bridge, consists of two concrete mooring islands protecting a wooden pier. Vessels should approach the terminal at HW.

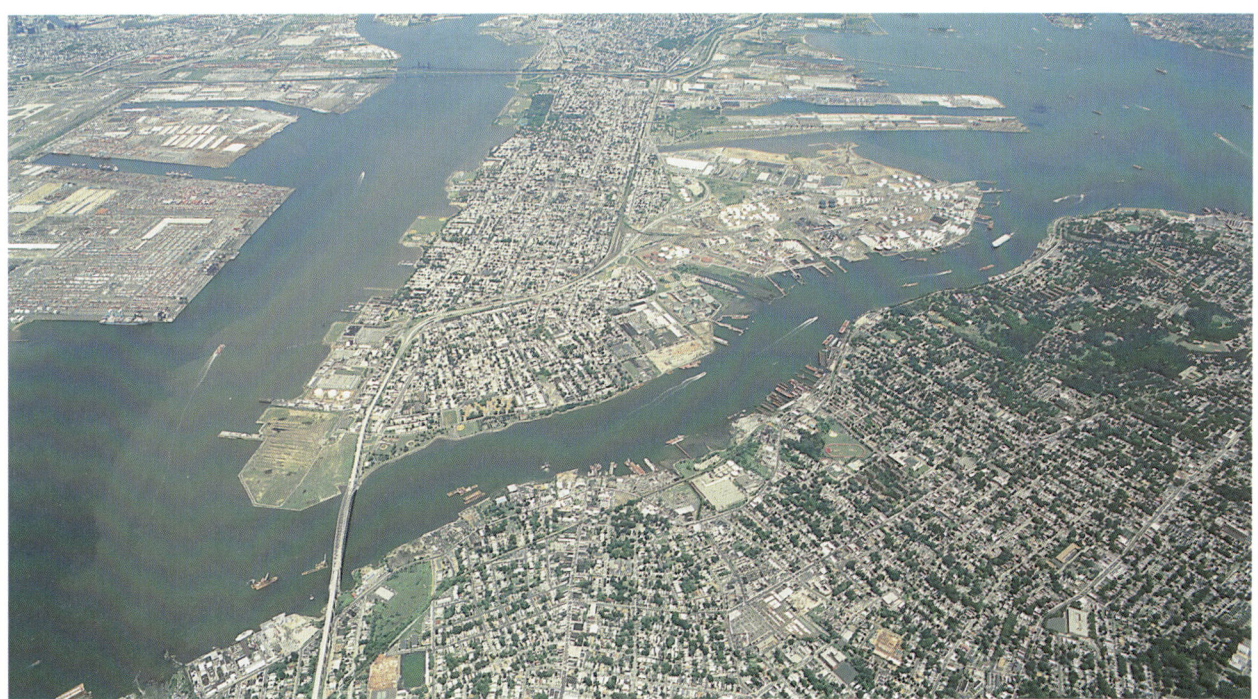

Kill van Kull and Newark Bay from S (7.161) & (7.169)
(Original dated 2001)

(Photograph - Joseph R Melanson of www.skypic.com)

Harbours
7.168

1 **Port Johnson** is situated on the N shore of Kill Van Kull, 1¼ miles E of Bayonne Bridge, between the two oil terminals. This port handles shipments of petroleum and other products.

2 **New Brighton** and **Port Richmond** are situated on the S shore of Kill Van Kull, 2 miles E and close E, respectively, of Bayonne Bridge. All types of repairs can be carried out on vessels of up to 10 000 tonnes at shipyards and floating docks on the S shore of Kill Van Kull.

NEWARK BAY AND ADJACENT WATERS

General information

Chart 3457
Description
7.169

1 **Newark Bay** lies N of the junction of Kill Van Kull and Arthur Kill and is entered between Bergen Point (40°39′N 74°09′W) and Shooters Island, 5 cables W. It extends 4 miles NNE to Kearny Point at the junction of the channels into Hackensack River (7.177) and Passaic River (7.176), which flow, respectively, into the E and W sides of the head of the bay.

2 The greater part of the bay is very shallow, but a dredged channel leads through the bay to the rivers and branch channels leading to the terminals on the W side of the bay.

Depths
7.170

1 The project depth in the main channel through Newark Bay leading to the branch channels to the Port Elizabeth Marine Terminal and Port Newark Terminal is 13·7 m (45 ft). For the latest controlling depths the charts and port authority should be consulted.

Tidal levels
7.171

1 Mean tidal range in Newark Bay is about 1·5 m.

Traffic regulations
7.172

1 **Safety and security zones.** The waters of Newark Bay, enclosing Port Elizabeth and Port Newark, from the South Elizabeth Channel to the New Jersey Turnpike Bridge (7.173) are a safety and security zone.

 For definition and general regulations concerning safety and security zones see Appendix V.

2 **Regulated Navigation Areas.** The waters of Newark Bay and its adjoining channels are Regulated Navigation Areas. Movement may be restricted during dredging operations and permission to enter or transit must be obtained from Vessel Traffic Services New York; see *Admiralty List of Radio Signals Volume 6(5)* and Appendix V for further information.

Vertical clearance
7.173

1 **Newark Bay.** New Jersey Turnpike Bridge, a fixed bridge with a vertical clearance of 41·1 m (135 ft), is situated 3½ miles above the entrance to Newark Bay and 7½ cables above Port Newark.

 A railway lift bridge, 2 cables above the New Jersey Turnpike Bridge, has a vertical clearance of 10·7 m (35 ft) when down and 41·1 m (135 ft) when open.

Ice
7.174

1 Ice sometimes closes Newark Bay during a part of January and February.

Directions
(continued from 7.166)

Newark Bay
7.175

1 From a position off Bergen Point (40°39′N 74°09′W) the main channel through Newark Bay, which is well marked with light-buoys and buoys (lateral), leads NNE for nearly 4 miles to a turning basin at the head of the bay, passing (with positions relative to Bergen Point):

2 ESE of Port Elizabeth Marine Terminal (7.180) (1½ miles N), thence:

  ESE of Port Newark Terminal (7.181) (2½ miles N).

Side channels
Passaic River
7.176

1 Passaic River, which flows into the NW end of Newark Bay, is used by vessels to Passaic at the head of navigation 13 miles above the mouth.

2 **Depths.** The project depth is 9·1 m (30 ft) from Newark Bay to a point 5 cables above the Lincoln Highway Bridge, which crosses the river 1½ miles above the turning basin at the channel entrance. Above this point the project depth reduces in stages and is 3 m (10ft) at Passaic. For the latest controlling depths the charts and port authority should be consulted.

3 **Passaic River.** There are more than 20 opening and fixed bridges between the mouth of the river and Passaic. The minimum vertical clearance of the fixed bridges is 30·5 m (100 ft).

Hackensack River
7.177

1 Hackensack River, which flows into the NE end of Newark Bay, is navigable for about 18 miles to the dams at New Milford.

 Depths. The project depth is 9·8 m (32 ft) from Newark Bay to a 7·6 m (25 ft) turning basin about 3 miles above the river mouth. Above this point depths of 3·4 m (11 ft) were reported in 1971. For the latest controlling depths the charts and port authority should be consulted.

2 **Vertical clearance.** There are more than 15 opening and fixed bridges, with a least vertical clearance of 10·7 m (35 ft), between the river mouth and Hackensack, 14 miles above the mouth. The least vertical clearance of overhead cables spanning the river is 27·1 m (89 ft).

Anchorages
Newark Bay
7.178

1 **Anchorage No 34,** situated on the W side of the entrance to Newark Bay, is centred 4 cables NNE of Shooters Island. The W part of this anchorage is designated as a special anchorage. See 1.49.

 Anchorage No 36, which is in two parts, is situated on the W side of the entrance of Newark Bay, S of the South Elizabeth Channel (7.180) and between the main channel and Port Newark Terminal, 1½ miles NNE.

2 **Anchorage No 37** is situated on the E side of the lower part of Newark Bay below the New Jersey Turnpike Bridge. The S part of this anchorage is designated as a special anchorage.

Anchorage No 38 is situated on the E side of the upper part of Newark Bay and below the first bridge on the E side of the lower part of Hackensack River.

Anchorage No 39 is situated between the entrance channels to the Hackensack River and Passaic River.

Terminals
7.179

1   Two major terminals, Port Elizabeth Marine Terminal and Port Newark Terminal, consisting of a number of smaller terminals are situated on the W side of Newark Bay. Both terminals are operated by the Port Authority of New York and New Jersey.

Port Elizabeth Marine Terminal
7.180

1   Port Elizabeth Marine Terminal is situated on the W side of Newark Bay, 1½ miles within the entrance.

Channels. South Elizabeth Channel fronts the berths on the SW side of the terminal, Elizabeth Pierhead Channel fronts the berths on the SE side of the terminal and Elizabeth Channel fronts the berths on the NE side of the terminal.

2   South Elizabeth and Elizabeth Pierhead Channels have project depths of 10·7 m (35 ft); Elizabeth Channel has a project depth of 13·7 m (45 ft). For the latest controlling depths the charts and port authority should be consulted.

Traffic Regulations. These channels are Regulated Navigation Areas. See 7.172.

3   **Berths.** There are 25 deep-draught berths at the terminal with depths alongside of 9·8 to 12·2 m.

Bay Avenue Terminal is a container terminal at the SE end of Elizabeth Channel; berths 70, 72, 74 and 76 at the SE end of Elizabeth Channel, have depths alongside of 11 m.

4   Maher Fleet Street Terminal is a container terminal on the S side of Elizabeth Channel; berths 52 to 66 (even numbers), depths alongside of 8·1 to 9·8 m.

Maher Tripoli Street Terminal and Maersk Sealand Terminal are container terminals situated on the E side and the SE end of Port Elizabeth Marine Terminal respectively.

Port Newark Terminal
7.181

1   Port Newark Terminal is situated on the W side of Newark Bay, 2½ miles within the entrance.

2   **Channels.** Elizabeth Channel, which lies between the two terminals, and has a project depth of 13·7 m (45 ft), fronts the berths on the SW side of Port Newark Terminal and Port Newark Pierhead Channel fronts the berths on the SE side. Port Newark Channel fronts the berths on the NW side and its E part links the terminal to the main channel in Newark Bay. These channels have a project depth of 12·2 m (40 ft). For the latest controlling depths the charts and port authority should be consulted.

Traffic Regulations. These channels are Regulated Navigation Areas. See 7.172.

3   **Berths.** There are 37 deep draught berths at the terminal with reported depths alongside of 9·8 to 10·7 m.

Port Newark Container Terminal, consisting of the Maersk and Universal Terminals, lies on the N side of Elizabeth Channel.

Several Ro-Ro berths, used mainly for the import of motor vehicles, are located on the N side of Port Newark Channel.

HUDSON RIVER

General information

Charts 2755, 2860 (see 1.17)
Scope
7.182

1   This section gives a brief description of the Hudson River from a position, (N limit of Chart 3454), 7½ miles N of The Battery (7.44), to the city of Albany.

Description
7.183

1   Hudson River, sometimes called North River in New York City, rises in Adirondack Mountains in the NE part of New York State, and flows in a S direction for 275 miles to its junction with East River at The Battery. The tidal part of the river extends to Albany, 125 miles above The Battery and then a further 7 miles to Troy Lock and Troy Dam from where traffic may join the New York State canal system.

2   This canal system leads W to The Great Lakes through the Erie Canal and Oswego Canal, and N to Lake Champlain through the Champlain Canal.

The river water is usually fresh as far S as Poughkeepsie, midway between Troy Dam and The Battery.

3   Navigation of the river is easy as far N as Kingston. 79 miles above The Battery, and then becomes more difficult because of numerous steep-to shoals and middle banks.

4   **No-discharge zone (NDZ).** All the waters of the Hudson River from the Battery to Troy (134 miles N) have been designated as a NDZ. See 1.44.

Depths
7.184

1   **Depths.** Project depth from the inner end of Hudson River Channel (7.138) to Albany is 9·8 m (32 ft). For the latest controlling depths the charts and port authority should be consulted.

Tidal levels
7.185

1   **Tidal levels.** Between The Battery and Albany the tidal range varies between about 1 and 1·5 m. See also information in *Admiralty Tide Tables*.

Pilotage
7.186

1   Hudson River Pilots embark N of Yonkers about 17 miles N of The Battery. Pilotage is compulsory.

Largest vessel
7.187

1   **Hudson River.** Maximum permissible size for navigation to Albany: length 229 m (750 ft); width 33·5 m (110 ft); draught 9·4 m (31 ft). Vessels with a draught of more than 8·5 m (28 ft) will be required to transit the river on a favourable tide as directed by the pilot.

2   **Erie Canal.** The controlling dimensions of the locks in this canal are length 91 m (300 ft), width 13 m (43 ft), 3·7 m (12 ft) over the sill; vertical clearance under bridges and cables of 4·6 m (15 ft).

Champlain Canal. The size of vessels is limited by a controlling depth of 3·7 m (12 ft) and a least vertical clearance of 5·2 m (17 ft).

Vertical clearance
7.188

1   The bridges between New York and Albany, which have a least vertical clearance of 41·1 m (135 ft), have either fixed or suspension spans. Overhead cables spanning the river have a least vertical clearance of 44·2 m (145 ft).

Buoyage
7.189
1 The lighted buoys marking the Hudson River are replaced during the winter by smaller lighted buoys or unlighted buoys.

Natural conditions
7.190
1 **Tidal streams:**
George Washington Bridge. In-going 1½ kn; out-going 2¼ kn.
Kingston. In-going 1¼ kn; out-going 1½ kn.
Albany. In-going ¼ kn; out-going ¾ kn.
The above figures will be affected by freshets, droughts and winds.
2 **Ice.** Even in extremely severe winters Coast Guard icebreakers and continuous river traffic maintain an open channel to Albany. The ice season usually starts in early January and ends in the middle of March. Normally shipping is affected between Tappan Zee and Albany. Aids to navigation are often covered or dragged off station by moving ice.

Albany

General information
7.191
1 **Albany** (42°40′N 73°45′W) is situated on the W bank of the Hudson River, 125 miles above The Battery.
The port of Albany is the terminus for deep-draught vessels on the Hudson River and serves as a transhipping point for large areas of New England. Waterborne commerce at the port is mainly in petroleum products, but many other products are also handled.
2 Albany, which in 2005 had an estimated population of 93 523, is the capital of New York State. It is also a port of entry.
Traffic. In 2005 the port was used by 4 vessels with a total dwt of 102 197 tonnes.
3 **Port Authority.** Albany Port District Commission, Administration Building, Port of Albany, Albany, NY 12202.
Internet. www.portofalbany.com

Limiting conditions
7.192
1 **Depths.** See 7.184.
Largest vessel. See 7.187.
Vertical clearance. See 7.188.
Natural conditions. See 7.190.
Largest berth. See 7.194.

Arrival information
7.193
1 **Anchorage.** The restricted width of the river is not sufficient to allow vessels to swing at anchor except in emergency. See 7.196.
Tugs are available.

Alongside berths
7.194
1 There are over 30 waterfront facilities and 1½ miles of wharves in Albany Port District. The major facilities have depths alongside of 8·5 to 10 m.

Port services
7.195
1 **Repairs.** All types of repairs can be carried out other than those that require docking, for which there are no facilities.
Other facilities: hospitals; oily waste disposal.
2 **Supplies.** Bunkering services are not available for deep-draught vessels. Diesel is available for small vessels. Water, stores and provisions are available.
Communications. Nearest airport Albany County Municipal, 19 km.

Anchorages and harbours

Anchorages
7.196
1 **General anchorages** begin 5 miles above The Battery (7.144) and extend upriver for about 10 miles.
Vessels proceeding from New York to Albany occasionally anchor overnight in the vicinity of Kingston, 79 miles above The Battery and 47 miles below Albany, to await daylight hours before passing through the constricted part of the river.
2 A buoyed anchorage 122 m wide and 732 m long is situated on the E side of the channel just above Stuyvesant, 15 miles below Albany. The anchorage has depths of 9·8 m (32 ft).
Special anchorages. There are numerous special anchorages on the river between New York and Albany. Their positions are best seen on the US charts of the river. See 1.49.

Newburgh
7.197
1 Newburgh is situated on the W bank of the river 53 miles above The Battery. It is a major petroleum distribution centre.
Berths. Most of the piers of the major oil companies are at the S end of the waterfront. Depths alongside range from 4·3 m at the N end of the waterfront to 10·7 m at the S end.

Poughkeepsie
7.198
1 Poughkeepsie is situated on the E bank of the river 65 miles above The Battery. It is an important industrial centre.
Berths. Tanker berths, with reported depths alongside of 4 to 6·1 m, are situated 1 mile S of the town.

Kingston
7.199
1 Kingston is situated on the W side of the river 80 miles above The Battery. Waterborne traffic consists mainly of building materials and oil products.
Berths. There is an oil terminal at Kingston Point from which tugs and barges transport oil products up and down the river.

Hudson
7.200
1 Hudson is situated on the E bank of the river 102 miles above The Battery. Waterborne commerce is in oil products.
Berths. The bulk petroleum pier has reported depths alongside of 3 m.

APPENDIX I

CODE OF FEDERAL REGULATIONS TITLE 33 — NAVIGATION AND NAVIGABLE WATERS

PART 26 — VESSEL BRIDGE-TO-BRIDGE RADIOTELEPHONE REGULATIONS

Appendix I contains extracts from the United States Bridge-to-Bridge Telephone Act. For a complete description of this part see 33 CFR 26.

§26.01 Purpose. (See 33 CFR 26)

§26.02 Definitions. (See 33 CFR 26)

§26.03 Radiotelephone required.

(a) Unless an exemption is granted under §26.09 (waters not applicable to this volume) and except as provided in paragraph (a)(4) of this section, this part applies to:
 (1) Every power-driven vessel of 20 m or over in length while navigating;
 (2) Every vessel of 100 gross tons and upward carrying one or more passengers for hire while navigating;
 (3) Every towing vessel of 26 ft (7·9 m) or over in length while navigating; and
 (4) Every dredge and floating plant engaged in or near a channel or fairway in operations likely to restrict or affect navigation of other vessels except for an unmanned or intermittently manned floating plant under the control of a dredge.
(b) Every vessel, dredge or floating plant described in paragraph (a) of this section must have a radiotelephone on board capable of operation from its navigational bridge, or in the case of a dredge from its main control station, and capable of transmitting and receiving on the frequency or frequencies within the 156-162 MHz band using the classes of emissions designated by the Federal Communications Commission for the exchange of navigational information.
(c) The radiotelephone required by paragraph (b) of this section must be carried on board the described vessels, dredges and floating plants upon the navigable waters of the United States.
(d) The radiotelephone required by paragraph (b) of this section must be capable of transmitting and receiving on VHF FM channel 22A (157.1 MHz).
(f) In addition to the radiotelephone required by paragraph (b) of this section each vessel described in paragraph (a) of this section, while transiting any waters within a Vessel Traffic Service Area, must have on board a radiotelephone capable of transmitting and receiving on the VTS designated frequency in Table 161.12 (c) (VTS and VMRS Centers, Call Signs/MMSI, Designated Frequencies and Monitoring Areas).
Note. A single VHF-FM radio, capable of scanning or sequential monitoring, (often referred to as dual watch capability) will not meet the requirements for two radios.

§26.04 Use of the designated frequency.

(d) On the navigable waters of the United States channel 13 (156.65 MHz) is the designated frequency required to be monitored in accordance with §26.05 (a), except

that in the area prescribed in §26.03 (e) (not listed - waters not applicable to this volume) channel 67 (156.375 MHz) is the designated frequency.
(e) On those navigable waters of the United States within a VTS area, the designated VTS frequency is an additional designated frequency required to be monitored in accordance with §26.05.
Note: As stated in 47 CFR 80.148 (b) a VHF watch on channel 16 (156.800 MHz) is not required on vessels subject to the Vessel Bridge-to-Bridge Radiotelephone Act and participating in a Vessel Traffic Service (VTS) system when the watch is maintained on both the vessel bridge-to-bridge frequency and a designated VTS frequency.

§26.05 Use of radiotelephone.

Section 5 of the Act states that the radio telephone required by this Act is for the exclusive use of the Master or person in charge of the vessel, or the person designated by the Master or person in charge to pilot or direct the movement of the vessel, who shall maintain a listening watch on the designated frequency. Nothing herein shall be interpreted as precluding the use of portable radiotelephone equipment to satisfy the requirements of this act.

§26.06 Maintenance of radiotelephone; failure of radiotelephone. (See 33 CFR 26)

§26.07 Communications.

No person may use the service of, and no person may serve as, a person required to maintain a listening watch under Section 5 of the Act, 33 U.S.C 1204 unless that person can communicate in the English language.

§26.08 Exemption procedures. (See 33 CFR 26)

§26.09 List of exemptions. (See 33 CFR 26)

§26.10 Penalties.

Section 9 of the Act states:
(a) Whoever, being the Master or person in charge of a vessel subject to the Act, fails to enforce or comply with the Act or the regulations hereunder; or whoever, being designated by the Master or person in charge of a vessel subject to the Act to pilot or direct the movement of the vessel fails to enforce or comply with the Act or the regulations hereunder is liable to a civil penalty of not more than $500 to be assessed by the Secretary.
(b) Every vessel navigated in violation of the Act or the regulations hereunder is liable to a civil penalty of not more than $500 to be assessed by the Secretary, for which the vessel may be proceeded against in any District Court of the United States having jurisdiction.
(c) Any penalty assessed under this section may be remitted or mitigated by the Secretary, upon such terms as he may deem proper.

APPENDIX II

CODE OF FEDERAL REGULATIONS TITLE 33 — NAVIGATION AND NAVIGABLE WATERS

PART 160 — PORTS AND WATERWAYS SAFETY — GENERAL

Appendix II contains extracts from Subpart C of the above regulations issued by the United States Department of Commerce. For a complete description of this part see 33 CFR 160.

Subpart C — Notification of Arrival, Hazardous Conditions, and Certain Dangerous Cargoes.

§160.201 General.

This subpart contains requirements and procedures for submitting Notices of Arrival (NOA) and Notice of Hazardous Condition. The sections in this subpart describe:

(a) Applicability and exemptions from requirements in this subpart;

(b) Required information in a NOA;

(c) Required changes to a NOA;

(d) Methods and times for submission of a NOA and changes to a NOA;

(e) How to obtain a waiver; and

(f) Requirements for submission of the Notice of Hazardous Conditions.

§160.202 Applicability.

(a) This subpart applies to US and foreign vessels bound for and departing from ports or places in the United States.

(b) This subpart does not apply to recreational vessels under 46 U.S.C. *4301 et seq.*

(c) Unless otherwise specified in this subpart, the owner, agent, master, operator, or person in charge of a vessel regulated by this subpart is responsible for compliance with the requirements in this subpart.

(d) Towing vessels controlling a barge or barges required to submit a NOA under this subpart must submit only one NOA containing the information required for the towing vessel and each barge under its control.

§160.203 Exemptions.

(a) Except for reporting notice of hazardous conditions, the following vessels are exempt from requirements in this subpart:

(1) Passenger and supply vessels when they are employed in the exploration for or in the removal of oil, gas, or mineral resources on the continental shelf.

(2) Oil Spill Recovery Vessels (OSRVs) when engaged in actual spill response operations or during spill response exercises.

(3) Vessels operating upon the following waters:

(i) Mississippi River between its sources and mile 235, Above Head of Passes;

(ii) Tributaries emptying into the Mississippi River above mile 235;

(iii) Atchafalaya River above its junction with the Plaquemine-Morgan City alternate waterway and the Red River; and

(iv) The Tennessee River from its confluence with the Ohio River to mile zero on the Mobile River and all other tributaries between those two points.

(b) If not carrying certain dangerous cargo or controlling another vessel carrying certain dangerous cargo, the following vessels are exempt from NOA requirements in this subpart:

(1) Vessels 300 gross tons or less, except for foreign vessels entering any port or place in the Seventh Coast Guard District as described in 33 CFR 3.35-1(b).

(2) Vessels operating exclusively within a Captain of the Port Zone.

(3) Vessels arriving at a port or place under force majeure.

(4) Towing vessels and barges operating solely between ports or places in the continental United States.

(5) Public vessels.

(6) Except for tank vessels, US vessels operating solely between ports or places in the United States on the Great Lakes.

(c) Vessels less than 500 gross tons need not submit the International Safety Management (ISM) Code Notice (Entry (7) in Table 160.206).

(d) [Suspended]

(e) [Suspended]

(f) US vessels need not submit the International Ship and Port Facility Code (ISPS) Notice Information (Entry (9) in Table 160.206).

§160.204 Definitions.

As used in this subpart:

Agent means any person, partnership, firm, company or corporation engaged by the owner or charterer of a vessel to act in their behalf in matters concerning the vessel.

Barge means a non-self propelled vessel engaged in commerce.

Carried in bulk means a commodity that is loaded or carried on board a vessel without containers or labels and received and handled without mark or count.

Certain dangerous cargo (CDC) includes any of the following:

(1) Division 1.1 or 1.2 explosives as defined in 49 CFR 173.50.

(2) Division 1.5D blasting agents for which a permit is required under 49 CFR 176.415, or for which a permit is required as a condition of a Research and Special Programs Administration exemption.

(3) Division 2.3 "poisonous gas", as listed in 49 CFR 172.101 that is also a "material poisonous by inhalation" as defined in 49 CFR 171.8, and that is in a quantity in excess of 1 metric ton per vessel.

(4) Division 5.1 oxidizing materials for which a permit is required under 49 CFR 176.415 or for which a permit is required as a condition of a Research and Special Programs Administration exemption.

(5) A liquid material that has a primary or subsidiary classification of Division 6.1 "poisonous material" as listed in 49 CFR 172.101 that is also a "material poisonous by inhalation" as defined in 49 CFR 171.8 and that is in a bulk packaging, or that is in a quantity in excess of 20 metric tons per vessel when not in a bulk packaging.

(6) Class 7, "highway route controlled quantity" radioactive material, or "fissile material, controlled shipment," as defined in 49 CFR 173.403.

(7) Bulk liquefied chlorine gas and bulk liquefied gas cargo that is flammable and/or toxic and carried under 46 CFR 154.7.

(8) The following bulk liquids:
   (i) Acetone cyanohydrin,
   (ii) Allyl alcohol,
   (iii) Chlorosulfonic acid,
   (iv) Crotonaldehyde,
   (v) Ethylene chlorohydrin,
   (vi) Ethylene dibromide,
   (vii) Methacrylonitrile, and
   (viii) Oleum (fuming sulphuric acid)

Charterer means the person or organisation that contracts for the majority of the carrying capacity of a ship for the transportation of cargo to a stated port for a specified period. This includes "time charterers" and voyage charterers".

Crewmember means all persons carried on board the vessel to provide navigation and maintenance of the vessel, its machinery, systems, and arrangements essential for propulsion and safe navigation or to provide services for other persons on board.

Great Lakes means Lakes Superior, Michigan, Huron, Erie, and Ontario, their connecting and tributary waters, the Saint Lawrence River as far Saint Regis, and adjacent port areas.

Gross tons means the tonnage determined by the tonnage authorities of a vessel's flag state in accordance with the national tonnage rules in force before the entry into force of the International Convention on Tonnage Measurement of Ships, 1969 ("Convention"). For a vessel measured only under Annex 1 of the Convention, gross tons means that tonnage. For a vessel measured under both systems, the higher gross tonnage is the tonnage used for the purposes of the 300 gross-ton threshold.

Hazardous condition means any condition that may adversely affect the safety of any vessel, bridge, structure, or shore area or the environmental quality of any port, harbor, or navigable waterway of the United States. It may, but need not, involve collision, fire, explosion, grounding, leaking, damage, injury or illness of a person on board, or manning shortage.

Nationality means the state (nation) in which a person is a citizen or to which a person owes permanent allegiance.

Operator means any person including, but not limited to, an owner, a charterer, or another contractor who conducts, or is responsible for, the operation of a vessel.

Persons in addition to crewmembers means any person onboard the vessel, including passengers, who are not included on the list of crewmembers.

Port or place of departure means any port or place in which a vessel is anchored or moored.

Port or place of destination means any port or place to which a vessel is bound to anchor or moor.

Public vessel means a vessel that is owned or demise (bareboat) chartered by the government of the United States, by a State or local government, or by the government of a foreign country and that is not engaged in commercial service.

Time charterer means the party who hires a vessel for a specific amount of time. The owner and his crew manage the vessel but the charterer selects the port of destination.

Voyage charterer means the party who hires a vessel for a single voyage. The owner and his crew manage the vessel but the charterer selects the port of destination.

§160.206 Information required in a NOA.

(a) Each NOA must contain all of the information items specified in Table 160.206.

TABLE 160.206. — NOA INFORMATION ITEMS

Required information	Vessels not carrying CDC	Vessels carrying CDC	
		Vessels	Towing vessels controlling vessels carrying CDC
(1) *Vessel information:*			
(i) Name;	X	X	X
(ii) Name of the registered owner;	X	X	X
(iii) Country of registry;	X	X	X
(iv) Call sign;	X	X	X
(v) International Maritime Organisation (IMO) international number or, if the vessel does not have an assigned IMO international number, substitute with official number;	X	X	X
(vi) Name of the operator;	X	X	X
(vii) Name of the charterer; and	X	X	X
(viii) Name of classification society.	X	X	X
(2) *Voyage information:*			
(i) Names of last five ports or places visited;	X	X	X
(ii) Dates of arrival and departure for last five ports or places visited;	X	X	X
(iii) For each port or place in the United States to be visited, list the names of the receiving facility, the port or place, the city, and the state;	X	X	X
(iv) For each port or place in the United States to be visited, the estimated date and time of arrival;	X	X	X
(v) For each port or place in the United States to be visited, the estimated date and time of departure;	X	X	X
(vi) The location (port or place and country) or position (latitude and longitude or waterway and mile marker) of the vessel at the time of reporting; and	X	X	X
(vii) The name and telephone number of a 24 hour point of contact.	X	X	X
(3) *Cargo information:*			
(i) A general description of cargo, other than CDC, onboard the vessel (e.g. grain, container, oil, etc.);	X	X	X
(ii) Name of each certain dangerous cargo carried, including cargo UN number, if applicable; and		X	X
(iii) Amount of each certain dangerous cargo carried.		X	X
(4) *Information for each Crewmember Onboard:*			
(i) Full name;	X	X	X
(ii) Date of birth;	X	X	X
(iii) Nationality;	X	X	X
(iv) Passport or mariners document number (type of identification and number);	X	X	X
(v) Position or duties on the vessel; and	X	X	X
(vi) Where the crewmember embarked (list port or place and country)	X	X	X
(5) *Information for each Person Onboard in Addition to Crew:*			
(i) Full name;	X	X	X
(ii) Date of birth;	X	X	X
(iii) Nationality;	X	X	X
(iv) Passport number; and	X	X	X
(v) Where the person embarked (list port or place and country)	X	X	X
(6) *Operational condition of equipment required by §164.35.*	X	X	X

Required information	Vessels not carrying CDC	Vessels carrying CDC	
		Vessels	Towing vessels controlling vessels carrying CDC
(7) *International Safety Management (ISM) Code Notice:*			
(i) The date of issuance for the company's Document of Compliance certificate that covers the vessel;	x	x	x
(ii) The date of issuance for the vessel's Safety Management Certificate; and	x	x	x
(iii) The name of the Flag Administration, or the recognized organization(s) representing the vessel flag administration, that issued those certificates.	x	x	x
(8) [Suspended]			
(9) *International Ship and Port Facility Code (ISPS) Notice:*			
(i) The date of issuance for the vessel's International Ship Security Certificate (ISSC), if any;	x	x	x
(ii) Whether the ISSC, if any, is an initial Interim ISSC, subsequent and consecutive Interim ISSC, or final ISSC;	x	x	x
(iii) Declaration that the approved ship security plan, if any, is being implemented;	x	x	x
(iv) If a subsequent and consecutive Interim ISSC, the reasons therefor;	x	x	x
(v) The name and 24 hour contact information for the Company Security Officer; and;	x	x	x
(vi) The name of the Flag Administration, or the recognised security organisation(s) representing the vessel flag Administration that issued the ISSC	x	x	x

(b) Vessels operating solely between ports or places in the continental United States need submit only the name of and date of arrival and departure for the last port or places visited to meet the requirements in entries (2)(i) and (ii) in Table 160.206 of this section.

(c) You may submit a copy of INS Form 1-418 to meet the requirements of entries (4) and (5) in Table 160.206.

(d) Any vessel planning to enter two or more consecutive ports or places in the United States during a single voyage may submit one consolidated Notification of Arrival at least 96 hours before entering the first port or place of destination. The consolidated notice must include the name of the port or place and estimated arrival and departure date for each destination of the voyage. Any vessel submitting a consolidated notice under this section must still meet the requirements of §160.208 of this part concerning requirements for changes to a NOA.

§160.208 Changes to a submitted NOA.

(a) Unless otherwise specified in this section, when submitted NOA information changes, vessels must submit a notice of change within the times required in §160.212.

(b) Changes in the following information need not be reported:

(1) Changes in arrival or departure times that are less than six (6) hours;

(2) Changes in vessel location or position of the vessel at the time of reporting (entry (2)(vi) in Table 160.206);

(3) Changes to crewmembers' positions or duties on the vessel (entry (5)(v) in Table 160.206).

(c) When reporting changes, submit only the name of the vessel, original NOA submission date, the port of arrival, the specific items to be corrected, and the new location or position of the vessel at the time of reporting. Only changes to NOA information need to be submitted.

§160.210 Methods for submitting a NOA.

(a) *Submission to the National Vessel Movement Center (NVMC).* Except as provided in paragraphs (b) and (c) of this section, vessels must submit NOA information required by §160.206 (entries 1-9 in Table 160.206) to the NVMC, United States Coast Guard, 408 Coast Guard Drive, Kearneysville, WV 25430, by:

(1) Electronic submission via the electronic Notice of Arrival and Departure (eNOAD) and consisting of the following three formats:

(i) A Web site that can be used to submit NOA information directly to the NVMC, accessible from the NVMC web site at http://www.nvmc.uscg.gov;

(ii) Electronic submission of Extensible Markup Language (XML) formatted documents via web service;

(iii) Electronic submission via Microsoft Infopath; contact the NVMC at sans@nvmc.uscg.gov or by telephone at 1-800-708-9823 or 304-264-2502 for more information.

(2) E-mail at sans@nvmc.uscg.gov. Workbook available at http://www.nvmc.uscg.gov;

(3) Fax at 1-800-547-8724 or 304-264-2684. Workbook available at http://www.nvmc.uscg.gov; or,

(4) Telephone at 1-800-708-9823 or 304-264-2502.

(c) *Seventh Coast Guard District.* Those foreign vessels 300 or less gross tons operating in the Seventh Coast Guard District must submit a NOA to the cognizant Captain of the Port (COTP).

(d) [Suspended]

221

§160.212 When to submit a NOA.

(a) *Submission of NOA.*

(1) Except as set out in paragraph (a)(2) of this section, all vessels must submit NOAs within the times required in paragraph (a)(3) of this section.

(2) Towing vessels, when in control of a vessel carrying CDC and operating solely between ports or places in the continental United States, must submit a NOA before departure but at least 12 hours before departure but at least 12 hours before entering the port or place of destination.

(3) Times for submitting NOAs are as follows:

If your voyage time is:-	You must submit a NOA:-
(i) 96 hours or more; or	At least 96 hours before entering the port or place of destination; or
(ii) Less than 96 hours	Before departure but at least 24 hours before entering the port or place of destination.

(b) *Submission of changes to NOA.*

(1) Except as set out in paragraph (b)(2) of this section, vessels must submit changes in NOA information within the times required in paragraph (b)(3) of this section.

(2) Towing vessels, when in control of a vessel carrying CDC and operating solely between ports or places in the continental United States, must submit changes to a NOA as soon as practicable but at least 6 hours before entering the port or place of destination.

(3) Times for submitting changes to NOAs are as follows:

If your remaining voyage time is:-	Then you must submit changes to a NOA:-
(i) 96 hours or more;	As soon as practicable but at least 24 hours before entering the port or place of destination;
(ii) Less than 96 hours but not less than 24 hours; or	As soon as practicable but at least 24 hours before entering the port or place of destination; or
(iii) Less than 24 hours	As soon as practicable but at least 24 hours before entering the port or place of destination;

(c) [Suspended]

§160.214 Waivers.

The Captain of the Port may waive, within that Captain of the Port's designated zone, any of the requirements of this subpart for any vessel or class of vessels upon finding that the vessel, route, area of operations, conditions of the voyage, or other circumstances are such that application of this subpart is unnecessary or impractical for purposes of safety, environmental protection, or national security.

§160.215 Notice of hazardous conditions.

Whenever there is a hazardous condition either aboard a vessel or caused by a vessel or its operation, the owner, agent, master, operator, or person in charge shall immediately notify the nearest Coast Guard Marine Safety Office or Group Office. (Compliance with this section does not relieve responsibility for the written report required by 46 CFR 4.05-10).

APPENDIX III

CODE OF FEDERAL REGULATIONS TITLE 33 — NAVIGATION AND NAVIGABLE WATERS

PART 161 — VESSEL TRAFFIC MANAGEMENT

Appendix III contains extracts from the above regulations issued by the United States Department of Commerce. For a complete description of this part see 33 CFR 161.

Subpart A — Vessel Traffic Services
General Rules

§161.1 Purpose and Intent.

(a) The purpose of this part is to promulgate regulations implementing and enforcing certain sections of the Ports and Waterways Safety Act (PWSA) setting-up a national system of Vessel Traffic Services that will enhance navigation, vessel safety, and marine environmental protection, and promote safe vessel movement by reducing the potential for collisions, rammings and groundings, and the loss of lives and property associated with these incidents within VTS areas established hereunder.

(b) Vessel Traffic Services provide the mariner with information related to the safe navigation of a waterway. This information, coupled with the mariner's compliance with the provisions set forth in this part, enhances the safe routing of vessels through congested waterways or waterways of particular hazard. Under certain circumstances, a VTS may issue directions to control the movement of vessels in order to minimize the risk of collision between vessels, or damage to property or the environment.

(c) The owner, operator, charterer, master or person directing the movement of a vessel remains at all times responsible for the manner in which the vessel is operated and maneuvered, and is responsible for the safe navigation of the vessel under all circumstances. Compliance with these rules or with a direction from the VTS is at all times contingent upon the exigencies of safe navigation.

(d) Nothing in this part is intended to relieve any vessel, owner, operator, charterer, master, or person directing the movement of a vessel from the consequences of any neglect to comply with this part or any other applicable law or regulations (e.g. the International Regulations for Prevention of Collisions at Sea, 1972 (72 COLREGS) or the Inland Navigation Rules) or of the neglect of any precaution which may be required by the ordinary practice of seamen, or by the special circumstances of the case.

§161.2 Definitions.

For the purposes of this part:

Cooperative Vessel Traffic Services (CVTS) means the system of vessel traffic management established and jointly operated by the United States and Canada within adjoining waters. In addition, CVTS facilitates traffic movement and anchorages, avoids jurisdictional disputes, and renders assistance in emergencies in adjoining United States and Canadian waters.

Hazardous Vessel Operating Condition means any condition related to a vessel's ability to safely navigate or maneuver, and includes, but is not limited to:

(1) The absence or malfunction of vessel operating equipment, such as propulsion machinery, steering gear, radar system, gyrocompass, depth sounding device, automatic radar plotting aid (ARPA), radiotelephone, Automatic Identification System equipment, navigation lighting, sound signalling devices or similar equipment.

(2) Any condition on board the vessel likely to impair navigation, such as lack of current nautical charts and publications, personnel shortage, or similar condition.

(3) Vessel characteristics that affect or restrict maneuverability, such as cargo arrangement, trim, loaded condition, underkeel clearance, speed, or similar characteristics.

Navigable waters means all navigable waters of the United States including the territorial sea of the United States, extending to 12 nautical miles from the United States baselines, as described in Presidential Proclamation No. 5928 of December 27, 1988.

Precautionary Area means a routing measure comprising an area within defined limits where vessels must navigate with particular caution and within which the direction of traffic may be recommended.

Navigable waters means all navigable waters of the United States, including the territorial sea of the United States, extending to 12 nautical miles from United States baselines, as described in Presidential Proclamation No 5928 of December 27, 1988.

Towing Vessel means any commercial vessel engaged in towing another vessel astern, alongside, or by pushing ahead.

Vessel Movement Center (VMC) means the shore-based facility that operates the vessel tracking system for a Vessel Movement Reporting System (VMRS) area or sector within such an area. The VMC does not necessarily have the capability or qualified personnel to interact with marine traffic, nor does it necessarily respond to traffic situations developing in the area, as does a Vessel Traffic Service (VTS).

Vessel Movement Reporting System (VMRS) means a mandatory reporting system used to monitor and track vessel movements. This is accomplished by a vessel providing information under established procedures as set forth in this part in the areas defined in Table 161.12 (c) (VTS and VMRS Centers, Call Signs/MMSI, Designated Frequencies, and Monitoring Areas).

Vessel Movement Reporting System (VMRS) User means a vessel, or an owner, operator, charterer, master, or person directing the movement of a vessel, that is required to participate in a VMRS.

Vessel Traffic Center (VTC) means the shore-based facility that operates the vessel traffic service for the Vessel Traffic Service area or sector within such an area.

Vessel Traffic Service (VTS) means a service implemented by the United States Coast Guard designed to improve the safety and efficiency of vessel traffic and to protect the environment. The VTS has the capability to interact with marine traffic and respond to traffic situations developing in the VTS area.

Vessel Traffic Service Area or VTS Area means the geographical area encompassing a specific VTS area of service. This area of service may be subdivided into sectors for the purpose of allocating responsibility to individual Vessel Traffic Centers or to identify different operating requirements.

> **Note:** Although regulatory jurisdiction is limited to the navigable waters of the United States, certain vessels will be encouraged or may be required, as a condition of port entry, to report beyond this area to facilitate traffic management within the VTS area.

VTS Special Area means a waterway within a VTS area in which special operating requirements apply.

VTS User means a vessel, or an owner, operator, charterer, master, or person directing the movement of a vessel, that is:

(a) Subject to the Bridge-to-Bridge Radiotelephone Act; or

(b) Required to participate in a VMRS within a VTS area (VMRS User).

VTS Users Manual means the manual established and distributed by the VTS to provide the mariner with a description of the services offered and rules in force for that VTS. Additionally, the manual may include chartlets showing the area and sector boundaries, general navigational information about the area, and procedures, radio frequencies, reporting provisions and other information which may assist the mariner while in the VTS area.

§161.3 Applicability.

The provisions of this subpart shall apply to each VTS User and may also apply to any vessel while underway or at anchor on the navigable waters of the United States within a VTS area, to the extent the VTS considers necessary.

§161.4 Requirement to carry the rules.

Each VTS User shall carry on board and maintain for ready reference a copy of these rules.

> **Note:** These rules are contained in the applicable U.S. Coast Pilot, the VTS User's Manual which may be obtained by contacting the appropriate VTS, and periodically published in the Local Notice to Mariners. The VTS User's Manual and the World VTS Guide, an International Maritime Organisation (IMO) recognised publication, contain additional information which may assist the prudent mariner while in the appropriate VTS area.

§161.5 Deviations from the rules.

(a) Requests to deviate from any provision in this part, either for an extended period of time or if anticipated before the start of a transit, must be submitted in writing to the appropriate District Commander. Upon receipt of the written request, the District Commander may authorize a deviation if it is determined that such a deviation provides a level of safety equivalent to that provided by the required measure or is a maneuver considered necessary for safe navigation under the circumstances. An application for an authorized deviation must state the need and fully describe the proposed alternative to the required measure.

(b) Requests to deviate from any provision in this part due to circumstances that develop during a transit or

immediately preceding a transit, may be made verbally to the appropriate VTS Commanding Officer. Requests to deviate shall be made as far in advance as practicable. Upon receipt of the request, the VTS Commanding Officer may authorize a deviation if it is determined that, based on vessel handling characteristics, traffic density, radar contacts, environmental conditions and other relevant information, such a deviation provides a level of safety equivalent to that provided by the required measure or is a maneuver considered necessary for safe navigation under the circumstances.

Services, VTS measures, and Operating Requirements

§161.10 Services.

To enhance navigation and vessel safety, and to protect the marine environment, a VTS may issue advisories, or respond to vessel requests for information, on reported conditions within the VTS area, such as:

(a) Hazardous conditions or circumstances;

(b) Vessel congestion;

(c) Traffic density;

(d) Environmental conditions;

(e) Aids to navigation status;

(f) Anticipated vessel encounters;

(g) Another vessel's name, type, position, hazardous vessel operating conditions, if applicable, and intended navigational movements, as reported;

(h) Temporary measures in effect;

(i) A description of local harbor operations and conditions, such as ferry routes, dredging, and so forth;

(j) Anchorage availability; or

(k) Other information or special circumstances.

§161.11 VTS measures.

(a) A VTS may issue measures or directions to enhance navigation and vessel safety and to protect the marine environment, such as, but not limited to:

(1) Designating temporary reporting points and procedures;

(2) Imposing vessel operating requirements; or

(3) Establishing vessel traffic routing schemes.

(b) During conditions of vessel congestion, restricted visibility, adverse weather, or other hazardous circumstances, a VTS may control, supervise, or otherwise manage traffic, by specifying times of entry, movement, or departure to, from or within a VTS area.

§161.12 Vessel operating requirements.

(a) Subject to the exigencies of safe navigation, a VTS User shall comply with all measures established or directions issued by by a VTS.

(b) If, in a specific circumstance, a VTS User is unable to safely comply with a measure or direction issued by the VTS, the VTS User may deviate only to the extent necessary to avoid endangering persons, property or the environment. The deviation shall be reported to the VTS as soon as is practicable.

(c) When not exchanging voice communications, a VTS User must maintain a listening watch as required by §26.04(e) of this chapter on the VTS frequency designated in Table 161.12(c) (VTS and VMRS Centers, Call Signs/MMSI, Designated Frequencies, and Monitoring Areas). In addition, the VTS User must respond promptly when hailed and communicate in the English language.

Note to §161.12(c): As stated in 47 CFR 80.148(b), a very high frequency watch on Channel 16 (156.800 Mhz) is not required on vessels subject to the Vessel Bridge-to-Bridge Radiotelephone Act and participating in a Vessel Traffic Service (VTS) system when the watch is maintained on both the vessel bridge-to-bridge frequency and a designated VTS frequency.

(d) As soon as practicable, a VTS User shall notify the VTS of any of the following:

(1) A marine casualty as defined in 46 CFR 4.05-1;

(2) Involvement in the ramming of a fixed or floating object;

(3) A pollution incident as defined in §151.15 of this chapter;

(4) A defect or discrepancy in an aid to navigation;

(5) A hazardous condition as defined in §160.203 of this chapter;

(6) Improper operation of vessel equipment required by Part 164 of this chapter;

(7) A situation involving hazardous materials for which a report is required by 49 CFR 176.48; and

(8) A hazardous vessel operating condition as defined in §161.2.

§161.13 VTS Special Area Operating Requirements.

The following operating requirements apply within a VTS Special Area:

(a) A VTS User shall, if towing astern, do so with as short a hawser as safety and good seamanship permits.

(b) A VMRS User shall:

(1) Not enter or get underway in the area without prior approval of the VTS;

(2) Not enter a VTS Special Area if a hazardous vessel operating condition or circumstance exists;

(3) Not meet, cross or overtake any other VMRS User in the area without prior approval of the VTS; and

(4) Before meeting, crossing or overtaking any other VMRS User in the area, communicate on the designated vessel bridge-to-bridge radiotelephone frequency, intended navigation movements, and any other information necessary in order to make safe passing arrangements. This requirement does not relieve a vessel of any duty prescribed by the International Regulations for Prevention of Collisions at Sea, 1972 (72 COLREGS) or the Inland Navigation Rules.

Subpart B — Vessel Movement Reporting System

§161.15 Purpose and intent.

(a) A Vessel Movement Reporting System (VMRS) is a system used to monitor and track vessel movements within a VTS or VMRS area. This is accomplished by requiring that vessels provide information under established procedures as set forth in this part, or as directed by the Center.

(b) To avoid imposing an undue reporting burden or unduly congesting radiotelephone frequencies, reports shall be limited to information which is essential to achieve the objectives of the VMRS. These reports are consolidated into three reports (sailing plan, position, and final).

§161.16 Applicability.

Unless otherwise stated, the provisions of this subpart shall apply to the following vessels and VMRS Users:

(a) Every power-driven vessel of 40 meters (approximately 131 feet) or more in length, while navigating;

(b) Every towing vessel of 8 meters (approximately 26 feet) or more in length, while navigating; or

(c) Every vessel certificated to carry 50 or more passengers for hire, when engaged in trade.

§161.17 Definitions.

As used in this subpart:

Center means a Vessel Traffic Center or Vessel Movement Center.

Published means available in a widely distributed and publicly available medium (e.g., VTS User's Manual, ferry schedule, Notice to Mariners).

§161.18 Reporting requirements.

(a) A Center may:

(1) Direct a vessel to provide any of the information set forth in Table 161.18(a) (IMO Standard Ship Reporting System);

(2) Establish other means of reporting for those vessels unable to report on the designated frequency; or

(3) Require reports from a vessel in sufficient time to allow advance vessel traffic planning.

(b) All reports required by this part shall be made as soon as is practicable on the frequency designated in Table 161.12(c) (VTS and VMRS Centers, Call Signs/MMSI, Designated Frequencies, and Monitoring Areas).

(c) When not exchanging communications, a VMRS User must maintain a listening watch as described in § 26.04(e) of this chapter on the frequency designated in Table 161.12(c) (VTS and VMRS Centers, Call Signs/MMSI, Designated Frequencies, and Monitoring Areas). In addition, the VMRS User must respond promptly when hailed and communicate in the English language.

Note: As stated in 47 CFR 80.148(b), a VHF watch on Channel 16 (156.800 Mhz) is not required on vessels subject to the Vessels Bridge-to-Bridge Radiotelephone Act and participating in a Vessel Traffic Service (VTS) system when the watch is maintained on both the vessel bridge-to-bridge frequency and a designated VTS frequency.

(d) A vessel must report:

(1) Any significant deviation from its Sailing Plan, as defined in §161.19, or from previously reported information; or

(2) Any intention to deviate from a VTS issued measure or vessel traffic routeing system.

(e) When reports required by this part include time information, such information shall be given using the local time zone in effect and the 24 hour military clock system.

§161.19 Sailing Plan (SP).

Unless otherwise stated, at least 15 minutes before navigating a VTS area, a vessel must report the:

(a) Vessel name and type;

(b) Position;

(c) Destination and ETA;

(d) Intended route;

(e) Time and point of entry; and

(f) Dangerous cargo on board, or in its tow, as defined in §161.203 of this chapter, and other required information as set out in §161.211 and §161.213 of this chapter, if applicable.

§161.20 Position Report (PR).

A vessel must report its name and position:

(a) Upon point of entry into a VMRS area;

(b) At designated points as set forth in Subpart C; or

(c) When directed by the Center.

§161.21 Automated reporting.

(a) Unless otherwise directed, vessels equipped with an Automatic Identification System (AIS) are required to make continuous, all stations, AIS broadcasts, in lieu of voice position reports, to those Centers denoted in Table 161.12(c) of this part.

(b) Should an AIS become non-operational, while or prior to navigating a VMRS area, it should be restored to operating condition as soon as possible, and, until restored a vessel must:

(1) Notify the Center;

(2) Make voice radio position reports at designated reporting points as required by §161.20(b) of this part; and

(3) Make any other reports as directed by the Center.

§161.22 Final Report (FR).

A vessel must report its name and position:

(a) On arrival at its destination; or

(b) When leaving a VTS area.

§161.23 Reporting exemptions.

(a) Unless otherwise directed, the following vessels are exempted from providing Position and Final Reports due to the nature of their operation:

(1) Vessels on a published schedule and route;

(2) Vessels operating within an area of a radius of three nautical miles or less; or

(3) Vessels escorting another vessel or assisting another vessel in maneuvering procedures.

(b) A vessel described in paragraph (a) of this section must:

(1) Provide a Sailing Plan at least 5 minutes but not more than 15 minutes before navigating within the VMRS area; and

(2) If it departs from its promulgated schedule by more than 15 minutes or changes its limited operating area, make the established VMRS reports, or report as directed.

APPENDIX IV

CODE OF FEDERAL REGULATIONS TITLE 33 — NAVIGATION AND NAVIGABLE WATERS

PART 164 — NAVIGATION SAFETY REGULATIONS

Appendix IV contains extracts from the above regulations issued by the United States Department of Commerce. For a complete description of this part see 33 CFR 164.

§164.01 Applicability.

(a) This part (except as specifically limited by this section) applies to each self-propelled vessel of 1600 or more gross tons (except as provided in paragraphs (c) and (d) of this section or for foreign vessels described in §164.02) when it is operating in the navigable waters of the United States except the St. Lawrence Seaway.

(c) Provisions of §164.11(a)2 and (c), §164.30, §164.33 and §164.46 do not apply to warships or other vessels owned, leased, or operated by the United States Government and used only in government non-commercial service when these vessels are equipped with electronic navigation systems that have met the applicable agency regulations regarding navigation safety.

(d) Provisions of §164.46 apply to some self-propelled vessels of less than 1600 gross tonnage.

§164.02 Applicability exception for foreign vessels.

(a) Except as provided in §164.46(a)(2), §§164.38 and 164.39 this part does not apply to vessels that:

  (1) Are not destined for, or departing from, a port or place subject to the jurisdiction of the United States; and

  (2) Are in:

    (i) Innocent passage through the territorial sea of the United States; or

    (ii) Transit through navigable waters of the United States which form a part of an international strait.

§164.03 Incorporation by reference.
(See 33 CFR 164.)

§164.11 Navigation underway: General.

The owner, master, or person in charge of each vessel underway shall ensure that:

  (a) The wheelhouse is constantly manned by persons who:

    (1) Direct and control the movement of the vessel; and

    (2) Fix the vessel's position;

  (b) Each person performing a duty described in paragraph (a) of this section is competent to perform that duty;

  (c) The position of the vessel at each fix is plotted on a chart of the area and the person directing the movement of the vessel is informed of the vessel's position;

  (d) Electronic and other navigational equipment, external fixed aids to navigation, geographic reference points, and hydrographic contours are used when fixing the vessel's position;

  (e) Buoys alone are not used to fix the vessel's position;

Note: Buoys are aids to navigation placed in approximate positions to alert the mariner to hazards to navigation or to indicate the orientation of a channel. Buoys may not maintain an exact position because strong or varying currents, heavy seas, ice, and collisions with vessels can move or sink them or set them adrift. Although buoys may corroborate a position fixed by other means, buoys cannot be used to fix a position: however, if no other aids are available, buoys alone may he used to establish an estimated position.

  (f) The danger of each closing visual or each closing radar contact is evaluated and the person directing the movement of the vessel knows the evaluation;

  (g) Rudder orders are executed as given;

  (h) Engine speed and direction orders are executed as given;

  (i) Magnetic variation and deviation and gyrocompass errors are known and correctly applied by the person directing the movement of the vessel;

  (j) A person whom he has determined is competent to steer the vessel is in the wheelhouse at all times (See also 46 U.S.C. 8702 (d), which requires an able seaman at the wheel on US vessels of 100 gross tons or more in narrow or crowded waters or during low visibility);

  (k) If a pilot other than a member of the vessel's crew is employed, the pilot is informed of the draft, maneuvering characteristics, and peculiarities of the vessel and of any abnormal circumstances on the vessel that may affect its safe navigation.

  (l) Current velocity and direction for the area to be transited are known by the person directing the movement of the vessel;

  (m) Predicted set and drift are known by the person directing the movement of the vessel;

  (n) Tidal state for the area to be transited is known by the person directing the movement of the vessel;

  (o) The vessel's anchors are ready for letting go;

  (p) The person directing the movement of the vessel sets the vessel's speed with consideration for:

    (1) The prevailing visibility and weather conditions;

    (2) The proximity of the vessel to fixed shore and marine structures;

    (3) The tendency of the vessel underway to squat and suffer impairment of maneuverability when there is small underkeel clearance;

    (4) The comparative proportions of the vessel and the channel;

    (5) The density of marine traffic;

    (6) The damage that might be caused by the vessel's wake;

    (7) The strength and direction of the current; and

    (8) Any local vessel speed limit;

(q) The tests required by §164.25 are made and recorded in the vessel's log; and

(r) The equipment required by this part is maintained in operable condition.

(s) Upon entering US waters, the steering wheel or lever on the navigating bridge is operated to determine if the steering equipment is operating properly under manual control, unless the vessel has been steered under manual control from the navigating bridge within the preceding 2 hours, except when operating on the Great Lakes and their connecting and tributary waters.

(t) At least two of the steering gear power units on the vessel are in operation when such units are capable of simultaneous operation, except when operating on the Great Lakes and their connecting and tributary waters.

(u) On each passenger vessel meeting the requirements of the International Convention for the Safety of Life at Sea, 1960 (SOLAS 60) and on each cargo vessel meeting the requirements of SOLAS 74 as amended in 1981, the number of steering gear power units necessary to move the rudder from 35° on either side to 30° on the other in not more than 28 seconds must be in simultaneous operation.

§164.13 Navigation underway: tankers.

(b) Each tanker must have an engineering watch capable of monitoring the propulsion system, communicating with the bridge, and implementing manual control measures immediately when necessary. The watch must be physically present in the machinery spaces or in the main control space and must consist of at least a licensed engineer.

(c) Each tanker must navigate with at least two licensed deck officers on watch on the bridge, one of whom may be a pilot. In waters where a pilot is required, the second officer must be an individual licensed and assigned to the vessel as master, mate, or officer in charge of a navigational watch, who is separate and distinct from the pilot.

(d) Except as specified in paragraph (e) of this section a tanker may operate with an auto pilot engaged only if all of the following conditions exist:

(1) The operation and performance of the automatic pilot conforms with the standards recommended by the International Maritime Organisation in IMO Resolution A.342(IX).

(2) A qualified helmsman is present at the helm and prepared at all times to assume manual control.

(3) The tanker is not operating in any of the following areas:

(i) The areas of the traffic separation schemes specified in subchapter P of this chapter.

(ii) The portions of a shipping safety fairway specified in part 166 of this chapter.

(iii) An anchorage ground specified in part 110 of this chapter.

(iv) An area within one-half nautical mile of any US shore.

(e) A tanker equipped with an integrated navigation system, and complying with paragraph (d)(2) of this section, may use the system with the auto pilot engaged while in the areas described in paragraphs (d)(3)(i) and (ii) of this section.

§164.15 Navigation bridge visibility. (See 33 CFR 164.)

§164.19 Requirements for vessels at anchor.

The master or person in charge of each vessel that is anchored shall ensure that:

(a) A proper anchor watch is maintained;

(b) Procedures are followed to detect a dragging anchor; and

(c) Whenever weather, tide, or current conditions are likely to cause the vessel's anchor to drag, action is taken to ensure the safety of the vessel, structures, and other vessels, such as being ready to veer chain, let go a second anchor, or get underway using the vessel's own propulsion or tug assistance.

§164.25 Tests before entering or getting underway.

(a) Except as provided in paragraphs (b) and (c) of this section no person may cause a vessel to enter into or get underway on the navigable waters of the United States unless no more than 12 hours before entering or getting underway, the following equipment has been tested:

(1) Primary and secondary steering gear. The test procedure includes a visual inspection of the steering gear and its connecting linkage, and, where applicable, the operation of the following:

(i) Each remote steering gear control system.

(ii) Each steering position located on the navigating bridge.

(iii) The main steering gear from the alternative power supply, if installed.

(iv) Each rudder angle indicator in relation to the actual position of the rudder.

(v) Each remote steering gear control system power failure alarm.

(vi) Each remote steering gear power unit failure alarm.

(vii) The full movement of the rudder to the required capabilities of the steering gear.

(2) All internal vessel control communications and vessel control alarms.

(3) Standby or emergency generator, for as long as necessary to show proper functioning, including steady state temperature and pressure readings.

(4) Storage batteries for emergency lighting and other systems in vessel control and propulsion machinery spaces.

(5) Main propulsion machinery, ahead and astern.

(b) Vessels navigating on the Great Lakes and their connecting and tributary waters, having once completed the test requirements of this sub-part, are considered to remain in compliance until arriving at the next port call on the Great Lakes.

(c) Vessels entering the Great Lakes from the St. Lawrence Seaway are considered to be in compliance with this sub-part if the required tests are conducted preparatory to or during the passage of the St. Lawrence Seaway or within one hour of passing Wolfe Island.

(d) No vessel may enter, or be operated on the navigable waters of the United States unless the emergency steering drill described below has been conducted within 48 hours prior to entry and logged in the vessel's logbook, unless the drill is conducted and logged on a regular basis at least once every three months. This drill must include at a minimum the following:

(1) Operation of the main steering gear from within the steering gear compartment.

(2) Operation of the means of communication between the navigating bridge and the steering compartment.

(3) Operation of the alternative power supply for the steering gear if the vessel is so equipped.

§164.30 Charts, publications and equipment: General.

No person may operate or cause the operation of a vessel unless the vessel has the marine charts, publications, and equipment as required by §§164.33 through 164.41 of this part.

§164.33 Charts and publications.

(a) Each vessel must have the following:

(1) Marine charts of the area to be transited, published by the National Ocean Service, US Army Corps of Engineers, or a river authority that:

(i) Are of a large enough scale and have enough detail to make safe navigation of the area possible; and

(ii) Are currently corrected.

(2) For the area to be transited, a currently corrected copy of, or applicable currently corrected extract from, each of the following publications:

(i) US Coast Pilot.

(ii) Coast Guard Light List.

(3) For the area to be transited, the current edition of, or applicable current extract from:

(i) Tide tables published by private entities using data provided by the National Ocean Service.

(ii) Tidal current tables published private entities using data provided by the National Ocean Service, or river current publication issued by the US Army Corps of Engineers, or a river authority.

(b) As an alternative to the requirements for paragraph (a) of this section, a marine chart or publication, or applicable extract, published by a foreign government may be substituted for a US chart and publication required by this section. The chart must be of large enough scale and have enough detail to make safe navigation of the area possible, and must be currently corrected. The publication, or applicable extract, must singly or in combination contain similar information to the US Government publication to make safe navigation of the area possible. The publication or applicable extract must be currently corrected, with the exception of tide and tidal current tables, which must be the current editions.

(c) As used in this section, "currently corrected" means corrected with changes contained in all Notices to Mariners published by National Imagery and Mapping Agency, or an equivalent foreign government publication, reasonably available to the vessel, and that is applicable to the vessel's transit.

§164.35 Equipment: All vessels.

Each vessel must have the following:

(a) A marine radar system for surface navigation.

(b) An illuminated magnetic steering compass, mounted in a binnacle, that can be read at the vessel's main steering stand.

(c) A current magnetic compass deviation table or graph or compass comparison record for the steering compass, in the wheelhouse.

(d) A gyrocompass.

(e) An illuminated repeater for the gyrocompass required by paragraph (d) of this section that is at the main steering stand, unless that gyrocompass is illuminated and is at the main steering stand.

(f) An illuminated rudder angle indicator in the wheelhouse.

(g) The following maneuvering information prominently displayed on a fact sheet in the wheelhouse:

(1) A turning circle diagram to port and starboard that shows the time and distance and advance and transfer required to alter course 90 degrees with maximum rudder angle and constant power settings, for either full and half speeds, or for full and slow speeds. For vessels whose turning circles are essentially the same for both directions, a diagram showing a turning circle in one direction, with a note on the diagram stating that turns to port and starboard are essentially the same, may be substituted.

(2) The time and distance to stop the vessel from either full and half speeds, or from full and slow speeds, while maintaining approximately the initial heading with minimum application of rudder.

(3) For each vessel with a fixed propeller, a table of shaft revolutions per minute for a representative range of speeds.

(4) For each vessel with a controllable pitch propeller, a table of control settings for a representative range of speeds.

(5) For each vessel that is fitted with an auxiliary device to assist in maneuvering, such as a bow thruster, a table of vessel speeds at which the auxiliary device is effective in maneuvering the vessel.

(6) The maneuvering information for the normal load and normal ballast condition for:

(i) Calm weather—wind 10 knots or less, calm sea;

(ii) No current;

(iii) Deep water conditions-water depth twice the vessel's draft or greater; and

(iv) Clean hull.

(7) At the bottom of the fact sheet, the following statement:

Warning.

The response of the (name of the vessel) may be different from that listed above if any of the following conditions, upon which the maneuvering information is based, are varied:

(1) Calm weather-wind 10 knots or less, calm sea;

(2) No current;

(3) Water depth twice the vessel's draft or greater;

(4) Clean hull; and

(5) Intermediate drafts or unusual trim.

(h) An echo depth sounding device.

(i) A device that can continuously record the depth readings of the vessel's echo depth sounding device except when operating on the Great Lakes and their connecting and tributary waters.

(j) Equipment on the bridge for plotting relative motion.

(k) Simple operating instructions with a block diagram, showing the changeover procedures for remote steering gear control systems and steering gear power units, permanently displayed on the navigating bridge and in the steering gear compartment.

(l) An indicator readable from the centerline conning position showing the rate of revolution of each propeller, except when operating on the Great Lakes and their connecting and tributary waters.

(m) If fitted with controllable pitch propellers, an indicator readable from the centerline conning position showing the pitch and operational mode of such propellers, except when operating on the Great Lakes and their connecting and tributary waters.

(n) If fitted with lateral thrust propellers, an indicator readable from the centerline conning position showing the direction and amount of thrust of such propellers, except when operating on the Great Lakes and their connecting and tributary waters.

(o) A telephone or other means of communication for relaying headings to the emergency steering station. Also, each vessel of 500 gross tons and over and constructed on or after June 9th 1995 must be provided with arrangements for supplying visual compass readings to the emergency steering station.

§164.37 Equipment: Vessels of 10,000 gross tons or more.

(a) Each vessel of 10,000 gross tons or more must have, in addition to the radar system under §164.35(a), a second marine radar system that operates independently of the first.

> **Note:** Independent operation means two completely separate systems, from separate branch power supply circuits or distribution panels to antennas, so that failure of any component of one system will not render the other system inoperative.

(b) On each tanker of 10,000 gross tons or more that is subject to 46 U.S.C. 3708, the dual radar system required by this part must have a short range capability and a long range capability; and each radar must have true north features consisting of a display that is stabilized in azimuth.

§164.38 Automatic radar plotting aids (ARPA). (See 33 CFR 164.)

§164.39 Steering Gear: Foreign Tankers. (See 33 CFR 164).

§164.40 Devices to indicate speed and distance.

(a) Each vessel required to be fitted with an Automatic Radar Plotting Aid (ARPA) under §164.38 must be fitted with a device to indicate speed and distance of the vessel either through the water, or over the ground.

§164.41 Electronic position fixing devices.

(a) Each vessel calling at a port in the continental United States, including Alaska south of Cape Prince of Wales, except each vessel owned or bareboat chartered and operated by the United States, or by a state or its political subdivision, or by a foreign nation, and not engaged in commerce, must have one of the following:

(1) A type I or II LORAN C receiver as defined in Section 1.2(e), meeting Part 2 (Minimum Performance Standards) of the Radio Technical Commission for Marine Services (RTCM) Paper 12-78/DO-100 dated December 20, 1977, entitled "Minimum Performance Standards (MPS) Marine Loran-C Receiving Equipment". Each receiver installed must be labeled with the information required under paragraph (b) of this section.

(2) A satellite navigation receiver with:

(i) Automatic acquisition of satellite signals after initial operator settings have been entered; and

(ii) Position updates derived from satellite information during each usable satellite pass.

(3) A system that is found by the Commandant to meet the intent of the statements of availability, coverage, and accuracy for the US Coastal Confluence Zone (CCZ) contained in the US "Federal Radionavigation Plan" (Report No. DOD-NO 4650.4-P, I or No. DOT-TSC-RSPA-80-16, I). A person desiring a finding by the Commandant under this subparagraph must submit a written application describing the device to the Assistant Commandant for Operations, 2100 Second Street, SW, Washington, DC 20593-0001. After reviewing the application, the Commandant may request additional information to establish whether or not the device meets the intent of the Federal Radionavigation Plan.

Note.—The Federal Radionavigation Plan is available from the National Technical Information Service, Springfield, Va. 22161, with the following Government Accession Numbers:

Vol 1, ADA 116468
Vol 2, ADA 116469
Vol 3, ADA 116470
Vol 4, ADA 116471

(b) Each label required under paragraph (a)(1) of this section must show the following:

(1) The name and address of the manufacturer.

(2) The following statement by the manufacturer: This receiver was designed and manufactured to meet Part 2 (Minimum Performance Standards) of the RTCM MPS for Marine Loran-C Receiving Equipment.

§164.42 Rate of turn indicator.

Each vessel of 100,000 gross tons or more shall be fitted with a rate of turn indicator.

§164.43 Automatic Identification System Shipborne Equipment (See 33 CFR 164.)

Each vessel required to provide automated position reports to a Vessel Traffic Service (VTS) must do so by an installed Automatic Identification System Shipborne Equipment (AISSE).

§164.46 Automatic Identification System (AIS) (See 33 CFR 164.)

§164.51 Deviations from rules: Emergency.

Except for the requirements of §164.53(b), in an emergency, any person may deviate from any rule in this part to the extent necessary to avoid endangering persons, property, or the environment.

§164.53 Deviations from rules and reporting: Non-operating equipment.

(a) If during a voyage any equipment required by this part stops operating properly, the person directing the movement of the vessel may continue to the next port of call, subject to the directions of the District

Commander or the Captain of the Port, as provided by 33 CFR 160.

(b) If the vessel's radar, radio navigation receivers, gyrocompass, echo depth sounding device, or primary steering gear stops operating properly, the person directing the movement of the vessel must report or cause to be reported that it is not operating properly to the nearest Captain of the Port, District Commander, or, if participating in a Vessel Traffic Service, to the Vessel Traffic Center, as soon as possible.

§164.55 Deviations from rules: Continuing operation or period of time.

The Captain of the Port, upon written application, may authorize a deviation from any rule in this part if he determines that the deviation does not impair the safe navigation of the vessel under anticipated conditions and will not result in a violation of the rules for preventing collisions at sea. The authorization may be issued for vessels operating in the waters under the jurisdiction of the Captain of the Port for any continuing operation or period of time the Captain of the Port specifies.

§164.61 Marine casualty reporting and record retention.

When a vessel is involved in a marine casualty as defined in 46 CFR 4.03-1, the master or person in charge of the vessel shall:

(a) Ensure compliance with 46 CFR 4.05, "Notice of Marine Casualty and Voyage Records," and

(b) Ensure that the voyage records required by 46 CFR 4.05-15 are retained for:

(1) 30 days after the casualty if the vessel remains in the navigable waters of the United States; or

(2) 30 days after the return of the vessel to a United States port if the vessel departs the navigable waters of the United States within 30 days after the marine casualty.

§164.70 Definitions. (See 33 CFR 164.)

§164.72 Navigational safety equipment, charts or maps, and publications required on towing vessels. (See 33 CFR 164.)

§164.74 Towline and terminal gear for towing astern. (See 33 CFR 164.)

§164.76 Towline and terminal gear for towing alongside and pushing ahead. (See 33 CFR 164.)

§164.78 Navigation underway: Towing vessels. (See 33 CFR 164.)

§164.80 Tests, inspections and voyage planning. (See 33 CFR 164.)

§164.82 Maintenance, failure and reporting. (See 33 CFR 164.)

APPENDIX V

CODE OF FEDERAL REGULATIONS TITLE 33 — NAVIGATION AND NAVIGABLE WATERS

PART 165 — REGULATED NAVIGATION AREAS AND LIMITED ACCESS AREAS — EXTRACTS

Appendix V contains extracts from the above regulations issued by the United States Department of Commerce. For a complete description of this part see 33 CFR 165. Regulations specific to this volume are given by title only where the area concerned falls wholly within pilotage waters; where the regulation affects an area outside pilotage waters, extracts from the regulation are given.

Subpart A — General

§165.5 Establishment procedures

(a) A safety zone, security zone, or regulated navigation area may be established on the initiative of any authorised Coast Guard official.

(b) Any person may request that a safety zone, security zone, or regulated navigation area may be established. Except as provided in paragraph (c) of this section, each request must be submitted in writing to either the Captain of the Port or District Commander.

(c) Safety Zones and Security Zones. If, for good cause, the request for a safety zone or security zone is made less than 5 working days before the zone is to be established, the request may be made orally, but it must be followed by a written request within 24 hours.

§165.7 Notification

(a) The establishment of these limited access areas and regulated navigation areas is considered rule making. The procedures used to notify persons of the establishment of these areas vary depending upon the circumstances and emergency conditions. Notification may be made by marine broadcasts, local notice to mariners, local news media, distribution in leaflet form, and on-scene oral notice, as well as publication in the Federal Register.

(b) Notification normally contains the physical boundaries of the area, the reasons for the rule, its estimated duration, and the method of obtaining authorization to enter the area, if applicable, and special navigational rules, if applicable.

§165.8 Geographic coordinates

Geographic coordinates expressed in terms of latitude or longitude, or both, are not intended for plotting on maps or charts whose referenced horizontal datum is the North American Datum of 1983 (NAD 83), unless such geographic coordinates are expressly labelled NAD 83. Geographic coordinates without the NAD 83 reference may be plotted on maps or charts referenced to NAD 83 only after application of the appropriate corrections that are published on the particular map or chart being used.

§165.9 Geographic application of limited and controlled access areas and regulated navigation areas.

(a) *General.* The geographic application of the limited and controlled access areas and regulated navigation areas

in this part are determined based on the statutory authority under which each is created.

(b) *Safety zones and regulated navigation areas.* These zones and areas are created under the authority of the Ports and Waterways Safety Act, 33 U.S.C. 1221-1232.

(c) *Security zones.* These zones have two sources of authority — the Ports and Waterways Safety Act, 33 U.S.C. 1221-1232, and the Act of June 15, 1917, as amended by both the Magnuson Act of August 9, 1950 ("Magnuson Act"), 50 U.S.C. 191-195, and sec. 104 of the Maritime Transportation Security Act of 2002.

(d) *Naval vessel protection zones.* These zones are issued under the authority of 14 U.S.C. 91 and 633 and may be established in waters subject to the jurisdiction of the United States as defined in §2.38 of this chapter, including the territorial sea to a seaward limit of 12 nautical miles from the baseline.

Subpart B — Regulated Navigation Areas

§165.10 Regulated navigation area.

A regulated navigation area is a water area within a defined boundary for which regulations for vessels navigating within the area have been established under this part.

§165.11 Vessel operating requirements (regulations).

Each District Commander may control vessel traffic in an area which is determined to have hazardous conditions, by issuing regulations:

(a) Specifying times of vessel entry, movement, or departure to, from, within, or through ports, harbors, or other waters;

(b) Establishing vessel size, speed, draft limitations, and operating conditions; and

(c) Restricting vessel operation, in a hazardous area or under hazardous conditions, to vessels which have particular operating characteristics or capabilities which are considered necessary for safe operation under the circumstances.

§165.13 General Regulations.

(a) The master of a vessel in a regulated navigation area shall operate the vessel in accordance with the regulations contained in Subpart F.

(b) No person may cause or authorize the operation of a vessel in a regulated navigation area contrary to the regulations in this Part.

Subpart C — Safety Zones

§165.20 Safety zones.

A safety zone is a water area, shore area, or water and shore area, to which, for safety or environmental purposes, access is limited to authorised persons, vehicles, or vessels. It may be stationary and described by fixed limits or it may be described as a zone around a vessel in motion.

§165.23 General regulations.

Unless otherwise provided for in this part:

(a) No person may enter a safety zone unless authorised by the Captain of the Port or the District Commander;

(b) No person may bring or cause to be brought into a safety zone any vehicle, vessel or object unless authorised by the Captain of the Port or the District Commander;

(c) No person may remain in a safety zone or allow any vehicle, vessel or object to remain in a safety zone unless authorised by the Captain of the Port or the District Commander; and

(d) Each person in a safety zone who has notice of a lawful order or direction shall obey the order or direction of the Captain of the Port or District Commander issued to carry out the purposes of this subpart.

Subpart D — Security Zones

§165.30 Security zones.

(a) A security zone is an area of land, water, or land and water which is so designated by the Captain of the Port or District Commander for such time as is necessary to prevent damage or injury to any vessel or waterfront facility, to safeguard ports, harbors, territories, or waters of the United States or to secure the observance of the rights and obligations of the United States.

(b) The purpose of a security zone is to safeguard from destruction, loss or injury from sabotage or other subversive acts, accidents, or other causes of a similar nature:

(1) Vessels,

(2) Harbors,

(3) Ports and

(4) Waterfront facilities in the United States and all territory, continental or insular, that is subject to the jurisdiction of the United States.

§165.33 General regulations.

Unless otherwise provided in the special regulations in Subpart F of this part:

(a) No person or vessel may enter or remain in a security zone without the permission of the Captain of the Port;

(b) Each person and vessel in a security zone shall obey any direction or order of the Captain of the Port;

(c) The Captain of the Port may take possession and control of any vessel in the security zone;

(d) The Captain of the Port may remove any person, vessel, article, or thing from a security zone;

(e) No person may board, or take or place any article or thing on board, any vessel in a security zone without the permission of the Captain of the Port; and

(f) No person may take or place any article or thing upon any waterfront facility in a security zone without the permission of the Captain of the Port.

Subpart E — Restricted Waterfront Areas

§165.40 Restricted Waterfront Areas.

The Commandant, may direct the COTP to prevent access to waterfront facilities, and port and harbor areas, including vessels and harbor craft therein. This section may apply to persons who do not possess the credentials outlined in 33 CFR 125.09 when certain shipping activities are conducted that are outlined in 33 CFR 125.15.

Subpart F — Specific Regulated Navigation Areas and Limited Access Areas

§165.100 Regulated navigation area; Navigable waters within the First Coast Guard District.

§165.101 Kittery, Maine; regulated navigation area.

§165.102 Security Zone; Walkers Point, Kennebunkport, Maine.

§165.103 Safety and Security Zones; LPG Vessel Transits in Portland, Maine, Captain of the Port Zone, Portsmouth Harbor, Portsmouth, New Hampshire.

§165.105 Security Zones; Passenger Vessels, Portland, Maine, Captain of the Port Zone.

§165.110 Safety and Security Zone; Liquefied Natural Gas Carrier Transits and Anchorage Operations, Boston, Massachusetts.

(b) *Location.* The following areas are safety and security zones:

(1) *Vessels underway.* All navigable waters of the United States within the Captain of the Port (COTP) Boston zone, as defined in 33 CFR 3.05-10, two miles ahead and one mile astern, and 500 yards on each side of any liquified natural gas carrier (LNGC) vessel while underway.

(2) *Vessels anchored in Broad Sound.* All waters within a 500 yard radius of any anchored LNGC vessel located in the waters of Broad Sound bounded by a line starting at position 42°25′N 070°58′W; then running SE to 42°22′N 070°56′W; then running E to 42°22′N 070°50′W; then running N to 42°25′N 070°50′W; then running W back to the starting point (NAD 83).

(c) *Regulations.*

(1) In accordance with the general regulations in §§165.23 and 165.33 of this part, entry into or movement within these zones is prohibited unless authorized by the Captain of the Port, Boston, or his authorised patrol representative.

§165.111 Safety Zone; Boston Harbor; Boston, Massachusetts.

§165.112 Safety Zone; USS Cassin Young, Boston, Massachusetts.

§165.114 Safety and Security Zones; Escorted Vessels - Boston Harbor, Massachusetts.

§165.115 Safety and Security Zones; Pilgrim Nuclear Power Plant, Plymouth, Massachusetts.

CAUTION. Mariners should be aware that there appears to be an error in the position quoted below as 41°56′40·5″N 70°41′04·5″W and that it appears that the correct position should be in the vicinity of 41°56′40·5″N 70°34′04·5″W. Mariners in doubt as to the correct position should contact the United States Coast Guard for clarification.

(a) *Location.* All waters of Cape Cod Bay and land adjacent to those waters enclosed by a line beginning at position:

41°57′05″N 70°34′42″W; then running SE to position:

41°56′40·5″N 70°41′04·5″W; then running SW to position:

41°56′32″N 70°34′14″W; then running NW to position:

41°56′55·5″N 70°34′52″W; then running NE back to position:

41°57′05″N 70°34′42″W.

(b) *The regulations:*

(1) In accordance with the general regulations in §§165.23 and 165.33 of this part, entry into or movement within these zones this zone is prohibited unless authorized by the Captain of the Port, Boston.

§165.116 Safety and Security Zones; Salem and Boston Harbors, Massachusetts.

§165.120 Safety Zone; Chelsea River, Boston Inner Harbor, Boston, Massachusetts.

§165.121 Safety and Security Zones; High Interest Vessels, Narragansett Bay, Rhode Island.

§165.122 Providence River, Providence, Rhode Island; regulated navigation area.

§165.130 Sandy Hook Bay, New Jersey; security zone.

§165.140 New London Harbor, Connecticut; security zone.

§165.141 Safety Zone; Sunken vessel EMPIRE KNIGHT, Boon Island, Maine.

(a) *Location.* The following area is a safety zone:

All waters of the Atlantic Ocean within a 1000 yard radius of the stern section of the sunken vessel EMPIRE KNIGHT, in approximate position 43°06′19″N 70°27′09″W (NAD 1983) and extending from the water's surface to the seabed floor.

(c) *The regulations:*

(1) The general regulations contained in 33 CFR 165.23 apply.

(2) All vessels and persons are prohibited from anchoring, diving, dredging, dumping, fishing, trawling, laying cable, or conducting salvage operations in this zone except as authorized by the Coast Guard Captain of the Port, Portland, Maine. Innocent transit through the area within the safety zone is not affected by this regulation and does not require the authorization of the Captain of the Port.

§165.150 New Haven Harbor, Quinnipiac River, Mill River.

§165.152 Coast Guard Station Fire Island, Long Island, New York; safety zone.

§165.153 Regulated navigation area; Long Island Sound Marine Inspection and Captain of the Port Zone.

(a) *Regulated Navigation Area location.* All waters of the Long Island Sound Marine Inspection and Captain of the Port (COTP) Zone, as delineated in 33 CFR 3.05–35, extending seaward 12 nautical miles from the territorial sea baseline, are established as a regulated navigation area (RNA).

(b) *Applicability.* This section applies to all vessels operating within the RNA excluding public vessels.

(c) *Definitions.* The following definitions apply to this section:

Commercial service means any type of trade or business involving the transportation of goods or individuals, except service performed by a combatant vessel.

Ferry means a vessel that:

(1) Operates in other than ocean or coastwise service;

(2) Has provisions only for deck passengers or vehicles, or both;

(3) Operates on a short run on a frequent schedule between two points over the most direct water route; and

(4) Offers a public service of a type normally attributed to a bridge or tunnel.

Public vessels means vessels owned or bareboat chartered and operated by the United States, or by a State or political subdivision thereof, or by a foreign nation, except when such vessel is engaged in commercial service.

Territorial sea baseline means the line defining the shoreward extent of the territorial sea of the United States drawn according to the principles, as recognized by the United States, of the Convention on the Territorial Sea and the Contiguous Zone, 15 U.S.T. 1606, and the 1982 United Nations Convention on the Law of the Sea (UNCLOS), 21 I.L.M. 1261. Normally, the territorial sea baseline is the mean low water line along the coast of the United States.

(d) *Regulations.*

(1) Speed restrictions in the vicinity of Naval Submarine Base New London and Lower Thames River. Unless authorized by the Captain of the Port (COTP), vessels of 300 gross tons or more may not proceed at a speed in excess of eight knots in the Thames River from New London Harbor channel buoys 7 and 8 (Light List numbers 21875 and 21880 respectively) north through the upper limit of the Naval Submarine Base New London Restricted Area, as that area is specified in 33 CFR 334.75(a). The U.S. Navy and other Federal, State and municipal agencies may assist the U.S. Coast Guard in the enforcement of this rule.

(2) Enhanced communications. Vessels of 300 gross tons or more and all vessels engaged in towing barges must issue securité calls on marine band or Very High Frequency (VHF) radio channel 16 upon approach to the following locations:

(i) Inbound approach to Cerberus Shoal; and

(ii) Outbound approach to Race Rock Light (USCG Light List No. 19815).

(3) All vessels operating within the RNA that are bound for a port or place located in the United States or

that must transit the internal waters of the United States, must be inspected to the satisfaction of the U.S. Coast Guard, before entering waters within three nautical miles from the territorial sea baseline. Vessels awaiting inspection will be required to anchor in the manner directed by the COTP. This section does not apply to vessels operating exclusively within the Long Island Sound Marine Inspection and COTP Zone, vessels on single voyage which depart from and return to the same port or place within the RNA, all towing vessels engaged in coastwise trade, vessels in innocent passage not bound for a port or place subject to the jurisdiction of the United States, and all vessels not engaged in commercial service whose last port of call was in the United States. Vessels requiring inspection by the COTP may contact the COTP via marine band or Very High Frequency (VHF) channel 16, telephone at (203) 468-4401, facsimile at (203) 468-4418, or letter, addressed to Captain of the Port, Long Island Sound, 120 Woodward Ave., New Haven, CT 06512.

(4) All vessels operating within the RNA that are bound for a port or place located in the United States or that must transit the internal waters of the United States, must obtain authorization from the Captain of the Port (COTP) before entering waters within three nautical miles from the territorial sea baseline. Vessels awaiting COTP authorization to enter waters within three nautical miles from the territorial sea baseline will be required to anchor in the manner directed by the COTP. This section does not apply to vessels operating exclusively within the Long Island Sound Marine Inspection and COTP Zone, vessels on a single voyage which depart from and return to the same port or place within the RNA, all towing vessels engaged in coastwise trade, vessels in innocent passage not bound for a port or place subject to the jurisdiction of the United States, and all vessels not engaged in commercial service whose last port of call was in the United States. Vessels may request authorization from the COTP by contacting the COTP via marine band or Very High Frequency (VHF) channel 16, telephone at (203) 468-4401, facsimile at (203) 468-4418, or letter addressed to Captain of the Port, Long Island Sound, 120 Woodward Ave., New Haven, CT 06512.

(5) Vessels over 1,600 gross tons operating in the RNA within three nautical miles from the territorial sea baseline that are bound for a port or place located in the United States or that must transit the internal waters of the United States must receive authorization from the COTP prior to transiting or any intentional vessel movements, including, but not limited to, shifting berths, departing anchorage, or getting underway from a mooring. This section does not apply to vessels in innocent passage not bound for a port or place subject to the jurisdiction of the United States.

(6) Ferry vessels. Vessels of 300 gross tons or more are prohibited from entering all waters within a 1200-yard radius of any ferry vessel transiting in any portion of the Long Island Sound Marine Inspection and COTP Zone without first obtaining the express prior authorization of the ferry vessel licensed operator, licensed master, COTP, or the designated COTP on-scene patrol.

(7) Vessels engaged in commercial service. No vessel may enter within a 100-yard radius of any vessel engaged in commercial service while that vessel is transiting, moored, or berthed in any portion of the Long Island Sound Marine Inspection and COTP zone without the express prior authorization of the vessel's licensed operator, master, COTP, or the designated COTP on-scene representative.

(8) Bridge foundations. Any vessel operating beneath a bridge must make a direct, immediate and expeditious passage beneath the bridge while remaining within the navigable channel. No vessel may stop, moor, anchor or loiter beneath a bridge at any time. No vessel may approach within a 25-yard radius of any bridge foundation, support, stanchion, pier or abutment except as required for the direct, immediate and expeditious transit beneath a bridge.

(9) This section does not relieve any vessel from compliance with applicable navigation rules.

§165.154 Safety and Security Zones; Long Island Sound Marine Inspection Zone and Captain of the Port Zone.

§165.155 Northville Industries Offshore Platform, Riverhead, Long Island, New York; safety zone.

§165.160 Safety and Security Zones; Liquified Hazardous Gas Vessel, Liquified Hazardous Gas Facility and Designated Vessel Transits, New York Marine Inspection Zone and Captain of the Port Zone.

§165.164 Security Zones; Dignitary Arrival/Departure New York, New York.

§165.165 Regulated navigation area; Kill Van Kull Channel, Newark Bay Channel, South Elizabeth Channel, Elizabeth Channel, Port Newark Channel and New Jersey Pierhead Channel, New York and New Jersey.

§165.169 Safety and Security Zones; New York Marine Inspection Zone and Captain of the Port Zone.

(a) *Safety and security zones.* The following waters within the New York Marine Inspection Zone and Captain of the Port Zone are safety and security zones:

(12) *Approaches to New York, Atlantic Ocean.* The following area is a security zone: All waters of the Atlantic Ocean between the Ambrose to Hudson Canyon Traffic Lane and the Barnegat to Ambrose Traffic Lane bound by the following points: 40°21′29.9″N 73°44′41.0″W; 40°21′04.5″N 73°45′31.4″W; 40°15′28.3″N 73°44′13.8″W; 40°15′35.4″N 73°43′29.8″W; 40°19′21.2″N 73°42′53.0″W; 40°21′29.9″N 73°44′41.0″W.

(b) *Regulations.*

(1) Entry into or remaining in a safety or security zone is prohibited unless authorized by the Coast Guard Captain of the Port, New York.

(4) The zone described in paragraph (a)(12) of this section is not a Federal Anchorage Ground. Only vessels directed by the Captain of the Port or his or her designated representative to enter this zone are authorized to anchor here.

(5) Vessels do not need permission from the Captain of the Port to transit the area described in paragraph (a)(12) of this section during periods when that security zone is not being enforced.

(c) *Enforcement.* Enforcement periods for the zone in paragraph (a)(12) will be announced through marine information broadcast or other appropriate method of communication. The Coast Guard is enforcing the zone whenever a vessel is anchored in the security zone or a Coast Guard patrol vessel is on scene.

§165.170 Safety Zone; Triathlon, Ulster Landing, Hudson River, New York.

Subpart G — Protection of Naval Vessels

§165.2010 Purpose.

This subpart establishes the geographic parameters of naval vessel protection zones surrounding US naval vessels in the navigable waters of the United States.

§165.2015 Definitions.

The following definitions apply to this subpart:

Large US naval vessel means any US naval vessel greater than 100 feet in length overall.

Naval vessel protection zone is a 500 yard regulated area of water surrounding large US naval vessels that is necessary to provide for the safety or security of these US naval vessels.

Official patrol means those personnel designated and supervised by a senior naval officer present in command.

Senior naval officer present in command is, unless otherwise designated by competent authority, the senior line officer of the US Navy on active duty, eligible for command at sea, who is present and in command of any part of the Department of Navy in the area.

US naval vessel means any vessel owned, operated, chartered, or leased by the US Navy; and any vessel under the operational control of the US Navy or a Combatant Command.

§165.2020 Enforcement authority.

(a) Coast Guard.

(b) Senior naval officer present in command.

§165.2025 Atlantic Area.

(a) This section applies to any vessel or person in the navigable waters of the United States within the boundaries of the US Coast Guard Atlantic Area which includes the First, Fifth, Seventh, Eighth, and Ninth US Coast Guard Districts.

Note to paragraph (a): The boundaries of the US Coast Guard Atlantic Area and the First, Fifth, Seventh, Eighth, and Ninth US Coast Guard Districts are set out in 33 CFR part 3.

(b) A naval vessel protection zone exists around US naval vessels greater than 100 feet in length overall at all times in the navigable waters of the United States, whether the large US naval vessel is underway, anchored, moored, or within a floating drydock, except when the large naval vessel is moored or anchored within a restricted area or within a naval defensive sea area.

(c) The Navigation Rules shall apply at all times within a naval vessel protection zone.

(d) When within a naval vessel protection zone, all vessels shall operate at the minimum speed necessary to maintain a safe course, unless required to maintain speed by the Navigation Rules, and shall proceed as directed by the Coast Guard, the senior naval officer present in command, or the official patrol. When within a naval vessel protection zone, no vessel or person is allowed within 100 yards of a large US naval vessel unless authorized by the Coast Guard, the senior naval officer present in command, or official patrol.

(e) To request authorization to operate within 100 yards of a large US naval vessel, contact the Coast Guard, the senior naval officer present in command, or official patrol on VHF-FM channel 16.

(f) When conditions permit, the Coast Guard, senior naval officer present in command, or the official patrol should:

(1) Give advance notice on VHF-FM channel 16 of all large US naval vessel movements;

(2) Permit vessels constrained by their navigational draft or restricted in their ability to maneuver to pass within 100 yards of a large US naval vessel in order to ensure a safe passage in accordance with the Navigation Rules; and:

(3) Permit commercial vessels anchored in a designated anchorage area to remain at anchor when within 100 yards of passing large US naval vessels; and:

(4) Permit vessels that must transit via a navigable channel or waterway to pass within 100 yards of a moored or anchored large US naval vessel with minimal delay consistent with security.

Note to paragraph (f): The listed actions are discretionary and do not create any additional right to appeal or otherwise dispute a decision of the Coast Guard, the senior naval officer present in command, or the official patrol.

CODE OF FEDERAL REGULATIONS TITLE 33 — NAVIGATION AND NAVIGABLE WATERS

PART 334 — Danger zones and restricted area regulations

Appendix VI contains extracts from the above regulations issued by the United States Department of Commerce.
For a complete description of this part see 33 CFR 334.
Regulations specific to this volume are given by title only where the area concerned falls wholly within pilotage waters; where the regulation affects an area outside pilotage waters, extracts of the regulation are given.

§334.1 Purpose.
The purpose of this part is to:
  (a) Prescribe procedures for establishing, amending and disestablishing danger zones and restricted areas.
  (b) List the specific danger zones and restricted areas and their boundaries; and
  (c) Prescribe specific requirements, access limitations and controlled activities within the danger zones and restricted areas.

§334.2 Definitions.
(a) **Danger zone.** A defined water area (or areas) used for target practice, bombing, rocket firing or other especially hazardous operations, normally for the armed forces. The danger zones may be closed to the public on a full time or intermittent basis, as stated in the regulations.
(b) **Restricted area.** A defined water area for the purpose of prohibiting or limiting public access to the area. Restricted areas generally provide security for Government property and/or protection to the public from the risks of damage or injury arising from the Government's use of that area.
   There are danger zones and/or restricted areas in the following areas:

§334.10 Gulf of Maine off Seal Island, Maine; Naval aircraft bombing target area.
(a) *The danger zone.* A circular area with a radius of 1·5 nautical miles, having its centre just easterly of Seal Island at latitude 43°53′00″ and longitude 68°44′00″.
(b) *The regulations:*
  (1) No aerial bombing practice will take place in the danger zone after 5:00 p.m. Mondays through Saturdays, at any time on Sundays, or during foggy or inclement weather.
  (2) Vessels or other watercraft will be allowed to enter the danger zone any time there are no aerial bombing exercises being conducted.
  (3) No live ammunition or explosives will be dropped in the area.
  (5) Prior to the conducting of each bombing practice, the area will be patrolled by a naval aircraft or surface vessel to ensure that no persons or watercraft are within the danger zone.
   Vessels may be requested to veer off when drops are to be made, however, drops will be made only when the area is clear. The patrol aircraft will employ the method of warning known as "buzzing" which consists of low flight by the airplane and repeated opening and closing of the throttle.

  (6) Any such watercraft shall, upon being so warned, immediately leave the designated area and, until the conclusion of the practice, shall remain at such distance that it will be safe from falling projectiles.

§334.20 Gulf of Maine off Cape Small, Maine; Naval aircraft practice mining range area.
(a) *The danger zone.* Within an area bounded as follows:
   43°43′·0N   69°46′·0W.
   43°38′·5N   69°46′·0W.
   43°38′·5N   69°49′·5W.
   43°42′·2N   69°49′·5W.
(b) *The regulations.*
  (1) Test drops from aircraft will be made within the area at intermittent periods from noon until sunset local time and only during periods of good visibility.
  (2) Testing will not restrict any fishing, recreational, or commercial activities in the testing area.
  (3) Aircraft will patrol the area prior to and during test periods to insure that no surface vessels are within the area. No test drops will be made while surface vessels are transitting the area.
  (4) No live ammunition or explosives will be dropped in the area.

§334.30 Gulf of Maine off Pemaquid Point, Maine; Naval Sonobuoy Test Area.
(a) *The area.* The test area or "Foul Area" encompasses a circular area one nautical mile in radius, the centre of which is located 7·9 nautical miles, bearing 187° magnetic from Pemaquid LIght.
(b) *The regulations:*
  (1) Sonobuoy drops will be made only in the designated area and when visibility is at least three miles.
  (2) Sonobuoy drop tests will normally be conducted at intermittent periods on a five day week basis, Monday through Friday. However, on occasions tests may be conducted intermittently on a seven day week basis.
  (3) Prior to and during the period when sonobuoys are being dropped, an escort vessel or naval aircraft will be in the vicinity to ensure that no persons or vessels are in the testing area. Vessels may be requested to veer off when sonobuoys are about to be dropped, however, drops will be made only when the area is clear.
  (5) No live ammunition or explosives will be dropped in the area.

§334.40 Atlantic Ocean in vicinity of Duck Island, Maine, Isles of Shoals; Naval aircraft bombing target area.
(a) *The danger zone.* A circular area with a radius of 500 yards having its centre on Shag Rock in the vicinity of Duck Island at latitude 43°00′12″, longitude 70°36′12″.
(b) *The regulations:*
  (1) No person or vessel shall enter or remain in the danger zone from 8:00 a.m. to 5:00 p.m. (local time) daily, except as authorized by the enforcing agency.

§334.45 Kennebec River, Bath Iron Works Shipyard, Bath, Maine; Naval restricted area.

§334.50 Piscataqua River at Portsmouth Naval Shipyard, Kittery, Maine; restricted areas.

§334.60 Cape Cod Bay south of Wellfleet Harbor, Massachusetts; Naval aircraft bombing target area.

(a) *The danger zone.* A circular area with a radius of 1000 yards having its centre on the aircraft bombing target hulk James Longstreet in Cape Cod Bay at latitude 41°49′46″, longitude 70°02′54″.

(b) *The regulations:*

(1) No vessel shall enter or remain in the danger zone at any time, except as authorized by the enforcing agency.

§334.70 Buzzards Bay and adjacent waters, Massachusetts; danger zones for naval operations.

(a) Atlantic Ocean in vicinity of Nomans Land:-

(1) *The area.* The waters surrounding Nomans Land within an area bounded as follows:

41°12′·5N 70°50′·5W.
41°15′·5N 70°51′·5W.
41°17′·5N 70°50′·5W.
41°16′·0N 70°47′·5W.
41°12′·5N 70°47′·5W.

(2) *The regulations.* No vessel or person shall at any time enter or remain within a rectangular portion of the area bounded on the north by latitude 41°16′·0, on the east by longitude 70°47′·5, on the south by latitude 41°12′·5, and on the west by longitude 70°50′·5, or within the remainder of the area between November 1 and April 30, inclusive, except by permission of the enforcing agency.

§334.75 Thames River, Naval Submarine Base New London; restricted area.

§334.78 Rhode Island Sound, Atlantic Ocean, approximately 4·0 nautical miles due south of Lands End in Newport, Rhode Island; restricted area for naval practice minefield.

§334.80 Narragansett Bay, Rhode Island; restricted area.

§334.81 Narragansett Bay, East Passage, Coddington Cove, Naval Station Newport, Newport, Rhode Island; Naval restricted area.

§334.82 Narragansett Bay, East Passage, Coasters Harbor Island, Naval Station Newport, Newport, Rhode Island; Restricted area.

§334.85 New York Harbor, adjacent to the Stapleton Naval Station, Staten Island, New York; restricted area.

§334.102 Sandy Hook Bay, Naval weapons station Earle, Piers and Terminal Channel, Middletown, New Jersey; restricted area.

APPENDIX VII

NAVIGATION RULES FOR UNITED STATES INLAND WATERS

Inland Navigational Rules Act of 1980 modifies the International Regulations for Preventing Collisions at Sea, 1972 for use in US Inland Waters, inshore of established lines of demarcation. These lines are shown, where appropriate, on Admiralty charts and described in this volume.

The Navigation Rules for US Inland Waters follow closely the *International Regulations for Preventing Collisions at Sea, 1972*, the Rules having corresponding numbers and usually corresponding paragraph numbers as well. This Appendix shows only those Rules for US Inland Waters or parts of those Rules, which differ from the *International Regulations*, except where the modifications are of no navigational significance. The modifications are shown in italic type; where matter has been omitted, this is indicated by the use of ' · · · '.

PART A - GENERAL

Rule 1

Application

The complete Rule has been rewritten:

(a) These Rules apply to all vessels upon the *inland waters of the United States, and to vessels of the United States on the Canadian waters of the Great Lakes to the extent that there is no conflict with Canadian law.*

(b)(i) *These Rules constitute special rules made by an appropriate authority within the meaning of Rule 1(b) of the International Regulations.*

  (ii) *All vessels complying with the construction and equipment requirements of the International Regulations are considered to be in compliance with these Rules.*

(c) Nothing in these Rules shall interfere with the operation of any special rules made by the *Secretary of the Navy* with respect to additional station or signal lights and shapes or whistle signals for ships of war and vessels proceeding under convoy, or by *the Secretary* with respect to additional station or signal lights and shapes for fishing vessels engaged in fishing as a fleet. These additional station or signal lights and shapes or whistle signals shall, so far as possible, be such that they cannot be mistaken for any light, shape, or signal authorized elsewhere under these Rules. *Notice of such special rules shall be published in the Federal Register and, after the effective date specified in such notice, they shall have effect as if they were a part of these Rules.* [1]

(d) Traffic separation schemes may be *established* for the purposes of these Rules. *Vessel traffic service regulations may be in effect in certain areas.*

(e) Whenever the *Secretary determines* that a vessel or class of vessels of special construction or purpose cannot comply fully with the provisions of any of these Rules with respect to the number, position, range, or arc of visibility of lights or shapes, as well as to the disposition and characteristics of sound-signalling appliances, without interfering with the special function of the vessel, *the* vessel shall comply with such other provisions in regard to the number, position, range, or arc of visibility of lights or shapes, as well as to the disposition and characteristics of sound-signalling appliances, as *the Secretary* shall have determined to be the closest possible compliance with these Rules. *The Secretary may issue a certificate of alternative compliance for a vessel or class of vessels specifying the closest possible compliance with these Rules. The Secretary of the Navy shall make these determinations and issue certificates of alternative compliance for vessels of the Navy.*

(f) *The Secretary may accept a certificate of alternative compliance issued by a contracting party to the International Regulations if he determines that the alternative compliance standards of the contracting party are substantially the same as those of the United States.*

[1] *Submarines may display, as a distinctive means of identification, an intermittent flashing amber (yellow) beacon with a sequence of operation of one flash per second for three (3) seconds followed by a three (3) second off-period. Other special rules made by the Secretary of the Navy with respect to additional station and signal lights are found in Part 706 of Title 32, Code of Federal Regulations (32 CFR 706).*

Rule 3
General Definitions

Paragraph (h) of the International Regulations is omitted, paragraphs (i), (j), (k) and (l) become (h), (i), (j) and (k) and new paragraphs (l) to (q) have been added:

(l) *"Western Rivers" means the Mississippi River, its tributaries, South Pass, and Southwest Pass, to the navigational demarcation lines dividing the high seas from harbors, rivers and other inland waters of the United States, and the Port Allen-Morgan City Alternate Route, and that part of the Atchafalaya River above its junction with the Port Allen-Morgan City Alternate Route including the Old River and the Red River;*

(m) *"Great Lakes" means the Great Lakes and their connecting tributary waters including the Calumet River as far as the Thomas J. O'Brien Lock and Controlling Waters (between mile 326 and 327), the Chicago River as far as the east side of the Ashland Avenue Bridge (between mile 321 and 322), and the Saint Lawrence River as far east as the lower exit of Saint Lambert Lock;*

(n) *"Secretary" means the Secretary of the Department in which the Coast Guard is operating;*

(o) *"Inland Waters" means the navigable waters of the United States shoreward of the navigational demarcation lines dividing the high seas from harbors, rivers, and other inland waters of the United States and the waters of the Great Lakes on the United States side of the International Boundary;*

(p) *"Inland Rules" or "Rules" mean the Inland Navigational Rules and the annexes thereto, which govern the conduct of vessels and specify the lights, shapes, and sound signals that apply on inland waters; and*

(q) *"International Regulations" means the International Regulations for Preventing Collisions at Sea, 1972, including annexes currently in force for the United States.*

PART B. STEERING AND SAILING RULES

Rule 9

Narrow Channels

Paragraphs (a)(i) and (ii) and (e)(i) have been rewritten:

(a)*(i)* A vessel proceeding along the course of a narrow channel or fairway shall keep as near to the outer limit of the channel or fairway which lies on her starboard side as is safe and practicable.

(ii) Notwithstanding paragraph (a)(i) and Rule 14(a), a power-driven vessel operating in narrow channels or fairways on the Great Lakes, Western Rivers, or waters specified by the Secretary, and proceeding downbound with a following current shall have the right-of-way over an upbound vessel, shall propose the manner and place of passage, and shall initiate the maneuvering signals prescribed by Rule 34(a)(i), as appropriate. The vessel proceeding upbound against the current shall hold as necessary to permit safe passing.

(e)(i) *In a narrow channel or fairway when overtaking, the power-driven vessel vessel intending to overtake another power-driven vessel shall indicate her intention by sounding the appropriate signal prescribed in Rule 34(c) and take steps to permit safe passing. The power-driven vessel being overtaken, if in agreement, shall sound the same signal and may, if specifically agreed to take steps to permit safe passing. If in doubt she shall sound the danger signal prescribed in Rule 34(d).*

Rule 10

Traffic separation schemes

Paragraph (a) has been rewritten:

(a) This Rule applies to traffic separation schemes ... and does not relieve any vessel of her obligation under any other Rule.

Rule 14

Head-on Situation

Paragraph (a) has been rewritten and new paragraph (d) added:

(a) *Unless otherwise agreed,* when two power-driven vessels are meeting on reciprocal or nearly reciprocal courses so as to involve risk of collision each shall alter her course to starboard so that each shall pass on the port side of the other.

(d) Notwithstanding paragraph (a) of this Rule, a power-driven vessel operating on the Great Lakes, Western Rivers, or waters specified by the Secretary, and proceeding downbound with a following current shall have the right-of-way over an upbound vessel, shall propose the manner of passage, and shall initiate the maneuvering signals prescribed by Rule 34(a)(i), as appropriate.

Rule 15

Crossing Situation

Existing Rule of the International Regulations becomes paragraph (a) and new paragraph (b) added:

(b) Notwithstanding paragraph (a), on the Great Lakes, Western Rivers, or water specified by the Secretary, a power-driven vessel crossing a river shall keep out of the way of a power-driven vessel ascending or descending the river.

Rule 18

Responsibilities Between Vessels

Paragraphs (d)(i) and (d)(ii) of the International Regulations have been omitted, paragraph (e) becomes paragraph (d).

PART C. LIGHTS AND SHAPES

Rule 21

Definitions

Paragraphs (a) and (b) have been rewritten and new paragraph (g) has been added:

(a) "Masthead light" means a white light placed over the fore and aft centerline of the vessel showing an unbroken light over an arc of the horizon of 225 degrees and so fixed as to show the light from right ahead to 22·5 degrees abaft the beam on either side of the vessel, *except that on a vessel of less than 12 meters in length the masthead light shall be placed as nearly as practicable to the fore and aft centerline of the vessel.*

(b) "Sidelights" mean a green light on the starboard side and a red light on the port side each showing an unbroken light over an arc of the horizon of 112·5 degrees and so fixed as to show the light from right ahead to 22·5 degrees abaft the beam on its respective side. In a vessel of less than 20 meters in length the sidelights may be combined in one lantern carried on the fore and aft centerline of the vessel, *except that on a vessel of less than 12 meters in length the sidelights when combined in one lantern shall be placed as nearly as practicable to the fore and aft centerline of the vessel.*

(g) *"Special flashing light" means a yellow light flashing at regular intervals at a frequency of 50 to 70 flashes per minute, placed as far forward and as nearly as practicable on the fore and aft centerline of the tow and showing an unbroken light over an arc of the horizon of not less than 180 degrees nor more than 225 degrees and so fixed as to show the light from right ahead to abeam and no more than 22·5 degrees abaft the beam on either side of the vessel.*

Rule 22

Visibility of Lights

Add at the end of paragraphs (a), (b) and (c) of the International Regulations:

...a special flashing light, 2 miles.

Rule 23

Power-driven Vessels Underway

Paragraphs (c)(ii) and (c)(iii) of the International Regulations have been omitted, paragraph (b) has been rewritten and new paragraph (d) has been added.

(b) An air-cushion vessel when operating in non-displacement mode shall, in addition to the lights prescribed in paragraph (a) of this Rule, exhibit an all-round flashing yellow light, *where it can best be seen.*

(d) A power-driven vessel when operating on the Great Lakes may carry an all-round white light in lieu of the second masthead light and sternlight prescribed in paragraph (a) of this Rule. The light shall be carried in the position of the second masthead light and be visible at the same minimum range.

Rule 24

Towing and Pushing

Paragraphs (a), (c), (d), (f), (g), and (h) have been rewritten, paragraph (i) becomes paragraph (j), and new paragraph (i) has been added:

(a) A power-driven vessel when towing *astern* shall exhibit:

  (i) Instead of the light prescribed in Rule 23(a)(i) or (a)(ii), two masthead lights in a vertical line. When the length of the tow, measuring from the stern of the towing vessel to the after end of the tow exceeds 200 meters, three such lights in a vertical line;

  (ii) sidelights;

  (iii) a sternlight;

  (iv) a towing light in a vertical line above the sternlight;

  (v) when the length of the tow exceeds 200 meters, a diamond shape where it can best be seen.

(c) A power-driven vessel when pushing ahead or towing alongside, except *as required by paragraphs (b) and (i) of this Rule,* shall exhibit:

  (i) instead of the light prescribed either in Rule 23(a)(i) or 23(a)(ii), two mastheads lights in a vertical line.

  (ii) sidelights; and

  (iii) *two towing lights in a vertical line.*

(d) A power-driven vessel to which paragraphs (a) or (c) of this Rule apply shall also comply with Rule 23(a)(i) and 23(a)(ii).

(f) Provided that any number of vessels being towed alongside or pushed in a group shall be lighted as one vessel, *except as provided in paragraph (iii):*

  (i) a vessel being pushed ahead, not being part of a composite unit, shall exhibit at the forward end, sidelights, *and a special flashing light;*

  (ii) a vessel being towed alongside shall exhibit a sternlight and at the forward end, sidelights, *and a special flashing light;*

  (iii) *when vessels are towed alongside on both sides of the towing vessels a sternlight shall be exhibited on the stern of the outboard vessel on each side of the towing vessel, and a single set of sidelights as far forward and as far outboard as is practicable, and a single special flashing light;*

(g) An inconspicuous, partly submerged vessel or object, *or combination of such vessels or objects being towed,* shall exhibit:

  (i) *if it is less than 25 meters in breadth, one all round white light at or near each end;*

  (ii) *if it is 25 meters or more in breadth, four all-round white lights to mark its length and breadth;*

  (iii) if it exceeds 100 meters in length, additional all round white lights between the lights prescribed in subparagraphs (i) and (ii) so that the distance between the lights shall not exceed 100 meters: *Provided, that any vessels or objects being towed alongside each other shall be lighted as one vessel or object;*

  (iv) a diamond shape at or near the aftermost extremity of the last vessel or object being towed...

  (v) *the towing vessel may direct a searchlight in the direction of the tow to indicate its presence to an approaching vessel.*

(h) Where from any sufficient cause it is impracticable for a vessel or object being towed to exhibit the lights...prescribed in paragraph (e) or (g) of this Rule, all possible measures shall be taken to light the vessel or object towed or at least to indicate the presence of the unlighted vessel or object.

(i) Notwithstanding paragraph (c), on the Western Rivers (except below the Huey P. Long Bridge on the Mississippi River) and on waters specified by the Secretary, a power-driven vessel when pushing ahead or towing alongside, except as paragraph (b) applies, shall exhibit:

  (i) sidelights; and

  (ii) two towing lights in a vertical line.

(j) Where from any sufficient cause it is impracticable for a vessel not normally engaged in towing operations to display the lights prescribed by paragraph (a),(c) or *(i)* of this Rule, such vessel shall not be required to exhibit those lights when engaged in towing another vessel in distress or otherwise in need of assistance. All possible measures shall be taken to indicate the nature of the relationship between the towing vessel and the vessel being towed as authorized by Rule 36, in particular by illuminating the *tow.*

Rule 25

Sailing Vessels Underway and Vessels under Oars

Paragraph (e) has been rewritten:

(e) A vessel proceeding under sail when also being propelled by machinery shall exhibit forward where it can best be seen a conical shape, apex downwards. *A vessel of less than 12 meters in length is not required to exhibit this shape, but may do so.*

Rule 27

Vessels Not Under Command or Restricted in Their Ability to Maneuver

Paragraphs (b)(iii), (c) and (d)(iii) have been rewritten:

(b)(iii) when making way through the water, *masthead lights,* sidelights and a sternlight and a sternlight in addition to the lights prescribed in sub-paragraph (b)(i);

(c) A power-driven vessel engaged in a towing operation such as severely restricts the towing vessel and her tow in their ability to deviate from their course shall, in addition to the lights or shapes prescribed in *subparagraphs (b)(i) and (ii) of this Rule,* exhibit the lights or shape *prescribed in Rule 24.*

(d)(iii) when at anchor, the lights or shapes prescribed in this paragraph instead of the lights or shape prescribed in Rule 30, *for anchored vessels.*

Rule 28

Vessels Constrained by their Draught

Rule 28 of the International Regulations has been omitted from the Inland Rules.

Rule 30

Anchored Vessels and Vessels Aground

Paragraph (d) has been rewritten and paragraph (g) has been added:

(*d*) A vessel aground shall exhibit the lights prescribed in paragraph (a) or (b) of this Rule and in addition, *if practicable,* where they can best be seen:
(i) two all-round red lights in a vertical line;
(ii) three balls in a vertical line.

(*g*) *A vessel of less than 20 meters in length, when at anchor in a special anchorage area designated by the Secretary, shall not be required to exhibit the anchor lights and shapes required by this Rule.*

PART D. SOUND AND LIGHT SIGNALS

Rule 34

Maneuvering and Warning Signals.

Paragraphs (a), (b) and (c) have been rewritten and new paragraphs (g) and (h) have been added:

(*a*) *When power-driven vessels are in sight of one another and meeting or crossing at a distance within half a mile of each other, each vessel underway, when maneuvering as authorized or required by these Rules:*
(i) *shall indicate that maneuver by the following signals on her whistle: one short blast to mean "I intend to leave you on my port side"; two short blasts to mean "I intend to leave you on my starboard side"; and three short blasts to mean "I am operating astern propulsion".*
(ii) *upon hearing the one or two blast signal of the other shall, if in agreement, sound the same whistle signal and take the steps necessary to effect a safe passing. If, however, from any cause, the vessel doubts the safety of the proposed maneuver, she shall sound the danger signal specified in paragraph (d) of this Rule and each vessel shall take appropriate precautionary action until a safe passing agreement is made.*

(*b*) *Any vessel may supplement the whistle signals prescribed in paragraph (a) of this Rule by light signals:*
(i) *these signals shall have the following significance:*
• *one flash to mean "I intend to leave you on my port side";*
• *two flashes to mean "I intend to leave you on my starboard side";*

• *three flashes to mean "I am operating astern propulsion";*
(ii) *the duration of each flash shall be about 1 second; and*
(iii) *the light used for this signal shall, if fitted, be an all-round white or yellow light, visible at a minimum range of 2 miles, synchronized with the whistle, and shall comply with the provisions of Annex I to these Rules.*

(*c*) *When in sight of one another:*
(i) *a power-driven vessel intending to overtake another power-driven vessel shall indicate her intention by the following signals on her whistle:*
• *one short blast to mean "I intend to overtake you on your starboard side";*
• *two short blasts to mean "I intend to overtake you on your port side", and*
(ii) *the power-driven vessel about to be overtaken shall, if in agreement, sound a similar signal. If in doubt she shall sound the danger signal prescribed in paragraph (d).*

(*g*) *When a power-driven vessel is leaving a dock or berth, she shall sound one prolonged blast.*

(*h*) *A vessel that reaches agreement with another vessel in a head-on, crossing, or overtaking situation, as for example, by using the radiotelephone as prescribed by the Bridge-to-Bridge Radiotelephone Act (85 Stat. 164; 33 U.S.C 1201 et seq.), is not obliged to sound the whistle signals prescribed by this Rule, but may do so. If agreement is not reached, then whistle signals shall be exchanged in a timely manner and shall prevail.*

Rule 35

Sound Signals in Restricted Visibility

Paragraph (c) has been rewritten and paragraph (d) of the International Regulations has been omitted. Paragraphs (e), (f), (g), (h), (i) and (j) become (d), (e), (f), (g), (h) and (i); and new paragraph (j) has been added:

(c) A vessel not under command; a vessel restricted in her ability to maneuver *whether underway or at anchor; ...,* a sailing vessel; a vessel engaged in fishing, *whether underway or at anchor;* and a vessel engaged in towing or pushing another vessel shall, instead of the signals prescribed in paragraphs (a) or (b) of this Rule, sound at intervals of not more than 2 minutes, three blasts in succession; namely one prolonged followed by two short blasts.

(j) *The following vessels shall not be required to sound signals as prescribed in paragraph (f) of this Rule when anchored in a special anchorage area designated by the Secretary:*
(i) *a vessel of less than 20 meters in length; and*
(ii) *a barge, canal boat, scow or other nondescript craft.*

Rule 36

The complete Rule has been rewritten:

Signals to Attract Attention

If necessary to attract the attention of another vessel, any vessel may make light or sound signals that cannot be mistaken for any signal authorized elsewhere in these Rules, or may direct the beam of her searchlight in the direction of the danger, in such a way as not to embarrass any vessel.

Rule 37

Distress Signals

While this Rule remains unaltered an additional signal is given in Annexe IV to the Inland Rules, namely:

(o) *A high intensity white light flashing at regular intervals from 50 to 70 times per minute.*

Rule 38

Exemptions

This rule has been completely rewritten in full:

Any vessel or class of vessels, the keel of which is laid or which is at a corresponding stage of construction before December 24, 1980, provided that she complies with the requirements of:

(a) The Act of June 7, 1897 (30 Stat. 96), as amended (33 U.S.C. 154-232) for vessels navigating the waters subject to that statute;

(b) Section 4233 of the Revised Statutes (33 U.S.C. 301-356) for vessels navigating the waters subject to that statute;

(c) The Act of February 8, 1895 (28 Stat. 645), as amended (33 U.S.C. 241-295) for vessels navigating the waters subject to that statute; or

(d) Sections 3, 4, and 5 of the Act of April 25, 1940 (54 Stat. 163), as amended (46 U.S.C. 526 b, c, and d) for motorboats navigating the waters subject to that statute; shall be exempted from compliance with the technical Annexes to these Rules as follows:

(i) The installation of lights with ranges prescribed in Rule 22, until 4 years after the effective date of these Rules, except that vessels of less than 20 meters in length are permanently exempt;.

(ii) The installation of lights with color specifications as prescribed in Section 7 of Annex 1 to these Rules, until 4 years after the effective date of these Rules, except that vessels of less than 20 meters in length are permanently exempt;

(iii) The repositioning of lights as a result of a conversion to metric units and rounding off measurement figures, are permanently exempt, and:

(iv) The horizontal repositioning of masthead lights prescribed by Annex I to these Rules:
  1. on vessels of less than 150 metres in length, permanent exemption.
  2. on vessels of 150 metres or more in length, until 9 years after the effective date of these Rules.

(v) The restructuring or repositioning of all lights to meet the prescriptions of Annex I to these Rules, until 9 years after the effective date of these Rules.

(vi) Power-driven vessels of 12 meters or more but less than 20 meters in length are permanently exempt from the provisions of Rule 23 (a)(i) and Rule 23 (a)(iv) provided that, in place of these lights, the vessel exhibits a white light aft visible all round the horizon; and:

(vii) The requirements for sound signal appliances prescribed in Annex III to these Rules, until 9 years after the effective date of these Rules.

APPENDIX VIII

CODE OF FEDERAL REGULATIONS TITLE 50 — WILDLIFE AND FISHERIES

Appendix VIII contains extracts from parts 222, 224 and 226 of the above regulations issued by the United States Department of Commerce.

For a complete description of these parts see 50 CFR.

Part 222 – Endangered and Threatened Marine Species

Subpart A — Introduction and General Provisions

§222.101 Purpose and scope of regulations.

The regulations of parts 222, 223, and 224 of this chapter implement the Endangered Species Act, and govern the taking, possession, transportation, sale, purchase, barter, exportation, importation of, and other requirements pertaining to wildlife and plants under the jurisdiction of the Secretary of Commerce and determined to be threatened or endangered pursuant to section 4(a) of the Act. These regulations are implemented by the National Marine Fisheries Service, National Oceanic and Atmospheric Administration, US Department of Commerce. This part pertains to general provisions and definitions. Specifically, parts 223 and 224 pertain to provisions to threatened species and endangered species, respectively. Part 226 enumerates designated critical habitat for endangered and threatened species.

Part 224 – Endangered Marine and Anadromous Species

§224.103 Special prohibitions for endangered marine mammals.

(c) Approaching Right Whales

   (1) *Prohibitions.* Except as provided under paragraph (c)(3) of this section, it is unlawful for any person subject to the jurisdiction of the United States to commit, attempt to commit, to solicit another to commit, or cause to be committed any of the following acts:

     (i) Approach (including by interception) within 500 yards (460 m) of a Right Whale by vessel, aircraft, or any other means;

     (ii) Fail to undertake required Right Whale avoidance measures specified under paragraph (c)(2) of this section.

   (2) *Right Whale avoidance measures.* Except as provided under paragraph (c)(3) of this section, the following avoidance measures must be taken if within 500 yards (460 m) of a Right Whale:

     (i) If underway, a vessel must steer a course away from the Right Whale and immediately leave the area at a slow safe speed;

     (ii) An aircraft must take a course away from the Right Whale and immediately leave the area at a constant airspeed.

   (3) *Exceptions.* The following exceptions apply to this section, but any person who claims the applicability of an exception has the burden of proving that the exception applies:

     (i) Paragraphs (c)(1) and (c)(2) of this section do not apply if a Right Whale approach is authorized by the National Marine Fisheries Service through a permit issued under part 222, subpart C, of this chapter (General Permit Procedures) or through a similar authorization.

     (ii) Paragraphs (c)(1) and (c)(2) of this section do not apply where compliance would create an imminent and serious threat to a person, vessel, or aircraft.

     (iii) Paragraphs (c)(1) and (c)(2) of this section do not apply when approaching to investigate a Right Whale entanglement or injury, or to assist in the disentanglement or rescue of a Right Whale, provided that permission is received from the National Marine Fisheries Service or designee prior to the approach.

     (iv) Paragraphs (c)(1) and (c)(2) of this section do not apply to an aircraft unless the aircraft is conducting whale watch activities.

     (v) Paragraph (c)(2) of this section does not apply to the extent that a vessel is restricted in her ability to manoeuvre, and because of the restriction, cannot comply with paragraph (c)(2) of this section.

Part 226 – Designated Critical Habitat

§226.101 Purpose and scope.

The regulations contained in this part identify those habitats designated by the Secretary of Commerce as critical under section 4 of the Act, for endangered and threatened species under the jurisdiction of the Secretary of Commerce.

§226.203 Critical habitat for Northern Right Whales.

   Northern Right Whale (*Eubalaena glacialis*)

   (a) Great South Channel. The area bounded by:
     41°40′N 69°45′W;
     41°00′N 69°05′W;
     41°38′N 68°13′W; and
     42°10′N 68°31′W.

   (b) Cape Cod Bay, Massachusetts. The area bounded by:
     42°04′·8N 70°10′W;
     42°12′N 70°15′W;
     42°12′N 70°30′W;
     41°46′·8N 70°30′W; and on the south and east by the interior shore line of Cape Cod, Massachusetts.

Northern Right Whale

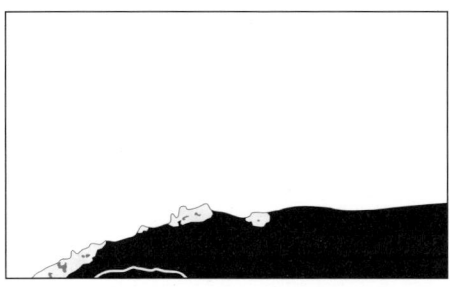

1. Whitish patches of raised and roughened skin (callosities) on top of the head.

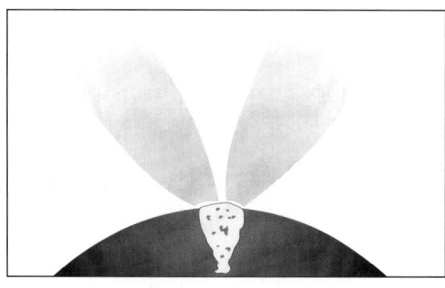

2. V - shaped blow easily visible from in front or behind the whale.

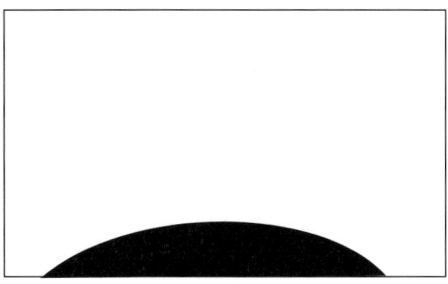

3. No dorsal fin on the back.

4. Tail flukes often lifted vertically when the whale dives.

5. All black tail on the top and underside.

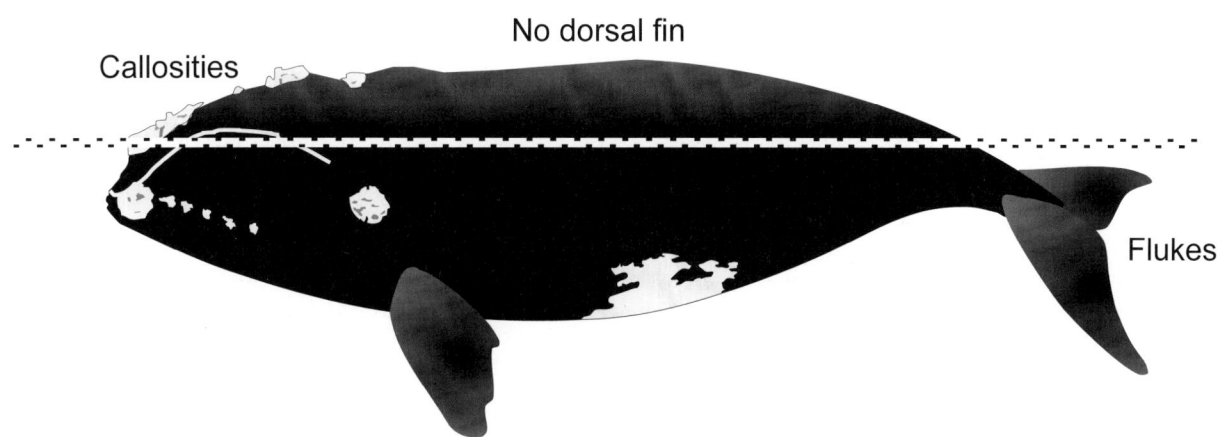

Callosities

No dorsal fin

Flukes

APPENDIX IX

CAPE COD CANAL - NAVIGATION REGULATIONS

Appendix IX contains extracts from the above regulations issued by the United States Department of commerce. For a complete description of this part see 33 CFR 207.

§207.20 Cape Cod Canal, Massachusetts; use, administration, and navigation.

(a) **Limits of canal.** The canal, including approaches, extends from the Canal Station Minus 100 in Cape Cod Bay, approximately one and six-tenths (1·6) statute miles seaward of the Canal Breakwater Light, through dredged channels and land cuts to Cleveland Ledge Light in Buzzards Bay approximately four (4) statute miles southwest of Wings Neck.

(b) **Supervision.**

(1) The movement of ships, boats and craft of every description through the canal and the operation and maintenance of the waterway and all property of the United States pertaining thereto shall be under the supervision of the Division Engineer, US Army Engineer Division, New England, Corps of Engineers, Waltham, Massachusetts, or the authorized representative of the division engineer, the Engineer-In-Charge of the Cape Cod Canal. The division engineer or the Engineer-In-Charge from time to time will prescribe rules governing the dimensions of vessels which may transit the waterway, and other special conditions and requirements which will govern the movement of vessels using the waterway.

(2) The Engineer-In-Charge, through the marine traffic controller on duty, will enforce these regulations and monitor traffic through the canal. The marine traffic controller on duty is the individual responsible for interpretation of these regulations with respect to vessels transiting the canal. Vessels transiting the canal must obey the orders of the marine traffic controller.

(3) The government has tugs stationed at the West Boat Basin for emergency use on an on-call basis. A patrol vessel is manned and operational 24-hours a day.

(c) **Communications.** There is a marine traffic controller on duty 24 hours a day, seven days a week, in the traffic control center located at the Canal Administrative Office. The primary method of communications between the canal and vessels transiting will be by VHF-FM Marine radio. The traffic controller can also be contacted by telephone.

(1) For radio communications, call the traffic controller on channel 16 to establish contact. The transmissions will then be switched to channel 12 or 14 as the working channel to pass information. Channel 13 is also available at the canal office; however, the use of channel 13 should be limited to emergency situations or whenever vessels do not have one of the other channels. All four channels are monitored continuously by the traffic controller. Radio discipline will be adhered to in accordance with FCC rules and regulations.

(2) For telephone communications with the traffic controller, call (508) 759–4431.

(3) Vessels shall maintain a radio guard on Marine VHF-FM channel 13 during the entire passage through the canal.

(4) All radio communications in the vicinity of the canal are tape recorded for future reference.

(d) **Vessels allowed passage.** The canal is open for passage to all adequately powered vessels properly equipped and seaworthy, of sizes consistent with safe navigation as governed by the controlling depths and widths of the channel and the vertical and horizontal clearances of the bridges over the waterway. The granting of permission for any vessel to proceed through the waterway shall not relieve the owners, agents and operators of full responsibility for its safe passage. No vessel having a greater draft forward than aft will be allowed to transit the canal. Craft of low power and wind driven are required to have and use auxiliary power during passage throughout the canal as defined in paragraph (a) of this section. Low powered vessels will be required to await slack water or favourable current for canal transit.

(e) **Tows.**

(1) Tows shall be made-up outside the canal entrances. All vessels engaged in towing other vessels not equipped with a rudder shall use two lines or a bridle and one tow line. If the vessel in tow is equipped with a rudder or a ship shaped bow, one tow line may be used. All tow lines of hawsers must be hauled as short as practicable for safe handling of the tows. No towboat will be allowed to enter the waterway with more than two barges in tow unless prior approval is granted by the Engineer-In-Charge; requests must be submitted 12 hours in advance of the passage.

(2) The maximum length of pontoon rafts using the canal will be limited to 600 feet, and the maximum width to 100 feet. Pontoon rafts exceeding 200 feet in length will be required to have an additional tug on the stern to insure that the tow is kept in line. The tugs used must have sufficient power to handle the raft safely.

(3) Dead ships are required to transit the canal during daylight hours and must be provided with the number of tugs sufficient to afford safe passage through the canal. (A dead ship will not be allowed to enter the canal unless prior approval is granted by the Engineer-In-Charge; requests must be submitted 12 hours in advance of the passage).

(f) **Dangerous Cargoes.** The master or pilot of any vessel or tow carrying dangerous cargoes must notify the Marine Traffic Controller prior to entering the canal. Dangerous cargoes are defined as those items listed in 33 CFR 126.10 when carried in bulk (i.e., quantities exceeding 110 US gallons in one tank) plus Class A explosives (commercial or military) as listed in 49 CFR 173.53 (commercial) and 46 CFR 146.29–100 (military), liquified natural gas and liquified petroleum gas. Transportation of dangerous cargoes through the canal shall be in strict accordance with existing regulations prescribed by law. In addition, vessels carrying dangerous cargoes shall comply with the following requirements.

(1) They must have sufficient horsepower to overcome tidal currents or they will be required to wait for favourable current conditions.

(2) Transits will be during daylight hours.

(3) No transit will be permitted when visibility conditions are unstable or less than 2 miles at the approaches and throughout the entire length of the canal.

(4) Transits must await a clear canal for passage.

(g) **Obtaining clearance.**

(1) Vessels under 65 feet in length may enter the canal without obtaining clearance. All craft are required to make a complete passage through the canal except excursion craft which may operate and change direction within the canal in accordance with procedures coordinated with the marine traffic controller on duty. When the railroad bridge span is in the closed (down) position, all vessels are directed not to proceed beyond the points designated by the stop signs posted east and west of the railroad bridge. Vessels proceeding with a fair tide (with the current) should turn and stem the current at the designated stop points until the railroad bridge is in the raised (open) position.

(2) Vessels 65 feet in length and over shall not enter the canal until clearance has been obtained from the marine traffic controller by radio. See paragraph (c) "Communications" for procedures. If a vessel, granted prior clearance, is delayed or stops at the mooring basins, state pier, or the Sandwich bulkhead, a second clearance must be obtained prior to continuing passage through the canal.

(3) Vessels will be given clearance in the order of arrival, except when conditions warrant one-way traffic, or for any reason an order of priority is necessary, clearance will be granted in the following order.

(i) First-To vessels owned or operated by the United States, including contractors' equipment employed on canal maintenance or improvement work.

(ii) Second-To passenger vessels.

(iii) Third-To tankers and barges docking and undocking at the Canal Electric Terminal.

(iv) Fourth-To merchant vessels, towboats, commercial fishing vessels, pleasure boats and miscellaneous craft.

(4) Procedures in adverse weather-Vessels carrying flammable or combustible cargoes as defined in 46 CFR 30.25 will be restricted from passage through the canal when visibility is less than ½ mile. Other vessels may transit the canal in thick weather by use of radar with the understanding that the United States Government will assume no responsibility: And provided, that clearance has been obtained from the marine traffic controller.

(h) **Traffic lights.** There are three sets of traffic lights showing red, green, and yellow that are operated on a continuous basis at the canal. The traffic lights apply to all vessels 65 feet in length and over. The traffic lights are a secondary system that is operated in support of the radio communications system. The traffic lights are located at the easterly canal entrance, Sandwich, and at the westerly entrance to Hog Island Channel at Wings Neck. A third traffic light is located at the Canal Electric Terminal basin on the south side of the canal in Sandwich, and applies only to vessels arriving and departing that terminal.

(1) Westbound traffic-When the green light is on at the eastern (Cape Cod Bay) entrance, vessels may proceed westward through the canal. When the red light is on, any type of vessel 65 feet in length and over must stop clear of the Cape Cod Bay entrance channel. When the yellow light is on, vessels 65 feet in length

and over and drawing less than 25 feet may proceed as far as the East Mooring Basin where they must stop. Prior to continuing passage through the canal, clearance must be obtained from the marine traffic controller.

(2) Eastbound traffic-When the green light is on at Wings Neck, vessels may proceed eastward through the canal. When the red light is on, vessels 65 feet and over in length and drawing less than 25 feet must keep southerly of Hog Island Channel Entrance Buoys Nos. 1 and 2 and utilize the general anchorage areas adjacent to the improved channel. Vessel traffic drawing 25 feet and over are directed not to enter the canal channel at the Cleveland Ledge Light entrance and shall lay to or anchor in the vicinity of Buzzards Bay Buoy No. 11 (FLW & Bell) until clearance is granted by the canal marine traffic controller or a green traffic light at Wings Neck is displayed. When the yellow light is on, vessels may proceed through Hog Island Channel as far as the West Mooring Basin where they must stop. Prior to continuing passage through the canal, clearance must be obtained from the marine traffic controller.

(i) **Railroad Bridge Signals.** The following signals at the Buzzards Bay Railroad Bridge will be given strict attention.

(1) The vertical lift span on the railroad bridge is normally kept in the raised (open) position except when it is lowered for the passage of trains, or for maintenance purposes. Immediately preceding the lowering of the span, the operator will sound two long blasts of an air horn. Immediately preceding the raising of the span, the operator will sound one long blast of an air horn. When a vessel or craft of any type is approaching the bridge with the span in the down (closed) position and the span cannot be raised immediately, the operator of the bridge will so indicate by sounding danger signals of four short blasts in quick succession.

(2) When the lift span is in the down (closed) position in foggy weather or when visibility is obscured by vapor, there will be four short blasts sounded from the bridge every two minutes.

(j) **Speed.** All vessels are directed to pass mooring and boat basin facilities, the state pier, and all floating plant engaged in maintenance operations of the waterway at a minimum speed consistent with safe navigation. In order to coordinate scheduled rail traffic with the passage of vessels, to minimize erosion of the canal banks and dikes from excessive wave wash and suction, and for the safety of vessels using the canal, the following speed regulations must be observed by vessels of all types, including pleasure craft. The minimum running time for the land cut between the East Mooring Basin (Station 35) and the Administration Office in Buzzards Bay (Station 388) is prescribed as follows; Head tide, 60 minutes; Fair tide, 30 minutes; and Slack tide, 45 minutes.

The minimum running time between the Administration Office (Station 388) and Hog Island Channel westerly entrance Buoy No. 1 (Station 661) is prescribed as follows: Head tide, 46 minutes; Fair tide, 23 minutes; and Slack tide, 35 minutes. The running time at slack water will apply to any vessel which enters that portion of the canal between Station 35 and 661, within the period of one-half hour before or after the predicted time of slack water as given in the National Ocean Service publication "Current Tables, Atlantic Coast,

North America." The minimum running time during a head tide or a fair tide shall apply to any vessel which enters that portion of the canal between Station 35 and 661 at any time other than designated above for time requirements at slack tide. Vessels of any kind unable to make a through transit of the land cut portion of the canal against a head current of 6 knots within a maximum time limit of 2 hours 30 minutes shall be required to obtain the assistance of a helper tug at the vessel owner's expense or await favourable tide conditions prior to receiving clearance from the marine traffic controller. In the event vessels within the confines of the canal fail to perform and are unable to make sufficient headway against the currents, the marine traffic controller may activate a helper tug in accordance with paragraph (k) of this section.

(k) **Management of vessels.**

(1) Vessels within the limits of the canal shall comply with applicable navigation rules.

(2) Vessels within the limits of the canal shall comply with the applicable requirements for the use of pilots established by the Coast Guard, including but not limited to those contained in 46 CFR 157.20–40. Vessels will not be granted clearance to enter the canal until the marine traffic controller has been notified of the name of the pilot who will be handling the vessel.

(3) The master of a vessel will be responsible for notifying the marine traffic controller as soon as an emergency situation appears to be developing. When in the opinion of the marine traffic controller an emergency exists, he/she can require the master to accept the assistance of a helper vessel. Whether or not assistance is provided by a government vessel or by a private firm under contract to the government, the government reserves the right to seek compensation from the vessel owners for all costs incurred.

(4) Right of Way – All vessels proceeding with the current shall have the right of way over those proceeding against the current. All craft up to 65 feet in length shall be operated so as not to interfere with the navigation of vessels of greater length.

(5) Passing of vessels – The passing of one vessel by another when proceeding in the same direction is prohibited except when a leading low powered ship is unable to make sufficient headway. However, extreme caution must be observed to avoid collision, and consideration must be given to the size of the ship to be overtaken, velocity of current and wind, and atmospheric conditions. Masters of vessels involved shall inform the marine traffic controller on duty of developing situations to facilitate coordination of vessel movement. Meeting or passing of vessels at the easterly end of the canal between Station Minus 40 and Station 60 will not be permitted, except in cases of extreme emergency, in order to allow vessels to utilize the center line range to minimize the effects of hazardous eddies and currents. Due to bank suction and tidal set, meeting and passing of vessels at the following location will be avoided:

(i) Sagamore Bridge.

(ii) Bourne Bridge.

(iii) Railroad Bridge.

(iv) Mass. Maritime Academy.

(6) Unnecessary delay in canal – Vessels and other type crafts must not obstruct navigation by unnecessarily idling at low speed when entering or passing through the canal.

(7) Stopping in the waterway – Anchoring in the Cape Cod Canal Channel is prohibited except in emergencies. For the safety of canal operations it is mandatory that the masters of all vessels anchoring in or adjacent to the Canal Channel (Cape Cod Bay to Cleveland Ledge Light) for any reason, immediately notify the marine traffic controller.

(8) Utilization of mooring and boat basins and the Sandwich Bulkhead – Vessels mooring or anchoring in the mooring or boat basins at the Sandwich bulkhead must do so in a manner not to obstruct or impede vessel movements to and from facilities. These facilities are of limited capacity and permission to occupy them for periods exceeding 24 hours must be obtained in advance from the marine traffic controller. Mooring in the West Boat Basin at Buzzards Bay, near the railroad bridge, is not permitted except in an emergency. Fishing boats, yachts, cabin cruisers and other craft utilizing the East Boat Basin on the south side of the canal at Sandwich, Massachusetts, are not permitted to tie up at the Corps of Engineers landing float or anchor in a manner to prevent canal floating plant from having ready access to the float. All vessels or barges left unattended must be securely tied with adequate lines or cables. The United States assumes no liability for damages which may be sustained by any craft using the bulkhead at Sandwich or the canal mooring or boat basin facilities. Vessels shall not be left unattended along the face of the government bulkhead. A responsible person with authority to authorize and/or accomplish vessel movement must remain onboard at all times.

(l) **Grounded, wrecked or damaged vessels.** In the event a vessel is grounded, or so damaged by accident as to render it likely to become an obstruction and/or hazard to navigation in the waterway, the division engineer or the division engineer's authorized representative shall supervise and direct all operations that may be necessary to remove the vessel to a safe locality.

(n) **Deposit of refuse.** No oil or other allied liquids, ashes, or materials of any kind shall be thrown, pumped or swept into the canal or its approaches from any vessel or craft using the waterway, nor shall any refuse be deposited on canal grounds, marine structures, or facilities.

(o) **Trespass to property.** Subject to the provisions of paragraph (q) of this section trespass upon the canal property is prohibited.

(p) **Bridges over the canal.** The government owns, operates and maintains all bridges across the canal which include one railroad bridge and two highway bridges. The division engineer or his/her authorized representative may establish rules and regulations governing the use of these bridges.

INDEX

Names without a paragraph number are for gazetteer purposes only

NOTES

NOTES

NOTES

NOTES

NOTES

NOTES

PUBLICATIONS OF THE
UNITED KINGDOM HYDROGRAPHIC OFFICE

A complete list of Sailing Directions, Charts and other works published by the United Kingdom Hydrographic Office, together with a list of Agents for their sale, is contained in the *Catalogue of Admiralty Charts and Publications*, published annually. The list of Admiralty Distributors is also on the UKHO website (www.ukho.gov.uk), or it can be obtained from:

The United Kingdom Hydrographic Office,
Admiralty Way,
Taunton, Somerset
TA1 2DN

Produced in the United Kingdom
by UKHO